EC Competition Law

The development of competition law in the EU can be explored through three interrelated perspectives: the extent to which controversies in economic thinking affect the design of the law; how changing political visions about the objectives of competition law have caused shifts in the interpretation of the rules; and the institution in charge of applying the rules. The economic and political debates on competition law show that it is a contested terrain, and the way courts and competition authorities apply the law reflects their responses to the objectives and economics of competition law. By characterising the application of competition law as a continuous response to policy and economic debates, the author casts fresh perspectives on the subject.

Written with competition law students in mind, Monti sets out economic concepts in a non-technical manner and explores the policy dimension of competition law by referring to key cases and contemporary policy initiatives.

EC Competition Law

GIORGIO MONTI

CAMBRIDGE
UNIVERSITY PRESS

CAMBRIDGE UNIVERSITY PRESS
Cambridge, New York, Melbourne, Madrid, Cape Town, Singapore, São Paulo

Cambridge University Press
The Edinburgh Building, Cambridge CB2 8RU, UK

Published in the United States of America by Cambridge University Press, New York

www.cambridge.org
Information on this title: www.cambridge.org/9780521700757

First published 2007

Printed in the United Kingdom at the University Press, Cambridge

A catalogue record for this publication is available from the British Library

ISBN 978-0-521-70075-7 paperback

Contents

Preface		*page* ix
Table of cases		xiii
Table of legislation		xxviii

1 Competition law: policy perspectives **1**
1 Introduction 1
2 A case study: the *de Havilland* decision of the European Commission 6
3 The demands of a workable competition policy 15
4 Conclusion 18

2 The core values of EC competition law in flux **20**
1 Introduction 20
2 Competition as economic freedom 22
3 The single market 39
4 Economic efficiency 44
5 The changing relationship among core values 48
6 The transformation thesis so far 51

3 Economics and competition law **53**
1 Introduction 53
2 Shared premises 55
3 The Structure–Conduct–Performance paradigm 57
4 The Chicago School 63
5 The post-Chicago paradigm 68
6 The effect of economics on law in US antitrust: a synthesis 73
7 European competition policy and economics 79
8 Economics in competition law: opportunities and limitations 87

4 Competition law and public policy **89**
1 Introduction 89
2 Environmental policy 91
3 Industrial policy 94
4 Employment policy 96

5 Consumer policy   99
6 Culture   102
7 National interests   110
8 Placing competition policy in the context of EU policies   113
9 The future of public policy considerations   122

5   Market power   **124**
1 Four concepts of market power   124
2 Dominance in EC competition law   127
3 Measuring market power   130
4 Market power in aftermarkets   148
5 Product differentiation and market power: the irrelevance of
  market definition   150
6 Market power in Article 81   153
7 From commercial power to market power   157

6   Abuse of a dominant position: anticompetitive exclusion   **159**
1 Introduction   160
2 Why penalise the abuse of a dominant position?
  BA/Virgin as a case study   162
3 Excluding rivals   173
4 Harm to other market participants   195
5 Market-partitioning abuses   198
6 Defences   203
7 Conclusion: Article 82 redux   211

**7   Abuse of a dominant position: from competition policy to
      sector-specific regulation**   **216**
1 Introduction   216
2 Exploitative abuse   217
3 Refusal to cooperate with competitors   223
4 Regulatory competition law   243

8   Merger policy   **245**
1 Introduction   246
2 Horizontal mergers: single-firm dominance   250
3 Market power without dominance?   256
4 Vertical mergers   264
5 Conglomerate mergers   271
6 Merger remedies   283
7 Widening the aims of merger policy?   291
8 A European merger policy?   300

9   Oligopoly markets   **308**
    1 Introduction   308
    2 Merger control   311
    3 Express collusion   324
    4 Tacit collusion   334
    5 Conclusion: unenforceable competition   344

10 Distribution agreements   **346**
    1 Introduction   347
    2 The economic debate   348
    3 Community policy towards vertical restraints   357
    4 Market integration in the regulation of distribution agreements   363
    5 Individual appraisal under Article 81   366
    6 Distributors' power   372
    7 The politics of distribution: the car sector   384
    8 Conclusion   390

11 Institutions: who enforces competition law?   **392**
    1 Introduction   392
    2 The background to modernisation   395
    3 The new enforcement structure   409
    4 Side effects   419
    5 Private enforcement   424
    6 The challenges of institutional resettlement   438

12 Competition law and liberalisation   **440**
    1 Introduction   441
    2 Initiating liberalisation   442
    3 Introducing competition in network industries   451
    4 Re-regulation   463
    5 Sector-specific competition law   474
    6 Public services   485
    7 More markets, more law   494

13 Conclusions   **497**
    1 Institutions   497
    2 Economics   500
    3 Politics   503

    Index   506

Preface

In the pages that follow I hope the reader finds a clear, yet challenging and controversial characterisation of competition law. The theme that underpins each chapter is that the substantive rules of competition law are best studied by avoiding exclusive reliance on legal method. Rather, other disciplines offer necessary assistance. I draw mostly on economics, but have also tried to incorporate some approaches used by political scientists. In brief, the gist of this book is that whether one looks at competition law doctrine as a whole, or at a single decision, one should ask three questions in order to understand it best: What is the policy behind it? What economic theory (if any) supports this policy? And who enforces the law? I think these questions receive different answers at different moments in the history of the development of competition law, and perhaps even conflicting answers at the same moment. Enforcers have diverging policy preferences, and different economic theories can be used to justify diametrically opposed conclusions as to the legality of a given practice. Asking these three questions, about the politics, the economics and the institution, reveals valuable information about the application of the law, its evolution and direction. The focus is on the competition law of the European Community, in the way it has been developed by the Commission and the European Courts; I hope that the method of analysis can be transplanted and applied to other legal systems and frame an inquiry into other competition laws.

The cover of the book (a painting by Lisa Graa Jensen entitled 'Big Spenders') illustrates a market in full flow, the domain of competition law. How are markets to be regulated? One of antitrust law's most eminent personalities, Richard Posner, published an influential book in 1976 under the title *Antitrust Law: An Economic Perspective*. This was a reaction against a populist streak of antitrust which considered that the rules were not just to ensure the big spenders had plentiful and cheap goods to buy, but were also designed to protect traders from each other, or to safeguard local markets like this against the competition from large out-of-town shopping malls. In the second edition in 2001 the subtitle was dropped because any other perspective had waned and there was no need to persuade the reader of the value of the economic perspective.[1] This

---

[1] R. A. Posner *Antitrust Law* 2nd edn (Chicago: University of Chicago Press, 2000) p. vii.

might be true for US competition law (and I try and explain why this might be so in chapter 3), but EC competition law has not yet become applied micro-economics. A range of policies, some misguided, some less so, affect the application of the law. EC competition law is nonetheless increasingly embracing economic analysis. On many occasions, members of the Directorate General for Competition suggest that the law is being reformed to embrace a 'more economics-oriented approach' or moving towards an application of 'mainstream economics'. However, these two utterances are unhelpful. The first one refers to there being 'more' economics, but this implies that other perspectives are also deployed to determine the application of EC competition law and quite what these are is never explained. The second claim is erroneous in that, bar some shared ground, there is no such thing as mainstream economics. Instead, there are different perspectives on how to regulate industrial behaviour, as I hope to illustrate with the review of how economists would regulate commercial practices. In sum, economists are still debating about how firms behave and about how to regulate firms. Trying to engage in these debates is more illuminating than believing that there are a set of economic postulates and formulae that one can apply to solve all competition cases. And exploring why certain economic prescriptions are followed by competition authorities and courts while others are not sheds light on how the competition rules are interpreted.

It follows, then, that to explain and assess EC competition law, we need to look at it from a range of perspectives. Some of the perspectives suggested in the book might be about to be buried (for example, the role of competition law in safeguarding the economic freedom of vulnerable firms) while others are today's spring chickens (for example, the still vacuous reference to consumer welfare). But both are worth considering to explain what has shaped the law and what might shape it in years to come. The study of competition law proposed here requires reflection on what economic theory is chosen and why, how the economic theories are translated into workable rules, how judges and competition authorities respond when economic paradigms shift, and how public policy considerations undermine or complement the application of competition law according to economic prescriptions.

I have tried to write this book in a way that is accessible to those whose background is law, economics or political science, and hopefully for a general audience interested in gaining a critical introduction to this topic. At times this has meant that I have simplified and perhaps exaggerated certain concepts to make them more accessible and I may have omitted certain critical qualifications, but the reader can chase up the footnotes to check the original sources and see the argument in full. I have also tried to make competition law sound exciting, because competition authorities seem bent on making the law dull by publishing guidelines on every substantive and procedural topic. Guidelines are probably the most problematic manifestation of a competition authority's powers today. As I show in the chapters that follow, some of the guidelines are attempts to make new law. This is in stark contradiction to the avowed purpose of guidelines, which is to enhance transparency. I struggle to see how a competition authority whose interpretation of the law should be subject to review by a court feels empowered to change the law by issuing guidelines. Moreover, a business will likely follow the guidelines to avoid being investigated by the competition authorities. In this way law is enforced by declarations that are not susceptible to the rule of law. And I struggle to see how transparency is enhanced when the change in policy is not even alluded to in guidelines but must be inferred by noting how the guidelines qualify earlier cases. Finally, guidelines hide the conflicts and differences of opinion about competition law. They present competition law as a seamless web of clear, consistent and complementary principles, obscuring the conundrums, contradictions and conflicts that require attention and debate.

A few notes on the text: First, the material is not arranged in the conventional manner that readers of other competition law books might anticipate. Instead, I have arranged topics so that certain cases and doctrines are brought together because of shared policy or economic goals. I hope nonetheless that the section headings are sufficiently clear for the reader to navigate through the text, while persuading the reader that the different perspective suggested in this book has value. Second, while I have tried to address the majority of the legal issues that are covered in undergraduate and postgraduate courses on EC competition law, the coverage is not always comprehensive, and at times I have preferred to draw the reader's attention to certain trends that are not part of the mainstream textbook presentations, to emphasise developments that are under-reported but significant if one is trying to understand how competition law is evolving. Those looking for a more conventional coverage of the law are well served by a variety of books, some (relatively inexpensive) addressed to students and some (extremely expensive) written by and for practitioners. Whether these two types of book are in different product markets is something the reader can ponder after reading chapter 5 on market definition. (This is a joke.) Third, several documents are only available electronically and, while I have cited the relevant home page where the document appears, as this seems to be academically correct, websites are updated very regularly and I advise the reader interested in finding any web-based document cited here to use internet search engines. This is much more efficient than trying to navigate some of the websites. Finally, I have refused to use the word 'undertaking' until chapter 12. Instead I use the word 'firm' to describe the entities that are the subjects of competition law. This seems to me more accurate. (Other language versions of the EC Treaty, and the UK's Enterprise Act 2002, refer to the subject of competition law as an enterprise, a more apt term.)

The following is a non-exhaustive list of debts, with the caveat that none of those mentioned are responsible for the errors and infelicities in the text. First, my thanks go to the staff at Cambridge University Press for their support for this project and their extraordinary patience. Second, I am grateful to all my LLB and LLM students who discussed some of the ideas in the pages that follow in seminars, and those who read some of the chapters in draft form and reassured me that what I wrote was comprehensible. I wish in particular to signal a word of thanks to the LLM class of 2002/03 for exemplary Thursday morning discussions. I am grateful to the SLS for the award of a research grant and to Tanneguy d'Honinuctun for excellent research assistance with the French law in chapter 11. I am also grateful to Hugh Collins who commented on chapter 11, Ester Reid who commented on chapter 1, and Ekaterina Rousseva for her thoughts on various chapters and for discussing and challenging several of the arguments. I am grateful to my parents for their unbounded support during my studies and beyond. And much gratitude of course goes to Ayako, who helped with the HHIs in chapter 9, was incommensurably patient and supportive during the writing process, and put up with my incessant scribbling on the margins of many books, cases and articles as the District Line lazily transported us to and from London.

I have taken into consideration developments up to 31 July 2006. A blog accompanies this book where recent cases and other developments are discussed, and readers are invited to add their comments. This is available at http://competitionlawboard.blogspot.com/index.html.

Table of cases

EUROPEAN COMMISSION COMPETITION DECISIONS

1998 Football World Cup [2000] OJ L55/5, 138

ACI [1994] OJ L224/28, 233
Air France/Alitalia (7 April 2004), 477
Asahi [1994] OJ L354/87, 101
Atlas [1996] OJ L239/23, 234, 458, 474, 484, 485
Austrian Airlines/Lufthansa [2002] OJ L242/25, 477, 478
Austrian ARA [2004] OJ L75/59, 412

Bass [1999] OJ L186/1, 367
Bayer/BPCL [1988] OJ L150/35, 95
Bayer/Gist Brocades, Decision 76/172 [1976] OJ L30/13, 28
Bayo-n-ox [1990] OJ L21/71, 43
Bertlesmann/Kirsch/Premiere [1999] OJ L53/1, 140, 142, 143
B&I plc/Sealink Harbours [1992] 5 CMLR 255, 232–3, 234
BiB/Open [1999] OJ L312/1, 270
Boosey & Hawkes: Interim Measures [1987] OJ L286/76, 241
BPB Industries plc [1989] OJ L10/50, 241
BPCL/ICI [1984] OJ L212/1, 95
British Midland/Aer Lingus [1992] OJ L96/34, 231–2, 244

Carlsberg [1984] OJ L207/26, 27–8, 30, 38–9, 50
Cartonboard [1994] OJ L243/1, 333
CECED [2000] OJ L187/47, 92, 93, 114, 120, 412
Coca-Cola [2005] OJ L253/21, 412
Cologne/Bonn Airports [1998] OJ L300/33, 236
Continental/Michelin [1988] OJ L305/33, 140

Daimler Chrysler [2002] OJ L257/1, 385
Deutsche Bahn [1994] OJ L37/34, 173
Deutsche Post AG [2001] OJ L125/27, 180, 185, 186, 199, 479–84
Deutsche Telekom [2003] OJ L263/9, 174, 472, 473, 474
Distillers [1978] OJ L50/16, 368

DSD [2001] OJ L166/1, 166, 211, 219
DSD [2001] OJ L319/1, 92
Dusseldorf Airport [1998] OJ L173/45, 236
Dutch Banks [1989] OJ L253/1, 27

Electrical and Mechanical Carbon and Graphite Products [2004] OJ L125, 334
Electronic Ticketing [1999] OJ L244/56, 235
ENI/Montedison [1987] OJ L5/13, 95
ENIC/UEFA, COMP/37.806, 112
Eurofix-Bauco/Hilti [1988] OJ L65/19, 147, 187–9, 190, 191, 192
Eurotunnel [1994] OJ L354/66, 233
Exxon-Shell [1994] OJ L144/21, 91, 92

Fenex [1996] OJ L181/28, 325
Fine Art Auction Houses (30 October 2002), 333
Finnish Airports [1999] OJ L69/24, 201
Ford/Volkswagen [1993] OJ L20/14, 2, 97
Frankfurt Airport [1998] OJ L72/30 (Art. 82 action), 236
Frankfurt Airport [1998] OJ L173/32 (Directive 96/97 action), 236

GE/Pratt & Whitney [2000] OJ L58/16, 46
GEC-Siemens/Plessey [1994] OJ L239/2, 96
Generics/Astra Zeneca (15 June 2005), 431
Glaxo [2001] OJ L302/1, 202
Graphite Electrodes [2002] OJ L100/1, 334
Grundig's EC Distribution System [1994] OJ L20/15, 101

Hamburg Airport [1998] OJ L300/41, 236
Hugin/Liptons [1978] OJ L22/23, 148–9

Inntrepreneur and Spring [2000] OJ L195/49, 36–7

Joint selling of the Media Rights to the German Bundesliga [2005] OJ L134/46,
    109, 412

Konica [1988] OJ L78/34, 43

Landing Fees at Brussels Airport [1995] OJ L216/8, 201
Langanese-Iglo [1993] OJ L183/19, 363
LdPE [1989] OJ L74/21, 330
London European/Sabena [1988] OJ L40/1, 234

Methylglucamine [2004] OJ L38/18, 333
Michelin 2 [2002] OJ L143/1, 183, 184, 185, 196, 198–9
Microsoft decision of 24 March 2004, 189–90, 191–5, 217, 229–31, 241,
    242–3, 244

Napier Brown/British Sugar [1988] OJ L284/41, 174, 194
National Sulphuric Acid Association [1980] OJ L260/24, 45–6

NDC Health/IMS Health Interim Measures [2003] OJ L268/69, 228, 242–3
Netherlands Express Delivery Services [1990] OJ L10/47, 481
Night Services [1994] OJ L259/21, 233
Nintendo [2003] OJ L255/33, 40

Olivetti/Canon [1988] OJ L52/60, 95–6
Opel [2001] OJ L59/1, 39, 385
Optical Fibres [1986] OJ L236/30, 95

Parfums Givenchy [1992] OJ L236/11, 361
Philips-Osram [1994] OJ L378/37, 91, 92
PO/Yamaha (16 July 2003), 365–6, 367
Polypropylene [1986] OJ L230/1, 42, 324

Rennet [1980] OJ L51/19, 27

Sabena/British Midlands [1995] OJ L216/8, 176
Sandoz [1987] OJ L222/28, 43
SAS/Maresk [2001] OJ L265/15, 39
Sea Containers/Stena Sealink [1994] OJ L15/8, 232
Simulcasting [2005] OJ L107/58, 412
Soda Ash: ICI [1991] OJ L152/40, 183, 185
Soda Ash: ICI [2003] OJ L10/33, 183
Soda Ash: Solvay [1991] OJ L152/1, 40, 183
Soda Ash: Solvay [2003] OJ L10/10, 183
Spanish International Express Courier Services [1990] OJ L233/19, 481
Stichting Bakstein [1994] OJ L131/15, 95, 96, 97
Stuttgart Airport [1998] OJ L300/25, 236
Synthetic Fibres [1984] OJ L207/17, 96, 97

T-Mobile Deutschland/O2 Germany [2004] OJ L75/32, 37–9, 50, 51, 474
TAT [1994] OJ L127/32, 455
Télévision par Satellite [1999] OJ L90/6, 32–3, 38, 50, 51
Tetra Pak 1 (BTG Licence) [1988] OJ L272/27, 176–7
Tetra Pak 2 [1992] OJ L72/1, 157, 180, 281

UEFA Champions League [2003] OJ L291/25, 107–9, 115, 117, 120, 234, 412
UK Agricultural Tractor Registration Exchange [1992] OJ L6819, 339

Vacuum Interrupters, Decision 77/160 [1977] OJ L48/32, 28
Van den Bergh Foods [1998] OJ L246/1, 367, 369, 372
VIFKA [1986] OJ L291/46, 27
Viho/Parker Pen [1992] OJ L233/27, 41
Virgin/British Airways [2000] OJ L30/1, 138, 143, 162–72, 184, 185, 232
Visa International [2002] OJ L318/17, 33

Vitamins [2003] OJ L16/1, 334
Volkswagen AG [1998] OJ L124/60, 39, 40, 385
Volkswagen AG [2001] OJ L262/14, 385

Whitbread [1999] OJ L88/26, 427

Zinc Phosphate [2003] OJ L153/1, 324, 327
Zinc Producer Group [1985] OJ L220/27, 309
Zoja v. Commercial Solvents [1972] OJ L299/51; [1973] CMLR D50, 224

EUROPEAN COMMISSION MERGER DECISIONS

ABB/Daimler Benz, M.580 [1997] OJ L11/1, 135, 319, 320
Aerospatiale-Alenia/de Havilland, M.53 [1991] OJ L334 42, 6–15, 16, 18, 252
Aerospatiale/MBB, M.17 [1991] OJ C59 13, 12
Agfa Gevaert/Du Pont, M.986 [1998] OJ L211/22, 256, 289
Air France/KLM, M.3280 (11 February 2004), 477, 478
Air Liquide/BOC, M.1630 (18 January 2000), 276–8, 281–2
Airtours/First Choice, M.1524 [2000] OJ L93/1, 136, 315
Alcatel/Telettra, M.042 [1991] OJ L122/48, 256, 299
Allied Signal/Honeywell, M.1601 [2001] OJ L152/1, 286
AOL/Time Warner, M.1845 [2000] OJ L268/28, 270
Apollo/Bakelite, M.3593 (1 April 2005), 267
Astra Zeneca/Novartis, M.1806 [2004] OJ L110/1, 251

Barilla/BPL/Kamps, M.2537 (25 June 2002), 264
BASF/Eurodiol/Pantochin, M.2314 [2002] OJ L132/45, 297–8
Bayer Healthcare/Roche (OTC Business), M.3544 (19 November 2004), 152
Blokker/Toys 'R' Us, M.890 [1998] OJ L316/1, 298
Boeing/Hughes, M.1879 (27 September 2000), 266
Boeing/McDonnell Douglas, M.877 [1997] OJ L336/16, 22–3, 139, 256, 289
Bombardier/ADtranz, M.2139 (3 April 2001), 288–9, 292
Bosch/Rexroth, M.2060 [2004] OJ L43/1, 284, 285
BP/E.ON, M.2533 (6 September 2001), 303
BSCH/A.Champalimaud, M.1616 (20 July 1999), 304
BskyB/KirschPayTV, JV.37 (21 March 2000), 142, 234, 270

C3D/Rhone/Go-Ahead, M.2154 (20 October 2000), 303
Carrefour/Promodes, M.1684 (25 October 2000), 373, 375, 376
Ciba-Geigy/Sandoz, M.737 [1997] OJ L201/1, 286
Coca-Cola/Amalgamated Beverages, M.794 [1997] OJ L218/15, 136

Danish Crown/Vestyske Slagterier, M.1313 [2000] OJ L20/1, 137–8, 292, 319,
    320, 324
Deutsche Post/Danzas/ASGm M.1549 (8 July 1999), 482
Deutsche Post/Danzas/Nedloyd, M.1513 (1 July 1999), 482

Deutsche Post/Securicor, M.1347 (23 February 1999), 482
DHL/Deutsche Post, M.1168 (26 June 1998), 482, 484
Dow Chemical/Union Carbide, M.1671 [2001] OJ L245/1, 136, 253, 254

EnBW/EDP/Cajastur/Hidrocantábrico, M.2684 (19 March 2002), 475–6
ENI/GDP/EDP, M.3440 (9 December 2004), 249
Enso/Stora, M.1225 [1999] OJ L254/9, 255–6, 316
E.ON/MOL, M.3696 (21 December 2005), 267

Fiat Geotech/New Holland, M.9 (18 February 1991), 252

GE/Instrumentarium, M.3083 [2004] OJ L109/1, 263
Gencor/Lonrho, M.619 [1997] OJ L11/30, 311, 314–15, 318, 320, 322, 323
General Electric/Honeywell, M.2220 [2004] OJ L48/1, 87, 129–30, 274–7, 291
Guinness/Grand Met, M.938 [1998] OJ L288/24, 272–4

HP/Compaq, M.2609 (13 February 2002), 251

Imetal/English China Clays, M.1381 (26 April 1999), 265
Interbrew/Bass, M.2044 (22 August 2000), 303

Johnson & Johnson/Guidant, M.3687 (25 August 2005), 152

Kesko/Tuko, M.784 [1997] OJ L110/53, 251, 373, 375
Kimberley-Clark/Scott, M.623 [1996] OJ L183/1, 133, 147, 150, 283

Lafarge/Blue Circle, M.2317 (1 March 2001), 265

MAN/Auwärter, M.2201 [2002] OJ L116/35, 311, 312, 316, 318
Mannersmann/Hoesch, M.222 [1993] OJ L114/34, 252
Mannersmann/Vallourec/llva, M.315 [1994] OJ L102/15, 14, 299, 311, 318
Masterfoods/Royal Canin, M.2544 (15 February 2002), 283
Mercedes-Benz/Kåssbohrer, M.477 [1995] OJ L211, 286
Metsälitto Osuuskunta/Vapo OY/JV, M.2234 (8 February 2001), 303
MSG/Media Services, M.469 [1994] OJ L364/1, 269, 299

Nestlé/Perrier, M.190 [1992] OJ L356/1, 133, 252, 283, 311, 314–15, 318, 320,
    324, 336, 354
Nestlé/Ralston Purina, M.2337 (27 July 2001), 285
New Holland/Case, M.1571 (28 October 1999), 289
Newscorp/Telepiú, M.2876 [2004] OJ L110/73, 142, 270, 287–8, 289
Newtell/Rubbermaid, M.1355 (13 January 1999), 136
Nordic Satellite Distribution, M.490 [1996] OJ L53/20, 269
Norske Skog/Parenco/Walsum, M.2498 [2002] OJ L233/38, 309, 345

Philips/Agilent Health Care Technologies, M.2256 (2 March 2001), 251, 263–4
Philips/Marconi Medical Systems, M.2537 (17 October 2001), 264
Piaggio/Aprilia, M.3570 (22 November 2004), 286–7, 289, 292, 299
Pirelli/BICC, M.1882 (19 July 2000), 140

Procter & Gamble/Gillette, M.1732 (15 July 2005), 294–6
Procter & Gamble/VP Schickedanz, M.430 [1994] OJ L354/32, 252, 283

Rewe/Meinl, M.1221 [1999] OJ L274/1, 373
RMC/Rugby, M.1759 (15 October 1999), 266
RTL/Veronica/Endemol, M.553 [1996] OJ L134/32, 143

Saint-Gobain/Wacker-Chemie/NOM, M.774 [1997] OJ L247/1, 298
SCA/Metsa Tissue, M.2097 [2002] OJ L57/1, 255
Secil/Holderbank/Cimpor, M.2054 (22 November 2000), 304
Sony/BMG, M.3333 (19 July 2004), 323
Steetley/Tarmac, M.180 (12 February 1992), 303
Sun Chemicals/TotalFinal/Coates, M.1742 (22 December 1999), 253, 254

Telefónica Sogecable/Cablevisión, M.709 (19 July 1996), 269
Telia/Sonera, M.2803 (10 July 2002), 266
Telia/Telnor, M.1439 [2001] OJ L40/1, 240, 286
Tetra Laval/Sidel, M.2416 [2004] OJ L43/13, 278, 282
Torras/Sarrió, M.166 (24 February 1992), 138
TotalFina/Elf, M.1628 [2001] OJ L143/1, 284

Unilever/Bestfoods, M.1990 (20 September 2000), 284
Unilever/Diversey, M.704 (20 March 1996), 252

VEBA/VIAG, M.1673 [2001] OJ L118/1, 475
Vivendi/Canal+/Seagram, M.2050 (13 October 2000), 142, 270–1, 287, 296
Vodafone Airtouch/Mannesmann, M.1795 (12 April 2000), 251, 253,
    254, 296
Volvo/Renault, M.1980 (1 September 2000), 262–3
Volvo/Scania, M.1672 [2000] OJ L143/74, 138, 140, 262, 263, 299

Worldcom/MCI, M.1069 [1999] OJ L116/1, 253–4, 286

EUROPEAN COURT OF JUSTICE

A. Ahlström Osakeyhtiö v. Commission (Woodpulp) Cases 89, 104, 114, 116,
    117 and 125–9/85 [1993] ECR I-1307, 330, 332
Aalborg Portland A/S and Others v. Commission, C-204/00P, C-205/00P,
    C-211/00P, C-213/00P, C-217/00P and C-219/00P [2004] ECR I-123,
    331, 426
ACF Chemiefarma v. Commission, Case 41/69 [1970] ECR 661, 326
Aéroports de Paris v. Commission, T-128/98 [2000] ECR II-3929, 200
Aéroports de Paris v. Commission, C-82/01P [2002] ECR I-2613, 200
Ahmed Saeed Flugreisen and Silver Line Reisebüro GmbH v. Zentrale zur
    Bekümpfung unlauteren Wettbewerbs eV, Case 66/86 [1989] ECR 803,
    447, 454
Air Inter SA v. Commission, T-266/94 [1994] ECR II-997, 455, 489

Airtours v. Commission, T-342/99 [2002] ECR II-2585, 311, 312, 315, 318, 318, 321, 323

AKZO Chemie BV v. Commission, C-62/86 [1991] ECR I-3359, 143, 179, 182, 207, 281

Albany International BV v. Stichting Bedriffspensionenfonds Textielindustrie, C-67/96 [1999] ECR I-5751, 449, 486, 490

Altmark Trans GmbH, C-280/00 [2003] ECR I-7747, 491

Ambulanz Glöckner v. Landkreis Südwestpfalz, C-475/99 [2001] ECR I-8089, 449, 489, 490, 491

Anic v. Commission, T-6/89 [1991] ECR II-1623, 339

AOK Bundesverband and Others v. Ichthyol-Gesellschaft Cordes, Hemani & Co., C-264/01, C-306/01 & C-355/01 [2004] ECR I-2493, 486

Atlantic Container Line, T-395/94 [2002] ECR II-875, 372

Atlantic Container Line AB and Others v. Commission, T191/98, T-212-214/98 [2003] ECR II-3275, 206, 372

Automec SRL v. Commission, T-64/89 [1990] ECR II-2223, 399

BAT and Reynolds, Cases 142/84 & 156/84 [1987] ECR 4487, 247

Bayer AG v. Commission, T-41/96 [2000] ECR II-3383, 42

Béguelin Import Co. v. SAGL Import Export, Case 22/71 [1971] ECR 949, 33

Belgische Radio en Televiste and Société Belge des Auteurs, Compositeurs et Editeurs de Musique v. SABAM, Case 127/73 [1974] ECR 51, 424

Bodson v. SA Pompes funèbres des règions libérées, Case 30/87 [1988] ECR 2479, 219

BP v. Commission, Case 77/77 [1978] ECR 1513, 240, 242

BPP Industries and British Gypsum v. Commission, T-65/89 [1993] ECR II-389, 160, 184, 193, 204, 205, 241

Brasserie de Haecht v. Wilkin-Janssen, Case 23/67 [1967] ECR 407, 31, 357

Brentjens' Handelsonderneming BV, C-115–17/97 [1999] ECR I-6025, 97, 111, 113, 121, 123

British Airways v. Commission, T-219/99 [2003] ECR II-5918, 162, 183, 184

British Airways v. Commission, C-95/04P (Opinion of 23 February 2006), 161, 212

British Leyland plc v. Commission, Case 226/84 [1986] ECR 326, 199–200

Bundesverband der Arzneimittel-Importeure eV and Commission v. Bayer AG, C-2/01 and C-3/01, judgment of 6 January 2004, 43–4

Bureau Européen des Unions des Consommateurs and National Consumer Council v. Commission, T-37/92 [1994] ECR II-285, 399

CCE de Vittel and Others v. Commission, T-12/93 [1995] ECR II-1247, 296

Centre belge d'études de marché-Télémarketing (CBEM) v. SA Compagnie luxembourgeoise de télédiffusion (CLT) and Information publicité Benelux (IPB), Case 311/84 [1985] ECR 3261, 145, 224–5

Cisal di Battistello Venanzio and C. Sas v. Istituto Nazionale contro gli infortuni sul lavoro (INAIL), C-218/00 [2002] ECR I-691, 488

Coca-Cola Company and Coca-Cola Enterprises Inc. v. Commission, T-125/97 and 127/97 [2000] ECR II-1733, 160, 258

Commission v. Anic Partecipazioni SpA, C-49/92 [1999] ECR I-4125, 326, 327, 328, 329

Commission v. Belgium, C-503/99 [2002] ECR I-4809, 306

Commission v. France, C-483/99 [2002] ECR I-4781, 306

Commission v. Italy, C-35/96 [1998] ECR 3581, 448

Commission v. Italy, C-174/04 (2 June 2006), 306, 307

Commission v. Netherlands, C-282/04 & 283/04 (judgment pending), 306

Commission v. Portugal, C-367/98 [2002] ECR I-4731, 306

Commission v. Spain, C-463/00 [2002] ECR I-4581, 306

Commission v. Tetra Laval BV, C-12/03P [2005] ECR I-987, 253, 254, 274, 278–80, 290

Commission v. UK, C-466/98 [2002] ECR I-9427, 456

Compagnie Maritime Belge v. Commission, C-395-6/96P [2000] ECR I-1365, 125, 338

Consorzio Industrie Flammiferi v. Autorità Garante della Concorrenza del Mercato, C-198/01 [2003] ECR I-8055, 448

Consten and Grundig v. Commission, Cases 56/64 and 58/64 [1966] ECR 299, 29, 39, 40–1, 44, 46, 51, 117, 353, 354, 357, 364, 396

Corbeau, C-320/91 [1993] ECR I-2533, 450–1, 488–9

Corsica Ferries France v. Gruppo Antichi Ormeggiatori del porto di Genova Corp, C-266/96 [1998] ECR I-3949, 489

Corsica Ferries Italy, C-18/93 [1994] ECR 1783, 201, 202

Costa v. ENEL, Case 6/64, 2, 451

Courage v. Crehan, C-453/99 [2001] ECR I-6297, 425, 427, 429, 439, 500

Criminal Proceedings against Arduino, C-39/99 [2002] ECR I-1529, 448

Criminal Proceedings against Bernard Keck and Daniel Mithouard, C-267/91 & C-268/91 [1993] ECR I-6097, 407

Dansk Røindustri A/S and Others v. Commission, C-189/02P, C-202/02P & C-205-208/02P (28 June 2005), 410

Delimitis v. Henninger Braü, C-234/89 [1991] ECR I-935, 29, 31, 36, 347, 348, 362

Deutsche Bahn v. Commission, T-229/94 [1997] ECR II-1689; [1999] ECR I-2387, 173

Distillers v. Commission [1980] ECR 2229, 51

Easyjet Airline Co. Ltd v. Commission, T-177/04 (4 July 2006), 478

Echirolles Distribution SA v. Association du Dauphiné and Others C-9/99 [2000] ECR I-8207, 104

ENS v. Commission, T-374/94, 375/94 & 388/94 [1998] ECR II-3141, 233

Entreprenøforeningens Affalds/Miljøsektion (FFAD) v. Københavns Kommune, C-209/98 [2000] ECR I-3743, 489

Europemballage Corp. and Continental Car Co. Inc. v. Commission, Case 6/72 [1972] ECR 215, 138, 160, 192, 247

Federación Española de Empresas de Tecnologia Sanitaria (FENIN) v. Commission, C-205/03 (11 July 2006), 486

Fédération Française des Sociétés d'Assurance and Others v. Ministère de l'Agriculture et de la Pêche, C-244/94 [1995] ECR I-4013, 487

Ford Werke AG v. Commission, Cases 25 & 26/84 [1985] ECR 2757, 42

France v. Commission, C-202/88 [1991] ECR I-1223, 201, 211, 446, 458

France v. Commission, C-381/93 [1994] ECR I-5145, 201

France v. Commission, C-159/94 [1997] ECR I-5815, 461

France v. Commission (Kali & Saltz), C-68/94 & 30/95 [1998] ECR I-1375, 249, 252, 296, 311, 312, 314, 318, 320, 323

Franzén, C-189/95 [1997] ECR I-5909, 444

Gencor v. Commission, T-102/96 [1999] ECR II-753, 251, 252, 311, 318

General Electric v. Commission, T-210/01 (14 December 2005), 266

General Motors v. Commission, C-551/03P (6 April 2006), 155

General Motors Continental NV v. Commission, Case 26/75 [1975] ECR 1367, 199

General Motors Nederland and Opel Nederland v. Commission, C-551/03 (25 October 2005), 328

Germany v. Commission, T-328/03, judgment of 2 May 2006, 37–9

Germany v. Parliament and Council (Tobacco Advertising), C-376/98 [2000] ECR I-8419, 445

Gøttrup-Klim e.a. Grovvareforeninger v. Dansk Landbrugs Grovvareselskab AmbA [1994] ECR I-5641, 34, 35, 373

Groupement d'achat Edouard Leclerc v. Commission, T-19/92 [1996] ECR II-1851, 150, 370

Guérin Automobiles v. Commission, C-282/95P [1997] ECR I-503, 424

Hercules v. Commission, T-7/89 [1991] ECR II-1711, 327

Herlitz v. Commission, T-66/92, 41

Hilti AG v. Commission, T-30/89 [1991] ECR II-1439, 145, 210–11

Hoffmann La Roche v. Commission, Case 85/76 [1979] ECR 461, 127, 135, 144, 147, 171, 183, 184, 185, 187, 191, 192, 207, 212, 341, 371, 372

Höfner and Elser v. Macrotron, C-41/90 [1991] ECR I-1979, 449, 489

Hugin Kassaregister AB and Hugin Cash Registers Ltd v. Commission, Case 22/78 [1979] ECR 1869, 148–9

Hüls AG v. Commission, C-199/92 [1999] ECR I-4287, 326

ICI v. Commission, [1995] ECR II-1846, 183

ICI v. Commission (Dyestuffs), Case 48–57/69 [1972] ECR 619, 40, 332

IMS Health GmbH & Co. OHG v. NDC Health GmbH & Co. KG, C-418/01 [2004] ECR I-5039, 227–9, 503

Independent Music Publishers and Labels Association (Impala) v.
    Commission, T-464/04 (13 July 2006), 323
Irish Sugar plc v. Commission, T-228/97 [1999] ECR II-2969, 173, 182, 196,
    208, 341
Istituto Chemioterapica Italiano SpA v. Commission, Cases 6/73 & 7/73 [1974]
    ECR 223, 192, 193, 224, 225, 232
ITT Promedia v. Commission, T-111/96, 431

Javico International and Javico AG v. Yves Saint-Laurent Parfums SA, C-306/
    96 [1998] ECR I-1983, 104
John Deere v. Commission, T-35/92 [1994] ECR II-957, 339
John Deere v. Commission, C-7/95P [1998] ECR I1-1311, 339

Lancôme v. Etos, Case 99/79 [1980] ECR 2511, 358
Langanese Iglo GmbH v. Commission, T-7/93 [1995] ECR II-1533, 363
Leclerc v. Au Blé Vert, Case 229/83 [1985] ECR 1, 104
Limburgse Vinyl Maatschappij NV, T-305/94 [1999] ECR II-9831, 326, 327
Lucuzeau v. SACEM, Cases 110/88 & 242/88 [1989] ECR 2811, 219

Manfredi and Others v. Lloyd Adriatico and Others, C-295-298/04 (13 July
    2006), 426, 427, 429
Manufacture française des pneumatiques Michelin v. Commission, T-203/01
    [2003] ECR II-4071, 204, 205
Masterfoods Ltd v. HB Ice Cream Ltd, C-344/98 [2000] ECR I-11369, 411
Matra Hachette v. Commission [1994] ECR II-595, 47, 97, 119, 156, 368
Meca-Medina and Majcen v. Commission, T-313/02 (30 September 2004);
    C-519/04P (18 July 2006), 114–15
Merci Convenzionali Porto di Genova SpA v. Siderurgica Gabrielli SpA, C-
    179/90 [1991] ECR I-5889, 201, 218, 448, 449, 489
Metro v. Commission (Metro 1), Case 26/76 [1977] ECR 1875, 370
Metro v. Commission (Metro 2), Case 75/84 [1986] ECR 3021, 362, 370
Metro SB-Großmärkte GmbH & Co. KG v. Commission [1977] ECR 1875, 96,
    119, 121
Métropole télévision (M6) and Others v. Commission [2001] ECR II-2459, 30,
    34, 126
Ministère Public v. Asjes, Cases 209–13/84 [1986] ECR 1425, 453, 454

Nederlandse Banden-Industrie Michelin NV v. Commission (Michelin 1),
    Case 322/81 [1983] ECR 3461, 127, 160, 195, 204, 205, 252
Netherlands and Others v. Commission, C-48/90 & C-60/90 [1990] ECR 565, 481
Nungesser v. Commissioner, Case 258/78 [1982] ECR 2015, 51

O2 (Germany) GmbH & Co. OHG v. Commission, T-328/03 (2 May 2006),
    411, 474
Oscar Bronner v. Mediaprint, C-7/97 [1998] ECR I-7791, 225–6, 231, 237, 238,
    241, 469, 478

Parker v. Commission, T-77/92 [1994] ECR II-531, 41

Pavel Pavlov and Others v. Stichting Pensioenfonds Medische Specialisten, C-180–4/98 [2000] ECR I-6451, 486

Philips v. Commission, T-119/02 [2003] ECR II-1433, 303

Piau v. Commission, T-193/02 (26 January 2005), 335

Portugal v. Commission, C-42/01 [2004] ECR I-6079, 304

Portugal v. Commission, C-163/99 [2001] ECR I-2613, 201

Poucet v. AGF and Camulrac and Pistre v. Cancava, C-159/91 & C-160/91 [1993] ECR I-637, 487

Procureur de la République and Others v. Bruno Giry and Guerlain and Others, Cases 253/78 & 1–3/79 [1980] ECR 2327, 398

Reisebüro Broede v. Gerd Sandker, C-3/95 [1996] ECR I-6511, 112

Remia BV and Others v. Commission [1985] ECR 2545, 33, 96

Rhône Poulenc v. Commission, T-1/89 [1991] ECR II-867, 326

RTE and ITP v. Commission (Magill), C-241/91P & 242/91P [1995] ECR I-743, 227–9, 231, 239

RTT v. GB-INNO-BM SA, C-18/88 [1991] ECR I-5941, 450, 451, 457, 464

SA Binon & Cie v. SA Agence et Messageries de la Presse, Case 243/83 [1985] ECR 2015, 369, 370

SA Musique Diffusion Française [1983] ECR 1825, 40

Sandoz v. Commission, C-277/87 [1990] ECR I-45, 42

Sarrió v. Commission, C-291/98P [2000] ECR I-9991, 329

Scandinavian Airlines System v. Commission, T-241/01 (13 July 2005), 39

SNCF and BR v. Commission, T-79-80/95 [1996] ECR II-1491, 233

Société Technique Minière v. Maschinenbau Ulm GmbH, Case 56/65 [1966] ECR 235, 36, 38, 104, 357, 361

Solvay SA v. Commission [1995] ECR II-1821, 183

Spain and Others v. Commission, C-281/90 & C-289/90 [1992] ECR I-5833, 458

Suiker Unie v. Commission, Cases 40–8, 50, 54–6, 111, 113, 114/73 [1975] ECR 1663; BPB [1993] ECR II-389, 183, 196, 326, 330, 331, 334

Syfait and Others v. Glaxosmithkline AEVE, C-53/03 (28 October 2004), 203

Tate & Lyle and Others v. Commission, T-202/98, T-204/98 & T-207/98 [2001] ECR II-2035, 329

Tetra Laval v. Commission, T-5/02 [2002] ECR II-4381, 160, 186, 215, 278–80

Tetra Pak v. Commission, T-83/91 [1994] ECR II-755, 191–2, 210–11

Tetra Pak v. Commission (Tetra Pak 2), C-333/94P [1996] ECR I-5951, 174, 192–5

Tetra Pak Rausing SA v. Commission, T-51/89 [1991] ECR II-309, 177

Thyssen Stahl v. Commission, T-141/94 [1999] ECR II-347, 326

Union royale belge des sociétés de football association ASBL v. Bosman, C-415/93 [1995] ECR 4921, 36, 107

United Brands Co. v. Commission, Case 27/76 [1978] ECR 207, 127, 128–9, 130, 135–6, 137–8, 140, 143, 147, 149, 150, 182, 196, 197, 201, 202, 203, 209, 219, 223, 241

UPS Europe SA v. Commission, T-127/98 [1999] ECR II-2633, 481

UPS Europe SA v. Commission, T-175/99 [2002] ECR II-1915, 194, 483

VAG-Händlerbeirat eV v. SYD-Consult, C-41/96 [1997] ECR I-3123, 408

Van den Bergh Foods Ltd v. Commission, T-65/98 [2003] ECR II-4653, 28, 32, 367

Van Landeswyck v. Commission, Cases 209/78 etc. [1980] ECR 3125, 156

VBVB and VBBB v. Commission C-43/82 and 63/82 [1984] ECR 19, 103, 104

Vereniging voor Energie, Milieu en Water and Others v. Directeur van de Dienst uitvoering en toezicht energie, C-17/03 (7 June 2005), 463

Viho Europe v. Commission, C-73/95 [1996] ECR I-5457, 41

Völk v. Vervaecke, Case 5/69 [1969] ECR 295, 154

Volkswagen v. Commission, T-62/98 [2000] ECR II-2707, 40

Volkswagen v. Commission, C-338/00P [2003] ECR I-9189, 40

Volvo v. Veng, Case 238/87 [1988] ECR 6211, 227, 387

Walt Wilhelm v. Bundeskartellamt, Case 14/68 [1969] ECR 1, 395

Wolf v. Meng, C-2/91 [1993] ECR I-5751, 448

Wouters and Others v. Alsgemeine Raad van de Nederlandse Order van Advocaten, C-309/99 [2002] ECR I-1577, 110–12, 113–15, 121, 123, 210

Züchner v. Bayerische Vereinsbank, Case 172/80 [1981] ECR 2021, 332

CANADA

Commissioner of Competition v. Superior Propane Inc. (2003) FC 529, 292

FRANCE

Conseil de la Concurrence, Decision 91-MC-03, 378

Cora Decision, 96–44 Carat, 18 June 1996, Recueil Lamy 698, 379

Court of Appeal of Paris, 23 October 1991, Gazette du Palais 26–28 January 1992, 378

Société Prodim v. Duval, Bulletin des arrêts de la Cour de Cassation 337, 291, 379

UNITED KINGDOM

Atlas Express Ltd v. Kafco (Importers and Distributors) Ltd [1989] QB 833, 126

Crehan v. Inntrepreneur [2004] EWCA Civ 637, 427

Donoghue v. Stevenson [1932] AC 562, 80

East v. Maurer [1991] 1 WLR 461, 33

Gorris v. Scott (1874) LR 9 Exch 125, 425

Inntrepreneur v. Crehan [2003] EWHC 1510 (Ch), 427
Inntrepreneur v. Crehan [2006] UKHL 38, 427

Mitchel v. Reynolds 24 ER 347 (1711), 35

UNITED KINGDOM CAT DECISIONS

Association of Convenience Stores v. OFT [2006] CAT 36, 391

ME Burgess, JJ Burgess and SJ Burgess (trading as JJ Burgess & Sons) v. Office
of Fair Trading [2005] 25 (funeral services), 140

Napp Pharmaceutical Holdings Ltd and Subsidiaries v. Director General of
Fair Trading [2002] CAT 1, 219

UNITED STATES

AA Poultry Farm Inc. v. Rose Acre Farm Inc. 881 F 2d 1396 (1989), 180
Advo Inc. v. Philadelphia Newspapers Inc. 51 F 3d 1191 (3d Cir 1995), 179
Alberta Gas Chemicals v. El Du Pont de Nemours 826 F 2d 1235 (3d Cir 1987),
66
Ash Grove Cement Co. v. FTC 577 F 2d 1368 (1978), 61, 66

Berkey Photo Inc. v. Eastman Kodak Co. 603 F 2d 263 (2d Cir 1979), 218
Broadcast Music Inc. v. CBS 441 US 1 (1979), 155
Brooke Group v. Brown & Williamson 509 US 209 (1993), 2, 68, 180, 205,
310, 335
Brown Shoe Company v. US 370 US 294 (1962), 12, 266
Brunswick Corp. v. Pueblo Bowl-O-Mat Inc. 429 US 477 (1977), 67

California v. ARC America 490 US 93 (1989), 433
California Dental Association v. FTC 526 US 756 (1999), 116, 122
California Retail Liquor Dealers Association v. Midcal 445 US 91 (1980), 448
Cargill Inc. v. Mountford of Colorada Inc. 479 US 104 (1986), 67
Chicago Professional Sport Ltd Partnership v. NBA 95 F 3d 953 (7th Cir 1996),
219
Chroma Lighting v. GTE Products Corp. 111 F 3d 653 (9th Cir 1997), 198
Coastal Fuels of Puerto Rico Inc. v. Caribbean Petroleum Corp. 79 F 3d 182
(1st Cir 1996), 135
Concord Boat v. Brunswick 207 F 3d 1039 (8th Cir 2000), 186
Continental TV Inc. v. GTE Sylvania Inc. 433 US 36 (1977), 80, 356
Copperweld Corp. v. Independence Tube Corp. 467 US 752 (1984), 80, 128

Corn Products Co. v. FTC 324 US 726 (1945), 62

Dr Miles Medical Co. v. John D Park & Son 220 US 373 (1911), 355

Eastman Kodak Co. v. Image Technical Services Inc. 504 US 451 (1992), 149, 157, 194

E.I. Du Pont de Nemours v. Federal Trade Commission 729 F 2d 128 (1984), 342

Federal Trade Commission v. H.J. Heinz Co. 246 F 3d 708 (2001), 257–8, 259

Federal Trade Commission v. H.J. Heinz Co. and Milnot Holding Corp. (14 July 2000), 257–8

Federal Trade Commission v. Procter & Gamble Co. 386 US 568 (1967), 281–2

Federal Trade Commission v. Staples 970 F Supp 1066 (DDC 1997), 70–1, 74, 151–2

Hanover Shoe Inc. v. United Shoe Machinery 392 US 481 (1968), 432

Illinois Brick Co. v. Illinois 431 US 720 (1977), 432

Image Technical Services Inc. v. Eastman Kodak Co. 125 F 3d 1195 (9th Cir 1997), 228

Independent Service Organisations Antitrust Litigation, Re, 203 F 3d 1322 (Fed Cir 2001), 228

Matsushita Electric Industrial Co. v. Zenith Radio 475 US 574 (1986), 68, 69–70, 74, 178

Miller Institutform of N. America 830 F 2d 606 (6th Cir 1987), 228

Monsanto v. Spary-Rite Services Corp. 465 US 752 (1984), 77

National Society of Professional Engineers v. US 435 US 679 (1978), 30

New York v. Kraft General Foods Inc. 926 F Supp 321 (SDNY 1995), 78

NYNEX Corp. v. Discon Inc. 525 US 128 (1998), 361

Olympia Equip. Leasing Co. v. Western Union Tel. Co. 797 F 2d 370 (7th Cir 1986), 73

Perma Life Mufflers v. International Parts Corp. 392 US 134 (1968), 430

SCM Corp. v. Xerox Corp. 64 F 3d 1195 (2d Cir 1981), 228

Sony Corporation of America v. Universal City Studios Inc. 464 US 417 (1984), 228

State of New York v. Kraft General Foods Inc. 926 F Supp 321 (1995), 133

State Oil v. Kahn 522 US 3 (1997), 80, 356

Traffic Scan Network Inc. v. Winston 1995 Trade Cas. (CCH) 71,044 (ED LA 1995), 179

US v. Addyston Pipe and Steel Co. 85 F 271 (6th Cir 1897), 35

US v. Aluminium Co. of America 48 F 2d 416 (2d Cir 1945), 217

US v. American Airlines 743 F 2d 1114 (5th Cir 1984), 329
US v. American Tobacco 221 US 106 (1911), 31
US v. AMR Corp. 140 F Supp 2d 1141 (D KS 2001), 73
US v. AMR Corp. 335 F 3d 1109 (10th Cir 2003), 73
US v. Arnold Schwein & Co. 388 US 365 (1967), 35
US v. Baker Hughes Inc. 908 F 2d 981 (DC Cir 1990), 66
US v. Container Corporation of America 393 US 333, 155
US v. EI du Pont de Nemours & Co. 118 F Supp 41 (D DE 1953); affd 351 US
    377 (1956), 134
US v. El Paso Natural Gas Co. 376 US 651 (1964), 282
US v. Griffith 334 US 100 (1948), 194
US v. Microsoft 253 F 3d 34 (DC Cir 2001), 128, 146, 190–1
US v. Oracle Corporation 33 F Supp 2d 1098 (2004), 125, 137, 153, 260–1, 264
US v. Philadelphia National Bank 374 US 321 (1963), 60
US v. Topco Associates Inc. 405 US 596 (1972), 500, 503
US v. Trans-Missouri Freight Association 166 US 290, 319 (1897), 24
US v. United Shoe Machinery Corp. 110 F Supp 295 (1953), 61, 78
US v. Von's Grocery Co. 384 US 270 (1966), 66
Utah Pie 386 US 685 (1967), 62–3, 68, 74

Verizon Communications Inc. v. Law Offices of Curtis V Trink LLP 540 US
    398 (2004), 217, 218, 244, 324, 473–4
Virgin Atlantic Airways v. British Airways 257 F 3d 256 (2001), 168–9
Volvo Trucks North America Inc. v. Reeder-Simco GMC Inc. 546
    US __ (2006), 198

Table of legislation

EC TREATY

Art. 2, 93
Art. 3, 94
Art. 3(1)(g), 2, 170
Art. 4, 1
Art. 6, 91, 93
Art. 10, 447–8
Art. 12, 201
Art. 16, 490, 493
Art. 28, 104
Art. 43, 306
Art. 49, 111–12, 200
Art. 51(1), 453
Art. 56, 305, 306
Art. 80, 234
Art. 81, 25–9, 45–6, 47, 80, 90–4, 97–9, 101–2, 104–5, 108, 116, 126, 141, 153–7,
    203, 210, 232, 233, 247, 301, 309, 325, 328, 330, 332, 334, 339–40, 366–72,
    393–4, 406, 420, 425, 426–9, 447–8, 474, 498, 503, 504
Art. 81(1), 25, 29–31, 32, 33, 36–9, 41, 46, 47, 48–50, 80, 114, 293, 359, 395–6,
    409, 411, 502
Art. 81(2), 25
Art. 81(3), 25–6, 29–31, 33, 45, 46–7, 48–50, 80, 89, 90–4, 96–7, 99, 100, 103,
    105, 108, 110, 114, 115, 119–22, 123, 203, 208–9, 212, 293, 340, 361–3,
    368–9, 371–2, 395–6, 404–5, 408, 409, 411–12, 420, 437, 458–9, 498, 502
Art. 82, 79, 127, 128, 141, 143, 156, 157, 160–2, 164, 168, 170–2, 182, 192,
    194–5, 208, 209, 211–15, 218–20, 236–7, 238, 240, 243, 246, 247, 251, 254,
    266, 279, 286, 335–8, 341–2, 371, 376, 393, 406, 420, 425, 426, 431,
    447–51, 463, 469, 480, 482, 483, 501, 502–3, 504
Art. 82(a), 160, 218
Art. 82(b), 160, 218
Art. 82(c), 160, 196, 218
Art. 82(d), 160

Art. 85, 411
Art. 86, 444–5, 457–8
Art. 86(1), 201, 444, 445, 448–51, 453
Art. 86(2), 210, 444, 445, 488, 489, 490–1
Art. 86(3), 200, 201, 445, 446, 452, 453, 456, 457, 461
Art. 87, 490
Art. 88, 490
Art. 95, 445, 457–8, 494
Art. 127, 96
Art. 127(2), 91
Art. 139, 97
Art. 151, 102
Art. 151(4), 91, 102, 104
Art. 152(1), 91
Art. 153, 99
Art. 153(2), 91
Art. 157(3), 91, 94
Art. 159, 91
Art. 174(3), 93
Art. 226, 306
Art. 251, 446
Art. 295, 444
Art. 296, 486

REGULATIONS

17/62, First Regulation implementing Articles 81 and 82 of the
    Treaty, OJ Special Edn 1962, 204/62, 21, 29, 52, 154, 395, 396,
    438, 480
  Art. 4, 29, 357
  Art. 9, 29
41/62 Exempting Transport from the Application of Council Regulation
    No. 17 [1962] OJ L124/2751, 453
1967/67 On the Application of Article 85(3) of the EC Treaty to Categories of
    Exclusive Distribution Agreements [1967] OJ L84/67, 398
123/85 On the Application of Article 85(3) to Certain Categories of Motor
    Vehicle Distribution and Servicing Agreements [1985] OJ L15/16, 384
4064/89, Merger Regulation [1989] OJ L395/1, 8, 247–9
  Art. 2, 6
  Art. 2(1)(b), 8
  Art. 2(3), 249, 311
2408/92 On Access for Community Air Carriers to intra-Community Air
    Routes [1992] OJ L240/8, 455

Art. 3, 455
Art. 8, 455
2409/92 On Fares and Rates for Air Services [1992] OJ L240/15, 455
95/93 On Common Rules for the Allocation of Slots at Community Airports
    [1993] OJ L14/6
Art. 4, 464
Art. 10(3), 455
Art. 10(7), 455
3089/93 On a Code of Conduct for Computerised Reservation Systems [1993]
    OJ L278/1
Recital 1, 235
Art. 3(2), 234–5
Art. 8(1), 236
1475/95 On the Application of Article 85(3) to Certain Categories of Motor
    Vehicle Distribution and Servicing Agreements
Recital 4, 384
1103/97 On Certain Provisions relating to the Introduction of the Euro [1997]
    OJ L162/1, 301
232/99 On a Code of Conduct for Computer Reservation Systems [1999] OJ
    L40/1, 234
1216/99 Amending Regulation 17/62 [1999] OJ L141/5, 21
2790/99 On the Application of Article 81(3) of the Treaty to Categories of
    Vertical Agreements and Concerted Practices [1999] OJ L336/21
Art. 2(1), 347
Art. 2(5), 384
Art. 3, 359
Art. 4, 355, 359, 360–1
Art. 4(b), 365
Art. 4(c), 365
Art. 5, 359, 361
Art. 6, 361, 430
Art. 7, 361
Art. 8(1), 362
2659/2000 On the Application of Article 81(3) of the Treaty to Categories of
    Research and Development Agreements [2000] OJ L304/7
Art. 4, 154
2887/2000 On Unbundled Access to the Local Loop [2000]
    OJ L336/4, 240
Recital 1, 219
Recital 3, 237
Art. 1, 237
Art. 3(3), 219
Art. 4(1), 219
Art. 4(4), 219

1400/2002 On the Application of Article 8(3) of the Treaty to Categories of
    Vertical Agreements and Concerted Practices in the Motor Vehicle
    Sector, 385
  Recital 2, 385
  Recital 9, 388
  Recital 11, 388
  Recital 14, 386
  Recital 15, 386
  Art. 1(b), 386
  Art. 3(1), 386
  Art. 3(4), 388
  Art. 3(5), 388
  Art. 3(6), 388
  Art. 4(1)(b)(i), 386
  Art. 4(1)(c), 389
  Art. 4(1)(g), 386
  Art. 4(1)(h), 387
  Art. 4(2), 387
  Art. 5(1)(a), 386
  Art. 5(1)(c), 386
  Art. 5(2)(b), 386
1/2003 On the Implementation of the Rules of Competition in Articles
    81 and 82 of the Treaty (Modernisation Regulation) [2003] OJ L1/
    1, 21, 47, 52, 119, 156, 213, 334, 366, 393–5, 404–9, 439, 471,
    498, 504
  Recital 7, 424, 436
  Recital 9, 407
  Recital 12, 336
  Recital 22, 412
  Recital 38, 413
  Art. 1(2), 394
  Art. 2, 46, 366
  Art. 3, 394, 406
  Art. 3(2), 407
  Art. 3(3), 407, 422
  Art. 6, 394, 424
  Art. 7, 336
  Art. 9, 412, 413, 420, 437, 498
  Art. 10, 413, 420
  Art. 11(2), 416
  Art. 11(3), 416
  Art. 11(4), 417

Art. 11(5), 417
Art. 11(6), 417
Art. 12, 417
Art. 14(7), 418
Art. 15, 438
Art. 16, 420
Art. 16(2), 417
Art. 17, 343
Art. 23(2), 410
Art. 35, 414
Art. 35(1), 420
358/2003 On the Application of Article 81(3) of the Treaty to Certain
    Categories of Agreements, Decisions and Concerted Pratices in the
    Insurance Sector [2003] OJ L53/8, 102
Recital 14, 102
Recital 15, 102
Art. 6(1)(e), 102
139/2004 On the Control of Concentrations between Undertakings (ECMR)
    [2004] OJ L24/1, 266–8, 300–7, 393
Recital 4, 292
Recital 14, 304
Recital 23, 292
Recital 25, 259, 312
Recital 26, 250
Recital 29, 292
Art. 1(2), 301
Art. 1(3), 301
Art. 1(4), 301
Art. 2(1)(b), 293
Art. 2(3), 250
Art. 3, 246
Art. 4(4), 302
Art. 4(5), 302
Art. 6, 249
Art. 7(1), 248
Art. 8, 249
Art. 9, 303, 304
Art. 9(7), 140
Art. 10(1), 249
Art. 18, 249
Art. 21, 300, 305
Art. 21(4), 143, 304
Art. 22, 302

DIRECTIVES

83/416 Concerning the Authorisation of Scheduled Inter-Regional Air Services for the Transport of Passengers, Mail and Cargo between Member States [1983] OJ L237/19, 453

87/601 On Fares for Scheduled Air Services between Member States [1987] OJ L374/12, 455

87/602 On the Sharing of Passenger Capacity between Air Carriers on Scheduled Air Services between Member States and on Access to Scheduled Air Services Routes [1987] OJ L374/12, 455

88/301 On Competition in the Markets in Telecommunications Terminal Equipment [1988] OJ L131/73, 456

    Recital 1, 457

    Recital 5, 457

    Recital 13, 457

    Recital 14, 457

    Art. 2, 457

90/388 On Competition in the Markets for Telecommunication Services [1990] OJ L192/10, 456

    Art. 2, 457

91/440 On the Development of the Community's Railways [1991] OJ L237/25, 173

92/53 On the Approximation of the Laws of the Member States relating to the Type-approval of Motor Vehicles and their Traders [1992] OJ L225/1, 199

94/62 On Packaging and Packaging Waste [1994] OJ L365/5, 92

94/96 Satellite Directive [1994] OJ L268/15, 456

95/96 Amending Directive 90/388 with regard to Cable TV [1995] OJ L256/49, 459

96/2 Mobile Directive [1996] L20/59, 456

96/19 Full Competition Directive [1996] OJ L74/13, 456

96/92 Concerning Common Rules for the Internal Market in Electricity [1987] OJ L27/20, 460

96/97 On Access to the Ground Handling Market at Community Airports [1996] OJ L272/36, 235–6

    Art. 1, 236

    Art. 4, 236

    Art. 6, 236

    Art. 6(1), 200

    Art. 7, 236

    Art. 9, 236

    Art. 20, 236

    Art. 21, 236

97/67 On Common Rules for the Development of the Internal Market of
    Community Postal Services and the Improvement of Quality of Service
    [1998] OJ L15/14
  Art. 3, 491
  Art. 7, 493
  Art. 7(1), 493
  Art. 9(4), 493
  Art. 14(2), 481
  Art. 22, 464
99/44 On Certain Aspects of Consumer Goods and Associated Guarantees
    [1999] OJ L171/17
  Art. 6, 101
2002/19 On Access to and Interconnection of Electronic Communication
    Networks and Associated Facilities (Access Directive) [2002] OJ L108/7,
    238, 239, 465
  Art. 4, 468
  Art. 5, 468
  Art. 9, 466
  Art. 10, 466
  Art. 11, 466
  Art. 12, 238, 466, 469
  Art. 12(1), 238, 466
  Art. 12(2), 238
  Art. 13, 466
  Art. 13(1), 221
2002/21 On a Common Regulatory Framework for Electronic
    Communications Networks and Services [2002] OJ L108/33
  Recital 25, 469
  Recital 27, 470
  Art. 3, 464
  Art. 3(4), 472
  Art. 3(5), 472
  Art. 7, 471
  Art. 7(3), 465
  Art. 7(4), 465
  Art. 8(1), 470
  Art. 8(1)(k), 459
  Art. 8(2), 470
  Art. 8(3), 470
  Art. 8(4), 470
  Art. 14(2), 130, 465
  Art. 14(3), 465

Art. 14(4), 465

Art. 15(1), 465

Art. 15(2), 465

Art. 15(3), 465

Art. 16(1), 465

2002/22 On Universal Services and Users' Rights relating to Electronic
    Communications Networks and Services (Universal Services Directive)
    [2002] OJ L108/51

Recital 4, 493

Recital 14, 493

Recital 21, 493

Art. 4, 492

Art. 5, 492

Art. 6, 492

Art. 7, 492

Art. 9, 222–3, 492

Art. 10(2), 492

Art. 11, 492

Art. 13, 493

Art. 17(1), 468

Art. 17(2), 468

Art. 20, 492

Art. 20(4), 492

Art. 21(1), 492

Art. 29(3), 492

Art. 30, 222, 468

Art. 30(2), 222

Annex 1, 492

2002/39 Amending Directive 97/67 with regard to Further Opening
    to Competition of Community Postal Services [2002] OJ
    L176/21, 483

2003/54 Concerning Common Rules for the Internal Market in Electricity
    [2003] OJ L176/37

Art. 3(3), 491

Art. 10(2)(d), 462

Art. 15(1), 462

Art. 15(2)(d), 462

Art. 17(d), 462

Art. 19, 462

Art. 20, 462

Art. 21, 460

NATIONAL LEGISLATION

Canada
Competition Act 1985
  s. 1, 19

Denmark
Competition Act 1990
  Art. 1, 311, 312, 318

France
Code de Commerce
  Art. L420(2), 378
  Art. L420(5), 407

Germany
Act Against Restraints of Competition
  s. 19, 407
  s. 33, 433
  s. 33(4), 435

Ireland
Competition Act 2002, 403

Italy
Law no. 287 (10 October 1990)
  Art. 1(1), 402
  Art. 1(4), 403
Law no. 52 (6 February 1996), 402

United Kingdom
Competition Act 1998
  s. 58A, 435
Contagious Diseases (Animals) Act 1869, 424
Enterprise Act 2002, 343, 422
  s. 58, 126
  s. 134, 343
  s. 134(4)(b), 343
  s. 134(6), 343
Fair Trading Act 1973, 343
  s. 88(2), 380
Monopolies and Restrictive Practices Inquiry and Control Act 1948, 343

United States

Celler–Kefauver Act 1950, 59
Clayton Act 1915, 59
    s. 2(a), 61
    s. 7, 67
Federal Telecommunications Act 1996, 473
Federal Trade Commission Act
    s. 5, 342
Robinson–Patman Act, 61, 62
    s. 13(1), 197–8
    s. 13(b), 205–6
Sherman Act 1890, 35, 128
    s. 1, 31, 168
    s. 2, 61, 67, 128, 168, 172, 175, 213, 473

1

Competition law: policy perspectives

Contents

1. Introduction   *page* 1
2. A case study: the *de Havilland* decision of the European
   Commission   6
   2.1 Politics   8
   2.2 Economics   9
   2.3 Institutions   13
3. The demands of a workable competition policy   15
   3.1 Predictability and a narrow approach to competition law   15
   3.2 Rules and standards   16
4. Conclusion   18

1 Introduction

The European Community's commitment to promoting competitive markets was a significant step when the EEC Treaty was agreed in 1957 because European economies had seen high levels of state control, legal cartels and protectionist policies.[1] Today, the EC's faith in the market is firmly established as the Community's economic policy is 'conducted in accordance with the principle of an open market economy with free competition'.[2]

---

[1] The US applied pressure for the enactment of competition laws in Europe in the post-war period, but there was considerable political reluctance to enforce these laws strictly. See H. Dumez and A. Jeunemaître 'The Convergence of Competition Policies in Europe: Internal Dynamics and External Imposition' in S. Berger and R. Dore (eds.) *National Diversity and Global Capitalism* (Ithaca: Cornell University Press, 1996) pp. 217–24. See also G. Marenco 'The Birth of Modern Competition Law in Europe' in A. von Bogdandy, P. Mavroidis and Y. Mény (eds.) *European Integration and International Coordination: Studies in Transnational Economic Law in Honour of C.-D. Ehlermann* (The Hague: Kluwer, 2002); W. Wells *Antitrust and the Formation of the Postwar World* (New York: Columbia University Press, 2002) chs. 5 and 6.

[2] Article 4 EC.

In a market economy, the consumer, not the state, dictates what goods and services are provided. Consumer demand drives production. Even if consumers are truly sovereign, however, a market economy will not eliminate all inefficiencies: scarcity means that society is unable to satisfy everyone's demand. Accordingly, competition law is not designed as a highly interventionist policy to guarantee the welfare of every segment of the economy, nor is it designed to compel or create incentives for firms to behave to promote economic welfare. Its aim is more modest: to condemn anticompetitive behaviour. In the Community, Article 3(1)(g) EC provides that the EC shall have 'a system ensuring that competition in the internal market is not distorted'. The system put in place by the EC Treaty provides for three principal rules to protect competition, which are addressed to firms: prohibiting firms from entering into agreements restrictive of competition (e.g. a price-fixing cartel); prohibiting dominant firms from harming the competitive process; prohibiting mergers that may harm competition. The rules are, in large part, enforced by the European Commission, with a dedicated Directorate General for Competition in charge of the operational tasks. The Treaty also imposes a number of obligations on Member States to reduce barriers to trade, which complement competition policy by creating a single European market.

It is not possible to go beyond these trite remarks about competition law without saying something controversial. For example, it is hard to provide a definition of 'competition' everyone will agree with, or to obtain consensus about the reasons for having competition law. The controversies over the role of competition law in regulating markets have been expressed in especially colourful language in the United States, with Professor Fox concluding that there is a 'battle for the soul of antitrust'.[3] The battle has been fought vigorously in academic journals but also in the courts. In some leading Supreme Court cases the clashes between plaintiff and defendant have often included eminent economists and law professors representing either side depending on their views of the purposes of competition law.[4] The controversies have been no less poignant in Europe: one author who observed the workings of the European Commission reported that 'fighting over competition policy was . . . endemic'.[5]

In entering this battlefield for normative supremacy, this book takes the following position: it is impossible to identify the 'soul' of competition law; the most that can be done is to show that there are different, equally legitimate

---

[3] E. M. Fox 'The Battle for the Soul of Antitrust' (1987) 75 *California Law Review* 917. (In the US competition law is referred to as antitrust law because the first statutes were designed to dismantle trusts which had been created by large companies as a means to collude to fix prices in industries such as railroads, oil, sugar and whisky.)

[4] See *Brooke Group v. Williamson* 509 US 209 (1993) where two eminent antitrust scholars were pitted against each other: Robert Bork (whose writings endorse the non-interventionist policy associated with the Chicago School) and Philip Areeda (who favoured a more aggressive antitrust policy).

[5] G. Ross *Jacques Delors and European Integration* (Cambridge: Polity Press, 1994) p. 130.

opinions as to what competition law should achieve. Moreover, within each country, the purposes of competition law can change over time, even without an amendment to the legislative texts. This is possible because of the open-textured nature of most antitrust legislation, which allows for considerable variety in interpretation. Understanding competition law thus is not only about dissecting legislative texts and judicial decisions according to settled canons of interpretation, but is also about understanding the particular forces that have influenced the direction of competition policy at particular times.

Professor Bork took a similar view. In his influential book *The Antitrust Paradox*, he opined that '[a]ntitrust policy cannot be made rational until we are able to give a firm answer to one question: What is the point of the law – what are its goals? Everything else follows from the answer we give ... Only when the issue of goals has been settled is it possible to frame a coherent body of substantive rules.'[6] However, in contrast to Bork's certainty about the possibility of answering that question, the position taken here is that while it is true that any specific decision in a competition case requires a prior resolution as to the aims of the law, to date no competition authority has deployed competition law in accordance with *one* unchanging set of aims – the goals of antitrust vary over time; even at the same time, the law can be pursuing different, even mutually contradictory, goals. The best way to understand competition law's evolution and its future is to gauge how differing answers to Bork's questions have arisen and how they have affected the shape of individual decisions and the direction of law.

As a result, before moving to consider the substantive rules, it is important to have an idea of the variety of aims which competition law enforcement might pursue. The body of rules we call 'competition law', and each decision reached, reflects a particular vision of what competition law is designed to do, or a compromise, which reflects the tensions among law makers as to the purposes of a particular rule. Only by understanding from which premises a particular rule or decision is coming can one then subject it to informed review. It is too simplistic to state that a decision is wrong because the person enforcing competition law got the 'economics' wrong when there is no consensus among economists as to what the right economic perspective is. Moreover, a decision might be economically irrational under any standard, but might be supported by political values that are widely respected.[7] Thus, competition law can be best understood, and subsequently criticised, if one

---

[6] R. Bork *The Antitrust Paradox* (New York: Free Press, 1993) p. 50. Along similar lines in Europe, see W. Möschel 'The Goals of Antitrust Revisited' (1991) 147 *Journal of Institutional and Theoretical Economics* 7: 'The decisive element for clarifying these vague legal concepts for application in the real world is the protective purpose which underlies each piece of legislation in this area [i.e. antitrust].'

[7] For example, allowing a merger with a failing firm because, even though the merger will strengthen the monopoly of the acquirer, it is seen as the best option to save as many jobs as possible. See pp. 296–8.

views the rules as a function of a number of considerations that animate its development.

In my view, it is helpful to think about the factors that influence the shape of competition law and the decisions that stem from those rules on the basis of the interaction of three components: a *political* decision about the aims of competition law; an *economic* theory about how markets behave, how and when they fail, and how market failures may be remedied; and the *institution* in charge of enforcing competition law.

When answering the political question, two extreme answers might be offered: either competition law is solely about promoting economic welfare by ensuring that firms behave in such a way as to minimise costs and maximise the benefits that consumers can obtain from the scarce resources that are available (in economic terms, the pursuit of productive, dynamic and allocative efficiency), or competition law can be used to pursue a variety of other public interest goals, for example to maximise economic freedom, preserve employment, promote national champions, facilitate restructuring, protect small firms, safeguard cultural values, conserve the environment, and so on. In between these two extremes of competition law as 'guardian of economic welfare' and as 'instrument of public policy' intermediate positions are possible whereby only a discrete set of public policy goals other than economic welfare are pursued.

In addressing the economic question, two extreme positions can be sketched. At one extreme we find economists who take a structural approach and suggest that the fewer firms there are in a particular industry, the more likely it is that there will be market failures. Thus a monopoly hinders the achievement of most policy goals which one might design for competition law, whilst a market with many buyers and many sellers operates so as to guarantee the welfare of consumers. At the other extreme there are those whose discourse is typically labelled the 'Chicago School', who take a less deterministic line – the structure of the industry is insufficient to predict whether firms are acting to promote the aims of competition law; one has to look at other features of the market to see if there are any pressures that 'discipline' firms. A monopolist in a market where potential entry by others is easy will not raise prices for fear of losing its position of dominance to other competitors, hence even a behemoth like Microsoft may not pose a risk for consumers when there are potential entrants able to punish it should it cease to satisfy consumers' interests. In this way, the market itself often resolves a possible reduction of competition. The former view was popular in the United States in the 1960s and the latter prominent in the 1980s. A structural approach would counsel for more aggressive competition law enforcement than a Chicago School approach, which places greater faith in the self-healing qualities of markets.

Finally, the institutional makeup affects the decisions reached. The most common method for enforcing competition law is through a system of administrative control by an agency (e.g. via the European Commission in the EC, the

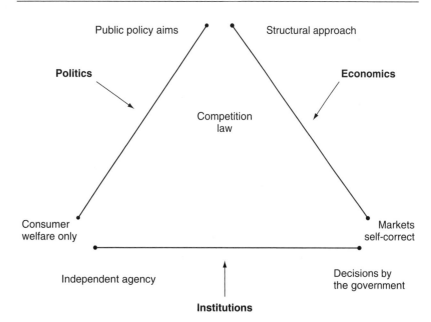

Figure 1.1 Influences on competition law

Office of Fair Trading and the Competition Commission in the UK, the Department of Justice and the Federal Trade Commission in the US). The composition as well as the powers of the competition agencies may be designed to achieve the kinds of goals which competition law seeks to attain – if competition law serves only the goal of consumer welfare then an agency independent of governmental influence is appropriate, but if competition law is also designed to pursue other public policies then an agency which is more accountable to government might be desirable. Conversely, the professional makeup of the institution may shape the economic and political direction of law enforcement. When US agencies hired and integrated economists in the 1960s, the agencies' approach became more economic and less legalistic.[8]

As I hope to show in this book, legislative provisions, or the legal reasoning of a court or a competition authority, the 'rules of competition' if you like, are less important than the three factors mentioned above which affect the shape and direction of the rules.

These three different forces may exert different pressures at different times in the history of competition law enforcement. Moreover, there are alliances: for instance, those who see competition as serving a multiplicity of goals and those who take a structural approach to the way firms behave tend to favour an aggressive competition policy. These alliances are most evident in the debates

---

[8] M. A. Eisner *Antitrust and the Triumph of Economics* (Chapel Hill: University of North Carolina Press, 1991).

in the United States: writings by supporters of the Chicago School indicate their preference for limited competition law intervention only in order to promote allocative efficiency, regardless of distributional concerns.[9] In contrast, those espousing more aggressive interventionism dictated by a view that markets are less than perfect also advocate the pursuit of a wider range of goals, including distributive justice considerations. Similarly, those advocating a minimalist policy scope favour a politically independent competition authority. These alliances should not come as a surprise – the distinction between institutional, economic and political discourses is an artificial one, for the three are closely interrelated.[10] Nevertheless, for analytical purposes, it is helpful to consider each independently.

2 A case study: the *de Havilland* decision of the European Commission

As a way of illustrating the perspective set out thus far, a controversial decision of the European Commission can be scrutinised to illustrate how the resolution of the relevant legal questions can be explained as a function of the three factors mentioned. After a short summary of the facts, we move on to explore how the decision can be mapped onto the threefold analytical structure proposed above.

In *de Havilland*, two companies active in the aerospace industry, Aerospatiale (a French firm) and Alenia (an Italian firm), proposed to acquire jointly the assets of de Havilland (a Canadian division of Boeing).[11] The proposed merger was notified to the European Commission for evaluation. The standard for assessment at the time was set out in Article 2 of the Merger Regulation, whereby a merger is prohibited if it would create a dominant position, and which would be likely to impede effective competition in the market.[12]

The Commission's formal assessment was that the merger should be blocked because it would create a dominant position. The Commission found that the merger would affect the market for regional turbo-propeller aircraft. Aerospatiale and Alenia jointly controlled ATR, which manufactured those aircraft, and both ATR and de Havilland were significant players in the market. After the merger, ATR's position would be strengthened further. Table 1.1, taken from the Commission's decision, shows the market shares of the parties and competitors in the relevant markets, EC-wide and worldwide.

The Commission found that the effect of the merger would be to create a firm with significant market power and with market shares considerably higher

---

[9] Bork *Antitrust Paradox*.

[10] See generally B. Clark *Political Economy: A Comparative Approach* 2nd edn (Westport: Praeger, 1998) chs. 1 and 7.

[11] Case M.53 *Aerospatiale–Alenia/de Havilland* [1991] OJ L334/42.

[12] Regulation 4064/89 on the Control of Concentrations between Undertakings [1989] OJ L257/13.

Table 1.1 Markets subdivided by seating capacity of turbo-propeller aircraft

20 to 39 seats		40 to 50 seats		60 seats plus		Overall 20 to 70 seats	
World	EC	World	EC	World	EC	World	EC
Embraer 36	Embraer 44	ATR 42	ATR 50	ATR 82	ATR 79	ATR 29	ATR 49
Saab 31	Saab 29	DHC 17	DHC 21	BAe 18	BAe 21	DHC 21	DHC 16
DHC 20	DHC 21	Fokker 19	Fokker 22			Saab 18	Fokker 12
Dornier 9	BAe 5	Saab 16	Casa 6			Embraer 13	BAe 8
BAe 5	Dornier 1	Casa 6	Saab 1			Fokker 9	Embraer 6
						BAe 4	Saab 5
						Casa 3	Casa 3
						Dornier 3	Dornier 1

Figures express market share in percentages; DHC = de Havilland; BAe = British Aerospace.

than those of its closest competitors (EC-wide the merged entity would have an overall market share of 65 per cent). Moreover, the new firm would be able to sell the whole range of turbo-propeller aircraft. Its dominance would lead it to behave against the interests of competitors, customers and consumers. Competition would break down – it would be the merged firm, not consumers, making the economic decisions of what and how much to produce – and this would lead to an increase in prices and a reduction in output. As a result of the anticompetitive effects that would ensue with the merger, the Commission prohibited it. However, if we go beyond this superficial review and dissect the case on the basis of the political, economic and institutional factors that underpin this decision, a richer subtext emerges.

2.1 Politics

This decision and its aftermath illustrate that there are divisions as to the purposes of competition law: the Commissioner in charge for competition at the time (Sir Leon (now Lord) Brittan) had been a key player in the implementation of the Merger Regulation and was adamant that the aim of competition law was to safeguard economic welfare and that in this case the resulting dominant firm would harm the interest of consumers. However, other Commissioners took a very different view. Martin Bangemann, Commissioner for industrial policy, was in favour of the merger, noting how it would strengthen European industry, which was challenged by strong foreign firms. In his view, the public interest lay in applying competition law to ensure the competitiveness of industry.[13] The decision on whether to block the merger was resolved by a vote of the College of Commissioners: a majority of nine (out of seventeen) voted to block the merger, although the two French members of the Commission abstained. The view that competition law was not to be used as an instrument of industrial policy was thus resolved in this case by the narrowest of margins.[14]

The political arguments in favour of allowing the merger for industrial policy reasons are not, as a matter of law, as far-fetched as one might think. Whilst the Merger Regulation is based upon considerations of economic welfare, the possibility of mergers being cleared on other grounds is not completely left out: it would have been possible for the Commission to reach a decision which allowed the merger based on the 'technical and economic progress' (Article 2(1)(b) of the Merger Regulation) which would ensue by having a strong European industry in this key sector of the economy, which would safeguard employment and strengthen the competitiveness of European industry. Moreover, the political argument in favour of using competition law

[13] 'The Captain of Industry – Martin Bangemann' *The Economist* 21 March 1992.
[14] Ross *Jacques Delors* p. 178.

to achieve goals other than efficiency could not be said to have been lost, given the narrow margins by which this merger was blocked.

The aftermath of this decision was a spate of accusations, especially by French politicians, as the merger would have benefited the French-based Aerospatiale. The most extreme position was probably that of Michel Rocard, a former Prime Minister, who called the decision a 'crime against Europe'.[15] More moderately, the French foreign minister said that the Commission should be using the Merger Regulation to create European firms strong enough to withstand the forces of globalisation and increased competition worldwide, a view shared by others around him. *Le Monde* noted the 'paradox of competition' whereby the creation of the single market and the implementation of a strong competition policy were not accompanied by an industrial policy which it saw as a necessary complement if European industry is to have sufficient 'muscle' to participate on the world stage.[16]

The controversies at the stage of decision-making, and the debates that appeared in the press in the aftermath of the decision, demonstrate that the battle for the soul of antitrust is alive and well in Europe, and that decisions in competition cases depend upon where on the political spectrum those in charge of the decision are located. It may be worth noting that Karel van Miert, who succeeded Lord Brittan as Commissioner for competition, was, at the time of *de Havilland*, Commissioner for transport, and he voted in favour of allowing the merger to go ahead.[17] One can only guess how differently the case might have been decided under his leadership.[18] *The Economist*'s suggestion that 'in the end, all competition decisions are subject to political debate'[19] is accurate: the political decision that competition law should not be used as a means of promoting European champions was the necessary prerequisite for the final decision to block the merger upon a narrow interpretation of the legislative text.

2.2 Economics

The economic analysis to gauge the anticompetitive risks of a merger requires three steps: (1) the identification of the relevant markets affected by the merger; (2) a determination of whether the merged firm would hold a dominant position in those markets; (3) a determination that dominance would

---

[15] *Le Monde* 11 October 1991, p. 26.   [16] *Le Monde* 9 October 1991.
[17] *Le Monde* 3 October 1991, p. 29.
[18] Many note that his leadership was less dogmatic than that of Brittan, and that he sought to apply competition policy with reference to the wider policies of the EC. L. McGowan 'Safeguarding the Economic Constitution: The Commission and Competition Policy' in N. Nugent (ed.) *At the Heart of the Union – Studies of the European Commission* 2nd edn (Basingstoke: Macmillan, 2000).
[19] 'War by Competition Policy: The de Havilland Row is just a Skirmish in the Battle between Economic Ideologies' *The Economist* 12 October 1991.

restrict competition. In reviewing these findings, not every economist was convinced by the Commission's analysis.

2.2.1 The relevant market

The most questionable part of the Commission's decision is its identification of the relevant market as that for turbo-propeller aircraft, indicating that jet-powered craft were in a separate product market. Evidence since the merger suggests that this was mistaken – a number of manufacturers began to develop smaller jet-propelled aircraft, which have quickly taken the place of turbo-propelled aircraft which have now been marginalised in Europe.[20] Moreover, already at the time the decision was reached, Lufthansa had bought fifty jets to compete on routes against turbo-propelled aircraft.[21] If one were to include jet aircraft in the relevant product market, then the high market shares upon which the decision on dominance was reached would be reduced significantly. According to Professor Utton, there was a methodological flaw in the Commission's approach to market definition. In his view, the Commission placed too much reliance on the views of customers and competitors and on the time required by manufacturers to switch from one range of aircraft to another. He thought that the real question that should have been asked was whether, if ATR/de Havilland were to raise prices for their aircraft, purchasers would switch to other (for example, larger) aeroplanes. If so, he estimated that the new firm would have held a market share of only 20 per cent and the merger would not have raised any competition concerns.[22]

2.2.2 Dominance

Having narrowed the market to one where de Havilland and ATR held high market shares, the Commission considered whether the merger would create a dominant position. A number of questions have been raised as to whether this would occur. First, some have criticised the decision for being too sceptical about the ability of other firms to respond to the new market conditions and adopting a static approach to the question of dominance. In their view, other manufacturers could pose a threat to ATR/de Havilland's position, limiting the possibility for it to exploit its increase in market share.[23] Second, criticism has

---

[20] P. D. Camesasca *European Merger Control: Getting the Efficiencies Right* (Antwerp: Intersentia, 2000) pp. 343–4.

[21] *The Financial Times* 7 October 1991, p. 2. Thus the argument that jet aircraft were in a different product market because they were considerably more expensive than turbo-propelled craft is irrelevant, for the real question is whether any increase in the price of turboprops would lead to substitution into the market for jets. See M. Motta *Competition Policy* (Cambridge: Cambridge University Press, 2004) pp. 109–10.

[22] M. A. Utton *Market Dominance and Antitrust Policy* (Cheltenham: Edward Elgar, 1995) p. 202.

[23] E. M. Fox 'Merger Control in the EEC: Towards a European Merger Jurisprudence' 1991 *Fordham Corporate Law Institute* 709, 738 (Hawk ed. 1992).

also been levelled at the Commission's views on potential competition – manufacturers from developing countries were played down; moreover, the fact that jet manufacturers were planning to design smaller jets to compete with turbo-propeller aircraft suggested a much more competitive market than the Commission described.[24] Consequently, even if one were to agree with the Commission's market definition, ATR/de Havilland's high market shares might not have given it much power to raise prices as other market players would have responded by lowering their prices and increasing their market share, at ATR/de Havilland's expense.

2.2.3 Significantly impeding competition

Finally, some of the consequences of this merger appeared positive, rather than negative. For instance, the Commission found that 'the higher market share could give ATR more flexibility to compete on price (including financing) than its smaller competitors. ATR would be able to react with more flexibility to initiatives of competitors in the market place.'[25] This suggests that the merged firm would be able to offer more competitive deals to its customers, and whilst this would be at the expense of competitors, it is not necessarily the case that competition would suffer as a result. On the contrary, lower prices would increase consumer welfare. Similarly, the fact that ATR was able to supply the entire range of commuter aircraft an airline might require would reduce costs to purchasers. As the Commission noted, '[f]rom the demand side, airlines derive cost advantages from buying different types from the same seller'.[26] Consequently, one might be tempted to conclude that the Commission was concerned about the merged entity's dominance because that position threatened the viability of competitors (a distributive goal) rather than the protection of economic welfare.

Some would go further and argue that the Commission used the efficiencies resulting from the merger as evidence that it should be blocked and suggest that this result is problematic because economic welfare would be enhanced by the transaction.[27] Following this perspective, one might suggest that the Commission in this case was pursuing an industrial policy, although not the type that Mr Bangemann had in mind: while it was not facilitating the creation of a strong European firm, the Commission was safeguarding the existence of other European firms which would be threatened by the bigger, more efficient firm resulting from the merger. In fact the Commission pointed out that British Aerospace and Fokker (two European firms) might be forced out of the market if the merger were cleared.[28] This might explain why the minority of

---

[24] *The Economist* 12 October 1991; *Financial Times* 7 October 1991, p. 23; *Le Monde* 4 October 1991, p. 4.

[25] *Aerospatiale–Alenia/de Havilland* [1991] OJ L334/42 para. 30.   [26] Ibid. para. 32.

[27] F. Jenny 'EEC Merger Control: Economies as an Antitrust Defense or an Antitrust Attack?' 1992 *Fordham Corporate Law Institute* 591, 603 (Hawk ed. 1993).

[28] *Aerospatiale–Alenia/de Havilland* [1991] OJ L334/42 para. 69.

the Advisory Committee on Concentrations concluded that the Commission's decision protected 'competitors, not competition',[29] a phrase which one comes across often in discussions about controversial competition cases.[30] On the other hand, some economists considered that the elimination of competitors was the most plausible reason for blocking the merger, for this would have foreclosed market access and consolidated ATR/de Havilland's position.[31] In the long run, ATR/de Havilland would have become the most powerful firm and would then have been able to distort competition.

More generally, some have suggested an inconsistency in the decisions of the Commission – for example, in another decision that year, *Aerospatiale/MBB*, the merged entity had a 50 per cent market share in civil helicopters but the merger was allowed without an in-depth investigation, the Commission taking an unusually positive view of the potential competition from United States manufacturers.[32] This contrasts with the pessimism shown towards potential competitors in *de Havilland*. Moreover, the *Aerospatiale/MBB* merger would cause some damage to two other European helicopter manufacturers (Augusta and Westland) but the impact of the merger on them was not considered, which contrasts with the Commission's concerns over Fokker and BAe in *de Havilland*. One author has even suggested that the *Aerospatiale/MBB* merger might have been allowed for industrial policy reasons (promoting a Euro-champion), which would cast into doubt the public commitment to reject industrial policy in *de Havilland*.[33]

These widely diverging opinions in all aspects of the competitive assessment of the merger illustrate how divided economists are in analysing markets and in predicting the potential impact of developments in the market. Had a different economic methodology been adopted, a very different decision would have been reached. It also shows how economics can be 'massaged' to suit a particular political viewpoint.

---

[29] [1991] OJ C314/7.

[30] I believe that the origin of this phrase is the Supreme Court judgment in *Brown Shoe Co. v. US* 370 US 294 (1962), where we find these obiter dicta by Chief Justice Warren: 'Taken as a whole, the legislative history illuminates congressional concern with the protection of *competition*, not *competitors*, and its desire to restrain mergers only to the extent that such combinations may tend to lessen competition' (at 320 (my emphasis)). However, later in his opinion, he qualified this statement: 'But we cannot fail to recognize Congress' desire to promote competition through the protection of viable, small, locally owned businesses. Congress appreciated that occasional higher costs and prices might result from the maintenance of fragmented industries and markets. It resolved these competing considerations in favor of decentralization. We must give effect to that decision' (at 344). The upshot is that the Supreme Court ended up protecting competition, not competitors.

[31] See P. Klemperer and A. J. Padilla 'Do Firms' Product Lines Include Too Many Varieties?' (1997) 28 *Rand Journal of Economics* 472.

[32] [1991] OJ C59/13.

[33] M. J. Reynolds 'The First Year of Enforcement under the EEC Merger Control Regulation: A Private View' 1991 *Fordham Corporate Law Institute* 649, 691 (Hawk ed. 1992).

2.3 Institutions

Lastly, the institutional makeup was crucial to the decision. Whilst the factual assessment of the merger was in the hands of the Commission's Merger Task Force, the final decision was not in the hands of the Directorate General for Competition (that is, it was not the decision of a specialised, independent agency), but in those of the College of Commissioners (composed of twenty Commissioners each with different portfolios representing all Community policies). Lord Brittan's task was not just to construct a persuasive economic and legal assessment, but also to lobby fellow Commissioners to back his position – there is evidence that in the days before the decision he did much to persuade other Commissioners, pointing out that jobs would be lost as a result of the merger (note that this was not lobbying in favour of the economic case against the merger). In contrast, the Commissioners in favour of the merger were not as active in lobbying for support, and this may have been the decisive reason why the merger was blocked.[34] Moreover, whilst Commissioners are not supposed to be swayed by domestic politics, it is no coincidence that the two Italian Commissioners voted in favour of the merger (which would have aided an Italian firm), while the French (whose national champion also had something to gain) abstained. The institutional makeup has two effects: first, the decision by a group of Commissioners each with a potentially conflicting agenda (because of their personal training, or because of the Commission policy they represent) means that there is considerable internal debate and division about the aims of competition law; second, national interests can affect the decisions of Commissioners, in spite of their supposed political independence.

This partly politicised institutional makeup is what made the decision an important one to establish the Commission's credibility as a regulator. This was the first merger the Commission blocked; in so doing it had to prove to the world that the regime set out to review mergers was impartial, and that political decisions to safeguard domestic interests were not going to threaten the decision-making process. Importantly, the Commission's 'credibility' seems to be appraised in the light of a particular type of decision: the view taken by Lord Brittan and other commentators is that EC merger law can only be credible if it espouses a narrow definition of the aims of competition law, concentrating on economic welfare. The fact that this approach is not dissimilar from that of the United States, Germany and the United Kingdom suggests that it is to these audiences that the Commission was trying to prove its credibility. More generally, it has been argued that one form of accountability for a competition authority's output is its reputation, which is measured by the approval that its decisions receive from the global legal and economic fraternity, which is composed of other competition authorities as well as expert

---

[34] Ross *Jacques Delors* p. 178.

groups, for instance the International Competition Network and the OECD's Joint Group on Trade and Competition which reviews national competition regimes on a regular basis. These constituencies favour a non-politicised, economics-based approach to competition law.[35]

In spite of what might have appeared to be a victory for the Commission's credibility and a strengthening of its position as a legitimate regulator, the aftermath of the decision led to a number of proposals, mostly from Germany, that competition cases were ill-suited for resolution within a political organ such as the Commission and were better resolved within the framework of an independent 'cartel office' which would guarantee decisions based solely on the 'right' competition criteria.[36] According to this view, the risks of an industrial policy decision might have been avoided in *de Havilland* but the narrowness of the Commission's victory led to fears that political decisions might occur in the future. In stark contrast, the European Parliament fielded proposals for amending the Merger Regulation to allow the Commission to use industrial policy as a basis for allowing mergers.[37] While neither camp had any success, it is clear that the institutional makeup of a competition authority has an impact on the decisions reached: while in *de Havilland* the supporters of a narrow approach to competition law were in a majority, some years later, in *Mannesmann/Vallourec/Ilva*, Karel van Miert (at this time the Commissioner for competition) objected to the merger but he was overruled by a narrow majority of the College of Commissioners for what seemed to many to be industrial policy reasons.[38] As *The Economist* noted: 'the creation of a single European market has turned the Commission itself into a political battle-ground, and many of the fiercest battles have been over competition policy'.[39] And more examples may be marshalled to illustrate this observation.[40]

In conclusion, this case study suggests that the open-ended nature of competition policy, the differing political and economic perspectives through which a market can be analysed, plus the institutional makeup of the decision-making authority all play a role in shaping the final outcome of a decision. The 'law' applied in *de Havilland* was shaped by a specific set of circumstances: a Commission with strong leadership by the competition Commissioner at the time, convinced that as a matter of politics, the aim of merger law is the protection of consumer welfare, not the protection of competitors; and an economic analysis relying on a structural and static economic assessment of

---

[35] See I. Maher 'The Rule of Law and Agency: The Case of Competition Policy' IEP WP 06/01 (available at www.chathamhouse.org.uk).

[36] S. Wilks and L. McGowan 'Disarming the Commission: The Debate over a European Cartel Office' (1995) 32 *Journal of Common Market Studies* 259.

[37] Resolution on de Havilland [1991] OJ C280/140.

[38] *Financial Times* 26 and 27 January 1994, noting that the parties sought to create a firm strong enough to compete against rivals in Japan and Eastern Europe.

[39] *The Economist* 14 March 1992.

[40] See, for example, Ross's explanation of why the Commission did not act to block the mergers relating to the *Fiat-Alcatel/CGE* deal, *Jacques Delors* pp. 132–5.

markets to analyse mergers. Change any one of these three variables, and a different decision can be obtained and for different reasons: a different leadership and industrial policy might have led to the merger being cleared in that it promoted a European champion; a different type of economic analysis might have led to the merger being cleared because it would not create a monopoly and would not thereby restrict competition!

Granted, *de Havilland* was a particularly controversial case because the economics of the market were in dispute, the amount of public support for the merger in some quarters was significant, and the Commission saw it as a test case for the Merger Regulation. However, this does not mean that the analysis suggested above does not apply to more 'usual' competition decisions – every competition case is based upon a particular political and economic vision, which, by reaffirming previous cases, confirms the maintenance of a specific perspective.

3 The demands of a workable competition policy

Taken to its extreme, the analytical structure proposed above can lead to the conclusion that competition law is indeterminate and that the exercise of discretion by those in power determines the results. This is not the thesis which is advanced here, because the competition authority enforcing the law is aware that absolute indeterminacy would make for unworkable policy as firms would not know what is lawful and unlawful and such unpredictability would in itself be counterproductive – firms would not try to compete too aggressively, lest their actions be struck down as illegal. Thus the market system (which competition law is supposed to maintain) would break down if the competition rules were too open-ended. A degree of predictability is necessary, and this puts a limit upon the ways in which competition law can be designed. Moreover, unless particular political and economic conceptions of competition law can be translated into laws which allow markets to work, then those ideas, however well intentioned, cannot be accepted, because a well-functioning market is the reason for having competition law. The market places limits as to the kind of competition policy that can be implemented.

However, this should not imply: (i) that because predictability is necessary then the only legitimate goal of competition law is the promotion of economic welfare, so that decisions are consistent because they all have one objective; or (ii) that competition law can be administered only by rules and not by open-ended standards.

3.1 Predictability and a narrow approach to competition law

As we have noted above, there are certain merger cases where the decisions seem to have supported some form of industrial policy. According to Cook and Kerse, this is a weakness in competition law because it: 'betrays the opportunities which exist, albeit exercised in highly unusual circumstances, for drafting a decision to justify a result which might seem desirable for industrial policy or other political reasons. It would, however, be wrong to suggest that this was other than a very exceptional case.'[41] The authors dislike the infiltration of policy and insist that it is an aberration. It might be argued that legal security for parties to mergers is strengthened by a narrower approach to competition issues, which allows the parties to predict with reasonable certainty what the Commission's final decision might be. It also helps them in presenting their case to the Commission. As soon as wider goals are being balanced, the final outcome is unpredictable.

However, what threatens to make competition law unworkable is not the pursuit of a wide range of public policy objectives, but the fact that market participants are unaware of the policies being pursued. The primary concern should not be the presence of policy considerations, but the lack of transparency in the decision-making process. Especially given the strong affirmation in *de Havilland* by the competition Commissioner that industrial policy plays no role in merger cases, to find that other merger decisions might have been affected by industrial policy concerns creates an unworkable legal system. The pursuit of other public policy objectives should not be objectionable *per se*, but the arbitrary and opaque pursuit of such objectives is problematic. At worst, such arbitrariness can result in a system which cannot properly be called a legal system.[42]

3.2 Rules and standards

One route to legal certainty would be to express all competition law in the form of rules. Rules have what has been called formal realisability: a determinate set of facts triggers the application of a law.[43] For example, the rule that a minor is not entitled to vote, or a rule that states that all mergers where the combined market share exceeds 50 per cent shall be blocked, is easily applicable because one fact is needed to trigger the rule. Rules maximise certainty by constraining discretion.

Rules make law workable, but they do so at the expense of over- and under-inclusion: most would think that a politically knowledgeable fifteen-year-old has more of a right to vote than an uninformed thirty-year-old. Similarly, a merger of firms in a competitive market with low entry barriers does not endanger competition even if the combined market share is higher than 50 per cent, while a merger in a highly concentrated market may be problematic even if the combined market share is less than 50 per cent. Thus, while a rule

---

[41] C. J. Cook and C. S. Kerse *EC Merger Control* 3rd edn (London: Sweet & Maxwell, 2000).

[42] I draw here on the account of the attributes which make a legal system possible by L. Fuller *The Morality of Law* rev. edn (New Haven: Yale University Press, 1969) ch. 2.

[43] I draw here on D. Kennedy 'Form and Substance in Private Law Adjudication' (1976) 89 *Harvard Law Review* 1685.

might make the law workable, there may be certain instances where the enforcement of the rule makes the market function poorly. Expressed more formally, if a rule prevents efficient behaviour (and is over-inclusive), this is called a *Type 1* error (or a false positive), while if a rule does not punish inefficient behaviour (and is under-inclusive) it is called a *Type 2* error (or a false negative). Of course a rule can lead to both types of error when applied to different facts, for example the rule that would block mergers only where the joint market share is above 50 per cent: some of those mergers may be beneficial, and some mergers below that market share may cause harm.

As a result, rules are inappropriate legal instruments when an application of the rule frustrates the purpose of the law, by causing either a Type 1 or a Type 2 error. In the context of competition law, this means that rules do not allow the market to develop in the most effective way possible. Accordingly, when rules fail, law is best administered by standards, which require the decision-maker to discover all relevant facts and 'to assess them in terms of the purposes or social values embodied in the standard'.[44] The application of a standard requires a wide-ranging inquiry to determine whether the conduct should be characterised as lawful or unlawful. In a merger case, this calls for an analysis of the market as a whole and a determination of whether the relevant Community interests would be enhanced by allowing or blocking the merger. The advantage of this method of analysis is that the decisions are more accurate; but they do not eliminate the risk of errors because we cannot ever have all the relevant information to do so. However, the risks that arise from this open-ended method of analysis are arbitrariness, opacity and a more costly legal process. Thus, the necessity of standards brings us back to the risk of unworkable competition policy, introducing two types of risk: an economic risk that the cost of applying the more sophisticated standard is greater than the reduction of the likelihood of Type 1 and Type 2 errors which would result by applying a simpler rule, and a political risk that the standard is interpreted differently in different contexts. Imagine, for instance, how much more costly, and uncertain, merger cases would be if the decision hinged upon whether the merger was in the 'public interest' or how controversial (and expensive to administer) we would find an electoral law which stated that only those with sufficient political knowledge can vote. This might suggest that abridged standards should be adopted, whereby rather than attempting to obtain all information about a market in order to make a decision, a judgement call is made based upon a limited set of factors. This reduces the costs of applying a standard while yielding greater accuracy than the application of a blunt rule. In subsequent chapters we will see how the law has devised abridged standards.

This discussion suggests that a workable system of competition law must operate with a mixture of rules and standards, opting for rules whenever the

---

[44] Ibid. See also L. Kaplow 'Rules Versus Standards: An Economic Analysis' (1992) 42 *Duke Law Journal* 557.

error costs can be tolerated, and setting out standards when the cost of implementing the standard is less than the error cost of a rule. One element that can lead to standards that are cheaper to apply and less prey to the whims of the decision-maker will be an express identification of the policies being pursued by the application of the laws. However, a tradeoff must often be made between cheap-to-enforce, rigid rules that risk producing error, and costly-to-enforce standards that can yield more precise results according to the goals of competition law.[45]

One additional reflection on tradeoffs is warranted. A competition authority is aware that in enforcing the law it will make mistakes: under-enforcement (a Type 2 error) or over-enforcement (a Type 1 error). Which type of error should an authority be most willing to make? From the perspective of safe-guarding the economic freedom of market players, US antitrust enforcement tolerates Type 2 errors more willingly because Type 1 errors chill competition.[46] This argument can be explained by reference to the *de Havilland* merger: if we make a Type 1 error and prohibit a good merger that would have led to greater efficiency, the efficiencies are lost forever. If we make a Type 2 error, and allow the merger even though it creates a dominant firm, we have in the first instance created a powerful firm that can exploit consumers, thus reducing efficiency. But in the long term, aircraft purchasers may try and find alternative sellers of aeroplanes to avoid paying the monopoly price, and other manufacturers may enter the market. Thus, even if we allow a monopoly to be created, the market, in the long term, will cure the anticompetitive effects. Conversely, if we stifle efficiency at the start, there is no way to recover the efficiencies.[47] Should EC competition law take the same view? We consider this question at several junctures in the chapters that follow and suggest that EC competition law favours Type 1 errors instead.

4 Conclusion

The European Commission's competition policy has been described as 'part jurisprudence and part political realism'.[48] This is so for every competition policy – competition decisions have a significant impact on the market and competition law may be used (some might say hijacked) to pursue a wide range of policy objectives. This does not mean that competition law is unworkable, merely that its enforcement will be affected by different policy priorities at

---

[45] See P. L. Joskow 'Transaction Cost Economics, Antitrust Rules, and Remedies' (2002) 18 *Journal of Law, Economics and Organization* 95. As will be seen, in the context of US antitrust the rules/standards dichotomy is rephrased in the tension between the per se approach (rule) and the rule of reason (standard).

[46] See W. J. Kolasky 'What is Competition? A Comparison of US and EC Perspectives' [2004] *Antitrust Bulletin* 29, 40–2.

[47] F. S. McChesney 'Talking 'Bout My Antitrust Generation' (2004) 27(3) *Regulation* 48, 50 (available at www.cato.org).

[48] By Lodewijk Briet, a member of Jacques Delors's *cabinet*, in Ross *Jacques Delors* p. 130.

different times. Moreover, advances in economics result in changes to the rules and standards that are applied.

What is missing from the competition laws of many jurisdictions, including the EC, is an authoritative statement of the role of competition policy.[49] Instead, the history of competition law reveals shifts in political and economic policy directions.[50] The aim of this book is to explore the changing paradigms that have informed competition law enforcement in the EC.

The book is structured in the following manner. First, we pursue in more detail the political and economic dimensions that animate competition law in the EC in chapters 2–4. This reveals that EC competition law is undergoing a transformation and is currently guided by an economic paradigm which places reliance on market power as a litmus test to identify risks to competition and an uncertain political resolution of the aims of competition law marked by a desire to abandon the use of competition law as a tool for public policy, and to deploy it exclusively as a means to achieve consumer welfare. Given the centrality of market power, chapter 5 is a review of how market power is measured, and in chapters 6–10 we consider how competition law has evolved in the context of different manifestations of market power. Up to this stage the book focuses on the application of competition law by the Commission to private firms. In chapter 11 we consider the changing institutional structure whereby the Commission seeks to delegate enforcement to National Competition Authorities and private litigants harmed by competition law infringements. In chapter 12 we consider the interaction between competition law and liberalisation of certain key economic sectors, noting the strategic way competition law is used to pursue the Community's industrial policy.

---

[49] In contrast, Section 1 of the Canadian Competition Act (RS 1985, c. C-34) provides a specific role for competition policy: 'The purpose of this Act is to maintain and encourage competition in Canada in order to promote the efficiency and adaptability of the Canadian economy, in order to expand opportunities for Canadian participation in world markets while at the same time recognizing the role of foreign competition in Canada, in order to ensure that small and medium-sized enterprises have an equitable opportunity to participate in the Canadian economy and in order to provide consumers with competitive prices and product choices.' However, it is not clear how much influence this text has had on competition law in Canada.

[50] For comprehensive historical accounts, see R. J. R. Peritz *Competition Policy in America: History, Rhetoric, Law* rev. edn (Oxford: Oxford University Press, 2000); D. J. Gerber *Law and Competition in Twentieth Century Europe – Protecting Prometheus* (Oxford: Oxford University Press, 1998).

2

The core values of EC competition law in flux

Contents

1. Introduction	*page* 20
2. Competition as economic freedom	22
2.1 Competing concepts of competition	22
2.2 The concept of competition in Article 81 EC	25
2.3 The rule of reason distraction	29
2.4 The contribution of the European Courts	31
3. The single market	39
3.1 Preventing market disintegration	39
3.2 Market integration and the notion of agreement	41
4. Economic efficiency	44
4.1 Efficiency in Article 81	45
4.2 Efficiency as a core value	46
5. The changing relationship among core values	48
5.1 Recasting the role of economic freedom	48
5.2 Market integration v. economic efficiency	50
6. The transformation thesis so far	51

1 Introduction

EC competition policy is currently undergoing a significant shift in economic theory and political ideology as well as in its institutional enforcement structure (a change along all three sides to the prism proposed in chapter 1).[1] In this chapter we suggest that, from a political perspective, competition policy in the EC originally promoted three 'core' values: competition (understood as the maintenance of economic freedom), the integration of the internal market and

---

[1] This argument builds upon my earlier work: G. Monti 'Article 81 EC and Public Policy' (2002) 39 *Common Market Law Review* 1057. For a similar analysis that reaches slightly different conclusions, see R. Wesseling *The Modernisation of EC Antitrust Law* (Oxford: Hart Publishing, 2000) ch. 3.

economic efficiency (as a means of enhancing consumer welfare). In the past, the first two values were pursued more assiduously than the last, while today economic efficiency and consumer welfare play a more significant role in motivating competition law enforcement. The effect is that the role of economic analysis in resolving competition cases takes centre stage.

In chapter 3 the history of economics in US antitrust allows us to see that there are different economic perspectives through which competition law can be enforced, and that shifts from one economic model to another are often instigated by changes in the policy consensus over how markets work.[2] This means that as the Community resolves to emphasise economic considerations, we must determine the normative foundations of the EC's approach before investigating how economics is used. At the end of chapter 3 we suggest that three themes underpin the economic approach favoured by the Community: consumer welfare, market power and pluralism. These themes prescribe an aggressive policy that is in line with post-Chicago economic theory. In the following chapters we explore the extent to which this economic paradigm is activated in the case law. In chapter 4 we suggest that the Commission wishes to complement the shift towards economics by banishing the use of competition law to achieve other public policy objectives. However, a significant number of public policy considerations affect decisions in competition cases, so that there is a tension between the wish to insulate competition law from politics and the increased role of public policy considerations.

The transformation of the political and economic paradigms began in the mid-1990s, but has accelerated in recent years. The reason for the speeding up is that institutionally, the locus of competition enforcement is shifting away from the Commission (which has to date been the principal enforcer of competition policy)[3] and towards National Competition Authorities, regulatory agencies and courts. These institutional changes are brought about in particular by Regulation 1/2003, which grants National Competition Authorities and courts the power and the obligation to apply EC competition law more fully than before.[4] This institutional change has led the Commission to suggest that there should be a reduction in the role of competition policy in promoting other values of Community interest, in the name of legal certainty and coherence on the one hand (for the fewer the goals of competition law the more consistent the decisions in the national authorities will be) and of institutional competence on the other (after all, a National Competition Authority cannot make industrial policy decisions in the interests of the Community as a whole). Instead, the

---

[2] See further M. S. Jacobs 'An Essay on the Normative Foundations of Antitrust Economics' (1995) 74 *North Carolina Law Review* 219.

[3] By virtue of Regulation 17/62, First Regulation implementing Articles [81] and [82] of the Treaty, OJ special edn 1962, No. 204/62 p. 87 (as amended by Regulation 1216/99 [1999] OJ L148/5).

[4] Regulation 1/2003 on the Implementation of the Rules on Competition laid down in Articles 81 and 82 of the Treaty [2003] OJ L1/1.

exclusive application of economics to resolve competition cases can ensure greater coherence among diverse institutions enforcing the law.

In general, these chapters show how, without any revision to the substantive law, the interpretation of competition law statutes is affected by economic, political or institutional paradigm shifts. Moreover, paradigm shifts on one of the three dimensions often stimulate changes in the other two.

2 Competition as economic freedom

2.1 Competing concepts of competition

We can distinguish three possible conceptions of competition. First, based on the natural meaning of the word, competition may exist when there is *rivalry* among firms. According to Professor Whish, '[c]ompetition means a struggle or contention for superiority, and in the commercial world this means a striving for the custom and business of people in the market place'.[5] This definition is helpful in so far as we do not confuse means and ends. Rivalry among firms is the means through which a number of socially desirable ends – e.g. economic efficiency, economic freedom or consumer welfare – are pursued.[6] To judge whether there is a distortion of competition it is more helpful to look to see whether the ends are met rather than whether firms are rivals, because it provides a more precise method to determine whether there is a market failure. The reason for this is that firms invent new ways of competing every day, and it would be wrong to presume that we can identify ideal states of 'rivalry' in the market.[7] Moreover, competition law does not prevent some forms of cooperation among firms (e.g. mergers), thus rivalry as the benchmark of competition is incomplete.[8]

Accordingly, most economists support a second conception of competition based on the effects of the behaviour of firms on economic welfare. This is preferable for two reasons: first, it provides a realistic benchmark by which to measure the presence of competition; second, it is more precise, because there can be rivalry but no competition. An example is in the market for aircraft. While the rivalry between Boeing and Airbus is well documented,[9] it is not

---

[5] R. Whish *Competition Law* 5th edn (London: Lexis Nexis, 2003) p. 2.

[6] See the important contribution to this debate by J. F. Brodley 'The Economic Goals of Antitrust: Efficiency, Consumer Welfare, and Technological Progress' (1987) 62 *New York University Law Review* 1020, 1023. The same means/ends analysis is used by R. A. Posner *Antitrust Law* 2nd edn (Chicago: University of Chicago Press, 2001) pp. 28–9.

[7] P. Nicolaides 'An Essay on Economics and the Competition Law of the European Community' (2000) 27 *Legal Issues of Economic Integration* 7, 18–19.

[8] P. J. Hammer 'Antitrust Beyond Competition: Market Failures, Total Welfare, and the Challenge of Intramarket Second-Best Tradeoffs' (2000) 98 *Michigan Law Review* 849, 922; F. A. Hayek *Individualism and Economic Order* (London: Routledge and Kegan Paul, 1949) p. 92.

[9] M. Lynn *Birds of Prey: The War Between Boeing and Airbus* (London: Mandarin Paperbacks, 1995).

clear that the market is competitive. This can be explained by reviewing an economic assessment carried out when in 1997 Boeing merged with a competing aircraft manufacturer, McDonnell Douglas.[10] McDonnell Douglas was not seen as a major player in the market; however, it was said that the prices for aircraft were higher when Boeing and Airbus competed for an order, than if McDonnell Douglas also offered its aircraft. The minor player had an effect on prices, to the benefit of consumers.[11] Therefore, after the merger, an important player would exit and prices might rise even if the rivalry between Boeing and Airbus remained unabated. Accordingly, the question about whether there is competition is not whether the market is characterised by rivalry, rather whether the market in question yields economic welfare. Defining competition by judging the effects on economic welfare (the *neoclassical* concept) is traditionally associated with economic approaches to competition law.

A third approach is the *economic freedom* conception of competition, which traces its roots to a political philosophy (ordoliberalism) developed in Germany and which influenced the birth of post-war German competition law.[12] Under the ordoliberal model, the aim of competition policy is 'the protection of individual economic freedom of action as a value in itself, or vice versa, the restraint of undue economic power'.[13] John Kay has recently suggested that an appropriate translation of ordoliberalism is 'disciplined pluralism'.[14] This label is useful because it embodies the two key notions of this economic philosophy: that the economic system should allow all individuals to participate unhampered by the economic power of others (pluralism); and that economic freedom is not guaranteed by an unregulated market – the risk of monopolies or cartels necessitates laws to sustain economic freedom (discipline). In this light the discipline of the market is as fundamental as contract law or property rights because it is a prerequisite for the success of the market. From this perspective, economic efficiency, as understood by the neoclassical approach, may be an indirect result, which is derived from the presence of economic freedom, but is not the aim of ordoliberalism. Indeed ordoliberals would prefer a state of inefficiency coupled with freedom to a totalitarian, but efficient, state of affairs.[15] Ordoliberal discourse is

---

[10] Case IV/M.877 *Boeing/McDonnell Douglas* [1997] OJ L336/16.

[11] B. Bishop 'Boeing/McDonnell Douglas' [1997] *European Competition Law Review* 417.

[12] K.-U. Kühn 'Germany' in E. M. Graham and J. D. Richardson (eds.) *Global Competition Policy* (Washington, DC: Institute for International Economics, 1997) pp. 138–40; D. J. Gerber *Law and Competition in Twentieth Century Europe – Protecting Prometheus* (Oxford: Oxford University Press, 1998) chs. 7 and 8.

[13] W. Möschel 'Competition Policy from an Ordo Point of View' in A. Peacock and H. Willgerodt (eds.) *German Neo-Liberals and the Social Market Economy* (London: Macmillan, 1989); W. Möschel 'The Proper Scope of Government Viewed from an Ordoliberal Perspective: The Example of Competition Policy' (2001) *Journal of Institutional and Theoretical Economics* 3.

[14] J. Kay *The Truth About Markets* (London: Penguin, 2003) p. 334.

[15] C. Watrin 'Germany's Social Market Economy' in A. Kilmarnock (ed.) *The Social Market and the State* (London: Social Market Foundation, 1999) pp. 91–5.

based on the values of personal liberty and equality; in contrast the neo-classical definition of competition is embedded in a utilitarian and laissez-faire economic philosophy, where intervention is called for as a second best, when the market fails to deliver economic efficiency, with no regard for the distributive consequences of the market order. Instead, the Kaldor–Hicks measure of economic efficiency, so fundamental to neoclassical thought, is incompatible with ordoliberal philosophy.[16] Translated to competition policy, ordoliberalism necessitates rules that safeguard economic freedom in the marketplace by imposing obligations of fair conduct and suppressing economic power. The kind of competition policy that results from this model will not normally deviate from a neoclassical model (both would declare cartels and abuses of monopoly power unlawful) but there may be cases where an agreement that increases economic welfare is prohibited if it reduces the economic freedom of other market players (threatening plural-ism), and activities of large firms are likely to be scrutinised more closely under an economic freedom model than by neoclassical economists.[17] This conception of competition is henceforth labelled the 'economic freedom' approach.[18]

The economic freedom approach has some affinities with the political content of US antitrust law in its early years. The Supreme Court at the end of the nineteenth century condemned large firms for exercising 'the great power that combined capital gave them by driving out of business the small dealers and worthy men'.[19] Some consider these values are inherent in the antitrust laws. Professor Pitofsky, for instance, summarised the political values of US antitrust law as follows: a concern that excessive concentration of economic power would breed antidemocratic political pressures; a desire to enhance individual and business freedom by reducing the range within which private discretion of the few in the economic sphere controls the welfare of all; a fear that a focus only on economic concerns will lead to excessive industrial concentration which will then require the state to play a more intrusive role in

---

[16] A Pareto-efficient position is reached when no change from that position could make someone better off without making at least one other person worse off. The Kaldor–Hicks conception of efficiency postulates that if a redistribution of resources increases total economic welfare, then it is desirable, regardless of individual losses. Taken to its extreme, it means that if slavery is a more efficient way of producing goods, employment contracts should be abandoned. In antitrust, an example is that a merger which creates a monopoly might be allowed if the gain in productive efficiency is greater than the reduction in allocative efficiency.

[17] For example, the prohibition of loyalty rebates and other forms of price discrimination main-tenance: see Kühn 'Germany' pp. 139–40.

[18] The notion of economic freedom taken here is different from that adopted by A. K. Sen 'Markets and Freedoms: The Achievements and Limitations of the Market Mechanisms in Promoting Individual Freedoms' (1993) 45 Oxford Economic Papers 519, who includes a wider range of distributive concerns.

[19] US v. Trans-Missouri Freight Association 166 US 290, 319 (1897).

economic affairs.[20] However, since the 1980s this view has waned as economic welfare has become more prominent in informing competition law. A comparable shift from ordoliberalism to consumer welfare is occurring in EC competition law now.

2.2 The concept of competition in Article 81 EC

Taking the above definitions, we can look more closely at the interpretation of the notion of competition offered by the Commission and Courts. Article 81 mentions the concept of competition twice and will serve as a case study.

Article 81

1. The following shall be prohibited as incompatible with the common market: all agreements between undertakings, decisions by associations of undertakings and concerted practices which may affect trade between Member States and which have as their object or effect the prevention, restriction or distortion of competition within the common market, and in particular those which:

   (a) directly or indirectly fix purchase or selling prices or any other trading conditions;
   (b) limit or control production, markets, technical development, or investment;
   (c) share markets or sources of supply;
   (d) apply dissimilar conditions to equivalent transactions with other trading parties, thereby placing them at a competitive disadvantage;
   (e) make the conclusion of contracts subject to acceptance by the other parties of supplementary obligations which, by their nature or according to commercial usage, have no connection with the subject of such contracts.

2. Any agreements or decisions prohibited pursuant to this article shall be automatically void.
3. The provisions of paragraph 1 may, however, be declared inapplicable in the case of:

   - any agreement or category of agreements between undertakings,
   - any decision or category of decisions by associations of undertakings,
   - any concerted practice or category of concerted practices,

   which contributes to improving the production or distribution of goods or to promoting technical or economic progress, while allowing consumers a fair share of the resulting benefit, and which does not:

   (a) impose on the undertakings concerned restrictions which are not indispensable to the attainment of these objectives;
   (b) afford such undertakings the possibility of eliminating competition in respect of a substantial part of the products in question.

---

[20] R. Pitofsky 'The Political Content of Antitrust' (1979) 127 *University of Pennsylvania Law Review* 1051. For similar sentiments, see G. Amato *Antitrust and the Bounds of Power* (Oxford: Hart Publishing, 1997) ch. 7.

This text is incompatible with a neoclassical definition of competition. Recall that from a neoclassical perspective competition is harmed when economic welfare is reduced. In this view, Article 81(3) is redundant – either an agreement restricts economic welfare, or it improves it, or has no effect on it.[21] The neoclassical economist only needs paragraphs (1) and (2) for the application of competition law according to the standards of economic welfare. Moreover, three of the four conditions for the application of Article 81(3) are hard to interpret from a perspective that focuses upon economic welfare. First, the agreement must promote technical and economic progress – does this mean productive and dynamic efficiency or other, wider public policy goals, like full employment or fairness? If it means the former, then it makes no sense because an agreement improving efficiency does not restrict competition, and if it means the latter this is not economically rational because inefficiency is tolerated in favour of other political interests. Second, the requirement that consumers must gain sits oddly with neoclassical thought: if an agreement improves productive efficiency (by reducing production costs, for example) but has a modest adverse impact on allocative efficiency (e.g. a slight price rise) then economic welfare (measured with the Kaldor–Hicks standard) is increased; there is no need to inquire whether consumers gain a benefit, so long as the overall wealth of society increases. The definition of competition in the EC contains elements of distributive justice, incompatible with the neoclassical model premised upon a utilitarian political philosophy. Third, the final requirement in Article 81(3), that the undertakings are not able to eliminate competition in respect of a substantial part of the products in question, does not translate well into economic jargon. Presumably it means that the firms who enter into the agreement must not be allowed to create a monopoly in the relevant product market. This would suggest that after the agreement there should still be other competitors in the market, but if an agreement generates economic welfare, the resulting market structure is irrelevant.[22]

The economic freedom interpretation of competition comes a little closer to explaining Article 81. In an early treatise on EC competition law, Arved Deringer took the view that 'competition is distinguished by two characteristics, namely, freedom of action of the individual enterprises and the possibility that market participants may make a choice'.[23] The market participants in question are those who enter into the agreement – by reducing the number

---

[21] See P. Nicolaides 'The Balancing Myth: The Economics of Article 81(1) and (3)' (2005) 32 *Legal Issues of Economic Integration* 123, 124.

[22] We find a similar condition in the US Merger Guidelines (1992, revised in 1997), which suggest that efficiencies will almost never justify a merger that creates a monopoly. Thus the fourth condition could be read as a per se rule based on the presumption that an agreement creating a monopoly has no redeeming efficiency virtues.

[23] A. Deringer *The Competition Law of the European Economic Community* (Chicago: CCH, 1968) para. 123.

of market players, one increases the 'degree of monopolisation' in the relevant market. In this view, a restriction of competition is a restraint between the parties to the agreement, and it is irrelevant whether the market is competitive, or whether the agreement's beneficial effects outweigh the harmful ones; such economic cost–benefit analysis is reserved for Article 81(3).[24] This position is reflected in a number of decisions of the Commission.[25] In discussing exclusive distribution agreements, for example, the Commission stated: 'the exclusive nature of a contractual relationship between a producer and a distributor is viewed as restricting competition since it limits the parties' freedom of action in the territory covered'.[26]

A particularly graphic example of the economic freedom approach is the *Carlsberg* decision.[27] The agreement was between Carlsberg and Grand Metropolitan (GM). GM undertook to buy a large quantity of lager from Carlsberg. The Commission held that the agreement restricted competition under Article 81(1), but that it merited exemption under Article 81(3). It is instructive to place alongside each other the reasons why the agreement was found to restrict competition and why it was exempted:

- GM's obligation to purchase a large quantity of lager from Carlsberg restricted its freedom to brew beer itself, or to find alternative suppliers, 'possibly on more favourable terms'.[28] . . . But it was exempted because the amount of lager which GM was committed to buy from Carlsberg represented only one third of its lager sales, which included a number of competing brands. Moreover, there were a large number of competing lager brands on the British market.
- Carlsberg's obligation to supply GM lager 'deprived Carlsberg of control over more than half of its present output which it would otherwise be able to sell to other breweries or on the free market through its agencies'.[29] . . . But it was exempted because it resulted in an increase in Carlsberg beer sold in the UK (whose market share was only 4 per cent), thanks to GM's extensive sales networks, and it resulted in Carlsberg's brewery in the UK operating at full capacity.[30]

Hence the agreement, far from reducing efficiency, actually increased it. In the Commission's words:

> Consumers are allowed a fair share of the benefits resulting from the above-mentioned improvements in production and distribution since, by making possible the brewing of Carlsberg beers in the United Kingdom, the agreement

---

[24] Ibid. paras. 125–6.

[25] See, for example: *Rennet* [1980] OJ L51/19; *VIFKA* [1986] OJ L291/46 (para. 12, but then exempted because efficient: paras. 18–19); *Dutch Banks* [1989] OJ L253/1 (para. 55, but then exempted because efficient: paras. 62–3).

[26] *Twenty-third Report on Competition Policy* (1993) para. 212.   [27] [1984] OJ L207/26.

[28] Ibid. para. II(A)(3)(i).   [29] Ibid. para. II(A)(3)(ii).   [30] Ibid. para. II(B)(8).

ensures that supplies of the beers there are more plentiful, fresher and also cheaper because of the saving of the considerable cost of transporting a heavy commodity like beer over large distances.[31]

The same analytical structure is found in many other decisions, an approach which would baffle any economist: the facts that explain why the agreement is declared anticompetitive under Article 81(1) are the same facts which are used by the Commission to show that the agreement yields economic benefits under Article 81(3)![32] And the Commission has gone further, considering also the restriction of the economic freedom of other market participants. Here the Commission is concerned about the risk that other market participants might be foreclosed from a market, for instance when a distribution agreement makes it more difficult for other manufacturers to find distributors who are able to sell their goods.[33]

Conceiving a restriction of competition in Article 81(1) as a restriction of economic freedom sheds some light on the significance of Article 81(3). Article 81(3) is also incompatible with the economic freedom model, but for different reasons than under a neoclassical light: if an agreement has an undesirable effect on economic freedom under Article 81(1), no exemption should be granted, as economic freedom is the sine qua non of competition policy.[34] The exemption provision in Article 81(3) is a way of reconciling an ordoliberal conception of competition with other values. But the use of other values in an agreement that restricts the economic freedom of firms may only be tolerated under the strict conditions provided in Article 81(3): that consumers benefit (a distributional concern), that economic freedom is not completely eliminated, and that the restriction of economic freedom is the least necessary to achieve those other public interest goals. This way the objective of economic freedom is sacrificed in part to other public interest goals.

In so far as Article 81(1) is concerned, the concept of a restriction of competition meant, in the early days, that the economic freedom of market

---

[31] Ibid. para. II(B)(10).

[32] See, for example, Decision 76/172 *Bayer/Gist Brocades* [1976] OJ L30/13 (a joint venture would restrict competition between the parties but would expand production, allowing sales by Gist Brocades to triple); Decision 77/160 *Vacuum Interrupters* [1977] OJ L48/32 (a joint venture would quash potential competition between the parties, but the new product would not have been developed without the joint venture). A Commission official has recently acknowledged the conceptual weakness of this approach, labelling it an 'intellectual detour' which was some-times used by the Commission to exert control over transactions: L. Gyselen 'The Substantive Legality Test Under Article 81(3) EC Treaty – Revisited in Light of the Commission's Modernization Initiative' in A. von Bogdandy, P. Mavroidis and Y. Mény (eds.) *European Integration and International Coordination: Studies in Transnational Economic Law in Honour of C.-D. Ehlermann* (The Hague: Kluwer, 2002).

[33] Case T-65/98 *Van den Bergh Foods Ltd v. Commission*, Judgment of 23 October 2003, paras. 80–119.

[34] In a similar fashion, Möschel regretted the cartel exceptions in the German Law. Möschel 'Competition Policy' p. 150.

participants was significantly impeded.[35] This does not mean that identifying a restriction of competition is easy. As Möschel puts it: 'the demarcation between practices which promote competition and those which hinder it has remained a field in which reasoned analysis and mere speculation exist in equal measure'.[36] However, the economic freedom paradigm offers us a perspective by which to reconcile the two paragraphs of Article 81, and seems to reflect the Commission's practice.

2.3 The rule of reason distraction

The Commission's interpretation of the concept of a restriction of competition was criticised vigorously by many, in particular because of the procedural consequences that resulted. Under Regulation 17/62, which set out the procedures for the application of competition law between 1962 and 2004, parties whose agreement would be automatically void for infringing Article 81(1) had to notify the agreement to the Commission and plead for an exemption under Article 81(3). The Commission had exclusive competence to apply Article 81(3).[37] The result of the Commission's interpretation of Article 81(1) using the economic freedom approach meant that several commercial contracts were potentially void unless exempted by the Commission and this realisation caused an avalanche of exemption notifications to the Commission from firms worried about the legality of their transactions, which led to severe delays in the processing of exemption applications and uncertainty as to the final result. At worst this cocktail of administrative inefficiency and unpredictability risked retarding the development of Community industry.

As a result, in the 1980s a number of commentators began to clamour for the EC to adopt a 'rule of reason' as a way of escaping from an overly aggressive stance under Article 81(1) and as a way of escaping the procedural delays of notification.[38] The rule of reason is a concept that arose early on in the history of US antitrust law, and while its precise scope is uncertain even in the United States, its advocates pointed out that the uncertainties were less problematic than the

---

[35] See the Commission's submissions in Cases 56 and 58/64 *Consten and Grundig v. Commission* [1966] ECR 299 p. 326; Case C-234/89 *Delimitis v. Henninger Braü* [1991] ECR I-935, Opinion of AG van Gerven, paras. 15 and 17. See J. Peeters 'The Rule of Reason Revisited: Prohibition on Restraints of Competition in the Sherman Act and the EEC Treaty' (1989) 37 *American Journal of Comparative Law* 521, 543; R. Joliet *The Rule of Reason in Antitrust* (The Hague: Nijhoff, 1967) p. 171.

[36] W. Möschel 'The Goals of Antitrust Revisited' (1991) 146 *Journal of Institutional and Theoretical Economics* 7, 9.

[37] Articles 4 and 9 of Regulation 17/62.

[38] The seminal contribution is Joliet *Rule of Reason*. See also V. Korah 'The Rise and Fall of Provisional Validity – The Need for a Rule of Reason in EEC Antitrust' (1981) *Northwest Journal of International Law and Business* 320; I. Forrester and D. Norall 'The Laicization of Community Law: Self-Help and the Rule of Reason' (1984) 21 *Common Market Law Review* 11. For a contrary view, see R. Whish and B. Sufrin 'Article 85 and the Rule of Reason' (1987) 7 *Yearbook of European Law* 12.

procedural delays and arbitrary decisions of the Commission at present. US antitrust law distinguishes between practices that are *per se* unlawful (and thereby condemned without any further analysis because experience teaches that certain kinds of practices have no redeeming benefits) and practices that are analysed under a *rule of reason* – that is, by a fact-specific inquiry to determine whether the agreements cause anticompetitive effects – to decide on their legality.[39]

Advocates of a rule of reason suggest that if the Commission were to apply this approach to determine whether an agreement infringes Article 81(1), parties would be spared the need to seek an exemption – the bulk of the substantive economic analysis would be carried out under Article 81(1) and so parties could implement an agreement without notification and the Commission would get involved, if at all, only after the agreement is implemented if it resulted in inefficiencies. And since most agreements would be efficiency enhancing, it was argued that the Commission would seldom be involved. Procedurally the rule of reason eliminates the need for *ex ante* scrutiny (avoiding the notorious delays), and substantively parties are able to identify for themselves, using economic analysis, whether the agreement causes anticompetitive effects necessitating notification. Applied to the *Carlsberg* decision we considered above, a rule of reason inquiry asks whether the agreement would have an adverse effect on the availability of competing beers and whether the agreement would cause the price of Carlsberg beer to increase. Upon finding that the agreement was not likely to harm consumers but reduce prices and increase the variety of beer offered to consumers, the agreement would be deemed not to infringe Article 81(1).

The arguments in favour of adopting a rule of reason have always been weak. First, its proponents for the most part advocate an exclusively economic analysis to competition policy and are in favour of the neoclassical conception of competition. Thus, their arguments do not fit within the political scope of EC competition policy, which, as we have suggested, embraces economic freedom as the basis for regulating markets. Second, from a legal perspective, an economic welfare interpretation of Article 81(1) would mean either that Article 81(3) is irrelevant (in which case the advocates of a rule of reason fail to offer a solution which is compatible with the legal text),[40] or that Article 81(3) provides for exemption in cases where an inefficient agreement may nonetheless yield desirable political benefits, a conclusion that is the exact opposite of what the advocates of a rule of reason wish to achieve, given their desire to focus exclusively on economic efficiency to test the legality of agreements.

The rule of reason suits US law because it is applied to a statute which proclaims that 'Every contract, combination in the form of trust or otherwise,

---

[39] For a modern judicial restatement, see *National Society of Professional Engineers v. US* 435 US 679 (1978). For commentary, see T. Calvani 'Some Thoughts on the Rule of Reason' [2001] *European Competition Law Review* 201; P. Manzini 'The European Rule of Reason – Crossing the Sea of Doubt' [2002] *European Competition Law Review* 392.

[40] Case T-112/99 *Métropole télévision (M6) and Others v. Commission* [2001] ECR II-2459 para. 74.

or conspiracy, in restraint of trade or commerce among the several States, or with foreign nations, is declared to be illegal.'[41] Read literally it suggests that every contract is prohibited, because every contract restrains trade in some way (if I promise to sell you my apple, I cannot then sell it to someone else, so trade is restricted for that good once the contract is made). The adoption of the rule of reason was necessary to create a mechanism to differentiate between desirable and undesirable agreements – a literal construction of the statute would lead to absurd results.[42] But the same legal method is unnecessary in the EC, because Article 81(3) provides the functional equivalent of the rule of reason.[43] Advocacy of a rule of reason shows a poor understanding of comparative law methods.[44]

2.4 The contribution of the European Courts

The European Courts' contribution to the interpretation of the notion of a restriction of competition rejects both the arguments of the advocates of the US-style rule of reason and the wide 'economic freedom' approach taken by some Commission decisions. While it is easy to say what the Courts have not done, it is less easy to provide an explanation of how they have interpreted the notion of a restriction on competition, because the case law is very opaque, and recent cases often restate bland pronouncements from earlier cases without adding any substance to them. The gist of the Courts' case law is to say that not all restrictions of economic freedom are restrictions of competition, and we can identify three strands of analysis that can lead to this conclusion.

2.4.1 Measuring restrictions of economic freedom

In some cases the Court takes the view that a restriction of the economic freedom of market players is a necessary element in the identification of a restriction of competition but is not sufficient: the degree to which economic freedom is restricted must be measured.[45] The Courts' contribution has been

---

[41] 15 USC 1 (colloquially known as s. 1 of the Sherman Act 1890).

[42] Thus, in US law, the rule of reason 'gives restraint of trade a meaning which would not destroy the individual right to contract or render difficult, if not impossible, any movement of trade in the channels of interstate commerce – the free movement of which it was the purpose of the statute to protect'. *US v. American Tobacco* 221 US 106, 180 (1911) (per White CJ).

[43] But with some differences in the method of analysis. See Peeters, 'Rule of Reason Revisited' pp. 535–6.

[44] As has been eloquently put: 'Incomparables cannot usefully be compared, and in law the only things which are comparable are those which fulfil the same function.' K. Zweigert and H. Kötz *An Introduction to Comparative Law* 2nd edn (Oxford: Clarendon Press, 1987) p. 31.

[45] For example, in *Delimitis* ([1991] ECR I-935 para. 15), when determining the legality of a beer supply agreement between a brewer and publicans, the ECJ held: 'it is necessary to analyse the effects of a beer supply agreement, taken together with other contracts of the same type, on the opportunities of national competitors or those from other Member States, to gain access to the market for beer consumption or to increase their market share and, accordingly, the effects on the range of products offered to consumers'. See also Case 23/67 *Brasserie de Haecht v. Wilkin-Janssen* [1967] ECR 407, 415–16.

to identify parameters by which such measurement takes place: the economic context in which the firms in question operate, the products covered and the market structure. A recent example of this is the Court of First Instance's (CFI's) review of the Commission's *Télévision par Satellite* decision. This was a joint venture among a number of French broadcasters and other firms to break into the satellite pay-TV market. The venture created a second competitor in the market for pay-TV in France, Télévision par Satellite (TPS), to compete against Canal + which held a strong market position in France. Two clauses were found to restrict competition. First, TPS had the right of first refusal over any special-interest channel created by the parents. According to the Commission, this clause, lasting for ten years, restricted the supply of special-interest channels: by giving TPS priority access to the parties' special-interest channels, entry by other competitors on the pay-TV market was made more difficult.[46] Second, TPS would have the exclusive right to transmit the general-interest channels of four parents (TF1, France 2, France 3 and M6) for the duration of the joint venture. The Commission held that this clause constituted 'a restriction of competition since it denies TPS's competitors access to attractive programmes'.[47] This assertion is not followed by any analysis as to the economic welfare effects; there is no indication that by foreclosing access consumers would suffer because TPS and Canal + would hold a duopoly as a result of which prices were likely to rise. In fact, the Commission, in granting an exemption, admitted that '*far from eliminating competition, the TPS agreements are pro-competitive.* Development of the pay-TV market has been strongly stimulated, particularly through the emergence of keen competition between CanalSatellite and TPS.'[48] Nevertheless, the fact that the agreement restricted the economic freedom of other potential market participants was sufficient to find that the agreement restricted competition for the purposes of Article 81(1).[49] In upholding this aspect of the decision, the CFI held that the Commission had not found a restriction of competition in the abstract, but had proved that the agreement foreclosed access to a lucrative market by other potential broadcasters, enough to show that the restriction of economic freedom was significant.[50] Thus the CFI upheld a decision where a restriction of competition was identified by finding that the economic freedom of certain

---

[46] [1999] OJ L90/6 paras. 101, 122, where this seems to be the implication. In other words, the contract did not mean that the special-interest channels would not be broadcast at all.

[47] Ibid. para. 107.   [48] Ibid. para. 135.

[49] But an exemption was granted when these clauses were amended. This reading is also confirmed by Case T-65/98 *Van den Bergh Foods v. Commission* [2003] ECR II-4653 para. 107, where the CFI stated that it is only within the specific framework of Article 81(3) that 'the pro and anti-competitive aspects of a restriction may be weighed'.

[50] *Métropole* [2001] ECR II-2459 paras. 78–9. Against the view taken here, see O. Odudu 'A New Economic Approach to Article 81(1)?' (2002) 27 *European Law Review* 100. He suggests that the Court's guidance is that an agreement infringes Article 81(1) when it reduces allocative efficiency. However, there is no express mention of economic criteria in the judgment or the decision.

market players had been hampered, and it did so because the market context showed that the foreclosure of rivals was likely as a result of the agreement.

A similar approach can be seen in the Commission's *Visa International* decision.[51] This concerned the default multilateral exchange fees set by Visa for transactions between a retailer's bank (which has accepted payment by Visa) and the cardholder's bank, when the former seeks to obtain the money resulting from the sale from the latter. The fee paid by the retailer's bank to the cardholder's bank for this service might be agreed between the banks, but absent such agreement the Visa default fee applied. The setting of a default fee was found to restrict competition because it 'restricts the freedom of banks individually to decide their own pricing policies, and distorts the conditions of competition on the Visa issuing and acquiring markets'.[52] The Commission stated expressly that the efficiency justifications (which led to the exemption of this agreement under Article 81(3)) had no role to play in Article 81(1),[53] merely noting that the impugned agreement would have affected the degree of price competition for acquiring banks and issuing banks, for their respective costs and revenues were largely fixed by the Visa agreement.

Under this approach one measures the degree to which economic freedom is limited by agreements, and assesses the consequences of the agreement (in the two cases above by considering the degree of market foreclosure or the degree of price competition). The question is whether the market operates with sufficient freedom, or whether the agreement restricts 'the free play of competition to an appreciable extent'.[54]

.2 Ancillary restraints

In a second strand of cases the Court explained that a restriction of economic freedom in a contract would not infringe Article 81 when it did not constitute the major part of the agreement but was necessary to allow for the implementation of an agreement that did not infringe competition.[55] For example, if a hairdresser were to sell his hairdressing salon in Manchester to another hairdresser, a non-compete clause would be included in the contract whereby the seller promises not to set up a competing salon after the sale. The reason for this is that the seller has developed good relations with customers (goodwill) and if he were to establish a competing hairdressing salon, all his customers would follow, leaving the buyer owning a salon but having no clients. The absence of a non-compete clause in the contract makes the sale worthless.[56] In the Commission's jargon the non-compete clause is an 'ancillary restraint'. The legal effect of this label is that if the major part of the agreement (the sale of the business) is not anticompetitive, then the ancillary restraint is lawful,

---

[51] [2002] OJ L318/17.   [52] Ibid. para. 66.   [53] Ibid. para. 59.
[54] Case 22/71 *Béguelin Import Co. v. SAGL Import Export* [1971] ECR 949 para. 16.
[55] Case 42/84 *Remia BV and Others v. Commission* [1985] ECR 2545.
[56] See the facts in *East v. Maurer* [1991] 1 WLR 461.

without any competition law analysis of the restraint. The application of this doctrine requires an analysis of two matters: determining first whether the restraint is subsidiary to the main transaction, and second whether the restraint is necessary for the commercial operation of the main transaction. The Court has given some guidance on the second aspect, indicating that the breadth of the restraint must be proportionate to the objective being achieved. In the hairdressing salon example therefore, a restriction on the seller not to set up a competing salon anywhere in the EU would be too wide (it should be limited to Manchester), and the duration of the non-competition clause must also be limited (the hairdresser must be able to return after the buyer has established himself on the market): the economic freedom of the seller may be limited but not eliminated. The Court has given less guidance about how to identify whether a clause is ancillary, although the case law suggests that a restraint is ancillary when it concerns the behaviour of the parties outside the framework of the agreement (e.g. in the agreement about the sale of a business, the non-compete clause is about restricting the seller's activities).

In one judgment, *Gøttrup-Klim*, the Court's language seemed to suggest a wider role for this doctrine.[57] The main part of the agreement was the operation of a purchasing cooperative, which small farmers joined. The cooperative was able to buy farming equipment at lower rates than the members individually because it bought in bulk and could secure discounts. The Court held that a restriction whereby its members were forbidden from joining other cooperatives could be lawful provided it was necessary for the effective operation of the cooperative. The Court found that the main agreement made way for more competition and the ancillary restraint might also have had beneficial effects on competition. This was because the cooperative's ability to obtain discounted prices from suppliers depended upon all members buying through it. If some members opted out, the cooperative would not buy as many goods and would lose its commercial muscle. The Court's judgment could be read to suggest that the agreement was assessed by considering its overall economic effects, rather than whether it restricted economic freedom. This interpretation would mean that the doctrine of ancillary restraints is a way of departing from the economic freedom model and approaching the assessment of agreements based on their overall effects on economic welfare. However, in subsequent cases the doctrine was not developed in this way. Instead, the doctrine serves to allow the enforcer to focus on the principal aspects of a transaction in determining its legality, while the ancillary restraints do not require scrutiny. If the main agreement is found not to restrict competition or is exempted, the ancillary restraint is valid automatically.[58] The doctrine is merely about administrative convenience, allowing the Commission to focus on the

---

[57] Case C-250/92 *Gøttrup-Klim e.a. Grovvareforeninger v. Dansk Landbrugs Grovvareselskab AmbA* [1994] ECR I-5641.
[58] *Métropole* [2001] ECR II-2459 para. 116.

principal effects of an agreement, but also to control minor aspects if the ancillary restraints are excessive in duration or scope.

The source of the ancillary restraints approach is revealing as it helps us to see a different source for the notion of economic freedom. It comes from the common law on restraints of trade. The law on restraints of trade forbids a contract term like the non-competition clause discussed above on two grounds: first because the clause deprives one party of his freedom to use his skills, and second because society suffers as it is unable to reap the benefits of that person's skills.[59] This doctrine is concerned about restrictions on a person's freedom to act, so it is not consistent with a neoclassical vision of the role of law. The common law, however, recognised that certain restraints were 'reasonable', for example non-competition clauses attached to contracts for the sale of a business.[60] Today we know that antitrust law is a novel form of economic regulation, but in the early years of the Sherman Act (the key US antitrust statute), at the end of the nineteenth century, American judges were divided as to whether the statute codified the common law on restraints of trade or whether it introduced a novel means to regulate agreements between firms, based on economic theories. Judge Taft, who supported the former interpretation, said that the Act, like the common law, did not prohibit restrictions of conduct like non-compete obligations when these were ancillary to the main subject matter of the agreement, and therefore reasonable.[61] He introduced the phrase 'ancillary restraint' in US antitrust law to describe restrictions that were reasonable and outside the scope of the Sherman Act. Today, however, this interpretation of the Sherman Act has waned, but the doctrine of ancillary restraints has remained in US jargon, playing a different role. It applies when restraints in joint ventures are assessed. In brief, ancillary restraints are lawful if two conditions are met: they are necessary for the transaction and they do not diminish the efficiency of the transaction.[62]

Therefore, 'ancillary restraints' in EC competition law is another misplaced label from the United States, like the rule of reason. In *Gøttrup-Klim* the European Court of Justice (ECJ) might have attempted to apply an approach which is similar to that of current US law on ancillary restraints, considering both whether the clause was necessary and whether it enhanced competition, but this has not been followed through. Instead, the EC's approach is simply to inquire whether the restriction is necessary for the commercial success of the main agreement. If it is, and if the agreement as a whole is lawful, the ancillary restraint is not assessed for its effects on the market: it is declared lawful even if

---

[59] H. Hovenkamp *Enterprise and American Law, 1836–1937* (Cambridge, MA: Harvard University Press, 1991) pp. 276–7.

[60] The seminal case is *Mitchel v. Reynolds* 24 ER 347 (1711).

[61] *US v. Addyston Pipe and Steel Co.* 85 F 271, 282 (6th Cir. 1897); *US v. Arnold Schwinn & Co.* 388 US 365 (1967) per Stewart J, noting the common law origins of the ancillary restraints doctrine.

[62] See E. Gellhorn and W. E. Kovacic *Antitrust Law and Economics in a Nutshell* 4th edn (St Paul, MN: West Publishing, 1994) pp. 254–9.

it restricts the parties' economic freedom. A better label might be 'collateral restraint' to distance the EC's approach from that of the US antitrust law.

2.4.3 Agreements creating competition

The most opaque strand of the ECJ's interpretation of Article 81(1) comes from a passage that is often repeated by the Court but never explained. One of the early obiter dicta is found in *Société Technique Minière*. In discussing the legality of an exclusive distribution contract (where a manufacturer nominates one distributor as exclusive distributor in a given geographical area) the Court said:

> The competition in question must be understood within the actual context in which it would occur in the absence of the agreement in dispute. In particular it may be doubted whether there is an interference with competition if the said agreement seems really necessary for the penetration of a new area by an undertaking.[63]

The first sentence appears to suggest that one can compare the state of the market with and without the agreement and if the market is better off with the agreement, then there is no infringement. However, this reading is too wide because it would allow one to balance a restriction of competition on the one hand with efficiencies on the other. This would introduce the US-style rule of reason that the Court has repeatedly rejected. Instead, the first sentence requires a narrower reading. The Court's causal inquiry is asking whether the competition created by the agreement would not exist but for the agreement. Exclusive distribution creates competition because it introduces a new product in the market (on the facts of this case, a German product on the French market where it would compete against similar French goods). The question is whether exclusive distribution is the cause of the increase, in which case the agreement is allowed. As Advocate General Lenz explained when reviewing the case law, 'the Court also regards restrictions of competition as compatible with Article [81(1)] if, taking all the circumstances of the particular case into account, it is apparent that without those restrictions the competition to be protected would not be possible at all'.[64] This interpretation is justified by the second sentence in *Société Technique Minière*, which is an example of the application of the test in the first sentence: if the agreement creates more competition by introducing new products on the market, then the restriction on other distributors is tolerated, provided that the restriction is necessary to create new competition.

The Commission applied this line of reasoning in *Inntrepreneur and Spring*.[65] The case concerned a beer supply agreement between the owner of a number of pubs (GPC) and its lessees. The agreement provided for a beer tie

---

[63] Case 56/65 *Société Technique Minière v. Maschinenbau Ulm GmbH* [1966] ECR 235, 250.

[64] Case C-415/93 *Union royale belge des sociétés de football association ASBL v. Bosman* [1995] ECR 4921 para. 268.

[65] [2000] OJ L195/49. The decision is an application of the principles established in *Delimitis* [1991] ECR I-935.

that gave GPC the discretion to select the beers sold in the pubs, except that each lessee was able to offer a 'guest beer' on its own initiative. The Commission noted that the agreement restricted intra-brand competition (that is, competition between two suppliers of the same brand of beer) between the beer supplier chosen by GPC and other wholesalers who offered the same brands to pubs, and while the tie also imposed some restriction on inter-brand competition (that is, competition between different brands of beer), this was not wholly eliminated by virtue of the 'guest beer' provisions allowing each landlord to select a competing beer. Moreover, the Commission found that the agreement did not raise entry barriers for other brewers; on the contrary, because GPC's purchasing was diversified and periodically revised, it offered 'a gateway for the already substantial number of brewers, and theoretically for all other national or foreign brewers, to the UK on-trade market'.[66] The upshot was that the agreement enhanced the competitive structure of the market by improving access for a wide range of brewers who would be able to market their beer in UK pubs. The partial restriction on wholesalers' economic freedom was more than offset by the significant market opening possibilities for brewers created by the agreement. This analysis is carried out without express reference to economic efficiency – the focus is on measuring how far the agreement restricts the freedom of market participants – and finding that overall economic freedom was enhanced by increasing market access allowed the Commission to decide that the agreement did not infringe Article 81(1). Underlying this analysis is the belief that by enhancing market access, consumers benefit from more choice and lower prices. Thus there is some recognition of the positive economic benefits of the agreement, although the analysis is premised upon creation of economic opportunities for other market players, not on an economic cost–benefit analysis.

However, the Commission failed to apply this approach in *T-Mobile/O2*, where the Court's quashing of the Commission decision helps develop this method.[67] The case concerns the German market for third generation (3G) mobile telecommunications. 3G phones allow the user to receive multimedia content and the provider has a statutory obligation to roll out network infrastructure throughout the country. However, roll out is costly, and 3G operators had paid handsomely for their licences but did not reap rewards as consumers so far have shown little interest in 3G phones. So they struggled to finance the construction of infrastructure. Accordingly, competing 3G operators cooperate by sharing each other's network infrastructure. This means that if one firm has built, say, a mast and an antenna, then it can enter into a contract to allow the other firm to share these facilities to provide its network. T-Mobile and O2 shared each other's networks but took their

---

[66] [2000] OJ L195/49 para. 60.
[67] *T-Mobile Deutschland/O2 Germany* [2004] OJ L75/32; reversed Case T-328/03 *O2 Germany v. Commission*, Judgment of 2 May 2006.

cooperation further, through roaming agreements: this means that O2 would use T-Mobile's facilities. Roaming was particularly important for O2, which was a new entrant to the market and had little network infrastructure. The agreements were temporary, giving O2 sufficient time to raise revenue to roll out the necessary infrastructure. The Commission found that sharing was acceptable but roaming restricted competition. By roaming, O2 would not roll out its network as quickly and so there would be a restriction of competition in network markets. Moreover, there would be restrictions at retail level as both T-Mobile and O2 would offer consumers phones with comparable network coverage, quality and transmission speeds. But the agreement was exempted because both parties would be able to provide better coverage, quality and transmission rates for 3G wholesale and retail services more rapidly. Given that O2 was the smallest operator, it was unlikely that without the agreement it would become an effective competitor on the market for 3G services. And enhanced market entry would provide incentives for all competitors to reduce costs and improve services. This reasoning in 2003 is hardly different from the reasoning in *Carlsberg* in 1984: the Commission assumes that without the agreement the market might work better, then, realising that the only way for the market to function is for the agreement to be implemented, it grants an exemption.

The CFI began by setting out the rule in *Société Technique Minière*: to consider the competition without the agreement and the impact of the agreement on actual and potential competition, emphasising that this is not a means to assess the pro-and anticompetitive aspects of the agreement. In applying this standard, the CFI first criticised the Commission for failing to consider competition without the agreement, because the Commission assumed that O2 would enter the market without roaming. But this assumption was not tenable in light of the evidence that suggested it was unlikely that O2 would enter without the ability to roam. This meant that the Commission did not perform 'the economic analysis of the effects of the agreement on the competitive situation'.[68] Second, the CFI criticised the Commission for failing to explain what the adverse impact of the agreement was. On the contrary, the CFI considered that it was arguable that the roaming agreement was 'enabling' the smallest players to compete with the other established firms.[69] In sum, the CFI condemned the Commission for failing to consider that the agreement created competition that would not have existed without it, as a result of which Article 81 would not be infringed.

Of these three approaches, the rule in *Société Technique Minière* is the most significant because it narrows the application of Article 81 considerably. Many contracts are designed to create new markets. For instance, had this test been applied to *TPS*, one could argue that without the joint venture Canal + would retain a monopoly, so the agreement created competition, introducing a new player. However, the Commission and the CFI took the view that without the

---

[68] *O2 v. Commission*, 2 May 2006, para. 79.   [69] Ibid. para. 108.

restrictions, the market for pay-TV in France would have been even more competitive, a pessimistic stance contradicted by its later statement that the joint venture was necessary to penetrate the market.

3 The single market

Since the birth of the Community, competition policy has been used as a mechanism for integrating the EC market, although the prime drivers for integration were other Treaty provisions, specifically those abolishing protectionist measures and allowing for the free movement of workers, goods, services and capital. The importance of competition law to create or maintain a single market is reflected in the priority given by the Commission to apply competition law to practices that disintegrate the internal market. These have been vigorously attacked since the early years and remain a priority for the Commission.[70] Yet the importance of market integration for the development of EC competition law cannot be fully grasped unless we explain not only how far the Commission goes to condemn agreements that partition the common market, but also how far it goes to interpret the rules of competition to catch practices that it believes threaten the integrity of the single market.

3.1 Preventing market disintegration

The main concern for the EC has been that private firms may re-create market divisions that were previously put in place by protectionist measures (e.g. quotas, tariffs and other import restrictions) devised by the Member States.[71] The integration of the market by dismantling state protectionism under EC law would be frustrated if private practices that have similar effects were not stymied. For instance, manufacturers that collude and assign to each other exclusive sales territories,[72] or a manufacturer that agrees to allocate each of its distributors an exclusive territory, prevent any parallel trade from other Member States, suffocate price competition, perpetuate different prices in different Member States and instil a degree of price rigidity which the single market was designed to remove. Some eminent scholars and the Commission have gone so far as to say that market integration is the 'first principle' of EC

---

[70] *First Report on Competition Policy* (1972) pp. 15–16; *Second Report on Competition Policy* (1973) p. 15; *Twenty-first Report on Competition Policy* (1991) pp. 40–1; C.-D. Ehlermann 'The Contribution of EC Competition Policy to the Single Market' (1992) 29 *Common Market Law Review* 257, 265–6.

[71] *Consten/Grundig* [1966] ECR 299 p. 340.

[72] E.g. *SAS/Maersk* [2001] OJ L265/15 (upheld Case T-241/01 *Scandinavian Airlines System v. Commission* (Judgment of 13 July 2005)) where one airline (Maersk) withdrew from the Copenhagen–Stockholm route where it competed with SAS, and reciprocally SAS withdrew from other routes leaving Maersk as the only carrier. In *Volkswagen AG* [1998] OJ L124/60 and in *Opel* [2001] OJ L59/1 the companies were found to have systematically forced their authorised dealers in one Member State not to make sales in other Member States.

competition policy.[73] This is supported by the fact that agreements whose objective is the partitioning of the internal market are especially grave because 'territories are hermetically sealed off, making interpenetrating of national markets impossible, thereby bringing to nought economic integration', thus 'jeopardising a fundamental principle of the Treaty'.[74] The level of the fine is correspondingly high for these types of infringement.[75]

However, it is arguable that in some cases the concern over practices that may disintegrate the market has been at the expense of economic efficiency and of market integration itself. The classical illustration of this is the seminal judgment of *Consten and Grundig*.[76] Grundig, a German firm, appointed Consten as exclusive distributor in France for its electrical consumer goods and took steps to ensure that there were no parallel imports of Grundig products from Germany into France. The Court agreed with the Commission's finding that the agreement was anticompetitive simply by virtue of the fact that it segmented the market, leaving Consten with a monopoly in Grundig products in France. The short-sightedness of this decision is illustrated by the fact that the Court failed to take into account that for a distributor like Consten to have the incentive to promote Grundig's (then unknown) goods on the French market in competition with existing brands, it required a degree of protection from those who might import the same goods from Germany. Without such protection, Consten might engage in extensive advertising only for its prices to be undercut by free riders selling cheaper imports – cheaper because the free rider would wait for Consten to advertise the goods, and it would have no advertising costs to recoup when it offered the goods for sale in France. Thus while the distribution agreement might have suffocated competition between retailers of the same brand (intra-brand competition) it would have enhanced the degree of competition between Grundig and other brands (inter-brand competition). But this cost–benefit analysis was not sufficient to convince the Court that an exemption should have been granted.

---

[73] B. E. Hawk 'The American (Antitrust) Revolution – Lessons for the EEC?' [1988] *European Competition Law Review* 53, 54; P. Pescatore 'Public and Private Aspects of Community Competition Law' 1986 *Fordham Corporate Law Institute* 428 (Hawk ed. 1987). The *Ninth Report on Competition Policy* (1980), which lists three aims of competition policy, identifies market integration as the 'first fundamental objective' (p. 9).

[74] *Nintendo* [2003] OJ L255/33 paras. 338 and 374 respectively (citing *SA Musique Diffusion Française* [1983] ECR 1825 para. 107). See also Case 48/69 *ICI v. Commission* [1972] ECR 619 paras. 115–16; *Re Soda Ash* [1991] OJ L152/1 para. 60.

[75] The highest fine was imposed in *Volkswagen* ([1998] OJ L124/60): €102 million for segregating the market, reduced to €90 million on appeal to the CFI (Case T-62/98 *Volkswagen v. Commission* [2000] ECR II-2707). The appeal against the CFI's decision was otherwise unsuccessful (Case C-338/00 P *Volkswagen v. Commission* [2003] ECR I-9189). See also *Nintendo* [2003] OJ L255/33 para. 374 and EC Commission Guidelines on the method of setting fines [2006] OJ C210/2 para. 23 (indicating that market partitioning abuses merit the highest fines).

[76] *Consten/Grundig* [1966] ECR 299. See V. Korah 'EEC Competition Policy – Legal Form or Economic Efficiency' (1986) 39 *Current Legal Problems* 85.

This judgment is often used as an illustration that market integration is more important than economic efficiency. An efficiency analysis would have found that the consumer benefits more if Consten is allowed to sell in France with the protection afforded by the contract. However, this case is also an illustration of the Community's irrational understanding of market integration. If protecting a distributor from parallel imports is necessary to give anyone the incentive to market products abroad, manufacturers like Grundig will find it difficult to export products in other Member States if they cannot offer a distributor territorial protection; thus the law could be making a negative contribution to market integration as the incentive to export is reduced. It is reported that Grundig's response to the decision was to buy Consten.[77] The effect was that Grundig became a vertically integrated firm owning production and distribution facilities, and so Grundig was able to seal off the French market from parallel importers because the relationship between it and the distributor falls outside Article 81: the two are one firm, so there can be no agreement. There is at least one other firm that has reacted to the Commission penalising its distribution agreement by buying its distributors.[78] Therefore the unexpected consequence of the Commission trying to integrate the market is to encourage some firms to find other ways of achieving the same ends. In sum, while market integration is an important end, it is not clear whether the enforcement policy in *Grundig* facilitates market integration in practice or whether it acts as a barrier to greater integration.

3.2 Market integration and the notion of agreement

The market integration goal not only affects the substantive assessment of competition issues, but also shapes the interpretation of other aspects of the competition rules. For instance, the meaning of 'agreement' in Article 81(1) has been extended to cover a wide range of tactics designed to thwart parallel imports. From a commercial perspective, because there remain significant price differences for many goods among Member States, a manufacturer has an incentive to price discriminate to reap higher margins in Member States where prices are high. This strategy would collapse if parallel importers were able to obtain goods sold cheaply in one Member State and resell them to another Member State where the price is higher. In particular, when transportation costs are low, this is a viable strategy. In order to thwart this, firms try to block parallel imports. However, knowing that agreements with distributors that expressly or impliedly prevent parallel imports are contrary to Article 81,

---

[77] V. Korah *Cases and Materials on EC Competition Law* 2nd edn (Oxford: Hart Publishing, 2001), p. 48.

[78] Parker Pen, also in response to the Commission making an adverse finding about its distribution contracts: *Viho/Parker Pen* [1992] OJ L233/27; affirmed in Case T-66/92 *Herlitz v. Commission* and Case T-77/92 *Parker v. Commission* [1994] ECR II-531 and II-549. See also Case C-73/95P *Viho Europe v. Commission* [1996] ECR I-5457.

manufacturers have attempted more subtle mechanisms to prevent cross-border trade so that there is no formal agreement between manufacturer and distributor, absent which Article 81 does not apply. However, many of their tactics have been caught by the Commission's ever expanding definition of what constitutes an agreement. It is trite law that an agreement can be found even if there is no contract, and that no formal record of an agreement is necessary for Article 81 to apply.[79] An agreement means 'a concurrence of wills between economic operators on the implementation of a policy, the pursuit of an objective, or the adoption of a given conduct on the market'.[80] However, when applying competition law to activities designed to hamper parallel trade, the case law has made two further extensions to the notion of agreement.

First, in cases of distribution networks, apparently unilateral terminations of supply of distributors that engage in parallel trade are seen as part of the distribution agreement. For example, in *Ford Werke AG*, Ford's German subsidiary manufactured right-hand-drive cars for use in the UK, but due to considerable price differences between Germany and the UK (on average prices in the UK were 20 per cent higher than in Germany),[81] many German wholesalers ordered right-hand-drive cars which they sold to British customers, undermining Ford's profits in the UK. In response Ford notified German dealers that it would stop supplying them with right-hand-drive cars. The Court held that this apparently unilateral refusal to supply right-hand-drive cars was an agreement, forming 'part of the contractual relations between the undertaking and its dealers. Indeed admission to the Ford dealer network implies acceptance by the contracting parties of the policy pursued by Ford with regard to the models to be delivered to the German market.'[82] In other words, German dealers had agreed to give Ford the discretion to decide which models would be sold on the German market, thereby implicitly agreeing to an export ban when Ford withdrew right-hand-drive cars from German wholesalers.[83]

In a second line of cases, the Commission draws inferences of agreement from the actions and reactions of manufacturers and dealers respectively. For instance, in *Sandoz*, the manufacturer shipped goods to its customers, and wrote the words 'export prohibited' on the label. While the export ban was not part of the contract between Sandoz and its customers, the Court held that it formed part of the contractual relations between the parties, and that the customers implicitly acquiesced to the export prohibition that Sandoz had requested.[84]

---

[79] E.g. *Polypropylene* [1986] OJ L230/1 para. 81.

[80] Case T-41/96 *Bayer AG v. Commission* [2000] ECR II-3383 para. 69.

[81] H. Ullrich 'Case Note on *Ford*' (1986) 23 *Common Market Law Review* 449, 456.

[82] Joined Cases 25 and 26/84 *Ford Werke AG v. Commission* [1985] ECR 2757 para. 21.

[83] Although, according to Ullrich ('Case Note on *Ford*'), the German dealers would have been better protected by an action for breach of contract under German law, which might have allowed supplies to resume and parallel imports to continue. Instead, the Court's judgment merely calls for Ford to redraw its contracts and still limit parallel imports.

[84] [1987] OJ L222/28; upheld by Case C-277/87 *Sandoz v. Commission* [1990] ECR I-45.

These two strands of case law make it very easy to block activities that impede parallel trade, but stretch the notion of 'agreement' beyond its natural meaning.[85] Moreover, in these cases the Commission imposes fines only upon the manufacturer, on the basis that the agreement benefited it and it was responsible for its operation, while the dealers, who had 'agreed' to the most significant breach of EC competition law, escape with no fine.[86]

However, the most audacious attempt by the Commission to expand the meaning of agreement to facilitate market integration has failed. In *Bayer/Adalat* the Commission observed that Bayer was concerned about parallel imports of one of its medicines from Spain to the UK. (As prices are fixed by local authorities, and UK prices were considerably higher, sales to the UK were particularly lucrative for parallel traders.) Bayer's reaction was to reduce the amounts of the pharmaceutical sold to Spanish wholesalers. The practical effect was a reduction in parallel imports without an agreement between Bayer and the Spanish wholesalers prohibiting the latter from exporting. However, the Commission insisted that the wholesalers were aware of the motives behind Bayer's reduction of supply and 'agreed' to reduce their exports for fear that otherwise their supplies would be cut further. This reasoning was rejected by the ECJ.[87] The Court held that there must be evidence to show that the manufacturer imposed an export prohibition which was then agreed by the customer; the mere fact that wholesalers knew that the manufacturer disapproved of parallel trade and was pursuing a policy to restrict parallel trade was insufficient to find an agreement,[88] otherwise, according to Advocate General Tizzano, 'we would reach the absurd result that an agreement can be reached by the tacit acceptance of a proposal that has never (even implicitly) been made!'.[89]

The caution displayed by the Court runs against the Commission's policy, and evidences how policy can guide the evolution of the law, but with limits – legal language can be stretched to accommodate policy ambitions but cannot be deprived of meaning simply to achieve a desired end. This decision also evidences a general trend in the Court's relationship with the EC Commission: in the early years the Court supported the Commission's adventurous interpretation of competition provisions, but since the 1990s, in particular with the

---

[85] The breadth of the current construction was acknowledged by AG Tizzano in Cases C-2/01P and C-3/01 *Bundesverband der Arzneimittel-Importeure eV and Commission of the European Communities v. Bayer AG*, Judgment of 6 January 2004. For a critique, see J. E. Thompson 'Case Note on *Sandoz* and *Tipp-Ex*' (1990) 27 *Common Market Law Review* 589.

[86] E.g. *Konica* [1988] OJ L78/34 para. 51; *Sandoz* [1987] OJ L222/28 para. 35; *Bayo-n-ox* [1990] OJ L21/71 para. 64.

[87] Case C-2/01P and C-3/01P *Bundesverband der Arzneimittel-Importeure eV and Commission v. Bayer* [2004] ECR I-23.

[88] Case T-41/96 *Bayer AG v. Commission* [2000] ECR II-3383 paras. 158–67.

[89] *Bayer*, Opinion of AG Tizzano, para. 61.

creation of a Court of First Instance, the Courts have become less supportive of policy-driven approaches.[90]

From an economic perspective, moreover, the Commission's market integration policy in a case like *Bayer* may be called into question. The pharmaceutical market works slightly differently from other markets: firms sell drugs mostly to governments who buy medicines for the national health systems. The price at which governments buy medicines differs because some pay higher prices in order to subsidise further research and development (R&D) by pharmaceutical companies, while others pay less in order to manage the health-care system more economically. In this market it has been argued that facilitating parallel trade is harmful, for three reasons. First, profits are transferred from the pharmaceutical companies (who would invest this money in R&D) to traders who profit merely by re-exporting medicines and add no value. Second, parallel trade prevents each Member State from running its own R&D policy by subsidising national pharmaceutical companies by buying medicines at higher prices, and thirdly the incentive to carry out R&D by pharmaceutical companies diminishes as profits fall. In the long term this can even raise the costs of running the health system, as new medicines are not developed.[91] This suggests that attempting to create a single market in pharmaceuticals merely by encouraging parallel trade is unsatisfactory and may be positively harmful. As with *Consten/Grundig*, the Commission's pursuit of market integration via competition law in this context appears counterproductive.

4 Economic efficiency

Economic welfare is one of the anticipated benefits of membership of the EC, and the Commission noted the contribution of competition policy to economic efficiency early on. In the *First Report on Competition Policy* we find this passage:

> Competition is the best stimulant of economic activity since it guarantees the widest possible freedom of action to all. An active competition policy pursued in accordance with the provisions of the Treaties establishing the Communities makes it easier for the supply and demand structures continually to adjust to technological development. Through the interplay of decentralised decision-making machinery, competition enables enterprises continuously to improve their efficiency, which is the sine qua non for a steady improvement in living standards and employment prospects of the Community.[92]

Note that the passage opens with an ordoliberal-inspired sentence about economic freedom, but then shifts to the economic benefits, hinting at allocative,

[90] A. Arnull *The European Union and its Court of Justice* (Oxford: Oxford University Press, 1999) ch. 12, noting this judicial trend.

[91] See P. Rey and J. S. Venit 'Parallel Trade and Pharmaceuticals: A Policy in Search of Itself' (2004) 29 *European Law Review* 153.

[92] *First Report on Competition Policy* (1972) p. 1.

productive and dynamic efficiencies. Moreover the last sentence reflects the belief that competitive markets yield a range of other economic benefits. But note that, according to the passage, efficiency is, on the one hand, a result of economic freedom and, on the other, not an end in itself. Thus, we must make a case for treating efficiency as a core value.

4.1 Efficiency in Article 81

Economic efficiency is recognised implicitly in Article 81(3) where agreements that restrict economic freedom may be exempted when there is evidence that they 'improve the production or distribution of goods or promote technical or economic progress'. This phrase can be interpreted to encompass all three types of efficiencies defined in the box below. In the Commission's decisions we find evidence of exemptions based on each of the three types of efficiency.

Typology of efficiencies

Allocative efficiency: existing goods and services are allocated to those who value them most, in terms of their willingness to pay. Resources thus allocated are used in the best way possible; no other distribution would increase aggregate welfare more.

Productive efficiency: this concept focuses on a particular firm or industry and considers whether a firm organises its resources in such a way that it exploits all economies of scale, exploits existing technology effectively, and cuts all superfluous costs, so that production is at minimum cost.

Dynamic efficiency: this is a measure of whether firms have the ability and the incentives to increase productivity and innovate, developing new products or reducing production costs which can yield greater benefits to consumers.

Allocative and productive efficiencies are static measures: a snapshot of the current market position. Dynamic efficiency instead looks at the potential that the economy has to develop further. A high degree of dynamic efficiency yields an increase in allocative and productive efficiencies: as new products are developed, more goods that consumers value are produced and resources are used better than they would be without the technological development.

In *National Sulphuric Acid Association* the Commission exempted a joint buying pool of major UK and Irish manufacturers of sulphuric acid whereby each agreed to purchase at least 25 per cent of their annual requirements of sulphur from the pool. The agreement was found to yield productive and allocative efficiencies: because of the large quantities that would be ordered by the association, transportation costs would be lowered, the distribution system would become more flexible and supplies would be guaranteed in times of shortage. The lower costs would in particular be passed on to smaller members who would not have had sufficient commercial strength to obtain sulphur at comparably low prices. The agreement maximised the amount of sulphuric acid even in times when sulphur was in short supply, and competition between pool members in the market for the sale of sulphuric acid intensified, for all manufacturers faced reduced costs that would be passed on to consumers.[93] Similar benefits were found in *GE/Pratt & Whitney*, a joint venture between two jet engine manufacturers to develop a new engine for the Airbus A380 generation of aircraft. While this agreement removed the possibility of both firms developing an engine independently, leaving customers only two choices (the other being Rolls Royce), the synergies resulting from joint production meant the new engine would be produced at lower cost, be cheaper to maintain and have lower gas and noise emissions. The agreement also yielded allocative efficiency as it allowed for the quicker production of an engine to compete against the one to be manufactured by Rolls Royce.[94]

It must be recalled, however, that while economic efficiency is relevant, it is not an end in itself. First, an exemption is only granted if the agreement and the individual restrictions in the agreement are indispensable to achieve the efficiencies.[95] So if the efficiencies can be obtained by causing less distortion, then the less harmful path must be chosen. Second, efficiencies must benefit the consumer. What the consumer may lose as a result of the restriction must be compensated by what the consumer gains as a result of the agreement.[96] The Commission takes the view that the greater the market power of the firms to the agreement, the greater the efficiencies. Lastly, efficiencies cannot justify an agreement that eliminates competition.[97]

4.2 Efficiency as a core value

It may be argued that efficiency should not be classified as a core value, because an agreement which restricts competition but is efficient requires an exemption, which is only granted if all the conditions in Article 81(3) are met, so if efficiency is a defence it can hardly qualify as a 'core' value. However, an alternative reading of Article 81 is possible, which shows that efficiencies are a core value. First, Article 81(1)'s approach to identifying a restriction of competition by measuring the restriction of economic freedom can be re-interpreted as a shortcut to create a presumption of illegality. Once the Commission can trigger that presumption, the burden is on the defendant to show efficiencies.[98] Procedurally, this allocates the burden of proof in a way that is administratively effective: the Commission is in a good place to observe

---

[93] [1980] OJ L260/24 paras. 39–47.   [94] [2000] OJ L58/16 paras. 77–84.

[95] EC Commission *Guidelines on the Application of Article 81(3) of the Treaty* [2004] OJ L101/97 paras. 73–82.

[96] In *Consten and Grundig* [1966] ECR 299 p. 348 the Court suggested that the improvements 'must in particular show appreciable objective advantages of such a character as to compensate for the disadvantages which they cause in the field of competition'. See *Guidelines on Article 81(3)*, paras. 83–104.

[97] *Guidelines on Article 81(3)*, paras. 105–16.   [98] Article 2, Regulation 1/2003.

the remaining degree of economic freedom, but it is the parties who have the best access to information about possible efficiencies. Second, Article 81(3) is not, strictly speaking, a defence. Rather, it acknowledges that positive economic benefits can outweigh the restriction of economic freedom. Indeed, every agreement may be exempted, provided the conditions of Article 81(3) are met.[99] Accordingly, Article 81 should be read holistically, not as embodying an offence/defence approach.[100]

The primacy of economic efficiency is strengthened even further by Regulation 1/2003, which provides that Article 81(3) has direct effect.[101] One consequence of this is that agreements may no longer be notified to the Commission for *ex ante* scrutiny – the application of Article 81(3) is considered only *ex post* if the agreement is challenged. This procedural change shows that the Commission gives less prominence to the risk that an agreement restricts economic freedom and is more concerned that inefficient agreements should be prohibited. The Commission will probably use competition law to challenge agreements that have negative economic effects, and will be unlikely to intervene against agreements that yield efficiencies. This will be particularly the case when determining whether an agreement that has existed for some years should be challenged – the question to consider at that stage is whether the agreement has provided efficient outcomes, and if so action against it is unlikely even if there is proof that it restricts economic freedom.

Moreover, the wider discourse about the development of the European Union's economic constitution supports the increased importance of economic efficiency. Not only has DG Competition's policy evolved to give economic efficiency greater priority, but the Community as a whole has shifted progressively away from establishing an internal market for the promotion of economic liberties towards seeing the internal market process as a means to create greater efficiencies in the EC, as testified most recently by the Lisbon strategy which seeks to make the EU the most competitive trading bloc in the world. Productive and dynamic efficiencies are key to the Union's overall economic policy.

The upshot is that the increased recognition of the significance of economic efficiency leads to a unitary assessment of Articles 81(1) and (3), whereby the restriction of economic freedom under Article 81(1) today operates as a preliminary filter to indicate that there may be an infringement of the competition rules, and the analysis of whether there is economic efficiency in

---

[99] Case T-17/93 *Matra Hachette v. Commission* [1994] ECR II-595. Thus, while the language of Article 81(3) seems to give the Commission a wide discretion (agreements *may* be exempted), it seems that if the conditions for Article 81(3) are met, the Commission *shall* grant an exemption.

[100] On the contrary, the Commission's *Guidelines on Article 81(3)*, para. 1, state that Article 81(3) is a defence.

[101] [2003] OJ L1/1.

Article 81(3) is a more thorough assessment of the economic realities of the agreement's impact – anticipated or actual.[102]

5 The changing relationship among core values

In a number of situations the core values complement each other: integrated markets increase economic freedom, which in turn creates stimuli for cost savings and other efficiencies. This enhances consumer sovereignty by creating an increasingly large pool of goods and services to choose from. However, the core values also sit uneasily with each other: in particular there are tensions when a practice that divides the common market is economically efficient, or when a practice that restricts economic freedom is efficient. How are these tensions resolved? We begin by exploring how the tension between economic freedom and efficiency has evolved, to the point that, in so far as Article 81(1) is concerned, economic freedom is no longer as important. Then we consider how the tension between market integration and efficiency is managed.

5.1 Recasting the role of economic freedom

In 2004 the Commission issued *Guidelines on the application of Article 81(3)* which it claims embody an economic approach to Article 81 as a whole.[103] The guidelines first marginalise the role of economic freedom in the application of Article 81(1), and emphasise market power as the basis for finding a restriction of competition. Second, the guidelines retain the value of economic freedom in the interpretation of Article 81(3).

5.1.1 A market-power screen

The guidelines contain an interpretation of Article 81(1) where the Commission abandons the emphasis on economic freedom that has characterised the case law: 'The objective of Article 81 is to protect competition on the market as a *means* of enhancing consumer welfare and of ensuring an efficient

---

[102] Alexander Schaub (a former Director General of DG Competition) compares this to the rule of reason approach in the US: 'Article 81(1) lays down a framework for assessing the effects of the agreement in its economic context including the structure of the effected market. *The required exercise is quite similar to the market power screen of the US rule of reason.* Article 81(1) does not provide a framework for weighing the pro and anticompetitive effects of an agreement. That is the role of Article 81(3), *which essentially is an efficiency defence* ... The analysis under Article 81(3) is quite similar to the second limb of the US rule of reason analysis, according to which it must be shown that the agreement generates efficiencies, that the restrictions of competition are reasonably necessary to achieve these efficiencies and that the pro-competitive effects outweigh the anticompetitive effects.' A. Schaub 'Continued Focus on Reform: Recent Developments in EC Competition Policy' 2001 *Fordham Corporate Law Institute* 31, 44–5 (Hawk ed. 2002) (emphasis added).

[103] L. Kjolbye 'The New Commission Guidelines on the Application of Article 81(3): An Economic Approach to Article 81' [2004] *European Competition Law Review* 566.

allocation of resources.'[104] This statement is a reflection of the neoclassical approach to competition policy and restates, almost *verbatim*, the views of the OECD.[105] This contrasts markedly with the economic freedom approach, where competition is an end in itself. The guidelines continue by noting that negative effects on competition are likely when the agreement strengthens market power or allows the parties to exploit their market power.[106] The Commission believes these observations 'reflect the economic approach which the Commission is applying'.[107]

However, the guidelines provide little detail on what degree of market power suffices to trigger the application of Article 81(1). Less market power is necessary for applying Article 81 than Article 82 (where the firm must dominate the market), but this does not get us much further. Moreover, the guidelines return to the economic freedom paradigm by stating that a restriction of competition is found either in a restriction between the parties or foreclosure of market access for competitors. Thus a restriction of competition is composed of two elements: a restriction of economic freedom plus market power. In this manner, the guidelines reflect the paradigm shift away from economic freedom and towards a neoclassical model, where the restriction of economic freedom when firms have market power creates a presumption of harm to economic welfare. The parties may rebut this by showing that the agreement yields the economic benefits referred to in Article 81(3). The upshot is that the guidelines introduce some economic analysis in Article 81(1) and leave some economic analysis in Article 81(3).[108] This approach is inspired by some of the case law of the Court of Justice we reviewed above, whereby restrictions on economic freedom must be measured to determine an infringement of Article 81.

The guidelines then continue: 'The assessment of restrictions ... under Article 81(1) is only one side of the analysis. The *other side*, which is reflected in Article 81(3), is the assessment of the positive economic effects of restrictive agreements.'[109] Hence, as suggested above, Articles 81(1) and (3) have the same status – the latter is not an exceptional, discretionary exemption, but an integral part of the analysis under Article 81. However, by breaking up the economic analysis into two parts, the Commission creates uncertainty because it is not clear how much economic analysis is required to prove a restriction. This is important because the burden of proof on Article 81(1) rests with the competition authority or plaintiff. If it were too easy to show a restriction of competition with a low market-power threshold, then the guidelines would mark no departure from the case law discussed above.

---

[104] *Guidelines on Article 81(3)*, para. 13 (my emphasis).
[105] 'The basic objective of competition policy is to protect competition as the most appropriate means of ensuring the efficient allocation of resources – and thus efficient market outcomes – in free market economies.' OECD *Competition Policy and Efficiency Claims in Horizontal Agreements* OECD/GD (96) 65 (1996).
[106] *Guidelines on Article 81(3)*, paras. 24–6, esp. para. 26.   [107] Ibid. para. 24.
[108] See also Nicolaides 'Balancing Myth', p. 144.   [109] *Guidelines on Article 81(3)*, para. 28.

One interpretation of the guidelines is that Article 81(1) contains a market-power screen, whereby a restriction of economic freedom is deemed to be likely to harm consumer welfare if the parties have market power. Then the burden shifts to the defendants to show that, in spite of market power, the agreement is efficient and consumers benefit from the restriction. On this interpretation, if market power is to have a true significance, the upshot should be that Article 81(1) is not infringed as often as in the past. For example, in applying the guidelines to the *Carlsberg* agreement, that firm's small share of the beer market in the UK should suffice to find that there is no infringement; likewise in the *TPS* agreement, the Commission should find no infringement because the joint venture was entering a market to compete against a dominant firm and would lack meaningful market power. It remains to be seen whether the guidelines lead to a less aggressive use of Article 81(1). The *T-Mobile/O2* decision discussed above suggests that the Commission has some way to go before relinquishing its wide interpretation of a restriction of competition, because the Commission saw a restriction when the smallest competitor entered into an agreement that was the only way for it to participate in the market.

5.1.2 Pluralism as the basis for efficiency

The value of economic freedom is not altogether eclipsed. Under Article 81(3) the agreement will not be tolerated if it eliminates competition, even if there are efficiency gains:

> Ultimately the protection of *rivalry and the competitive process is given priority over potentially pro-competitive efficiency gains* which could result from restrictive agreements ... [R]ivalry between undertakings is an essential driver of economic efficiency, including dynamic efficiencies in the shape of innovation. In other words, the *ultimate aim of Article 81 is to protect the competitive process.*[110]

This means that the Commission considers that, in the long term, rivalry (and thereby economic freedom) yields greater economic benefits than efficiencies generated by the elimination of rivalry. Thus, while Article 81(3) exemptions tolerate some restriction of economic freedom, its elimination is not tolerated. However, this is not because economic freedom is a value important in itself. Rather, it is because without some economic freedom, efficiencies, and the gains to consumers, cannot materialise.

5.2 Market integration v. economic efficiency

It is difficult to offer a general synthesis of the way the tension between market integration and economic efficiency is managed.[111] The position is particularly

---

[110] Arnull, *The EU and its Court of Justice*, para. 105 (my emphasis).

[111] For a general overview, see A. Albors-Llorens 'Competition Policy and the Shaping of the Single Market' in C. Barnard and J. Scott (eds.) *The Law of the Single European Market:*

ambiguous in the case of agreements regulated by Article 81: on the one hand, there are decisions that illustrate how market integration is promoted for its own sake, at the expense of efficiency;[112] on the other, there are decisions that show that some degree of market disintegration can be tolerated if efficiencies result from the agreement.[113] A particularly clear example of the latter trend is the Commission's new policy on distribution agreements, which we review in more detail in chapter 10. The Commission now provides that absolute territorial protection may be conferred for a period of one year when the distributor is asked to promote a new product or to enter a new geographical market.[114] This is a long way from the position in *Consten and Grundig* where absolute territorial protection was always condemned. In contrast, the Commission's current position 'overrules' the judgment in *Consten* because it suggests that it would take a different view of a similar agreement today. For example, if a company were to develop a new type of MP3 player today and wished to market this aggressively in a foreign country, it would be able to appoint a single distributor and prevent parallel imports to give the distributor the best incentive to market this product successfully. This was the opportunity the Court denied Grundig.

A commonly held view is that the value of market integration should recede now that the single market is, more or less, a reality. However, the Commission's policy to date retains the value of market integration at the forefront, but with increased sophistication – while efficient market-partitioning practices are increasingly tolerated, inefficient market-partitioning agreements are punished severely.[115] However, as we have seen, it can be argued that in the pharmaceutical sector the Commission's policy of market integration can be characterised as misguided from an economic perspective.

6 The transformation thesis so far

For a long time in the history of Community competition law, the core values of market integration and economic freedom had a higher status than economic efficiency – decisions like *Consten and Grundig* show market integration taking priority over economic efficiency, and exemptions as recent as those in *TPS* and *T-Mobile/O2* show economic freedom to be dominant over economic efficiency.

Unpacking the Premises (Oxford: Hart Publishing, 2002); J. Baquero Cruz *Between Competition and Free Movement* (Oxford: Hart Publishing, 2002) pp. 98–103.

[112] E.g. *Consten and Grundig* [1966] ECR 299; Case 30/78 *Distillers v. Commission* [1980] ECR 2229. In *Distillers* the Commission gave the firm a period of grace during which it could limit parallel trade to promote the goods abroad. A. Jones and B. Sufrin *EC Competition Law: Text, Cases and Materials* 2nd edn (Oxford: Oxford University Press, 2004) pp. 678–9.

[113] E.g. Case 258/78 *Nungesser v. Commission* [1982] ECR 2015.

[114] *Guidelines on Vertical Restraints* [2000] OJ C291/1 para. 119 point 10.

[115] See Monti 'Article 81 EC' pp. 1064–9.

However, today, efficiency is an increasingly important value. Compare the 1972 *Report on Competition Policy* cited above with the 2002 *Report*: 'Competition policy then serves a twofold aim: addressing market failures resulting from anticompetitive behaviour by market participants and from certain market structures, on the one hand, and contributing to an overall economic policy framework across economic sectors that is conducive to effective competition, on the other.'[116] The passage speaks the language of economics, not the language of political freedom that we saw in the earlier report. The increased importance of economic efficiency is a result of a change both in substantive analysis and in procedure. At the substantive level, the Commission increasingly uses economic analysis to determine the welfare effects of practices under scrutiny. At a procedural level, Regulation 1/2003 creates an environment where the prohibition of agreements under Article 81 is only likely when the agreement has actual adverse effects on economic welfare (as opposed to the previous system where agreements were blocked *ex ante* when anticompetitive effects were predicted). Thus the procedural changes complement and accelerate the move towards a more economics-oriented approach to competition policy, moving EC competition law closer to the neoclassical model.

This transformation changes the meaning of the notion of 'restriction of competition'. Originally interpreted as a substantial interference with economic freedom, a restriction of economic freedom now serves only to establish a presumption that the agreement reduces efficiency to the detriment of consumers, a presumption which can be aided when the firms have market power.

---

[116] *Thirty-second Report on Competition Policy* (2002) p. 11.

3

Economics and competition law

Contents

1. Introduction	*page* 53
2. Shared premises	55
3. The Structure–Conduct–Performance paradigm	57
3.1 Principles	57
3.2 Policy prescriptions	59
4. The Chicago School	63
4.1 Principles	63
4.2 Policy prescriptions	65
5. The post-Chicago paradigm	68
5.1 Principles	68
5.2 Policy prescriptions	71
6. The effect of economics on law in US antitrust: a synthesis	73
6.1 Economics translated into law	73
6.2 Institutions, politics and the translation of economics into law	75
7. European competition policy and economics	79
7.1 A lack of economic analysis	79
7.2 Contemporary EC competition policy: what sort of economic approach?	82
8. Economics in competition law: opportunities and limitations	87

1 Introduction

Competition law in the EC is now presented, by DG Competition, as a set of rules dominated by an economic paradigm that focuses on consumer welfare. Now we explore further what an economic approach to competition law may entail. The aim of this chapter is to present an analysis of the relationship between competition law and economic learning. Given the Community's recent conversion to economics, we use US law to learn some lessons. The central argument is that, depending on which economic premises one begins with, the prescriptions for competition law change, sometimes quite drastically. This means that embracing economics is only the starting point. It is now imperative to identify which economic approach the Commission takes. The significance of economic paradigms, from an American perspective, was noted by Professor Baker in the following terms: 'While lawyers including judges are in control of prosecutorial choices and judicial decisions . . . it is fair to say that, from a longer term perspective, decade-to-decade, or era-to-era, antitrust has been shaped more importantly by the arguments of economists.'[1] This position is too sanguine, as there is also a political dimension that drives the adoption of economic theories.[2] A novel economic theory should be consistent with the judicial and enforcement policy of the time in order to have a chance of success, and transitions to new economic paradigms are often preceded by policy commitments that go in a similar direction. In short, economic paradigms change when political paradigms shift.

This chapter offers a thumbnail sketch of three economic models that have been present in the evolution of antitrust law in the United States (the *SCP*, the *Chicago* and the *post-Chicago* paradigms), outlining their different analytical positions and how these translate into antitrust policy by reviewing how the law on mergers and predatory pricing changes as courts and competition authorities embrace new economic approaches. The lesson to be taken from this study is that the economic models and the underlying policy climate influence each other. Moreover, a competition law dispute can be won when the adjudicator accepts one's economic analysis. Accordingly, it is also important to consider what legal standards judges and administrators adopt when deciding whether to accept a novel economic paradigm as a basis for their decision, an issue touched upon in section 6 below. The strong bond between economics and antitrust is not present in the history of EC competition law. The reasons for this, and the emergence of an economics-oriented paradigm, were broached in the previous chapter and are considered more fully in the final section of this chapter, identifying the constituent features of the economic model characterising contemporary EC competition policy.

---

[1] J. B. Baker 'A Preface to Post-Chicago Antitrust' in A. Cucinotta, R. Pardolesi and R. Van den Bergh (eds.) *Post-Chicago Developments in Antitrust Law* (Cheltenham: Edward Elgar, 2002) p. 68. Note also this aphorism: 'The ideas of economists and political philosophers, both when they are right and when they are wrong, are more powerful than is commonly understood. Indeed the world is ruled by little else. Practical men, who believe themselves to be quite exempt from any intellectual influence, are usually the slaves of some defunct economist. Madmen in authority, who hear voices in the air, are distilling their frenzy from some academic scribbler of a few years back.' J. M. Keynes *A General Theory of Employment, Interest and Money* (London: Macmillan, 1936) p. 383.

[2] See M. S. Jacobs 'An Essay on the Normative Foundations of Antitrust Economics' (1995) 74 *North Carolina Law Review* 219.

2 Shared premises

Differences among economic models should not be exaggerated, most pre-scriptions for competition policy share a number of common features, and survey evidence in the US shows that economists on all sides support com-petition policy more than any other economic policy:[3] its public support led one to describe antitrust as an American religion.[4] The differences are about how to apply economics to regulate markets. Principally, the need for com-petition law intervention arises when there is a market failure – so long as markets remain competitive, consumers benefit from low prices and innova-tive products because firms are driven by the desire to maximise profits and sell as many goods as is economically feasible at the lowest price. The market system is perceived to be the ideal mechanism through which the fundamental economic questions are answered: what goods to produce, how many to produce and how to distribute them. As we saw in chapter 2, for economists competition is a word that identifies a state of affairs 'in which consumer interests are well served rather than as a process of rivalry'.[5] Or as Bork put it, 'Competition, for the purposes of antitrust analysis, must be understood as a term of art signifying any state of affairs in which consumer welfare cannot be increased by judicial decree.'[6]

When there is competition, economic benefits accrue without the aid of government intervention and without firms intending to generate economic welfare: firms act to maximise profits by satisfying consumer demand, and as if by an invisible hand, this leads to the most effective use of scarce resources. Markets fail when the way for firms to maximise profits is no longer to reduce price and maximise output, but rather to limit production and raise prices. This leads to an inefficient use of existing resources so that society is worse off. Competition laws are then needed to cure that market failure and restore competitive markets. So far, we have focused on how competition can enhance allocative efficiency. However, as Professor Vickers noted, competition is also a means to achieve productive efficiency, in three ways: first, competitive pres-sures give firms greater incentives to reduce costs to avoid being taken over or rendered insolvent by more efficient competitors; second, and related, com-petition is a means of selecting the more efficient firms, which will thrive; third, the competition to innovate is a source of productive efficiency.[7] So competi-tion may also be a means to achieve dynamic efficiency.

---

[3] F. McChesney 'In Search of the Public Interest Model of Antitrust' in F. McChesney and W. Shughart (eds.) *The Causes and Consequences of Antitrust: The Public Choice Perspective* (Chicago: University of Chicago Press, 1995) p. 27.

[4] A. Shonfield *Modern Capitalism: The Changing Balance of Public and Private Power* (Oxford: Oxford University Press, 1965) p. 329.

[5] *University Life Insurance Co. v. Unimarc Ltd* 699 F 2d 846, 853 (7th Cir. 1983) Posner J.

[6] R. Bork *The Antitrust Paradox* (New York: Free Press, 1978) p. 52.

[7] J. Vickers 'Concepts of Competition' (1995) 47 *Oxford Economic Papers* 1.

From these shared concerns, some examples of market failure draw almost unanimous disdain. A cartel of all manufacturers of a product capable of monopolising a market results in allocative inefficiency: output is reduced, leading to the waste of resources. A monopoly reduces allocative efficiency and may also show productive inefficiency – as it faces no challenge, it has no incentive to minimise costs and organise its resources effectively. Moreover, economists tend to be utilitarian. That is, their interest is in the total welfare of society, so if a monopoly is more productively efficient than a market populated by several firms, then if the gains in productive efficiency are greater than the losses of allocative efficiency, economists would approve of the monopoly.[8]

Economists also agree that the costs of market failure are difficult to measure. An oft-cited study concluded that the deadweight loss of monopoly was 0.1 per cent of gross national product (GNP).[9] This would make the benefit of competition law very small indeed. However, later studies found that the loss was between 4 and 13 per cent of GNP, and it has been suggested that without competition law the cost would be more significant.[10] However, the more significant social costs of monopoly are the reduction of productive and dynamic efficiency – a firm with market power might use its extra profits (which from an economic perspective are mostly transfers of wealth) to thwart the entry of rivals in the market. This behaviour is wasteful, as the increased revenues do not go into increasing productive efficiency of the dominant firm; instead they destroy the economic resources of the rivals.[11] Another kind of economic loss is labelled 'X-inefficiency'.[12] This is a term used to indicate that the dominant monopolist has no incentives to reduce production costs or to invent new goods, happy to lead the 'quiet life' at the expense of introducing greater economic welfare. Arguably, dynamic efficiency may also suffer if the monopolist's rent-seeking behaviour creates disincentives for other firms to enter the market with innovative products. According to many, these kinds of losses are more significant than the reductions in allocative efficiency and, while the link between these efficiencies and antitrust policies remains to be fully uncovered, the evidence to date justifies the presence of antitrust laws as a means of delivering allocative, productive and dynamic efficiency.[13]

---

[8] The clearest exposition is in the division between economists and lawyers over the efficiency defence in merger cases. See pp. 292–6.

[9] A. C. Harberger 'Monopoly and Resource Allocation' (1954) 44 *American Economic Review* 77.

[10] W. K. Viscusi, J. E. Harrington Jr and J. M. Vernon *Economics of Regulation and Antitrust* 4th edn (Cambridge, MA: MIT Press, 2005) pp. 90–2.

[11] R. A. Posner 'The Social Costs of Monopoly and Regulation' (1975) 83 *Journal of Political Economy* 807.

[12] H. Leibenstein 'Allocative Efficiency vs. "X-Efficiency"' (1966) 56 *American Economic Review* 392.

[13] F. M. Scherer 'Antitrust, Efficiency, and Progress' (1987) 62 *New York University Law Review* 998.

Moving beyond these shared starting points (inefficiencies are the evil to be penalised and usually inefficiencies will be found where there is market power) economic analyses of competition policy diverge, for example in defining what 'market power' means and in identifying what other practices reduce efficiency. The following sections review three economic paradigms which have affected US antitrust law. For each there is a sketch of the basic principles that characterise the paradigm followed by illustrations of how those principles have been applied in US antitrust law – this will show how American antitrust has responded to changes in economic learning. The discussion also offers a flavour of the policy debates that affect the evolution of antitrust law, in an attempt to understand how the shift from one economic paradigm to another occurs.[14]

3 The Structure–Conduct–Performance paradigm

3.1 Principles

The Structure–Conduct–Performance (hereinafter SCP) paradigm was prominent in the 1950s and 1960s. It suggests that by observing the structure of a market, inferences can be drawn as to how firms conduct themselves, and this allows one to evaluate the market's economic performance. On this basis, certain market structures can be identified as being the cause of anticompetitive conduct, which in turn leads to poor economic performance.

Market structure is a term used to define the characteristics within which firms operate in a given product market. The principal characteristics are the number of firms and their size. Also relevant is the market power of the firms' customers, the ease with which new firms can enter the market and old ones can exit it.

Conduct describes the way in which the firms behave: what criteria they use to set prices (collusion, independently, or on the basis of consumer demand); how they decide on advertising and research and development expenditure.

Performance is the yardstick by which the conduct of firms is measured. The standard measure for this is whether the firms enhance economic welfare. This is normally done by measuring productive, allocative and dynamic efficiency. In addition to these benchmarks, performance might also be judged on the basis of whether there is full employment of human resources and whether there is an equitable distribution of income.[15]

---

[14] The three paradigms identified here have been used by other authors in similar ways. See e.g. W. E. Kovacic and C. Shapiro 'Antitrust Policy: A Century of Economic and Legal Thinking' (2000) 14 *Journal of Economic Perspectives* 43 and see the illuminating reflections in Jacobs 'Normative Foundations'.

[15] The wider conception of progress is taken by F. M. Scherer and D. R. Ross *Industrial Market Structure and Economic Performance* 3rd edn (Boston, MA: Houghton Mifflin, 1990) p. 4.

The theory predicts that the more closely the market in question approaches conditions of monopoly the worse its performance (because anticompetitive coordination among firms is easier the smaller their number), and the more closely the market approaches the conditions of perfect competition the better its performance. In so doing it builds upon previous work in welfare economics, which had led to a taxonomy of market structures. The principal ones are defined in the box below.

> *Perfect competition*: many sellers producing homogeneous goods where the profits are primarily determined by consumer demand and consumer choice is based uniquely on price. Each seller's market share is too small to have any impact on the price of the goods in question.
>
> *Monopolistic competition*: many sellers producing differentiated products, whereby consumer choice is dictated by considerations other than price (e.g. additional services, geographical location of sellers, or the image of the product).
>
> *Oligopoly*: a small number of sellers where each seller's profits are affected significantly by the actions of the others in the market.
>
> *Monopoly*: one seller in the market.

In the market for cafés in London for example, the SCP paradigm would define this as a market with the attributes of monopolistic competition, where brand image creates an entry barrier which forecloses competition even from lower-priced sellers, thereby reducing economic welfare.[16] Moreover, competitors misallocate resources by devoting their revenue to advertising or introducing loyalty schemes to raise entry barriers rather than to efficiency-enhancing innovations.

Proponents of this paradigm made two predictions. The first was that high levels of concentration mean firms have market power, which facilitates anticompetitive behaviour. Concentration levels measure how many firms there are in an industry: the fewer firms, the more highly concentrated the market. Thus, monopoly and oligopoly market structures are less efficient than market structures with more players. The second prediction was that if entry barriers are high the price–cost margin of the leading firms increases.[17] This was supported by empirical studies which illustrated a weak, but significant, link between the level of concentration and profit rates, and studies showing that firms in markets with high barriers to entry had significantly higher rates of return than firms in markets with lower entry barriers.[18] Moreover, the argument about large economies of scale (a minimum efficient scale is the smallest output a firm can produce to minimise its long-run costs, thus a market with

---

[16] J. S. Bain *Barriers to New Competition: Their Character and Consequences in Manufacturing Industries* (Cambridge, MA: Harvard University Press, 1956) p. 142.

[17] L. W. Weiss 'The SCP Paradigm and Antitrust' (1979) 127 *University of Pennsylvania Law Review* 1104, 1105.

[18] Bain *Barriers to New Competition*.

large economies of scale requires large output in order to operate profitably so that the market can only support a small number of firms) did not justify the currently high levels of concentration in US industries – firms could be smaller and still be productively efficient.[19] In addition, entry barriers could be raised artificially by existing firms, for example by product differentiation or making entry of a new product more difficult by creating brand loyalty.[20] In sum, high concentration leads to inefficiency: firms in oligopoly and monopoly markets limit output and raise prices; firms insulated from competition by high entry barriers have no incentives to produce efficiently, and there are no incentives to innovate when inefficient behaviour is profitable.[21]

The implication of the SCP paradigm for competition policy is that we can identify which market structures lead to anticompetitive results and devise a competition law that is designed to modify or prevent market structures that are linked with poor economic performance.[22] The policy recommendation that flows from the SCP paradigm is that special attention should be given to those market structures most likely to reduce consumer welfare – monopoly and oligopoly. Following this recommendation could yield a very aggressive antitrust policy as some scholars believed that anticompetitive behaviour could manifest itself even with fairly low levels of concentration.[23] Moreover, the paradigm sees the structure of an industry as the cause of market failure, remedies are designed primarily to alter the structure of the market, and to prevent incumbents from raising entry barriers. It follows that small industry deserves protection from larger firms: large numbers of small firms yield greater economic welfare than a small number of large firms.

3.2 Policy prescriptions

3.2.1 Mergers

Evidence of the SCP paradigm's influence can be seen in the field of merger legislation, most clearly in the Celler–Kefauver Act of 1950 which amended the merger provisions in the Clayton Act of 1915 in two respects. First, the Clayton Act covered only mergers by stock acquisition, and the 1950 Act extended the scope to mergers that took place by asset acquisition. Second, merger control was extended to all mergers, not just those between competitors. Underpinning these changes is a strong legislative desire to take a tougher line against mergers, for both economic reasons – given the economic

---

[19] J. S. Bain 'Economies of Scale, Concentration, and the Condition of Entry in Twenty Manufacturing Industries' (1954) 44 *American Economic Review* 15; Bain *Barriers to New Competition* pp. 53–113.

[20] Bain *Barriers to New Competition* pp. 114–43.

[21] F. M. Scherer *Innovation and Growth: Schumpeterian Perspectives* (Cambridge, MA: MIT Press, 1984) p. 247.

[22] P. R. Ferguson and G. J. Ferguson *Industrial Economics: Issues and Perspectives* 2nd edn (London: Macmillan, 1994) p. 13.

[23] Bain *Barriers to New Competition* pp. 1–42.

inefficiency of increased concentration – and political concerns that economic concentration would threaten democratic government.[24] Merger enforcement was also affected by the SCP paradigm, no more so than in the 1968 Department of Justice (DOJ) Merger Guidelines (drafted by Donald Turner, an influential advocate of the SCP paradigm and at the time Chief of the Antitrust Division at the DOJ)[25] which provide an implementation of the SCP paradigm into antitrust law. The Guidelines proclaim: 'Market structure is the focus of the Department's merger policy chiefly because the conduct of the individual firms in a market tends to be controlled by the structure of that market.'[26] The Supreme Court was also influenced by the SCP paradigm, developing legal standards based on the concentration of the industry, the market shares of the merging firms, the trend in concentration and the effect of the merger on concentration.[27] The Guidelines formalised the Court's approach by setting out concentration 'thresholds' as presumptive indicators of likely anticompetitive effect.

Vertical mergers are also a concern under the SCP approach. (A merger is vertical when an upstream and a downstream business merge.) The most aggressive SCP-led policy against vertical mergers was in the cement sector between 1967 and 1985.[28] This was led by the Federal Trade Commission (FTC). (In the US two federal agencies apply the antitrust laws: the Department of Justice and the FTC.) This industry saw eighty vertical mergers between cement and concrete manufacturers between 1940 and 1959, and the FTC's fear was that the combined effect of further concentration would be the foreclosure of the market as new cement manufacturers find it difficult to sell because many ready-mixed concrete firms are vertically integrated, and entry in the ready-mixed concrete market is also more difficult.[29] The FTC policy was to block all vertical mergers that created foreclosure risks.[30] The policy was based on a report which stated that the primary reason for vertical mergers in this sector was to 'foreclose the impact of rivals' aggressive price and non

---

[24] For a fuller analysis, see R. J. R. Peritz *Competition Policy in America: History, Rhetoric, Law* rev. edn (Oxford: Oxford University Press, 2000) ch. 4 esp. pp. 195–9.

[25] Earlier, he had co-authored an authoritative work on antitrust law, heavily reliant on the work of Bain: C. Kaysen and D. Turner *Antitrust Policy: An Economic and Legal Analysis* (Cambridge, MA: Harvard University Press, 1959).

[26] Department of Justice Merger Guidelines (1968) (available at www.usdoj.gov/atr/hmerger/ 11247.htm).

[27] *US v. Philadelphia National Bank* 374 US 321 (1963).

[28] See H. Dumez and A. Jeaunemaître 'The Unlikely Encounter between Economics and a Market: The Case of the Cement Industry' in M. Callon (ed.) *The Laws of the Markets* (Oxford: Blackwell, 1998); R. N. Johnson and A. M. Parkman 'Spatial Competition and Vertical Mergers; Cement and Concrete Revisited – A Comment' (1987) 77 *American Economic Review* 750.

[29] M. E. McBride 'Spatial Competition and Vertical Integration: Cement and Concrete Revisited' (1983) 73 *American Economic Review* 1011.

[30] Enforcement Policy with Respect to Vertical Mergers in the Cement Industry 71 FTC 1623 (1967); rescinded in Enforcement Policy with Respect to Vertical Mergers in the Cement Industry 50 Fed Reg 21,507 (1985).

price strategies'.[31] The result of the FTC's policy was that all action taken against vertical mergers resulted in divestiture or a consent decree (a settlement with the FTC) that achieved dissolution. Typical of the enforcement actions is the *Ash Grove* case.[32] Ash Grove had acquired two ready-mixed cement manufacturers in a market where it was the third largest of ten cement firms, where the top two accounted for 68.1 per cent of the market and it had a market share of 13–18 per cent. The Court of Appeals rejected the value of Ash Grove's evidence that there was price competition in the market even after its acquisitions, and its conclusions represent an apt summary of the concerns animating the SCP paradigm:

> Price competition in an unconcentrated market is indeed a sign of healthy competition. However, a brief flurry of price competition in a heavily concentrated market which has the effect and possibly the purpose of destroying independent competitors is not a sign of a healthy market. Once the independents [i.e. smaller cement firms] are eliminated there is no guarantee of continued low pricing from the large integrated suppliers who have acquired captive customers.[33]

Here the Court anticipates market failure as industry becomes increasingly concentrated, and the only way of preventing a further deterioration of competition is to stop mergers that eliminate the source of competitive behaviour: small, independent competitors.

3.2.2 Predatory pricing

There are two statutes that may be used to regulate predatory pricing: section 2 of the Sherman Act forbids 'monopolization or attempts to monopolize' while section 2(a) of the Clayton Act (as amended by the Robinson–Patman Act) prohibits price discrimination 'where the effect of such discrimination may be substantially to lessen competition or tend to create a monopoly in any line of commerce . . .'.[34] In the application of these provisions, the SCP paradigm was instrumental in introducing more rigorous economic analysis. The early s. 2 Sherman Act case law focused upon behaviour that courts viewed as reproachable, but in the 1950s the courts introduced the current two-pronged analysis: (1) proof that there is monopoly power; (2) showing that the monopoly power was acquired or maintained by predatory or exclusionary conduct.[35] The SCP paradigm was influential in providing economic tools to assess the existence of market power, by positing the necessity to define the relevant market and to assess the level of concentration and the barriers to entry. In this era it became common for economists to give evidence in court as to the existence of

---

[31] Federal Trade Commission *Economic Report on Mergers and Vertical Integration in the Cement Industry* (Washington, DC: USGPO, 1966) p. 97.
[32] *Ash Grove Cement Co. v. FTC* 577 F 2d 1368 (1978).
[33] Ibid. 1379–80.   [34] 15 USC §§ 2 and 13 respectively.
[35] *US v. United Shoe Machinery Corp.* 110 F Supp 295 (1953).

monopoly power, although courts did not integrate economic methodology in their reasoning formally and judgments of the time are often worded using common law rhetoric.[36]

The economics of predatory pricing at that time are well encapsulated in the 1955 report of the Attorney General's National Committee to Study the Antitrust Laws: '[p]redatory price cutting designed to eliminate a smaller business rival ... is a practice which inevitably frustrates competition by excluding competitors from the market or deliberately impairing their competitive strength'.[37] Predatory pricing affects the structure of the market by reducing the number of competitors, leading to increased concentration. Politically at the time, the aim of antitrust was not only to curb the direct elimination of competitors, but more widely to prevent trends towards concentration, which gave credence to the conclusion that the Robinson–Patman Act 'does not require that the discrimination must have harmed competition, but only that there is a reasonable possibility that they (sic) "may" have such an effect'.[38] There is a consonance between the political ideals and the economic analysis, which the majority opinion in *Utah Pie* illustrates. The case concerned the market for frozen dessert pies in Salt Lake City. Utah Pie, a local family-run manufacturer, was a recent entrant whose presence in Salt Lake City saved it substantial transportation costs, allowing it to undercut the prices of three large, national producers. Each of the three national producers engaged in a variety of practices to oust the local pie manufacturer which were condemned under the Robinson–Patman Act. The Supreme Court found that each sold pies in Salt Lake City at prices lower than in other markets which were considerably closer to their manufacturing plants.[39] There was also evidence that each of the three national manufacturers used this tactic intending to oust Utah Pie.

Justice White's majority opinion shows a concern for the protection of small family-owned businesses, but also an interpretation of the law which is in tune with the SCP paradigm: first, by noting how the three large national manufacturers considered that Utah Pie's presence was an 'unfavourable factor' which posed a constant 'check' on their performance, suggesting that with its elimination the more concentrated market would lead to higher prices;[40] second, although the evidence did not show that Utah Pie was likely to leave the market soon, he held that the practices of the three defendants were likely to render Utah Pie a less competitive force and that one may penalise 'price

---

[36] J. W. Meehan Jr and R. J. Larner 'The Structural School, Its Critics, and Its Progeny: An Assessment' in R. J. Larner and J. W. Meehan Jr (eds.) *Economics and Antitrust Policy* (New York: Quorum, 1989) p. 184.

[37] Report of the Attorney General's National Committee to Study the Antitrust Laws 165–6 (1955), cited in *Brooke Group Ltd v. Brown & Williamson Tobacco Corp.* 509 US 209 (1993) footnote 14.

[38] *Corn Products Co. v. FTC* 324 US 726, 742 (1945).

[39] 386 US 685, 690 (1967).   [40] Ibid. 697.

discrimination that *erodes* competition as much as price discrimination that is intended to have *immediate* destructive impact'.[41]

Foreshadowing many of the Chicago School arguments, the dissent in *Utah Pie* noted that before the alleged predation Utah Pie had a market share of 66.5 per cent, which was eroded to 45.3 per cent by the price war, leaving Utah Pie with a commanding lead (the next largest seller had 29.4 per cent of the market). The dissent could not agree that the antitrust laws were designed to protect a monopoly from effective price competition.[42] From this perspective (which ignores the wider market power of the three national producers and exaggerates the market power of the plaintiff) the activities in question were making markets more competitive, reducing prices and introducing new competitors in Salt Lake City. The majority, adopting a longer-term perspective, foresaw instead a market which would be dominated by the three national firms, with Utah Pie destined to dwindle without the rescue of the antitrust laws.

4 The Chicago School

4.1 Principles

Chicago scholars launched three central challenges to the SCP approach. First, the connection between industry concentration and anticompetitive effects was refuted. Stigler pointed out that anticompetitive behaviour in a concentrated industry was hard to obtain. It requires agreement over the prices to charge and on how to share the market; moreover firms must have a mechanism to deter cheating: each participant in a cartel has an incentive to deviate from the high prices to reap higher profits. Without these measures, anticompetitive behaviour is unlikely, and because agreement on how to manage coordination is so costly, the likelihood of any successful coordination is minimal.[43] Therefore, one cannot presume coordinated anticompetitive behaviour in all concentrated industries. Furthermore, the statistical correlation between high concentration and high profit rates was not necessarily caused by anticompetitive behaviour, but could be the result of economic efficiency.[44] Finally, economies of scale did justify high levels of concentration: the SCP paradigm's work was criticised for taking into consideration only production costs, while if one took into account distribution costs then large plants could be justified on the basis of economies of scale.[45] Thus, there is no ideal market structure that leads to optimum performance.[46]

---

[41] Ibid. 703 (emphasis added).   [42] Ibid. 706.

[43] G. J. Stigler 'A Theory of Oligopoly' (1964) 72 *Journal of Political Economy* 44.

[44] H. Demsetz 'Industry Structure, Market Rivalry and Public Policy' (1973) 3 *Journal of Law and Economics* 1–9; H. Demsetz 'Two Systems of Belief about Monopoly' in H. J. Goldschmid, H. M. Mann and J. F. Weston (eds.) *Industrial Concentration: The New Learning* (Boston, MA: Little Brown, 1974) pp. 164–84.

[45] See the debate between McGee and Scherer in Goldschmid et al. *Industrial Concentration*.

[46] F. Easterbrook 'Workable Antitrust Policy' (1986) 84 *Michigan Law Review* 1696, 1700.

Second, many Chicagoans pointed out that market structure could be affected by performance in the market – the SCP model omitted the possibility of endogenous effects on structure. The gist of this argument is the simple observation that if a firm with a large market share chooses to behave anti-competitively by cutting output, this will invite new entrants, which will improve competition.[47] *Conduct affects structure.*

Third, the Chicago School questioned the SCP's definition of 'barriers to entry'. Bain's definition of an entry barrier for the SCP paradigm was this: 'the extent to which, in the long run, established firms can elevate their selling prices above the minimal average costs … without inducing potential entrants to enter the industry'.[48] Under this definition, economies of scale, product differentiation and cost advantages due to the control of superior resources are entry barriers. For Chicagoans, none of these qualify as entry barriers. Instead, a barrier to entry for Chicagoans is a cost 'which must be borne by a firm which seeks to enter an industry but is not borne by firms already in the industry'.[49] Chicago's criticism of the SCP definition of entry barriers is that the latter saw entry barriers whenever entry was more *difficult*, whilst the question for the Chicago paradigm is whether entry is more *costly* for the new entrant. For Chicagoans the only entry barriers are property rights conferred by government (e.g. if the incumbent owns the patent to a product necessary for entry, then the only way for new entry to occur is through a licence from the incumbent – the cost of the licence for the new firm is a cost not borne by the patent owner). Eliminate Bainian entry barriers, and the spectre of concentrated markets vanishes. As Professor Posner put it, '[o]nce "barrier to entry" was redefined … the plausibility of supposing that barriers to entry are common, or commonly substantial, diminished sharply. The deconcentrators [those arguing in favour of aggressive policy against concentrated markets] are thus arguing from an abandoned premise.'[50]

Put together, these three critiques led to the basic principle of the Chicago approach: markets normally cure themselves and competitive outcomes are likely without significant government intervention. 'Competition is hardier than you think. The desire to make a buck leads people to undermine monopolistic practices.'[51] In addition to questioning the very basis of the causal connection between structure, conduct and performance, the Chicago School argued that courts or government agencies are often unable, through legal intervention, to effect any improvement in welfare – on the contrary, legal

---

[47] Demsetz 'Two Systems'; W. M. Landes and R. A. Posner 'Market Power in Antitrust Cases' (1981) 94 *Harvard Law Review* 937.

[48] J. S. Bain *Industrial Organisation* 2nd edn (New York: Wiley, 1968) p. 252.

[49] G. J. Stigler *The Organization of Industry* (Homewood, IL: R. D. Irwin, 1968) p. 67.

[50] R. A. Posner 'The Chicago School of Antitrust Analysis' (1979) 127 *University of Pennsylvania Law Review* 925, 947.

[51] Easterbrook 'Workable Antitrust Policy' p. 1701.

intervention may lead to inefficient results, and the costs of error (e.g. reducing competition, creating disincentives to invest) reduce economic welfare.[52]

Armed with these alternative models of economic behaviour, Chicagoans criticised much of the application of competition law as misguided. In their view, the test for antitrust violations is not whether conduct injures competitors or excludes rivals, but whether the practices in question allow firms to reduce output and raise prices. The standard by which to judge antitrust violations shifts from an inquiry into market power (the leading work representing the SCP paradigm argued that the chief purpose of antitrust policy was the 'limitation of market power')[53] to an inquiry about whether the practice in question is efficient.[54]

4.2 Policy prescriptions

In contrast to the SCP proponents, antitrust enforcement is much less intrusive under the Chicago School model. The orthodox Chicago position of the 1960s and 1970s identified explicit price fixing and large horizontal mergers as the only antitrust problems.[55] These views have informed enforcement since the 1980s.

4.2.1 Mergers

The 1968 Merger Guidelines were rewritten in the 1980s by a Chicagoan DOJ led by William Baxter. Under his leadership, the Guidelines were designed to reflect a concern over market power (not market structure, as under the SCP paradigm), which he defined as the ability of a seller or group of sellers in concert profitably to raise prices above competitive levels, generating allocative inefficiencies.[56] This narrower focus led to less severe enforcement than under the 1968 Guidelines.[57] Moreover, the Guidelines no longer use market concentration as the sole tool to determine anticompetitive risks, but consider in more detail other factors which make anticompetitive effects less likely – notably ease of entry – which reduced the number of mergers raising competition risks.[58] Moreover, it was noted that actual enforcement was even more lenient than the Guidelines.[59] These amendments, combined with a judiciary

[52] F. Easterbrook 'Ignorance and Antitrust' in T. M. Jorde and D. J. Teece (eds.) *Antitrust, Innovation and Competitiveness* (New York: Oxford University Press, 1992).

[53] Kaysen and Turner *Antitrust Policy* p. 82.

[54] For a succinct review of the Chicago position, see H. Hovenkamp 'Antitrust Policy After Chicago' (1985) 84 *Michigan Law Review* 213, 226–9.

[55] Posner 'Chicago School' p. 933; Easterbrook 'Workable Antitrust Policy' p. 1702.

[56] W. F. Baxter 'Responding to the Reaction: The Draftsman's View' (1983) 71 *California Law Review* 618, 622.

[57] F. M. Scherer 'Merger Policy in the 1970s and 80s' in Larner and Meehan *Economics and Antitrust Policy*.

[58] For a comparison of the 1968 and 1982 Guidelines, see T. E. Kauper 'The 1982 Horizontal Merger Guidelines: Of Collusion, Efficiency, and Failure' (1983) 71 *California Law Review* 497.

[59] M. A. Eisner *Antitrust and the Triumph of Economics* (Chapel Hill: University of North Carolina Press, 1991) p. 204.

viewing entry barriers as generally low,[60] reduced the scope of merger enforcement, and between 1981 and 1984 the Federal Trade Commission approved nine of the largest mergers in the US.[61]

More specifically, the fear that vertical mergers would 'foreclose' markets was condemned as erroneous. The acquisition of downstream firms would not generate anticompetitive effects unless the acquiring company obtained market power in the up- or downstream market. Absent market power, vertical mergers were likely to yield efficiencies by lowering costs. True, vertical integration would prevent non-integrated upstream manufacturers from selling to the downstream firm, which was now vertically integrated, but absent very high levels of concentration 'there would merely be a realignment of existing market sales without any likelihood of a diminution in competition'.[62] In 1985 the FTC rescinded its restrictive approach to vertical mergers in the cement industry, accompanied by economic studies that found no evidence that the FTC's policy had improved competition in the sector.[63] The *Ash Grove* case was criticised for failing to take into account the fact that new entry was possible because of lower transportation costs, and for the court's refusal to acknowledge the fact that falling prices suggested that the market was competitive.[64] The DOJ Guidelines reflected this by revisiting the Guidelines and refusing to scrutinise vertical mergers. The Guidelines see anticompetitive risks only when a vertical merger has horizontal effects – for example, if it raises entry barriers by forcing new entrants to enter at both up- and downstream levels, if it facilitates collusion by making it easier to monitor prices, or if the acquired firm is a disruptive customer who made horizontal collusion more difficult. In fact, the Guidelines display almost a U-turn: under the SCP paradigm the trend to vertical integration was seen as increasing foreclosure risk, but the 1984 Guidelines provide that 'an extensive pattern of vertical integration may constitute evidence that substantial economies are afforded by vertical integration'.[65]

During the SCP's era, the Government won all merger cases that went to the Supreme Court.[66] The Chicago era is characterised by few appeals because of reduced enforcement, and by the Supreme Court refusing to block mergers. Of particular interest, because the clash between majority and dissent illustrates the gap between the SCP and the Chicago paradigm, is *Cargill Inc. v. Montford of Colorado Inc.*[67] The second and third largest beef packers in the US had

---

[60] E.g. *US v. Baker Hughes Inc.* 908 F 2d 981 (DC Cir. 1990).   [61] Eisner *Antitrust* p. 221.

[62] *Alberta Gas Chemicals v. E. I. Du Pont de Nemours* 826 F 2d 1235, 1246 (3d Cir. 1987).

[63] R. N. Johnson and A. M. Parkman 'The Role of Ideas in Antitrust Policy toward Vertical Mergers: Evidence from the FTC Cement-Ready Mixed Concrete Cases' [1987] *Antitrust Bulletin* 841; McBride 'Spatial Competition'.

[64] Johnson and Parkman 'Role of Ideas' pp. 872–3.

[65] Department of Justice Merger Guidelines (1984) para. 4.24 (available at www.usdoj.gov/atr/public/guidelines/2614.htm).

[66] Stewart J remarked bitterly that the 'sole consistency that I can find is that in litigation under Section 7 the Government always wins'. *US v. Von's Grocery Co.* 384 US 270, 301 (1966).

[67] 479 US 104 (1986).

agreed a merger, and the fifth largest sought to enjoin it, fearing it would substantially lessen competition, contrary to s. 7 of the Clayton Act.[68] The plaintiff considered that the merged entity would reduce prices at a level just above cost, which would squeeze its profits. The majority held that the plaintiff had no right to seek an injunction because he would not suffer antitrust injury, that is the kind of injury that the antitrust laws were designed to prevent: he would merely suffer as a result of price competition which the courts should encourage.[69] Higher concentration is of no consequence as the pricing behaviour of the newly merged entity would not be unlawful.

The dissent, accusing the majority of frustrating the purpose of merger law, and relying upon a structural analysis, took the opposite view: the Court should consider whether the increased concentration resulting from the merger might have an adverse effect on competition, focusing on the structure, not on the subsequent conduct of the merged entity.[70] Accordingly, 'when the proof discloses a reasonable probability that competition will be harmed as a result of a merger, I would also conclude that there is a reasonable probability that a competitor of the merging firms will suffer some corresponding harm in due course'.[71] In this view the plaintiff did not have to prove exactly how he would be harmed, but would be able to block the merger merely by showing that the merger lessened competition by increasing market concentration. This case shows how even a technical legal doctrine on standing to sue is affected directly by the shift in economic analysis.[72]

4.2.2 Predatory pricing

The Chicago School is sceptical about the ability of firms to increase monopoly power unilaterally,[73] so their policy prescription would be to abandon many cases under s. 2 of the Sherman Act. This had an effect once the Reagan administration replaced members of the DOJ and FTC with persons sympathetic to the Chicago paradigm: the DOJ dropped its long-standing lawsuit against IBM and settled the AT&T investigation, while the FTC dismissed its claim against the cereal manufacturers and against DuPont, which had been accused of monopolising the market for titanium dioxide.[74] Monopoly behaviour, in the Chicago view, is likely to attract new entry, thus the market is the best cure against concentrated markets. Turning to predatory pricing, Chicagoans suggested that this strategy was hardly likely to obtain in real life. Successful predatory pricing is very risky, for the prey might not exit, and even if it did the predator would have to recover the losses sustained during a

---

[68] 15 USCA § 18.

[69] 479 US 104, 117 following *Brunswick Corp. v. Pueblo Bowl-O-Mat Inc.* 429 US 477 (1977).

[70] Ibid. 123.   [71] Ibid. 129.

[72] Recall how the technical meaning of agreement is affected in EC competition law by the desire to use competition to integrate the markets (pp. 41–4). Politics and economics force the legal interpretation.

[73] Posner 'Chicago School' p. 928.   [74] Meehan and Larner 'Structural School' p. 191.

predatory campaign, but this could only occur if the predator increased prices after the prey exited; however, this price hike would invite new entrants which would restore competitive pricing. Only a monopolist shielded by impenetrable entry barriers would be able to recoup his losses. Otherwise, below-cost pricing is evidence of competition on the merits, and should not be penalised.[75] In addition to predatory pricing being implausible, there is also a high risk that the courts could punish competitive pricing and 'because cutting prices in order to increase business often is the very essence of competition ... mistaken inferences ... are especially costly because they chill the very conduct the antitrust laws are designed to protect'.[76]

However, the Supreme Court, which embraced the Chicago School position, did not go so far as to proclaim that predatory pricing cannot exist: it raised the evidentiary burden. Plaintiffs must prove two things: that the defendant has set price below cost and that it has a reasonable chance to recoup its losses in the aftermath of predatory pricing.[77] This makes predatory pricing lawsuits risky: measuring costs is an inherently difficult exercise, and proving prospects of post-predation recoupment is very hard, demanding that the plaintiff foresee future effects, in situations when the market conditions may change and in an antitrust environment where entry barriers are presumptively low. These requirements also have the effect of limiting claims of predatory pricing to those cases where the predator has a near-monopoly. This approach casts doubt over the validity of *Utah Pie* as a precedent: the Court in these new cases made no reference to intent, a crucial element in *Utah Pie*, and the Court would have found it economically implausible for three large firms to try to price Utah Pie out of the market, for they had no monopoly profits to gain, as they would still be competing against each other after Utah Pie exited.[78] It is unsurprising that predatory pricing claims have almost become extinct as a result of this new judicial standard.

5 The post-Chicago paradigm

5.1 Principles

The post-Chicago paradigm relies on complex tools to determine whether there is a market failure, and the specific features of an industry are crucial to determining market failures.[79] The principal indicator of market failure is the

---

[75] J. McGee 'Predatory Price Cutting: The *Standard Oil* Case' (1958) 1 *Journal of Law and Economics* 137; J. B. Baker 'Predatory Pricing after *Brooke Group*: An Economic Perspective' (1994) 62 *Antitrust Law Journal* 585, 586–7.

[76] *Matsushita Electric Industrial Co. v. Zenith Radio Corp.* 475 US 574, 594 (1986).

[77] *Brooke Group Ltd v. Brown & Williamson Tobacco Corp.* 509 US 209 (1993).

[78] *Brooke Group* (ibid.) rejected the likelihood of recoupment when an allegation of predatory pricing was made against firms in an oligopoly market.

[79] Reviews of this increasing literature can be found in: J. B. Baker 'Recent Developments in Economics that Challenge Chicago School Views' (1989) 58 *Antitrust Law Journal* 645;

presence of market power, defined by the ability to set prices above marginal cost. In this light, most firms hold a degree of market power because price is set at marginal cost only where there is perfect competition. To some extent the potential for market failure is present in all markets, but is not presumed to occur by considering market structure, as in the SCP paradigm. It is rather the way in which firms act that can cause market failures, and the greater a firm's market power the greater the range of activities it is able to engage in to stifle competition. To simplify what is a rich vein of economic thinking, the new industrial economic approach to market failure is concerned with the *strategic means* by which market power is exercised or created. Strategic behaviour may be defined as conduct designed to reduce the attractiveness of competitors' offers.[80] The focus is on the conduct of firms in imperfectly competitive markets, and how that conduct affects the reactions of other firms in the market. This paradigm shuns the wide generalisations that characterise both the SCP concern that all structurally imperfect market structures pose risks, and the Chicago view that markets are sufficiently robust to quash many anticompetitive strategies, in favour of fact-intensive investigations to determine what market characteristics create a realistic risk of market failure when the defendant behaves strategically to undermine its competitors.

While the Chicago paradigm was a rejection of the SCP canon, the post-Chicago paradigm is an attempt to build on the insights of Chicago by adding different analytical tools that question some of the conclusions reached by the Chicago School. The post-Chicago paradigm demands that markets should be studied in more detail before determining whether a practice is pro- or anticompetitive. The likelihood of market failure increases in the post-Chicago paradigm because of their recognition that strategic behaviour, which may appear pro-competitive viewed statically (e.g. product improvement), may, if considered strategically, lead to the elimination of competition and to monopoly pricing.

One of the key methodological departures of this paradigm is the rising importance of empirical fact-finding. Two examples illustrate this. In *Matsushita Electric Industrial Co. v. Zenith Radio Corp.*[81] the plaintiff's claim that Japanese manufacturers had engaged in a predatory pricing conspiracy was dismissed by a slim Supreme Court majority on the basis that predatory pricing schemes are rarely tried and even more rarely successful. The decision was seen as a victory for the Chicago paradigm.[82] However, the empirical evidence relied upon by the dissenting justices demonstrates that predatory

---

H. Hovenkamp 'The Reckoning of Post-Chicago Antitrust' in Cucinotta et al. *Post-Chicago Developments.*

[80] R. S. Markovitz 'The Limits to Simplifying Antitrust – A Reply to Professor Easterbrook' (1984) 63 *Texas Law Review* 41, 44 (adopted also by Hovenkamp 'Antitrust Policy after Chicago' p. 260).

[81] 475 US 574 (1986).

[82] W. H. Page 'The Chicago School and the Evolution of Antitrust: Characterization, Antitrust Injury, and Evidentiary Sufficiency' (1989) 75 *Virginia Law Review* 1221, 1287–90.

pricing was a plausible claim on the facts: there was coordinated below-cost pricing, US competitors were being eliminated, and Japanese manufacturers were engaged in price fixing at home as a way of recouping the losses suffered as a result of below-cost exports.[83] Increased empirical attention to the specific circumstances in an industry had an impact in the *Federal Trade Commission v. Staples* merger decision.[84] The nub of the dispute centred on market definition: the parties to the merger (Staples and Office Depot, the two largest office superstore chains in the US) claimed that the relevant market was the sale of consumable office products through all retail outlets, where the firms held a combined market share of 5.5 per cent, so their merger posed no anticompetitive risks. However, the FTC defined the market as one for consumable office supplies sold through office superstores. From a Chicago School approach, this narrow market makes little sense: a pen is a pen wherever it is purchased, and as consumers shop around for the cheapest deal, any attempt by office superstores to raise prices will lead to a loss of sales to other retail outlets. This intuition about the consumer's shopping skills was however denied by the facts: there were three main office superstores in the US and in geographical areas where Staples faced no competition prices were 13 per cent higher than in markets where Staples competed with Office Depot and Office Max; similarly Office Depot's prices were well over 5 per cent higher in areas where it faced no competition. Moreover, the FTC constructed econometric models that demonstrated how little impact other retail outlets have on the pricing decisions of office superstores, and that if all three office superstores were to merge, prices would increase by 8.49 per cent. This econometric evidence led the FTC to conclude that the prices of goods in office superstores are affected primarily by the other office superstores, and that non-superstore competition is not a significant check on prices. Thus, pre-merger the three superstores already enjoyed a degree of market power, which the merger would enhance by eliminating a particularly aggressive competitor. The decision is significant for its use of econometric studies to identify a competition risk which on a cursory analysis, biased by presumptions about consumer reactions to higher prices, appeared unrealistic.[85]

Armed with fact-specific empirical evidence, the post-Chicago paradigm suggests that in addition to inefficient behaviour, firms with market power can cause market failures by taking steps to exclude entry: by deterring future entrants or by eliminating competitors. In the *Staples* decision, for example, the concern was that by eliminating one important competitor in a market

---

[83] L. Constantine 'An Antitrust Enforcer Confronts the New Economics' (1989) 58 *Antitrust Law Journal* 661, 666–7.

[84] 970 F Supp 1066 (DDC 1997).

[85] The decision was facilitated by scanner technology which made the data about different prices readily available. S. Dalkir and F. R. Warren-Boulton 'Prices, Market Definition, and the Effects of Merger: *Staples–Office Depot* (1997)' in J. E. Kwoka Jr and L. J. White (eds.) *The Antitrust Revolution* 3rd edn (Oxford: Oxford University Press, 1999).

with high entry barriers, Staples was seeking to gain greater freedom to price anticompetitively in areas where it faced little competition from Office Max. Thus the merger was not an attempt to 'monopolise' the market in the traditional sense, rather a strategic decision to facilitate future anticompetitive behaviour in some local markets.

5.2 Policy prescriptions

5.2.1 Mergers

Post-Chicago economics identified a wider range of mergers that might lead to anticompetitive behaviour. One of its most prominent contributions is the analysis of unilateral effects in mergers, which we review in chapter 8.[86] In evaluating vertical mergers, post-Chicago economists have suggested that the benevolent approach of the Chicago paradigm fails to see that under certain circumstances, vertical mergers may have anticompetitive effects. For example, in a market with two upstream and two downstream firms producing differentiated products, a vertical merger between two firms leaves the remaining upstream firm in a position of market power vis-à-vis the remaining downstream firm. The non-integrated upstream firm may have no incentive to compete aggressively with the integrated firm – perhaps because expanding output would be costly, in which case it may choose to align its prices to those of the vertically integrated firm, which may lead to anticompetitive effects.[87] This approach does not rely on foreclosure, but on strategic responses by the non-integrated upstream and the vertically integrated firms. It requires detailed economic modelling and empirical testing to determine under what circumstances such strategic response is likely. Another hypothesis is that if firm A (e.g. a manufacturer of computer cartridges) acquires the supplier of a large upstream component manufacturer (e.g. a manufacturer of ink), then if the ink manufacturer is in a strong position and also sells to firms competing with A, it can raise the price of ink to A's competitors, weakening them and strengthening A's position on the market.[88]

5.2.2 Predatory pricing

Post-Chicago scholars see predatory pricing as a rational strategy, but only in specific circumstances, where a dominant firm is able to engage in strategic behaviour to harm competitors to safeguard its dominant position. For example, they argue that predatory pricing may be a strategy designed to create a

---

[86] See pp. 256–64. See also J. B. Baker 'Contemporary Empirical Merger Analysis' (1997) 5 *George Mason Law Review* 411; J. B. Baker and T. F. Bresnahan 'The Gains for Merger or Collusion in Product-Differentiated Industries' (1985) 33 *Journal of Industrial Economics* 427.

[87] J. A. Ordover, G. Saloner and S. C. Salop 'Equilibrium Vertical Foreclosure' (1990) 80 *American Economic Review* 127.

[88] M. H. Riordan and S. C. Salop 'Evaluating Vertical Mergers: A Post Chicago Approach' (1995) 63 *Antitrust Law Journal* 513.

reputation for predatory behaviour, which makes competitors and new entrants fear a more significant predatory pricing campaign. The effect is that competitors do not attempt to compete too aggressively and potential entrants are deterred from entering.[89] For instance, Professor Baker suggests that a firm present in many different geographical markets that faces a new entrant in one of these markets may opt to reduce its prices in those areas where the new competitor is entering (thus the costs of predatory pricing are limited to a small number of goods sold). This tactic injures the current competitor, and also intimidates others who are threatened by the dominant firm's price cuts. Other firms in the market will not risk engaging in price competition against the dominant firm, for risk of suffering defeat in a price war, and other entrants may be deterred from entering. 'The primary new theoretical development is the identification of a new type of predator, which cuts price in a handful of markets and creates a reputation as an aggressive competitor. This type of predator recoups the costs of predation not merely in the markets in which it engaged in a price war, but also in other markets to which its reputation has spread, by intimidating rivals in those markets to act less aggressively toward it.'[90] This kind of analysis differs from the SCP's concern over the elimination of rivals and increased concentration and refutes the Chicago School which suggests that predatory pricing schemes are only worthwhile if the predator is able to monopolise the market after the predatory pricing campaign, by observing subtler advantages that can be gained from a predatory strategy.

Post-Chicago enforcement policy is demonstrated by the DOJ's unsuccessful lawsuit against American Airlines. American Airlines was faced with a number of low-cost carriers operating competing services on a number of routes to and from Dallas Fort Worth airport. In response, American Airlines reduced prices and increased the number of flights along those routes on which it faced competitors. This led to the low-cost carriers exiting the market. After their exit, American Airlines raised prices back to the levels that existed before entry. The DOJ's case was based upon two allegations of predatory behaviour: first that the lower prices were themselves predatory, and secondly that American's behaviour had also had an anticompetitive effect on other routes because it had established a reputation for predation which would deter others from competing with American Airlines. The DOJ's concerns were shared by the Department of Transportation, which proposed guidelines to prohibit exclusionary conduct in the airline industry. Its proposal recognised that the costs of a predatory strategy could be recovered because of 'reputation effects', which would deter others from competing against the incumbent, allowing the predator to be free to recoup losses.[91] This approach did not fare well in the

---

[89] M. R. Burns 'Predatory Pricing and the Acquisition Costs of Competitors' (1986) 94 *Journal of Political Economy* 266, who uses this theory to explain the growth of American Tobacco.

[90] Baker 'Predatory Pricing' p. 592.

[91] Department of Transport *Unfair Exclusionary Conduct in Airline Transportation Industry Policy* Trade Reg Rep No. 50,163 (13 May 1998).

courts, however. Not only did the judge consider that the DOJ had failed to marshal enough evidence to sustain its claim, but he expressed serious reservations about the theoretical basis of 'reputation effects':

> The government's theory of liability by reputation is not the law, and should not be. A fundamental principle of antitrust law is that it be capable of effective and accurate administration, and not chill the competition it seeks to foster. The government's reputational liability approach would violate this principle, permitting claims of predation based solely upon the subjective and unverifiable complaints of a defendant's competitors.[92]

This passage evidences the difficulties that post-Chicago theories face: the practices which are challenged appear to be pro-competitive responses which competition law should encourage, the consumer harm appears too remote for the court to take seriously, even though the court acknowledged that the strength of post-Chicago theories meant that it would not approach predatory pricing claims with the 'incredulity that once prevailed'.[93]

6 The effect of economics on law in US antitrust: a synthesis

6.1 Economics translated into law

As the examples above illustrate, decisions in competition cases require an economic model to determine the legality of behaviour.[94] Judge Posner explains the relevance of a credible economic theory of harm in blunt terms:

> If firm A through lower prices or a better or more dependable product succeeds in driving competitor B out of business, society is better off, unlike the case where A and B are individuals and A kills B for B's money. In both cases the 'aggressor' seeks to transfer his victim's wealth to himself, but in the first case we applaud the result because society as a whole benefits from the competitive process. That Western Union [the defendant] wanted to 'flush these turkeys' [the plaintiffs] tells us nothing about the lawfulness of its conduct.[95]

The relationship between economic paradigm shifts and US antitrust law is complex, but it is fair to generalise by stating that changes in economic theory tend to lead to changes in enforcement – both in terms of legal methods and in terms of policy priorities. Thus, in the SCP-dominated 1960s and 1970s we see aggressive antitrust enforcement, whilst the Chicago School has been dominant since the 1980s, where we see minimalist antitrust enforcement, and post-Chicago ideas have been embraced with hesitation since the 1990s. A merger which would have been blocked in the 1960s is not even seen as posing

---

[92] *US v. AMR Corp.* 140 F Supp 2d 1141, 1219 (D KS 2001); aff'd 335 F 3d 1109 (10th Cir. 2003).
[93] *US v. AMR Corp* 335 F 3d 1109, 1116 (10th Cir. 2003).
[94] See R. Schmalensee 'The Use of Economic Models in Antitrust: The *ReaLemon* Case' (1979) 127 *University of Pennsylvania Law Review* 994.
[95] *Olympia Equip. Leasing Co. v. Western Union Tel. Co.* 797 F 2d 370, 379 (7th Cir. 1986).

anticompetitive risks in the 1980s, while some transactions which escaped scrutiny in the 1980s might be reviewed more stringently today.[96] In the context of predatory behaviour, *Utah Pie* would be decided differently in the 1980s and post-Chicagoans would argue that *Matsushita* was a prima facie case of predatory pricing that infringed the antitrust laws.

There are time lags between a paradigm shift in economic thinking and its effects on law: the risks of concentration were first noted in the 1930s but it was only some decades later that this turned into antitrust policy;[97] the seminal works of the Chicago paradigm were written during the judicial high-water mark of the SCP paradigm; and post-Chicago literature emerged in the 1980s.[98] The reason for time lags stems from a reluctance to embrace an economic theory before it is well established and the need for scholars to translate economic theories into workable antitrust policy – judges are often not able to comprehend the significance of economic theories, hence the importance of scholars who can act as intermediaries for judges, translating the insights of economics into language and methods which judges can apply.

The legal translation of economics often requires some simplification. Economic analysis of a business practice is often composed of a range of variables which makes policy conclusions impossible unless matters are simplified by the adoption of a smaller set of variables which makes adjudication feasible.[99] An example is the presumption in EC competition law that a firm is dominant when its market share is 50 per cent or more. From an economic perspective, market shares are not a useful indicator of dominance, but they offer a clear filter for courts to sift those cases where competitive concerns exist and those where enforcement is less important. Obviously, simplification leads to the risk of over- or under-enforcement, but carrying out a full economic analysis to identify dominance would consume too many resources. This explains the resilience of the basic structure of the Merger Guidelines in the United States: enforcement still begins by an analysis of the market structure, as the SCP paradigm would recommend. In spite of the Chicago School revolution, it is still convenient to begin an analysis of mergers by calculating the degree of concentration as a means of filtering unimportant transactions. This suggests that the longevity of an economic paradigm might have

---

[96] Thus the *Staples* merger would probably not have raised competition concerns under a Chicago paradigm.

[97] Kaysen and Turner *Antitrust Policy* was the major work of the period advocating deconcentration as a major policy goal.

[98] The role of strategic behaviour in antitrust economics was already being disputed during a conference on Antitrust Law and Economics held in 1978 (the papers and debates are reproduced in Goldschmid et al. *Industrial Concentration*), the year that saw the publication of Bork's *Antitrust Paradox*. See also O. E. Williamson 'Symposium on Antitrust Law and Economics' (1979) 127 *University of Pennsylvania Law Review* 918.

[99] A view taken by many. For a succinct synthesis, see T. J. Muris, Chairman of the FTC, 'Improving the Economic Foundations of Competition Policy' (2003) 12 *George Mason Law Review* 1, Winter Antitrust Symposium, 15 January 2003 (available at www.ftc.gov).

something to do with the ease by which the economics can be translated into workable legal rules, rather than with its scientific truth or accuracy. As Muris puts it, an efficient rule 'will minimize the sum of failures to capture anticompetitive conduct and interventions that challenge or chill pro-competitive conduct, along with the costs of understanding and following the legal rules and of litigation'.[100] In contrast, an economic theory which cannot be translated into efficient rules will not affect the development of competition law. This explains the reason why some post-Chicago theories fail to take hold. According to Professor Hovenkamp:

> It now seems quite clear that Chicago School economic orthodoxy is no longer the best, or certainly not the only, analytic tool for evaluating markets. But the sad fact is that judges have not come close to developing antitrust rules that take this messier, more complex economics into account. An even sadder fact is that in many instances judges may not be capable of doing so.[101]

The reason for this is that many of the post-Chicago economic theories cannot yet offer a model that allows the judge to draw up a rule that has the following three attributes: first, it distinguishes in a convincing manner between pro- and anticompetitive behaviour; second, the courts are able to provide a remedy which they believe will improve consumer welfare; third, the rule is sufficiently simple to apply in the courtroom. An economic theory, or a novel economic paradigm, must pass these tests before it can be accepted.[102] If it is too easy to offer an alternative, pro-competitive explanation of a particular kind of conduct, or if the welfare consequences of imposing a remedy are unclear, or the rule is too complex for courts to understand, courts refuse to follow the economic theory which would proscribe that conduct.

6.2 Institutions, politics and the translation of economics into law

While economic arguments had been a feature of antitrust law since the 1940s,[103] it was not until the 1960s that systematic use of economic arguments became the norm. In a revealing essay, Oliver Williamson points out how the DOJ in the 1960s under Donald Turner (the first Assistant Attorney General of the Antitrust Division with a PhD in economics) was reshaped, with an increased injection of economists, lawyers fluent in economics, the creation of the post of Special Economics Assistant (later replaced by the Economic Policy Office (EPO) as the number of economists surged) and a number of

---

[100] Ibid.

[101] H. Hovenkamp 'Post-Chicago Antitrust: A Review and Critique' (2001) *Columbia Business Law Review* 257, 271.

[102] In a similar vein, Muris ('Improving the Economic Foundations') argues that economics can only be successful if they are embodied in *administrable* rules.

[103] F. M. Rowe 'The Decline of Antitrust and the Delusions of Models: The Faustian Pact of Law and Economics' (1984) 72 *Georgetown Law Journal* 1511, 1520–2.

other structural changes to the organisation that led to an increased emphasis upon economic analysis in bringing antitrust cases.[104] The institutional makeup of the agency changed to give greater profile to economists and their analytical methods. As Eisner noted, while in the 1960s economics became more prominent, it was in the 1970s that increased attempts were made to integrate the economic theories into law enforcement; the aim of the EPO was to make economists more directly involved with the litigation and thereby to integrate economists with the work of a legalistic DOJ. As George Hay, one of those responsible for instituting the EPO, put it: 'the whole idea was to convince the lawyers that it was in their interest to have us [economists] work with them, not to shoot down their cases'.[105] By the mid-1970s the EPO was able to assist in determining policy by carrying out market studies, and its economists were integrated at every stage of litigation.[106]

But the reception of new economic ideas is not uniform – some areas of competition policy are more receptive to new economic thinking than others. Merger policy is the most flexible category, because it is to a great extent led by antitrust agencies who, through the promulgation of amended guidelines, can respond quickly to changes in economic fashion, especially when the leadership of both DOJ and FTC is shaped by the incumbent administration which appoints persons in tune with the dominant political and economic perspectives. In particular, DOJ appointees are members of the executive and are expected to represent the government's policy goals. The President also appoints the head of the FTC, but as this is an independent agency, direct political control is less strong.[107] Making new law by redrafting guidelines, which do not require governmental approval or court sanction, does not shackle the enforcers to precedent. This was exemplified above by the frequency with which merger guidelines are rewritten and by the decision of the FTC to resile from its aggressive policy over vertical mergers during the Reagan era. It also shows that when there is prosecutorial discretion (mergers are seldom privately litigated) then policy shifts depend on changes in the administration – see for instance the surge of collusion cases and the reduction in merger challenges almost as soon as the Chicago School gained ascendancy.[108] These factors speed up the arrival of new economic thinking when government agencies are the principal enforcers. However, Eisner, in a thorough study of the antitrust agencies, has taken a different view of the causal relationship between politics and policy change. In his view the successful injection of economics as a method into the antitrust authorities facilitated the switch from SCP to Chicago, and the change occurred because of the way economics had become embedded within the agencies, not due to changes in the political winds. In his words: 'politics, in essence, lagged behind policy. Ideas gained a certain independence from politics, once they were integrated into

---

[104] O. E. Williamson 'Economics and Antitrust Enforcement: Transition Years' [2003] *Antitrust* 61.
[105] Cited in Eisner *Antitrust* p. 138.   [106] Ibid. p. 140.   [107] Ibid. pp. 41–2.   [108] Ibid. p. 148.

institutions.'[109] However, this position should not undermine the determining influence that politics and political appointments can have in shaping the direction of the agencies: consider for instance the way that the Democrats' complaints in the 1990s about the direction of antitrust policy (too lenient on mergers, inadequate enforcement of predatory pricing) later translated into stricter approaches in those areas by the Clinton administration.[110] Bluntly, if you employ Chicagoans to run the competition authority, you get a different enforcement policy than if you hire post-Chicagoans. Their professionalism does not immunise them completely from their normative assumptions about how markets should be regulated.

Turning our attention to practices which are mostly disputed in the courts, or in areas with well-established precedents, economic theory has much less bite. For example, the Chicago School's prescription (which we will review in chapter 10) that all vertical agreements are pro-competitive never led any court to declare that resale price maintenance should be considered lawful, although Chicago-inspired courts did construct rules to circumvent this rule, for instance by holding that resale price maintenance agreements could not be inferred simply because the supplier terminated a discounting dealer.[111] For a judge, the duty to observe precedent (even by drawing artificial distinctions) is valued so highly that she would be very reluctant to displace precedent because economic paradigms have changed – even the most 'realist' of judges will work within the formal framework of the law.[112] However, the composition of the courts can affect the power of paradigms: the Chicago School paradigm became dominant as Chicago-leaning scholars were appointed to federal courts (e.g. Judges Bork, Posner and Easterbrook) and to the Supreme Court (e.g. Justices Scalia and Thomas). They made a significant contribution to the development of antitrust policy.[113] Divisions among the judiciary (some Chicagoan, some anti-Chicago) also account for the mixed fortunes of post-Chicago theories.[114] Kovacic went as far as to claim that 'a president can determine how economics and particular economic views affect antitrust litigation by his choice of judicial nominees',[115] a position he supported by

---

[109] Ibid. p. 233.

[110] L. J. White 'Antitrust Activities during the Clinton Administration' in R. W. Hahn (ed.) *High-Stakes Antitrust – The Last Hurrah?* (Washington, DC: AEI-Brookings Joint Center for Regulatory Studies, 2003) pp. 11–12.

[111] *Monsanto v. Spary-Rite Services Corp.* 465 US 752 (1984).

[112] On realism/formalism, see J. N. Adams and R. Brownsword 'The Ideologies of Contract Law' (1987) 7 *Legal Studies* 205.

[113] W. E. Kovacic 'Reagan's Judicial Appointees and Antitrust in the 1990s' (1991) 60 *Fordham Law Review* 49.

[114] This gives rise to contradictory methodologies. See, for a brief overview, E. M. Fox 'Post-Chicago, Post-Seattle and the Dilemma of Globalization' in Cucinotta et al. *Post-Chicago Developments.* A similar clash occurred in the late 1970s when a still SCP-led FTC was facing a hostile, Chicago-oriented judiciary. See J. C. Miller III *The Economist as Reformer: Revamping the FTC, 1981–1985* (Washington, DC: American Enterprise Institute, 1989).

[115] W. E. Kovacic 'The Influence of Economics on Antitrust Law' (1992) 30 *Economic Inquiry* 294, 296.

showing how Reagan appointees to the Court of Appeals were more tolerant of mergers, exclusionary practices and vertical restraints than Carter appointees.[116] However, on the whole, enforcement agencies are able to accommodate economic paradigm shifts more quickly and more completely than courts.

Courts also receive relatively less guidance from economic experts than competition agencies. Assistance has occurred episodically, in some cases the court appointing economists to help them understand the markets.[117] In the long term one might see more systematic use of experts. In the context of medical evidence in tort cases, Justice Breyer has recommended that pre-trial hearings can be used to sift through the scientific evidence so that judges have a better opportunity to understand and identify the relevant facts. In the US the CASE (Court Appointed Scientific Experts) programme of the American Association for the Advancement of Science is designed to facilitate greater connections between judges and scientific experts by allowing judges to find independent experts for their cases.[118] These institutions could be exploited to allow economics to play a wider role in adjudication and this would speed up legal change as novel economic theories are argued more frequently in courts.

In sum, politics and institutions are relevant points of reference when trying to understand developments in the economics of competition law. Moreover, the SCP and Chicago paradigms tally with changing political trends – SCP's concern over concentrated markets supplements the liberal concern about the protection of small business's freedom to compete, and Chicago's emphasis on the strength of markets tallied with Reagan's vision: 'Mr Reagan had promised to restore the economy to its former vigor by getting out of the business of business. A vision of antitrust as conservative microeconomic policy, which would sanction antitrust only when it could create a more efficient allocation of resources … fit nicely with the political philosophy … of the administration.'[119] The post-Chicago paradigm as yet lacks a political flag. Many of its proponents claim to be working *within* the Chicago policy orientation, viewing economic efficiency as the ultimate goal, but deploying more complex economic analysis to identify market failure. Possibly because of its lack of a distinctive political agenda, the post-Chicago paradigm may not enjoy the real-world success of the earlier paradigms.

[116] Ibid.
[117] For example, a leading economist, Carl Kaysen, assisted the district court judge in *US v. United Shoe Machinery Corp*. 110 F Supp 295 (D MA 1953), aff'd per curiam, 347 US 521 (1954). See C. Kaysen 'In Memoriam: Charles E. Wyzanski, Jr' (1987) 100 *Harvard Law Review* 713, 713–15. In *New York v. Kraft General Foods Inc*. 926 F Supp 321, 351–2 (SDNY 1995) a court-appointed expert economist was deployed to evaluate a merger case.
[118] See www.aaas.org/spp/case/case.htm.
[119] P. D. Quick 'Business: Reagan's Industrial Policy' in J. L. Palmer and I. V. Sawhill (eds.) *The Reagan Record: An Assessment of America's Changing Domestic Priorities* (Cambridge, MA: Ballinger Publishing, 1984).

In a sophisticated attempt to redirect antitrust away from the Chicago paradigm, Professor Brodley argued that antitrust should be concerned about both economic efficiency and consumer welfare (defined as direct consumer benefits from competition). In this model of 'antitrust welfare', Brodley called, *inter alia*, for increased scrutiny over exclusionary tactics (in line with post-Chicago thinking) on the basis that this behaviour reduces productive and dynamic efficiencies and also leads to a reduction in consumer welfare.[120] This compelling restatement suggests a wider policy ambition for antitrust than the Chicago School – a concern about consumer welfare understood in a distributive sense, and a prioritisation of enforcement towards actions which reduce productive and dynamic efficiency rather than those which reduce allocative efficiency. This attempt to marry a liberal political vision with contemporary advances in economics is unsuccessful because many argue that economic thinking is incompatible with distributive concerns.[121] Economics is now so embedded in the rationale for antitrust policy in the US that any attempt to combat the dominant paradigm must do so with the language of economics. Listen to the certainty expressed by the FTC's Chairman: 'Policy discourse no longer focuses on whether economics should guide antitrust policy. That debate was settled long ago. The pressing question today is how. Which theories from the vast, diverse body of industrial organisation economics should courts and enforcement agencies use to address antitrust problems? ... How are economic ideas to be translated into operational rules?'[122]

7 European competition policy and economics

7.1 A lack of economic analysis

It is trite to say that, historically, EC competition law has not been affected by economic paradigms to the degree that US antitrust has. There are many reasons which may in part explain the lack of economic sophistication by the European Commission and the Courts.

From a legal perspective, most Member States have civil law traditions that have been traditionally less receptive to economic analysis of law.[123] Economic

---

[120] J. F. Brodley 'The Economic Goals of Antitrust: Efficiency, Consumer Welfare, and Technological Progress' (1987) 62 *New York University Law Review* 1020. An alternative, but roughly similar, approach is proposed by Hovenkamp 'Antitrust Policy after Chicago' 224–6, who argued that as post-Chicago economics are so complex, antitrust should rely less on economics and more on political values.

[121] For a characterisation of the debate, see E. M. Fox and L. A. Sullivan 'Antitrust – Retrospective and Prospective: Where Are We Coming From? Where Are We Going?' (1987) 62 *New York University Law Review* 936.

[122] Muris 'Improving the Economic Foundations'.

[123] See D. J. Gerber 'Law and the Abuse of Economic Power in Europe' (1987) 62 *Tulane Law Review* 57, who noted that the civil law training also led to a degree of reluctance in the early years to enforce the more vague aspects of EC competition law (e.g. Article 82 EC).

analysis requires case-by-case reasoning, considering the potential effects of imposing or not imposing liability. This type of legal reasoning suits the common law more easily than the civil law – in the former, consequentialist reasoning is a regular feature which animates the development of the law in a number of areas.[124] The roots of US antitrust law were English cases on restraints of trade, some of which are premised upon a rough economic utilitarian calculus. Accordingly, swings in economic thinking have allowed the US courts to overrule precedents inconsistent with modern economics.[125] On the contrary, the civil law culture favours reasoning according to legal categories, resolving problems by a literal interpretation of the statutes. The civilian method does not mean that legal reasoning cannot be adventurous, but one finds fewer references to the practical implications of the rules, and more to the integrity of the legal system as a whole. Furthermore, as was illustrated in the previous chapter, Article 81 EC does not allow an interpretation which is consonant with the shared tenets of the economic paradigms summarised above. It will be recalled that Article 81(1), read literally, is closer to the 'economic freedom' model and Article 81(3) does not espouse a neoclassical calculation, but rather favours distributive justice: an agreement's overall efficiency is an insufficient basis for legality, consumers must receive some benefit from the agreement. This is closer to Brodley's 'antitrust welfare' model than to the economic welfare model of economists. Accordingly, it is impossible to interpret Article 81 using economic paradigms based upon a utilitarian political philosophy which would allow the exclusive use of economic tools to determine the legality of industrial behaviour. It was easier to use economics in the comparable provision in US law, which is more open-textured.

From an institutional perspective, DG Competition (formerly DG IV) was, in the early days, populated more by lawyers than economists (by a ratio of seven to one), thus favouring a (civilian) legal discourse over an economic discourse. According to some, this creates a bias against the use of economics and in favour of decisions that are legally defensible.[126] However, this argument is too simplistic. The use of economics may create risks that decisions are not legally defensible if the economic theory is not accepted by judges, but the

---

[124] For example, in the law of tort, a decision whether or not to impose a duty of care is often based upon whether the imposition of liability would have a detrimental effect on the defendant's tasks. The interest in compensating the injured claimant is balanced against the interests of society in ensuring that the defendant is not deterred from carrying out socially useful acts. This can be seen in the classic negligence case *Donoghue v. Stevenson* [1932] AC 562. See the discussion of consequentialist reasoning by N. McCormack *Legal Reasoning and Legal Theory* (Oxford: Oxford University Press, 1978). See also P. S. Atiyah *The Rise and Fall of Freedom of Contract* (Oxford: Oxford University Press, 1979) for an analysis of the impact of political economy on judges.

[125] See notably *State Oil v. Khan* 622 US 3 (1997); *Copperweld Corp. v. Independence Tube Corp.* 467 US 752 (1984); *Continental TV Inc. v. GTE Sylvania Inc.* 433 US 36 (1977).

[126] S. Wilks and L. McGowan 'Competition Policy in the European Union: Creating a Federal Agency?' in G. B. Doern and S. Wilks (eds.) *Comparative Competition Policy* (Oxford: Oxford University Press, 1996) p. 259.

same risk occurs if the judge does not accept the Commission's legal analysis. There is a more significant concern: lawyers prefer rules to standards.[127] Economic standards require the decision-maker to investigate often ambiguous welfare consequences of industrial behaviour, while rules allow judges to determine, based on a few easily observable facts, whether a practice is lawful or not. A young and inexperienced Commission would have been attracted to a rule-based approach, rather than risk making errors by misapplying economic theories.

From a political perspective, the goals of EC competition law were never purely economic – Robert Bork has no intellectual twin in Europe. The law's ordoliberal origins favoured economic freedom over efficiency and the Community's concern over other goals (in particular market integration) reduced the potential impact of economics.[128] However, this should not be taken to mean that political ideas prevent the use of economic analysis. After all, US antitrust policy shows a synthesis between politics and economics: the SCP paradigm was in tune with the political desire to protect small traders, while the Chicagoan paradigm is closely associated with the laissez-faire philosophy of the 1980s. In the EC, the concern about economic freedom was motivated by a fear that without such freedom, the market would descend again into the cartelised state which contributed to the rise of totalitarianism in Europe, and the concern over market integration was a corollary to the importance placed by the EC Treaty on creating a single market. In the EC also, the political and the economic visions worked in parallel to devise a particularly European approach to competition law, divorced from the microeconomic debates that engulfed the US courts.

In sum, it is not easy to pinpoint a single reason why economic analysis played a less significant role in the early years of EC competition policy than it did during the same period in the United States. Equally, it is possible to identify a variety of reasons why the use of economics has increased over the years. First, as the Commission has gained better experience of the market it regulates, a switch from rules to economic standards is facilitated; second, greater experience has allowed the Commission to identify practices that rarely have anticompetitive effects.[129] Lack of economic analysis is often seen as an indicator of decisions that lack predictability and transparency; thus increasingly demands were made for the EC to adopt an economic approach to competition policy.[130] Pressure from business, from the United States and from academic circles has probably also had an influence. Many have pointed

---

[127] See also Eisner *Antitrust* pp. 153–4.

[128] R. van den Bergh 'The Difficult Reception of Economic Analysis in European Competition Law' in Cucinotta et al. *Post-Chicago Developments*.

[129] For example, vertical restraints, which we consider in chapter 10.

[130] M. Furse 'The Role of Competition Policy: A Survey' [1996] *European Competition Law Review* 250, 258. Cf. T. Frazer 'Competition Policy After 1992: The Next Step' (1990) 53 *Modern Law Review* 609.

out that the use of economic analysis surged after the enactment of the Merger Regulation, which incorporated an economic welfare standard. But perhaps an equally important event in the 1990s was the establishment of formal communication channels with US antitrust authorities, and the economic tools deployed by the Americans will have affected the perspective of the Commission.[131] Moreover, looking at the composition of DG Competition, there are more economists: between 1999 and 2004 the Commissioner for competition, Mario Monti, was an economist (the first Commissioner for competition with that qualification); and in 2004 the Commission appointed a chief economist and a team of ten economists. Of the current A-grade staff, approximately 24 per cent have an economics background.[132] The increase in economists mirrors what occurred in the United States antitrust agencies in the late 1960s.

A variety of factors have contributed to the Commission's shift to an economics-based approach. However, as we noted when reviewing economics in the US, there is no such thing as *the* economic analysis of competition law, rather there are various paradigms that compete for supremacy. The question we consider in the next section is whether we can identify a *European* economic paradigm.

7.2 Contemporary EC competition policy: what sort of economic approach?

The Commission's increased reliance on economic analysis was gradual. In 1996 it published the *Green Paper on Vertical Restraints*, which marks the beginning of a legal and cultural change in EC competition policy – the Green Paper is the first serious and sustained attempt to deploy economic analysis to competition law. This passage from the Green Paper shows how, in the transition to economics, the Commission was cautious:

---

[131] Agreement between the Government of the United States of America and the Commission of the European Communities regarding the Application of their Competition Laws [1995] OJ L95/47. This was followed by the Agreement between the European Communities and the Government of the United States of America on the Application of Positive Comity Principles in the Enforcement of their Competition Laws [1998] OJ L173/26, the Administrative Arrangement on Attendance in 1999 (Bulletin of the EU 3-1999, Competition (18/43)); and the Best Practices on Cooperation in Merger Investigations agreed in 2002. Under these agreements there has been significant cooperation, especially in the field of merger control, with the two agencies sharing information and carrying out certain analyses jointly. This explains, at least in part, why the increased economic sophistication in market definition began with mergers. Annual reports document the nature of cooperation between the agencies: see Report from the Commission to the Council and European Parliament on the Application of the Agreements between the European Communities and the Government of the United States of America and the Government of Canada regarding the Application of their Competition Laws COM(2002)505 final.

[132] A-grade staff are case handlers and those involved in policy development and management. Of the 344 A-grade staff, 83 have training in economics and 184 in law. Source: http:// europa.eu.int/comm/competition/index_en.html.

economic theory cannot be the only factor in the design of policy ... Firstly strict economic theory is just one of the sources of policy. In practice the application of economic theory must take place in the context of the existing legal texts and jurisprudence. Secondly, economic theories are necessarily based on simplifying assumptions often obtained in the context of stylised theoretical models that cannot take into account all the complexities of real life cases.[133]

Since this document, the Commission has repeatedly indicated its willingness to take a 'more economics-oriented approach' to EC competition policy and the scepticism represented in the above passage has waned.[134] There seem to be three themes in the EC's economic approach: that competition policy should be enforced to benefit consumers; that competitive risks grow with increased market power; that economic freedom, and a plurality of market players, guarantees economic benefits.

7.2.1 Consumer interests

The shared consensus among economists is that contemporary EC competition policy is concerned about maximising consumer welfare, while economists prefer a standard based on total welfare.[135] To explain the difference between these two standards, a diagram and a very simplified example may help:

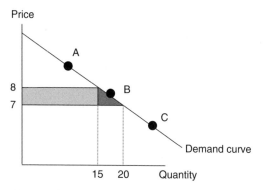

Figure 3.1 The consumer interest

Three consumers are represented on the demand curve, A, B and C. Each point represents how much each customer is willing to pay for a good, say a set of earphones. As prices fall, more consumers are willing to buy the earphones. Say there are two companies that make earphones, and before the two decide to enter into a cooperative agreement, the price for the earphones is €7 and twenty units are sold. At this stage all consumers willing to pay €7 or more for

---

[133] *Green Paper on Vertical Restraints in EC Competition Policy* COM(96)721 para. 86.

[134] G. Monti 'New Directions in EC Competition Law' in T. Tridimas and P. Nebbia (eds.) *European Union Law for the Twenty-First Century* vol. II (Oxford: Hart Publishing, 2004).

[135] S. Bishop and M. Walker *The Economics of EC Competition Law* 2nd edn (London: Sweet & Maxwell, 2002) paras. 2.22–2.27; M. Motta *Competition Policy* (Cambridge: Cambridge University Press, 2004) pp. 18–22.

the goods are satisfied, while consumer C is already priced out of the market. He has to settle for other goods because he is unable or unwilling to pay the market price. Scarcity means every market has persons in C's position. Now, assume that the two companies that make earphones agree to create a joint venture that will henceforth be the same manufacturer of earphones. This leads to a monopoly in the market. The expectation of monopoly is an increase in price, say from €7 to €8. A and B suffer in different ways. B suffers the most because she cannot buy the earphones at the inflated price. The resources she would have used to buy the goods will be spent on something else that gives her less utility. Consumer A can still buy the earphones, in fact he would have been willing to pay more than €8, so to him the price increase is not as painful.

Economists say that the monopoly is undesirable because of the harm it causes to consumers like B (the entire harm is the area of the darkly shaded triangle). These consumers are forced to leave their preferred market, misallocating resources: fewer earphones are produced and more goods that consumers want less keenly are made. Economists are unconcerned about the extra money that consumers like A have to pay (the entire extra that all consumers pay is represented by the lightly shaded area). This excess is merely a transfer of resources from the consumer to the producer; it is not a loss of utility for society as a whole. A competition authority interested in safeguarding the interests of consumers instead would say that the merger is bad for A and B, as both suffer higher prices.

Having explained the difference between a consumer welfare and a total welfare approach, does it make any difference that EC competition policy has opted for the consumer standard? It seems that there are two differences. The first is that in certain circumstances the consumer welfare standard is stricter than the total welfare standard. Consider if after the joint venture between the two earphones manufacturers, the joint venture is able to produce earphones more cheaply, because by sharing technical know-how the firm reduces production costs: the merger generates productive efficiencies. But because they have market power, they do not use the cost savings to cut prices. However, the benefit of productive efficiencies remains: economic resources are saved and the savings can be injected into society to generate welfare in other ways (e.g. the companies can use the savings to develop new, better earphones). Economists trade off the loss of consumer utility to consumers like B with the savings due to the productive efficiency and consider whether, overall, resources were saved or lost: if the gain in productive efficiency outweighed the welfare loss (the small, darkly shaded triangle), then the joint venture is efficient overall. Plus consumers as shareholders or as subscribers to pension funds that invest in firms have an interest in the productive efficiencies of firms. In contrast, a focus only on consumer welfare will not tolerate this kind of cost–benefit analysis: the price increase is sufficient to condemn the joint venture. In sum, a total welfare standard tolerates practices which the consumer welfare standard would not allow.

There is a second dimension of the consumer welfare standard that we must consider. This arises when we think of consumer welfare in the subjective terms that the Commission mentions. According to the Commission, the consumer is looking for low prices, high-quality products, a wide selection of goods and services, and innovation.[136] Once this wider conception of the consumer interest arises, the consumer welfare standard becomes fuzzy. Consider the joint venture above again: the improvement in productive efficiency might stimulate research into better products, the consumer of today may suffer, but the consumers of tomorrow will be offered the benefit of a better product. Should such inter-generational considerations be relevant? Or let us say that pre-merger the earphones of one company had poor sound quality while the earphones of the other offered better sound isolation. Post-merger the good qualities of both earphones are combined, but prices rise. Are consumers better off given that they have access to a better product, even if it is more expensive and some cannot afford it? Moreover, some consumers may have valued the lower price, others would have valued the better quality. Examples may be multiplied of scenarios where some consumers will be better off, and some will lose out. For instance, if competition law safeguards small inner city shops at the expense of allowing large out-of-town shopping centres to expand, the consumers of the out-of-town shopping malls lose as prices fail to fall, while the consumers who are unable to afford trips far from their homes benefit. In these circumstances, the total welfare standard seems to offer greater certainty by considering simply whether economic resources are deployed most effectively, while a consumer welfare standard that looks to the subjective interests of consumers appears nebulous. Once a standard that applies distributive criteria is deployed, the question of how the distribution is to be carried out arises, and the diversity of consumer interests makes this a difficult question to answer.

Moreover, it is not easy to obtain all the evidence about consumer preferences – the diversity of viewpoints, and the diffusion of consumer concerns across so many goods and services, makes it difficult to identify the consumer interest. Even more problematically, the diffusion of the consumer interest leads to the free-rider problem: if thousands of consumers are affected by the anticompetitive behaviour of a firm, why should one complain when there are others who could do so as well? And, if consumer interests are so diverse and so unlikely to come to the fore, policy-making will not be affected by the interests of consumers but will be more easily captured by the more established pressure groups: manufacturers and workers.[137] A response to these problems may be

---

[136] E.g. *Guidelines on the Assessment of Horizontal Mergers* [2004] OJ C31/5 para. 8; *Guidelines on the Application of Article 81(3) of the Treaty* [2004] OJ C101/97 footnote 84 (defining consumer harm as higher prices or lower quality, less variety or lower innovation than would otherwise have occurred).

[137] M. Trebilcock 'Winners and Losers in the Modern Regulatory State: Must the Consumer Always Lose?' (1975) 13 *Osgoode Hall Law Journal* 618.

the creation of consumer organisations to represent the interests of consumers systematically. In fact it may be argued that by attempting to represent the interests of consumers, the EC is seeking to escape the risk of decisions being pro-producer and anti-consumer, thus redressing a bias in its decision-making institutional structure. This is particularly evidenced by the creation of a new post in DG Competition in December 2003: the Consumer Liaison Officer. His role is to 'ensure a permanent dialogue with European consumers, whose welfare is the primary concern of competition policy, but whose voice is not sufficiently heard when handling individual cases or discussing policy issues'.[138] If the relationship between DG Competition and consumer evolves as the Commission anticipates, it will mean that EC competition law may create standards of consumer welfare based on consumer preferences, and this may well skew policy away from a strictly economics-based approach.

7.2.2 Market power

At the root of the Commission's economic approach is the recognition that competition problems arise more frequently when firms hold market power.[139] Hence stricter standards apply when the firm has a dominant position, and considerably looser standards are applied when the firm is small in a market with many other small competitors. This approach has affinities with the SCP paradigm, being premised upon market structure as a measure of presumptive legality/illegality. The advantage of focusing on market power is to allow the enforcement agency 'to distinguish more clearly between innocuous and seriously anticompetitive behaviour'.[140] Thus a simple economic tool allows the Commission to set its enforcement priorities in line with anticipated anticompetitive effects that result from a particular practice, given the degree of market power.[141]

Market power as a basis for designing competition policy fits well with the consumer interest focus: consumers are likely to suffer greater harm when the market is monopolised than when there are more competitors on the market. As we saw in chapter 2, the Commission's reform of the law on agreements between firms has been premised upon a market-power analysis. Moreover, as we will see in chapters 8 and 9, contemporary merger policy adopts some of the analytical methods of the post-Chicago paradigm that were illustrated earlier in order to identify market power.

---

[138] See http://europa.eu.int/comm/competition/publications/competition_policy_and_the_citizen/consumer_liaison/.

[139] 'The market power approach is more flexible and more in line with economic reality.' A. Schaub 'Continued Focus on Reform: Recent Developments in EC Competition Policy' 2001 *Fordham Corporate Law Institute* 31 (Hawk ed., 2002).

[140] P. Nicolaides 'An Essay on Economics and the Competition Law of the European Community' (2000) 27 *Legal Issues of Economic Integration* 7, 9.

[141] This approach is reflected in the *Guidelines on Vertical Restraints* [2000] OJ C291/1 and the *Guidelines on the Applicability of Article 81 of the EC Treaty to Horizontal Cooperation Agreements* [2001] OJ C3/2.

7.2.3 Pluralism

Finally, a value that underlies EC competition policy is a belief that a plurality of market participants guarantees better economic performance. This draws upon the SCP paradigm but is also premised upon the ordoliberal values of EC competition policy. As was shown in chapter 2, when efficiency threatens economic freedom, the Commission favours economic freedom. In the *GE/Honeywell* merger, for example, which we will consider in detail in chapter 8, the Commission preferred to block a merger in spite of the efficiencies which the parties and many commentators considered would result from the merger on the basis that the merger would suffocate other market players. In the Commission's words: 'By being progressively marginalised, as a result of the integration of Honeywell into GE, Honeywell's competitors would have been deprived of a vital source of revenue and seen their ability to invest for the future and develop the next generation of aircraft systems substantially reduced/eliminated, to the detriment of innovation, competition and *thus* consumer welfare.'[142] Pluralism is no longer favoured merely for its own sake (as per the ordoliberal theory) but as a means to increased consumer welfare. Similarly, in the context of the rules of predatory pricing (discussed in chapter 6), the EC standard is different from that of the Chicago School (which requires that the plaintiff show that after the predatory pricing campaign the predator would be able to monopolise the market and recover the cost of predation) and favours a standard based upon the risk that predatory pricing would lead to the exit of competitors, something more closely associated with post-Chicago theories of predation, but also closely associated with the value of pluralism seen under the SCP paradigm.[143]

8 Economics in competition law: opportunities and limitations

Now that EC competition policy is redirected towards an increased use of economic analysis two factors need discussion: first, whether the kind of economic analysis espoused by the Commission is appropriate; and second, whether the translation of economic theory into legal standards is successful. This is the task of the next chapters but some preliminary remarks are appropriate at this stage.

In deciding whether the economic standard chosen is desirable, one must consider not only whether the standard leads to better results (this inquiry can easily be skewed by the analytical position we take – the preference for consumer welfare over total welfare is one symptom of this), but more importantly whether the standards are suited to the political ambitions of the EC. The preference for pluralism over efficiency, and the emphasis on consumer

---

[142] *Thirty-first Report on Competition Policy* (2001) p. 98 (my emphasis).
[143] See further chapter 6.

welfare, while problematic from the perspective of a puritanical economist, should be welcomed from the perspective of one interested in the development of a competition policy for the EC in so far as these respond better to the Community's economic policy. This also suggests that from the perspective of EC competition law, the refusal to apply economic theory to certain business practices might be justified on the basis of other legitimate public policy reasons. The conversion to economics does not necessitate an abandonment of the political content of competition policy. Rather, a redefinition of the relationship between the economic and political aims of competition policy is necessary, so as to ensure that the economic analysis is based upon the normative foundations of EC competition law. It is tempting to suggest that while post-Chicago theories have not been completely successful in the United States, they might find a more hospitable home in the EC as the values espoused by the Community call for more aggressive enforcement of competition law than in the US.

Translating economics into rules of law raises a number of issues broached in chapter 1. It is important to bear in mind that any legal standard will of necessity simplify the economic theory upon which it is based, and lead to risks of error: either the standard is too strict so that the risk of Type 1 errors (prohibiting efficient behaviour) is increased or the standard is too loose whereby the risk of Type 2 errors (inefficient behaviour is not prohibited) arises. The court or authority has to decide which error it prefers to make. Moreover, the design of the law has to take into account the cost of enforcing a rule: a more sophisticated rule that avoids error may not be worthwhile if the cost of deploying the rule is greater than the benefits gained from avoiding the risks of error. Given the Community's preference for pluralism, it may be more willing to make Type 1 errors, preserving market structures that it believes are a source of competition in the long term, rather than Type 2 errors which eliminate that source.

4

Competition law and public policy

Contents

1. Introduction	*page* 89
2. Environmental policy	91
3. Industrial policy	94
4. Employment policy	96
4.1 Protecting/promoting employment	96
4.2 Protecting the working conditions of employees	97
5. Consumer policy	99
6. Culture	102
6.1 Book prices	103
6.2 Sports broadcasting	105
7. National interests	110
8. Placing competition policy in the context of EU policies	113
8.1 Methods	113
8.2 Institutional legitimacy	118
8.3 Limitations: eliminating public policy considerations?	119
9. The future of public policy considerations	122

1 Introduction

In the previous chapters we noted the Commission's move towards using consumer welfare as the benchmark for testing the legality of agreements. A second, related move that we consider in this chapter is a commitment to avoid using non-economic considerations in making decisions when applying competition law. As in chapter 2, this move is examined by reference to the interpretation of Article 81, in particular subsection (3). Recently, the Commission has claimed that the purpose of Article 81(3) is: 'to provide a legal framework for the economic assessment of restrictive practices and not to allow the application of the competition rules to be set aside because of political considerations'.[1] By statements such as these, the Commission is repositioning competition policy quite considerably, suggesting that other non-economic values (except the single market, which the Commission sees as a means of achieving greater efficiency) have no role in the decision-making process. In a thoughtful contribution that complements this position, Alexander Schaub (a former Director General of DG Competition) said that while the *ultimate* objective underlying the political decision to have competition policy is the promotion of the public interest widely defined (e.g. in terms of prosperity, employment and social cohesion), the day-to-day enforcement of competition law should not be preoccupied with achieving these political benefits directly – public interest goals should not be translated into 'criteria for law enforcement' but are achieved by preventing distortions of competition in the internal market.[2] Schaub supports this conclusion by drawing on the view that the basic aim of competition policy is the indirect pursuit of public policy gains, and by arguing that if competition policy were used to contribute directly to wider public policy aims, the pursuit of the public interest might fail, and it would be a move away from the free market principles that underpin the EC. This approach is different from the previous policy. In the *Twenty-first Report on Competition Policy* the Commission set out the following vision of the relationship between competition law and other EC policies: 'This link between Community objectives and competition policy is a two-way process. It is inconceivable that competition policy could be applied without reference to the priorities fixed by the Community. But it is also important to realize how an effective competition policy will help to attain these goals.'[3] In this perspective, the relationship between competition law and other Community objectives is reciprocal: on the one hand, competition helps achieve other Community goals, while on the other, competition policy can be applied by direct reference to other Community goals.

Therefore, to claim that competition law should not be affected by other public policy goals is at the very least a resolution of some of the internal differences between members of DG Competition, and at most a potentially significant delimitation of its powers. Indeed, the Commission in 1993 had noted how a competition policy that did not have an impact on other Community policies would be marginalised and of less relevance.[4] Moreover, this policy change is problematic from a legal perspective. First, as Frazer noted,[5] it is not easy to carry out an 'efficiency re-write' of Article 81 because the language of Article 81(3) includes other non-economic values, including a

---

[1] EC Commission *White Paper on Modernisation of the Rules Implementing Articles [81] and [82] of the Treaty* COM(99)101 final para. 57.

[2] A. Schaub 'Working Paper VII' in C.-D. Ehlermann and L. Laudati (eds.) *European Competition Law Annual 1997: Objectives of Competition Policy* (Oxford: Hart Publishing, 1998).

[3] *Twenty-first Report on Competition Policy* (1991) p. 13.

[4] Ibid. p. 14.

[5] T. Frazer 'Competition Policy after 1992: The Next Step' (1990) 53 *Modern Law Review* 609, 616.

consumer benefit) and some form of
or economic progress'). Second, as will
enounces the commitment to a purely
le 81, accepting that other factors may
ce. Third, the Treaty itself *compels* the
iderations through the inclusion in the
ese clauses demand that in the imple-
ne area, the effect in other fields must be
Treaty Establishing a Constitution for
his holistic approach: part III of the
nd functioning of the Union, begins by
sure consistency between the different
his Part, taking all of the Union's objec-
s legitimate to consider how agreements
other Community policies. And as the
ment of an agreement under Article 81
tion to a variety of Community policies,
ethodology. We conclude this chapter by
used to take public policy factors into

y because it represents most clearly the role
es in shaping competition law. In pursuing
sion has encouraged 'voluntary agreements
ectives while respecting the competition
lement EC environmental regulation. As a
n exempted under Article 81(3) when they
es and reduced environmental risks,[9] or led
and to better prospects for realising energy
grammes.[10] In these decisions, environmen-
ason for exemption – the agreements also
by reduced production costs, the use of new

127(2) (employment); 151(4) (culture); 152(1) (health);
(industrial policy); 159 (economic and social cohesion).
stitution for Europe (Cm 6429, 2004).
Parliament and Council of 24 September 1998 on the
y and Action in relation to the Environment and
ustainability' [1998] OJ L275/1, Art. 3(1)(f). This ambi-
s *Communication on the Sixth Environmental Action*
5–19.
67 and 68 (environmental risks would be reduced because
to transport a noxious chemical).
ra. 25.

technology and increases in production capacity.[11] More recently, an agreement's contribution to Community environmental policy was given greater prominence in *DSD*,[12] where the Commission granted an individual exemption on the basis that the agreement, in addition to generating economies of scale, gave 'direct practical effect to environmental objectives' laid out in Community law by a directive on packaging waste.[13]

The Commission's commitment to fostering environmental objectives through competition law is reflected in part 7 of the *Guidelines on Horizontal Agreements* which describes the Commission's policy on environmental agreements among competitors.[14] The guidelines provide that the Commission exempts agreements which 'reduce environmental pressure' so long as the 'net contribution to the improvement of the environmental situation overall outweighs increased costs'.[15] The Commission takes into account not only economic efficiency, but also sustainability, widening the kinds of benefits that are taken into account under Article 81(3) in order to grant an exemption. This approach finds its clearest expression in the *CECED* decision (upon which the test in the guidelines appears to be based) where the Commission exempted an agreement among washing machine manufacturers to phase out machines with high electricity consumption.[16] While this meant that cheaper models would no longer be available and some manufacturers would be at a disadvantage if they lacked the technology to develop more energy efficient machines, the Commission noted the considerable environmental benefits of this agreement in its reduction of negative externalities. The Commission found that cost savings for consumers (in the form of lower electricity bills) were greater than the price increase in the electrical goods subject to the agreements, and the Commission's methodology appears to allow it to decide that an agreement may be exempted solely on the basis of improved environmental conditions, provided that these outweigh the reduction in competition.[17] In two subsequent notifications similar to *CECED*, the Commission issued a comfort letter (an informal statement that the agreement is unlikely to infringe Article 81) where it explained that when reviewing an environmental agreement the Commission will consider the cost savings for consumers of the goods in question, and then estimate the 'benefits which the society at large derives from improved environmental conditions'.[18] This suggests that the environmental benefits to society as a whole (not only the benefits to buyers of electrical goods) are relevant, and the environmental benefits to society are sufficient to grant an exemption.

---

[11] *Exxon–Shell* [1994] OJ L144/21 para. 67; *Philips–Osram* [1994] OJ L378/37 paras. 25–6.

[12] [2001] OJ L319/1 paras. 143–5.

[13] Directive 94/62 on Packaging and Packaging Waste [1994] OJ L365/5.

[14] Commission Notice – *Guidelines on the Applicability of Article 81 of the EC Treaty to Horizontal Cooperation Agreements* [2001] OJ C3/2 para. 179.

[15] Ibid. paras 196, 198.   [16] [2000] OJ L187/47.   [17] See especially para. 56 (ibid.).

[18] M. Martínez López 'Commission Confirms its Policy Line in respect of Horizontal Agreements on Energy Efficiency of Domestic Appliances' (2002) 1 *Competition Policy Newsletter* 50, 52.

These decisions epitomise the problems in understanding the role of Community policy considerations in competition law decisions: in the early cases the agreement's contribution to environmental gains is added as an embellishment, noting how an efficient agreement also has other benefits. This suggests that the environmental effects are unnecessary for exemption. However, some of the later cases suggest that the environmental benefits are part of the assessment of the agreement's overall benefits, indicating that an agreement like *CECED* might not gain exemption merely on the strength of the anticipated cost savings, giving the environmental impact assessment a decisive role to play in the decision to exempt. And the Commission has been criticised because, by acknowledging that environmental considerations are a factor that moves the Commission to exempt an agreement, the recent decisions run against the interpretation of Article 81(3) given by the Commission in its *Guidelines on the Application of Article 81(3)*, which provide that efficiencies are the sole benefit that counts when exemptions are granted.[19]

If *CECED* represents the current policy, there are two methods to analyse the combination of economic and ecological considerations. The first, drawing on ecological modernisation theories, suggests that the environment has an economic value. The environmental costs and benefits of a practice are as economically relevant as its impact on other aspects of economic efficiency.[20] In this light, *CECED* widens the notion of economic efficiency to take into account an agreement's positive impact on sustainable development. The decision deploys a cost–benefit analysis that incorporates assessment of an agreement's environmental impact, which is in line with the Community's general approach to environmental regulation.[21] This is consistent with the Commission's duty to promote a 'sustainable development of economic activities', and to integrate environmental protection requirements into the definition and implementation of Community policies.[22] This interpretation would support the Commission's current view that Article 81(3) is exclusively about efficiency by widening the meaning of economic efficiency.

A second method to interpret the role of environmental protection in competition cases is to suggest that the duty imposed by Article 6 EC to integrate environmental protection in the Community policies and activities

---

[19] See G. van Gerven 'The Application of Article 81 in the New Europe' 2003 *Fordham Corporate Law Institute* 429–30 (Hawk ed. 2004).

[20] For an authoritative elaboration of this point, see D. Pearce and E. B. Barbier *Blueprint for a Sustainable Economy* (London: Earthscan, 2000) ch. 1, esp. p. 20. See also M. Hajer *The Politics of Environmental Discourse: Ecological Modernisation and the Policy Process* (Oxford: Oxford University Press, 1995) p. 31; R. Hollander and G. Curran 'The Greening of the Grey: National Competition Policy and the Environment' (2001) 60 *Australian Journal of Public Administration* 42, 43–5.

[21] Article 174(3) line 3 EC. Restated in the *Communication on the Sixth Environmental Action Programme* p. 12. For a review of this type of approach, see N. Hanley and C. L. Spash *Cost Benefit Analysis and the Environment* (Aldershot: Edward Elgar, 1993).

[22] Articles 2 and 6 EC respectively. See H. Vedder *Competition Law and Environmental Protection in Europe* (Groenigen: Europa Law Publishing, 2003).

referred to in Article 3 EC means that environmental protection is normatively superior to competition law, and may thereby act as a 'trump' to justify even anticompetitive agreements if these are necessary to safeguard the environment. Thus, a cleaner environment may be the basis for an exemption, regardless of any efficiency considerations. Under this reinterpretation one could arguably also reach the conclusion that an agreement that reduces costs, and increases productive and allocative efficiency, may be prohibited if it has an adverse effect on the environment. This interpretation can be used to cast doubt upon the Commission's current commitment to expunge non-competition considerations from Article 81(3).

Whichever of these two methods is selected, from a practical perspective, an agreement's environmental impact can affect the assessment of an agreement's legality in two ways: on the one hand, an agreement's positive contribution to other Community policies can serve as a further basis for exemption, and on the other, it is arguable (but there is no precedent to support this) that an agreement's negative impact on the environment might be a basis for a decision not to exempt under Article 81(3) because an agreement which increases pollution does not yield economic progress.

3 Industrial policy

In the field of industrial policy, the interaction between two potentially conflicting fields, competition and competitiveness, has been expressly mediated by Article 157 EC: while this provision empowers the Commission to ensure that European industry is competitive, it also provides that this 'shall not serve as a basis for the introduction by the Community of any measure which could lead to a distortion of competition'.[23] The reason for this is that the Community believes that competition in the internal market is the best source for industrial strength in world markets, and so promoting competitiveness cannot be achieved through means that reduce competition. 'European companies will not be competitive in world markets without competition at home.'[24] This indicates that the contribution that competition policy makes to the EC's industrial policy is largely negative: it prevents firms from collusion and other forms of anticompetitive behaviour that restrict the opportunities for other firms to develop and grow, thereby creating an environment which favours economic development.[25]

However, at times the Commission has used competition law to facilitate the development of EC industry in a different way, stating that it 'has taken into account the need to underpin the restructuring of Community industry

---

[23] Article 157(3) EC.
[24] *Twenty-first Report on Competition Policy* (1991) para. 43.
[25] *White Paper on Growth Competitiveness and Employment* COM(93)700 final; *Twenty-fourth Report on Competition Policy* (1995) paras. 14–17.

so as to increase its competitiveness'.[26] The Commission's policy in this context has had two dimensions: on the one hand, it has intervened to exempt a number of 'crisis cartels', that is agreements among competitors in difficulty that are designed to facilitate the remedying of structural problems and ensure the firms' return to profitability (a policy pursued principally in the early 1980s following a period of economic stagnation in Europe), and on the other, it has exempted agreements designed to strengthen Community industry vis-à-vis global competitors (a policy pursued primarily during the build-up to the single market deadline of 1992).

In the restructuring decisions, the Commission said that agreements designed to reduce overproduction when demand is low yield three benefits: (1) efficiency; (2) softening the impact on employment; (3) facilitating and speeding up restructuring which would lead to enhanced competitiveness of European industry.[27] These three considerations, cumulatively, provide a sufficient degree of 'technical or economic progress' to outweigh the restriction of competition, a restriction which in any event would be temporary.[28] In its decisions, the Commission has principally focused on the variety of ways in which cooperative agreements enhance efficiency, but the other two factors have strengthened the decision to exempt: in both *BPCL/ICI* and *ENI/Montedison* the Commission held that the resolution of the industry's structural problems via a reciprocal agreement is faster and better than what the parties could have arranged independently.[29] The industry's return to competitiveness is regularly noted,[30] most emphatically in *Bayer/BPCL* where the technological improvements were particularly valued because the industry sector was 'threatened' by imports from outside the EC.[31]

In the decisions in the run up to the 1992 deadline, agreements which enhanced the strength of European industry vis-à-vis competitors from other countries regularly gained exemption. In *Optical Fibres*, one of the reasons for exemption was the fact that the joint venture facilitated the transfer of new technology from the United States into the EC, which the Commission deemed 'essential to enable the European companies to withstand competition from non-Community producers, especially in the USA and Japan, in an area of fast moving technology'.[32] The same line was taken in *Olivetti/Canon*, where the agreement was exempted because it would 'contribute to improving the

---

[26] *Twenty-fourth Report on Competition Policy* (1995) para. 16.

[27] *Twelfth Report on Competition Policy* (1982) paras. 38–40, restated verbatim in the *Twenty-third Report* (1994). See R. B. Bouterse *Competition and Integration: What Goals Count?* (Deventer: Kluwer, 1994) ch. 5 for an earlier study.

[28] E.g. *Stichting Baksteen* [1994] OJ L131/15 para. 36.

[29] *BPCL/ICI* [1984] OJ L212/1 para. 37; *ENI/Montedison* [1987] OJ L5/13 para. 31.

[30] E.g. *Stichting Baksteen* [1994] OJ L131/15 para. 26; *Twelfth Report on Competition Policy* (1982) para. 39.

[31] [1988] OJ L150/35 para. 27.

[32] *Optical Fibres* [1986] OJ L236/30 para. 59. The Commission identified AT&T and Sumitomo as the firms EC industry should catch up with.

technological patterns of the EEC industry and ultimately its competitivity (sic)'.[33] However, without the efficiencies that would result due to the introduction of the new technology, the agreements would not have been exempted.

These decisions demonstrate that the promotion of industrial policy is not a sufficient condition for exempting an agreement. Nonetheless, the anticipated industrial policy benefits are noted when explaining the reason to exempt. Compared to the environmental agreements, industrial policy arguments have less weight – they might tip the balance in marginal cases, but are not as decisive as considerations of environmental policy.

4 Employment policy

4.1 Protecting/promoting employment

The relevance of an agreement's effects on employment in the application of EC competition law has increased. In 1977 the ECJ explained, in a particularly opaque passage, that an agreement's beneficial effect on employment, 'since it improves the general conditions of production, especially when market conditions are unfavourable, comes within the framework of the objectives to which reference *may* be had pursuant to Article [81(3)]'.[34] However, the Commission now must take employment into account because Article 127 EC requires that the impact of employment *shall* be considered for all Community measures. Accordingly, exemptions have been granted to agreements which in addition to efficiencies led to stability in the labour market.[35] Employment considerations were also relevant in the 'crisis cartel' cases considered above. The Commission used the impact of the restructuring plan on employment as a factor that contributes to satisfy the conditions in Article 81(3), when the coordination of closures 'helps to mitigate, spread and stagger their impact on employment'.[36] Specifically, the Commission said that coordinated closures that allow for restructuring to be 'carried out in acceptable social conditions, including the redeployment of employees', contribute to improving production and promoting technical and economic progress.[37] Moreover, in some restructuring agreements, the exemption under Article 81(3) was made conditional upon the parties promising to re-deploy or retrain

---

[33] *Olivetti/Canon* [1988] OJ L52/60 point 54. See also *GEC–Siemens/Plessey* [1990] OJ C239/2, where the competitiveness of firms in the US and Japan persuaded the Commission to exempt an agreement which would strengthen EC industries.

[34] Case 26/76 *Metro SB–Großmärkte GmbH & Co. KG v. Commission* [1977] ECR 1875 para. 43. The analysis was restated in Case 42/84 *Remia BV and Others v. Commission* [1985] ECR 2545 para. 42.

[35] *Metro* [1977] ECR 1875.

[36] The position is set out in the *Twelfth Report on Competition Policy* (1982) para. 39 and repeated verbatim in the *Twenty-third Report on Competition Policy* (1994) para. 85.

[37] *Stichting Baksteen* [1994] OJ L131/15 paras. 27–8; identical analysis in *Synthetic Fibres* [1984] OJ L207/17 para. 37.

their staff, suggesting that without measures designed to soften the blow on employment, the agreements might not have been approved.[38]

However, in some decisions, the relevance of employment considerations is less clear. One particularly controversial decision in this respect is *Ford/ Volkswagen*, granting an exemption to a joint venture to build a new car manufacturing plant in a poor area of Portugal.[39] It is not clear from the text of the decision whether or not the improved employment prospects were a relevant consideration, leading Professor Amato to the conclusion that the decision displayed an 'ambiguous relevance/irrelevance . . . to the social profile of the affair'.[40] And while the CFI's decision suggests that the agreement's positive impact on employment was irrelevant to the Commission's decision to exempt,[41] many are persuaded that the agreement's impact on employment was a relevant factor.[42] The ambiguity of the relevance of employment considerations is even more profound than that which surrounds the consideration of environmental or industrial policy.

4.2 Protecting the working conditions of employees

As if these doubts were not enough, the Court of Justice has added another layer of complexity by indicating that, in certain circumstances, employment considerations mean that an agreement does not fall within Article 81 at all, even though competition is restricted. This occurred in the *Brentjens* case that arose from a dispute over pension arrangements in the Netherlands where a compulsory pension fund was established for those who are employed in firms engaged in wholesale trade in building materials. The fund was set up by a decision of the organisations representing employers and workers in this sector in the context of a collective agreement. The restriction of competition was evident: as the complainant noted, first, the compulsory scheme prevented the firms in this sector from obtaining cheaper pension schemes elsewhere and, second, the agreement excluded all insurers from a substantial part of the insurance market.[43] However, the Court justified the scheme by making reference to certain provisions of EC law (Article 139 EC and the Agreement on Social Policy)[44] to indicate that another Community ambition is the

---

[38] *Synthetic Fibres* [1984] OJ L207/17 para. 18; *Stichting Baksteen* [1994] OJ L131/15 para. 12.

[39] 'This would not be enough to make an exemption possible unless the conditions of Article 85(3) were fulfilled, but it is an element which the Commission has taken into account.' [1993] OJ L20/14 para. 36.

[40] G. Amato *Antitrust and the Bounds of Power* (Oxford: Hart Publishing, 1997) p. 61.

[41] Case T-17/93 *Matra Hachette v. Commission* [1994] ECR II-595 para. 139.

[42] E.g. J. Faull and A. Nikpay *The EC Law of Competition* (Oxford: Oxford University Press, 1999) para. 2.131, claiming that job creation 'was a relevant consideration in the granting of the exemption'.

[43] Joined Cases C-115/97, C-116/97 and C-117/97 *Brentjens' Handelsonderneming BV* [1999] ECR I-6025 para. 47.

[44] Article 1 of the Agreement on Social Policy [1992] OJ C191/91.

development of a policy in the social sphere (i.e. employment). In particular, the Commission is empowered to promote close cooperation between Member States in the social field, especially in matters relating to the right of association and collective bargaining between employers and workers. The Court observed that a restriction of competition was possible as a result of collective agreements between associations representing employers and workers, but that the social policy objectives pursued by such agreements would be undermined if Article 81 were to apply to instances when management and labour cooperate to improve conditions of work and employment. Therefore, 'an interpretation of the provisions of the Treaty as a whole which is both effective and consistent [means] that agreements concluded in the context of collective negotiations between management and labour in pursuit of such objectives must, by virtue of their nature and purpose, be regarded as falling outside the scope of Article [81(1)] of the Treaty'.[45] The Court did not say that any collective agreement fell outside Article 81, but noted that the agreement in this instance was designed to guarantee a certain level of pension for all workers; accordingly it improved their working conditions. It is hard to explain this judgment because one can legitimately argue that the policy factors could have been taken into consideration at the Article 81(3) stage rather than by finding that Article 81 did not apply.[46] Moreover, it is not easy to circumscribe the limits of the Court's approach. On the one hand, it can be argued that the case is limited to collective agreements whose aim is to improve working conditions. This can be supported by the Advocate General's remarks that in national law collective agreements have a special status that restricts the scope of application of national competition law.[47] On the other hand, the Court's sweeping reasoning supports a wider reading whereby an agreement that contributes to any policy in the social sphere might be excluded from the application of Article 81.[48]

Whether the narrow or the wide approach is taken, the judgment creates another mechanism for reconciling the core values of competition law with other Community policies: to exclude the application of Article 81 when this would undermine the pursuit of (some) other Community objectives. This approach is clearly more vigorous than that under Article 81(3) where the Commission evaluates the agreement's overall effects, with more or less attention to relevant Community values. Under the approach taken by the Court in this case, the other Community values go so far as to exclude the application of

---

[45] [1999] ECR I-6025 para. 57.

[46] In its submissions, the Commission argued that Article 81(3) would not suffice to grant an exemption. Not only is this questionable, but it is not a sufficient reason on which to base the argument that Article 81 should therefore not apply.

[47] AG Jacobs [1999] ECR I-6025 paras. 109–11.

[48] But AG Jacobs rejects this wider reading on the basis that the exclusion of the application of competition law is normally expressly provided in the Treaty for specific sectors, e.g. agriculture and military equipment (para. 123). Nor has the Court excluded the application of competition law in other sectors on the basis of the presence of other Community interests.

competition law outright. However, there is no way of identifying which other Community policies have such importance that they can displace the application of competition law. Why, for example, is environmental protection not something that trumps the application of Article 81?

5 Consumer policy

As we saw in chapter 3, the protection of consumer interests has recently gained prominence in EC competition law. To a degree, the interests of consumers should always have played a role in Article 81(3): an exemption may only be granted if consumers receive a fair share of the benefits of the agreement. However, in the early years the consumer benefit requirement was addressed superficially – the Commission often assumed that provided the agreement did not eliminate competition completely, consumers would be protected.[49] Moreover, the notion of the consumer in EC competition law is wider than that in national consumer law (in the French version of the Treaty, reference is made to 'utilizateurs', i.e. all users, not just consumers). It covers all those who purchase goods from the firm accused of infringing competition law – thus a downstream manufacturer, a distributor, or the person buying goods in a shop all count as consumers. This wider definition is justified by the core aims pursued by competition law: the interests of market participants who buy from the parties to an anticompetitive agreement must be safeguarded, accordingly the consumer interest is implicitly incorporated in the economic freedom value.[50]

However, recently the attention of the Commission has been on the *final* consumer, and the Commission reflects more carefully about how the final consumer may or may not gain from the behaviour of firms. This is consistent with an increased 'Europeanisation' of consumer law and policy following the Treaty of European Union.[51] In the context of competition law, the increased interest in the final consumer is evidenced by the creation of the position of Consumer Liaison Officer in 2003, whose task is to act as a contact point for consumer organisations, to alert consumer groups to cases where their input

---

[49] A. Evans 'European Competition Law and Consumers: The Article 85(3) Exemption' [1981] *European Competition Law Review* 425.

[50] See generally K. Mortelmans and S. Watson 'The Notion of Consumer in Community Law: A Lottery?' in J. Lonbay (ed.) *Enhancing the Legal Position of the European Consumer* (London: British Institute of International and Comparative Law, 1996).

[51] Article 153 EC (inserted in the Maastricht Treaty) allows the Commission to take consumer interests into account, in particular through internal market legislation, but also to have regard to the consumer interest in defining and implementing all Community policies and activities. There have been numerous directives addressing various aspects of consumer law. See generally H. Collins *The Law of Contract* 4th edn (London: Lexis Nexis, 2002) pp. 40–2. In the context of EC legislation in the field of consumer law, the consumer is more narrowly defined as 'a natural person who is acting for purposes which can be regarded as outside his trade or profession' (Article 2 Directive 85/577 on Contracts Negotiated Away From Business Premises [1985] OJ L372/31).

might be useful, and to intensify contacts between DG Competition and other Directorates General whose portfolio includes consumer interests.[52] Similarly, the rhetoric from the 'European Competition Days' (a yearly event organised by DG Competition to explain the role of competition law to European citizens) emphasises the benefits that the final consumer obtains from the enforcement of competition law.[53] The focus on the final consumer is such that some have suggested that the standard by which EC competition law operates is not efficiency, or economic freedom, but consumer welfare.[54] The speeches of the former Commissioner (Mario Monti) indicate that under his steward-ship competition policy focused on 'consumer interests' narrowly defined to include only the final consumer.[55] The interests of the final consumer are varied: they include low prices, high-quality products, a wide selection of goods and services, and innovation.[56] At times it will be fairly easy to see how the enforcement of competition law can safeguard the consumer interest: blocking a cartel will lower prices; allowing an agreement which reduces production costs that yield lower prices also benefits consumers. In most cases prohibiting inefficient agreements and allowing efficient ones will lead to consumers benefiting. This need not always be the case: for instance, an agreement between two firms may lead to cost savings that are achieved by reducing certain services that some consumers value, simply to cut costs (e.g. shutting down local branches in favour of large out-of-town shops). This may reduce prices but inconvenience certain consumers who have further to travel to obtain the goods. How can one in this scenario decide what the best solution is for consumers? At least in the context of Article 81(3), this kind of question can be avoided because all that needs to be shown is that the consumer gains a share of the benefits; thus, provided that some efficiencies are passed on to consumers, there is no need to worry about the fact that some consumers are less satisfied. Nevertheless, the fact that an agreement can lead to some con-sumers gaining and others losing requires further consideration if one is to take the 'consumer welfare' objective seriously.[57]

While competition law and consumer law are designed to remedy market failures, they do so in slightly different ways.[58] Competition law safeguards

---

[52] Press release IP/03/1679, 9 December 2003.

[53] The competition day takes place during each presidency of the EU (the first was in Lisbon in 2000).

[54] S. Bishop and M. Walker *The Economics of EC Competition Law* 2nd edn (London: Sweet & Maxwell, 2002) pp. 23–7.

[55] E.g. M. Monti 'Foreword' in *Thirty-first Report on Competition Policy* (2001); M. Monti 'Competition Enforcement and the Interests of Consumers', speech at the European Competition Day in Athens, 14 February 2004; M. Monti 'The Future for Competition Policy in the European Union', speech at Merchant Taylors' Hall, London, 9 July 2001.

[56] *Guidelines on the Assessment of Horizontal Mergers under the Council Regulation on the Control of Concentrations between Undertakings* [2004] OJ C31/5 para. 8.

[57] See ch. 3, pp. 83–6.

[58] For an overview, see J. Stuyck 'European Consumer Law After the Treaty of Amsterdam: Consumer Policy In or Beyond the Internal Market?' (2000) 37 *Common Market Law Review* 367.

economic freedom so that consumer sovereignty can be exercised, while consumer law is associated with a wider, and deeper, range of measures to protect the consumer from dangerous products, unfair contract terms, lack of information, or abusive sales tactics. In other words, competition law regulates the market process in general, while consumer law regulates the specific transaction between seller and consumer.[59] Accordingly, might an agreement be exempted not just as a means of safeguarding consumer sovereignty, but also as a way of safeguarding wider consumer interests? In *Asahi*, the Commission exempted an agreement that, in addition to stimulating the development of new products (thereby encouraging dynamic efficiency), also led to safer consumer goods.[60] However, as with employment factors, the relevance of consumer safety in the decision to exempt is uncertain: is it a mere embellishment or is it a decisive factor that tips the balance in favour of exemption?

A definitive answer is hard to give: at times the consumer interests are noted in passing, at other times consumer policy objectives appear so important as to condition the interpretation of Article 81 to facilitate the attainment of goals normally associated with consumer law. An example is the regulation of consumer guarantees. There has been some standardisation as to the form of these guarantees to protect consumers,[61] but under EC competition law, additional steps have been taken in this respect. Already by the 1970s the Commission was of the view that a manufacturer's guarantee must extend to all of its goods, and not only to those purchased through its distribution network. While the Commission was concerned about the potential for market segregation caused by guarantees limited to those goods bought in the Member State where the guarantee was issued, the interest of consumer choice was an element that underpinned the Commission's approach.[62] The effect was to create an obligation on manufacturers who decide to include a guarantee, to offer a *Community-wide* guarantee system, a degree of harmonisation that goes well beyond the minimal harmonisation achieved to date under EC consumer law.[63] In *Grundig* for example, a selective distribution network was exempted because the manufacturer had agreed, among other things, to introduce a uniform Europe-wide comprehensive warranty, and that pending its arrival it undertook to ensure that customers could benefit from their warranties in the Member State where they reside even if the goods were purchased abroad.[64] Here Article 81 is used to impose standard terms in consumer contracts designed to protect the consumer in a manner resembling consumer law.

---

[59] See generally N. W. Averitt and R. H. Lande 'Consumer Sovereignty: A Unified Theory of Antitrust and Consumer Protection Law' (1997) 65 *Antitrust Law Journal* 713.

[60] *Asahi* [1994] OJ L354/87 paras. 24–6.

[61] Article 6 Directive 1999/44/EC on Certain Aspects of the Sale of Consumer Goods and Associated Guarantees [1999] OJ L171/12.

[62] The case law is reviewed in J. Goyder 'Consumer Guarantees and Competition Issues' in Lonbay *Enhancing the Legal Position*.

[63] EC Commission Notice – *Guidelines on Vertical Restraints* [2000] OJ C291/1 para. 49.

[64] *Grundig's EC Distribution System* [1994] OJ L20/15 para. 19.

A similar approach is found in the Block Exemption on agreements in the insurance sector.[65] This allows competing insurers to cooperate by agreeing upon non-binding standard policy conditions. This increases competition by facilitating the entry of new insurance providers who face lower costs by using standard terms, and also benefits consumers directly because consumer organisations can use these standard terms as a benchmark to compare insurance policies offered by different insurers and advise consumers.[66] But, in addition, the Block Exemption also stipulates that the standard policies cannot include certain provisions to protect consumers from unfair, but not necessarily anticompetitive, behaviour, which creates a significant imbalance between the rights and obligations arising from the contract.[67] For example, no exemption is available if the insurer can modify the terms of the contract without the consent of the policyholder.[68] This again incorporates consumer law standards into competition law norms.

It may be argued that using competition law to supplement consumer protection legislation is a misuse of powers by the EC. On the other hand, it confirms the increasing importance of the consumer interest in EC competition law, and more specifically it illustrates a different mechanism for incorporating Community policies in competition cases: the declaration of the agreement's legality under Article 81 is made conditional on the parties modifying the agreement in ways that protect the consumer. This suggests that an agreement which is efficient but which may harm consumer interests may not be exempted unless modified to guarantee consumer benefits. This 'conditional legality' approach (whereby an exemption is available only if the parties undertake to take certain steps designed to accomplish other Community policies) is present also in decisions affecting cultural policy, discussed below.

6 Culture

The Community's cultural policy is different from the policies we have discussed so far because there is no 'European' culture to defend, only national cultures. Article 151 provides that the Community's task is to 'contribute to the flowering of cultures of the Member States'. Accordingly, EC law safeguards national cultural values.[69] In common with other policy fields, Article 151(4) is a cross-sectional clause whereby 'the Community shall take cultural aspects into account in its actions under other provisions of this Treaty, in

---

[65] Commission Regulation (EC) No. 358/2003 of 27 February 2003 on the Application of Article 81(3) of the Treaty to Certain Categories of Agreements, Decisions and Concerted Practices in the Insurance Sector [2003] OJ L53/8.

[66] Ibid. Recital 14.   [67] Ibid. Recital 15.   [68] Ibid. Art. 6(1)(e).

[69] C. Schmid 'Diagonal Competence Conflicts between European Competition Law and National Regulation – A Conflict of Laws Reconstruction of the Dispute on Book Price Fixing' (2000) 8 *European Review of Private Law* 155, 164.

particular in order to respect and to promote the diversity of its cultures'. However, while in the context of other cross-sectional clauses the Commission is reconciling two Community interests (e.g. competition v. industrial policy), in the context of culture the balance is between a *Community* policy (competition) and a *national* policy (cultural diversity). This raises a considerable problem in that Article 81(3) does not allow for exemptions when national interests are at stake; thus, when an agreement restricts competition but protects national cultures, it is doubtful if the cross-sectional clause is sufficient to justify the grant of an exemption. This legal doubt might explain in part the unconvincing approach taken by the Commission when confronting the competition versus culture debate in the book publishing sector, and the cautious avoidance of that debate in considering the collective sales of broadcasting rights to football games.

6.1 Book prices

In the field of book pricing the legal issue confronting the Commission is whether a nationwide agreement to fix the resale prices of books can be tolerated. The agreements function in this way: national book publishers agree to fix prices for their books and individual publishers impose a price restriction on the booksellers at retail level. In general terms resale price maintenance agreements have an anticompetitive object, and are prohibited because they suffocate price competition at retail level.[70] However, in the market for books there are arguments for applying a different policy. The gist of these is that publishers use popular books as a means of subsidising the sales of less popular ones. Without resale price maintenance booksellers would sell popular books for very little and raise the price for less popular works. The effect from a cultural perspective would be that the diversity of what is published is diminished as no retailer wishes to sell expensive, unpopular books. Some have gone so far as to suggest that without resale price maintenance the effect would be to threaten freedom of expression guaranteed by Article 10 of the European Convention on Human Rights.[71] The price-fixing agreement among publishers serves a public interest, while restricting competition. Regulating these agreements from a Community perspective was controversial because often the agreements had the support of the government and in some cases price fixing is supported by national legislation.[72] Moreover, the Council supported the use of resale price maintenance as a means of

---

[70] D. G. Goyder *EC Competition Law* 4th edn (Oxford: Oxford University Press, 2003) pp. 177–9. See further ch. 10.

[71] See the arguments presented in Joined Cases 43 and 63/82 *VBVB and VBBB v. Commission* [1984] ECR 19 para. 33.

[72] For example, in France. See also European Parliament Resolution with Recommendations to the Commission on the Drawing-up of a Directive of the European Parliament and of the Council on the Fixing of Book Prices [2003] OJ C180 E/476.

safeguarding the cultural value of books, and asked the Commission to consider its competition policy in the light of Article 151(4).[73]

The solution reached by the Commission and the Courts is highly formalistic. They have held that in so far as a price-fixing system has no effect on trade between Member States, then Article 81 does not apply (because it only forbids agreements whose anticompetitive effects have a cross-border element) but that as soon as price fixing affects trade between Member States, then it is prohibited, and no exemption may be granted for 'cultural' reasons.[74]

We can explore the practical implications of this position by considering the Commission's analysis of the agreement between publishers and booksellers in Germany.[75] In this instance, resale price maintenance is allowed for books published in Germany destined for the national market. However, resale price maintenance is not allowed for books published abroad, or published in Germany but set to be exported, except if the only reason the book is being exported is in order to re-import it and circumvent the resale price maintenance agreement. This system does not infringe Article 81 because, according to the Commission, it does not affect trade between Member States. This approach is comparable to that taken by the Court of Justice in reviewing book resale price maintenance legislation under Article 28 EC. In that context too, resale price maintenance laws for books are only lawful if they do not prevent the free movement of goods.[76]

There are three problems with this approach. The first is the assertion that purely national schemes do not affect trade between Member States. In both the free movement and competition case law the Court has regularly said that measures affect trade between Member States when the effect is 'direct or indirect, actual or potential'.[77] Moreover, the effect has in some cases been described as an effect on 'the pattern of trade between member States'.[78] This test has been applied so aggressively that it is unconvincing that national price-fixing schemes have no inter-state effects. The second difficulty comes from comments made by the then Commissioner for competition in announcing that the German scheme was lawful: 'by clearing the German price fixing system the Commission, in a perspective of subsidiarity, also takes account

---

[73] Council Decision on Cross-Border Fixed Book Prices in European Linguistic Areas [1997] OJ C305/2.

[74] The position has remained constant since the early cases: see Joined Cases 43 and 63/82 *VBVB and VBBB v. Commission* [1984] ECR 19 paras. 44–5.

[75] *Sammelrevers and Einzelreverse* [2000] 5 Common Market Law Reports 346; the final draft is available in English at (2002) 2 *Competition Policy Newsletter* 37. Similar conclusions were reached in respect of the resale price maintenance agreement in the Netherlands (IP/99/668, 9 September 1999).

[76] Case 229/83 *Leclerc v. Au Blé Vert* [1985] ECR 1; Case C-9/99 *Echirolles Distribution SA v. Association du Dauphiné and Others* [2000] ECR I-8207.

[77] Case 56/65 *Société Technique Minière v. Maschinenbau Ulm GmbH* [1966] ECR 235, 249.

[78] Case C-306/96 *Javico International and Javico AG v. Yves Saint Laurent Parfums SA* [1998] ECR I-1983 para. 25.

of the national interest in maintaining these systems which are aimed at preserving cultural and linguistic diversity in Europe'.[79] This statement is controversial because if an agreement has no effect on trade, this is because of its commercial effects and has nothing to do with national public policy considerations. As a result, this statement raises the question of whether the EC massages the meaning of 'effect on trade' to achieve certain policy objectives. If so, it demonstrates another technique for taking policy considerations into account: pretending that one of the conditions for the application of Article 81 is not met. In contrast, the previous competition Commissioner, Karel van Miert, had taken the view that cultural considerations could be taken into account under Article 81(3),[80] which might have been a more transparent way of balancing the restriction of competition and the public interest in preserving diversity in book publishing, although this would have fallen foul of today's more restrictive interpretation of Article 81(3) by the Commission. The third problem is whether the German scheme the Commission has approved is sufficient to secure the cultural interests the parties wished to defend. In this context it has been argued that as soon as German traders realise that re-imports are not covered by resale price maintenance, then e-commerce will mean that national price-fixing agreements will lose much effectiveness.[81] Drawing these three strands together, it seems that the Community's policy is an unhelpful attempt to carve out a compromise without confronting the difficult question about how to balance competition and culture in the books sector.

6.2 Sports broadcasting

The non-economic dimension of sport is that it performs a social function, forging identities and bringing people together.[82] This has become relevant in the debates over the regulation of the sale of broadcasting rights to football matches. The Commission's regulation of this market is an illustration of how competition, industrial policy and cultural policy interact to inform the Commission's approach. As a preliminary matter, it is worth noting that the Council of Ministers invited the Commission 'to continue and to make more effective its contribution to the development of the audiovisual sector based on an approach that integrates the cultural, competitive and industrial dimensions of the sector'.[83] This suggests that the Council considers that the

---

[79] Press release IP/02/461, 22 March 2002.

[80] Answer to MEP's written question on 28 April 1998; [1999] 4 Common Market Law Reports 394.

[81] See V. Emmerich 'The Law on the National Book Price Maintenance' (2001) 2 *European Business Organization Law Review* 553; S. B. Hornsby 'Public and Private Resale Price Maintenance Systems in the Publishing Sector: The Need for Equal Treatment in European Law' (1985) 10 *European Law Review* 381, 393–4.

[82] Declaration 29 on Sport attached to the Treaty of Amsterdam.

[83] Council Resolution of 21 January 2002 on the Development of the Audiovisual Sector [2002] OJ C32/4, 5.

application of Commission policies has to remain holistic; competition enforcement should be sensitive to the cultural and industrial dimensions of this economic sector.

The context within which the Commission intervenes in this sector is the following: on one side, the liberalisation of the broadcasting sector combined with developments in technology mean that new broadcasting media are on the market (e.g. pay-TV and broadcasting via mobile phones or via the Internet). This has led to increased competition to acquire broadcasting rights to sports events because these are the kinds of programmes that are key to the success of a new broadcaster. The Commission takes the view that popular sports and Hollywood feature films are 'premium content', necessary to attract consumers to new broadcasting services.[84] The competition problems arise because football clubs in a league allow their football associations to sell the broadcasting rights of each league collectively, and the rights are often sold exclusively to one broadcaster. Therefore, there is a small pool of sellers holding desirable content, which grants them considerable commercial leverage. The Commission's main concern is that the manner in which broadcasting rights are sold means that broadcasters who are unable to obtain some of the rights to popular sports events may exit the market; this is a particular concern for those wishing to broadcast via mobile phones, using 3G technologies, and those wishing to broadcast over the Internet. Thus, from an economic perspective there are worries about the lack of competition in broadcasting (in case the market becomes dominated by a small number of powerful pay-TV outlets) and about the failure of new broadcasting technologies (as without attractive content, owners of 3G licences will be unable to sell their services).

If these were the sole relevant factors, an economic approach would condemn collective selling as tantamount to a cartel among football clubs, and rule that the collective sale of exclusive broadcasting rights is an agreement whose effect is to foreclose market access to competing broadcasters. However, from a cultural perspective, an additional complication arises: 'competition' in the world of sport means something different from competition in the economic sense. Sport demands a contest between equals, and in the football context this means that all teams in a given league have roughly the same potential to win the contest. To achieve this, it is important that all clubs have broadly comparable revenues to train new players and attract established stars.[85] Joint sales of broadcasting rights by the football teams allow for the revenue to be distributed among the clubs in a more equitable manner than if each team were to sell broadcasting rights to its matches individually. If the latter were to occur, matches involving more popular teams would sell for much more than

---

[84] A. Schaub 'Sports and Competition: Broadcasting Rights of Sports Events' (speech, 26 February 2002).

[85] For a perceptive discussion, see S. Weatherill 'Sport as Culture in EC Law' in R. Craufurd-Smith (ed.) *Culture and European Union Law* (Oxford: Oxford University Press, 2004).

matches involving less popular teams. The disparity in revenue would enrich popular teams, allowing them to buy better players and making matches less enjoyable as the result would in many cases be predictable. This would reduce popular support for, and interest in, sport.

That there is a social and cultural value in maintaining competitive leagues was acknowledged by the Declaration on Sport attached to the Amsterdam Treaty and the Helsinki Report on Sport.[86] The latter declares ambitiously that there is a 'European approach to sport', which sees it as an instrument of social cohesion and education. These rhetorical flourishes suggest a political willingness to moderate the role of competition to take into account the cultural value of sport. The argument has similarities to that used in the book sector: the restriction of competition allows the revenue generated from the sale of matches likely to draw a wide audience to subsidise the poorer clubs, thereby keeping the league competitive and unpredictable. In the years leading up to the recent decisions about collective selling, the Commission appeared willing to take the cultural dimension into account.[87] The Commission drew legal support from the *Bosman* ruling where the Court said that national restrictions on the right of workers to move freely could be justified having regard to the social importance of sporting activities and the need to maintain a balance between teams to preserve equality and uncertainty as to the results.[88] This statement was used to support the view that the application of Article 81 could be affected by the social and cultural values of sport.

However, in the formal decisions, there is little reference to solidarity among the football clubs, but considerable reference to economic efficiency instead. In the *UEFA Champions League* decision, the Commission obtained, by negotiating with the parties over a period of two years, an agreement whereby football broadcasting rights are sold in a set of different packages.[89] In brief, the league sells two live TV packages of 47 of the 125 matches, plus a highlights programme. The remaining matches are either sold one by one by UEFA or, if it is unable to sell these, the individual club may sell them. In addition, packages for Internet broadcasts for 3G mobile phones are also for sale. In approving this novel selling arrangement, the Commission is eager to support the development of new technologies, suggesting that the exempted agreement supports the EC's industrial policy in this sector. In particular, while the Commission exempts the collective sale of two live packages on the basis that collective sales are more efficient because the buyers have one point

---

[86] COM(1999)644. S. Weatherill 'The Helsinki Report on Sport' (2000) 25 *European Law Review* 282.

[87] *Twenty-ninth Report on Competition Policy* (1999) paras. 140–1; M. Monti 'Competition and Sport: The Rules of the Game', speech, 26 February 2001; Schaub 'Sports and Competition'.

[88] Case C-415/93 *Union Royale Belge des Sociétés de Football Association ASBL and Others v. Jean-Marc Bosman and Others* [1995] ECR I-4921 para. 106.

[89] The statement of objections was sent on 20 July 2001 (IP/01/1043) and the Decision was reached in July 2003.

of sale and because UEFA's collective selling allows for the maintenance of a strong brand name for the product, the agreement would not have been exempted without UEFA creating other packages designed to facilitate market access by those broadcasting via new technologies: the Commission utilises competition law to support emerging industries. The approach taken is highly interventionist because it prescribes to which groups of business the relevant rights should be sold.

Without wishing to doubt the potential benefits of developing Internet and 3G broadcasting, the legitimacy of the Commission's prescriptive approach can certainly be called into question. As we discuss in chapter 7, it is accepted that firms holding a monopoly over an essential resource should have obligations to make that resource available to others (e.g. the owner of a natural monopoly like the rail network infrastructure should allow firms wishing to offer train services access to the network) but there was no question about UEFA holding a monopoly over any market. The Commission's decision, however, indicates that premium sports content is 'essential' for the commercial success of new broadcasters, taking the view that UEFA has some market power. Therefore the Commission is using Article 81 to make markets more competitive, something which is not necessarily within its powers, although it is consistent with the industrial policy orientation of the decision.

Notably absent from the reasons granting exemption in *UEFA Champions League* is any reliance on the specific cultural characteristics of sport. The parties mentioned the cultural benefits of joint selling but the Commission held that, on the facts, it was unnecessary to consider this point because the agreement deserved exemption in light of its efficiencies.[90] Arguably in the context of this sports competition, the redistribution of income among clubs is not a high priority. The UEFA Champions League competition is composed of the top teams in each national league and all are fairly wealthy, so redistribution of income is not as essential in this scenario as it would be when rights to a national league are sold. Nevertheless, the Commission accepted that solidarity among clubs could be taken into consideration in deciding whether to exempt collective selling in this passage:

> Any need to take the specific characteristics of sport into account, such as the possible need to protect weaker clubs through a cross-subsidisation of funds from the richer to the poorer clubs, or by any other means, *must* be considered under Article 81(3) of the Treaty.[91]

This suggests, in line with the earlier rhetoric from Commission officials, that in appropriate circumstances, exemptions may be granted which sacrifice economic competition in favour of allowing a 'competitive' sports league.

---

[90] *Joint Selling of the Commercial Rights of the UEFA Champions League* [2003] OJ L291/25 paras. 164–7.
[91] Ibid. para. 129 (my emphasis).

It is therefore particularly unfortunate that in handling the collective sale of broadcasting rights for the German League (a scenario where income redistribution might have been more relevant) the Commission chose to settle the case rather than issue a fully reasoned conclusion.[92] This leaves one uncertain as to whether in settling the case the Commission took into account income redistribution.

Similarly to the *UEFA Champions League* decision, the settlement with the German Football League entails an unbundling of broadcasting rights, with several packages available to broadcasters and packages for Internet and mobile phone broadcasts.[93] Commenting on this decision, the competition Commissioner, Neelie Kroes, made the following observations:

> [t]his decision benefits both football fans and the game. Fans benefit from new products and greater choice. Leagues and clubs benefit from the increased coverage of their games. Readily available premium content such as top football boosts innovation and growth in the media and information technology sectors. Moreover, open markets and access to content are an essential safeguard against media concentration.[94]

These comments reinforce the industrial policy dimension of the Commission's policy in this area but also introduce a novel cultural policy observation: the maintenance of media pluralism. This might be an oblique reference to the Commission's concerns about collective selling of the Premier League matches in the UK where BskyB has had no serious rivals in the broadcasting market,[95] but it is also a reflection of a more widespread concern that the Commission has over newly developing technologies. The Commission wishes to see several market players offering competing services, thereby affording consumers greater choice. Choice has an economic rationale in that greater choice improves consumer welfare, but in the broadcasting sector, choice also implies a wish to ensure the plurality of broadcasting outlets as a means of safeguarding diversity of expression as a value in itself.

The upshot of the Commission's regulatory approach to the football broadcasting sector is that it attempts to create a situation where a variety of policy interests are catered for: first, by allowing leagues to sell all matches collectively it retains a redistributive element (allowing the cultural function of sport to continue); second, by forcing packages of broadcasting rights to be sold separately it guarantees competition among broadcasters (allowing for cultural diversity and pluralism); and third, by creating mechanisms whereby Internet

---

[92] *Joint Selling of the Media Rights to the German Bundesliga* [2005] OJ L134/46.

[93] Memo 05/16, Details of broadcasting rights commitments made by the German Football League, 19 January 2005.

[94] IP/05/62 Competition: German Football League commitments to liberalise joint selling of Bundesliga media rights made legally binding by Commission decision of 19 January 2005.

[95] See D. McAuley 'Exclusively for All and Collectively for None: Refereeing Broadcasting Rights Between the Premier League, European Commission and BskyB' [2004] *European Competition Law Review* 370.

and 3G broadcasters have opportunities to buy some rights, the industrial policy goal of introducing this novel technology is achieved. The process shows competition law being used to achieve other public policy goals. However, the process is defective in two ways: first, in relation to the industrial policy objective the Commission forces sellers to behave in specific ways (e.g. to create packages for Internet and 3G broadcasters) which seem to be beyond what is allowed under Article 81; and second, in relation to the cultural value of sport, the role of this is hidden because it does not form part of the reasoning in the only published decision (even though it is expressly mentioned as a relevant factor) and the other dispute has been settled so the relevance of income redistribution was not confronted directly, generating some uncertainty over its relevance.

7 National interests

So far, we have considered how an anticompetitive agreement which contributes to other Community policies has been appraised. In the context of agreements that sustain cultural objectives, the Commission's policy is problematic, in part because Article 81(3) does not appear to tolerate an exemption on the basis of national culture. In the book-pricing sector the Commission avoided confronting the application of Article 81(3), and in the broadcasting sector the relevance of cultural policy was not set out clearly. Many of the Commission's interventions in the cultural sector predate a significant ruling of the Court of Justice, *Wouters*.[96] This case provides a method by which an anticompetitive practice may be tolerated if it provides a necessary means to support a legitimate national policy, which may apply in cases of culture, or other national policies.

The dispute in *Wouters* arose because of a decision by the Netherlands Bar Association forbidding multi-disciplinary partnerships between lawyers and accountants. The Bar Association was formed by statute and authorised to devise rules for the practice of the profession. The rule in question was held to be a decision by an association of undertakings with a clear anticompetitive effect: a novel means of providing services for clients was stifled.[97] Lawyers and accountants challenged the rule because they wished to establish such practices. Whether the decision was anticompetitive because it restricted economic freedom, or anticompetitive because it harmed consumers, both kinds of harm were present. The rule, however, was supported on the basis that it safeguarded the proper practice of the legal profession, maintaining a sound justice system and protecting the rights of clients. In particular, the Court noted that a lawyer operating in the Netherlands has obligations of professional conduct, which

---

[96] Case C-309/99 *Wouters and Others v. Algemene Raad van de Nederlandse Orde van Advocaten* [2002] ECR I-1577.
[97] Ibid. paras. 86–90.

accountants do not have, and the advisory role of a lawyer may be in conflict with the supervisory capacity of the accountant. The Court thus concluded: 'The Bar of the Netherlands was entitled to consider that members of the Bar might no longer be in a position to advise and represent their clients independently and in the observance of strict professional secrecy if they belonged to an organisation which is also responsible for producing an account of the financial results of the transactions in respect of which their services were called upon and for certifying those accounts.'[98] The ratio decidendi of the judgment is that if a restriction of competition is necessary to safeguard the proper practice of the legal profession, then competition law does not apply to the measure, and the restriction of competition is tolerated. Public policy trumps the application of competition law.

The successful application of the *Wouters* rule leads to the same result that we saw with the *Brentjens* judgment but with one significant difference. In *Wouters* the Court demands that the restriction of competition should be necessary to achieve the non-economic policy objective, while in *Brentjens* there is no comparable proportionality test, one merely has to show that there is a causal relationship between the measure that restricts competition and the welfare of employees. The only distinguishing feature between the two cases that may justify a more lax approach might be explained by the fact that whereas in *Brentjens* the balance is between two Community policies (competition v. the interests of employees safeguarded by collective agreements), the Court considers that less stringent requirements should apply than when a Member State's policy conflicts with one of the central policies of the Community.

While the *Wouters* judgment is a novelty in the field of competition law, the basis of the Court's approach is well established in the case law of the internal market. There the Court has long recognised that in applying the rules on free movement (say, for example, the rule about the free movement of services in Article 49 EC) Member States may restrict the free movement of services if they impose certain restrictions that apply uniformly to all economic actors which are designed to protect a national interest. In the Court's jargon, a Member State may invoke such 'mandatory requirements' to justify the restriction on the free movement of services. (Academic commentators have often referred to this approach as the application of a 'rule of reason'. This is confusing because what they mean has nothing to do with what the US Supreme Court means by that phrase in applying antitrust law.) For example, in one case the Court was faced with a German law that prevented a person from carrying out judicial debt collection work without the assistance of a lawyer. This affected foreign providers adversely and prima facie infringed their freedom to provide services. However, the Court held that the restriction may be justified if the rule is

---

[98] Ibid. para. 105.

necessary to ensure that clients are adequately advised of their legal position.[99] So the Court has already recognised that the integrity of the legal system is a justification for restricting the application of the EC's internal market law, and *Wouters* extends this approach so that the application of EC competition law is suspended when necessary to uphold the integrity of a national legal system. Accordingly, while the Court has long resisted the application of a US rule of reason (balancing pro-and anticompetitive effects of an agreement) it has now extended the application of the 'European rule of reason' (balancing national policy and Community law) from the free movement to the competition field.[100]

This interpretation of *Wouters* means that any restriction of competition necessary to safeguard a national public policy consideration may be allowed to stand. Against this interpretation, it has been argued that *Wouters* stands for the proposition that a restriction of competition is tolerated when necessary for the proper performance of an economic service, a restriction 'ancillary to a regulatory function'.[101] This is a narrower interpretation, which requires that the restriction be necessary for the proper functioning of a market. This is the interpretation given by the Commission in rejecting a complaint about a rule established by UEFA forbidding one person from owning two football clubs in a league. The Commission applied *Wouters* to rule that the prohibition was necessary for the proper functioning of the market in question: the organisation of football competitions. If two teams are owned by the same person, the public's perception that the games between them would be fair diminishes and this devalues the product in the eyes of consumers.[102] The approach has analogies with the doctrine of 'ancillary restraints' we considered in chapter 2.

A competition lawyer would find the analogy with ancillary restraints more compelling, while an EC lawyer would find the analogy with mandatory requirements more apt. There are two major differences between the two views. One is that the doctrine of ancillary restraints applies in circumstances where the agreement, viewed as a whole, is economically beneficial. In contrast, the rule on mandatory requirements allows for market rules to be suspended for a greater good even if the agreement as a whole is anticompetitive. The

---

[99]   Case C-3/95 *Reisebüro Broede v. Gerd Sandker* [1996] ECR I-6511.

[100]   This is the view I took in G. Monti 'Article 81 EC and Public Policy' (2002) 39 *Common Market Law Review* 1057. Unfortunately, the 'European rule of reason' label has been misunderstood. A. P. Komninos 'Non-Competition Concerns: Resolution of Conflicts in the Integrated Article 81 EC', Working Paper (L) 08/05 Oxford Centre for Competition Law and Policy (available at www.competition-law.ox.ac.uk/competition/portal.php) says that the *Wouters* approach is constitutional in nature and rejects the 'European rule of reason' label. However, his interpretation of *Wouters* is in substance identical to mine, so the difference is one of labels.

[101]   R. Whish *Competition Law* 5th edn (London: Lexis Nexis, 2003) p. 122.

[102]   Case COMP/37.806 *ENIC/UEFA* (2002), available at http://europa.eu.int/comm/competition/antitrust/cases/decisions/37806/en.pdf.

second is that the rule on mandatory requirements applies to actions which sustain state policies, whereas the ancillary restraints rule applies to agreements that sustain markets. The two interpretations are not mutually inconsistent, and the decision can be a basis for both approaches.

8 Placing competition policy in the context of EU policies

The upshot of the decisions reviewed above is that a variety of Community policies have influenced the Commission's competition decisions. It is worthwhile drawing together the general themes that emerge from the above policy-by-policy analysis. The first task is to generalise from the above what methods are used to relate competition law to other Community policies. The second is to consider whether these methods are legitimate. The third is to evaluate the Commission's recently expressed wish to distance competition law from other public policy fields.

8.1 Methods

Six methods have been used to integrate public policy considerations in competition decisions. Each is summarised below.

The first method is exclusionary in nature: the Community resolves the tension between competition and another policy by deciding that the other policy takes precedence, and as a result competition law does not apply. There are two clear manifestations of this in the case law discussed above: the first is in the competition v. employees' rights debate in *Brentjens*, the second in the reconciliation between competition policy and national public policy in *Wouters*. While *Wouters* and *Brentjens* reach a similar conclusion, it is important to keep the two approaches separate because there is one distinctive feature. In *Wouters*, as we saw above, the Court deployed a proportionality test, so that a restriction of competition is justified when necessary to achieve the public policy objective. In *Brentjens* there is no proportionality test: the fact that the agreement is designed to safeguard the interests of employees is sufficient to find that competition law does not apply.

It is likely that both approaches will be applied more widely, although their scope remains to be defined fully. The *Brentjens* approach, for example, might be deployed when other EC policies have greater weight than competition law, so that the pursuit of those is normatively superior to other policies – thus the successful development of dialogue between management and labour could be said to be so important that its pursuit cannot be undermined by other Community policies. The difficulties of this view are that it is not at all clear which Community policies have such importance that the application of competition law should be excluded. If the Treaty is our guide, it may legitimately be argued that environmental policy, which is given such high priority, should warrant the non-application of Article 81, yet environmental agreements are exempted. While the legal effect of exemption under Article 81(3) and exclusion of competition law is the same (under both the agreement is allowed to stand even if it restricts competition), the method of analysis is different and there are some not insignificant procedural issues which suggest that the two approaches cannot be applied interchangeably: the burden of proof for finding a breach of Article 81(1) rests with the complainant, the burden under Article 81(3) with the defendant; Article 81(3) exemptions have in the past been made conditional upon certain contractual modifications (e.g. the obligation to retrain staff which we saw in the crisis cartel cases above) while the non-application of Article 81(1) does not allow for any post-assessment changes.

Anti-doping and antitrust

The breadth of *Wouters* is illustrated by the recent judgment in *Meca-Medina*. Two athletes were given bans for doping offences. They alleged that the doping rules, fixed by the International Olympic Committee, were anticompetitive, in breach of Article 81. According to the Court of First Instance, the Commission was entitled to reject this allegation because the rule was about sport, not about trade, so the competition rules did not apply.[103] However, the ECJ took a different line and subjected the anti-doping rules to the *Wouters* test. The key passage is worth quoting in full:

> Not every agreement . . . which restricts the freedom of action of the parties or of one of them necessarily falls within the prohibition laid down in Article 81(1) EC. For the purposes of application of that provision to a particular case, account must first of all be taken of the overall context in which the decision of the association of undertakings was taken or produces its effects and, more specifically, of its objectives. It has then to be considered whether the consequential effects restrictive of competition are inherent in the pursuit of those objectives and are proportionate to them.
>
> As regards the overall context in which the rules at issue were adopted, the Commission could rightly take the view that the general objective of the rules was, as none of the parties disputes, to combat doping in order for competitive sport to be conducted fairly and that it included the need to safeguard equal chances for athletes, athletes' health, the integrity and objectivity of competitive sport and ethical values in sport.
>
> In addition, given that penalties are necessary to ensure enforcement of the doping ban, their effect on athletes' freedom of action must be considered to be, in principle, inherent itself in the anti-doping rules.
>
> Therefore, even if the anti-doping rules at issue are to be regarded as a decision of an association of undertakings limiting the appellants' freedom of action, they do not, for all that, necessarily constitute a restriction of competition incompatible with the common

---

[103] Case T-313/02 *Meca-Medina and Majcen v. Commission*, judgment of 30 September 2004.

> market, within the meaning of Article 81 EC, since they are *justified* by a legitimate objective. Such a limitation is inherent in the organisation and proper conduct of competitive sport and its very purpose is to ensure healthy rivalry between athletes.[104]
>
> The parties argued that disqualification damaged their earnings as they would be unable to win prize money or obtain sponsorship. The Court held that the restriction of their economic freedom was justified because the doping rules pursued a variety of other public interest goals. The Court's application of the *Wouters* test can be explained in both ways discussed at pp. 111–13. On the one hand, it extends the rule that certain public policies justify the non-application of Article 81 (namely athletes' health and the integrity and ethical values of sport). On the other hand, more restrictively, the ruling may stand for the proposition that the proper conduct of an activity (in this case, long-distance swimming) may justify a restriction of competition.

The second method is to *redefine economic efficiency* to include other public policy considerations. This occurred in the recent environmental agreements where reduced pollution was characterised as an economic benefit. This method is also the approach preferred by the Commission in its Guidelines on Article 81(3).

The third approach is to use non-economic benefits as factors that *tip the balance* in favour of granting an exemption. This approach is visible in some early environmental agreements and in cases where industrial policy considerations arise. It is the most opaque approach. In some decisions we reviewed above, the benefits to other Community policies are merely mentioned, without any attempt to integrate them into the decision to exempt, while in others they appear necessary to gain exemption.

The fourth approach is to grant *conditional exemptions* and to use remedies to achieve the public policy goal. In this scenario an agreement is exempted only if the parties agree to take steps that help in securing certain Community objectives. The most radical exemplification of this is in the *UEFA* decision where the Commission's exemption was on the condition that it regulates who buys the exclusive rights as a means of supporting the development of new technologies. Similar steps were taken in the crisis cartel cases to insist upon retraining as a condition for exemption, and in exempting certain agreements affecting consumer contracts the Commission required the insertion of clauses designed to protect the consumer's weaker position. Luc Gyselen offers a valuable insight in respect of the fourth approach. In reviewing the *Ford/ Volkswagen* case (where, as we saw above, an exemption was granted to a joint venture that would aid employment in a poor European region), he suggests that the Commission's 'intellectual detour' into Article 81(3) was used to impose certain conditions on the joint venture between the two car

---

[104] Case C-519/04P *Meca-Medina and Majcen v. Commission*, judgment of 18 July 2006, paras. 42–5 (my emphasis).

manufacturers.[105] The conditions were designed, first, to avoid any anticompetitive 'spillover' (whereby any cooperation between Ford and Volkswagen could facilitate collusion in other markets) and, second, to achieve supplementary pro-competitive benefits at the production level. The second aim confirms the analysis which we have offered of other Commission decisions where remedies are used to achieve other policies in the Community interest. Here the remedy was designed to increase the economic benefits by making the market more competitive. As we will see in chapters 8 and 12, the Commission has deployed a similar method in merger cases, where parties are allowed to merge on the condition that they undertake additional commitments designed to improve the functioning of the market. It is appropriate to ask whether this approach is defensible. First, from a practical perspective, the approach appears 'dirigiste' in character. That is, it assumes that the Commissioners know more about how to make the business work than the businessmen involved and are able to guide them to achieve greater efficiencies. This assumption is most likely imprudent. Second, this approach seems unlawful. A basic objection is that the remedy is disproportionate: if the agreement as designed by the parties already merits exemption under Article 81(3), there is no need to require further amendment. A further objection is that the Commission misuses its powers: the aim of Article 81 is to maintain competitive markets, not to make markets work better. Only if we agree that competition law is about sustaining an activist industrial policy can we argue that the Commission's approach is within its powers and proportionate.

The fifth approach we have seen is to rule *formalistically* that an agreement does not fall within Article 81 because trade between Member States is not affected. This is how the Commission avoided confronting the 'culture question' in the books sector. In chapter 12 we shall see an additional illustration of this approach where the Court decides that an economic actor is not performing an economic activity and is therefore not an 'undertaking', thereby falling outside the scope of Articles 81 and 82 EC. This is used to facilitate the provision of certain public services by shielding them from the application of competition law.

The sixth method is to find that the non-competition consequences of the agreement are of such importance that if an agreement is inefficient but contributes to another Community policy, it is exempt. Conversely if an agreement is efficient but harms a particularly important policy, then it is not exempt. The second interpretation of *CECED* set out above falls within this approach: if the environmental effects are more relevant than the competition effects, then the analysis under Article 81(3) will be skewed towards the ecological effects. Traces of this approach are also present in those exemption

---

[105] L. Gyselen 'The Substantive Legality Test Under Article 81(3) EC Treaty – Revisited in Light of the Commission's Modernization Initiative' in A. von Bogdandy, P. Mavroidis and Y. Mény (eds.) *European Integration and International Coordination: Studies in Transnational Economic Law in Honour of C.-D. Ehlermann* (The Hague: Kluwer, 2002) pp. 189–90.

decisions which impose additional commitments on the parties in the decision to exempt (e.g. a duty to retrain staff or a duty to license the broadcast rights more widely). The other interest (employment or industrial policy) has such weight that it enlarges the scope of considerations relevant for exemption. The converse approach (banning an efficient agreement when it runs counter to another aim of the Treaty) can be seen in *Consten and Grundig* which we discussed in chapter 2, where efficiencies were not admissible once the agreement was found to disturb the creation of a single market.

Luc Gyselen, a former senior member of DG Competition, has taken a slightly different interpretation of the case law discussed in this chapter and his views are worthy of attention.[106] First, he suggests that in the industrial policy cases comments about the employment benefits are mere 'obiter dicta'. It is not particularly clear what he means. To English ears, obiter dicta are parts of a judgment that, while not necessary to reach a conclusion in the case, are statements of law which are persuasive. An example of obiter dicta is the passage we have cited above from the *UEFA* decision where the Commission states that although in this case reference to the cultural value of sport was not necessary, it is a relevant consideration in appropriate cases. If we adopt the common law definition of obiter dicta, it means that the Commission's statements about an agreement's positive employment benefits mean that in other cases the Commission would be willing to exempt solely on the basis of desirable non-economic effects. This would go well beyond the role which we have ascribed to the Commission's decisions. However, it is clear from reading the entirety of Gyselen's essay that this is not what he meant to say. He wishes to say that these statements are just present but have no legal relevance. This does not answer the question of why these remarks are present in the first place. These statements are in documents that are justiciable and have value as guides to business about what the Commission decides. If *ex post* we are told that the Commission does not mean what it writes, this casts grave doubts about the entirety of the decisions. Second, turning to the Treaty Articles that we have argued compel the consideration of other policies in competition cases, Gyselen says that the Treaty requires the 'integration' of other policies in competition policy and that an agreement cannot be exempted merely because it contributes to a Community policy but is anticompetitive. This may be so, but the difficulty we have tried to explore in this chapter is that this 'integration' seems to be accomplished by different methods, and that in some cases some policy factors seem more important than in others.

Each of the six approaches we have identified confers a different weight upon the public policy interest concerned, and no approach is used exclusively in one policy area. It is therefore also difficult to say that certain policies play a more significant role than others. The institutional setting within which Article 81(3) decisions are reached may explain this uncertain state of play.

---

[106] Ibid. pp. 185–6.

8.2 Institutional legitimacy

Until now, competition law has been enforced by a centralised system, with considerable policy-making discretion and autonomy.[107] In addition to the courts, there are two other main players that constrain DG Competition's policy autonomy: the College of Commissioners (which must vote on each decision) and the Member States (particularly in the form of the Advisory Committee, but also through less formalised channels). This distinguishes competition policy from other policy areas of the EC where there is considerably greater involvement by other important political players (e.g. the Council, the European Parliament).[108] According to some, its powers to regulate the behaviour of firms and its autonomy make DG Competition a European federal agency,[109] albeit subject to its decisions being ratified by the College of Commissioners.

This institutional makeup explains to a large extent the difficulties about the role of public policy factors in EC competition policy: other Commissioners may press for competition policy to be adapted to a wider range of public interest goals. Internal differences among the Commissioners, due to their policy portfolios and the ideological position taken by the Directorate General in question, may lead to clashes about how to handle a particular agreement – we saw this in chapter 1 when reviewing *de Havilland* and it is likely that similar disputes occur in some Article 81 cases.[110] This institutional makeup is a logical corollary of the nature and structure of the EC Treaty, which locates competition policy within the wider aims of the Treaty. Challenges to EC competition policy on the basis that it is politicised miss the mark – it is *designed* to be politicised, albeit within the limits of Community competence.[111] Hence there will be instances where the Commission's decision will be a compromise solution that the text of the decision may fail to reflect.[112]

---

[107] S. Wilks and L. McGowan 'Competition Policy in the European Union: Creating a Federal Agency?' in G. B. Doern and S. Wilks (eds.) *Comparative Competition Policy* (Oxford: Oxford University Press, 1996).

[108] Though some have argued that by establishing rigorous procedures the Commission has reduced the risk of regulatory capture. See J. From 'Decision-making in a Complex Environment: A Sociological Institutionalist Analysis of Competition Policy Decision-making in the European Commission' (2002) 9 *Journal of European Public Policy* 219.

[109] F. Jacobs 'Jurisdiction and Enforcement in EEC Competition Cases' in D. Rowe, F. Jacobs and P. Jackson (eds.) *Enterprise Law of the Eighties* (London: American Bar Association, 1981) p. 205; M. Cini and L. McGowan *Competition Policy in the European Union* (London: Macmillan, 1998) p. 53.

[110] See generally A. Stevens with H. Stevens *Brussels Bureaucrats? The Administration of the European Union* (Basingstoke: Palgrave, 2001) ch. 9.

[111] The critiques of the political nature of competition decisions in the EC come mostly from German commentators who would favour a cartel office operating independently of the Commission. See C.-D. Ehlermann 'Reflections on a European Cartel Office' (1995) 32 *Common Market Law Review* 471.

[112] A point also made by Wolf Sauter, who observed that the 'real reasons' for a Commission decision may not be expressly articulated in the Official Journal. W. Sauter *Competition Law and Industrial Policy in the EU* (Oxford: Oxford University Press, 1997) p. 123.

Some Commissioners may be swayed because the agreement is efficient, others only if it also promotes employment or other policy factors. Thus, uncertainty is inherent in the deliberative process of the Commission. This can in part explain the diverse methods deployed to take public policy considerations into account and the ambiguity in drafting of the Commission's decisions, but it cannot excuse the Commission's failure to articulate a consistent and transparent method. Perhaps matters are too complex to hope for a clearer solution; in fact the Court when called upon to adjudicate the application of Article 81(3) has steered clear of intervening, granting the Commission wide berth by saying that it has a wide margin of appreciation.[113] Moreover, when confronting some of the controversial cases, the Court has rendered extremely ambiguous judgments. Not only has the Court been unwilling to intervene in the Commission's exercise of discretion, it has also invented its own approach to reconcile conflicting interests, excluding the application of Article 81 when more powerful interests have to be attained.

Should the role of Community policies in competition decisions change, now that National Competition Authorities will handle the bulk of competition cases as a result of Regulation 1/2003? By and large, national authorities will be independent of domestic politics, so immune from regulatory capture. The Commission's answer is in the affirmative: Article 81(3) shall henceforth only exempt efficient agreements.

8.3 Limitations: eliminating public policy considerations?

The Commission has long recognised the need to identify priorities in its policy, consistency in its enforcement and transparency in its decision-making process.[114] In its view, an essential step to achieve these objectives is to narrow down the meaning of Article 81(3). The recently published *Guidelines on the Application of Article 81(3) EC* achieve the narrowing down in two ways. First, they interpret the phrase 'technical or economic progress' narrowly so that it only includes economic efficiency, postulating that the purpose of the first condition of Article 81(3) is 'to define the types of efficiency gains that can be taken into account'.[115] Secondly, they marginalise the role of non-efficiency considerations:

> Goals pursued by other Treaty provisions can be taken into account to the extent that they can be *subsumed* under the four conditions of Article 81(3).[116]

If this is read as if it were a statutory provision, the key is the verb 'subsume'.[117] Literally, to subsume means to place an idea or a term in a wider category.

---

[113] Whish *Competition Law* pp. 162–3.
[114] E.g. *Twenty-third Report on Competition Policy* (1993) p. 52.
[115] *Guidelines on the Application of Article 81(3) of the Treaty* [2004] OJ C101/97 para. 50.
[116] Ibid. para. 42 (emphasis added). The Commission cites in support *Matra Hachette* [1994] ECR II-595 para. 139 and *Metro* [1977] ECR 1875 para. 43.
[117] In the French version the term 'integrated' is used instead.

Under this reading, employment, cultural and industrial policy considerations become irrelevant because they cannot be subsumed under the 'efficiency' gains of Article 81(3). Under this approach, most of the policy aims indicated above could not be integrated into an 'efficiency' analysis. This seems to be the intention of the Commission's Guidelines. The anticipated benefit that the Commission envisages is that the degree of discretion in the hands of the national courts and National Competition Authorities is reduced: the pursuit of legal certainty and uniformity in decision-making is superior to the use of competition law as an instrument to achieve the Treaty's objectives, and the institutional changes cause a political reorientation.

However, the Commission's approach embraces a fairly wide conception of the economic effects of an agreement, which is not restricted to allocative, productive and dynamic efficiency. The Guidelines distinguish between *cost* efficiencies of an agreement (whereby costs are reduced as a result of the cooperation) and *qualitative* efficiencies. In considering qualitative efficiencies, the Commission uses the example of an R&D agreement between two tyre manufacturers that leads to the creation of a safer tyre. Increased safety is a relevant objective benefit. The Commission's decision in *CECED* also suggests that qualitative environmental benefits are relevant. And this decision is particularly interesting because the washing machine manufacturers did not agree to innovate; they merely agreed to eliminate a product line. There are no dynamic or productive efficiencies that result from the agreement – its only benefits are a reduction of externalities. Under this approach then, any gain can be taken into consideration provided that we can translate it into a benefit for consumers. If so, we can subsume consumer safety and environmental improvements under Article 81(3), but not all industrial policy considerations: supporting a strategic industry which is inefficient, or preserving jobs, can yield social benefits but these are not related to the aim of enhancing the final consumer's interests. On the other hand, exempting an agreement with a condition that helps to facilitate the entry of new products, like 3G phones in *UEFA*, is an economic benefit. The advantage of this approach is that by focusing on economic advances that benefit the consumer, a transparent method may emerge to determine whether the agreement deserves exemption. Moreover, by excluding certain industrial policy considerations, it removes the risk that National Competition Authorities can use Article 81(3) in a political manner to sustain national interests. As we saw in chapter 2, the institutional changes are accelerating a move towards using competition law in a narrow sense, focusing on consumer welfare.

However, this approach suffers from three weaknesses. First, it risks being insensitive to certain interests which we may wish to preserve even if there is a reduction in economic efficiency or consumer welfare – pluralism in publishing or a healthy sports sector might be values which we wish to preserve at the expense of consumer welfare. It might be said that if there are policies of a non-economic nature that should be safeguarded, then these should simply be excluded from the application of EC competition law, as in *Brentjens* in the case of EC policies or *Wouters* in the case of national policies. This might make for a neater methodology, but we would then, in effect, return substantially to the status quo, although using different methods to integrate public policy cosiderations: agreements that have a consumer benefit 'flavour' are exempted under Article 81(3) and agreements with benefits of a non-economic nature are excluded from the application of competition law.

Second, this approach raises what has been called the problem of characterisation:[118] is an agreement by certain manufacturers not to use a particularly harmful chemical in the workplace justifiable on the basis of the employees' safety (which would not count under the total welfare approach), or can we say that the agreement is a way of responding to a market failure, i.e. the employer's ignorance of the harmful effects of the chemical, and the agreement's contribution to a productive workforce (which would then count under the Guidelines as an economic benefit)? Given that virtually any benefit might be translated into an economic value, this might frustrate the Commission's intention by reintroducing all non-competition factors into the scheme of Article 81(3) EC. In fact, even the preservation of employment has been said to have economic value in certain circumstances. This argument has been made by Lars Kjolbye, a Commission official.[119] Basing himself upon dicta in *Metro I*, he argues that in markets where there is fluctuating demand, an employer will need to lay off workers when demand is low and take them on when demand increases. If an agreement 'stabilises' employment this is beneficial because it reduces training costs and the loss of valuable skills. Thus stabilising employment is an economic benefit. This sounds like a plausible argument on the facts of *Metro I*: a distribution agreement obliged wholesalers to undertake to take set quantities of the manufacturer's goods. The effect was to stabilise production and thus employment at the manufacturer's plant. However, it might be argued that this is a somewhat simplistic way of looking at markets because by stabilising the workforce one also makes it less flexible. It might be preferable to force businesses to face fluctuations of demand so that they are better able to respond to these natural market trends than to make firms and employees inflexible. Moreover, stabilising production of goods in an unstable market seems economically inefficient because in a downturn useless stock will be produced. The argument ultimately strays into the terrain of macroeconomics and it cannot be Kjolbye's intention to give a competition authority the power to determine aspects of employment policy. However, for the sake of argument, let us accept the line that so long as one is able to make an effect of the agreement sound economic in nature then

[118] L. A. Sullivan and W. S. Grimes *The Law of Antitrust: An Integrated Handbook* (St Paul, MN: West Publishing, 2000) p. 205.

[119] L. Kjolbye 'The New Commission Guidelines on the Application of Article 81(3): An Economic Approach to Article 81' [2004] *European Competition Law Review* 570.

it will be 'subsumed' into Article 81(3). If so, it can even be argued, as another Commission official has done, that diversity in book publishing is an economic benefit because this leads to wider consumer choice of books at affordable prices as the popular books subsidise the unpopular ones.[120] If every public interest can be made to 'sound' like an economic benefit, then the Guidelines achieve nothing but restating the status quo where public policy factors have some relevance some of the time but nobody exactly knows how much relevance. In response, it may be argued that by forcing parties to characterise the anticipated benefits of their agreement in economic terms, to show how their agreement resolves a market failure, this approach structures the analysis of non-competition factors in an open, transparent manner and it should be possible for national courts and authorities to adjudicate upon these matters. If this argument is accepted, then the approach in the Guidelines is not too different from the approach in US antitrust law.[121]

The third problem with excluding non-economic considerations is that it is not consistent with the Commission's past and present policy on exemptions, because the Commission is still speaking of benefits beyond the core values: for example, the recent reference to sport's cultural role and the pluralism of the publishing sector. Moreover, the Court has adopted a rule whereby competition law is excluded or infringement justified when certain public policy considerations are deemed to be of greater importance. So public policy considerations seem to retain a role in spite of the Commission's guidelines to the contrary. Finally, the approach fails to take into account that the Commission will remain competent to apply Article 81, and in this institutional setting it is less easy to escape the relevance of the impact of competition law on other Community policies. Might we see the Commission reach decisions taking into account public policy considerations in a way that National Competition Authorities do not?

9 The future of public policy considerations

This chapter presented the second major plank of the paradigm shift in the interpretation of competition law. In chapters 2 and 3 we noted a shift away from economic freedom and towards economic efficiency, in this chapter a move away from taking public policy considerations into account and towards, again, a focus upon the economic effects of agreements, in particular the effects on consumers. Thus, while the EC remains wedded to a model of 'disciplined pluralism' whereby intense concentrations of economic power are viewed with suspicion, increasing importance is given to exempting agreements on the basis of economic efficiency as a means to obtain the tangible economic benefits upon which the EC project is built.

---

[120] Gyselen 'Substantive Legality Test'.
[121] E.g. *California Dental Association v. FTC* 526 US 756 (1999) – an agreement may be justified if it resolves an information problem even though it facilitates price coordination.

This suggests that the future relevance of non-economic public policy considerations is bleak. These may justify the non-application of competition law under the *Wouters* and *Brentjens* formulae, but exemptions under Article 81(3) are destined to be based upon proof of economic benefits, even though this phrase seems so elastic that the difference between the current system and that of the past decisions is likely to be more about the presentation of the benefits rather than about the nature of the process.

5

Market power

Contents

1. Four concepts of market power   *page* 124
2. Dominance in EC competition law   127
3. Measuring market power   130
   3.1 Market definition: the hypothetical monopolist test   132
   3.2 Market definition in EC competition law   135
   3.3 Market shares   143
   3.4 Entry barriers   144
4. Market power in aftermarkets   148
5. Product differentiation and market power: the irrelevance
   of market definition   150
6. Market power in Article 81   153
   6.1 Safe harbours   154
   6.2 Quasi per se rules   155
   6.3 An evolving market power analysis   156
7. From commercial power to market power   157

1 Four concepts of market power

At the heart of the EC's current economic approach to competition law is the view that market power offers a helpful preliminary filter to identify the sources of competition problems. However, the identification of market power is problematic because only firms in perfectly competitive markets are unable to raise price (because any price increase by one firm will lead to consumers switching to another competitor who sells at a lower price), but since perfect competition is a hypothetical model, it means all firms have some market power.[1] This is why in the relatively competitive retail market for beer one

---

[1] In all markets, firms face a downward sloping demand curve, while in a perfectly competitive market the demand curve is flat.

brewer can comfortably advertise beer as 'reassuringly expensive' as a means of competing against others.[2] Since the brief of a competition authority is not to create perfect competition but to deter certain forms of behaviour that harm economic welfare, only 'significant' manifestations of market power fall within the ambit of competition law. However, even with this qualification, the meaning of market power remains elusive.

There are four ways to think about market power. The first equates market power with the ability to increase price (the neoclassical approach), the second equates market power with commercial power, the third sees market power as the ability to exclude rivals so as to gain the power to increase price, and the fourth sees market power as a formal jurisdictional test.[3]

The first draws upon economic considerations. To an economist, market power means the ability of a firm 'to price profitably above the competitive level'.[4] And market power is a worry when it is both significant and durable.[5] This approach has been accepted by the US courts: it is the 'reduction in output and elevation of price that has been the historic concern of antitrust'.[6] However, market power is also a relative concept: the greater the power, the more harm the firm can inflict. Therefore certain infringements, like excessive or predatory pricing, are penalised only when the firm in question has significant market power, while other kinds of infringement, like anticompetitive distribution agreements, may be penalised even if the firm has less market power, provided it is able to cause damage to competitors or consumers. Different thresholds of market power apply depending on the infringement in question,[7] and, as a rule of thumb, the number and the degree of anticompetitive risks posed increases with higher levels of market power.

A second way of defining market power is to inquire whether the firm has greater commercial power than others on the market. This approach sometimes finds its way into the discussion of certain contract law doctrines, like economic duress, where one party has a 'situational monopoly' over the other contracting party.[8] For example, when a small basket-weaving company has a major contract to supply a large retailer and enters into a contract with a

---

[2] The beer in question is Stella Artois.

[3] For more details on these four models, see G. Monti 'The Concept of Dominance' (2006) 2 *European Competition Journal* (Special Issue) 31.

[4] D. W. Carlton and J. M. Perloff *Modern Industrial Organization* 2nd edn (New York: Harper Collins, 1994) p. 8.

[5] G. Werden 'Demand Elasticities in Antitrust Analysis' (1998) 66 *Antitrust Law Journal* 363, 373–80.

[6] *US v. Oracle Corporation* 331 F Supp 2d 1098, 1114 (2004).

[7] L. A. Sullivan and W. S. Grimes *The Law of Antitrust: An Integrated Handbook* (St Paul, MN: West Publishing, 2000) pp. 26–7. This point was suggested by Advocate General Fennelly in *Compagnie Maritime Belge and Others v. Commission* [2000] ECR I-1365 para. 137, where he noted that some firms are 'super-dominant' in that they hold a 'position of such overwhelming dominance verging on monopoly' so that they are subject to 'particularly onerous special obligations'.

[8] M. J. Trebilcock 'Economic Criteria of Unconscionability' in B. J. Reiter and J. Swan (eds.) *Studies in Contract Law* (Toronto: Butterworth, 1980).

transport firm to carry the baskets, the transport company is able to renego-
tiate a much higher price at the last minute, which the small company must
accept in order to stay in business.[9] Opportunistic behaviour is undesirable
and there may be good moral and commercial reasons for controlling the
distributor's behaviour, but this is not usually seen as a scenario that requires
the intervention of competition law because, so long as the market for baskets
and transport is competitive, there is no consumer harm. Nevertheless, as we
will see below, the Community definitions of market power may be wide
enough to encompass this kind of power also, because this definition reflects
a concern about economic freedom, and a worry that a firm that has commercial power can harm the interests of others.

A third definition of market power, which we label post-Chicago, provides
that a firm has market power when it is able to devise strategies that can harm
rivals and so give it, in the future, the power to raise prices and reduce
output.[10] This approach is wider than the neoclassical definition, but it has
the same aim: to penalise firms whose strategies can have undesirable economic effects. On the other hand, this definition is also related to the definition
of market power taken by those wishing to safeguard economic freedom,
because it focuses on the power to harm competitors. However, in contrast
to the commercial power definition, the post-Chicago approach sees the power
to harm competitors as a means by which the firm can subsequently gain
power to harm consumers.

A fourth approach is to interpret market power as a jurisdictional concept.
This has been applied in Article 81; for example, the Commission has stipu-
lated that certain types of agreement are lawful provided the parties' market
shares are below a given threshold. As we discuss more fully in section 7 below,
when parties to a horizontal agreement like the *Métropole* joint venture have
market shares below 10 per cent, the Commission may declare that the agreement does not restrict competition appreciably.[11] Market shares provide a
relatively simple means to measure market power even though they are
insufficient to provide an accurate picture. Therefore, to base a determination
of legality upon market shares can lead to Type 2 errors, as inefficient behaviour is not punished. Conversely, the risk of anticompetitive harm when
market shares are low is limited, so the savings in enforcement costs compensate the risk of Type 2 errors. Using market shares as a means to establish
jurisdiction creates safe harbours so that firms below the relevant threshold
know that certain prohibitions do not apply to them. The jurisdictional
approach acknowledges that there may be market power below the level set

---

[9] *Atlas Express Ltd v. Kafco (Importers and Distributors) Ltd* [1989] QB 833.

[10] T. G. Krattenmaker, R. H. Lande and S. C. Salop 'Monopoly Power and Market Power in
Antitrust Law' (1987) 76 *Georgetown Law Journal* 241.

[11] Commission Notice on Agreements of Minor Importance which do not Appreciably Restrict
Competition under Article 81(1) of the Treaty Establishing the European Communities [2001]
OJ C368/13 para. 7(a).

by the safe harbour, but trades off under-enforcement for cheaper and more effective application of the law. As the Community has had little to say about substantive definitions of market power in the context of Article 81, we move to consider this concept in the framework of Article 82 and merger control, and then return to Article 81.

2 Dominance in EC competition law

In applying Article 82, and for most merger cases, the Commission must identify dominance. The way that the Courts have interpreted this notion allows us to understand what concept of market power prevails in EC competition law. Thinking about market power in the context of the meaning of dominance is also helpful because this concept is currently in transition: the Commission wishes to move away from the current emphasis upon commercial power and towards identifying dominance with substantial market power based on economic theories.[12] We begin with the seminal cases.

In *Michelin*, the Court held that Article 82 'prohibits any abuse of a position of economic strength enjoyed by an undertaking which enables it to hinder the maintenance of effective competition on the relevant market by allowing it to behave to an appreciable extent independently of its competitors and customers and ultimately of consumers'.[13] This passage represents the standard test for dominance.[14] The Court's reference to the ability to behave independently 'to an appreciable extent' is relevant for two reasons: first, because it means that Article 82 does not apply to the sort of market power that most firms have due to markets not being perfectly competitive; second, because total control of the market is unnecessary to identify dominance. As the Court in *Hoffmann La Roche* explained, dominance

> does not preclude some competition, which it does where there is a monopoly or a quasi-monopoly, but enables the undertaking which profits by it, if not to determine, at least to have an appreciable influence on the conditions under which that competition will develop, and in any case to act largely in disregard of it so long as such conduct does not operate to its detriment.[15]

Dominance indicates a degree of market power which is considerably greater than that of other firms on the market and which can be used to harm the economic freedom of other market players by excluding them from the

---

[12] DG Competition discussion paper on the application of Article 82 of the Treaty to exclusionary abuses (December 2005), pt 4.

[13] Case 322/81 *Nederlandsche Banden-Industrie Michelin NV v. Commission* [1983] ECR 3461 para. 30. This is an oft-repeated formulation: see also Case 27/76 *United Brands Co. v. Commission* [1978] ECR 207 para. 65; Case 85/76 *Hoffmann La Roche v. Commission* [1979] ECR 461 para. 38.

[14] Van Bael and Bellis *Competition Law of the European Community* 4th edn (The Hague: Kluwer Law International, 2005) p. 117.

[15] *Hoffmann La Roche* [1979] ECR 461 para. 39.

market. An antitrust authority less concerned with economic freedom would opt for a higher degree of dominance in order to safeguard the ability of large firms to act aggressively on the market in the pursuit of their interests. Thus, in the US the *Microsoft* court defined monopoly in the neoclassical way: 'a firm is a monopolist if it can profitably raise prices above the competitive level'.[16] In fact if anyone's economic freedom is preserved by the US standard, it is the defendant's. As the Supreme Court put it: 'Congress authorised Sherman Act scrutiny of such firms only when they pose a danger of monopolization. Judging unilateral conduct in this manner reduces the risk that the antitrust laws will dampen the competitive zeal of a single aggressive entrepreneur.'[17] The ECJ's definitions of dominance are not consistent with a neoclassical interpretation of market power, as the degree of dominance required to trigger the application of Article 82 is lower than that necessary to trigger the application of the comparable provision in the United States (section 2 of the Sherman Act).[18]

If dominance is not defined in a neoclassical way, the question remains whether the Community approach is about commercial power or strategic power in the post-Chicago sense. Answering this question is tricky because these two forms of market power overlap somewhat: both look to whether the firm in question is able to harm competitors. However, while commercial power is found as soon as this ability is identified, strategic power requires a second step: determining whether the harm in question would give the firm the power to raise prices. As matters stand, it seems more plausible to suggest that commercial power is the basis upon which market power is identified in the case law. This can be justified in three ways. First, in chapter 2 we saw that EC competition law has been premised upon the protection of economic freedom. Therefore, firms that have the power to undermine the economic freedom of others require control. Second, in chapter 6 we will see that the aim of some of the 'abuse' doctrines is to protect the economic freedom of other market participants, as such a definition of dominance which emphasises the commercial power of certain firms to harm the economic freedom of others is necessary. Third, the leading cases demonstrate an emphasis upon commercial power, or as John Temple Lang has put it, 'the ability to contain competition'.[19]

In *United Brands*, for example, the firm was found to be dominant in the market for bananas in part because of certain commercial attributes that competitors lacked: it owned several banana plantations and a fleet of ships to transport bananas from Latin America to Europe, so that it was not

---

[16] *US v. Microsoft* 253 F 3d 34, 50 (DC Cir. 2001).

[17] *Copperweld Corp. v. Independence Tube Corp.* 467 US 752, 767–8 (1984).

[18] G. J. Werden 'Competition Policy on Exclusionary Conduct: Toward an Effects-based Analysis?' (2006) 2 *European Competition Journal* (Special Issue) 53, 56; Monti 'Concept of Dominance' p. 48.

[19] J. Temple Lang 'Some Aspects of Abuse of a Dominant Position in EC Antitrust Law' (1979) 3 *Fordham International Law Forum* 1, 12.

susceptible to strikes, and this guaranteed it 'commercial stability and well being'.[20] Moreover, its research and development projects designed to prevent the spread of illness in banana plantations and its work on increasing productivity were also deemed to point to dominance, as well as its procedures for quality control and advertising.[21] These attributes suggest United Brands was efficient, but count against it as evidence of dominance. In addition, the Court rejected the significance of the fact that there was 'fierce' competition in the banana market because United Brands would be able to hold competitors off: its 'economic strength has thus enabled it to adopt a flexible overall strategy directed against new competitors establishing themselves on the whole of the relevant market'.[22] The Court favoured this evidence and rejected the relevance of the losses United Brands was incurring during the time it carried out the acts that the Court characterised as abuse of dominance. The Court's approach is inconsistent with a neoclassical conception of market power and also with a post-Chicago perspective: dominance is found in the firm's commercial strength irrespective of market outcomes.

A similar approach can be found even in recent cases, for example in the Commission's decision that General Electric (GE) held a dominant position in the market of large jet engines.[23] The Commission noted that GE's market shares were twice as large as the next competitor. It then pointed out that certain commercial links made GE more powerful: GE had a finance arm (GE Capital) which could be deployed to foreclose rivals; loans could be offered to airlines in exchange for the lender buying GE aircraft.[24] GE Capital also facilitated risky investments by GE in the engine sector.[25] GE also owned GECAS, an aircraft leasing company that bought 10 per cent of the world's aircraft. GECAS only bought GE-powered aeroplanes. The Commission reasoned that companies leasing planes from GECAS could be asked to use GE-powered aircraft for all their fleet.[26] The Commission boosts these findings with quotes from *Forbes* and *Fortune* magazines that show, with colourful language, that GE is a most successful company, and the Commission equates commercial success with dominance.[27] The same facts were considered by the US Department of Justice, but it saw no evidence of dominance. The DOJ emphasised the competition from GE's rivals which were investing in new products, and the fact that GE seemed to be losing ground to them. Moreover, the DOJ noted that GE's market shares were high because some years ago it had been successful in securing a contract to supply engines for the Boeing 737, the

---

[20] *United Brands* [1978] ECR 207 para. 81.
[21] Similar considerations were also taken into account in *Hoffmann La Roche* [1979] ECR 461 para. 48.
[22] *United Brands* [1978] ECR 207 para. 121.
[23] Case M.2220 *General Electric/Honeywell* [2004] OJ L48/1.   [24] Ibid. paras. 112–17.
[25] Ibid. para. 110.   [26] Ibid. paras. 121–39.
[27] Ibid. para. 167, quoting from *Forbes* ('Instead of selling engines, [Jack Welch] is selling power, since some clever financing helped GE win the business'); para. 117 (*Fortune*).

most successful aircraft in the world. If the sales from the contract were excluded, then GE's market share became less threatening (down from 51 per cent to 44 per cent).[28] The contrast between the evidence that the US and EC authorities consider relevant is telling. The Americans see the presence of rivalry and falls in market share as proof that the firm under scrutiny seems unable to reduce output and increase price. In contrast, the EC sees the commercial resilience of the firm in question, and its clever use of its comparative advantages to remain in the market, as proof of dominance. Dominance then is the power to affect the competitive process by limiting the economic opportunities of rivals.

However, in December 2005, the Commission signalled a change in direction in the framework of its reassessment of Article 82.[29] It suggested that henceforth dominance should be associated with 'substantial market power' (SMP) and identified in neoclassical terms as the power to reduce output and increase price.[30] If this policy shift is put into practice, it could have significant implications for the scope of application of Article 82 and the merger rules because findings of dominance would be fewer. It is unlikely, for example, that the Commission would be able to find dominance in the two major cases discussed above: *United Brands* and *General Electric*. In neither of those decisions did the evidence point to the power to reduce output and increase price; on the contrary the market was competitive.

Now we move on to consider how one would measure market power. The first thing that will strike the reader is that, while the Commission and Court have shunned a neoclassical definition of market power when defining dominance, the Community begins its analysis of market power using tools that are suitable to determine market power from a neoclassical perspective. This is so because the methodology we describe is standard in antitrust law and it affords the Commission the flexibility to look for commercial power.

3 Measuring market power

Theoretically there is a precise, direct way of measuring market power as understood in the neoclassical sense: the Lerner index.[31] This measures the

---

[28] W. J. Kolasky 'Conglomerate Mergers and Range Effects: It's a Long Way from Chicago to Brussels' (speech, 9 November 2001, available at www.usdoj.gov/atr/public/speeches/9536.pdf).

[29] DG Competition discussion paper on Article 82, paras. 21–8.

[30] This concept has already become part of Community law in the field of electronic communications (Article 14(2) Directive 2002/21 on a Common Regulatory Framework for Electronic Communications Networks and Services [2002] OJ L108/33). Having equated SMP with dominance in that sector, the Commission's approach in the discussion paper on Article 82 is to restate the converse of that proposition: dominance means SMP for all economic sectors. This broadly follows the suggestion made in S. Bishop and M. Walker *The Economics of EC Competition Law* 2nd edn (London: Sweet & Maxwell, 2002) pp. 183–5.

[31] A. Lerner 'The Concept of Monopoly and the Measurement of Monopoly Power' (1934) 1 *Review of Economic Studies* 157.

difference between the price at which a firm sells its goods and its marginal cost. The greater the difference between the two, the more market power. However, this approach has little practical value because marginal costs are difficult to calculate.[32] Moreover, firms with market power may have high costs (as they face no competition, they may have few incentives to minimise production costs) and their prices will be just slightly above their inefficiently high costs, so the index underestimates their power. Instead, an indirect method is used to measure market power, based upon a calculation of the firm's market shares and of barriers to entry. According to this approach, if a firm has very high market shares and entry for new competitors is blocked (say government licensing regulations limit the number of competitors), then it holds market power because it is free to raise prices without fearing that its position may be undermined by new entrants.

A simple example will illustrate the operation and the potential controversies of measuring market power by this method: assume an ice cream seller in Hyde Park is the sole seller of strawberry flavoured ice creams. Does he have market power? It may be argued that he has a 100 per cent share of the market in strawberry flavoured ice cream in Hyde Park, holding an undisputed dominant position. The ice cream seller may retort that he competes against other ice cream sellers who supply other flavours, so that the relevant market is that for all flavours of ice cream. In this wider market his market share is likely to be much less than 100 per cent. He might go further, and argue that consumers are looking for refreshment, thus chilled drinks would also be substitutes for ice cream, reducing his market share even further. Moreover, he might argue that Hyde Park is surrounded by a number of streets with numerous shops, many selling ice cream of all flavours, thus consumers are free to leave the park momentarily (there being no entry charges) and find cheaper ice cream. All these observations serve the same purpose: widening the definition of the relevant market so as to diminish the defendant's market share. Moreover, he can also argue that there is nothing stopping a new business entering the park and selling strawberry ice cream. These observations suggest that entry into the market is easy, so that he has no market power, because a price increase on his part will invite other competitors and bring prices down again.

This example demonstrates that the identification of market power is intimately connected with how we define the market. It also synthesises the dynamics of litigation over market definition. First, the party enforcing the law opts for a narrow product and geographical market (strawberry flavoured ice cream sold in Hyde Park, giving the defendant a market share of 100 per cent), while the defendant tries to widen the market so as to reduce the chances of being found dominant (all refreshments sold in Hyde Park and the vicinity,

---

[32] For detailed analysis, see W. M. Landes and R. A. Posner 'Market Power in Antitrust Cases' (1981) 94 *Harvard Law Review* 937, 939–43.

whereby the market share would dwindle to insignificance). In economic jargon, a market is defined by reference to *demand* substitutability (what other goods and what other locations people think are in the same market as the defendant) and *supply* substitutability (which producers could easily switch to sell the same products as the defendant or move into his geographical area). Having established an agreed market and a share of that market, the next question is whether that market share is stable, or whether the market is so contestable that even with a large market share the defendant is unable to monopolise – this is a question of *entry barriers*. If it is easy for new ice cream sellers to enter the market, then the market shares do not tell the full story, for the market power they represent is temporary and likely to evaporate as soon as that power is exploited. Having sketched the issues, we turn to consider how the law applies economic insights to determine market power. First we consider the process of market definition (sections 3.1 and 3.2), then the role of market shares (section 3.3) and finally entry barriers (section 3.4).

3.1 Market definition: the hypothetical monopolist test

The leading market definition test was first incorporated in the US Merger Guidelines in 1982, and now forms part of the approach deployed by the EC Commission. Applied to the ice cream example above, the test asks: *if* the defendant has a hypothetical monopoly in the strawberry flavoured ice cream market in Hyde Park, would he be likely to 'impose at least a "small but significant and nontransitory" increase in price, assuming the terms of sale of all other products are held constant'?[33] If the answer is yes, the relevant market is that of strawberry flavoured ice cream sold in Hyde Park because a price rise would be profitable. If the price rise would not be profitable, because most consumers would switch to other fruit flavours or leave the park and buy strawberry flavoured ice cream in the vicinity, the test is repeated by widening the market, say all fruit flavoured ice cream sold in Hyde Park and its vicinity, and considering whether a hypothetical monopolist of fruit flavoured ice cream would be able to increase the price; if not, the market is widened again, by adding the next best substitute, say all ice cream flavours, and asking the same question. This process continues until we find a market where a hypothetical monopolist would be able to raise the price of the product profitably. As a general simplification, the question the hypothetical monopolist test asks is this: *is this a market worth monopolising?*[34]

It is important to bear in mind that the hypothetical monopolist test will not usually be applied directly; rather it is a 'conceptual tool' that allows one

---

[33] Department of Justice and Federal Trade Commission *Horizontal Merger Guidelines* (1992, revised 1997) para. 1.0 (in the jargon this is known as the hypothetical monopolist test or the SSNIP test – small substantial, non-transitory increase in price).

[34] Bishop and Walker *Economics* pt 4.05.

to assess the empirical evidence that is available.[35] US antitrust authorities commonly ask customers (e.g. the strawberry ice cream eating public) directly how they would respond to price increases, thereby identifying the next best substitute.[36] Other empirical evidence may include the following: own price elasticity (which is a measure of the change in the quantity of the firm's product demanded following a small price increase – the greater the decrease in quantity demanded the less likely that the product is in a market all of its own); cross-price elasticity of demand (which measures how a change in the price of one good affects demand for another); and price correlation studies (which assess the price changes of goods over time, and suggest that two products are in the same market if the prices change with the same rhythm).[37] Some examples can help put some flesh on these approaches.

In *Kraft* a US court had to determine whether the 'adult' variety of ready-to-eat breakfast cereal was a separate market from children's ready-to-eat cereals. The court reviewed a number of empirical studies on the purchasing patterns of cereals and noted that there was no evidence of a separate market. Instead consumers readily substituted along the whole spectrum of cereals offered, and the Court concluded, relying on cross-elasticity of demand studies, that: 'Any substantial price increase for any one type of ready to eat cereal would lead to significant demand-side substitution of many other ready to eat cereals.'[38]

In *Nestlé/Perrier* the Commission decided that mineral water was a distinct market. In part it relied on price correlation studies which indicated that there was no relationship between the prices of mineral waters and those of soft drinks – at one point the former were rising and the latter falling but there was no marked effect on consumption. The Commission concluded: 'This price evolution seems to indicate that even strong and sustained reductions of soft drink prices in real terms would not force source water suppliers to also reduce their own prices, nor would it affect their ability to increase them.'[39]

In *Kimberly-Clark/Scott* the Commission reasoned that private label and branded tissues were in the same market on the basis that the price correlation was significant and that consumers switched between them when there were promotional campaigns.[40]

---

[35] P. Crocioni 'The Hypothetical Monopolist Test: What it Can and Cannot Tell You' [2002] *European Competition Law Review* 354, 355.

[36] J. Langerfeld 'The Merger Guidelines as Applied' in M. Coates and A. Kleit (eds.) *The Economics of the Antitrust Process* (Boston: Kluwer Academic Publishers, 1996) pp. 43–5.

[37] For a more detailed explanation, see M. Motta *Competition Policy* (Cambridge: Cambridge University Press, 2004) pp. 106–10; J. Church and R. Ware *Industrial Organization – A Strategic Approach* (Boston: Irwin McGraw Hill, 2000) ch. 19.

[38] *State of New York v. Kraft General Foods Inc.* 926 F Supp. 321, 333 (1995).

[39] Case IV/M.190 *Nestlé/Perrier* [1992] OJ L356/1 paras. 13 and 16.

[40] Case IV/M.623 *Kimberly-Clark/Scott* [1996] OJ L183/1 para. 48.

The hypothetical monopolist test is not designed to give the absolutely correct answer to the market definition question. Inherent in its operation are a number of arbitrary choices. For instance, why choose a 5 per cent price increase, and not a higher or a lower one?[41] Which products do we begin our analysis with? What geographical market do we start with? Nevertheless, by asking the same questions for each case, whether about ice cream or sophisticated computer software, or the services offered by accountancy firms, the test yields consistency.[42]

One specific criticism of this test is that markets are defined too widely when, at the time the hypothetical monopolist test is applied, the firm under investigation already has market power in the neoclassical sense; that is, it can raise prices well above cost. In the jargon, this is known as the 'cellophane fallacy', after the Supreme Court decision in *du Pont*.[43] The Government had charged du Pont with monopolising the cellophane market. However, the Court found that the relevant market was wider than cellophane and included a range of other wrapping materials, and it held that du Pont had no monopoly power. This was based upon observations that consumers replaced cellophane with other products – a high cross-elasticity of demand. However, the consensus among economists is that the Supreme Court was wrong because it carried out its analysis of cross-elasticity at a time when du Pont was selling its cellophane at a monopoly price and, of course, at that high price consumers would switch to other products given a further increase because the monopolist would already have set prices at a level where further price increases would cease to be profitable. The cross-elasticity test should have been carried out when du Pont was pricing competitively and checks made to see whether a small increase above the competitive price would have led to consumers switching – asking if consumers would have switched if there was a small increase in monopoly price would of course have led to many more consumers switching. The US Guidelines attempt to avoid making this error by using a competitive price when the circumstances in the market lead to suspicion that current prices are inflated by the presence of market power.[44]

Overall, the advantage of the hypothetical monopolist test is that it provides for a consistent and predictable framework – although each market definition analysis remains intimately fact specific. The Commission had begun to use this methodology under the Merger Regulation, and in 1997 it published a *Notice*

---

[41] Some think 5 per cent is too high: R. Pitofsky 'New Definitions of Relevant Market and the Assault on Antitrust' (1990) 90 *Columbia Law Review* 1805, 1824.

[42] W. F. Baxter 'Responding to the Reaction: The Draftsman's View' (1983) 71 *California Law Review* 618, 624.

[43] *US v. EI du Pont de Nemours & Co.* 118 F Supp 41 (D DE 1953) aff'd 351 US 377 (1956). For a detailed examination, see Bishop and Walker *Economics* pts 4.34–4.43.

[44] US Merger Guidelines para. 1.11. The EC *Notice on the Definition of the Relevant Market for the Purposes of Community Competition Law* [1997] OJ C372/5 recognises this problem (para. 19) but does not resolve it. However, determining what a competitive price might be is controversial (see Crocioni 'Hypothetical Monopolist Test' p. 359, and ch. 7 pp. 218–20).

on the Definition of the Relevant Market for the Purposes of Community Competition Law[45] which indicated its increased willingness to deploy the hypothetical monopolist test in all competition cases.[46] In what follows we assess how this approach contrasts with that which was originally taken by the EC.

3.2 Market definition in EC competition law

3.2.1 Product market definition

The early case law placed little reliance on economic assessment of the relevant market, as evidenced by the notorious *United Brands* decision, where the banana market was identified as a relevant market distinct from other fresh fruits.[47] The Court used a mixture of controversial criteria to come to this conclusion. First, it noted that a distinct group of consumers – the young, the old and the sick – would not find other fruits equally substitutable, because for them the banana was an easier fruit to eat. This is erroneous for there was no evidence that United Brands would be able to target this particular group of consumers with higher prices – they and all other consumers shop in the same place, thus the market for those consumers is not one worth monopolising because it is logistically impossible to do so. Second, *United Brands* also encapsulated a qualitative set of criteria for defining the relevant market, encompassing products considered interchangeable because of their character-istics, price and intended use.[48] In the case of bananas these are: 'softness, seedlessness, ease of handling and regular availability'. There is a risk that this standard allows one to add infinite descriptive words before a noun to create narrow markets (e.g. organic, seedless, preservative-free, home-made straw-berry ice cream). Finally, the Court also took into consideration econometric evidence to consider whether the bananas competed with other fruit. On this point, there was some controversy over the weight given by the econo-metric studies which were relied upon: according to the defendant, these showed that other fruits competed with bananas, while the Court considered that the studies demonstrated that the competition was not suffi-ciently intense to place bananas in a wider market.[49] Overall, the problem with

---

[45] [1997] OJ C372/5.

[46] There is nothing to prevent the test from applying only to mergers. See G. J. Werden 'Market Delineation under the Merger Guidelines: Monopoly Cases and Alternative Approaches' (2000) 16 *Review of Industrial Organization* 211, citing *Coastal Fuels of Puerto Rico Inc. v. Caribbean Petroleum Corp.* 79 F 3d 182 (1st Cir. 1996), where the hypothetical monopolist test was applied in a monopolisation case to identify the relevant geographical market. See also *US v. Kodak* 63 F 3d 95 (1995).

[47] [1978] ECR 207.

[48] Market Definition Notice, para. 8. See also *Hoffmann La Roche* [1979] ECR 461 para. 24; Case M.580 *ABB/Daimler Benz* [1997] OJ L11/1 para. 13.

[49] Some argued that in the summer months bananas were more easily replaceable with other fresh fruit: W. C. Baden Fuller 'Article 86 EEC: Economic Analysis of the Existence of a Dominant Position' (1979) 4 *European Law Review* 423.

the *United Brands* approach was that the Court did not establish a clear methodology and at its centre rested a number of subjective considerations, with the risk of inconsistent decisions.[50]

In contrast, the 1997 Market Definition Notice places the quantitative, hypothetical monopolist test discussed above at the centre of the assessment of the relevant product market, relegating the qualitative criteria to an initial stage to limit the field of investigation.[51] The test draws very closely upon the US Merger Guidelines:

> The question to be answered is whether the parties' customers would switch to readily available substitutes or to suppliers located elsewhere in response to a hypothetical small (in the range 5% to 10%) but permanent relative price increase in the products and areas being considered. If substitution were enough to make the price increase unprofitable because of the resulting loss of sales, additional substitutes and areas are included in the relevant market. This would be done until the set of products and geographical areas is such that small, permanent increases in relative prices would be profitable.[52]

However, the kind of evidence that the Commission will consider in order to carry out the hypothetical monopolist test is not always convincing.[53] On the one hand, the Commission looks at past evidence of substitution between products, and is also open to a variety of econometric and statistical approaches (e.g. cross-elasticity and price correlation studies, which we have explained above),[54] as well as marketing studies that have been carried out prior to the investigation and which seek to identify consumer preferences. Moreover, the Commission will look at switching costs that consumers may face (e.g. switching from one software product to another may be costly as files cannot easily be transferred to work on the new software package).[55] On the other hand, the Commission also considers the views of competitors and customers. The evidence of these groups is not always reliable – often they will offer evidence that supports their interests in the resolution of the dispute (e.g. competitors might fear the efficiency of a merger and want the transaction blocked). The limits of consumers' views were recently exposed in an American case. The US Department of Justice argued that only three firms were present in the market for certain computing services, and lined up a number of highly sophisticated business managers to testify that they saw the market in the same

---

[50] For instance, the Commission concluded that cola flavoured soft drinks are in a separate market from other soft drinks (Case M.794 *Coca-Cola/Amalgamated Beverages* [1997] OJ L218/15), but home storage products (food and non-food) are in the same product market (Case M.1355 *Newtell/Rubbermaid* (13 January 1999) para. 11).

[51] Market Definition Notice paras. 15–19, 36.   [52] Ibid. para. 17.   [53] Ibid. paras. 38–42.

[54] See Case M.1524 *Airtours/First Choice* [2000] OJ L93/1 para. 22 for a more recent example.

[55] E.g. Case M.1671 *Dow Chemical/Union Carbide* [2001] OJ L245/1 para. 27, where the Commission reports the results of a SSNIP test and notes that the reasons consumers gave for not switching if prices rose were high costs of adapting the production process to use a different product, or technical inability to switch to other products.

way, but the court rejected their views because they only represented the consumers' preferences and none of the witnesses explained how they would react if the firms in question raised prices by 10 per cent. The court went on to explain the limited value of consumers' views: 'customer testimony of the kind plaintiffs offered can put a human perspective or face on the injury to competition that plaintiffs allege. But unsubstantiated customer apprehensions do not substitute for hard evidence.'[56] In contrast to this detailed scrutiny of the value of consumer views, the Commission Notice indicates that there is no 'rigid hierarchy of different sources of information or types of evidence'.[57] This is unfortunate as the quality of evidence can often be related to its source.

After the publication of the Market Definition Notice, we might expect that reasoning like that in *United Brands* would not be repeated. The broadly comparable *Danish Crown* case suggests this is the case. It concerned a merger of two Danish farmers' cooperatives and the question arose whether beef, pork, veal, sheep, lamb and poultry were part of a fresh meat market or whether each type of meat was in a different market, in particular whether beef and pork were in separate markets. While we find comments analogous to those in *United Brands* (namely that consumers perceive these meats differently on the basis of attributes such as flavour, taste, nutritional value, tenderness, cost, ease of use),[58] these criteria are backed up by considerable empirical evidence (e.g. information from wholesalers and supermarkets about consumer demand, and data about consumer preferences). Moreover, the Commission carried out a hypothetical monopolist test asking buyers whether a 5–10 per cent increase in the price of pork or beef would lead them to buy other meats. The replies received from caterers, wholesalers and supermarkets indicated that there was only a slight degree of substitution between the different types of meat.[59] In addition, the Commission relied upon data showing that the price elasticities for pork and beef were low, indicating that the price of one meat did not affect consumption of other meats significantly.[60]

In addition to a new methodology, one element of the *United Brands* test has been *de facto* overruled –the reference to the fact that certain customers prefer one product to another. According to the Market Definition Notice, if a product has no substitutes for a group of individuals the Commission will consider that there is a separate market only when such a group can be subjected to price discrimination,[61] thus reacting directly to the economic criticism levelled against *United Brands*. This novel approach is visible in *Danish Crown* where sales of meat to caterers (restaurants, canteens and government offices) were treated as a different market from that for sales of meat to retail outlets (supermarkets and butchers). This distinction was justified on a number of grounds: for caterers the origin of the meat is less

[56] *Oracle* 331 F Supp 2d 1098, 1131 (2004).   [57] Market Definition Notice para. 25.
[58] Case M.1313 *Danish Crown/Vestjyske Slagterier* [2000] OJ L20/1 para. 24.
[59] Ibid. para. 26.   [60] Ibid. para. 29.   [61] Ibid. para. 43.

important (there have been more imports of meat from other EU countries by caterers); no arbitrage is possible between the two buyers because distribution and packaging is different (e.g. meat sold to supermarkets is already cut and packaged with all the information the consumer needs); retailers need to buy all kinds of meat so as to offer clients diverse cuts, while caterers tend to buy larger quantities of one cut of meat.[62] Accordingly, the catering market and the retail market are both worth monopolising separately, as the sales to one kind of customer are distinct from those to another.

In spite of these advances, some have criticised the Market Definition Notice for containing an unfortunate mix of old-style subjectivity (based on product characteristics) and modern economic analysis.[63] Moreover, in certain cases the Commission has retained an emphasis on qualitative criteria.[64] For instance in *Volvo/Scania*, while the Commission relied on sophisticated economic analysis to define the relevant geographical market, it defined the relevant product much more superficially: it distinguished between '5–16 tonne trucks' and '16 tonne and over trucks' on the basis that these were physically different, but paid no heed to the question of whether the consumers of the larger trucks might consider buying more smaller trucks if the price of the heavier ones rose, nor did it examine possible supply substitutability between the two sizes of trucks.[65] Thus, flexibility is preferred over consistency in approach: while quantitative methods are used, the trend is to use a mixture of qualitative (product characteristics, price, intended use) and quantitative evidence in determining the relevant market.

The Commission's focus, both in its case law and in the Notice, is on *demand* substitution. Less attention is paid to the reaction of other firms.[66] The Commission distinguishes between supply substitution whose 'effects are equivalent to those of demand substitution in terms of effectiveness and immediacy' and supply substitution that takes longer to materialise.[67] The former is incorporated into the relevant market definition, the latter is taken into account only at a second stage to determine whether there are entry barriers (see section 3.4 below).[68] A more precise approach is taken in the

---

[62] Ibid. n. 30 para. 38.

[63] P. D. Camesasca and R. J. van den Bergh 'Achilles Uncovered: Revisiting the European Commission's 1997 Market Definition Notice' [2002] *Antitrust Bulletin* 143, 158; J. Faull and A. Nikpay *The EC Law of Competition* (Oxford: Oxford University Press, 1999) para. 4.146.

[64] For example, in the same year the Commission did not apply the SSNIP test in *Virgin/British Airways* [2000] OJ L30/1 but did so in *1998 Football World Cup* [2000] OJ L55/5.

[65] Case M.1672 *Volvo/Scania* [2001] OJ L143/74.

[66] Curiously, in one of the few cases the Commission lost on market definition, it was criticised for failing to identify supply substitutes: Case 6/72 *Europemballage Corp. and Continental Can Co. Inc. v. Commission* [1972] ECR 215. For criticism, see Bishop and Walker *Economics* paras. 4.26–4.32.

[67] Market Definition Notice paras. 20–3. In Case IV/M166 *Torras/Sarrió* (24 February 1992) the Commission speculated that supply substitution between two types of paper was easy (para. 18).

[68] For criticism on the practicality of this distinction, see Camesasca and van den Bergh 'Achilles Uncovered' pp. 159–62.

US Guidelines – potential competitors are considered as participants in the relevant market if, in response to a small but significant and nontransitory price increase, they can enter the market 'within one year and without the expenditure of significant sunk costs of entry and exit'.[69] Supply responses that do not meet these two criteria are assessed at a second stage when determining entry barriers into the relevant market. Accordingly, the US approach uses the hypothetical monopolist test also to define supply substitutability. Although some might take the view that supply substitutes should be considered more fully when determining the relevant market,[70] the important issue is that competitive constraints from supply substitutes are taken into account at some point in the inquiry, and whether this occurs at the stage of market definition or at a second stage, or – as is the case now – partly when defining the market and partly at the entry barrier stage, the economic analysis of market power and the legal result will be comparable.[71] Nonetheless, the distinction in the Notice is unsatisfactory in its reference to potentially arbitrary criteria of immediacy and effectiveness.

3.2.2 Geographical market

A geographical market comprises an area where the 'conditions of competition are sufficiently homogeneous and which can be distinguished from neighbouring areas because the conditions of competition are appreciably different in those areas'.[72] As with the product market, the Commission Notice indicates that the hypothetical monopolist test can be applied, considering whether customers would switch to other geographical markets should there be a price increase.[73] A range of considerations can affect the application of the hypothetical monopolist test, principally the costs of transport: a market is worth monopolising when transportation costs from outside the region are high relative to the price of the product; accordingly the market for aircraft is justifiably global,[74] while markets for perishable products tend to be narrower given the increased costs of transport involved.[75] Consumer preferences are

---

[69] US Horizontal Merger Guidelines para. 1.32.

[70] See Bishop and Walker *Economics* para. 4.58; Motta *Competition Policy* pp. 104–5, arguing that if there is a presumption of market power based on market shares, it is not easy to displace this when assessing ease of entry.

[71] One difference is where the application of a Block Exemption depends exclusively upon market shares, then here the failure to include supply substitutes may disqualify a firm from the benefit of the Block Exemption, even though it may lack market power. See further ch. 10.

[72] Market Definition Notice para. 8.

[73] Ibid. paras. 16–17. So the criticism that the Commission adopts a different approach for geographical market definition (Camesasca and van den Bergh 'Achilles Uncovered') is erroneous.

[74] *Boeing/MDD* [1997] OJ L336/16.

[75] For example, 'glucose syrups and blends need to be kept at a constant high temperature to avoid crystallisation, the costs of transport are significant and the logistic issues are important'; accordingly certain markets are national or regional: Case IV/M.2502 *Cargill/Cerestar*, 18 January 2002, para. 17.

also relevant, as are language considerations in the case of broadcasting markets.[76] For certain consumer goods, when on-line purchasing is not an option, it is probable that markets are local and cover only a small territory.[77]

The geographical size of the market increases with deeper legislative integration by the EU: 'The measures adopted and implemented in the internal market programme to remove barriers to trade and further integrate the Community markets cannot be ignored when assessing the effects on competition of a concentration or a structural joint venture.'[78] This observation is evidenced by the *Pirelli/BICC* merger decision where the liberalisation of the electricity markets meant that utility companies now source their requirements outside their Member States – thus a merger between two Italian firms producing power cables had a wider geographical dimension than Italy for, post liberalisation, the competitive constraints arose from other Member States.[79] However, barriers to trade may remain in spite of Community legislation and this will reduce the geographic scope of the market. Thus in *Volvo/Scania* one reason why the market for trucks was found to be regional and not EC-wide was because technical regulations for trucks differed among the Member States, meaning that a purchaser operating a truck from Sweden could not buy a truck from another Member State where the technical specifications were incompatible with those in Sweden. In this case, EC directives designed to harmonise technical specifications had not been successful in integrating the market.[80]

One general criticism of the geographical market definition is that often the focus is on the regions where the infringement of competition law takes place – thus when Michelin (a firm that has a global presence) was accused of abusing a dominant position in the Belgian market, little analysis was carried out to determine competitive pressures from outside the border.[81] In contrast, when a joint venture agreement between Michelin and Continental was reviewed, the Commission had no qualms in identifying a European market, and at times even referred to the tyre market as a global one.[82] Some see nothing problematic with this and suggest that in cases of restrictive practices the focus is on the market where the firm 'may be able to engage in abuses which hinder effective competition',[83] while in cases of mergers or joint ventures the area is that where the firms are 'involved in the supply and demand of the products or services' concerned.[84] Accordingly, 'the definition of the relevant geographic market must ... take into account the geographic scope of the conduct

---

[76] E.g. *Bertelsmann/Kirch/Premiere* [1999] OJ L53/1 para. 22.

[77] E.g. *M. E. Burgess, J. J. Burgess and S. J. Burgess (trading as J. J. Burgess & Sons) v. Office of Fair Trading* [2005] CAT 25 (funeral services).

[78] Market Definition Notice para. 32.   [79] Case M.1882 *Pirelli/BICC*, 19 July 2000.

[80] *Volvo/Scania* [2001] OJ L 143/74 para. 56.   [81] Bishop and Walker *Economics* para. 4.70.

[82] *Continental/Michelin* [1988] OJ L305/33 paras. 19 and 5 respectively.

[83] *United Brands* [1978] ECR 207 para. 44.

[84] Article 9(7) Council Regulation (EC) No. 139/2004 of 20 January 2004 on the Control of Concentrations between Undertakings [2004] OJ L24/1.

in question'.[85] While doctrinally accurate, this approach can be challenged – if Michelin chooses to abuse its considerable market power in Belgium, it is legitimate to ask whether it is possible for competitors in other markets to enter the Belgian market, or for buyers of its tyres to exit Belgium and purchase elsewhere. Merely because under Articles 81 and 82 one is often judging the legality of past behaviour, this does not mean that an analysis of the consumers' options is irrelevant. A static approach that defines the geographical market merely by identifying the area where the practice takes place can lead to unnecessarily narrow market definitions.[86]

3.2.3 Policy-driven market definition?

From a litigation perspective, the party alleging an antitrust infringement usually advocates a narrow market definition to maximise the defendant's market power. The reason market definition is so highly contested is because if the Commission is successful with its market definition, the defendant is likely to lose on the merits, especially in cases of abuse of dominance where many practices are banned outright when carried out by a dominant firm, and in mergers, where a finding of dominance often creates a presumption that the merger is anticompetitive. But there is another possible motivation for narrow market definition – the accomplishment of public policy aims – and sometimes one can see the enforcer's policies at play when markets are being defined.[87] Consider for example media pluralism.[88] This is normally safeguarded under national legislation: in Germany, for example, media mergers are scrutinised by the Commission for the Establishment of Concentration in the Media,[89] and in the UK special rules apply to mergers in the media sector, because the Government does not believe that reliance on general competition law is sufficient to protect pluralism.[90] Moreover, under the Merger Regulation, Member States are allowed to take appropriate measures to protect the plurality of the media even if the merger has a Community dimension.[91] In the 1990s attempts were made to regulate media ownership at Community level, with the Commission being of the view that 'the single market cannot be

---

[85] L. Ritter, W. D. Braun and F. Rawlinson *European Competition Law: A Practitioner's Guide* 2nd edn (The Hague: Kluwer Law International, 1999) p. 37.

[86] See T. E. Kauper 'The Problem of Market Definition under EC Competition Law' (1997) 20 *Fordham International Law Journal* 1682, 1690, noting that the US courts apply a dynamic approach which leads to wider markets.

[87] In a similar vein, see ibid. For an additional set of examples, see G. Monti 'Article 82 and New Economy Markets' in C. Graham and F. Smith (eds.) *Competition, Regulation and the New Economy* (Oxford: Hart Publishing, 2004).

[88] See generally M. Ariño 'Digital War and Peace: Regulation and Competition in European Digital Broadcasting' (2004) 10 *European Public Law* 135.

[89] See www.kek-online.de.

[90] Section 58 Enterprise Act 2002. Quite how to safeguard pluralism effectively is a matter of debate. See E. Barendt 'Structural and Content Regulation in the Media: UK Law and Some American Comparisons' (1997–8) III *Yearbook of Media and Entertainment Law* 75.

[91] Article 21(4) Regulation 139/2004.

put into practice at the expense of pluralism'.[92] This initiative failed through a mix of difficulties, ranging from questions about the EC's legislative competence and divisions among the EC institutions to political foot-dragging.[93] However, as Levy notes, the Commission's appraisal of media mergers which escape the clutches of national laws and are analysed under the Merger Regulation has defended media pluralism, possibly beyond what any directive on media ownership could have achieved.[94]

The relationship between market definition and pluralism can be seen in the Commission's definition of pay-TV markets as separate from free-to-air TV because the Commission was concerned with ensuring that the consumer is able to choose between more than one pay-TV platform. In *Bertelsmann/Kirch/Premiere* the Commission blocked a transaction where Kirch would increase its shareholding in Premiere (Germany's leading pay-TV supplier), and exit from the pay-TV market, leaving only one pay-TV platform. One of the Commission's concerns was that there would not be any programme platform competition left on the German market.[95] However, provided that other pay-TV operators are cleared to compete, mergers in the pay-TV market are allowed (for example, *Vivendi/Canal+/Seagram*).[96] These decisions rely on unconvincingly narrow market definitions, using methods that eschew the kind of economic analysis that the Commission has promised in its Market Definition Notice. In fact, the Commission noted that free-to-air TV exerts considerable competitive pressure on pay-TV: in the *BskyB/Kirch* and *Newscorp/Telepiù* decisions, it was clear that free-to-air TV was one of the main reasons for the financial difficulties faced by the pay-TV firms under scrutiny.[97] Moreover, when the German regulator reviewed the *Bertelsmann/Kirch/Premiere* merger it felt that pay-TV was subject to sufficient competitive pressure from free-to-air TV.[98] However, by considering pay-TV as a separate market, it is then easy to find dominance, assuming that consumers will be hurt by the presence of only one pay-TV operator, and block the merger.

At times, it seems as if the media decisions on market definition are also affected more by concerns about the development of an industrial segment

[92] Communication to Parliament and Council: Follow-up to the Consultation Process Relating to the Green Paper on 'Pluralism and Media Concentration in the Internal Market – An Assessment of the Need for Community Action' (COM(94)353 final) p. 7.

[93] See generally D. Levy *Europe's Digital Revolution* (London: Routledge, 1999) pp. 50–9; A. Harcourt 'Regulating Media Concentration: The Emerging Policy of the EU' (1996) 7 *Utilities Law Review* 202; G. Doyle 'From "Pluralism" to "Ownership": Europe's Emergent Policy on Media Concentrations Navigates the Doldrums' (1997) 3 *Journal of Information, Law and Technology*, http://elj.warwick.ac.uk/jilt/commsreg/97_3doyl/.

[94] Levy *Europe's Digital Revolution* p. 98.   [95] [1999] OJ L53/1 paras. 66–7.

[96] Case M.2050 *Vivendi/Canal+/Seagram*, 13 October 2000.

[97] Case JV.37 *BskyB/Kirch*, 21 March 2000; Case M.2876 *Newscorp/Telepiù* [2004] OJ L110/73.

[98] I. Nitsche *Broadcasting in the European Union: The Role of Public Interest in Competition Analysis* (The Hague: Asser Press, 2001) pp. 126–7.

than by the promotion of consumer welfare or of pluralism. For example, in the *Holland Media Group* case, the Commission said that in addition to creating a dominant position, the alliance 'could even be counterproductive to the development of digital TV in the Netherlands'.[99] This suggests that a mixture of pluralism and industrial policy considerations are in play. The concern over pluralism plays a significant role in these decisions and it was tacitly acknowledged by one Commission official's comments on *Bertelsmann/Kirch/Premiere*: 'new media cases … tend to escape the traditional national legislation designed to control the media and assure pluralism, thus giving the Community, as an inherently Europe-wide mechanism, a central role'.[100]

Market definition can be strategic in two ways: first, as a litigation strategy, it serves to facilitate a finding of market power; second, market definitions can give the competition authority the competence to achieve other public policy aims of Community interest. In the cases just reviewed, two policies are at play: safeguarding pluralism (however imperfectly)[101] and enhancing the development of new technology. These can also be seen in the football broadcasting rights decisions we examined in chapter 4, where such rights are identified as a distinct market as a means to facilitate the growth of alternative media, like 3G and the Internet.[102]

3.3 Market shares

Once the market is defined, the firm's market share in the relevant market can be calculated. Market shares are a proxy for market power, not a precise measure. In EC law, when it comes to determining whether a firm holds a dominant position for the purposes of applying Article 82, the Court has indicated that a market share of 50 per cent gives rise to a presumption of dominance,[103] and the case law suggests that a firm may dominate a market with market shares as low as 40 per cent.[104] In contrast, the US courts suggest that market shares of 70 per cent are enough to trigger the presumption of monopoly, and some courts have suggested that a market share of less than 50 per cent cannot confer monopoly power.[105] As we suggested earlier, the lower

---

[99] Case M.553 *RTL/Veronica/Endemol* [1996] OJ L134/32 para. 110.
[100] H. Ungerer 'EU Competition Law in the Telecommunications, Media and Information Technology Sectors' speech, New York City, 27 October 1995, para. 88 (available at http://europa.eu.int/comm/competition/speeches/).
[101] See Ariño 'Digital War and Peace' for a critique of the role of competition law in the pursuit of pluralism.
[102] See pp. 105–10.
[103] Case C-62/86 *AKZO Chemie BV v. Commission* [1991] ECR I-3359 para. 60.
[104] E.g. *United Brands* [1978] ECR 207 and *British Airways/Virgin* [2000] OJ L30/1.
[105] See H. Hovenkamp *Federal Antitrust Policy* (St Paul, MN: West Publishing, 1994) pp. 244–5; ABA Section of Antitrust Law *Antitrust Law Developments* 4th edn (Chicago: ABA, 1997) pp. 355–6 for a review of the US cases.

dominance threshold in the EC is compatible with a competition policy designed to protect economic freedom because even firms that do not dominate the market absolutely are able to disrupt its functioning because of their commercial power. A lower threshold is also compatible with a strategic, post-Chicago, approach to market power because firms holding a large share of the market are more likely to be able to devise strategies that harm smaller competitors. In contrast, the high market shares deployed in the US signal a commitment to a neoclassical definition of market power. While the Community begins with a neoclassical economic tool to identify the relevant market, it then uses the results to measure market power in a manner that is unrelated to neoclassical economics.

For completeness, two technical matters should be clarified. The first is that the market share of the dominant firm is insufficiently informative, and should be compared to the shares of competitors. The significance of a 40 per cent market share wanes if the second largest firm has a share of 39 per cent. In contrast, a large firm with a number of small fringe firms is more likely to have market power.[106] A related issue is that the stability of market shares over time suggests dominance, while fluctuating market shares indicate lively competition.[107] The second matter is about how to calculate market shares. For fungible goods market shares are calculated by the volume of sales; however, for other branded goods there is a preference to compute market shares by value, because this gives more prominence to the seller of expensive goods and reflects market power more accurately. In each case the aim is to identify the market share measurement that is the most accurate reflection of the firm's future market power.[108]

3.4 Entry barriers

Market shares tell us little about market power if entry into the relevant product market is easy. In contestable markets (characterised by opportunities to enter and exit markets with ease), the incumbent has no market power, for it is continuously threatened by firms ready to enter the relevant market. As we noted in chapter 3, there is controversy on the correct economic approach to the identification of barriers to entry. However, this is mostly because the economics scholarship is not useful when applied to competition law. Economists are divided into two camps: some, following Bain, define entry barriers as those factors which allow existing firms to raise prices without inducing entry. Others, following Stigler, define entry barriers as those costs that a new entrant must face which were not incurred by incumbents when

---

[106] The ECJ has recognised this point: see *Hoffmann La Roche* [1979] ECR 461 para. 48.

[107] Ibid. para. 44, noting that retaining large shares suggests dominance.

[108] Commission Market Definition Notice paras. 53–5. For an exhaustive catalogue of methodologies, see A. Lindsay *The EC Merger Regulation: Substantive Issues* (London: Sweet & Maxwell, 2003) pp. 152–81.

they entered.[109] Under Stigler's approach entry barriers would be limited to intellectual property rights, or other kinds of government regulation;[110] while following Bain's approach a wider range of factors would be considered to be entry barriers, in particular certain structural features of the market. For example, large economies of scale indicate that anyone participating in the market has to produce a large number of goods in order to break even, accordingly there may not be enough space in the market for more firms unless they operate at suboptimal scale (for example, assume that to produce widgets profitably each manufacturer has to make 1,000, but that total demand for widgets is 1,200: it would be uneconomical for a second firm to enter the market); product differentiation (especially if the dominant firm has a strong reputation, it will be costly to induce consumers to switch), absolute cost advantages due to superior access to technology, or location constitute Bainian entry barriers.[111] The 'Stiglerian' approach does not classify these factors as entry barriers because it is based on the premise that one should worry only about factors that deter efficient entry, and not about factors that merely deter entry by anyone. For instance, in response to those who see large economies of scale as an entry barrier in a market where demand is for 1,200 units and where the minimum efficient scale is 1,000 units, then no firm can profitably enter to make 200 units, but this is because the market is operating efficiently as it is. New entry would mean that one firm operates at suboptimal levels. Moreover, there is scope to compete 'for' the market in this instance. That is, a new entrant can try and conquer the sale of 1,000 units from the incumbent. Likewise, product differentiation and cost advantages are aspects of production which can be reproduced by the new entrant, and while greater costs make entry more risky, the same risk had been faced by the incumbent firm. In sum, Stigler criticises Bain for saying that an entry barrier is that which makes entry risky, while an entry barrier should be defined as that which makes entry more costly.

However, the economic debate between Stigler and Bain over what is an entry barrier is not particularly helpful in the application of competition law. First, it confuses the question of determining market power with the question of whether the person holding that market power should be penalised. Whether a monopoly should be condemned is a secondary question,

---

[109] J. S. Bain *Barriers to New Competition: Their Character and Consequences in Manufacturing Industries* (Cambridge, MA: Harvard University Press, 1956); G. J. Stigler *The Organization of Industry* (Homewood, IL: R. D. Irwin, 1968).

[110] For example, the patents in Case T-30/89 *Hilti AG v. Commission* [1991] ECR II-1439; the exclusive monopoly right granted by the state in Case 311/84 *Centre belge d'études de marché – Télémarketing (CBEM) v. SA Compagnie luxembourgeoise de télédiffusion (CLT) and Information publicité Benelux (IPB)* [1985] ECR 3261 paras. 16–18.

[111] For a helpful explanation, see W. K. Viscusi, J. E. Harrington Jr and J. M. Vernon *Economics of Regulation and Antitrust* 4th edn (Cambridge, MA: MIT Press, 2005) pp. 168–72; R. Schmalensee 'Ease of Entry: Has the Concept Been Applied Too Readily?' (1987) 56 *Antitrust Law Journal* 41, 43–4.

depending for example upon whether its behaviour lowers economic efficiency, so the criticism that Bain classifies certain efficiencies as entry barriers misses the mark.[112] Second, the debate is also unhelpful because the concern of competition law is not how the market will behave in the long run, but on whether in the short run the firms are able to raise prices and reduce output.

In both US and EC competition law, less effort is spent defining entry barriers and more is devoted to asking whether new entry is timely, likely and sufficient to counter the reduction in output and increase in price.[113] First, entry must be likely to occur in time to quell anticompetitive behaviour; second, entry should be profitable, taking into account the sunk costs that entry entails; third, entry must be of a sufficient scale to reduce the market power of the existing firms.[114] In the context of a merger, the question is whether, if the merger creates a dominant position, the firm can exploit this or whether entry barriers are so low that others can enter and prevent high prices. In abuse cases, the same question arises: are the high market shares truly indicative of the power to reduce output and raise price, or would a new entrant be able to establish an effective competitive counterpoint should prices rise? From this perspective, the Bain approach is preferable because it suits the purposes of competition law inquiries: examining the probability of fast, effective entry that would deter anticompetitive behaviour. In the US *Microsoft* litigation the Court of Appeals used a definition close to the Bainian model: 'factors (such as certain regulatory requirements) that prevent new rivals from timely responding to an increase in price above the competitive level'.[115] This legal standard takes into account the important issue that the speed and degree of entry is relevant for competition law and the Stigler/Bain debate is unhelpful in the context of this kind of inquiry.[116] This approach avoids defining entry barriers and considers matters from the perspective of incentives.

However, the approach taken by competition authorities is risky because it can lead to a slippery slope whereby any factor making entry more risky or difficult becomes an entry barrier without detailed scrutiny, an approach that exaggerates market power. In the EC for example, factors like a big technological lead over others, an effective sales network, or a successful advertising campaign that brings customer loyalty are entry barriers because they give the

---

[112] Hovenkamp *Federal Antitrust Policy* pp. 468–9, arguing that if there was a rule of no-fault monopoly whereby liability would be imposed purely based on dominance, then the Stiglerian approach would make sense, for one would not want to punish efficient monopolies.

[113] *Guidelines on the Assessment of Horizontal Mergers under the Council Regulation of Concentrations between Undertakings* [2004] OJ C31/5 pt VI; DG Competition discussion paper on Article 82, paras. 35–7.

[114] US Horizontal Merger Guidelines, section 3.

[115] *US v. Microsoft* 253 F 3d 34, 51 (DC Cir. 2001).

[116] See D. W. Carlton 'Why Barriers to Entry are Barriers to Understanding' (2004) 94 *American Economic Review* 466.

firm technical and commercial advantages over rivals.[117] The objection to treating these as entry barriers without more is that if capital markets are efficient then there is nothing to stop other firms from matching the incumbent in terms of research and development and advertising, allowing for quick entry. In this respect, the US Guidelines are crucially different from the EC's approach: in the EC something like advertising is an entry barrier *per se*, under the US Guidelines the question is whether the sunk costs of advertising by a new competitor can be recouped via successful entry, or whether the risk of failure is so great as to dissuade entrants. For instance, in *Kimberly-Clark/Scott* the Commission said: 'Any new entrant to the branded product market sector who does not enjoy the strength of an existing major brand would have to compete with the financial strength and resources of the combined Kimberly-Clark/Scott entity. Moreover, advertising expenditure and market share is self-reinforcing. On the one hand, there is the virtuous circle where high market share allows high profitability to engage in sustained advertising to support the brand. On the other hand, there is a vicious circle where low market share means low profits and inadequate resources to implement the necessary advertising campaign to boost flagging sales.'[118] In contrast, under the US Guidelines, the approach is different. The competition authority would ask: is it worth obtaining enough resources to mount a credible advertising campaign that would allow the new brand to establish itself on the market and recoup the sunk advertising costs? Only if entry is too risky, because the incumbent's brand loyalty is so strong that no amount of advertising can displace the existing firms, will there be an entry barrier.[119]

However, striking a balance between a too wide and a too narrow conception of entry barriers is not easy, perhaps because entry barriers, like market definition, can be prey to political interests. According to Pitofsky for example, some formulations of market power and entry barriers by the American courts in the 1980s reflected a Chicago-inspired position, which rejected aggressive antitrust scrutiny. In his review of a number of significant decisions, he demonstrates how the courts tended to place emphasis on the hypothetical future possibilities of entry into the relevant market and failed to focus on the history of entry into the markets, which suggested that entry was unlikely.[120] Similarly, the Community's wider conception of entry barriers might be motivated by a policy designed to make it as easy as possible for firms to participate in the marketplace, guaranteeing 'disciplined pluralism'. The Community's approach may also be justified in light of economic evidence that entry in the EC market is in fact difficult, where entry has been by

---

[117] E.g. *Hoffmann La Roche* [1979] ECR 461 para. 48; *United Brands* [1978] ECR 207 para. 122; *Eurofix-Bauco/Hilti* [1988] OJ L65/19 para. 69.

[118] Case IV/M.623 *Kimberly-Clark/Scott* [1996] OJ L183/1 para. 145.

[119] E. Mensch and A. Freeman 'Efficiency and Image: Advertising as an Antitrust Issue' [1990] *Duke Law Journal* 321.

[120] Pitofsky 'New Definitions' p. 1805; but see Schmalensee 'Ease of Entry'.

small-scale firms that occupy niche markets without challenging the larger firms,[121] suggesting that the differences in the way markets work in the US and the EU may require different regulatory norms.[122]

4 Market power in aftermarkets

Certain goods need spare parts or maintenance. For example, consumers buy one printer, but make several purchases of ink cartridges throughout the lifetime of the printer; consumers buy a photocopier and require servicing when it breaks down. Is the market for the additional goods and services consumers need after the initial purchase a separate product market for the purposes of competition law? In an early decision, *Hugin*, the Court held that spare parts were separate products.[123] Hugin held a 12–13 per cent share of the cash register market; however, in the market for the repair of Hugin cash registers, it held a monopoly, for only its spare parts could be used to fix broken cash registers. Hugin refused to supply spare parts to independent repairers (*inter alia* Liptons) and was accused of abusing its dominant position in the 'aftermarket' of parts for Hugin cash registers. The Commission concluded that the 'aftermarket' constituted a relevant product market, but this approach is controversial. Bishop and Walker have voiced scepticism about the possibility of market power in aftermarkets when the firm faces strong competition in the primary market: 'we should expect competition in the primary market to have competed away any excess profits that might in theory be attached to the 100 per cent share of the spare parts market'.[124] That is, if Hugin were to sell its spare parts at high prices, consumers of Hugin cash registers would switch and buy other cash registers where the manufacturer sells cheaper spare parts.

It is arguable that the approach in *Hugin* is evidence of a policy-oriented market definition: the injured party was not the consumer (no evidence was available that Hugin set anticompetitive prices for repair services to its customers, in fact Advocate General Reischl deemed this evidence irrelevant)[125] but small, independent repairers who were being denied access to the market. The Commission's decision is replete with passages explaining the effect of the refusal to supply parts. (For example, 'Liptons has accordingly been forced gradually to withdraw from these businesses in which it had invested time and money and had established a strong basis for profitable expansion.')[126] From

---

[121] P. Geroski and A. Jaquemin 'Industrial Change, Barriers to Mobility and European Industrial Policy' (1985) 1 *Economic Policy* 170, 182–3.

[122] See generally P. A. Hall and D. Soskice 'An Introduction to Varieties of Capitalism' in P. A. Hall and D. Soskice (eds.) *Varieties of Capitalism* (Oxford: Oxford University Press, 2001).

[123] *Hugin/Liptons* [1978] OJ L22/23. The Commission lost the appeal because the Court held that there had been no effect on trade between Member States, but the conclusion on the definition of the relevant product market and its abuse has not been called into question: Case 22/78 *Hugin Kassaregister AB and Hugin Cash Registers Ltd v. Commission* [1979] ECR 1869.

[124] Bishop and Walker *Economics para.* 4.81.   [125] [1979] ECR 1869, 1911.

[126] *Hugin/Liptons* [1978] OJ L22/23, p. 32.

the perspective of allocative efficiency, Liptons' presence or absence might be irrelevant; however, drawing on the core values of EC competition law, specifically economic freedom, there is a justification in defining the market narrowly so as to guarantee market players like Liptons access to the market. Yet even from the economic freedom perspective, one might chastise the decision because the independent repairers would not have gone out of business, they would have redirected their focus to servicing other cash registers, in what was a highly competitive market.[127]

However, it would be wrong to say that the approach in *Hugin* is wrong from either an economic or a policy perspective, because there is a justifiable economic basis for the *Hugin* decision, although it is far removed from the Court's ratio decidendi. Post-Chicago economic theory suggests that there may be a separate market in spare parts if certain conditions obtain: (1) the primary product (the cash register) is expensive as compared to the spare parts; (2) the primary product has a long lifetime; (3) the costs of the secondary product (the after sales repair service) are uncertain. In these situations it is profitable for the firm selling the primary product to exploit the fact that the consumer lacks information about the total cost of spare parts over the lifetime of the product, or is 'locked in' because switching to another primary product is more expensive than buying spare parts for the original.[128] In these scenarios there might be market power in aftermarkets, justifying the Court's narrow market definition in *Hugin*.[129] The aftermarket is worth monopolising because a small increase in the price of Hugin parts sold to their current owners is tolerated so long as the extra costs are less than the cost of switching to a different machine where the spare parts are cheaper. The Commission's Market Definition Notice acknowledges this kind of analysis, which has also been accepted by the US Supreme Court.[130] Again therefore, as with *United Brands*, the Notice *de facto* overrules the Court's earlier approach in favour of a standard which is in line with contemporary economics – here reaching the same conclusion as the Court, but on the basis of a policy designed to maximise consumer welfare, not a policy designed to safeguard the economic freedom of independent repairers.

This more economically inspired standard was applied in *Pelikan/Kyocera*.[131] Pelikan complained that its attempts to sell toner cartridges that fit on printers made by Kyocera were being stifled by a number of tactical practices by

---

[127] E. M. Fox 'Monopolization and Dominance in the United States and the European Community: Efficiency, Opportunity and Fairness' (1986) 61 *Notre Dame Law Review* 981, 1003.

[128] Information costs and switching costs are the reasons the US Supreme Court is willing to find power in aftermarkets: see *Eastman Kodak Co. v. Image Technical Services Inc.* 504 US 451, 472–80 (1992).

[129] These matters were already noted by AG Reischl in *Hugin* [1979] ECR 1869, 1905, 1908 and are present in the Market Definition Notice para. 56. The issue is dealt with much more clearly in OFT *Guidelines: Market Definition* (December 2004) pp. 21–3.

[130] *Kodak* 504 US 451 (1992).   [131] *Twenty-fifth Report on Competition Policy* (1996) p. 140.

Kyocera to ensure that consumers bought the manufacturer's own cartridges. However, the Commission found that there was no separate market for toner cartridges for printers because consumers were well informed about the prices of the replacement part and took this into account when choosing which printer to buy. Therefore Kyocera had no dominant position it could abuse.

However, the post-Chicago aftermarket theory is controversial: it rests on specific market circumstances that appear unrealistic for some, or unduly patronising to others. For instance, it assumes that the buyer is uninterested in working out the total cost (including the anticipated maintenance costs) of the goods she buys, or unable to work this out. In particular, in a competitive market for primary products, sellers are often keen to compete by offering inexpensive secondary products. Moreover, the exercise of market power in aftermarkets is limited if the manufacturer is concerned about adverse effects on its reputation: if its aftermarket prices are too high, consumers may cease purchasing the primary product. In the long run then, exercising power in an aftermarket is counterproductive.[132]

5 Product differentiation and market power: the irrelevance of market definition

It cannot be denied that sellers of branded goods are able to set prices that are higher than the competitive price – Armani jeans are more expensive than unbranded jeans even if the only difference is the label. Economists use the notion of 'monopolistic competition' to describe markets with differentiated products, for each manufacturer has a degree of market power, but not to the extent that a monopolist holds market power. In these markets, which represent most of the goods that final consumers buy, competition is often not based uniquely on price but also on other attributes of the product, be it brand image or quality. The question for competition policy is whether a firm selling branded goods can ever have enough market power to behave anticompetitively and to cause damage to the values that competition laws seek to protect. In some decisions, the relevance of brand image was noted: for example, the Commission noted that there was low substitutability in the minds of consumers between luxury cosmetics and other ranges of cosmetics, so that the former were a separate market;[133] and in *United Brands*, the firm's strong brand was evidence of dominance, although in other cases the facts showed that brands were irrelevant to consumer choice.[134] However, the risk of using a strong brand as the only source for identifying market power for the

---

[132] See generally C. Shapiro 'Aftermarkets and Consumer Welfare – Making Sense of *Kodak*' (1995) 63 *Antitrust Law Journal* 483; S. Borenstein, J. K. MacKie-Mason and J. S. Netz 'Antitrust Policy in Aftermarkets' (1995) 63 *Antitrust Law Journal* 455.

[133] Case T-19/92 *Groupement d'achat Edouard Leclerc v. Commission* [1996] ECR II-1851 para. 186.

[134] Case M.623 *Kimberley-Clark/Scott* [1996] OJ L183/1 para. 48.

application of competition law is that we could find market power in every imperfectly competitive market.[135] Nonetheless, there seem to be certain circumstances where market failures may result in the context of branded goods primarily because of product differentiation.

Considering product differentiation as the source of market power arises in the relatively novel notion of 'unilateral effects' in merger analysis, which we introduced in chapter 4 and will consider more fully in chapter 8.[136] The US Merger Guidelines suggest that in markets with differentiated products, competition between some brands may be keener than among others. While the relevant market may include all similar products, the degree of competition between brands A and B is greater than that between brands A and C or B and C. In these circumstances, a merger between brands A and B may allow the merged entity to raise the price of one or both products, knowing that consumers are unwilling to switch to other brands.[137] This approach was applied in the FTC's case against the merger between Heinz and Beech-Nut, the second and third largest manufacturers of jarred baby foods. The leading firm, Gerber, had a 65 per cent share of the market and was the undisputed leader, while Heinz and Beech-Nut trailed with 17.4 per cent and 15.4 per cent of the market respectively. However, the FTC observed that there was strong competition between the Heinz and Beech-Nut brands, and that a merger would eliminate this, leading to higher prices by the merged entity. While there was no market power in the traditional sense of high market shares, the Court identified a risk to consumer welfare, without needing to define a market. Market power was identified directly.[138]

The kind of market power found in the *Heinz* case could be identified using the traditional tools we explained above. The evidence suggested that supermarkets bought Gerber no matter what because it was a must-stock brand. Then the supermarket chose either Heinz or Beech-Nut as a second choice. Accordingly, the relevant market from the perspective of the supermarket was the second brand of baby food. If one applied the SSNIP test one would find that if Gerber were to raise prices, it would not lose sales, but that if Heinz did, it would lose sales to Beech-Nut (and vice versa), and if, after the merger, the Heinz/Beech-Nut entity raised prices, it would be profitable as the supermarket had no other product to offer as a second choice brand. However, this exercise is unnecessary: we do not need to define the market or to compute market shares when the data tell us that anticompetitive effects are foreseeable

---

[135] T. C. Arthur 'The Costly Quest for Perfect Competition: *Kodak* and Nonstructural Market Power' (1994) 69 *New York University Law Review* 1; *Kodak* 504 US 451 (1992), Scalia J's dissent.

[136] See pp. 256–64.

[137] US Horizontal Merger Guidelines para. 2.21. See also G. J. Werden 'Expert Report in *United States v. Interstate Bakeries Corp. and Continental Baking Co.*' (2000) 7 *International Journal of the Economics of Business* 139.

[138] *FTC v. H. J. Heinz Co.* 246 F 3d 708 (2001).

if Heinz and Beech-Nut join forces.[139] In recent cases the Commission has begun to move away from defining a market in order to identify market power, and towards testing directly whether the firm in question has market power. This can occur in the context of goods characterised by product differentiation because the Commission is able to obtain the data necessary to identify consumer preferences. Two merger cases exemplify the application of this emerging method to determine market power by the Commission.

In *Bayer Healthcare/Roche* the parties to the merger sold anti-acid over-the-counter medicines (medicines that treat heartburn and acid-related gastric disorders): Bayer had the 'Talcid' brand and Roche the 'Rennie' brand. In Germany their combined market share was 30–35 per cent and the Commission considered whether the two medicines were particularly close substitutes so that they might raise prices. It considered replies from customers, competitors and pharmacists to conclude that the two products were poor substitutes: Rennie was considered as a relatively 'simple' drug, marketed through mass consumer advertising, while Talcid was in closer competition with a range of other medicines marketed through pharmacist endorsement.[140] In the Austrian market Rennie had a market share of 40–50 per cent and was the clear market leader, while Talcid had a market share of 10–15 per cent. However, the combined market share of 55–60 per cent overstated the effect of the merger because in this country too Rennie was positioned at the more casual end of the market, and Talcid was a distant substitute, so an increase in the price of Talcid would not result in more sales of Rennie: consumers would substitute for other high-end drugs.[141]

In *Johnson & Johnson/Guidant* the parties were active in the market for endovascular stents (specialised medical equipment). The merger would have reduced the number of firms from three to two. Competition was largely based upon brand reputation. Considering the three major firms, the Commission, relying upon a survey of doctors, discovered that the products of the merging firms were each other's closest competitors. That is, doctors would substitute Johnson & Johnson most readily with Guidant's product and vice versa: 62 per cent said Guidant was the best substitute for J&J and in 78 per cent of the responses it was the first or second best.[142] Moreover, there was no comparable closeness of substitution with the other brands. This evidence indicated that a merger would remove J&J's strongest and closest competitor. The effect would be to eliminate head-to-head competition, causing higher prices and a slower rate of innovation.[143]

In the first case closeness of competition was considered even when the market shares did not suggest there would be a dominant position in order to test whether the branded goods might be close competitors, while in the second case the close substitutability was

[139] M. G. Schildkraut '*Oracle* and the Future of Unilateral Effects' (2004) 19 *Antitrust* 20.

[140] Case M.3544 *Bayer Healthcare/Roche* (*OTC Business*), 19 November 2004, paras. 33–9.

[141] Ibid. paras. 40–5.

[142] Case M.3687 *Johnson & Johnson/Guidant*, 25 August 2005, para. 266.   [143] Ibid. paras. 312–13.

> helpful in predicting that the merger would lead to an impediment of effective competition. The method deployed in these two cases made it unnecessary to prove dominance indirectly by reference to market shares. This method does not remove the need to consider entry barriers, or the ability of competitors to rebrand their goods to try and compete against the firm that has market power.

The application of this novel method requires caution. In *US v. Oracle* for example, the Department of Justice argued that in a market for a certain type of business software, Oracle and PeopleSoft (the two entities seeking to merge) were each other's closest competitors. The evidence showed that when Oracle competed against PeopleSoft, consumers would get discounts that were 9–14 per cent greater than when Oracle sold the good with no competitors vying for the same customer. However, the Court held that this evidence was insufficient on its own. It merely indicated that Oracle and PeopleSoft 'often meet on the battlefield and fight aggressively' but it did not show whether the same aggressive competition also obtained when Oracle was facing other competitors.[144] The evidence must show that in markets where one of the two closest competitors is absent, the other is able to raise prices because it feels no competitive pressure from anyone else. The evidence must also show that when Oracle and PeopleSoft go head to head, there is not also a third supplier who is forcing the prices down.

There is nothing in the method just described that suggests it should be limited to merger cases, where the competition authority is predicting the future effects on the market should the merger go ahead. It is equally possible to apply this approach in situations where the competition authority is reviewing the previous conduct of a firm – if anticompetitive effects are shown to exist, then it can be presumed that the firm in question has market power, without the need to identify a product and a geographical market.[145] This method allows a competition authority to identify firms that hold significant market power and are able to exploit it by monopolisation: reducing output and increasing price. Foreseeable consumer harm is proven directly without the need to identify a relevant market.

6 Market power in Article 81

As noted above, when applying Article 81, there has been little substantive analysis of market power. However, three themes emerge from the case law and Commission documents, which show that different policy concerns have animated the Commission's decisional practice.

---

[144] *Oracle* (2004) 331 F Supp 2d 1098, 1169.

[145] For an assessment of the US case law that deploys this approach, see J. A. Keyte and N. R. Stoll 'Markets? We Don't Need No Stinking Markets! The FTC and Market Definition' (2004) 49 *Antitrust Bulletin* 593.

6.1 Safe harbours

First, the Commission has applied a jurisdictional concept of market power, and devised safe harbours using market shares. The lowest safe harbour is found in the Notice on Agreements of Minor Importance.[146] In the Notice the Commission begins by stating that agreements between firms where the market share is below a certain threshold do not appreciably restrict competition. In agreements between competitors the threshold is an aggregate market share of 10 per cent (e.g. a joint venture agreement where one firm has 4 per cent and the other 3 per cent of the relevant market); in agreements between firms who are not competitors (e.g. a distribution agreement) then provided neither party has a market share exceeding 15 per cent the agreement benefits from the Notice. However, the Notice goes on to say that there are certain types of agreement that do not benefit from this exclusionary rule. In the context of agreements between competitors, the following agreements are forbidden even if the joint market shares are below the 10 per cent threshold: (1) agreements fixing prices; (2) agreements limiting output or sales; (3) agreements which allocate markets or customers.[147]

The Notice fails to take account of the case law of the Court of Justice, which suggests that some agreements are between firms of such little economic significance that competition law should not apply at all.[148] According to one view, there are two low market share thresholds in EC competition law. First there is a 'very low' market share threshold (below 1 per cent) where firms have absolute freedom to enter into whatever agreements they please and then there is a 'quite low' market share threshold established in the Notice (above 1 per cent and up to the thresholds in the Notice) where firms have some freedom but cannot implement agreements that are egregiously unlawful.[149]

The next thresholds are found in Block Exemption Regulations, and the format is the same as the Notice.[150] That is, the Regulations provide that undertakings with market shares below a given amount, and which enter into agreements that do not include certain terms that are expressly forbidden, have their agreements exempted automatically. We analyse one of these Regulations in depth in chapter 10.

The rationale behind this approach is that under Regulation 17/62 the Commission operated a system whereby parties were compelled to notify agreements to gain exemption, and the Commission was snowed under with trivial contracts that were unlikely to harm competition but were being notified so the parties could obtain legal security. The Notice on Agreements of Minor Importance and the Block Exemptions are responses to this problem:

---

[146] Notice on Agreements of Minor Importance [2001] OJ C368/13.   [147] Ibid. para. 11.
[148] Case 5/69 *Völk v. Vervaecke* [1969] ECR 295, 302.
[149] Faull and Nikpay *EC Law of Competition* paras. 2.66–2.70.
[150] E.g. Article 4, Regulation 2659/2000 on the Application of Article 81(3) of the Treaty to Categories of Research and Development Agreements [2000] OJ L304/7.

they presume that firms below the thresholds have insufficient market power to harm competition. The approach might cause Type 2 errors (a failure to punish certain harmful conduct) but the administrative cost savings vastly outstrip the risk of a few harmful agreements escaping scrutiny. The institutional inability to cope with notification led to the safe harbour approach. One criticism of the safe harbour approach, which we will consider more fully in chapter 10, is that the list of contract terms that take the agreement outside the safe harbour is too long, and that if the Commission was serious about leaving those without market power alone, it should provide that they have absolute freedom to enter into whatever contracts they wish, even fixing prices.

6.2 Quasi per se rules

A second significant consideration is that under Article 81 certain kinds of agreements are unlawful without the need to carry out a market-power test. The rationale for this is that certain types of agreement 'would always or almost always tend to restrict competition and decrease output'.[151] In US antitrust jargon, this is known as the rule of per se illegality. Price-fixing agreements by competitors are per se illegal, regardless of the market power the firms have, and regardless of any pro-competitive justification the firms might be able to provide. Justice Thurgood Marshall explains the reason for per se illegality:

> Per se rules always contain a degree of arbitrariness. They are justified on the assumption that the gains from imposition of the rule will far outweigh the losses and that significant administrative advantages will result. In other words, the potential competitive harm plus the administrative costs of determining in what particular situations a practice may be harmful must far outweigh the benefits that may result. If the potential benefits in the aggregate are outweighed to this degree, then they are simply not worth identifying in individual cases.[152]

The per se rule is one of administrative convenience. We know that most price-fixing agreements among competitors are likely to harm consumers. By banning all of them, the risk of Type 1 errors (over-enforcement preventing pro-competitive behaviour) is low, and the administrative costs of analysing in detail each price-fixing case are greater than the reduction of Type 1 errors.

In EC competition law, something resembling the per se rule can be seen when the Commission penalises agreements whose 'object' is the restriction of competition. The Court has held that if an agreement is designed with the intention to restrict competition,[153] or if the restriction is foreseeable, or 'obviously capable'[154] of restricting competition, then the agreement is unlawful for the purposes of Article 81(1) without market analysis (except perhaps if

---

[151] *Broadcast Music Inc. v. CBS* 441 US 1, 19–20 (1979).
[152] *US v. Container Corporation of America* 393 US 333, 341 (1969).
[153] Case C-551/03P *General Motors v. Commission*, judgment of 6 April 2006, paras. 77–8.
[154] Ibid. Opinion of AG Tizzano para. 77.

the market share is 'very low' as discussed in section 6.1). This approach can be found most frequently when parties enter into agreements that divide the market or in cartel cases. However, the Community does not apply a strict per se approach. The CFI has held that every agreement may in theory be exempted under Article 81(3),[155] therefore even agreements that are prohibited because they run against the core values of EC competition law may be exempted. As we noted in chapter 4 for example, price-fixing and cartel-like arrangements may be exempted when other Community policies justify this.

6.3 An evolving market power analysis

In cases that do not benefit from an automatic presumption of legality (safe harbours) or an automatic presumption of illegality (quasi per se illegality), the Commission's approach has evolved. Before Regulation 1/2003 the application of Article 81(1) did not require a finding of market power. As we saw in chapter 2, so long as a restriction of competition is identified as a restriction of economic freedom, market power does not come into consideration. Under this wide reading of Article 81(1), the role of market power was relegated to Article 81(3). That is, the party seeking to obtain an exemption bore the burden of proving that the agreement did not eliminate competition (the final condition in Article 81(3)). In most cases, proof that the parties lacked market power was sufficient to allow the Commission to infer that the agreement did not eliminate competition, and agreements where the firm had market power were not exempted.[156] The Commission's original approach under Article 81 did contain a market-power inquiry, but the burden was placed on the defendant seeking exemption to show that there was no market power.

The emerging approach instead contains a market-power inquiry in Article 81(1). If the market power of the parties defined in neoclassical terms was used as a threshold question in the application of Article 81, very few agreements that we reviewed in chapters 2 and 4 would be caught. It remains to be seen how far the methods outlined above to identify market power for the purposes of Article 82 and the Merger Regulation will be applied regularly in Article 81 cases and how far market power in this way will play a role in Article 81(1).

In sum, under Article 81, there seem to be two concepts of market power. Very low degrees of market power (where market shares are a jurisdictional threshold) determine the non-application of the prohibition of Article 81. For firms whose market shares exceed the safe harbours (or whose contracts contain clauses that are inadmissible under the safe harbours) then a more detailed analysis of market power is used to determine the anticompetitive

---

[155] Case T-17/93 *Matra Hachette v. Commission* [1994] ER II-595.
[156] E.g. Cases 209/78 etc. *Van Landewyck v. Commission* [1980] ECR 3125 (agreement affecting 80 per cent of the relevant market not exempted).

effects of an agreement, unless the object of the agreement is a restriction of competition, in which case no market-power analysis is required.

7 From commercial power to market power

The relevance of the discussion in this chapter is captured by this assessment by the US Supreme Court: '[b]ecause market power is often inferred from market share, market definition generally determines the result of the case'.[157] As the EC moves towards an enforcement policy based upon an economic approach, the identification of market power and the tools necessary for that task are of growing importance. However, there is a tension: on the one hand, the Commission is increasingly using market definition tools that rely on economic analysis and which are premised upon discovering whether a firm has market power in the neoclassical sense. On the other, the Court's case law in Article 82 suggests that the meaning of market power is associated with commercial power. The means to define markets that the Commission is developing seem to be inconsistent with the notion of market power being used by the Courts and the Commission itself. This apparent tension can be resolved by indicating that Community competition law is in transition. There is a political commitment to embrace economic methods, but this is developing against a background of decades of enforcement premised upon the economic freedom model. However, until a transition is made to a particular economic theory of competitive harm (whether neoclassical or post-Chicagoan) there will be tensions and contradictions in the Community's application of competition law.

There are two more specific lessons that emerge from this chapter. The first is about the role of economic analysis in identifying market power. There is no doubt that since the coming into force of the Merger Regulation, market definition has become more sophisticated: it is in the merger cases before the Market Definition Notice that the Commission began to use the hypothetical monopoly test, and where it is now pioneering novel methods that allow the direct identification of market power, dispensing with market definition and market shares. The merger decisions tend to embody a more economics-based approach than decisions about past infringements.[158] However, as we have seen, the Commission does not apply the hypothetical monopolist test regularly. More generally, the market definition plus market share approach is an interesting illustration of the resilience of certain economic paradigms.

---

[157] *Kodak v. ITS* 54 US 451 (footnote 15).

[158] Kauper 'Problem of Market Definition' p. 1700. See also J. S. Venit 'Brave New World: The Modernisation and Decentralisation of Enforcement under Articles 81 and 82 of the EC Treaty' (2003) 40 *Common Market Law Review* 545, making similar suggestions. There are of course certain pre-1997 non-merger cases where the Commission does deploy an economic approach to market definition. See, for example, references to demand elasticities in *Tetra Pak 2* [1992] OJ L72/1 para. 93.

Judging market power by market shares is an approach closely associated with the SCP paradigm, which was challenged by the Chicago School. Nonetheless, market share analysis remains at the heart of competition law inquiry because it provides a relatively simple rule of thumb to identify markets where competition is at risk. The chapter also suggests that the Commission has been less than enthusiastic in applying Chicagoan approaches (for example, there is a wider list of conditions that constitute entry barriers in EC competition law than the Chicago School identifies), but has accepted some of the insights of the post-Chicago paradigm, for instance aftermarkets and direct proof of market power.

The second lesson from this chapter is about the role that policy plays in the definition of the relevant market. As shown in chapter 2 with reference to the meaning of 'agreement', even technical legal issues may be resolved on the basis of the underlying policies that animate the law. In this chapter we have seen some decisions where the Commission's definition of the relevant market can be characterised as 'strategic'. That is, the market is identified in order to achieve a specific regulatory objective: pay-TV is seen as a separate market even when the application of the hypothetical monopolist test may suggest otherwise because the Commission wishes to apply competition law to promote the development of this industry, or to safeguard pluralism. Accordingly, even if a more economics-oriented approach to market power is developed, there are instances where market definition is used to facilitate the achievement of wider, public policy ambitions.

6

Abuse of a dominant position: anticompetitive exclusion

Contents

1. Introduction   *page* 160
2. Why penalise the abuse of a dominant position? *BA/Virgin* as a case study   162
    2.1 Neoclassical analysis   163
    2.2 A post-Chicago paradigm: anticompetitive exclusion   164
    2.3 The economic freedom paradigm   166
    2.4 Which standard was applied in *BA/Virgin*?   167
    2.5 The protective scope of Article 82   170
3. Excluding rivals   173
    3.1 Raising rivals' costs   173
    3.2 Below-cost pricing   177
    3.3 Above-cost discounts   182
    3.4 Distribution agreements foreclosing entry   183
    3.5 Leverage   186
4. Harm to other market participants   195
5. Market-partitioning abuses   198
    5.1 Market disintegration as an aggravating factor   198
    5.2 Market disintegration as the reason for the finding of abuse   199
6. Defences   203
    6.1 Economic justification   204
    6.2 Meeting competition   205
    6.3 Economic efficiency   208
    6.4 Public policy   210
7. Conclusion: Article 82 redux   211
    7.1 Novel policy directions   211
    7.2 A unifying economic paradigm?   213

1 Introduction

Dominance is not unlawful, but 'where an undertaking is in a dominant position it is in consequence obliged, where appropriate, *to modify its conduct so as not to impair effective competition on the market regardless of whether the Commission has adopted a decision to that effect*'.[1] This dual obligation on dominant firms, to avoid acts that harm competition and to modify their practices if they are likely to harm competition, forces them to observe the markets they operate in and to monitor the effects of their commercial practices, which may become illegal if market circumstances change. Every act of a dominant firm is laden with risk, in particular when even commercial behaviour regarded as normal may constitute abuse within the meaning of Article 82.[2]

Article 82

Any abuse by one or more undertakings of a dominant position within the common market or in a substantial part of it shall be prohibited as incompatible with the common market insofar as it may affect trade between Member States.

Such abuse may, in particular, consist in:

(a) directly or indirectly imposing unfair purchase or selling prices or other unfair trading conditions;

(b) limiting production, markets or technical development to the prejudice of consumers;

(c) applying dissimilar conditions to equivalent transactions with other trading parties, thereby placing them at a competitive disadvantage;

(d) making the conclusion of contracts subject to acceptance by the other parties of supplementary obligations which, by their nature or according to commercial usage, have no connection with the subject of such contracts.

Anatomically, Article 82 contains a general section, which prohibits the abuse of a dominant position, followed by a non-exhaustive list of examples of behaviour that may constitute abuse.[3] In contrast with Article 81, there is no stated purpose in the language of Article 82.[4] Other language versions of the Treaty offer no further guidance. For example, the French version speaks of 'exploitation in an abusive manner' ('exploiter de façon abusive'). In an early

---

[1] Case T-5/02 *Tetra Laval v. Commission* [2002] ECR II-4381 para. 157 (my emphasis). See also Case 322/81 *Nederlandse Banden-Industrie Michelin v. Commission* [1983] ECR 3461 (*Michelin 1*) para. 57; Cases T-125 and 127/97 *The Coca-Cola Company and Coca-Cola Enterprises Inc. v. Commission* [2000] ECR II-1733 paras. 80–5.

[2] Case T-65/89 *BPB Industries and British Gypsum v. Commission* [1993] ECR II-389 para. 69.

[3] Case 6/72 *Europemballage Corporation and Continental Can Company Inc v. Commission* [1973] ECR 215 para. 26.

[4] Case T-203/01 *Manufacture française des pneumatiques Michelin v. Commission* [2003] ECR II-4071 (*Michelin 2*) para. 237.

analysis, Joliet, drawing on the list of examples of abuse set out in Article 82 and the French language version of the Treaty, suggested that this provision was intended to catch 'instances where dominant market power is exploited, used, or exercised *to the detriment of suppliers and purchasers*'.[5] So even if the list of abuses is illustrative, any additions to the abuse doctrine must harm suppliers or purchasers. However, already in the late 1960s the Commission was pressing for a wider concept of abuse, to encompass activities designed to harm or oust *competitors*.[6] The language of Article 82 therefore created ample discretion for the decision-maker to determine its protective scope by reference to the kind of policy objectives it favoured – be it the protection of consumer interests or the protection of economic freedom of other market participants. The analysis of the abuse doctrine in this chapter begins with an exploration of the possible protective scope of Article 82.[7]

The abuse doctrine has four possible roles. The first is to protect the market from dominant firms when these reduce output and raise prices. The second is to protect the market from dominant firms when these harm competitors so as to obtain the power to reduce output and increase prices. These two roles are based upon economic theories. The former represents a neoclassical approach, while the second is representative of post-Chicago theories that firms behave strategically to gain market power. A third role for the abuse doctrine is to protect other market participants from the acts of dominant firms. Under an economic freedom model, dominant firms are the major reason for competition policy. They have the commercial power to harm others: competitors, customers or consumers. A fourth role for the abuse doctrine is to protect the internal market. These last two roles are explicitly political, and correspond to two of the core values of EC competition law.

The first three interpretations correspond to the concepts of dominance discussed in chapter 5, which suggests that the concept of dominance one embraces colours the meaning and scope of the abuse doctrine. In section 2, these models are considered in more detail with the help of a case study. Based on what was said in chapter 5, the reader will be aware that dominant firms are controlled for their power to harm the competitive process, so that dominance means the power to harm consumers, customers and competitors. Therefore, of the concepts of abuse noted above, the third is the one that represents the Commission's position most logically. However, as we noted in chapter 5, currently the Commission is carrying out a review of Article 82 so as to bring it

---

[5] R. Joliet *Monopolization and Abuse of Dominant Position* (Liège: Université de Liège, 1970) p. 247.

[6] Concentration of Enterprises in the Common Market: memorandum of the EC Commission to the Governments of the Member States (1 December 1965) at 29.

[7] The notion of a protective scope is drawn from two sources. First, it occurs in the interpretation of statutes under the tort of breach of statutory duty in England, and also in the interpretation of statutory liability under the French or German Civil Codes. Second, this concept was used by AG Kokott in Case C-95/04P *British Airways v. Commission* (Opinion of 23 February 2006) para. 69, a passage which is considered below.

in line with 'mainstream economics'.[8] The motivation for this review is two-fold: first, reform is necessary as a matter of coherence (if Article 81 has been recast so as to focus on consumer welfare rather than economic freedom, so should Article 82); second, reform is necessary because no aspect of EC competition law has incurred the wrath of commentators more than the Commission's application of Article 82. The Commission's first 'reform' document was published in December 2005;[9] however, the seeds for the reform of Article 82 are already inherent in the case law, which suggests that the Commission's reform programme envisages incremental change rather than radical revolution.

The reform process is designed to affect the concept of dominance and the concept of abuse. As we suggested in chapter 5, dominance is being redefined to mean substantial market power to harm consumer interests. This suggests that the protective scope of Article 82 should also be refocused so as to apply only to practices that harm consumers. That is, if we switch from an ordoliberal to an economic conception of market power, we should make the same shift when considering the abuse doctrine. Both the concept of dominance and the protective scope of the abuse doctrine should be moulded by considerations of consumer welfare. The effect is to restrict the protective scope of Article 82.

2 Why penalise the abuse of a dominant position? *BA/Virgin* as a case study

The role of the abuse doctrine can be examined by considering a recent controversial decision, *British Airways/Virgin*. The dispute centred on rebate schemes that British Airways (BA) provided for travel agents. (A rebate is a retrospective discount.) Travel agents buy tickets from the airlines and sell these to travellers. They make profits by a commission, which BA pays on the basis of the number of tickets they sell. BA offered travel agents additional financial incentives in the form of rebates if they sold more of its tickets. In 1993 Virgin complained to the Commission about BA's marketing schemes whose effect, it claimed, was to reduce the incentives for travel agents to sell tickets of competing airlines. The Commission defined the relevant market as that for air travel agency services in the United Kingdom. It found that BA was the dominant purchaser of these services. BA's market share in the total of air ticket sales handled by travel agents was between 39 and 46 per cent, while its competitors had market shares below 10 per cent.[10] Combined with the fact that BA offered flights to many more destinations compared to its competitors,

---

[8] P. Lowe 'DG Competition's Review of the Policy on Abuse of Dominance' 2003 *Fordham Corporate Law Institute* 163, 165 (Hawk ed. 2004).

[9] DG Competition discussion paper on the application of Article 82 of the Treaty to exclusionary abuses (December 2005).

[10] Case T-219/99 *British Airways v. Commission* [2003] ECR II-5917 para. 211.

BA was an 'obligatory business partner of travel agents'.[11] Travel agents could not operate without selling BA flights as part of their portfolio. In this market context, should one penalise BA for introducing financial incentives designed to reward travel agents if they sell even more of its tickets?

2.1 Neoclassical analysis

From a neoclassical perspective, a monopoly reduces economic welfare because, unhindered by actual or potential competitors, it is able to reduce output, thereby leading to a price increase. Consumers unable to buy at the higher price suffer a loss in utility. The same consequence can occur when the largest firm faces some competition from fringe firms. On the assumption that the fringe firms are unable to expand their output significantly, the dominant firm takes the output capacity of the fringe into account and realises that for the residual demand the fringe cannot meet, it holds a monopoly. Thus the monopoly price is set by reference to the residual demand.[12] For example, suppose that there are 100 customers and the fringe firms can supply at most ten customers. The dominant firm is in competition vis-à-vis those ten customers but holds a monopoly over the rest of the market. Arguably a firm in a dominant position reduces welfare less than a monopolist – it cannot reduce output by as much as it would wish because of the supply by the fringe firms, but the more significant the dominant firm's market power, the greater the deadweight loss.[13]

A neoclassical economist reading *British Airways/Virgin* would see that BA's rebate schemes with travel agents were found to be abusive because they were loyalty inducing, reducing the opportunities of travel agents to sell their services to other airlines and preventing other airlines' access to the market.[14] Here the concern was not that flights would be more expensive: in fact the rebates' effect on ticket prices was not even considered. Moreover, it is likely that travel agents would offer better deals and more services to consumers so as to sell more tickets and win the rebate. The rebate can be seen as a strategy to give distributors greater incentives to market BA's tickets. This attitude suggests that EC competition law is concerned with behaviour that excludes other participants from the market, and fails to consider the welfare effects of this – a competitor, and not competition, is protected.[15] Under a neoclassical approach, the rebates offered by BA, the dominant firm, appear efficiency enhancing provided that the prices set are not below cost. On this

---

[11] Ibid. para. 217.

[12] D. W. Carlton and J. M. Perloff *Modern Industrial Organization* 2nd edn (New York: Harper Collins, 1994) pp. 160–1.

[13] M. A. Utton *Market Dominance and Antitrust Policy* (Cheltenham: Edward Elgar, 1995) p. 64.

[14] *Virgin/British Airways* [2000] OJ L30/1.

[15] E. M. Fox 'We Protect Competition, You Protect Competitors' (2003) 26 *World Competition* 149.

view, Article 82 should play no role in controlling the way dominant firms attempt to compete with rivals.[16]

2.2 A post-Chicago paradigm: anticompetitive exclusion

Recent research in economics has indicated that an alternative paradigm can be used to explain why BA's tactics may merit punishment, drawing upon literature suggesting that strategies designed to injure rivals can reduce consumer welfare. As Ordover and Saloner explain: 'the hallmark of these strategies is that, invariably, they reduce the expected level of profits that incumbent's rivals – present and future – can hope to earn'.[17] The strategies are anticompetitive because they dissuade rivals from entering a new market or force rivals to exit, and in the long run allow dominant undertakings to raise prices, having removed all significant competitors. Often the strategies in question (e.g. lower prices, increased advertising, distribution agreements including loyalty rebates, non-cooperation with the newcomer) are exactly the kind of procompetitive response that we would expect from a firm whose market position is challenged. Thus a distinction needs to be drawn between responses by competitors that increase welfare (competition on the merits) and those that reduce it (anticompetitive exclusion). A simple example of anticompetitive exclusion is Ordover and Willig's theory of predatory product innovation: an incumbent may design a new product aimed at diverting sales away from the rival. If this is successful, and provided re-entry is costly, the incumbent is then able to raise prices to an anticompetitive level, for he now dominates the market. The new product's introduction is deemed predatory when the recovery of the costs incurred in developing the new product can only occur if the competitor exits the market, and not from the sales of the product.[18] The behaviour makes no business sense but for its exclusionary effect. The example is somewhat unpersuasive because if consumers value product innovation a firm will not innovate unless it anticipates profits.[19] Nevertheless, it exemplifies the gist of the theories of anticompetitive exclusion: an apparently procompetitive reaction by the dominant firm excludes rivals and gives the incumbent the power to enjoy greater profits once rivals exit. The harm to economic welfare is noted once rivals have left, but the root cause of the harm

---

[16] See R. Epstein 'Monopoly Dominance or Level Playing Field? The New Antitrust Paradox' (2005) 72 *University of Chicago Law Review* 49, who argues that exclusionary behaviour by dominant firms should not be regulated by US antitrust law.

[17] J. A. Ordover and G. Saloner 'Predation, Monopolization and Antitrust' in R. Schmalensee and R. D. Willig *Handbook of Industrial Organization* vol. I (Amsterdam: North-Holland, 1989) ch. 9 p. 538.

[18] J. A. Ordover and R. D. Willig 'An Economic Definition of Predation: Pricing and Product Innovation' (1981) 91 *Yale Law Journal* 8.

[19] For a critique of this approach, see M. Motta *Competition Policy* (Cambridge: Cambridge University Press, 2004) pp. 454–6.

lies in the strategy implemented by the dominant firm which raises the costs of existing rivals and deters potential rivals from entering.

If we analyse BA's strategy of offering incremental rebates to travel agents that sell more BA tickets under this paradigm, it may be described as a mechanism for *raising rivals' costs*.[20] BA's rivals have to offer similar, if not more generous, financial incentives to travel agents in order to remain in the market. Thus, the cost of competing against BA is increased through BA's marketing scheme. This strategy can be successful provided three conditions are satisfied: first, the incumbent must be willing to pay to exclude the entrant more than the entrant is willing to pay to stay in the market – that is, BA must be willing to pay travel agents better rebates than Virgin; second, the new entrant must be unable to find alternative means of entering the market; third, the excluding firm must have market power so that it can exploit the disadvantage suffered by its rival.[21] According to this view, a legal test for determining whether BA's tactics are in breach of competition law would be the following:[22]

1. Whether the dominant firm's conduct raises rivals' marginal costs;
2. If the firm that has adopted the cost-raising strategy can subsequently increase prices after rivals' costs have been increased;
3. Whether rivals have any effective counterstrategies to render the incumbent's tactics worthless;
4. Whether the incumbent can justify its strategy as increasing economic welfare.

In a similar vein, Richard Posner has agreed that it is legitimate to enforce competition laws against dominant firms which exclude competitors from the market, provided that the excluded firm is as efficient as or more efficient than the dominant firm and provided that the exclusionary practices carried out by the dominant firm cannot be justified as efficient.[23] The two provisos ensure that the purpose of competition law remains the maximisation of efficiency – the exclusion of a competitor is not punished unless the welfare effects are negative.

The methodology suggested by these two tests requires a detailed analysis of the market in question, considering the viability of alternative distribution channels and the costs faced by the incumbent and the challenger. The

---

[20] T. G. Krattenmaker, R. H. Lande and S. C. Salop 'Monopoly Power and Market Power in Antitrust Law' (1987) 76 *Georgetown Law Journal* 241.

[21] Ordover and Saloner 'Predation, Monopolization and Antitrust' p. 566.

[22] Krattenmaker et al. 'Monopoly Power'.

[23] R. A. Posner *Antitrust Law* 2nd edn (Chicago: University of Chicago Press, 2001) pp. 194–5. Some readers might balk at seeing Posner cited under a 'post-Chicago' heading, given that he is best known for adopting a 'Chicago School' approach. However, I use the 'post-Chicago' label to indicate a paradigm of economic thought. It is a historical label denoting an epoch of economic thinking rather than an ideological label. Posner's important book adopts some of the insights of contemporary economic thinking. As such it is post-Chicagoan.

post-Chicago approach shares the goals of the neoclassical paradigm but differs by identifying a wider range of methods that may be deployed by a dominant firm to reduce economic welfare.

2.3 The economic freedom paradigm

Finally, a wider conception of anticompetitive exclusion is also possible. The standard of the post-Chicago paradigm is limited in two ways: first, it is concerned only with the exclusion of competitors, not with the exclusion of or harm to firms operating at other levels of trade; second and more significantly, it is premised upon a 'total welfare' analysis whereby the exclusion or elimination of a competitor is not the harm that competition law seeks to address. The real harm is the dominant firm exploiting its market power once the rival is gone. However, from the perspective of 'economic freedom' that we set out in chapter 2, the concept of abuse can be extended to protect market participants from abusive tactics of dominant firms. This wider protection is justified by economic and political means. From an economic perspective, competition law should protect all firms that are threatened by a dominant firm's activities, not only firms that are as efficient as the dominant firm. First, it is not easy to determine whether a firm threatened with elimination is (or will become) more efficient than the incumbent dominant firm: unless other firms are given an opportunity to establish themselves on the market, new firms will find it hard to enter.[24] Second, when a new firm enters it is likely that the dominant firm will be more efficient – it will have an established distribution network, experience of the market, and generally lower costs. Unless the new entrant is afforded some breathing space, it will struggle to enter.[25]

Accordingly, safeguarding pluralism is an important means of guaranteeing healthy markets, and the discipline of Article 82 is necessary for this reason. From this perspective, the standard of proof in the post-Chicago paradigm is too high. From a political perspective, a tougher line against dominant firms can be justified in another way: the economic power of a dominant firm is akin to the political power of the state. Hence, public law standards of control should be extended from their traditional arena (administrative power) to regulate analogous manifestations of economic power.[26] On this basis one might be more comfortable with a rule prohibiting the *existence* of dominance, but it would be problematic to enforce such a rule. From a slightly different

---

[24] But see the articulate objections to this line of argument in E. Elhauge 'Why Above-Cost Price Cuts to Drive Out Entrants are not Predatory – and the Implications for Defining Costs and Market Power' (2002) 112 *Yale Law Journal* 681 part IV.

[25] A position articulated by the Commission in *DSD* [2001] OJ L166/1 para. 121, where it recognised that it would be economically realistic for a new entrant to start with a small operation.

[26] See G. Amato *Antitrust and the Bounds of Power* (Oxford: Hart Publishing, 1997) p. 66 for a similar argument.

perspective, this wider conception of abuse of dominance has been said to have affinities with private law doctrines of duress and undue influence, as it is designed 'to protect businesses and individuals in their freedom to trade'.[27] According to this liberal conception, the ability to participate in the market free from unacceptable constraints is a right to be safeguarded regardless of utilitarian considerations about the welfare effects of such protection.

2.4 Which standard was applied in *BA/Virgin*?

The neoclassical conception of abuse cannot explain the *BA/Virgin* decision, but the post-Chicago and the economic freedom paradigms can offer an explanation for the Commission's finding. The Commission's decision demonstrates an uneasy tension – sometimes favouring a consumer welfare view premised upon some post-Chicago ideas, sometimes supporting the economic freedom paradigm. The reasons why the loyalty rebates BA offered to travel agents were condemned were the following: (1) they removed the travel agent's freedom to select its customers, and this 'regardless of any possibility for the travel agents or competing airlines to minimise or avoid [the] effects' of the loyalty schemes;[28] (2) by offering discriminatory commissions to travel agents they distorted competition among them;[29] (3) they harmed all BA's actual and potential competitors, and 'therefore harm competition in general and so consumers, rather than only harming certain competitors who cannot compete with BA on merit'.[30] The first two grounds are based on economic freedom conceptions, penalising a dominant firm for interfering with the freedom to trade of other market participants, while the third ground is premised upon a conception of abuse much closer to the post-Chicago theories by noting that consumer welfare is reduced when the dominant firm's exclusionary tactics harm competitors who are as efficient as BA, and implicitly tolerating the exclusion of less efficient competitors.

There is a similar ambiguity in the CFI's ruling that upholds the Commission's decision. The CFI held that as a result of BA's tactics: '[a]gents were thereby deterred from offering their travel agency services to airlines in competition with BA whose entry into or progress in the UK market for travel agency services was thereby necessarily hindered'.[31] Some aspects of the CFI's reasoning suggest that the Court was concerned about the exclusion of 'as efficient competitors'. For example, the Court notes that none of BA's rivals sold as many tickets as BA and therefore they did not have the level of revenue to give them a 'sufficiently broad financial base to allow them to establish a reward scheme similar to BA's in order to counteract the exclusionary effect of that scheme against them'.[32] And the CFI added that BA was

---

[27] H. Collins *The Law of Contract* 3rd edn (London: Butterworths, 1997) p. 146.
[28] *Virgin/BA* [2000] OJ L30/1 para. 102.   [29] Ibid. para. 111.   [30] Ibid. para. 106.
[31] [2003] ECR II-5917 para. 287.   [32] Ibid. para. 278.

unable to offer any economic efficiency justification for the rebate schemes, leaving it to infer that the reward schemes were designed to oust rivals.

On the other hand, the CFI retains a focus on the economic freedom model, by considering the losses of travel agents' independence, and also in deciding that the actual effects of BA's practices are irrelevant. With respect to the latter point, BA noted in its appeal that the market shares of its competitors had increased in spite of the rebate scheme, which might indicate that there is no anticompetitive exclusion resulting from the rebate schemes. The Court's response was twofold. First, as a matter of law the CFI ruled that 'it is not necessary to demonstrate that the abuse in question had a concrete effect on the markets concerned. It is sufficient in that respect to demonstrate that the abusive conduct of the undertaking in a dominant position tends to restrict competition, or, in other words, that the conduct is capable of having, or likely to have, such an effect.'[33] Having proven that BA had market power and that its competitors lacked the resources to compete against it, then it follows that BA's practices are able to have adverse effects. This can be criticised for penalising a firm that has financial resources to devise effective marketing strategies. More generally, the Court indicated that there is an infringement of Article 82 when a firm attempts to oust rivals, because 'the fact that the hoped-for result is not achieved is not sufficient to prevent a finding of abuse'.[34] The Court's second response was that the growth of competitors was modest and that without the rebates 'it may legitimately be considered that the market shares for those competitors would have been able to grow more significantly'.[35] It is remarkable how a competition authority and court claim to know more about how markets might develop than most business analysts. It is passages like these that fortify the criticisms that the Commission and Courts are devoted to safeguarding competitors through the use of Article 82.[36]

It is instructive to contrast the Commission's analysis with the ruling on similar facts in the United States.[37] Virgin embarked on private litigation and complained that BA's incentive agreements with travel agents (which, like the schemes in the UK, provided for commissions or discounts when certain thresholds for sales had been met) were in breach of section 1 of the Sherman Act (prohibiting agreements in restraint of trade), but this argument was dismissed because the court found that Virgin had failed to show that consumers had suffered. On the contrary, the loyalty agreements were pro-competitive: the reward of customer loyalty was found to be competition on the merits, a conclusion which is the exact opposite of that taken by the European Commission. Virgin claimed that the incentive schemes were in breach of section 2 of the Sherman Act (the rough equivalent of Article 82),

---

[33] Ibid. para. 293.   [34] Ibid. para. 297.   [35] Ibid. para. 298.
[36] The same approach was taken in *Michelin 2* [2003] ECR II-4071 paras. 239–40.
[37] *Virgin Atlantic Airways v. British Airways* (2001) 257 F 3d 256.

constituting predatory pricing or as leveraging, but failed. Tellingly, the court began its opinion by restating the concepts underlying antitrust law under current US doctrine: 'Foremost among them is the notion that competition fosters consumer welfare. Since competition, which is the very essence of business, results in lower prices for consumers, it is a positive aspect of the marketplace. Thus, what the antitrust laws are designed to protect is competitive conduct, not individual competitors.'[38] The philosophy espoused in this passage is very different from that animating the bulk of the Commission's decision on similar facts.

Before drawing lessons from this case study, some background to the *BA/ Virgin* dispute is necessary to obtain a more complete understanding of this case. First, BA's strategy should be placed in the overall context of the relationship between the two airlines in the 1990s. In January 1991 the Civil Aviation Authority allowed Virgin to operate flights from Heathrow and since that time BA had engaged in a 'dirty tricks' campaign against Virgin. BA was particularly concerned that Virgin was competing against BA on its most profitable routes (London–New York and London–Tokyo), thereby causing a significant dent in BA's profits even if BA flew to considerably more destinations than Virgin. This campaign included espionage and attempts to discredit Virgin, which resulted in an expensive lawsuit for defamation that BA settled.[39] In addition, BA deployed a strategy known as 'switch selling' whereby travel agents would contact passengers booked on Virgin flights and offer a comparable BA flight in addition to bonus 'air miles' on BA's frequent flyer programmes. Agents that managed to switch a passenger received a £5 Marks & Spencer gift voucher.[40] BA's rebate agreements with travel agents were part of this campaign, and the press characterised BA's rebate schemes as 'bribes' to travel agents to sell BA tickets over those of its competitors.[41] Second, the Commission's action against British Airways should be seen in the wider context of the liberalisation of air transport.[42] The gist of the Commission's policy is to facilitate the entry of new airlines and to offer greater choice for consumers. British Airways was a former flag carrier. That is, the UK government had owned and financed BA, affording it a commercial advantage over new entrants. These two features may explain the Commission's aggressive stance against British Airways. However, the assumption that a recently privatised firm is laden with money does not always hold: in fact BA had been cutting costs deeply in the years leading up to privatisation, in particular given the global commercial strength of other flag carriers.[43]

---

[38] Ibid. at 259.

[39] See generally M. Gregory *Dirty Tricks: British Airways' Secret War Against Virgin Atlantic* (London: Little, Brown, 1994).

[40] Ibid. p. 223.

[41] 'Virgin Wins Luxembourg Appeal on Dirty Tricks in BA Sales', *Guardian*, 18 December 2003.

[42] See ch. 12.   [43] Gregory *Dirty Tricks* pp. 19–26.

2.5 The protective scope of Article 82

In spite of the last two observations, which indicate that the Commission's interest in regulating BA was to ensure that markets were liberalised, the decision in *BA/Virgin* represents the current approach to Article 82 and we can draw three lessons from it. The first is that the 'economic freedom' paradigm has a strong influence in regulating dominant firms. BA's 'dirty tricks' and its rebate schemes are comparable in that they represent attempts to harm competitors. Associating anti-competitive behaviour with 'ungentle-manly' commercial conduct also colours much of the reporting of the dirty tricks affair. Article 82 is a kind of 'business tort' where firms with market power have obligations to deal fairly when faced with competition. The 'economic freedom' conception underpinning Article 82 allows the abuse doctrine to prohibit behaviour perceived to be unacceptable.[44] A particularly eloquent formulation of this point of view has been set out by Advocate General Kokott, and it is worth quoting extensively:

> The starting-point here must be the protective purpose of Article 82 EC. The provision forms part of a system designed to protect competition within the internal market from distortions (Article 3(1)(g) EC). Accordingly, Article 82 EC, like the other competition rules of the Treaty, is not designed only or primarily to protect the immediate interests of individual competitors or con-sumers, but to protect the *structure of the market* and thus *competition as such (as an institution)*, which has already been weakened by the presence of the domi-nant undertaking on the market. In this way, consumers are also indirectly protected. Because where competition as such is damaged, disadvantages for consumers are also to be feared.
>
> The conduct of a dominant undertaking is not, therefore, to be regarded as abusive within the meaning of Article 82 EC only once it has concrete effects on individual market participants, be they competitors or consumers. Rather, a *line of conduct* of a dominant undertaking is abusive as soon as it *runs counter to the purpose* of protecting competition in the internal market from distortions (Article 3(1)(g) EC). That is because, as already mentioned, a dominant under-taking bears a particular responsibility to ensure that effective and undistorted competition in the common market is not undermined by its *conduct*.[45]

So competition is not an end result (the neoclassical view), but a process, or an institution that is protected because it has an intrinsic value. The protection of consumers is an indirect benefit and not the focus of the law.

The second lesson is that while the decision might be rooted in an economic freedom paradigm, there is also some attempt to justify the adverse finding using economic analysis; in particular there are affinities between certain parts of the CFI's analysis and recent economic thinking about the adverse effects of

---

[44] Ibid. p. 222.

[45] Case C-95/04P *British Airways v. Commission*, Opinion of AG Kokott, 23 February 2006, paras. 68–9 (emphasis in the original).

exclusionary practices. The roots for the reform of Article 82 are inherent in the current abuse doctrine. However, one major limitation in redefining the protective scope of Article 82 is the Court's general statement on the nature of abuse in the seminal cases, which has been regularly repeated by the judiciary:

> Article [82] covers practices which are likely to affect the structure of a market where, as a direct result of the presence of the undertaking in question, competition has already been weakened, and which, through recourse to methods different from those governing normal competition in products or services based on traders' performance, have the effect of hindering the maintenance or development of the level of competition still existing on the market.[46]

This passage suggests a two-stage inquiry: first the identification of abnormal conduct, second the effect on competition. The first limb is problematic in that it suggests that there are certain forms of conduct that are a priori abusive in character. As we will find below, proof that a firm engages in such practices is often sufficient to find an abuse. If abusive conduct is capable of having exclusionary effects, then there is no need to investigate whether these effects materialise.[47] The presence of such a strict abuse doctrine prevents major reform. However, the second limb of the test (the effect on competition) affords the Commission considerable flexibility. As we noted in the context of Article 81, the Commission has reinterpreted the concept of a restriction of competition so that it means a reduction in consumer welfare rather than a restriction of economic freedom. A similar reinterpretation of the above definition of abuse opens the possibility of rethinking the protective scope of Article 82.

The third lesson is about the relationship between Article 82 enforcement and the Community's policy. This has two dimensions. The first relates to the use of Article 82 in industries which have been liberalised recently, where the concern is to facilitate market access to new entrants that lack the competitive advantages of the incumbents. The effect is that the Commission favours aggressive enforcement of Article 82 in these markets. The second, related, consideration is that in recent years, market access is not valued as a good in itself, rather it is perceived to be the means by which consumer welfare is enhanced.

These observations suggest conflicting roles for Article 82, which should inform the Commission's current wish to revisit its enforcement strategy. From an economic perspective, Article 82 can make economic sense if the post-Chicago exclusionary theories are examined more fully in the decision-making process. This requires less emphasis on 'economic freedom' than the

---

[46] *Michelin 1* [1983] ECR 3461 para. 70. Often a similar passage from *Hoffmann La Roche* (para. 91) is cited, but it has been noted that the English version was translated erroneously. See Kallaugher and Sher 'Rebates Revisited: Anti-Competitive Effects and Exclusionary Abuse under Article 82' [2004] *European Competition Law Review* 263, 269–70.

[47] *Michelin 2* [2003] ECR II-4071 paras. 239–42.

current law. Such an approach would be consonant with the receding importance of economic freedom we noted in chapter 2 when considering Article 81.
From a policy perspective, however, there are three tensions if this route is
followed. The first is that it may be legitimate to apply tougher abuse standards
in industries which have been recently liberalised as a means of making
markets more competitive. The second tension is with the Commission's
interest in using competition law to promote consumer welfare. This can
afford the Commission considerable discretion to regulate markets. As we
noted above, the US judges were unimpressed with Virgin's claim because
they saw prices falling as a result of BA's actions, while the Commission noted
that consumers would gain if they were able to obtain a more diverse range of
airlines offering flights. Both saw consumer interests in a different light. The
Commission's broad definition of 'consumer welfare' (which we explained in
chapter 4) gives it the power to regulate markets in an intrusive manner which
risks undermining the adoption of economic standards. The third source of
tension comes from the fact that by reducing the protective scope of Article 82
the Commission loses the power to use this provision to regulate markets
where there may be a Community interest in intervening, for example to
protect small traders or to promote the integration of the market.

 These tensions suggest that one major challenge in deploying an economics-
based standard to the abuse provision is that other policy considerations
militate in favour of a different, more aggressive, role for Article 82. In fact,
until now the concept of abuse has been shaped by reference to a range of
diverse values. Therefore this chapter is organised by exploring how different
values have informed enforcement, and how the shift away from economic
freedom and towards consumer welfare might be accomplished, together with
the limits of this reform process.[48] Section 3 considers how the abuse concept
applies to the exercise of market power designed to restrict the output of rivals
by raising their costs.[49] Here there is a tension in the case law because, on the
one hand, it appears that the rules are framed according to post-Chicago
economic theories, while, on the other hand, at times it seems as if the rules
are designed to protect market participants. Section 4 is about how the abuse
doctrine applies to the exercise of market power to harm other market participants who are not competitors of the dominant firm, an approach which is
most closely associated with the economic freedom model. Section 5 shows
how the abuse concept has been used to support market integration.

---

[48] While occasional reference to US antitrust law is made, direct comparison between s. 2 of the
   Sherman Act and Article 82 is undesirable as the two provisions reflect differing regulatory
   philosophies. There may be overlaps and similarities on occasion but not systematically. Thus
   the list of abuses does not correspond fully to a list one would make of monopolisation under
   s. 2, which is primarily concerned with the abuses analysed in section 3. For an exploration of the
   differences, see T. E. Kauper 'Whither Article 86? Observations on Excessive Prices and Refusals
   to Deal' 1990 *Fordham Corporate Law Institute* (Hawk ed. 1989), especially pp. 651–5.
[49] Krattenmaker et al. 'Monopoly Power'.

3 Excluding rivals

The most common concern in EC competition law has been practices that force rivals out of markets and/or prevent the entry of new rivals.[50] These are at the centre of the Commission's reform process, where the tension between the economic freedom and post-Chicago models of abuse is most acute. We start by exploring the theory of 'raising rivals' costs' so as to provide a framework for exploring how far the current abuse doctrine requires reform if one wishes to depart from the economic freedom model.

3.1 Raising rivals' costs

In certain markets competitors are in a situation of economic dependence vis-à-vis the dominant firm. *Deutsche Bahn* provides an apt illustration.[51] The dominant firm held a statutory monopoly over the supply of rail transport services in Germany. These services were used by transport firms to move containers from ports in Northern Germany, Belgium and the Netherlands. Deutsche Bahn sold its services in a discriminatory manner: it charged less to Transfrecht (the transport firm that operated from the German port which was 80 per cent owned by Deutsche Bahn) and more to operators transporting containers from Belgium and the Netherlands. The impact of this was an increase in container traffic to Hamburg and a decrease of traffic through the Dutch and Belgian ports. Deutsche Bahn promoted its services at the expense of those of the Dutch and Belgian rail operators and also promoted the interests of its transport subsidiary. The Commission considered this a particularly serious abuse because it negated the EC's aim to develop international combined transport services in the EC.[52] This is a clear example of how a dominant firm can raise costs for its rivals, possibly causing them to leave the market, thereby allowing the dominant firm to increase prices once rivals have been eliminated.

A rival's costs may also be raised when there is no economic dependence. For instance, in *Irish Sugar* the Commission found a breach of Article 82 when Irish Sugar (dominant in the industrial sugar market in Ireland with a market share of 88 per cent) sold its product at discriminatory prices, setting a higher price to sugar packers who competed against it downstream, thereby 'restrict[ing] competition by rival sugar packers on the retail sugar market'.[53]

---

[50] Van Bael and Bellis *Competition Law of the European Community* 4th edn (The Hague: Kluwer International, 2005) pp. 904–5, noting that it is ironic that while a literal interpretation of Article 82 should have led the Commission to concentrate on exploitative abuse, its enforcement priorities have been towards exclusionary abuses.

[51] [1994] OJ L37/34, upheld in Case T-229/94 *Deutsche Bahn v. Commission* [1997] ECR II-1689; ECJ Case C-436/97P [1999] ECR I-2387.

[52] See Directive 91/440 on the development of the Community's railways [1991] OJ L237/25; *Twenty-fourth Report on Competition Policy* (1994).

[53] Case T-228/97 *Irish Sugar plc v. Commission* [1999] ECR II-2969 para. 167.

Both practices have the same effect – excluding a competitor from the dominant firm's market.[54]

Rivals' costs can also be raised indirectly through contractual agreements with customers that make it more expensive for competitors to lure customers away from their contracts with the dominant firm. For example, a long-term contract with a penalty clause can raise rivals' costs, because in order for the rival to induce the customer to switch, his price has to make it worthwhile for the customer to break the current contract, pay the penalty clause and buy the product from the new entrant. This scenario deters entry by raising costs and consolidates the incumbent's dominance.[55] While the penalty clause benefits both the dominant firm and the consumer (the monopolist can lower prices because he will collect rents when the penalty clause is enforced), prices would be even lower if other entrants could compete – the penalty clause excludes more efficient entrants. The consumer signs the contract because of uncertainty on his part about the entry of a cheaper supplier: after all, if all other consumers sign the long-term contract with the incumbent, then the new entry will not materialise.

A dominant firm will often use both direct and indirect means to eliminate a competitor, as evidenced by British Sugar's diversified strategy to raise Napier Brown's (NB) costs.[56] NB was a sugar merchant competing with British Sugar which dominated the retail market and which was also the largest producer of sugar in the UK, holding a dominant position upstream of NB. British Sugar's efforts to exclude NB included refusals to supply NB with industrial sugar, a move that would 'precipitate NB's withdrawal from the retail sugar market' and a discriminatory refusal to supply beet-origin sugar. Moreover, British Sugar raised NB's costs directly by reducing its retail sugar price by a margin greater than its costs of processing industrial sugar, a price neither NB, nor any other efficient firm, would be able to match because they bought industrial sugar from British Sugar and would have to include the cost of processing this in their retail price. In addition, British Sugar raised NB's costs indirectly by offering a rebate to buying groups who committed themselves to buying exclusively from it.

From an economic perspective, these practices can be challenged because they raise the cost to the dominant firm's rivals, reducing their output, allowing the dominant firm to act like a monopolist once competitors exit. Professors Krattenmaker and Salop have proposed a two-step analysis for exclusionary

---

[54] See also *Deutsche Telekom* [2003] OJ L263/9, where the wholesale price of the essential facility owned by the dominant firm was higher than its retail price, preventing profitable entry at the retail level: discussed further in ch. 12.

[55] J. F. Brodley and C. A. Ma 'Contract Penalties, Monopolizing Strategies, and Antitrust Policy' (1993) 45 *Stanford Law Review* 1161, drawing upon P. Agihon and P. Bolton 'Contracts as a Barrier to Entry' (1987) 77 *American Economic Review* 388, and illustrating this with reference to Case C-333/94P *Tetra Pak v. Commission* [1996] ECR I-5951.

[56] *Napier Brown/British Sugar* [1988] OJ L284/41.

practices: first, whether the conduct in question 'unavoidably and significantly increases the costs of its competitors' and, second, whether raising rivals' costs 'enables the excluding firm to exercise monopoly power – that is, to raise price above the competitive level'.[57] The anticompetitive conduct takes place in two stages: in the first stage rivals' costs are raised, in the second, the newly acquired power is exploited. One significant difficulty in translating this method into competition law enforcement is that competition authorities intervene at the first stage. If intervention is delayed until the second stage (only punishing the exploitation of a dominant position, and not the exclusion of rivals) then any remedy is unlikely to restore the market to the status quo ante, as competitors have already exited and new entrants may take time to have an impact. It is imperative for the enforcement action to take place at the time when the dominant firm is excluding rivals. At this stage one should establish whether the practices of the dominant firm are likely to eliminate rivals and give the aggressor the power to raise prices. This creates the risk of Type 1 errors in that the competition authority might punish efficiency-enhancing conduct by dominant firms: often the conduct in question seems to benefit consumers by bringing lower prices. A particularly demanding task is to distinguish harmful from beneficial means of competing.

We have illustrated various strategies for raising rivals' costs that have been deployed by dominant firms in the EC; however, the Community's practice in these cases eschews the kind of analysis proposed by Krattenmaker and Salop. The EC penalises the dominant firm only upon a showing that the costs to rivals have been raised, and often it does so without even quantifying expressly by how much those costs have increased. This is not because the EC presumes that the dominant firm will exploit its dominant position upon proof of anticompetitive exclusion, rather that exclusion in itself is an abuse of dominance, suffocating the economic freedom of market players. However, the Commission's approach requires only slight analytical modifications so as to fit within the economics-oriented framework explained above. First the Commission should quantify the degree of exclusion that the practices are likely to have, and consider whether there are any entry barriers. The Commission should have evidence to show that the exclusion of the rival is sufficient to confer upon the dominant firm the power to raise prices after exclusion. This kind of evidence is not impossible to obtain and would eliminate the risk that Article 82 is used to protect a competitor whose existence on the market is not necessary to guarantee consumer welfare. To exemplify the different kinds of factual evidence that would be required, we may consider the Commission's decision on tariffs for piloting in the Port of

---

[57] T. G. Krattenmaker and S. C. Salop 'Anticompetitive Exclusion: Raising Rivals' Costs to Achieve Power over Price' (1986) 96 *Yale Law Journal* 209, 214. The authors' analysis is based upon cases alleging a breach of s. 1 of the Sherman Act but they suggest that the same type of analysis applies, *mutatis mutandis*, to s. 2 Sherman Act cases (p. 292).

Genoa.[58] The Commission found that the Corporation of Pilots of the Port of Genoa had an exclusive right to offer piloting services and thus a monopoly. Piloting rates discriminated against certain transport firms, with the effect that four firms were quoted rates 65 per cent lower than their competitors. In analysing the anticompetitive impact of this discrimination, the Commission concluded that the effect was to place 'any other operating company or company wishing to gain access to the route at a competitive disadvantage'.[59] This does not go far enough to prove adverse effects because, on the routes in question, there remained a number of competitors. The Commission should investigate further whether the favoured undertakings were behaving in a cartel-like manner, taking advantage of the high entry barriers created by the price discrimination, and whether the price discrimination practised by the port authorities had the effect of excluding potential competitors that would have broken up any anticompetitive behaviour by the four favoured firms.

It is likely that the Commission will be able to find evidence that the rivals' exclusion strengthens the market power of the protected firms, and also evidence that the practices are having an adverse effect on competitors. For instance, in its decision on landing fees in Brussels,[60] the discriminatory fees favoured Sabena over British Midland, which at the time was a new company making heavy inroads into Sabena's market. It would be possible to find evidence establishing that by eliminating British Midland, Sabena's prices would increase, perhaps noting how Sabena's prices changed upon British Midland's entry into the market. Moreover, it would be important to consider not only whether British Midland's costs were raised but also whether there were any other competitors whose costs were equally raised, thereby estimating the true degree of foreclosure achieved by the discriminatory practices so as to gauge the risk of anticompetitive pricing. Instead, in both of these cases the Commission was more interested in showing that the measures were protectionist, designed to favour national firms.[61] While the Commission's concerns over market integration might have led, incidentally, to a result that is consistent with economic welfare, a more explicitly effects-based examination of the facts would render these decisions compatible with an economics-based analysis of abuse. The risk the Commission runs, of course, is that if the economic evidence shows that the discriminatory tactics have no foreclosure effects, then the dominant firm is free to carry out what has been considered the most egregious breach of EC competition law: partitioning the internal market.

A decision which is in line with the approach canvassed above is *Tetra Pak 1.* Here, Tetra Pak, dominant in the market for UHT milk packaging, acquired Liquipak. Liquipak held an exclusive licence over a new method of UHT milk packaging which, prior to the merger, was being developed jointly with Elopak. With the merger, the exclusive licence belonged to Tetra Pak. The effect of the merger was to prevent Elopak from entering the market, where Tetra held a

---

[58] [1997] OJ L301/27.   [59] Ibid. para. 13.   [60] [1995] OJ L216/8.   [61] Ibid., especially para. 17.

market share of 91.8 per cent in UHT machines and where there were no other likely competitors given the high costs of entry. The Commission concluded that the acquisition of the licence was an abuse because it 'raised considerably or even insurmountably the barriers to entry. The effect of blocking or delaying the entry of a new competitor is all the more serious in a market such as the present one already dominated by Tetra because a new entrant is virtually the only way at the present time in which Tetra's power over the market could be challenged.'[62] Here the Commission's analysis is preferable to that in the other decisions because there is evidence that Elopak would have entered but for Tetra's acquisition of the licence, and that there were no other competitors likely to penetrate the market. Having raised the only rival's costs, Tetra Pak obtained the power to exploit its dominance.[63]

In sum, if the Commission wishes to condemn exclusionary tactics using a more economics-oriented framework, then a dominant firm's tactics which exclude rivals should not be condemned merely upon proof of anticipated exclusion or possible exclusion, or the fact that the conduct is not competitive on the merits. To safeguard economic freedom to such levels is counterproductive because it allows inefficient firms to remain in the market, excluding more efficient market participants. By attempting to promote economic freedom one might stifle it. On the contrary, economic freedom would be maximised by penalising dominant firms only when the evidence shows that the exclusionary tactics may facilitate monopoly pricing. That is, drawing on the second limb of the abuse test set out at page 171, the Commission should prove how far objectionable conduct is likely to have anticompetitive effects.

3.2 Below-cost pricing

Below-cost pricing can exclude or discipline competitors, increasing the market power of the dominant firm. In contrast to the above exclusionary tactics, where harm is caused by targeting the rival (e.g. by dealing with it so as to raise its costs), below-cost pricing harms rivals by encouraging consumers to switch away from the products offered by the rival. In the jargon this technique is known as *predatory pricing* and defined as 'a response to a rival that sacrifices part of the profit that could be earned under competitive circumstances were the rival to remain viable, in order to induce exit and gain consequent additional monopoly profit'.[64] The main challenge in penalising such practices is that it is hard to distinguish between fair, aggressive pricing (which is an

---

[62] *Tetra Pak 1 (BTG Licence)* [1988] OJ L272/27 para. 47.

[63] For completeness, it should be noted that after the Commission issued a statement of objections, Tetra Pak renounced exclusivity over the licence, but a decision was issued in the interest of establishing a precedent. The nature of the abuse was not raised in the appeal, Case T-51/89 *Tetra Pak Rausing SA v. Commission* [1991] ECR II-309.

[64] Ordover and Willig 'Economic Definition of Predation' p. 9.

essential ingredient of competitive markets) and unfair, predatory pricing. Part of the difficulty in this area is due to fuzzy terminology: literally, to describe a tactic as predatory implies an act of aggression against the competitor, but if this is the case then predatory pricing encompasses *any* pricing strategy which has exclusionary effects; the label is too broad. Accordingly, the discussion here will focus upon *below-cost* pricing, and other sections explore other pricing strategies that might have exclusionary effects.

The US Supreme Court has expressed doubts about the likelihood that firms would engage in below-cost pricing, by considering the Chicago School's critiques. First, a decision to engage in below-cost pricing is very costly, as it is unclear how long the prices have to be set below cost in order to drive out competitors. Second, the last firm standing must be able to raise prices to an anticompetitive level so as to recoup the losses it has suffered. Almost inevitably high prices invite new entrants, reducing the predator's profits, making the strategy unworkable. Given the considerable cost, uncertainty and risk present in any decision to engage in a below-cost pricing campaign, the Supreme Court reached the conclusion that 'predatory pricing schemes are rarely tried, and even more rarely successful'.[65]

This scepticism has been called into question. Consider the following snapshot of scenarios where below-cost pricing is possible.[66] First, when the dominant firm has vast resources with which to finance an aggressive pricing campaign, and the prey only enough resources to fight the predator for a short time, then below-cost pricing is rational. Second, a bout of below-cost pricing may suffice to establish a 'reputation' for below-cost pricing, thereby deterring entry.[67] Here the dominant firm needs to reduce price in only one market, making the victim believe that it is capable of a more widespread pricing tactic. Third, a 'cost signalling' strategy can be designed to make the prey believe that the dominant firm has lower production costs than the prey. Fourth, below-cost pricing might be a tactic to 'soften up' a potential takeover target, lowering its value before launching a takeover bid.[68] The success of these four tactics relies on informational asymmetries: in the first, the dominant firm knows how many resources the prey has, while in the 'reputation' and 'softening up' models, the prey is ignorant of the true costs or motivation of the predator. In the reputation model, it is unnecessary for the dominant firm to be able to

---

[65] *Matsushita Elec. Industrial Co. v. Zenith Radio* 475 US 574 (1986). For a Chicago view, see F. H. Easterbrook 'Predatory Strategies and Counterstrategies' (1981) 48 *University of Chicago Law Review* 263.

[66] For a summary but more formal economic exposition, see J. Church and R. Ware *Industrial Organization – A Strategic Approach* pp. 647–58 (Boston: Irwin McGraw Hill, 2000).

[67] P. Milgrom and J. Roberts 'Predation, Reputation and Entry Deterrence' (1982) 27 *Journal of Economic Theory* 280; D. Kreps and R. Wilson 'Reputation and Imperfect Information' (1982) 27 *Journal of Economic Theory* 253; G. Saloner 'Predation, Merger and Incomplete Information' (1987) 18 *RAND Journal of Economics* 165.

[68] M. R. Burns 'Predatory Pricing and the Acquisition Costs of Competitors' (1986) 94 *Journal of Political Economy* 266.

drive the competitor out of business, but the competitor believes that the dominant firm is able to afford an extensive predatory pricing campaign and this suffices to deter entry. These strategies can lead to the competitor exiting the market, or to it refusing to make new investment and innovate, and at the same time may deter other potential entrants, effects that benefit the dominant firm and reduce economic welfare.[69]

However, these economic insights have had little impact upon legal standards.[70] Courts have suggested that below-cost pricing is abusive when the prices of the dominant firm fall below a certain measure of cost.[71] In the EC, prices below average variable cost (AVC) are always predatory, while prices below average total cost (ATC) (variable costs plus fixed costs, i.e. costs that do not vary according to quantities produced) but above AVC may be predatory when there is evidence of a plan to drive out a competitor.[72] The justification for a cost-based standard is that a firm setting a price which does not cover its variable costs is acting irrationally because it fails to recover any of its production costs. The inference is that it is choosing to suffer a temporary loss as a means of ousting a competitor. When prices are above AVC and below ATC the firm is recovering its marginal costs, which can be a rational short-term strategy, thus an inference of predatory pricing cannot be reached without evidence that the prices are set with the aim of ousting a competitor. Evidence of exclusionary intent includes prices that are unnecessarily low to compete with the other firms, and low prices charged only to customers that are loyal to the competitor while prices to the dominant firm's loyal customers remain high.[73]

If we refer back to the economic models summarised above, there are a number of problems in the decision to use cost as the means to determine predatory pricing. First, the cost-based standard might be over-inclusive because it fails to determine whether the elimination of a rival will reduce economic welfare. Thus it creates the risk of Type 1 errors: after all, consumers benefit when a firm sets low prices, and if the low prices do not lead to monopoly prices in the long term (that is, the dominant firm is unable to exclude competitors with its pricing strategy) then there is no consumer harm.

[69] P. Milgrom 'Predatory Pricing' in J. Eatwell et al. (eds.) *The New Palgrave Dictionary of Economics* (London: Macmillan, 1987) pp. 937, 938.

[70] Although predation by reputation has now been accepted as a credible strategy by some US courts: *Advo Inc. v. Philadelphia Newspapers Inc.* 51 F 3d 1191 (3d Cir. 1995); *Traffic Scan Network Inc. v. Winston* 1995 Trade Cas. (CCH) 71,044 (ED LA 1995). However, in both the facts did not support the reputation theory.

[71] This approach was pioneered by Philip Areeda and Donald F. Turner in their seminal paper 'Predatory Pricing and Related Practices Under Section 2 of the Sherman Act' (1975) 88 *Harvard Law Review* 697.

[72] Case C-62/86 *AKZO Chemie BV v. Commission* [1991] ECR I-3359 paras. 71–2. Note that neither the Commission nor the Advocate General used this approach. Most authors take the view that prices below AVC raise a presumption of abuse; however, the language of the Court is absolute.

[73] Ibid. paras. 108, 115 respectively.

This is why the US Supreme Court has required that there must be evidence that the predator is able to recoup its losses for a finding of below-cost pricing to stick. This requires a showing that after the below-cost price predatory campaign the predator is able to set supracompetitive prices, or exploit some other advantage so as to recover the losses sustained during the predatory pricing campaign. The amount thus recovered must be 'sufficient to compensate for the amounts expended on the predation, including the time value of the money invested in it'.[74] According to the Court, recoupment is only feasible if the market structure facilitates it: the market should be concentrated and entry barriers high. This requirement sharpens the accuracy of the cost-based test, by minimising the cost of Type 1 errors. Second, the cost-based standard also raises practical questions as to which cost should be taken into account; in the United States the Supreme Court has declined to give guidance and a variety of different tests are used by Federal Circuits. In the EC the AVC standard is generally applied but is modified when it is necessary to take into consideration specific features of an industry.[75] When the cost benchmark is decided, there is the practical difficulty of measuring such costs, so the operational costs of this test are high. Third, the inclusion of an 'intention' requirement in the EC test is ambiguous, for surely most firms wish to see rivals disappear. As the United States Court of Appeals, Seventh Circuit, in *AA Poultry Farms Inc. v. Rose Acre Farms Inc.*, noted: 'Firms "intend" to do all the business they can, to crush their rivals if they can ... Entrepreneurs who work hardest to cut their prices will do the most damage to their rivals, and they will see good in it ...'[76] As a result, looking for evidence that the dominant firm planned the rival's demise is unhelpful: that information tells us nothing more than that the dominant firm sees the rival as a competitor to be concerned about. Finally, the gap between economic theory and legal standards is even wider in the EC because there is no obligation to show that predatory pricing will be successful. In *Tetra Pak 2* the appellants had pressed the Court to find that, in addition to below-cost pricing, the Commission should have to prove that the defendant had a reasonable prospect of recouping the losses incurred during the below-cost pricing campaign, but the ECJ was unwilling to take this step. In its view, 'it must be possible to penalise predatory pricing whenever there is a risk that competitors will be eliminated'

---

[74] *Brooke Group Ltd v. Brown & Williamson Tobacco Corp.* 509 US 209, 226 (1993).

[75] For example, in *Deutsche Post AG* [2001] OJ L125/27 paras. 8–10. Here Deutsche Post had a statutory public service obligation to be the carrier of last resort for parcels, which meant that it had to keep a parcel delivery infrastructure in place even without it operating. The Commission ruled that a price would be predatory if it was below the *incremental cost* of producing the individual service where the firm is accused of pricing predatorily, without including in this cost the running costs of the public service obligation. The effect of this was that in operating the new parcel service, Deutsche Post need not recover any of the variable costs that would have to be spent anyway given its public service obligation. The practical impact of this is that Deutsche Post is able to charge a price below the AVC as calculated following the *AKZO* rule.

[76] 881 F 2d 1396 at 1401–2 (1989).

because 'the aim pursued, which is to maintain undistorted competition, rules out waiting until such a strategy leads to the actual elimination of competitors'.[77] Again here, there is confusion between the elimination of a competitor and the elimination of competition – the disappearance of one firm does not necessarily lead to a reduction in consumer welfare.

The Court's aggressive below-cost pricing standard is more suited to the protection of economic freedom, but fits uncomfortably with economic standards. However, even from an economic freedom perspective the law is too aggressive as it focuses on the harm to a competitor without reflection on whether the competitive process is stifled. A possible compromise is to design a standard that only penalises conduct likely to harm the competitive process, and which is also in line with the Commission's wish to apply competition law to protect consumer welfare, thereby protecting both economic freedom and efficiency. An example might be the model proposed by Professors Bolton, Brodley and Riordan. They suggest a five-step inquiry to test whether below-cost pricing is occurring: (1) a facilitating market structure; (2) a scheme of predation and supporting evidence; (3) probable recoupment; (4) price below cost; and (5) absence of a business justification or an efficiencies defence.[78] The first three steps form part of a first tier of analysis, allowing a court to dismiss an action if the threshold requirements for successful predation are not met. This creates a mechanism to identify the plausible claims at least expense, and leaves for a second stage more complex factual issues. It also allows for an aggressive policy against below-cost pricing, embracing post-Chicago theories. The significant step for this purpose is the second. After establishing that the alleged predator has market power, the authors propose to investigate whether in the circumstances it would be rational for the firm to engage in a predatory pricing campaign. In the context of predation designed to send a signal to the prey so as to discipline it, the authors suggest that the following evidence would serve to demonstrate the plausibility of a predatory strategy based on reputation effects: (a) there must be two markets (either two geographical markets or two product markets) so that the predator can select one market to engage in its predatory strategy and there is a second market where the effects of predation are felt – i.e. the prey is discouraged from entering the other market; (b) if the reputation effect is such that potential entrants fear further predatory pricing by the firm, there should be evidence that recoupment is possible; (c) there should be evidence that the predator is deliberately pursuing a predatory strategy (for example, repetition of localised predation, or the dissemination of information to show unsuccessful entry caused by predation); (d) knowledge by entrants and potential entrants that the market is dominated by a firm with

---

[77] *Tetra Pak 2* [1996] ECR I-5951 para. 43. The Advocate General was even more categorical. In his view predatory pricing is in itself anticompetitive (para. 78).

[78] P. Bolton, J. F. Brodley and M. H. Riordan 'Predatory Pricing: Strategic Theory and Legal Policy' (2000) 88 *Georgetown Law Journal* 2239.

a reputation for predatory pricing. These facts serve to identify whether the market in question is susceptible to predatory pricing designed to create a reputation for predation. Once the market conditions demonstrate that the dominant firm is acting in a predatory manner, the cost standard is invoked. Even though economists agree that prices above total cost could be predatory, the predatory pricing test must afford a sufficient degree of certainty, especially when it comes to pricing decisions, which every firm will make on a regular basis. The test is necessarily under-inclusive (creating a risk of Type 2 errors) but above-cost predatory tactics are tolerated because it allows for a more workable rule (lowering costs of compliance).

An approach like this can serve to bring the law on below-cost pricing closer to identifying markets where below-cost pricing strategies are more likely to occur and be successful, allowing the abuse doctrine to evolve towards a standard based on consumer welfare, while at the same time offering dominant firms a rule which gives them a degree of certainty. Note that while embracing a post-Chicago theory reduces the protective scope of Article 82, this does not mean that the scope for growing the abuse doctrine is stifled. For example, the Community has not yet used the notion of 'reputation effects' in predatory pricing cases, but the model considered above would allow the Commission to apply Article 82 to these practices in a rigorous manner.[79] And by catching only conduct that damages the competitive process, the standard safeguards economic freedom more effectively than the current law.

3.3 Above-cost discounts

From an economic perspective, predatory pricing could entail above-cost prices also, but the model suggested above required below-cost pricing because it tolerates a Type 2 error for ease of compliance. There is also a risk that penalising above-cost discounts can lead to Type 1 errors: after all, above-cost discounts are efficient. The Commission however also penalises a firm that offers above-cost discounts but only if it does so in a selective manner when it finds evidence that the selective prices are designed to drive a competitor out of the market. Discounts have been found abusive when offered to customers who are likely to switch to a competitor's goods – these might be targeted at certain geographical areas, or at specific customers.[80] The findings of abuse have been restricted to firms that hold a particularly strong position on the market, suggesting that discriminatory discounts by dominant firms with less significant degrees of market power are not abusive. Moreover, in all cases the dominant firm used selective pricing as one tactic among others to exclude

---

[79] There is a hint of recognition that a dominant firm may create a 'reputation' for certain kinds of conduct in Case 27/76 *United Brands v. Commission* [1978] ECR 207 para. 192.

[80] For example, the 'border rebates' in *Irish Sugar* [1999] ECR II-2969 and the selectively low prices in *AKZO* [1991] ECR I-3359.

competitors, which facilitated the finding that the pricing was designed to exclude new firms. However, even when limiting the scope of the 'selective above-cost pricing abuse' in these ways, the law penalises efficient conduct: if the prices are not below cost, an equally efficient competitor should match the discounts and render the strategy worthless. Accordingly, the law protects the economic freedom of all firms, even those that are less efficient than the defendant.

3.4 Distribution agreements foreclosing entry

The Commission regularly condemns distribution agreements by dominant firms when their effect is to foreclose entry by potential competitors. The most stringent attack has been on discount and rebate schemes offered to distributors. The Commission's investigations are characterised by an extremely detailed examination of the kind of discount and rebate scheme in question, and the cases defy easy classification.[81] However, the Commission's approach is basically a two-step one.[82] First, the detailed analysis of the distribution contracts is designed to answer one question: do the rebates induce loyalty? The answer is inevitably in the affirmative, and is explained in this way: the distributor, before the discount, is already buying a large amount of goods from the dominant firm. As a result, a rebate offered if the distributor buys even more of its supplies from the dominant firm must induce loyalty. Second, loyalty-inducing rebates may be justified only if the discount reflects genuine cost savings. So far no firm has been able to offer such justification.

Applying the first limb, the Commission has found abuse in volume rebates (conditional on the customer obtaining all annual requirements exclusively from one firm);[83] target rebates (conditional on the customer reaching a set number of purchases);[84] and top slice rebates (discount only if the customer buys more than the usual amounts).[85]

Having shown that rebates are loyalty inducing, the rebate is abusive from the day the contract is signed. There is no need to prove likely effects; proof of

---

[81] For a more detailed analysis, see A. Jones and B. Sufrin *EC Competition Law: Text, Cases and Materials* 2nd edn (Oxford: Oxford University Press, 2004) pp. 419–50; L. Gyselen 'What is an Abuse of a Dominant Position? Rebates: Competition on the Merits or Exclusionary Practice?' in C.-D. Ehlermann and I. Atanasiu (eds.) *European Competition Law Annual 2003: What is an Abuse of a Dominant Position?* (Oxford: Hart Publishing, 2006). The Commission's discussion paper on Article 82 provides yet another means of classifying rebates.

[82] *BA v. Commission* [2003] ECR II-5917 para. 271.

[83] Case 85/76 *Hoffmann La Roche v. Commission* [1979] ER 461 para. 89; Joined Cases 40–8, 50, 54–6, 111, 113 and 114/73 *Suiker Unie v. Commission* [1975] ECR 1663; Case T-65/89 *BPB Industries and British Gypsum v. Commission* [1993] ECR II-389 para. 71.

[84] *Michelin 2* [2002] OJ L143/1.

[85] E.g. *Soda-Ash: Solvay* [1991] OJ L152/40; *Soda-Ash: ICI* [1991] OJ L152/40, annulled because of procedural irregularities (*Slovay SA v. Commission* [1995] ECR II-1821; *ICI plc v. Commission* [1995] ECR II-1846) but a new decision was adopted on the same ground as the earlier ones: *Soda-Ash: Solvay* [2003] OJ L10/10; *Soda-Ash: ICI* [2003] OJ L10/33.

the first two factors shows that rebates have an anticompetitive 'object' and so are unlawful: 'it is not necessary to demonstrate that the abuse in question had a concrete effect on the markets concerned. It is sufficient in this respect to demonstrate that the abusive conduct ... tends to restrict competition, or in other words, that the conduct is capable of having, or is likely to have, such an effect.'[86] Even unsuccessful attempts are abusive, provided they are *intended* to exclude competitors.[87] Moreover, in the few decisions where harm is discussed, the Court assumes that these tactics reduce consumer welfare without detailed analysis.[88] The level of concern over exclusivity agreements is so strong that the Commission is unwilling to excuse such an agreement even if it is a response to demands of powerful buyers.[89]

The Commission's policy has been criticised for deploying a per se prohibition against many discounting practices which are normal business behaviour.[90] Granted the dominant firm is able to offer discounts, but only if these reflect the dominant firm's cost savings (which would be the case with a discount purely linked with the volume of purchases which would allow the dominant firm to plan production in advance), or because the purchaser confers additional benefits on the dominant firm (e.g. prompt payment, or advertising the firm's goods).[91] Dominant firms may not use price strategically. This is unnecessarily restrictive because it ignores the possibility that a rebate scheme could be the most effective means of giving incentives to distributors to market goods aggressively, and therefore it is a cost-saving strategy. Alternatives might entail visits to distributors to inspect their practices, which are more costly and can breed ill feeling between contracting parties. However, there is an intuitive logic behind the Commission's per se approach, in that exclusivity agreements are important when launching a new product, and dominant firms, by their very dominance, do not need to promote their goods as much as new entrants. Furthermore, some might see the strict approach as a reflection of the economic freedom value in EC competition law whereby any restriction of economic freedom is chastised, an approach which is inconsistent with the economics-based approach that animates contemporary competition law.[92]

---

[86] *Virgin/BA* [2000] OJ L30/1 para. 293; similarly, *Michelin 2* [2002] OJ L143/1 para. 239.

[87] *BA v. Commission* [2003] ECR II-5917 para. 294.

[88] E.g. *Hoffmann La Roche* [1979] ECR 461 para. 90.

[89] *BPB v. Commission* [1993] ECR II-389 paras. 68 and 70 (affirmed by ECJ C-310/93P).

[90] D. Ridyard 'Exclusionary Pricing and Price Discrimination Abuses under Article 82 – An Economic Analysis' [2002] *European Competition Law Review* 286.

[91] *Hoffmann La Roche* [1979] ECR 461 para. 90; *BA v. Commission* [2003] ECR II-5917 para. 246 ('Quantity rebates are thus deemed to reflect gains in efficiency and economies of scale achieved by the dominant undertaking'). See the Commission's discussion of a settlement reached with Coca Cola, *Nineteenth Report on Competition Policy* (1989) pp. 65–6.

[92] Kallaugher and Sher 'Rebates Revisited' are among the many to suggest that the economics-based transformation of Article 81 no longer justifies an economic-freedom-based approach under Article 82.

A simple way of reforming the law, as with other tactics that raise rivals' costs, can be to require that the Commission show that the rebates have an adverse effect on competition, by measuring the degree of foreclosure that results from the rebate. To date, this has not been proven. In *Soda Ash–ICI* we are merely informed that all major customers benefited from the rebates, but this is insufficient to show that ICI's competitors were excluded from the market.[93] Similarly, in *Hoffmann La Roche*, we know that the dominant firm entered into advantageous contracts with twenty-two of its biggest buyers, but there is no additional information about the degree of foreclosure caused by Roche's practices, nor about the minimum amount of sales necessary for competitors to remain in the market.[94] Moreover, in *BA/Virgin* evidence that the complainant's market share had increased during the period of the alleged abuse was deemed irrelevant, and in *Michelin 2* the market share of the dominant firm had been falling during the period of the abuse but this was not considered. The dicta in the leading rebate case, *Hoffmann La Roche*, suggest that the key to the abuse is the condition of loyalty and not the amount of goods that must be purchased exclusively from the dominant firm.[95] Moreover, the Commission never considers the fact that the victim is often not only in competition with the dominant firm, but also with other market players, and their impact is not taken into account. Nor does the Commission consider whether a rival is able to match the discount of the dominant firm or take other steps to increase its market share. Measuring foreclosure would bring the law in line with the approach taken for vertical restraints under Article 81.[96] Moreover, the value of economic freedom would be boosted by this approach because rebates that have no effect on competitors are allowed (so prices to consumers fall).

However, Kallaugher and Sher have argued that merely quantifying foreclosure is insufficient without further proof that the increased entry barriers are likely to lead to anticompetitive harm.[97] They show that in at least one decision, *Deutsche Post*, the Commission has done this.[98] Their suggestion

---

[93] [1991] OJ L152/40 para. 17.

[94] See E. M. Fox 'Monopolization and Dominance in the United States and the European Community: Efficiency, Opportunity and Fairness' (1986) 61 *Notre Dame Law Review* 981, 1011. Nor indeed is there any information on whether these discounts were forced upon Roche by powerful buyers.

[95] *Hoffmann La Roche* [1979] ECR 461 para. 89.

[96] See ch. 10. An analogous proposal would suggest that rebate cases should be assessed under Article 81 instead. See E. Rousseva 'Modernising by Eradicating: How the Commission's New Approach to Article 81 EC Dispenses with the Need to Apply Article 82 to Vertical Restraints' (2005) 42 *Common Market Law Review* 587.

[97] Kallaugher and Sher 'Rebates Revisited'. The same position is taken by S. Bishop and M. Walker *The Economics of EC Competition Law* 2nd edn (London: Sweet & Maxwell, 2002), according to whom an abuse should be found when the practice causes a reduction in total output (para. 6.36).

[98] *Deutsche Post AG* [2001] OJ L125/27 paras. 37–8 (for further detail on this decision see ch. 12 pp. 478–84).

tallies with the approach taken in the US courts. In *Concord Boat v. Brunswick*, for example, competitors of the leading manufacturer of boat engines challenged its rebate scheme but lost because they were unable to show that in the ten years during which the rebates were granted, there had been adverse effects on the market: the dominant firm's market share was receding and new entry had taken place.[99] However, based upon the Community's conception of consumer welfare, this additional step is not necessary. The Community is keen to see the entry of new competitors, on the assumption that their entry enhances consumer interests. The economic approach embraced by the Community is not a total welfare approach based upon maximising efficiency, but a standard premised upon facilitating market access by a plurality of firms. If so, the requirement to measure foreclosure is sufficient. Accordingly, in *Deutsche Post* the relevant finding which should become compulsory for all the commercial contracts is the following:

> Successful entry into the mail-order parcel services market requires a certain critical mass of activity (some 100 million parcels or catalogues) and hence the parcel volumes of at least two cooperation partners in this field. By granting fidelity rebates to its biggest partners, DPAG has deliberately prevented competitors from reaching the 'critical mass' of some 100 million in annual turnover.[100]

In this passage the Commission measures the degree of foreclosure, finding that the dominant firm prevented any entry into the relevant market by offering rebates to all major customers. Conversely, had the rebates been offered to only one customer, leaving the remainder free to utilise other parcel delivery firms, then the rebate should not be deemed unlawful. Under the economic freedom paradigm, modified to ensure consumer welfare via the presence of a plurality of sellers, it is unnecessary to go further and speculate whether the market would be more efficient with more participants.

3.5 Leverage

The practices detailed above harm or threaten to harm competitors in the same market as that of the dominant firm. However, the dominant firm may extend its power into other markets, thereby excluding competitors from a market it does not (yet) dominate. Leveraging is a general term that encompasses a variety of strategies that a firm might use to extend its market power from one market to another, for instance by tying, rebates or predatory pricing.[101] Two issues arise: first whether one should be concerned about leverage, and second whether Article 82 is an adequate legal tool to address this practice.

---

[99] 207 F 3d 1039 (8th Cir. 2000).   [100] *Deutsche Post* [2001] OJ L125/27 para. 37.
[101] *Tetra Laval* [2002] ECR II-4381 para. 156.

3.5.1 Why is leveraging anticompetitive?

Leveraging may take many forms, one of which is tying, with the *Hilti* case providing a classical example.[102] A simplified version of the facts illustrates the economics of leveraging. Hilti manufactures a popular nail gun used in the building trade. To operate it the user has to purchase a cartridge and nails. The cartridge explodes when the nail is 'shot'. Once the nails are used up, a new cartridge and a new set of nails is needed. Cartridges and nails are used in fixed proportions. Hilti was dominant in three separate markets: nail guns, cartridges and nails. The Commission accused Hilti of abuse because it tied the sale of cartridges to that of its nails. That is, consumers wishing to buy a cartridge from Hilti had to buy Hilti nails. The effect of this tactic was to make entry of competing nail manufacturers more difficult.[103]

An economist looking at this factual matrix would say that Hilti is not guilty of anticompetitive practices because there is no evidence that, having eliminated all competing nail manufacturers, prices will increase: Hilti, the monopolist in the cartridges market which seeks to create a monopoly in the market for nails, is unable to obtain any extra profits through leverage because it cannot earn any extra profits on the sale of nails.[104] This conclusion can be explained with a simple example. Let us say that consumers are willing to buy the Hilti gun if the price for the spare parts (nails plus cartridge) is €6. At a higher price, the consumer switches to another nail gun, so €6 is the monopoly price for the two components. Say the market for cartridges is monopolised by Hilti and the market for nails is competitive, and the competitive price for nails is €1 and nails and cartridges are sold separately. In these circumstances, the monopolist will sell the cartridge at €5. If the cartridge price is set higher, consumers switch to another nail gun, making €5 the monopoly price for the cartridge. Tying cannot raise price, because the monopoly price for the tied goods is €6, whether or not there are competing nail manufacturers. So whether the monopolist ties or not, his monopoly profits are the same.

Now, let us say that a new, efficient, nail producer enters the market and sells nails at €0.50. Should this worry Hilti to such an extent that it will want to tie the sale of its cartridge to that of its nails? The answer is no, in fact Hilti should welcome this new, low-cost entrant because it allows Hilti to increase the price of the cartridge to €5.50 (the total price for the consumer is still €6, now Hilti pockets an extra €0.50). If an efficient nail manufacturer comes along, Hilti should shut down its inefficient nail production plant and benefit from the

---

[102] *Eurofix Bauco v. Hilti* [1988] OJ L65/19.

[103] Effects similar to this may be created less explicitly, for example by offering a discount if the customers agree to buy all their requirements (cartridge and nails) from the dominant firm (*Hoffmann La Roche* [1997] ECR 461), or by withdrawing a guarantee if the customer does not use the supplier's components: *Novo/Nordisk, Twenty-sixth Report on Competition Policy* (1996) pp. 142–3.

[104] A. Director and E. H. Levi 'Law and the Future: Trade Regulation' (1956) 51 *Northwestern University Law Review* 281.

efficient supplier's existence. The upshot of this example is that Hilti has no economic reason to tie the sale of the cartridge to its nails. The maximum price that Hilti can set for nails and cartridges is €6, so it cannot make greater profits by selling both goods. In fact, as the example shows, its profits increase when a more efficient nail seller arrives. Therefore, leverage may injure competing nail manufacturers, but has no adverse welfare consequences.[105] This is the Chicago School position on tying. On this view, tying can only be explained on grounds of efficiency: for instance, it allows the manufacturer to ensure that consumers have the most suitable nails for the gun they buy (removing information costs), or it is actually cheaper for the manufacturer to make the two together than for the buyer to assemble the goods (e.g. shoes are sold in pairs).[106] As a result, it has been argued that the justification given by Hilti, that tying was designed to ensure that the nail gun operated safely, was probably plausible.[107] Moreover, unless the manufacturer has no safety concerns, it will prefer not to tie the cartridge to the nails, because in a more competitive nail market each nail manufacturer will try to make nails that work best with the Hilti gun, and this will increase demand for the monopolised product.

However, this analysis should not be taken to mean that tying is always pro-competitive and that leverage is an unrealistic strategy. Change the facts in Hilti slightly: assume that there are only two firms manufacturing nails for nail guns, and a number of nail gun manufacturers, with Hilti dominant. If Hilti ties sales of its cartridge to those of its nails, this reduces the amount of nails that the rival can sell. Perhaps this causes the rival nail producer to exit the market because the number of sales is too small and Hilti's practices prevent the competitor from realising economies of scale. This then gives Hilti a monopoly in the market for nails, and it can then exploit its monopoly vis-à-vis the consumers who use other nail guns, because now even those who do not use the Hilti nail gun must buy nails from Hilti. Tying is profitable because it gives Hilti monopoly power over customers that it had no market power over before. In this example, leveraging works in the same way as predatory pricing: it weakens rivals as a means of generating more market power for the dominant firm. Generalising from these two hypotheses, we can say that tying is not an effective leveraging strategy when the two goods are bought in fixed proportions and when there are no economies of scale, but that if goods are not bought in fixed proportions and there is a minimum efficient scale, then leveraging is a profitable strategy.

So far we have suggested that leverage is a profit-maximising strategy because when the dominant firm excludes all competition on the tied market it can then set monopoly prices vis-à-vis buyers of that product who do not buy other products made by the dominant firm (e.g. nails to those who buy

---

[105] H. Hovenkamp *Federal Antitrust Policy* (St Paul, MN: West Publishing, 1994) pp. 371–2.
[106] See further M. L. Katz and C. Shapiro 'Systems Competition and Network Effects' (1994) 8 *Journal of Economic Perspectives* 653, noting that in network markets technical tying can lead to efficiencies.
[107] B. Nalebuff 'Bundling, Tying and Portfolio Effects' (DTI Economics Paper No. 1, 2003) vol. 2 ch. 3.

other nail guns). However, leveraging can also give the dominant firm power to increase prices towards its own customers when the dominant firm leverages into an 'aftermarket'. As we noted in chapter 5, there are certain circumstances where consumers who buy goods do not think about the subsequent costs of spare parts or repair services.[108] In these contexts there is a market for the primary product (e.g. the nail gun in Hilti) and a separate market for the secondary products (e.g. the cartridge and the nails). *Hilti* was not analysed in these terms, but we can use the facts to think about why tying would be profitable if the purchaser of the nail gun did not think about the costs of the spare parts when he bought the gun. Having acquired the gun, this person is locked into the market for spare parts. Now it is profitable to raise the price of nails. Here, in contrast to the Chicago School model, there are two monopoly prices. An example may assist. Let us say that there is a monopoly producer of guns and spare parts and the price for the gun is €100, the cartridges and nails cost €6 and the lifespan of the gun is 100 cartridges, and the consumer notes that the total price for this system is €700 (if the consumer thinks in these terms, then there is no aftermarket). Assume a new entrant comes in selling the cartridge and nails for €3. A Chicago economist would suggest that the monopoly should not tie the gun and the nails but just raise the price of the gun and maintain the same amount of profit. (On the numbers above, the gun can be sold for €400, and the consumer still gets a 'system' of gun plus parts for €700.) However, this suggestion only works if the consumer thinks about the gun and the spare parts as one 'system', one single product. If, however, the consumer's choice of gun depends only on the price of the gun and the consumer does not take into account the price of the parts, then the price of the gun cannot go up in response to entry in the spare parts market. The gun's monopoly price is set independently from the monopoly price of the spare parts. Thus, when the new, more efficient entrant comes into the parts market, the incumbent loses profits on that market and cannot compensate by increasing the price of the gun. In these circumstances, leveraging to gain monopoly in the parts market is profitable because it is a new, distinct market which is worth monopolising.

Leveraging, therefore, can help extend a dominant position from one market to another. However, the effect this has on consumers can be more than just a higher price. In the Commission's decisions two additional harmful effects are identified: the consumer's reduced choice and the harm to innovation. These aspects are explored in some detail in the *Microsoft* decision.[109] Microsoft was

---

[108] See pp. 148–50.

[109] Decision of 24 March 2004. In what follows we assume that the Commission's findings of fact are correct. Much of the literature which criticises the Commission's decision is premised upon the view that the Commission did not understand the market. This may be true, but what is of more general interest is how the Commission, in contrast with the earlier tying cases, examined the adverse effects of tying. (The literature includes: K.-U. Kühn, R. Stillman and C. Caffarra 'Economic Theories of Bundling and their Policy Implications in Abuse Cases: An Assessment in the Light of the *Microsoft* Case' (2005) 1 *European Competition Journal* 85; Nalebuff 'Building'; M. Dolmans and T. Graf 'Analysis of Tying under Article 82 EC' (2004) 27 *World Competition* 225.)

found to have abused Article 82 in tying its operating system with Windows Media Player (WMP), making market access for competing media player software more difficult. The Commission reasoned that because consumers would find WMP pre-installed, they would use it and not install other competing media player software. The effect is that content providers (e.g. music companies) would wish to format their music so it could play on WMP and fail to format music to be played on other media player formats, thereby giving Microsoft a competitive advantage that had nothing to do with the quality of WMP but everything to do with Microsoft's dominance of the operating systems market.[110] The Commission's concern was that this would stifle competition in innovation in this market. According to the Commission, the 'normal competitive process' is for several firms to participate to invent better and better media player software, and tying would foreclose market access because nobody would be interested in investing resources in competing software which cannot be sold as a result of the tie.[111] More generally, the Commission also feared that tying in this market would reduce investment in other types of software because the profitability of new software developments would be stifled if Microsoft were to design a competing product and tie it to the operating system.[112] In the Commission's colourful language, tying

> shields Microsoft from effective competition from potentially more efficient media player vendors which could challenge its position. Microsoft thus reduces the talent and capital invested in innovation of media players, not least its own, and anticompetitively raises barriers to market entry. Microsoft's conduct affects a market which could be a hotbed for new and exciting products springing forth in a climate of undistorted competition.[113]

While readers with greater technological awareness than this author will be able to contest the truth of the facts upon which this analysis is built, the most significant aspect of the decision is the Commission's choice to explore the ways in which tying would cause harm to consumer welfare. The methodology is much closer to the economic models of leveraging than that displayed by the Commission in its earlier tying case law (e.g. *Hilti*). In contrast to the earlier cases where it was not clear what specific harm the consumer or society suffered when cartridges and nails were sold jointly, here the economic welfare losses of tying are set out in detail.

So far we have explored leverage from a dominated market *into* a new market. However, some have suggested that another common reason for tying is to practise 'defensive leverage':[114] that is, using tying to protect the monopoly position in the market which is already dominated. The facts of *US v. Microsoft* help explain how this may occur. Microsoft dominated the

---

[110] *Microsoft*, 24 March 2004, para. 891.   [111] Ibid. para. 980.
[112] Ibid. para. 983.   [113] Ibid. para. 981.
[114] R. C. Feldman 'Defensive Leveraging in Antitrust' (1999) 87 *Georgetown Law Journal* 2079.

operating systems market and tied sales of its internet browser (Explorer). The effect was to exclude other browsers. Competing browsers would have given consumers the opportunity of surfing the web and downloading applications that Microsoft would normally sell with its operating system. In the long term, this meant that consumers did not need to buy a Microsoft operating system because they would just use the Internet to obtain the software they wished. Documentary evidence obtained from Microsoft showed that this was precisely what the company feared. Thus, tying the operating system with the internet browser was necessary to maintain Microsoft's dominance in the operating systems market.[115]

Another defensive strategy can be suggested in leveraging in aftermarkets. Change the facts of *Hilti* slightly: assume that at first Hilti has a monopoly in the market for both cartridges and nails and is faced with a new entrant selling cartridges. In this context, tying is a strategy that allows the monopolist to eliminate the new entrant. Either the new entrant starts to manufacture both nails and cartridges, or it must exit the market because nobody wishes to buy an empty cartridge.[116] In this respect the abuse in the nail market is designed to protect the monopoly in the cartridge market. This is akin to the raising of rivals' costs strategies we have seen earlier.

In sum, there are plausible economic reasons for being worried about leveraging. However, it must be borne in mind that from an EC perspective, the anticompetitive nature of tying is not based only upon concerns over efficiency. In *Tetra Pak 2* for example, tying is characterised as an abuse because it 'deprives the customer of the ability to choose its sources of supply and denies other producers access to the market'.[117] It is important to note that this passage embodies two distinct concerns. First, the harm to consumers is associated with the *exploitation* of a dominant position.[118] However, the Commission, until *Microsoft*, never investigated in detail what the nature of this harm entailed, so that it seems as if 'consumer choice' is beneficial in itself; thus even if it were shown that prices would be higher with more competitors in the market, the Commission would still find an abuse. Second, the passage refers to the exclusionary potential of tying but there is no attempt to test how far the exclusion of rivals harms consumers.

The themes of this discussion are similar to those we have broached earlier: there are competing economic theories about when tying harms consumer welfare, but the Commission's decisions (except for *Microsoft*) are not based

---

[115] For a helpful account, see M. D. Whinston 'Exclusivity and Tying in *US v. Microsoft*. What We Know, What We Don't Know' (2001) 15 *Journal of Economic Perspectives* 63. See also G. Monti 'Article 82 and New Economy Markets' in C. Graham and F. Smith (eds.) *Competition, Regulation and the New Economy* (Oxford: Hart Publishing, 2004) pp. 36–40.

[116] M. D. Whinston 'Tying, Foreclosure and Exclusion' (1990) 80 *American Economic Review* 837.

[117] Case T-83/91 *Tetra Pak v. Commission* [1994] ECR II-755 para. 137 (see also *Hoffmann La Roche* [1979] ECR 461 paras. 89–90).

[118] *Eurofix Bauco v. Hilti* [1988] OJ L65/19 para. 75.

upon any of these models. Embracing economic analysis does not mean that the decisions in *Hilti* and *Tetra Pak 2* would be different, but it requires a different analytical method to establish the anticompetitive effects of the practices in question.

3.5.2 Extending the concept of abuse

Having determined that, whether for economic or political reasons, some forms of leveraging are of concern, we must confront one legal issue. Leveraging occurs in a different way from the other abuses. In the case of 'defensive leveraging', the firm dominant in market A carries out activities in market B to protect market A. In cases where leveraging is used to extend dominance into another market, the dominant firm has two options. First, assume that market A is a raw material and the dominant firm is the sole manufacturer; it can then leverage into market B by refusing to supply the raw material to other downstream firms. Here the abuse is committed in the dominated market, but the effects are felt in the non-dominated market. Second, consider the situation where a tie of products A and B leads to the elimination of competitors in market B. Here, dominance in market A is abused to gain power in market B. Can competition law apply when dominance and the benefits from the abuse occur in separate markets?

Leveraging claims have been greatly facilitated by two early rulings of the ECJ: *Commercial Solvents* and *Continental Can*. In the first the Court held that Article 82 applies to an abuse in one market causing anticompetitive effects in a downstream market. The second judgment was even more sweeping as the ECJ ruled that Article 82 could block as abusive a merger by which a dominant firm increased its dominance, while denying any need to show that the dominant position had to be used to achieve the abuse.[119] These two cases sever causal links between the dominant position and the abuse – making it possible to develop Article 82 to address leveraging practices. These two rulings came at a time when the Court of Justice was widening the reach of Community law more generally, and there is a risk that reading them literally would extend the scope of Article 82 too far, so it is worth considering how the later case law has interpreted them.

In *Tetra Pak 2*, Advocate General Colomer reconsidered the seminal cases and proposed a helpful analytical structure we reproduce schematically opposite.[120] He had no qualms in saying that the abuse doctrine could apply in the first three categories, as the case law had already established this. This is sufficient to allow

---

[119] Joined Cases 6 and 7/73 *ICI and Commercial Solvents v. Commission* [1974] ECR 223; Case 6/72 *Europemballage Corporation and Continental Can v. Commission* [1973] ECR 215. The same point was repeated in *Hoffmann La Roche* [1979] ECR 461 para. 91, where the Court held that abuse does not imply that the dominance is the means by which the abuse is brought about.

[120] *Tetra Pak* [1996] ECR I-5951 paras. 34–62. For a similar tabular analysis, see R. Whish *Competition Law* 5th edn (London: Lexis Nexis, 2003) pp. 200–2.

Table 6.1 Dominance, abuse and anticompetitive effects

	Dominance	Abuse	Effects
1	Dominance in market A	Abuse in market A	Effect in market A
2	Dominance in market A	Abuse in market A	Effect in market B where firm has no dominance
3	Dominance in market A	Abuse in market B where the firm is not dominant	Effect is to strengthen dominance in market A
4	Dominance in market A	Abuse in market B where the firm is not dominant, and where B is a market related to A	Effects felt in market B
5	Dominance in market A	Abuse in an unrelated market B	Effects in market B

some leveraging claims. The second category allows the Commission to catch leveraging when it is practised by a refusal to supply,[121] and also when leveraging is accomplished through tying: the tie is an abuse of dominance in the dominated market which allows the firm to make gains in the non-dominated market. The third category allows the Commission to catch 'defensive' leveraging, as the CFI ruled in *British Gypsum*.[122] Here the firm was dominant in the market for plasterboard (market A) and offered preferential treatment to customers on the separate market for plaster (market B) who were loyal to it on the market for plasterboard. The conduct on the plaster market was designed to safeguard the firm's position on the dominated market.

Consider now the fourth and fifth categories. Can we extend the abuse doctrine when the abuse and the benefits take place in non-dominated markets? The Advocate General in *Tetra Pak 2*, with whom the Court agreed, held that the abuse doctrine could apply to category four, but not to category five. The facts of *Tetra Pak 2* are necessary to understand the Court's wish to draw a line between categories four and five. Tetra Pak was dominant in the market for aseptic packaging (which is used for packaging liquid and semi-liquid food products), which consists of two distinct markets: that for aseptic packaging machines and that for aseptic cartons that can be used on the machines. Its market shares in these two markets were very high (92 per cent and 89 per cent). Tetra Pak also had a strong, but not dominant, position in the markets for non-aseptic packaging (52 per cent of the market for non-aseptic machines and 48 per cent of the market for non-aseptic cartons). Two of the abuses carried out by Tetra Pak took place in the non-aseptic markets: it tied the sale

---

[121] *Commercial Solvents* [1974] ECR 223.

[122] Case T-65/89 *BPB Industries and British Gypsum v. Commission* [1993] ECR II-389, upheld on appeal in Case C-310/93P *BPB Industries and British Gypsum v. Commission* [1995] ECR I-865.

of machines to the sale of cartons and it engaged in below-cost pricing of non-aseptic machines in the UK.

The Court found that the abuse doctrine could apply to acts committed on the non-dominated market because there was a close relationship between the aseptic and non-aseptic sectors. The Court noted that there were 'associative links' between the two packaging systems: many customers bought both systems and Tetra Pak's closest competitor was active in both markets.[123] Moreover, the combined market shares gave Tetra Pak 78 per cent of the total packaging market, seven times more than its nearest competitors, and its 90 per cent share of the aseptic market made it a 'favoured' supplier of non-aseptic systems.[124] As a result, it was as if Tetra Pak held a dominant position on the packaging market taken as a whole.[125] The Court was careful to suggest that all the special circumstances that were found in this market were necessary to justify the application of Article 82 to acts in a market where the firm has no dominance and which are designed to benefit the firm on that non-dominated market.

This ruling does not allow for the application of Article 82 where a firm, dominant in the market for, say, postal services, decides to enter the market for toothpaste and engages in below-cost pricing on the toothpaste market, using its high profits in the postal services market to finance an aggressive pricing campaign. This limitation is not entirely logical. On the one hand, it is normally the case that a dominant firm will try to leverage its market power in a closely related market, because that is commercially the most advantageous way to extend one's market power. A manufacturer of a technologically complex product will try to leverage its position in the market for repair,[126] a seller of goods which require specialist transportation might sell its goods only by delivery contracts so that it can strengthen its position in the market for delivery,[127] but this is not necessarily the case: a conglomerate firm dominant in a wide range of products might set predatory prices in a market it seeks to dominate and recoup those losses in another, wholly unrelated market where it holds a dominant position. Similarly the Court's ruling may preclude a finding of leverage where a firm dominant in one geographical market attempts to extend that dominance in another geographical market, by predatory or discriminatory pricing. However, this practice has been witnessed in the US. For instance, in *US v. Griffith* a regional cinema firm had the only cinema in certain cities and used this monopoly position to force film distributors to grant it favourable dates for films in towns where it competed with other cinemas.[128] Comparable attempts to conquer new geographical markets should be covered by Article 82 given that their potential anticompetitive effects are no different from other leveraging strategies.

---

[123] *Tetra Pak 2* [1996] ECR I-5951 para. 29.   [124] Ibid. para. 28.   [125] Ibid. para. 31.
[126] E.g. *Eastman Kodak Co. v. Image Technical Services Inc.* 504 US 451 (1992).
[127] *Napier Brown/British Sugar* [1988] OJ L284/41.   [128] *US v. Griffith* 334 US 100 (1948).

However, Advocate General Colomer in *Tetra Pak 2* suggested that it would be undesirable to extend the abuse doctrine where there is no link between the dominated market and that where the abuse occurs. In his view the presence of dominance on an unrelated market does not necessarily give a firm an advantage. If on market B there are two multinationals that are in competition, Company 1 which is dominant in market A and Company 2 which has a significant market share in a range of other markets but no dominance, then it seems unfair to deprive Company 1 of the advantages it can reap from its dominant position, while leaving Company 2 free to draw upon its resources from other markets to mount aggressive pricing campaigns in market B. To apply competition law to Company 1 would deprive it of the ability to compete under conditions of equality, and would not contribute to maintaining undistorted competition.[129] This argument is not particularly compelling because if a firm has a monopoly and has exploited it to gain significant revenue which it then invests in a new market, then it is not in the same position as other competitors in that new market. Arguably in this context, however, competition law should prohibit the firm's excessive prices in the dominated markets, rather than its ventures in new markets. Nevertheless, if a dominant firm has a special responsibility not to hinder the competitive process, it might be argued that this extends to any of its corporate activities.[130]

4 Harm to other market participants

A dominant firm also abuses its dominant position when it restricts the freedom of non-competitors. This occurs in distribution agreements where the harm is the distributors' inability to exercise their commercial freedom to look elsewhere for goods, to diversify their business and to look for other suppliers. Often, the primary basis for penalising the dominant firm is the foreclosure of competitors, but regular mention is also made of the injury which distributors suffer. For example, in *Michelin* the ECJ held that abusive discounts 'tend to remove or restrict the buyer's freedom to choose his sources of supply' and as a result 'bar competitors from access to the market'.[131] The general principle animating the protection of other market participants was explained by Arved Deringer:

> The purpose of the competition rules is to preserve the freedom of choice of those who transact business in the market as well as the free interplay of supply and demand in competition. The exploitation is therefore an abuse where the

---

[129] AG Colomer in *Tetra Pak 2* para. 42.

[130] For example, the CFI in Case T-175/99 *UPS Europe SA v. Commission* [2002] ECR II-1915 para. 55 suggested that if a firm subsidises a merger through excessive profits made in a sector where it has a statutory monopoly, this might give grounds for challenging the merger.

[131] *Michelin 1* [1983] ECR 3461 para. 73.

dominant position is used to restrain or eliminate the freedom of decision in competition either of competitors or the consumers.[132]

A dominant firm may be penalised for causing harm to distributors *independently* of any effect on consumer welfare. As the ECJ put it in *United Brands*, it is important to preserve 'the independence of small and medium sized firms in their commercial relations with the firm in a dominant position'.[133] The most remarkable exemplification of this approach can be found in the *Michelin 2* decision. The Commission found that specialised tyre dealers were 'placed despite themselves in a situation of economic dependence that makes Michelin an unavoidable partner'.[134] Having established such power over retailers, the Commission went on to condemn a raft of rebate schemes as unfair – some rebates were awarded so late that dealers were forced to sell at a loss, placing them in a precarious situation also with respect to subsequent negotiations with Michelin.[135] Moreover, the Commission found that dealers' experience of Michelin's bonus scheme was arbitrary. For example, the contracts with dealers included a 'service bonus' linked to the quality of service offered by the dealer to his customers, and the level of quality was something that Michelin would measure. This was condemned because it 'allowed the manufacturer's representative to put strong pressure on the dealer as regards future commitments and allowed him, if necessary, to use the arrangement in a discriminatory manner'.[136] In these passages the Commission is condemning unfair contractual practices that harm distributors, not anticompetitive practices.

Article 82(c) provides a specific example of abuse that is designed to protect customers of the dominant firm, whereby abuse may consist in 'applying dissimilar conditions to equivalent transactions with other trading parties, thereby placing them at a competitive disadvantage'. This provision is often applied in cases where anticompetitive rebates are found, because the rebates discriminate among dealers, thereby placing them at a competitive disadvantage vis-à-vis each other.[137] For example, in *Irish Sugar* the seller (dominant in the sugar market) granted rebates to sugar manufacturers who exported their processed products, but the rebates varied among customers and were not awarded to manufacturers who sold in Ireland. The discrimination was two-fold: between different exporters, and between exporters and non-exporters. The Courts assume that if there is discrimination then the distributor who receives the higher price is placed at a competitive disadvantage.[138] This assumption stems from the economic freedom roots of the abuse doctrine.

---

[132] A. Deringer *The Competition Law of the European Economic Community* (Chicago: CCH, 1968) para. 533 pp. 166–7.

[133] *United Brands* [1978] ECR 207 para. 193.   [134] [2002] OJ L143/1 para. 204.

[135] Ibid. paras. 218–25.   [136] Ibid. paras. 250–3.

[137] *Suiker Unie* [1975] ECR 1663 paras. 522–5; *BA v. Commission* [2003] ECR II-5917 para. 235.

[138] *Irish Sugar* [1999] ECR II-2969 para. 138.

Another manifestation of the Community's concern with the protection of customers is found in *United Brands*. The dominant firm's termination of the contract with its Danish supplier (Olesen), on grounds that Olesen had failed to promote United Brands' bananas effectively, was declared a breach of Article 82. The Court articulated a general principle that a firm with a well-known product was not entitled to cease supplying a long-standing customer who abides by normal commercial practice if his orders are in no way out of the ordinary. While the Court also noted that *consumers* might suffer harm as a result, it is hard to see how this damage would result on the facts of the case, since Olesen did not disappear from the market, and since there is no evidence that consumer prices rose. It has been suggested that United Brands' abuse was the request that Olesen distribute UBC's bananas on an exclusive basis, but the judgment is cast in wider terms. Perhaps the Court's concern is about the signal that UBC's termination might send to other distributors who would now be more careful and seek not to upset UBC's practices. In this light the termination might be a strategic move to discipline all distributors and force them to remain loyal to UBC. However, this possible strategy is not explored, and UBC is punished for terminating a contract with a long-standing customer without justification.[139]

That competition law should regulate contractual practices vis-à-vis contracting parties appears odd at first sight – it seems as if competition law is taking the place of contract law, where we also find principles that seek to protect weaker contracting parties. However, this kind of regulation is intimately related to the economic freedom paradigm that guides competition policy in the EC. On the other hand, Professor Gerber has argued that these decisions manifest a concern about 'relational' market power whose exercise could harm economic welfare as well as individuals subjected to that power.[140] Of course it is possible to articulate ways in which discriminatory treatment of dealers might harm economic welfare: if some are forced to exit from the market, intrabrand competition is reduced; if enough leave the market, the distribution network may become inefficient. However, no theory of economic harm is presented in the case law, whose reasoning fits more comfortably within the economic freedom paradigm.

An American reader might see little to distinguish some of the case law summarised above from that under the Robinson–Patman Act.[141] This statute prohibits price discrimination when this would harm competitors. In a majority of Appellate Circuits, defendants are not able to plead that even though price discrimination caused damage to one buyer, the market is still competitive because Congress intended 'to protect individual competitors, not just

---

[139] *United Brands* [1978] ECR 207 (a discreet mention of the signalling theory is in para. 192).

[140] D. J. Gerber 'Law and the Abuse of Economic Power in Europe' (1987) 62 *Tulane Law Review* 57, 93–4.

[141] 15 USCA s. 13(1).

market competition'.[142] This Act has been roundly criticised as inappropriate in a sound competition system but shows it is possible for a system of competition law to embrace both economic and populist considerations, in so far as the legislative intent to do so is clear. The US thus shares a tension similar to that currently facing the EC: the majority of the case law is concerned with monopoly that harms consumers, but certain strands have a wider protective scope. The case law also shows, however, a reluctance by the Supreme Court to afford this statute too much scope, by interpreting it, so far as possible, in a manner broadly consistent with antitrust policy, and so it has recently refused to apply it when the firm accused of price discrimination was active in a competitive market.[143]

5 Market-partitioning abuses

Market integration is a core value for EC competition policy and the abuse doctrine extends to these practices. Infringements that 'jeopardize the proper functioning of the single market, such as the partitioning of national markets' are very serious and deserve the highest fines.[144] We distinguish between two types of cases: first those where the disintegration of the market is a factor that aggravates an abuse, and second those where market disintegration is the reason for a finding of abuse, and where the principles underpinning Article 82 are extended to facilitate the integration of the common market.

5.1 Market disintegration as an aggravating factor

Many of the decisions reviewed above are based not only on damage to market players, but also on market-partitioning effects. For instance, the rebate schemes in *Michelin 2* were penalised for their loyalty-inducing effects and for their market-partitioning effects. The latter were explained as follows: the rebates were available only from purchases made via Michelin France and not from other subsidiaries; moreover the high level of prices in France before the rebates discouraged purchases in France from abroad, especially as the rebates were not available to dealers outside France. The upshot was that dealers in the French market were even more dependent upon Michelin France.[145] It is easy to see how sealing off the French market from imports would serve to facilitate

---

[142] *Chroma Lighting v. GTE Products Corp.* 111 F 3d 653, 657 (9th Cir. 1997).

[143] *Volvo Trucks North America Inc. v. Reeder-Simco GMC Inc.* 546 US __ (2006). The ratio decidendi was that Volvo had not engaged in discrimination, by giving the concept a very restrictive meaning, but obiter it also noted a lack of market power, suggesting that even if the plaintiff's discrimination argument was correct, the court would resist an interpretation of the Act that would protect existing competitors; rather the law should stimulate competition.

[144] *Guidelines on the Method of Setting Fines Imposed Pursuant to Art. 15(2) of Regulation 17* [1988] OJ C9/3.

[145] *Michelin 2* [2002] OJ L143/1 paras. 240–6.

anticompetitive behaviour, for Michelin's dominance is consolidated. Less clear is the anticompetitive effect on dealers outside France. Clearly their freedom to select Michelin tyres from the French subsidiary is restricted but there is no explanation of any adverse welfare effects on markets outside France, though such proof is unnecessary given the importance attached to the ability to buy goods across borders. Similarly in *Deutsche Post*, the gist of the abuse was a rebate scheme that foreclosed access to the German parcel delivery market, but because the excluded competitors were from outside Germany, this aggravated the abuse: 'this walling off of a national market affects the development of trade to an extent highly inimical to the Community's interests'.[146]

5.2 Market disintegration as the reason for the finding of abuse

As we shall see in the following chapter, the EC is chary of taking action in excessive pricing cases. Of the few decisions targeting excessive pricing by dominant firms, the real motivation seems to have been the concern that prices contribute to the partitioning of the single market. Some decisions targeted the car industry where, until 1993, national approval systems were in place to ensure that imported vehicles conformed to domestic safety standards.[147] In some Member States manufacturers had the exclusive right to issue certificates of conformity for cars manufactured abroad. In *British Leyland* for example, the fee for the issue of a certificate of conformity set by British Leyland for imported Metro models was three times higher than the fee for Metro models sold directly in the UK. It is apparent from the ECJ's judgment that the principal concern was the fact that the higher fee would stifle the export of Metro models from mainland Europe to the UK. The ECJ held that the 'fee level suggests that it was fixed solely with a view to making the re-importation of left hand drive vehicles less attractive'.[148] Moreover, the higher fees were only part of British Leyland's market-partitioning strategy, which included the refusal to issue certificates of conformity. The ECJ used the parties' intention as a way of explaining why the prices were excessive, a formulation which would not sit easily in standard determinations of excessive pricing under Article 82. Moreover, the Commission manufactured a narrow market definition to allow it to apply Article 82, stating that British Leyland had an administrative

---

[146] *Deutsche Post* [2001] OJ L125/27.

[147] The EC has agreed a uniform set of technical requirements: Council Directive No. 92/53/EEC of 18 June 1992 amending Directive 70/156/EEC on the Approximation of the Laws of the Member States relating to the Type-Approval of Motor Vehicles and their Trailers [1992] OJ L225/1 (as amended). See F. Verboven 'International Price Discrimination in the European Car Market' (1996) 27 *RAND Journal of Economics* 240.

[148] Case 226/84 *British Leyland plc v. Commission* [1986] ECR 3263. See also Case 26/75 *General Motors Continental NV v. Commission* [1975] ECR 1367, but here the Commission's claim was not successful.

monopoly in the issue of certificates of conformity in its own cars! However, the market for cars was in no way dominated by British Leyland and when it argued that its practices had not had a real impact on imports of Metro cars from Belgium, the EC rejected this evidence as irrelevant because its tactics *might* have had an adverse effect on imports, and that was sufficient for an infringement.[149] All this evidences a concern over market integration, and the abuse doctrine is moulded to allow for such a finding.

More recently, the policy of market integration has appeared in decisions where the Commission investigates sectors that have been liberalised by Community law. For instance, in a Directive on access to the groundhandling market at Community airports (that is, the provision of services like cleaning, refuelling and baggage handling), the EC had sought to allow free access to competing groundhandling services, in accordance with the Treaty's provisions on the free movement of services (Article 49 EC).[150] In France, access for groundhandlers at Orly Airport is regulated by Aéroports de Paris and it charged different fees to different operators, whereby the highest fees were paid by AFS, a company based in the UK. This benefited the French operator (OAT, a subsidiary of Air France), whose running costs were considerably lower. The Commission found that the price discrimination was an abuse which in the first instance harmed OAT's competitors, and in the second instance caused harm between competing air transport services because the higher groundhandling costs would be passed on to them.[151] Overall then, the price discrimination 'impaired the smooth functioning of the single air transport market'.[152]

Two aspects of this ruling are of note. The first is that competition law is used to ensure the functioning of the internal market which the Community sought to create by legislative means. Second, the dominant firm was not present in the markets where the abuses took place.[153] This unusual aspect deserves some explanation. The source of the Court's approach lies in a series of cases designed to thwart protectionist measures by Member States developed in the context of Article 86 EC which we will consider more fully in chapter 12.[154] This provision gives the Commission powers to issue decisions

---

[149] *British Leyland* [1986] ECR 3263 para. 20.

[150] See Article 6(1) of Directive 96/67 [1996] OJ L272/36 and see further ch. 7 pp. 235–7.

[151] *ADP/AFS* [1998] OJ L230/10, point 126, affirmed by the European Courts: Case T-128/98 *Aéroports de Paris v. Commission* [2000] ECR II-3929, Case C-82/01P *Aéroports de Paris v. Commission* [2002] ECR I-2613.

[152] *Twenty-eighth Report on Competition Policy* (1998) p. 144.

[153] In fact, in its defence ADP had also claimed that it had no commercial interest in harming AFS, but this was deemed irrelevant by the Court, because intention is not a necessary element to prove the existence of an abuse: Case T-128/98 *Aéroports de Paris v. Commission* [2000] ECR II-3929 paras. 173–5.

[154] Article 86(3) reads: 'The Commission shall ensure the application of the provisions of this Article and shall, where necessary, address appropriate directives or decisions to Member States.'

in respect of public-sector firms when these infringe the Treaty rules, specifically the competition rules, and the rule against discrimination (Article 12 EC). It will often be the case that a publicly owned firm is placed in the role of gatekeeper to a market, as ADP was. If so, it has an obligation under EC law to ensure equality of opportunity between various economic operators, regardless of whether it is present in the market.[155] For example, in another case in the airline industry, in Portugal this time, airport charges were administered by a public company. The Commission found that the charges were significantly lower for the two Portuguese-based airlines, and that the public company had abused its dominant position in the market for aircraft landing and take-off services (without access to which no aircraft could operate in Portugal). The charge in question was levied pursuant to a state measure, which meant that Portugal was in breach of Article 86(1), read in conjunction with Article 82.[156] This approach was necessary to attack protectionist actions by Member States keen to shield domestic industry from the effects of the single market. This line of attack is consistent with the ECJ's approach to national *legislation* which discriminates in favour of local transport firms and is thereby in breach of Article 49 EC.[157]

In *Aéroports de Paris*, we find the principles described above extended to complement the single market rules, by creating non-discrimination obligations on firms (public or private) that are in a position to regulate access to transport markets. The implications of this kind of approach are controversial. On the one hand, these decisions lead to more competitive markets, thus the imposition of a non-discrimination obligation on the firm controlling access is desirable. On the other hand, the reasoning of the Court is based not upon the beneficial economic consequences, but on the need to safeguard the rights of economic operators in the Community. The provisions ensuring free movement of goods, persons, services and capital are 'fundamental Community provisions and *any restriction*, even minor, of that freedom is prohibited'.[158] Competition law then is stretched to ensure that these fundamental freedoms are not hampered by the behaviour of the dominant firms, even when these firms have no presence in the relevant market.

This approach resonates with the economic freedom rationale for competition law and the Court seems to suggest that the same reasoning applies to the non-discrimination obligation in Article 82. Advocate General van Gerven in particular espoused this view: 'It appears implicitly from the Community case-law, in particular the judgments in *United Brands* and *Merci*, that the Court

---

[155] Case C-202/88 *France v. Commission* [1991] ECR I-1223 para. 51.
[156] Case C-163/99 *Portugal v. Commission* [2001] ECR I-2613; see also *Finnish Airports* [1999] OJ L69/24. The first decision concerned *Landing Fees at Brussels National Airport* [1995] OJ L216/8, based on Article 86(3) EC. All these decisions rest on the seminal judgment in Case C-18/93 *Corsica Ferries Italy* [1994] ECR I-1783.
[157] Case C-381/93 *Commission v. France* [1994] ECR I-5145 para. 21.
[158] Case C-49/89 *Corsica Ferries France* [1989] ECR 4441 para. 8 (emphasis added).

does not interpret that phrase [Article 82(c)] restrictively with the result that it is not necessary that the trading partners of the undertaking responsible for the abuse should suffer a competitive disadvantage. . .'[159] The risk of this kind of assertion is that the wide approach to non-discrimination obligations under Article 82, which applies in the restricted circumstances when a gatekeeper is entrusted with the task of guaranteeing access to a newly liberalised market, is translated into a rule of *general* application where the economic benefits are not as clear. For example, *United Brands* was found to have abused its dominant position in the banana market by setting different prices in each Member State, thereby creating an obstacle to the free movement of goods.[160] However, Bishop noted that such price discrimination does not necessarily reduce economic welfare, in fact in his view it is usually efficient to price discriminate, on the basis that more sales can be achieved, to the benefit of consumers (for instance by selling more cheaply in poorer Member States). Moreover, the judgment also fails to achieve the aim of market integration. The dominant firm, which is not allowed to price discriminate, sets a uniform average price, thereby increasing the prices of bananas in those poor countries where United Brands was selling more cheaply, resulting in a worse misallocation of resources than previously.[161] In this view, while market integration might have motivated the decision, its effects are inconsistent with that objective. Partly as a response to this strong critique, it has been suggested that the reasoning in *United Brands* should not be read to prohibit all geographical price discrimination by dominant firms, but to apply when this practice is combined with other mechanisms put in place by the dominant firm to prevent arbitrage, thereby damaging competition among distributors. For instance, in *United Brands* the dominant firm had imposed other restrictions on export.[162] However, even this limitation does not escape the criticism that the decision is based upon dubious economic grounds and fails to create the right incentives for market integration.

This review of how market integration is pursued under Article 82 suggests that using competition policy to integrate the single market is a subtle task, beyond merely ensuring that goods and services are allowed to move freely without contractual restrictions by dominant firms. In addition, obligations are also imposed upon dominant firms that are in a position to regulate access to foreign markets. Moreover, the importance accorded to the goal of market integration is such that an abuse will be found even if there have not been any

---

[159] Case C-18/93 *Corsica Ferries Italy* [1994] ECR I-1783.

[160] The same approach is found in Article 81 cases, e.g. *Glaxo* [2001] OJ L302/1.

[161] B. Bishop 'Price Discrimination under Article 86: Political Economy in the European Court' (1981) 44 *Modern Law Review* 282.

[162] M. Waelbroeck 'Price Discrimination and Rebate Policies under EU Competition Law' 1995 *Fordham Corporate Law Institute* 147 (Hawk ed. 1996). However, others suggest that if a dominant firm imposes different prices in two Member States forming part of the same geographical market, this may count as an abuse.

actual effects on the movement of goods, raising free movement to a fundamental right, so that there is no need to show adverse economic effects. However, a more cautious approach is warranted: market disintegration should be the basis of an abuse only in cases where the dominant firm is a gatekeeper to a market – in this context competition law complements the free movement principles and it can be assumed that market access will increase economic welfare. In other cases, like *United Brands*, market segmentation should not be a sufficient basis for a finding of abuse because we cannot presume that economic welfare is diminished as a result of the dominant firm's actions.

The blind adherence to market integration shown in *United Brands* is reminiscent of some other Commission initiatives we explored in chapter 2, for example in the pharmaceutical sector, where the interpretation of the concept of 'agreement' was driven by the wish to integrate markets. The politics of integration has a profound effect on the interpretation of competition law. It remains to be seen whether the case law reviewed in this section will be abandoned now that the Commission has announced an interest in focusing on consumer welfare. If the reform of Article 81 is any guide, it is unlikely that the Commission will abandon its policy: the pursuit of market integration has remained a core value and the Commission has continued to use Article 81 as a means to integrate markets because it takes the view that integrated markets are the means to generate greater economic welfare.

6 Defences

It might seem strange to indicate that there are defences to a finding of abuse because there is no provision in the text of Article 82, especially if we contrast it with Article 81, where Article 81(3) might be said to provide a defence for an otherwise unlawful agreement. Nevertheless, the Court has said that certain practices are abusive unless objectively justified. In technical terms, this seems to reverse the burden of proof from the Commission to the defendant. However, there is little to support this conclusion. It is best to say that there is a space within the context of the definition of abuse for the dominant firm to bring evidence to show that the acts in question do not constitute an abuse.[163] This is the way in which the concept of 'defences' is understood in this section. One of the more interesting features of the Commission's discussion paper on Article 82 is the extensive discussion of defences. This is remarkable because, at least in so far as the case law of the Court is concerned, no firm has yet managed to defend itself successfully. In what follows a taxonomy of defences is set out which departs somewhat from that in the Commission's discussion paper.

---

[163] In a similar vein, see Opinion of AG Jacobs in Case C-53/03 *Syfait and Others v. Glaxosmithkline AEVE* (28 October 2004) para. 72. On defences generally, see the excellent paper by E. Rousseva 'The Concept of "Objective Justification" of an Abuse of a Dominant Position: Can it Help to Modernise the Analysis under Article 82 EC?' (2006) 2 *Competition Law Review*.

6.1 Economic justification

The abuse doctrine applies to distribution agreements in two main circumstances: when these are loyalty inducing and/or when they discriminate among dealers.[164] The Court has regularly suggested that price incentives may be objectively justified on economic grounds. For example, in *Michelin 2* the CFI stated that: 'a rebate system in which the rate of the discount increases according to the volume purchased will not infringe Article 82 EC unless the criteria and rules for granting the rebate reveal that the system is not based on an economically justified countervailing advantage but tends, following the example of a loyalty and target rebate, to prevent customers from obtaining their supplies from competitors'.[165] The gist of the Court's approach is to consider whether the rebate was linked to any cost savings that the dominant firm made, so that 'if increasing the quantity supplied results in lower costs for the supplier, the latter is entitled to pass on that reduction to the customer in the form of a more favourable tariff'.[166] On the facts, Michelin failed to show that the rebates were in proportion to the cost savings it had made.

While in almost all cases the dominant firm has failed to justify its discounting policy, several informal settlements suggest that economic justification is not a dead letter in the context of distribution agreements. For example, in the aftermath of *BA/Virgin* the Commission and British Airways agreed on a set of principles that would allow BA (and indeed any other dominant airline) to continue to offer some forms of rebate to travel agents. The principles suggest that the commissions which travel agents receive can be differentiated if these differences reflect: (1) the differing costs of distribution through different travel agents; or (2) differences in the services that travel agents provide. Rebates may be granted at a rate reflecting savings on BA's costs or an increase in the value of services that the travel agent provides. Moreover, commissions must relate to sales made by travel agents in a period not exceeding six months, there must be no sales targets, and the commission paid on any ticket is designed to reward the agent for making the extra sale, not for achieving a given sales target.[167] In a dispute arising from Coca Cola's distribution agreements on the Italian market, the Commission reached a settlement whereby Coca Cola amended its rebate policy and was allowed to offer rebates to distributors that purchased a series of sizes of the same product and to distributors that agreed to carry out additional services (e.g. rearranging and resupplying shelves or carrying out promotional activities). On the contrary, the Commission objected to rebates granted in exchange for exclusivity and rebates conditional on the purchase of other products.[168] A similar settlement

---

[164] E.g. *Michelin 1* [1983] ECR 3461 para. 85.   [165] *Michelin 2* [2003] ECR II-4071 para. 59.

[166] Ibid. para. 98.

[167] The Commission set out its policy on commissions paid by airlines to travel agents in IP/99/504 (14 July 1999).

[168] Coca Cola (IP/88/615, 13 October 1988).

was reached with Interbrew regarding its beer distribution agreements whereby it agreed to eliminate the loyalty-inducing aspects of its distribution system and to redesign its system of financial incentives given to wholesalers that engage in promotional activities. These incentives are to be made available to any wholesaler, and they may not be conditional on buying beer exclusively from Interbrew.[169] And in the aftermath of a finding of abuse in the plasterboard sector, the firm submitted and obtained negative clearance for a series of rebate schemes which were granted in exchange for extra benefits that were received (e.g. additional customer services, reductions in advertising costs and accessing new markets).[170]

In these four cases the Commission guided the parties towards designing distribution agreements that were economically justified. However, there are drawbacks to this procedure whereby objectively justified distribution agreements are obtained by negotiation. First, the Commission has the upper hand in the bargaining process: the fines for an infringement are high and the Court's jurisprudence is strict, so parties prefer to settle rather than face the almost certain adverse finding by the Commission. This allows the Commission to extract settlements that may be more severe than necessary to avoid anticompetitive effects. Second, the early settlements are highly fact specific so they may not be relied upon as precedents in subsequent cases in different markets.[171] Perhaps as a way of offering wider guidance, the settlement with BA provides something akin to a 'Block Exemption' for all dominant airlines. This is a creative approach that provides legal security for several firms but it deprives other dominant airlines of the freedom to negotiate the kinds of distribution agreement that they think is suitable.

6.2 Meeting competition

In the United States, there is a 'meeting competition' defence in the Robinson–Patman Act. The Act forbids price discrimination but provides that such discrimination is lawful when it is applied in order to meet competition from other firms. As we have seen in earlier chapters, references to phrases taken from US antitrust law have done more harm than good in the development of EC competition law, so one should be cautious about this phrase. In particular, the Robinson–Patman Act has been read restrictively in recent years, with the Supreme Court suggesting that its interpretation should be aligned to that of section 2 of the Sherman Act.[172] Given this, the lower courts'

---

[169] 'Commission Closes Probe concerning Interbrew's Practices towards Belgian Beer Wholesalers' IP/04/574 (30 April 2004).

[170] *British Gypsum* [1992] OJ C321/9. Four schemes were granted negative clearance.

[171] For example, in *Michelin 2* [2003] ECR II-4071 the applicant sought to rely on some earlier statements by the Commission on the rebate schemes agreed between British Gypsum and the Commission (see paras. 82–4).

[172] *Brooke Group* 509 US 209 (1993).

case law on the defence may provide little insight. Moreover, the statutory defence applies a standard that does not fit neatly into EC competition policy. The Act provides that the defence applies if the discount offered by the defendant was 'made in good faith to meet an equally low price of a competitor, or the services or facilities furnished by a competitor'.[173] The good faith requirement imports a novel concept into EC competition law which seems unnecessary given that the principle of 'proportionality' can offer a comparable standard. Nevertheless, one can appreciate the sentiment behind this kind of defence: a firm should be able to defend its position in the market when challenged by others. In EC competition law, a non-dominant firm is free to defend itself provided it does not infringe Article 81, but in the context of dominant firms the defence is more complex because a dominant firm's very existence presupposes that it has market power, and any attempt to defend its position means that it will retain the power to harm consumers. However, this defence has been supported because it is necessary to mitigate the harshness of the abuse doctrine, in particular when it comes to discounts offered by dominant firms.[174] The Court has regularly said that a dominant firm is free to defend itself from challenges to its position, but it has yet to identify a scenario where the defence applied. This is because, as Ekaterina Rousseva has put it, the meeting competition defence is a sham.[175] This is clear by considering the Court's oft-repeated phrase:

> the fact that an undertaking is in a dominant position cannot disentitle it from protecting its own commercial interests if they are attacked, and that such an undertaking must be conceded the right to take such reasonable steps as it deems appropriate to protect its interests, provided however that the purpose of such behaviour is not to strengthen this dominant position and abuse it . . . However, the justifications permitted by the case-law in respect of Article [82] of the Treaty cannot result in creating exemptions from the application of that provision. The sole purpose of those grounds of justification is to enable a dominant undertaking to show not that the practices in question should be permitted because they confer certain advantages, but only that the purpose of those practices is reasonably to protect its commercial interests in the face of action taken by certain third parties and that they do not therefore in fact constitute an abuse.[176]

The 'meeting competition defence' is evidence that the practice in question is not an abuse of a dominant position. However, what is puzzling from the Court's case law is that the fact that a dominant firm appears to react to the challenges of competitors can easily become evidence that it intends to abuse

---

[173] 15(1) USC 13(b).

[174] See J. Faull and A. Nikpay *The EC Law of Competition* (Oxford: Oxford University Press, 1999) p. 172; R. O'Donoghue 'Over-Regulating Prices: Time for a Rethink on Pricing Abuses under Article 82 ?' in Ehlermann and Atanasiu *European Competition Law Annual 2003*.

[175] Rousseva 'Concept of "Objective Justification"'.

[176] Joined Cases T-191/98, T-212/98 to T-214/98 *Atlantic Container Line AB and Others v. Commission* [2003] ECR II-3275 paras. 1113–14.

its dominant position. For example, in *AKZO* the dominant firm set a price below ATC but above AVC in what it said was an attempt to win new customers in response to the aggressive tactics deployed by ECS. However, the Court held that the low prices were evidence of an intention to damage ECS because they were 'well below' those charged by the competitor, which 'shows that AKZO's intention was not solely to win the order, which would have induced it to reduce its prices only to the extent necessary for this purpose'.[177] Moreover, *AKZO* seems to suggest that even 'reasonably low prices' would constitute an abuse if these were not offered on a non-discriminatory basis. The Court held that because AKZO gave deeper discounts to ECS customers, this 'shows that AKZO's intention was not to pursue a general policy of favourable prices, but to adopt a strategy that could damage ECS'.[178]

So a dominant firm can quote low prices, but not too low: an impracticable standard. It is not clear from the judgment if AKZO would have avoided a finding of abuse had the price been slightly lower than that charged by ECS but still below ATC and above AVC, or whether AKZO could merely 'match' the prices charged by ECS. And anyway, it is lawful to set low prices only provided these are available on a non-discriminatory basis. AKZO complained that these prohibitions prevented it from ever doing anything in response to competitors' inroads into its market. It said that if ECS approaches an AKZO customer, then it has two choices: either align its prices to those of ECS and offer the same prices to all other comparable customers (i.e. to offer non-discriminatory discounts) or lose the customer. The Court's reply reveals the poverty of its reasoning. In the Court's view AKZO can make 'defensive adjustments, even aligning itself on ECS's prices, in order to keep the customers that were originally its own'.[179] So a dominant firm can give a selective discount (presumably provided the price is not below AVC) only if the price is aligned to that of ECS (so that it is not lower) and only in order to retain a customer. It is not clear how one can be sure of keeping an order if the price must be the same as that of the competitor, nor is it always going to be possible for the dominant firm to find out which of its customers is being targeted by ECS unless the customer informs AKZO. (And in this context it is worth recalling that a dominant firm would probably abuse its dominant position if it inserted a clause in its contracts which entitled the customer to inform the dominant firm of competing offers from others which the dominant firm promises to match).[180] Moreover, if a dominant firm can reduce prices to meet competition, this can deter competitors' incentives to offer lower prices.[181] Thus, not only is the meeting competition defence a sham because there is no defence, but the process of meeting competition is doomed to fail if the response entails below-cost pricing.[182]

[177] *AKZO* [1991] ECR I-3359 para. 102.   [178] Ibid. para. 115.   [179] Ibid. para. 156.
[180] *Hoffmann La Roche* [1979] ECR 461.   [181] Bishop and Walker *Economics* para. 6.43.
[182] Discussion paper on Article 82, para. 83.

However, what of above-cost discounts? As we suggested above, there is little reason to consider above-cost selective discounts as an abuse of a dominant position; however, they have been found abusive when the firm is very powerful and when the firm's conduct partitions the internal market and thus harms one of the core values of EC competition law. In *Irish Sugar*, the defendant sought to justify its discriminatory rebates on the ground that it was responding to competition and the Court said that this was what had to be proven:

> Thus, even if the existence of a dominant position does not deprive an undertaking placed in that position of the right to protect its own commercial interests when they are threatened, the protection of the commercial position of an undertaking in a dominant position with the characteristics of that of the applicant at the time in question must, at the very least, in order to be lawful, be based on criteria of economic efficiency and consistent with the interests of consumers. In this case, the applicant has not shown that those conditions were fulfilled.[183]

Thus, firms that have a significant dominant position have a much harder task than other dominant firms when justifying their responses to competitors' challenges: the response must be efficient and in the interest of consumers. This is very different from the criteria set out in *AKZO* or in the rebate cases. In those cases there is no need to show a benefit to consumers. However, even in this context the Commission has yet to find a single instance where aggressive competition in response to new entry can be justified.

6.3 Economic efficiency

The discussion paper on Article 82 suggests that there can be an efficiency defence in Article 82, modelled upon Article 81(3). This defence differs from the other two we have considered so far in that it would allow the dominant firm to bring to the table certain benefits that result from its actions to justify what may otherwise constitute an abuse. This defence is not consistent with the CFI's dicta in *Atlantic Container* cited above, which suggest that the only way to escape a finding of abuse is to prove that the conduct is not an abuse. Nevertheless, the law must be capable of evolution, and it is worth setting out the Commission's case. Moreover, there is good reason why economic efficiency should play a role in Article 82: the core values of EC competition law are shifting. The current core aims are the promotion of consumer interests and the creation of efficiencies. If so, dominant firms must be able to continue those activities which promote these values even if they cause some harm to the competitive process.

The Commission's suggestion is to apply the same four conditions as under Article 81(3). This requires proof of the following: efficiency; that there is no other way of achieving the efficiency so that the abuse is indispensable; that

[183] *Irish Sugar* [1999] ECR II-2969 para. 189.

the efficiencies benefit consumers; that the abuse does not eliminate competition. The third and the fourth conditions are worth a closer look. In the Commission's eyes consumer benefit is not sufficient: the dominant firm must show that the efficiencies 'outweigh the likely negative effects on competition and therewith the likely harm to consumers that the conduct might otherwise have'.[184] According to the Commission, this occurs when the efficiencies enhance the ability and the incentive of the dominant firm to act to the benefit of consumers. This incentive will not exist when there is little competitive pressure on the firm. This suggests that the efficiency defence is likely to be more successfully invoked when the degree of market power is on the low side. The fourth condition supplements this as the Commission repeats the approach in Article 81(3) by stating that the protection of rivalry and the competitive process is more important than efficiencies, so that if the dominant firm's efficient conduct eliminates all competitors, then the defence will not apply. It is hard to see how these two conditions can be met in a realistic manner. If a firm's dominance is based on its ability to reduce output and increase price, what incentive will it ever have to pass on efficiency gains to consumers? The only way for the defence to play a meaningful role is if we define the concept of dominance as meaning the presence of commercial power to respond to competition. Thus, in a case like *United Brands* where the firm's dominance is proven by its ability to defend its position, an efficiency defence might provide a means to justify otherwise abusive behaviour. However, as we indicated in chapter 5, the correct view is to find that firms that merely have commercial power should not be found dominant. Thus, an 'Article 82(3)' defence has a purpose only when the Commission interprets Article 82 too broadly. If Article 82 is reduced in scope by tightening the concept of dominance and narrowing the notion of abuse, then an efficiency defence is unnecessary.

In the discussion paper, the scope of application of the efficiency defence is limited to rebate and tying abuses. It has been argued that rebates should be justified because they provide dealers with an incentive to market the products more intensely, which is to the benefit of consumers. However, the Commission has not accepted this argument. A rebate can only be efficient when it is granted to a dealer who has market power, and when the rebate convinces the dealer to reduce prices.[185] In the context of tying, the Commission's interpretation of the efficiency defence is almost identical to the Commission's interpretation of the application of Article 81(3) in the *Guidelines on Vertical Restraints*.[186] This suggests that an alternative way of applying the efficiency defence could be to apply Article 81 when a firm

---

[184] Discussion paper on Article 82, para. 87. The same interpretation has been given of this condition in Article 81(3): see *Guidelines on Article 81(3)* [2004] OJ C101/97 para. 85.
[185] Discussion paper on Article 82, para. 174.
[186] Compare ibid. para. 206 with *Guidelines on Vertical Restraints*, para. 222.

engages in tying or rebates. The Commission, as we will see in chapter 10, has already established a framework to consider efficiencies in the context of distribution agreements, so rather than trying to invent an efficiency defence, it might be simpler to avoid applying Article 82 in cases of vertical restraints.[187]

6.4 Public policy

In chapter 4, we noted how in certain circumstances the ECJ has ruled that Article 81 was inapplicable even if the agreement was a patent restriction of competition because the agreement was necessary to promote or safeguard a Community or a national public interest.[188] There is no comparable case law on Article 82; however, the same principles which the Court recognised for Article 81 should apply here, *mutatis mutandis*. First, the EC Treaty provides that if a firm is entrusted with the provision of a service of general economic interest, then it is exempt from the Treaty obligations in so far as this is necessary to provide the service in question, on the basis of Article 86(2), which we consider in more detail in chapter 12. This provision has led to a statutory exemption for several state-created monopolies. Second, when the Court in *Wouters* decided that Article 81 was inapplicable, it did so by reference to its case law on the internal market, suggesting that there is a general principle of Community law whereby the Treaty obligations are inapplicable when their enforcement would undermine legitimate national concerns. Moreover, as some have suggested, *Wouters* is about the relationship between competition law as a whole and other public interest considerations, and is authority for the proposition that there are circumstances where other public interest considerations trump the application of competition law.[189]

An example of the unsuccessful attempt to rely on public policy considerations in the Article 82 context is the argument put forward by Hilti and Tetra Pak that tying agreements were necessary to protect the consumer from harm that could result if the product that these companies sold (nail guns and packaging machines respectively) was not used together with the firms' own brand of parts (nails and cartons respectively). The Court of First Instance held that the tie was a disproportionate way to safeguard the interests of consumers. In both cases the Court said that there are national laws that are designed to protect consumers from unsafe goods, and it was not up to the firm in question to choose to protect consumers unilaterally, because to do so would allow the firm to regulate the market, a job which was for the relevant regulatory authorities. The most that the dominant firm could do was to notify the national authorities of its concerns about the risks to consumers should they

---

[187] As already suggested by Rousseva 'Modernising by Eradicating'.

[188] See ch. 4 pp. 110–13.

[189] A. P. Komninos 'Non-Competition Concerns: Resolution of Conflicts in the Integrated Article 81 EC', Working Paper (L) 08/05 Oxford Centre for Competition Law and Policy (available at www.competition-law.ox.ac.uk/competition/portal.php).

utilise certain components.[190] These two decisions confirm that the dominant firm may take steps to safeguard a public interest when this is the only way to achieve this, but that when there are other, less restrictive measures in place to protect the public interest, then the firm's actions do not merit reprieve.[191]

7 Conclusion: Article 82 redux[192]

7.1 Novel policy directions

The key policy that has underpinned the Community's regulation of dominant firms is to protect the economic freedom of other market participants. The early case law's focus was upon considerations of fairness to those who traded with the dominant firm, while the case law since the 1980s has placed more emphasis upon the elimination of rivals.[193] In ensuring that dominant firms do not thwart the freedom of rivals or other firms, the Court of Justice has expanded the meaning of abuse to ease the burden of proving an infringement, and some recent decisions of the CFI have continued this trend by indicating that an abuse may be found even before the exclusion of rivals can be felt. In *DSD* the Commission summed up its perception of Article 82 in this way:

> The Court has stated in this matter that 'a system of undistorted competition, as laid down in the Treaty, can be guaranteed only if equality of opportunity is secured as between the various economic operators'.[194] Such equality of opportunity is particularly important for new market entrants on a market in which competition is already weakened by the presence of a dominant undertaking and other circumstances. In particular, small competitors should not be the victims of behaviour by a dominant firm, facilitated by that firm's market power, which is designed to exclude those competitors from the market or which has such exclusionary effect.[195]

Equal access to the market is a right valuable in itself, without the need to demonstrate that economic gains flow from its guarantee. However, economic benefits are perceived to flow on the basis that greater numbers of market participants create the disciplined capitalism which lies at the heart of the Community's economic constitution. In addition, the case law suggests that other policies are in play in the application of the abuse doctrine, in particular the protection of a single market. Economic efficiency and consumer benefits

---

[190] Case T-30/89 *Hilti AG v. Commission* [1991] ECR II-1439 paras. 115–19; Case T-83/91 *Tetra Pak International SA v. Commission* [1994] ECR II-755 paras. 138–40.

[191] In a similar vein, Rousseva 'Concept of "Objective Justification"'.

[192] Redux means to be brought back, restored. The title is inspired by John Updike's *Rabbit Redux*.

[193] T. E. Kauper 'The Problem of Market Definition under EC Competition Law' (1997) 20 *Fordham International Law Journal* 1682.

[194] Case C-208/88 *France v. Commission* [1991] ECR I-1271 para. 51.

[195] *DSD* [2001] OJ L166/1 para. 114.

might be an 'indirect' result of the application of Article 82,[196] but they are not the central goals of the abuse doctrine.

The current protective scope of Article 82 is at odds with the changing paradigm of EC competition policy, which has the interests of the consumer at its centre. In some of the case law the Commission and Courts have begun to move towards considering how abuse harms consumer interests, so that the Commission's reform of Article 82 should be seen as an incremental reconsideration of the abuse doctrine.

There is no major 'legal' obstacle to an incremental shift away from the current law. First, as we have noted, the classical and oft-repeated definition of abuse can be reinterpreted in much the same way that Article 81 has been re-read. The fact that abuse 'has the effect of hindering the maintenance of the degree of competition still existing in the market or the growth of that competition'[197] can be interpreted afresh as meaning that abuse has to foreclose rivals. This is the clever re-reading which the Commission offered in its discussion paper on Article 82, and which tallies with the reinterpretation of Article 81 in the Guidelines on the application of Article 81(3). Second, there is nothing in Article 82 itself that limits the protective scope of that provision. Third, it is possible to embrace a more extensive list of 'defences' so as to afford the dominant firm the opportunity of justifying what appears to be anticompetitive behaviour. The law is sufficiently elastic for incremental reform to occur as the policy priorities shift.

The first of the major challenges is whether the Commission is truly committed to relying solely upon an economic paradigm. The implications of this could be that the scope of the abuse doctrine is curtailed significantly and many of the findings of abuse in the seminal cases would no longer be representative of the law. It is submitted that the Commission is not willing to transform Article 82 to such an extent as to abandon some of the fundamental notions that underpin the abuse doctrine. First, it does not accept a total welfare analysis of markets. Conduct which is economically efficient can be prohibited when that conduct would harm the competitive process. Ultimately the economic freedom roots are too strong to give way to a full economic analysis. Second, as noted earlier, the Commission's consideration of 'consumer' welfare can give it the discretion to attack conduct which is not harmful to consumers' economic interests but which the Commission thinks is harmful (rebates that lower prices but reduce choice are harmful to consumer welfare because there is less choice). Third, changing the scope of application of Article 82 risks damaging the interests of the Community. In many cases discussed above the aggressive use of Article 82 has been deployed in markets which have been recently liberalised, and action has been taken to accelerate competition. This policy might be threatened if we reduce the protective scope of Article 82.

[196] AG Kokott in *BA v. Commission* (Opinion of 23 February 2006) para. 68.
[197] *Hoffmann La Roche* [1979] ECR 461 para. 91.

These are policy barriers that limit a complete application of economic standards.

The second challenge is institutional. Under Regulation 1/2003 enforcement of EC competition law is decentralised, and this makes it more difficult for a policy change to occur given that there are several loci of enforcement. Had the Commission remained the sole enforcer of Article 82, it would be relatively unproblematic to announce a change of direction in its policy and publish guidelines that explain its new policy priorities. However, with decentralisation it is trickier to ensure that all enforcers apply new principles. The technique that was used in Article 81 was to publish a number of exemption decisions in a range of sectors and to publish Guidelines to aid national authorities. It remains to be seen whether the Commission will embark on a comparable strategy by bringing fresh Article 82 cases and applying novel methods. The discussion paper has already been published in the form of Guidelines, so a similar pattern of coordination is emerging.

The third challenge is whether, bearing in mind the Commission's reluctance to rely solely upon economic analysis, it should deploy a unified economic standard for the abuse doctrine. We consider this in the section below.

7.2 A unifying economic paradigm?

The Commission's reconsideration of the abuse doctrine chimes with a similar debate in the United States over the role of s. 2 of the Sherman Act, and competing economic models have been presented.[198] Those who propose a unified test to identify exclusionary behaviour share the following starting points. First, exclusionary tactics are a two-stage strategy: in the first stage the dominant firm embarks on a strategy to harm competitors, and once it has damaged them by eliminating them, or by raising their costs, or by deterring them from entering the market, then in the second stage the dominant firm will exploit its newly acquired market power. Second, the law must punish only exclusionary behaviour that reduces consumer welfare. The aim is to protect consumers, not competitors. Third, because economists view exclusionary behaviour as a strategy that takes time to play out, then competition law must intervene before this strategy is successful. That is, we want to catch exclusionary behaviour before there has been exclusion. The reason is that if we intervene after the dominant firm has eliminated competitors, there is no remedy for the market failure, so intervention can only be effective if it prevents the elimination of competitors. However, early intervention creates a risk of being over-inclusive. Thus, what we need is a test that allows us to predict with some precision whether the dominant firm's conduct will harm

---

[198] See T. O. Barnett 'The Gales of Creative Destruction: The Need for Clear and Objective Standards for Enforcing Section 2 of the Sherman Act' (speech, 20 June 2006) (available at www.usdoj.gov) introducing the Section 2 Hearings.

competition. Taking these premises as given, commentators have suggested three approaches.[199] One is to ask whether the conduct is likely to harm consumer welfare. Two other approaches suggest that the harm to consumer welfare question can be asked in a less direct manner, either by asking whether the dominant firm's conduct can eliminate a competitor that is at least as efficient as the dominant firm, or by asking whether the dominant firm's conduct makes no economic sense but for its tendency to harm competition (the 'sacrifice test').[200] Below, I explore each of these tests briefly in the context of predatory pricing.

The no-economic-sense test is proposed by several American commentators and it asks whether the conduct makes no economic sense but for the tendency to harm competition.[201] Put another way, it asks whether it is possible to explain that the conduct of the dominant firm can benefit consumers. If there is no consumer welfare explanation, then the behaviour is harmful. The test clearly applies to predatory pricing: prices below AVC when recoupment is possible make no economic sense unless the prey exits the market. The as-efficient-competitor test instead provides that the abuse doctrine should prohibit conduct that is capable of eliminating rivals who are no less efficient than the dominant firm. This standard works comfortably with below-cost pricing but does not require proof of recoupment: if the dominant firm prices below cost and can do so because it has superior financial resources (e.g. a deep pocket) then its behaviour can eliminate a rival who is as efficient as it (that is, a firm with identical production costs). In sum, the as-efficient-competitor test probably allows one to find abuse more easily than the no-economic-sense test, and sits comfortably with the current EC doctrine, based as it is on foreclosure. These methods are preferable to attempts to determine harm to consumers directly. The difficulty with a consumer welfare standard is about what standard of proof one selects. Must one show that the conduct tends to harm consumers, or must one show that harm to consumers is highly probable? A low standard of proof leads one to make Type 1 errors, but too high a standard of proof can cause Type 2 errors.

However, there is another perspective through which to consider the reform of Article 82 if one is minded to look for a common denominator. These cases, broadly speaking, have three limbs: dominance, abuse and a lack of objective justification. The three tests above try to refine the second and the third limbs. The no-economic-sense test in particular seems to invite the defendant to prove why its conduct makes economic sense. These models often ignore the

---

[199] The following discussion is based largely on J. Vickers 'Abuse of Market Power' (2005) 115 *Economic Journal* F244.

[200] For a succinct explanation, see G. J. Werden 'Competition Policy on Exclusionary Conduct: Toward an Effects-based Analysis?' (2006) 2 *European Competition Journal* (Special Issue on Article 82) 53.

[201] See e.g. A. D. Melamed 'Exclusive Dealing Agreements and Other Exclusionary Conduct – Are there Unifying Principles?' (2006) 73 *Antitrust Law Journal* 375.

starting point: Article 82 is infringed only when a firm is dominant. The reason this is ignored is because for economists dominance is irrelevant. Exclusionary conduct either is or is not deleterious for consumers. However, because in EC competition law Article 82 can be invoked only if the firm is dominant, then reform of the dominance test might affect how we think about abuse. As I suggested in chapter 5, dominance is found too easily, merely upon proof of commercial strength. If dominance instead meant the power to reduce output and increase price, then the scope of Article 82 would be reduced significantly, applying only to firms who already have the power to harm consumers. Then, in this regime we might be willing to tolerate a strict 'abuse' doctrine where proof of likely foreclosure is sufficient to find an abuse. Applied to predatory pricing, this allows the competition authority to take into consideration post-Chicago theories of predation (e.g. predation by reputation) and it justifies not asking whether recoupment is feasible because the firm is already able to price above cost before the abuse. As the Commission states repeatedly, rivalry is the key to a healthy competitive process. Foreclosure that stymies rivalry could be a blunt test to apply at the start of all abuse cases, but the risk of Type 1 errors is reduced by shrinking the scope of application only to firms with real market power.

7

Abuse of a dominant position: from competition policy to sector-specific regulation

Contents

1. Introduction	*page* 216
2. Exploitative abuse	217
2.1 Excessive prices under Article 82	218
2.2 Price controls by bespoke regulators	220
3. Refusal to cooperate with competitors	223
3.1 From economic freedom to consumer welfare	224
3.2 Refusal to license intellectual property rights	227
3.3 Essential facilities: from competition to regulation	231
3.4 Essential facilities outside Article 82	234
3.5 The duty to cooperate with rivals: a synthesis	239
3.6 Defences	240
3.7 Remedies	242
4. Regulatory competition law	243

1 Introduction

In chapter 6 we considered a range of tactics through which the dominant firm reacted to the challenges posed by existing competitors, or tried to exclude competitors to expand its market power. The behaviour of dominant firms we study in this chapter is motivated by different considerations. In section 2 we examine how competition law regulates excessive prices and reductions of productive efficiency, the traditional harms associated with monopoly power. In section 3 we examine situations where a dominant firm is able to prevent the entry of new competitors, by refusing to engage in cooperative contractual relationships with them.

The reason for considering these two types of abuse together is that when a competition authority intervenes in these scenarios its objective is the creation of a more competitive market. This is a slightly different task from that performed when tackling the abuses in chapter 6. When a firm engages in predatory pricing, raises rivals' costs or leverages its position, it does so to damage rivals and to maintain or augment pre-eminence in the market. Competition law prevents the firm from damaging the competitive process. Instead, when a firm raises prices, it means that the competitive process has already been destroyed, and the firm is exploiting the position it is in. Regulating the dominant firm's prices makes it perform 'as if' it were in a competitive market. The same applies in situations where a dominant firm refuses to cooperate with potential rivals: perhaps it owns some key technology without which market access is impossible. If a competition authority requires the firm to share that technology, it is forced to subsidise the entry of competitors so as to create a more competitive market. We must question whether the role of competition law is to improve markets, or whether its role should be limited to deterring firms from damaging the operation of markets. In the United States, courts are chary of imposing such obligations: 'The Sherman Act is indeed the Magna Carta of free enterprise, but it does not give judges carte blanche to insist that a monopolist alter its way of doing business whenever some other approach might yield greater competition.'[1]

A second similarity in the two forms of abuse considered in this chapter lies in the nature of the remedy: in the abuses discussed in chapter 6 a fine and a prohibitory injunction may suffice to put an end to anticompetitive conduct and deter the firm, but in the abuses considered here, a mandatory injunction is necessary as is regular supervision so that the dominant firm continues to behave in ways that make markets work better. We should question whether a competition authority should get involved in regulating industries so closely. In an early monopolisation case in the US, Judge Learned Hand's classic dictum suggests caution in attacking a winning firm: 'The successful competitor, having been urged to compete, must not be turned upon when he wins.'[2] This dictum finds little resonance in the doctrines we consider below.

A third reason for treating these two forms of abuse separately is that access and prices are also regulated by legal means other than Article 82, so that we find that concepts developed to regulate dominant firms are transplanted from their antitrust soil and grafted onto sector-specific regulation, and used to achieve a related but distinct set of policy ambitions.

2 Exploitative abuse

Many say that the best prize for a monopolist is the quiet life that the firm enjoys after having achieved dominance. Surrounded by entry barriers, it has no need to innovate or to cut costs. However, in some circumstances sloth can be an abuse of a dominant position. This arises in particular where the dominant firm enjoys its dominance by virtue of a state-granted monopoly.

---

[1] *Verizon Communications Inc. v. Law Offices of Curtis V. Trinko LLP* 540 US 398, 415 (2004).
[2] *US v. Aluminum Co. of America* 148 F 2d 416, 430 (2d Cir. 1945).

In *Merci Convenzionali Porto di Genova*, a contractual dispute arose between a shipper and dock workers in the Italian port of Genoa. The shipper claimed that the dock workers had delayed unloading his goods, causing loss. During the litigation it transpired that the dock workers had a statutory monopoly. The Court of Justice referred to Article 82(a), (b) and (c) and suggested that the dock workers' failures might constitute an infringement of these provisions either because the firm asks for payment for services that have not been requested, or because the prices are excessive, or because the firm refused 'to have recourse to modern technology, which involves an increase in the cost of the operations and a prolongation of the time required for their performance'.[3]

In spite of these findings, which are derived from a literal interpretation of Article 82, the Commission has avoided developing the abuse doctrine to penalise lazy monopolists. Instead, as we explore more fully in chapter 12, inefficiency can be the basis upon which the state's decision to confer a monopoly on a firm is challenged. A little more effort has been devoted to regulating excessive pricing, and we explore the Commission's strategy below.

2.1 Excessive prices under Article 82

Whilst economics textbooks identify output reduction and price increases as the main objection against monopoly, competition authorities have attacked excessive prices very rarely.[4] There are several reasons for this. First, reduced output and higher prices are the hallmarks of monopoly, but to challenge all monopolists would imply that holding a dominant position is unlawful *per se*. Second, penalising a firm for excessive pricing can remove incentives to reduce costs and innovate. As the Supreme Court explained, the 'opportunity to charge monopoly prices – at least for a short period – is what attracts "business acumen" in the first place; it induces risk taking that produces innovation and economic growth'.[5] Third, high prices invite entrants that challenge the dominant firm to obtain profits.[6] Fourth, it is difficult to determine an abusive price. Every firm has enough market power to price above marginal cost, so the competition authority has the delicate if not impossible task of distinguishing

---

[3] Case C-179/90 *Merci Convenzionali Porto di Genova SpA v. Siderurgica Gabrielli SpA* [1991] ECR I-5889 para. 19.

[4] For an illuminating account, see M. Motta and A. de Streel 'Exploitative and Exclusionary Excessive Prices in EU Law' in C.-D. Ehlermann and I. Atanasiu (eds.) *European Competition Law Annual 2003: What is an Abuse of a Dominant Position?* (Oxford: Hart Publishing, 2006).

[5] *Verizon* 540 US 398, 407 (2004). See also L. Gyselen 'Abuse of Monopoly Power within the Meaning of Article 86 of the EEC Treaty: Recent Developments' 1989 *Fordham Corporate Law Institute* 597, 598–9 (Hawk ed. 1990).

[6] *Berkey Photo Inc. v. Eastman Kodak Co.* 603 F 2d 263, 294 (2d Cir. 1979). In contrast, the Office of Fair Trading has argued that excessive prices constitute abuse only when there is no present or foreseeable competitor that could force a price reduction by the dominant firm. See *Napp Pharmaceutical Holdings Ltd* CA98/2/2001 [2001] UKCLR 597 (para. 203), which may suggest that certain national competition authorities will be more eager than the Commission to regulate high prices.

between tolerably high and excessively high prices. Fifth, if competition authorities began to compute appropriate price levels they would stray from their core
task and become regulators.[7] Some of these difficulties were evidenced when the
Commission accused United Brands of setting excessive prices for bananas and
recommended that prices be dropped by 15 per cent. In reply the parties noted
that this injunction made little sense: the banana market was so volatile that it
was impossible to comply with the Commission's order. Further resolution of
this difficulty was avoided when the ECJ overturned the Commission's decision
on this point. However, the Court failed to articulate a clear standard for
identifying excessive pricing, merely stating that a price is excessive if it bears
no relation to the economic value of the product, a criterion applied by
comparing the cost of production with the selling price.[8] This is highly uninformative because even non-dominant firms are able to price above cost, and it
fails to resolve the question of how much above cost the price must be for it to
be excessive.

When references were made to the ECJ from national courts to clarify the
standard by which to identify excessive prices, the Court was short on detail:
during the disputes in France between the collecting society (SACEM) and
discotheques, the ECJ's contribution to the question of excessive pricing was
to suggest that if the fees charged by SACEM were appreciably higher than those
charged by collecting societies in other Member States, this would be an indication that prices were excessive; but this indicator is insufficient.[9] Moreover, the
Court complicated matters by suggesting that the difference between price and
cost should be based on the costs of an efficient operator, and not necessarily the
costs of the defendant whose dominance may have led to increased production
costs.[10] However, this standard is even more difficult to apply. Accordingly,
there is no workable policy to identify and penalise excessive pricing.[11]

---

[7] 'The antitrust laws do not deputize district judges as one-man regulatory agencies', *Chicago
Professional Sport Ltd Partnership v. NBA* 95 F 3d 953, 957 (7th Cir. 1996); D. F. Turner 'The
Definition of Agreement Under the Sherman Act: Conscious Parallelism and Refusal to Deal'
[1962] 75 *Harvard Law Review* 655, 681.

[8] Case 27/76 *United Brands v. Commission* [1978] ECR 207.

[9] Case 395/87 *Ministère Public v. Tournier* [1989] ECR 2521 para. 38; Joined Cases 110/88, 241/88
and 242/88 *Lucazeau v. SACEM* [1989] ECR 2811 para. 25. The same point that prices in one
market could be compared with those in another was made in Case 30/87 *Bodson v. SA Pompes
funèbres des régions libérées* [1988] ECR 2479.

[10] This is implicit in *SACEM* [1989] ECR 2811 at para. 42.

[11] But it has applied this norm, e.g. in *DSD* [2001] OJ L166/1, where one firm monopolised the
market for waste collection and entry barriers were so high that no new entry was expected.
Moreover, the relevant German environmental laws had not made provision for preventing
monopoly pricing. However, in this instance the excessive pricing abuse was part of a broader
exclusionary strategy by DSD (see e.g. para. 102). In the UK context see *Napp Pharmaceutical
Holdings Limited and Subsidiaries v. Director General of Fair Trading* [2002] CAT 1, where a
finding of excessive pricing was made in respect of a firm with a market share of 96 per cent and
high entry barriers where the Pharmaceutical Price Regulations Scheme agreed by firms and the
Secretary of State for Health under the Health Act 1999 made no provisions to check excessive
pricing.

There has been little Commission enforcement against excessive pricing; instead the Commission has announced a preference to apply Article 82 to exclusionary abuses.[12] Nevertheless, the Commission has been active in regulating prices in newly liberalised sectors, in particular in the field of telecommunications. The reason for this is strategic, in two ways. First it is a means of obtaining support for its deregulatory agenda. As one senior Commission official noted, the Commission's actions against excessive prices are 'aimed particularly at passing on rapidly the advantages of liberalisation in terms of price reductions and service developments to consumers – a major objective in order to show as rapidly as possible the effective consumer benefits and to secure sustained public support for liberalisation'.[13] Second, the Commission's strategy has not been to reach decisions under Article 82, but to launch investigations and use these to put pressure on firms and National Regulatory Authorities in charge of telecommunications to achieve price reductions. In 1998 for example, it commenced fifteen cases, one against each Member State, alleging that interconnection charges for calls from mobile to fixed phones were excessive, but these were dropped as firms agreed to reduce charges or the Commission agreed that National Regulatory Authorities would address the price concerns.[14] It reached a similar result when it challenged certain charges of Deutsche Telekom to competitors: the Commission dropped the case once satisfied that the National Regulatory Authority would regulate prices.[15]

2.2 Price controls by bespoke regulators

The role of price control by bespoke regulators is different from that achieved under Article 82. Three examples of price control drawn from the field of telecommunications can help us to see the differences.

First, we can consider two important features of telecommunications: access to the local loop and interconnection. The local loop is an (upstream) infrastructure that connects each house to the telecommunications network. This is normally the property of the former state monopoly telephone provider who is now in competition with several other providers of (downstream) telecommunication services. New competitors must have access to the local loop to provide services because it is uneconomical to duplicate this part of the network. For instance, a new entrant wishing to provide internet services in competition with the former state monopoly must be able to connect his services to the local loop that is still owned by the incumbent. The second characteristic of telecommunications is that it is a network market, where

---

[12] *Twenty-fourth Report on Competition Policy* (1994) para. 207.
[13] H. Ungerer 'Use of EC Competition Rules in the Liberalisation of the European Union's Telecommunications Sector: Assessment of Past Experiences and Some Conclusions' (2001) 2 *Competition Policy Newsletter* 16, 19–20.
[14] Press Release IP 98/1036 of 26 November 1998.   [15] Press Release IP 98/430 of 13 May 1998.

interconnection between users of different networks is essential for the success of a new entrant – the entrant's users must be able to communicate with users of other networks. Interconnection prices must be competitive or else consumers will not buy the services of new entrants.

In both of these scenarios, when the owner of the local loop is also the largest provider of telephone services, it has no incentive to facilitate entry of competitors, and so the law may impose access remedies and regulate the prices of access to the local loop and interconnections. Note that in these two contexts (markets exhibiting natural monopoly characteristics and network effects) the regulatory ambition of the Community is not merely to prevent anticompetitive behaviour, but to inject more competition by facilitating the entry of new firms by regulating access and price.

The Community imposes duties on National Regulatory Authorities (NRAs) to regulate price, subject to guidance established by the Commission. In regulating prices for access to the local loop the NRA must take into account a variety of policy objectives: first, that prices foster fair and effective competition; second, to ensure economic efficiency and maximum benefit of users; third, to monitor that prices are cost-oriented. Cost-orientation means that the local loop provider can cover costs plus a reasonable return, so that he has the incentive to develop and upgrade the local loop. Moreover, the price should give incentives to the requiring firms to develop competing infrastructure so as to eliminate their dependence on the incumbent's local loop.[16] The effect of these rules is that prices should be low enough to encourage new entrants, but high enough to encourage the incumbent to maintain the network and stimulate the construction of competing networks. This is a tricky mix of policies, and NRAs have yet to devise the most effective pricing structure.[17] Similar guidance applies when NRAs regulate interconnection prices where account must be taken of the operator's investments so as to allow a reasonable rate of return.[18] This achieves two aims: to ensure that the firm that grants interconnection has incentives to develop and maintain the infrastructure, and to inject competition by facilitating entry.

These two examples show that there are similarities with Article 82, but also divergences. The reason for intervention (market power) is comparable, but the differences lie in the timing of intervention (which may be *ex ante*, to prevent excessive prices), in the institution (a specialised body, not a competition authority or a court), and in the variety of policy goals (not just protecting

[16] Articles 3(3), 4(1) and (4), Recital 11, Regulation 2887/2000 on Unbundled Access to the Local Loop [2000] OJ L336/4.

[17] J. Delgado, J. Fehrenbach and R. Klotz 'The Price of Access: The Unbundling of the Local Loop in the EU' in P. A. Buigues and P. Rey (eds.) *The Economics of Antitrust and Regulation in Telecommunications: Perspectives for the New European Regulatory Framework* (Cheltenham: Edward Elgar, 2004).

[18] Article 13(1) Directive 2002/19 on Access to, and Interconnection of, Electronic Communication Networks and Associated Facilities (Access Directive) [2002] OJ L108/7.

buyers from high prices) that must be taken into consideration when determining an appropriate price.

A second example can be found in Article 30 of the Universal Service Directive.[19] This provides that consumers should be able to switch from one telecommunications provider to another and retain their telephone numbers. Consumers are more likely to switch if they can hold on to their telephone numbers so this facility is very important to encourage new telephone service providers, as it lowers entry barriers. However, switching is not costless. If a subscriber wishes to change from, say, Vodafone (in the jargon, the donor operator) to Orange (in the jargon, the recipient operator), Vodafone incurs costs to ensure that the number is portable. It will charge Orange to recover these costs when the consumer switches. The consumer may well pay nothing directly, but if the charges set by the donor operator are too high, then some of the costs result in higher bills for users of the recipient operator, and consumers will not switch. Article 30(2) empowers the NRA to ensure that the prices are cost-oriented and that if the consumer has to pay for this, the level is not such as to act as a disincentive for the use of number portability. The Belgian regulator recently made use of this provision to regulate the wholesale charges of donor operators. In Belgium, Belgacom, the major provider of mobile phone services, had a market share greater than 50 per cent and faced competition from two relatively new entrants (Mobilstar and Base). Given Belgacom's market position, it had an incentive to hamper number portability. The Court of Justice, in approving the Belgian NRA's approach to price regulation, noted especially that when the donor is a large firm, then effective price controls are crucial to guarantee a competitive market.[20] This example is a little different from the previous one. While the regulator is concerned about injecting more competition in the market, the power to intervene does not depend on finding a firm with a dominant position. On the facts of the Belgian case, the former state monopoly did have a dominant position but this is not a precondition for price regulation under the directive. Moreover, the prices controls applied to all firms, as any of the three could be donor operators.

A third example is price controls that apply in relation to goods and services the state decides should be available to all at affordable rates. In Community law, these are labelled universal services. The Universal Service Directive imposes an obligation on NRAs to monitor retail rates to ensure that they are affordable for those on low incomes or with special needs.[21] In this context, the link with Article 82 is non-existent. The market is not regulated

---

[19] Directive 2002/22 on Universal Service and Users' Rights relating to Electronic Communications Networks and Services (Universal Service Directive) [2002] OJ L108/51.

[20] Case C-438/04 *Mobistar SA v. IBPT*, judgment of 13 July 2006, para. 29.

[21] Article 9 Universal Service Directive.

to achieve efficiency or consumer welfare: retail prices are controlled to achieve fairness.

This brief overview of price controls in electronic communications indicates a doctrinal and policy overlap between Article 82 and sector-specific regulation carried out at national level on the basis of a common EU-wide framework. Both share an interest in economic efficiency and consumer welfare. Regulation is wider in its ambit, however: not only is it designed to promote competition rather than merely prevent its deterioration, but other goals (e.g. development of the industry and fair access to basic services) are also pursued.

3 Refusal to cooperate with competitors

In certain circumstances, dominant firms have an obligation to facilitate the entry of other firms, in particular of competitors, but there is no certainty about when this duty arises. The case law can be read to suggest that there are four related doctrines. The first (which we have observed in chapter 6, and which was identified in *United Brands*) is that a dominant firm cannot rescind a contract with a firm that is not in competition with it unless there is justification.[22] The second doctrine (considered in section 3.1 below) began life by suggesting that a dominant firm must facilitate the existence of competitors. As with the first doctrine, this is grounded in the economic freedom paradigm, but there are signs that the Court is shifting away from this rationale and imposing a duty to help rivals only when this would increase consumer welfare. The third doctrine (considered in section 3.2) applies when the dominant firm refuses to share intellectual property rights with competitors. Here, the obligation to share is imposed only if a stricter test is met, which is consonant with the trend towards a consumer welfare model. This is because the person wishing to obtain access to information protected by intellectual property rights must show that this information will be used to provide a new product and benefit consumers. The fourth doctrine (considered in section 3.3) emerges from decisions where the obligation to cooperate with rivals was imposed in markets where Member States have granted monopoly rights to privileged firms, and which the EC has sought to liberalise. Here, the Commission imposed obligations to cooperate with rivals with scant regard to the limitations set out by the ECJ in the case law considered in sections 3.1 and 3.2. Subsequently, the fourth doctrine has led to legislation to ensure market access as a means of securing the injection of greater competition into newly liberalised economic sectors (discussed in section 3.4). After considering the difficulties of moving towards a unified doctrine (section 3.5), we explore what defences are available to justify a refusal to cooperate with rivals (section 3.6) and finally consider how the obligation to cooperate is enforced (section 3.7).

---

[22] See pp. 196–7.

3.1 From economic freedom to consumer welfare

The Court's first significant judgment on refusals to supply illustrates the prominence of the economic freedom approach. In *Commercial Solvents* a firm dominant in the market for a raw material (aminobutanol) chose to extend its activities in the downstream market for a derivative of that raw material (ethambutol, an anti-tubercular drug). In so doing it ceased supplying Zoja, a firm operating in the market of the derivative. The Commission was concerned that this would eliminate 'one of the principal producers of ethambutol in the Common Market . . . mak[ing] a heavy blow at the maintenance of effective conditions of competition within the Common Market'.[23] Similarly, the ECJ upheld the finding of abuse on the basis that Zoja would be eliminated as a competitor.[24] The Court and Commission focused on Zoja's potential elimination as the evidence of competitive harm, to the extent that a number of commentators have suggested that the decision sought to protect a small European firm against the might of its American supplier. This criticism is given further credence by the fact that other firms were present in the ethambutol market: American Cyanamid and two smaller firms. There was little to suggest that the price of ethambutol would rise.[25] Moreover, it was alleged, although not considered, that aminobutanol was available from other sources and that ethambutol could be manufactured with other chemicals; thus Zoja was not necessarily going to leave the market, although it would have to make some adjustments to stay.[26]

The Court returned to consider refusals to contract in *Telemarketing*. The RTL television station held a dominant position in the market for advertisements directed at the French-speaking community in Belgium. It had allowed CBEM to broadcast telemarketing advertisements (where the advertisement has a telephone number which the customer can ring to order the product advertised). RTL subsequently refused to allow such advertisements unless the telephone numbers were those of its telemarketing subsidiary, and not those of CBEM. The Court said that there would be an abuse when the dominant firm holds a dominant position in a service that is indispensable for the other firm, and where the refusal would eliminate all competition from the competitor.[27] The abuse here (unlike that in *Commercial Solvents*) would necessarily eliminate CBEM from the market and would allow RTL to dominate the downstream market – the restriction of economic freedom was clearer here than in

[23] *Zoja v. Commercial Solvents* [1972] JO L299/51; [1973] CMLR D50.
[24] Joined Cases 6 and 7/73 *Istituto Chemioterapico Italiano SpA v. Commission* [1974] ECR 223 para. 25.
[25] Unless the Commission was concerned that Commercial Solvents and American Cyanamid were going to collude, an allegation made by Zoja ([1972] JO L299/51; [1973] CMLR D50 para. 1.bb).
[26] *Istituto Chemioterapico Italiano* [1974] ECR 223 recital 15.
[27] Case 311/84 *Centre belge d'études de marché – Télémarketing (CBEM) v. Compagnie luxembourgeoise de télédiffusion (CLT)* [1985] ECR 3261 para. 26.

Commercial Solvents because the dominant firm's refusal to cooperate eliminated all competitors from the market, not only one firm.

The Court returned to consider this matter in *Oscar Bronner*, where the factual matrix was slightly different in that there had been no prior contract between the dominant firm and the firm requesting access.[28] The dispute arose when Mediaprint, a major newspaper publisher in Austria, devised a home delivery service for its newspapers and refused to deliver the plaintiff's newspapers through this service. The Court characterised this dispute as one where an upstream product (the home delivery service) was used to facilitate the sales of the downstream product (newspapers) and the question was whether the refusal to give the plaintiff access to the distribution system constituted an abuse. The Court held that there would be an abuse where: (1) a firm in a dominant position in one market (e.g. the market for newspaper deliveries) refuses to supply a firm with which it is in competition in a neighbouring market with raw materials or services which are 'indispensable to carrying on *the rival's business*' and (2) where the refusal is 'likely to eliminate all competition *on the part of that undertaking*'[29] and (3) where there is no objective justification for the refusal. In setting out this three-stage test the Court seems concerned about injury to a rival (note the singular in the italicised passages above) not about injury to consumer welfare. In this light, all three judgments (*Telemarketing*, *Commercial Solvents* and *Bronner*) reflect a concern about ensuring that market players remain on the market, rather than about ensuring that markets are efficient or that consumers benefit. The Court's stance is at odds with the advice offered by Advocate General Jacobs in *Bronner*. He stated that 'the primary purpose of [Article 82] is to prevent distortion of competition – and in particular to safeguard the interests of consumers – rather than to protect the position of particular competitors'.[30] In his Opinion, consumer harm does not result from the elimination of a competitor unless the dominant firm has gained or would gain a dominant position in the downstream market. On the facts of this dispute, there would be no abuse unless the refusal gave the firm a monopoly in the newspaper market. Referring to the recent increase in sales of Bronner's newspapers, he indicated that this was inconsistent with the view that Mediaprint's upstream distribution network was essential to compete in the downstream market.[31] The Advocate General also reinterpreted *Commercial Solvents* as an instance where, absent Zoja, consumers would face a monopoly supplier of the anti-tubercular drug in question, which had no substitutes.[32] Thus, in his view, unless the refusal to supply creates a monopoly,

---

[28] Some authors argue that there are two distinct doctrines, one applying to a termination of an existing relationship and another applying to the refusal to enter into a fresh supply contract. The debate is reviewed in C. Ritter 'Refusals to Deal and Essential Facilities: Does Intellectual Property Require Special Deference Compared to Tangible Property?' (2005) 28 *World Competition* 281, 282–5.

[29] Case C-7/97 *Oscar Bronner v. Mediaprint* [1998] ECR I-7791 para. 38.

[30] Ibid. para. 58.   [31] Ibid. para. 67.   [32] Ibid. paras. 59–60.

there can be no consumer harm and so no need to apply Article 82. The Advocate General's consumer welfare orientation contrasts with the economic freedom approach of the Court.

However, the *Bronner* judgment is difficult to interpret because while in formulating the test for abuse the Court embraces the economic freedom themes of the previous case law, in later paragraphs the Court follows the Advocate General's definition of indispensability under the first step of the test. Thus, rather than considering whether Mediaprint's network is indispensable for Bronner, it considers the wider question of whether creating an alternative distribution network is economically viable, assessed objectively, not subjectively. In this respect the Court follows the Advocate General's advice that an obligation to cooperate would only arise if it is 'extremely difficult not merely for the undertaking demanding access but *for any other undertaking to compete*'.[33] The Court's judgment is confusing: in the early parts it displays concerns about the elimination of *the* competitor seeking access, but in defining the notion of indispensability it asks whether *any* actual or potential competitor would find Mediaprint's distribution network indispensable, an objective test which is more consistent with an economic analysis which asks whether the refusal to supply creates a monopoly in the downstream market. Reading the Court's judgment as a whole, *Bronner* restricts the dominant firm's obligation to supply to cases where the dominant firm's property is truly indispensable so that a refusal leads to the creation of a dominant position in a second market. Therefore today a case like *Commercial Solvents* would be analysed in a different manner, by looking at Zoja's alternatives for staying in the market and considering whether patients would have alternative suppliers should Zoja be forced from the market. *Bronner* indicates a shift away from the economic freedom model. The concern remains with the risk of foreclosing market access, but the Court now only finds an abuse when the firms that risk foreclosure are as efficient as the dominant firm and still unable to enter the market. In these circumstances, foreclosure of efficient rivals harms consumer welfare by depriving the market of a worthy participant.

This line of cases suggests that a dominant firm has an obligation to continue to cooperate, or to begin to cooperate, with actual or potential competitors. This empowers the competition authority to facilitate the growth of markets. One aspect of the *Bronner* decision which is uncertain is whether anyone has a right to secure the cooperation of the dominant firm once it has been shown that the dominant firm's good or service is indispensable to create a competitive downstream market, or whether the right to access is limited in some ways. The salience of this question will become relevant when we consider the third doctrine below, where access to assets protected by intellectual property rights is made subject to stricter conditions.

[33] Ibid. para. 46.

3.2 Refusal to license intellectual property rights

Ownership of an intellectual property (IP) right does not necessarily mean one has a monopoly, it only allows the owner to exclude others from using that property, so an author's copyright over a book on competition law does not create a monopoly in the market for competition law books, much as each author would like that to be the result. On the other hand, a patent right over the only medicine to cure a particular ailment confers on the owner a dominant position.

In the principal cases where the IP right conferred a dominant position on the owner, the Court has required, as with the doctrine examined above, evidence that the refusal to license the IP right eliminates all competition on the part of the firm requiring access and that the IP right should be indispensable to carrying on that business in that there are no actual or potential substitutes, so that competition in the downstream market where the IP rights are exploited is eliminated.[34] In addition, the person seeking a licence of the IP right must point to *exceptional circumstances* that justify the request.[35] In *Volvo* (a reference to the ECJ for a preliminary ruling upon Volvo's refusal to supply third parties with a licence for the manufacture of car spare parts) the Court suggested that 'arbitrary' refusals to independent repairers would constitute an abuse.[36] Unfortunately, the Court did not elaborate upon what this meant; however, as competition law tends to protect independent repairers it is likely that the Court had in mind a scenario where the refusal would harm small enterprises.[37] (The Court also suggested that it would be abusive to sell the parts at excessive prices, or to refuse to sell parts for old models, forcing consumers to scrap their cars, although these forms of abuse have nothing to do with refusals to license.)[38] In the *Magill* case, the exceptional circumstances related to consumer welfare. Three broadcasters refused to license their copyright-protected TV listings (a list of what's on TV on their channels) to a firm wishing to compile all the TV listings for Irish terrestrial channels so that the consumers could buy a comprehensive weekly TV guide rather than three separate weekly guides produced by the broadcasters. The refusal was held to be an abuse of a dominant position because: (i) it prevented the emergence of a new product for which there is a potential consumer demand, (ii) it reserved the market for TV guides to the three broadcasters, and (iii) there was no objective justification for the refusal.[39] The Court took the same approach in *IMS Health*.[40] In this case the dominant firm had a monopoly in the provision

---

[34] Case C-418/01 *IMS Health GmbH & Co. OHG v. NDC Health GmbH & Co. KG* [2004] ECR I-5039 para. 37.

[35] Case 238/87 *Volvo v. Veng* [1988] ECR 6211 para. 9; Joined Cases C-241/91P and C-242/91P *RTE and ITP v. Commission (Magill)* [1995] ECR I-743 para. 50; *IMS Health* [2004] ECR I-5039 para. 35.

[36] *Volvo* [1988] ECR 6211 para. 9; Case 53/87 *CICRA v. Renault* [1988] ECR 6039 para. 16.

[37] See pp. 148–50.   [38] *Volvo* [1988] ECR 6211 para. 9.

[39] *Magill* [1995] ECR I-743 paras. 52–8.   [40] [2004] ECR I-5039.

of market reports, which it sold to pharmaceutical companies. It was dominant because it was able to arrange the data according to a geographical set of criteria (a so-called brick structure) over which it had a copyright. Pharmaceutical companies would only buy market studies when the data were arranged according to that brick structure. The Court applied the ruling in *Magill* and advised that there would be an abuse only if the firm requesting the copyright licence intended to produce new services, not offered by the copyright owner, for which there is potential consumer demand.[41] While the three conditions in the *Magill* test are cumulative, they are but an illustration of a factual matrix where, exceptionally, a duty to license may be imposed.

The reason why the Courts impose an obligation to license only in exceptional circumstances is because there is a presumption that a refusal to license IP rights benefits the economy. The grant of an IP right is designed 'to motivate the creative activity of authors and inventors by the provision of special rewards',[42] and the imposition of a duty to license would weaken this incentive system, depriving customers of new products.[43] The reason for this presumption is that IP rights sacrifice a degree of allocative efficiency in favour of promoting dynamic efficiency by creating a financial incentive to invest. On this view IP law and competition law pursue the same objective.[44] Therefore, the use of competition law to impose obligations upon holders of IP rights to license these would undermine the economic rationale for IP rights and harm consumers. However, the presumption that a refusal to license is economically efficient may be rebutted, and the ECJ's case law suggests that in exceptional cases where the consumer surplus from entry outweighs the dynamic efficiency considerations, then the refusal to license is abusive. (In *Magill* this was certainly the case as the copyright in question could hardly be said to be a reward for the broadcaster's ingenuity, and in *IMS Health* the German courts limited the scope of the copyright, allowing competitors to enter the market with alternative brick structures, which allowed the Commission to close the case.)[45] The 'new product' test in *Magill* is an imaginative (if imperfect) way of carrying out this cost–benefit analysis: if the new entrant wishes to offer something new for which there is consumer demand, then it suggests that the

---

[41] Ibid. para. 49.

[42] *Sony Corporation of America v. Universal City Studios Inc.* 464 US 417, 429 (1984).

[43] *Miller Institutform of N. America Inc.* 830 F 2d 606, 609 (6th Cir. 1987); *SCM Corp. v. Xerox Corp.* 64 F 2d 1195, 1209 (2d Cir. 1981). The American case law suggests that a refusal to license will never amount to a violation of antitrust law (*In re Independent Service Organisations Antitrust Litigation* 203 F 3d 1322 (Fed. Cir. 2000)) but there may be an infringement if the reliance on IP rights is a pretext (*Image Technical Services Inc. v. Eastman Kodak Co.* 125 F 3d 1195, 1218 (9th Cir. 1997)). However, the position is unclear: see P. D. Marquardt and M. Leddy 'The Essential Facilities Doctrine and Intellectual Property Rights: A Response to Pitofsky, Patterson and Hooks' (2003) 70 *Antitrust Law Journal* 847, who suggest that a refusal to license can be an antitrust offence in leveraging cases.

[44] *Image Technical Services* 125 F 3d 1195, 1218.

[45] *NDC Health/IMS Health: Interim Measures* [2003] OJ L268/69.

consumer benefits exist. Moreover, if the entrant is offering something distinct from that which the IP holder is offering, the risk that future inventions will be chilled by the imposition of a licence is reduced as the IP holder's monopoly is not challenged, only his refusal to allow others to offer alternative services. Indeed, it may be argued that dynamic efficiency is improved because the new entrant can exploit the IP right in novel ways. The Court in *IMS Health* remarked explicitly that in applying the *Magill* test one was balancing the economic freedom of the IP owner with the interests of consumers.[46] Of course it may be argued that, when the IP right is granted, the legislature has already balanced the likely restriction of competition against the innovation incentives, and the application of competition law seems to carry out the balance de novo. However, it might be argued that IP law creates Type 2 errors. That is, it has no safety valve should the grant of an IP right turn out to be excessively generous. Competition law cures that error risk when, exceptionally, the grant of an IP right does more harm than good.

The Court in *Magill* and *IMS Health* does not address the issue of what a new product is – arguably if the requiring party wishes to offer the same product that is already on the market but says he can offer it more cheaply, this would be insufficient because the lower production costs may merely reflect the fact that the incumbent has sacrificed considerable resources in developing his product, expenses which the new entrant does not need to incur, so he would be 'free riding' on the dominant firm's sunk costs. On the other hand, consumer demand can be evidence of a new product, or one might apply the SSNIP test discussed in chapter 5 to determine if the product that the requiring firm wishes to make is likely to occupy a unique place in the market.

Once the 'new product' requirement established in *Magill* is understood as only one example of an exceptional circumstance where the consumer benefit outweighs the risk that there will be a diminution of dynamic efficiencies,[47] the Commission is free to discover other circumstances where consumer welfare would be enhanced by imposing an obligation to deal. The *Microsoft* case provided the Commission with the opportunity to find a new setting where

---

[46] [2004] ECR I-5039 para. 48, following AG Tizzano's advice at para. 62.

[47] On the contrary, some suggest that the 'new product' requirement is a necessary element for the finding of an abuse, and as a result the *Microsoft* decision is open to challenge (see D. Geradin 'Limiting the Scope of Article 82 EC: What the EU Can Learn from the US Supreme Court's Judgment in *Trinko* in the Wake of *Microsoft*, *IMS* and *Deutsche Telekom*' (2004) 41 *Common Market Law Review* 1519, and J. Killick '*IMS* and *Microsoft* Judged in the Cold Light of *IMS*' (2004) 1(2) *Competition Law Review* 38–40, who also argues that the *IMS* test requires that competition be eliminated immediately as a result of the refusal, so that proof of likely elimination is insufficient). Supporting the view that the *Magill/IMS Health* 'new product' requirement is not necessary and that other exceptional circumstances may be found, see S. Anderman 'Does the *Microsoft* Case Offer a New Paradigm for the "Exceptional Circumstances" Test and Compulsory Copyright Licenses under EC Competition Law?' (2004) 1(2) *Competition Law Review* 13–14. It seems clear that since *Magill* is but an application of *Volvo*'s general principle that exceptional circumstances make a refusal to license anticompetitive, the 'new product' requirement is not a necessary part of the test.

consumers would benefit by the application of Article 82, and is significant because the Commission attempts to balance the benefits and costs for consumers directly.[48] Microsoft is dominant in the market for PC operating systems, with a market share of 90 per cent and high entry barriers. It is also dominant in a downstream market for 'group servers' (that is, programmes that allow sharing of printers among office staff or security on a local network, e.g. a university network). Microsoft refused to provide information about its operating system to firms wishing to market group servers in competition with Microsoft. Without such information the competitor's group servers would be unable to 'interoperate' with computers running with Microsoft's operating system. In short, the facts are that the competitor wants the dominant firm to provide it with information to allow the competitor to sell goods to consumers that have already bought the dominant firm's downstream product and which will work together with the competitor's upstream product. The Commission found that Microsoft's refusal to license caused harm to consumers because they would be unable to buy innovative products manufactured by Microsoft's competitors, and would suffer even more once this refusal reduced the incentives for competitors to innovate.[49] The refusal harmed consumers and stifled technological development.[50] One of Microsoft's counterarguments was that to order it to cooperate with rivals would undermine dynamic efficiency. The Commission rejected this view, and turned it on its head, holding that Microsoft's refusal was itself the reason why dynamic efficiency in the market was stymied:

> Microsoft's research and development efforts are indeed spurred by the innovative steps its competitors take in the work group server operating system market. Were such competitors to disappear, this would diminish Microsoft's incentives to innovate. By contrast, were Microsoft to supply Sun and other work group server operating systems with the interoperability information at stake in this case, the competitive landscape would liven up as Microsoft's work group server operating system products would have to compete with implementations interoperable with the Windows domain architecture. Microsoft would no longer benefit from a lock-in effect that drives consumers towards a homogeneous Microsoft solution, and such competitive pressure would increase Microsoft's own incentives to innovate.[51]

In other words, the Commission imposes an obligation to license when 'exceptional circumstances' suggest that there is a public interest in remedying the harm suffered by consumers. In reaching this conclusion the Commission makes a prima facie case that the obligation to license causes benefits that

---

[48] *Microsoft*, decision of 24 March 2004.   [49] Ibid. para. 694.

[50] Ibid. paras. 701, 711–12. It is not clear from the decision how much weight was placed on the fact that Microsoft had in the past supplied some interoperability information, and that therefore its conduct could be characterised, at least in part, as the disruption of previous levels of supply. See paras. 556 and 578–84, which suggest that these facts are 'of interest'.

[51] Ibid. para. 725.

outweigh the potential reduction in incentives to innovate. It is then up to the defendant to suggest that this presumption is inaccurate. Lack of certainty is inherent in this approach, which requires a holistic appraisal of all the facts.[52] Moreover, there is a distinct logic underpinning the reasoning cited above: innovation is the result of competition, and a firm that is not challenged will not innovate. The result is that when a refusal to license excludes the firms that are responsible for innovation, there is a loss in dynamic efficiencies. This position is central to the Commission's understanding of how markets work: rivalry is the key to efficiency.[53] In contrast to the 'indirect' way of balancing competition and innovation offered by the 'new product' rule in *Magill*, the Commission here balances innovation and competition directly and therefore provides a dominant firm with an 'innovation defence', the scope of which we explore further below.

3.3 Essential facilities: from competition to regulation

When markets that were formerly monopolised by national law are being opened to competition, the Commission takes a more aggressive stance towards non-cooperative behaviour. This is evidenced by the language of the *British Midland/Aer Lingus* decision: Aer Lingus (the Irish flag carrier dominant on the flight route between London and Dublin) refused to interline with a new entrant, British Midland, on the London–Dublin route. (Interlining is a practice which allows a travel agent to offer passengers a ticket providing for transportation on different carriers.) The result was that British Midland struggled to establish itself as a carrier on the London–Dublin route. The Commission report shows that British Midland's 'determination to succeed' allowed it to obtain a significant share of the market.[54] However, Aer Lingus's refusal was abusive because 'British Midland would have incurred lower costs, it would have earned higher revenues, its services would have been more attractive to its passengers and it would have been a stronger and more successful competitor than it now is.'[55] There is no evidence that consumer welfare was reduced, only that British Midland's market opportunities were reduced. The decision appears to be a policy intervention in a newly liberalised market where 'airlines making use of the *new opportunities for competition* should be given a *fair chance* to develop and sustain their challenge to established carriers'.[56] However, this decision would not pass the more stringent requirements set out in *Bronner* (no indispensability), nor the additional test in the IP cases (no new product is offered, no other exceptional circumstances seemed to exist). Nor is this decision simply about safeguarding economic

---

[52] In favour of the approach, see F. Lévêque 'Innovation, Leveraging and Essential Facilities: Interoperability Licensing in the EU *Microsoft* Case' (2005) 21 *World Competition* 71.

[53] See ch. 2 p. 50 and ch. 3 p. 87.

[54] [1992] OJ L96/34 paras. 29–30.   [55] Ibid. para. 29.

[56] *Twenty-second Report on Competition Policy* (1992) para. 218 (emphasis added).

freedom as a value in itself, it is more specifically about ensuring that the Commission's liberalisation of the air transport market is successful. This is evidenced by the fact that the majority of cases where the more aggressive stance is taken are in newly liberalised markets. The reader might note the similarity with *BA/Virgin*: there too harm to Virgin and losses incurred by BA were deemed irrelevant once it was found that the object of BA's rebates was to hinder the development of the competitive process.[57]

In some of the cases in markets that are being liberalised, the Commission made use of a different phrase than commonly found in this type of abuse: it held that the dominant firm controlled an *essential facility*, which others had a right to use. The first cases where this concept was deployed concerned the port of Holyhead, owned by Stena Link Seaports. Holyhead was identified as a relevant market as the most convenient place to operate ferries from the north of the UK towards Dublin. The Commission said that the owner of the port, who also offered transport services, controlled an essential facility (the port) and would infringe Article 82 by using 'its power in one market in order to protect or strengthen its position in another related market, in particular, by refusing to grant access to a competitor, or by granting access on less favourable terms than those of its own services, and thus imposing a competitive disadvantage on its competitor'.[58] Consequently, Stena was obliged to redesign its schedules to allow competing operators to carry out their services conveniently. It was asked to behave as if it were an independent port authority, without giving favourable treatment to its ferries. The *Commercial Solvents* case law justified this approach, so it is not clear what was gained by describing the harbour as an essential facility. The essential facility concept is drawn from US case law; however, it is hard to draw direct comparisons in this area given that much of what would be covered by the notion of essential facilities in the US falls to be considered under traditional refusal-to-supply case law in the EC.[59] Moreover, it is risky to draw comparisons when the essential facilities doctrine is so unsettled in the United States that it is impossible even for US commentators to say exactly what the doctrine covers.[60] The Commission uses the essential facilities phrase in a distinctly 'European' way, as a means of carving out additional regulatory space beyond that afforded by the refusal-to-supply line of authority. The essential facilities doctrine gave the Commission more leeway in two respects.

---

[57] See pp. 167–9.

[58] *B&I Line plc/Sealink Harbours* [1992] 5 CMLR 255 para. 41; see also the related decision in *Sea Containers/Stena Sealink* [1994] OJ L15/8 para. 66, where a duty was imposed to grant non-discriminatory access to a new entrant.

[59] For a comparative analysis, see J. S. Venit and J. J. Kallaugher 'Essential Facilities: A Comparative Law Approach' 1994 *Fordham Corporate Law Institute* 315 (Hawk ed. 1995).

[60] The most astute commentary remains that of P. Areeda 'Essential Facilities: An Epithet in Need of Limiting Principles' (1990) 58 *Antitrust Law Journal* 841.

First, it was imposed in situations where the indispensability criterion was not met. In the port cases for example, little attention was paid to working out how indispensable the particular port was. The Holyhead disputes are a striking illustration of how an indispensability analysis would have led to a different result: travel from Holyhead to Ireland by ferry is convenient because the ferry journey is shorter than the comparable ferry journey from, say, Liverpool. This might suggest that the port of Holyhead is a separate market from that in Liverpool (planning restrictions making the construction of additional harbour facilities impossible). However, this does not take into account that the journey to Holyhead for most customers is across a tortuous road in Wales, while travel to Liverpool is via a convenient motorway – the total journey time to Ireland differs little if one takes into consideration the travel time to the port. In fact, while the Commission's decisions permitted Sea Containers to operate from Holyhead, it never took up this possibility – instead it operated a service from Liverpool, advertising the convenience of travel to Liverpool.[61]

Second, the essential facilities doctrine empowers the Commission to impose obligations to cooperate without a finding of abuse. The Commission acts *ex ante* to guarantee that potential competitors have market access, trying to prevent the firms from committing abuses in the future, specifically in markets that are being liberalised. The implication of this is that the essential facilities doctrine is designed to improve competition.[62] Vivid examples of this are three exemption decisions under Article 81 concerning new railway services that would be offered as a result of the liberalisation of the railways and the opening of the channel tunnel. Consortia including national railway operators established joint ventures to offer new international transport services, including combined transport services and night trains to a number of European destinations. The Commission exempted these agreements subject to the condition that national railway operators afford access to the railway infrastructure to any other firm wishing to enter these markets and compete against the consortia that had been established.[63] The Commission characterised railway infrastructure as an essential facility, access to which was indispensable to provide international transport services.[64] Note how closely this follows the

---

[61] S. Bishop and D. Ridyard '*Oscar Bronner* – Legitimate Refusals to Supply' in J. Grayston (ed.) *European Economics and Law* (Bembridge: Palladian Law Publishing, 1999) pp. 24–6.

[62] *Oscar Bronner* [1998] ECR I-7791 (Opinion of AG Jacobs para. 34).

[63] *ACI* [1994] OJ L224/28; *Eurotunnel* [1994] OJ L354/66; *Night Services* [1994] OJ L259/21.

[64] *Twenty-fourth Report on Competition Policy* (1994) para. 182. However, two of these decisions were overruled by the CFI. Of particular importance is the *Night Services* annulment (Joined Cases T-374, 375 and 388/94 *ENS v. Commission* [1998] ECR II-3141), which calls into question how the facilities could be essential given that the relevant product market included all forms of transport, and not only rail transport (paras. 212–13), and condemns the Commission for failing to consider whether the facilities in question were truly essential. *Eurotunnel* was annulled because it was vitiated by an error of fact (Joined Cases T-79 and 80/95 *SNCF and BR v. Commission* [1996] ECR II-1491 paras. 59–60). However, the Court did not question the legal basis of the Commission's decision to impose *ex ante* obligations on the basis of an Article 81(3) exemption.

theme of the *Stena* decision, where the Commission also obliged the owner of the facility to manage it as if he did not compete in the downstream markets. This *leitmotiv* returns in a number of telecommunication and broadcasting decisions, where agreements, mergers and joint ventures have been exempted on the condition that the parties agree to facilitate access of new entrants.[65]

3.4 Essential facilities outside Article 82

In some situations, obligations on holders of essential facilities to manage them without favouring their own downstream operations are imposed outside of the competition rules, but are inspired by the principles developed in Article 82. Two fields exemplify this: air transport (where we explore access to computer reservation systems and access to airport grounds to provide ground-handling services) and electronic communications (where we revisit access to the local loop).

3.4.1 Air transport

A computer reservations system (CRS) stores and retrieves information about flights. It was originally operated by airlines but is now available to travel agents. All airlines value the possibility of having their flights listed on a CRS as it increases sales. Understandably CRS owners (who were major airlines) were reluctant to give competing airlines access to their system. Accordingly, a Regulation on a code of conduct for computerised reservation systems (CRS), based upon Article 80 EC, imposes a duty upon CRS service providers to 'allow any air carrier the opportunity to participate, on an equal and non-discriminatory basis, in its distribution facilities within the available capacity of the system concerned'.[66] This Regulation was probably a response to the decision in *London European/Sabena* where, in finding Sabena in breach of Article 82 for failing to give London European access to its CRS, the Commission held that such systems were 'essential for a company wishing to compete with companies already on the market'.[67] The Regulation generalises the obligation to grant access to all CRS 'to *achieve* undistorted competition

---

[65] E.g. *Atlas* [1996] OJ L239/23; Case COMP/JV.37 *BSkyB/KirchPayTV* (Art. 6(1)(b) decision): joint venture approved on the condition that access to broadcasting markets is open to third parties; *SWIFT* (*Twenty-Seventh Report on Competition Policy* (1997) pp. 120–2): undertaking by SWIFT to grant access to its international telecommunications network which offers reliable and secure data communication and processing to financial institutions located all over the world; *Joint Selling of the Commercial Rights of the UEFA Champions League* [2003] OJ L291/25: exemption conditional on grant of broadcasting rights in the manner specified by the Commission.

[66] Article 3(2) Council Regulation 3089/93 of 29 October 1993 amending Regulation 2299/89 on a Code of Conduct for Computerised Reservation Systems [1993] OJ L278/1. (The Code was amended again by Council Regulation 323/1999 of 8 February 1999 amending Regulation 2299/89 on a Code of Conduct for Computer Reservation Systems (CRSs) [1999] OJ L40/1.)

[67] [1988] OJ L317/47 para. 14.

between air carriers and between computer reservation systems, thereby protecting the interests of consumers'.[68] The Commission's interest is in improving economic welfare *ex ante*, a wider ambition than merely preventing a restriction of competition *ex post*. Moreover, the aim is to allow competition in two markets: first, entry of new airlines whose flights can be listed on competitors' CRS systems; second, competition between CRS providers.

Note that the obligation to cooperate applies without proof of dominance, so the Code of Practice has given the Commission the power to enforce access rights independently of EC competition law, but with similar remedial powers (in addition to the power to require access, also the power to impose fines of up to 10 per cent of turnover on firms who infringe the Code). In *Electronic Ticketing*, for example, the Commission responded to a complaint by one CRS operator, SABRE. It noted that Lufthansa was offering financial incentives to travel agents to issue electronic tickets. However, electronic tickets could only be issued using the START/Amadeus CRS (partly owned by Lufthansa). This practice was squeezing SABRE out of the market. SABRE complained that Lufthansa refused to give it sufficient information to allow it to sell electronic tickets on Lufthansa flights. Lufthansa's financial inducements were found contrary to the Code of Practice, which prohibits an airline that owns a CRS from giving inducements that favour the use of its CRS.[69] As the Commission explained, the aim of the Code of Practice is to prevent 'a parent carrier of a system vendor from distorting competition between CRSs by the granting of incentives to subscribers (travel agents) to use its own system'.[70] Lufthansa defended its practice by indicating that the incentives were necessary to promote this new form of ticket. The Commission was sceptical about this (offering scant justification for its diffidence) and relied on a literal reading of the Code to prohibit Lufthansa's actions. This decision would never have been reached applying Article 82: even if START/Amadeus might have been dominant in Germany, there was no evidence that access to Lufthansa's flights was indispensable for SABRE, and there was evidence that Lufthansa would, after testing its new type of ticket, have made e-ticketing possible through all CRS systems. The Code then, while inspired by Article 82, creates obligations that are much more wide-ranging.

Access to the airport grounds is crucial for providers of groundhandling services (e.g. check in, baggage handling, catering services) and Community law obliges Member States to grant access to competing groundhandling firms. Groundhandling may be provided by independent firms (third-party handling) or by the airline (self-handling). A Directive on access to groundhandling services was agreed in 1996 and provides for the market to be opened gradually, starting with access to the larger airports by 1999 and setting 2001 as the date by which there should be at least one new authorised supplier of

---

[68] Recital 1 Regulation 3089/93 (emphasis added).   [69] Article 8(1) Regulation 3089/93.
[70] *Electronic Ticketing* [1999] OJ L244/56 para. 48.

services unrelated to the managing body of the airport or the major airlines using the airport.[71] The Directive also seeks to unbundle the provision of groundhandling services from the operation of airlines, or the management of the airport, by requiring separate accounts for each activity.[72] This is designed to avoid cross-subsidies to assist the groundhandling service provider when faced with competition from new entrants. The legislation recognises that some services cannot be duplicated economically (e.g. baggage sorting, de-icing, water purification and fuel-distribution systems) and these are excluded from the access requirements; moreover, Member States may seek additional exemption from the liberalisation obligations when 'specific constraints of available space or capacity, arising in particular from congestion and area utilization rate, make it impossible to open up the market and/or implement self-handling to the degree provided for in this Directive'.[73] In these circumstances, Member States must notify the Commission of the proposed restriction of competition, and the Commission may refuse to approve the derogation from the obligations under the Directive. The Commission has denied or circumscribed exemptions granted by Germany to many of its airports.[74] In addition to this administrative process, individual providers whose access is denied may appeal against the decision to a national public authority independent of the airport's management body or a court, and political retaliation is possible via a reciprocity clause whereby a Member State may suspend the obligations under the Directive vis-à-vis a Member State which denies its suppliers access to groundhandling markets.[75]

While dedicated sector-specific rules are in place to facilitate market access, this has not excluded the application of Article 82 to groundhandling. At times both lines of attack have been pursued: for instance, when concerned about the provision of groundhandling services at Frankfurt airport, the Commission acted both under the relevant sector-specific Directive and under Article 82 in finding that the restrictions in the supply of groundhandling services were unlawful.[76] While the Article 82 decision was addressed to the airport authorities and the decision based on the sector-specific Directive was addressed to the Member State, the common result from both is a commitment to improve market access for competing groundhandling services (in this case to allow airlines to supply their own groundhandling services immediately, and to allow

---

[71] Articles 1, 6 and 7 Directive 96/67 on Access to the Groundhandling Market at Community Airports [1996] OJ L272/36.

[72] Ibid. Article 4.   [73] Ibid. Article 9.

[74] *Stuttgart Airport* [1998] OJ L300/25; *Cologne/Bonn Airport* [1998] OJ L300/33; *Hamburg Airport* [1998] OJ L300/41; *Dusseldorf Airport* [1998] OJ L173/45.

[75] Articles 21 and 20, Directive 96/97.

[76] *Frankfurt Airport* [1998] OJ L72/30 (Article 82 action); *Frankfurt Airport* [1998] OJ L173/32 (action under Directive 96/67). See E. M. Armani 'One Step Beyond the Application of the Essential Facility Theory' (1999) 3 *EC Competition Policy Newsletter* 15; K. Karlsson and J. J. Callaghan 'Air Transport Liberalisation Comes Down to the Ground: Recent Developments in Groundhandling Sector' [1999] *European Competition Law Review* 86.

third party access from 1999). On the one hand, the overlap between sector-specific access rules and Article 82 may be justified in that the Commission is free to apply Article 82 to all airports, not just those covered by the Directive; moreover, the continued use of Article 82 is necessary to prevent the dominant firm from using other restrictive practices to raise entry barriers (as the operator of Frankfurt airport had planned, by entering into long-term ground-handling supply contracts with some airlines).[77] On the other hand, there is a risk of politicising Article 82 if we look at the remedies imposed in the Frankfurt airport case: when a refusal to grant access is seen as an abuse, the dominant firm must grant access immediately unless there is some practical difficulty in so doing. There is no room for political bargains. However, in this case the Commission agreed that the access remedy should not be imposed with immediate effect but that access should be granted gradually. Bending Article 82, so that it is consistent with the political necessity for slow liberalisation to allow former monopolies time to adjust, distorts the application of Article 82.

3.4.2 Electronic communications

As we saw above, access to the local loop is essential for the provision of new telecommunication services (e.g. internet access and multimedia applications), so as to intensify competition and stimulate technological innovation.[78] In addition to empowering NRAs to monitor the price of access, the Regulation on local loop unbundling imposes a duty on the owner to meet reasonable requests for access on transparent, fair and non-discriminatory conditions. Requests may only be refused if the grant of access is not technically possible. The justification for this wide-ranging duty is on the basis that 'these operators rolled out their . . . infrastructures over significant periods of time protected by exclusive rights and were able to fund investment costs through monopoly rents'.[79] Following this cost–benefit analysis there is no risk that extensive obligations to share the facility will undermine dynamic efficiency, although as we noted earlier prices are regulated to make sure the owner has an incentive to maintain the infrastructure. Some have gone so far as to say that the Regulation 'borrows a number of concepts from the essential facilities doctrine and effectively codifies them'.[80] But on the other hand the Regulation is premised upon an explicit cost–benefit analysis, which is largely absent from the Court's case law on refusals to supply. In *Bronner*, for example, no account is taken as to whether imposing an obligation to share one's distribution network would create disincentives for others to develop successful distribution networks, nor are access prices regulated to achieve industrial policy objectives.

---

[77] Press Release IP/98/794.   [78] Article 1 Regulation 2887/2000.
[79] Recital 3 Regulation 2887/2000.
[80] A. F. Bavasso 'Essential Facilities in EC Law: The Rise of an "Epithet" and the Consolidation of a Doctrine in the Communications Sector' [2002] *Yearbook of European Law* 63, 85.

The distinctiveness of the essential facilities doctrine under sector-specific regulation can also be detected by considering the access remedy available to NRAs under Article 12 of the Access Directive. This provides that competitors may gain access to specific network elements: for example, in Germany the NRA found that Deutsche Telekom was dominant in the market for broadband networks, and it imposed an obligation designed to facilitate the entry of competitors offering alternative broadband services via Deutsche Telekom's network.[81] When determining access, the NRA must first decide whether the firm has substantial market power (akin to dominance) and, if so, it is able to impose an obligation to grant access to competitors without proof of any wrongdoing. In granting the remedy the NRA must take into account a range of factors, including: whether the denial of access would 'hinder the emergence of a sustainable competitive market at the retail level, or would not be in the end-user's interests'; the technical and economic viability of using or installing competing facilities; the feasibility of granting access in relation to available capacity; the owner's initial investment and the risks involved in making that investment; the need to safeguard long-term competition; and the provision of pan-European services.[82] It is not easy to match these considerations with the Article 82 refusal-to-supply test in *Oscar Bronner*. That test requires proof of (1) indispensability; (2) elimination of competition without access; (3) lack of objective justification. The indispensability criterion seems to be present in the Access Directive (the NRA must consider alternative routes to market access) and capacity constraint is akin to an objective justification. The key difference is the second limb: in Article 82 a refusal to supply must eliminate competition downstream, while under the Directive lack of access must hinder the emergence of sustainable competition, and the Commission has also to consider the development of pan-European services, a much more ambitious set of considerations than under the *Bronner* test. Moreover, the NRA is bound to take into account the dominant firm's investment in that facility (which might make the NRA less willing to award the access remedy). In sum, the criteria for granting access are different and, from a practical perspective, the firm wishing to obtain access may well pursue two actions in parallel: demand access from the NRA and demand an access remedy under Article 82.

What is codified in these sector-specific rules is the Commission's essential-facilities approach which is used to achieve a different kind of regulatory ambition that applies in newly liberalised sectors: obligations are imposed *ex ante* on owners of essential facilities; the obligation is to manage the essential facility in a way that does not favour the owner's own downstream business; and the aim is to ensure that markets become more competitive and develop according to the Community's industrial policy. From this perspective, essential facilities represent a particular European response to regulating newly liberalised markets by accelerating the transition from monopoly to

---

[81] Case DE2006/0457 (Press Release IP/06/1110).   [82] Article 12(1) and (2) Access Directive.

competition. It represents a doctrine developed solely by the Commission, and distinct from that created by the Court of Justice, which is transposed into directives.

3.5 The duty to cooperate with rivals: a synthesis

The case law on refusals to supply is untidy because there seem to be three standards that are applied: the *conventional case law* (dealing with goods/ services that are not protected by the state, either by IP laws or by state monopolies) where the early judgments demonstrated a concern over economic freedom, while more recent pronouncements edge towards a consideration of consumer welfare; the *IP case law* where consumer welfare has been at the heart of the test since the *Magill* decision; and the *liberalisation case law* where a more aggressive approach applies, justified by the fact that the sector had been protected by state exclusive rights.[83] There is also a fourth strand where essential facilities are found and regulated outside the scope of Article 82, but where the legislation seems to borrow some of the criteria established in Article 82 in order to create competitive markets. Some tidying up is required.

The first two categories should be assessed with the same cost–benefit analysis approach that prevails in the IP cases and is also part of the test in the Access Directive: considering whether the services provided by the entrant compensate consumers for the loss of dynamic efficiency. This is because to limit the cost–benefit analysis to IP rights cases is unconvincing.[84] First, the argument about creating incentives to invent and invest also applies when the dominant firm's invention is not protected by IP rights. This is exemplified in *Oscar Bronner* where Mediaprint's investment in an efficient distribution network, while not protected by any IP rights, seems to deserve some protection from competition law on the basis that otherwise incentives to invest in efficient distribution networks diminish.[85] Second, if we take the incentives argument seriously then an obligation to cooperate with competitors should only be imposed when the increase in allocative and dynamic efficiency caused by cooperation is greater than the reduction in dynamic and productive efficiency due to reduced incentives. The Court can take this path regardless of the nature of the property right in question. In so doing it would be able to focus more precisely upon the consumer interest. Granted, an explicit consideration about whether the imposition of an obligation to license benefits consumers more than it harms them is difficult, so that the competition authority may over- or under-enforce this rule.[86]

[83] E.g. EC *Commission Proposal for a Directive on Market Access to Port Services* COM(2001)35 final p. 3, noting state protection of port services.

[84] For a similar attack on the distinction between refusals to supply and refusals to license IP rights, see Ritter 'Refusals to Deal' pp. 585–98.

[85] A point noted by AG Jacobs in *Bronner* [1998] ECR I-7791 para. 57.

[86] Geradin 'Limiting the Scope of Article 82'.

The liberalisation case law based on the essential-facilities label is less easy to explain from a doctrinal perspective because some of the decisions do not fit squarely with the refusal-to-supply doctrine articulated by the Courts. As a result there is a separate essential-facilities doctrine which shares some of the features of the refusals-to-supply doctrine but operates in a different field (liberalised network markets), with a different approach (*ex ante* regulation, often with the support of national regulatory authorities, and sometimes through the imposition of access conditions in merger and joint venture notifications), and with a different regulatory ambition (improving competition in the relevant market, developing the industrial sector in question). The development of the essential-facilities strand of case law can best be viewed from a strategic perspective: the Commission used Article 82 to facilitate subsequent sector-specific regulation of the markets. Thus the use of essential-facilities rhetoric in the Article 82 case law is a preparatory step to facilitate legislation to impose access in newly liberalised sectors. This was seen in the field of CRS and groundhandling, where an Article 82 decision was followed by legislation generalising the decision, and in the field of access to port services, where a small number of decisions granting access to ports was followed by political agreement on a Directive on market access to port services which establishes a regulator for each port to grant access that is to be independent from service providers, and imposes obligations on Member States to guarantee access subject only to capacity constraints and environmental or public service considerations.[87] Finally, in telecommunications the Directive on access to the local loop was anticipated by a merger decision where access to the essential facility (the local loop) was a condition for clearing the transaction, as well as by a soft law communication suggesting that refusal to give access to this market would infringe Article 82.[88] Transposing essential-facilities-based obligations into legislation administered by NRAs can facilitate the imposition of obligations to allow access to new entrants.

3.6 Defences

3.6.1 Objective justification

Terminating an existing contractual relationship is sometimes justified, when the reason for terminating is some form of 'force majeure' like a shortage of goods that prevents the dominant firm from supplying.[89] However, even in

---

[87] Common Position (EC) No. 61/2002 adopted by the Council on 5 November 2002 with a view to adopting Directive 2002/.../EC of the European Parliament and of the Council of . . . Concerning Market Access to Port Services [2002] OJ C299/E1; Proposal for a Directive on Market Access to Port Services COM(2004) 654 final.

[88] Case M.1439 *Telia/Telnor* [2001] OJ L40/1 (the merger was not finally consummated); EC Commission Notice on the Application of the Competition Rules to Access Agreements in the Telecommunications Sector [1998] OJ C265/2 paras. 87–98.

[89] E. Rousseva "The Concept of "Objective Justification" of an Abuse of a Dominant Position: Can it Help to Modernise the Analysis under Article 82 EC?' (2006) 2 *Competition Law Review*, citing Case 77/77 *BP v. Commission* [1978] ECR 1513.

times of shortage, the dominant firm has an obligation to continue to supply what goods it has in a fair manner, so when the dominant plaster producer reduced supplies to customers who also bought plasterboard from it, the Commission considered this to be an abuse of dominance.[90] The case law also makes it hard for a dominant firm to terminate a contract when it is dissatisfied with the other party's performance, or when the contracting party starts a business in competition with it, finding that these terminations are usually a disproportionate response.[91] In *United Brands* the Court noted that terminating a distributor who does not comply with United Brands' wishes can be a strategy to deter other distributors from deviating, and as a result it can be a means to consolidate one's control over the distribution network.[92] It is likely that considerations of this nature would also apply to a refusal to supply de novo, so that the owner of a port could refuse to give access to a firm whose ships are too large for the harbour, or the owner of IP rights could refuse to license these to a firm which is not creditworthy. A similar defence applies in sector-specific regulation. However, the scope of these defences seems very narrow indeed.

3.6.2 Innovation

When discussing refusals to license intellectual property rights the Court has adopted an indirect method to decide whether the benefits from the obligation to license (in terms of allocative efficiency) are greater than the adverse effects on innovation, the new product requirement. In *Microsoft*, the Commission went further and considered what effect a licensing obligation would have on allocative and dynamic efficiency directly. It held that an obligation to license would increase both allocative and dynamic efficiencies because it would boost the ability of Microsoft's competitors to innovate. In the discussion paper on Article 82, the Commission expands the approach pioneered in *Microsoft* to cases of refusal to supply goods, suggesting a convergence between the three categories of cases discussed above. The discussion paper suggests that this defence, which we might call the 'innovation defence', is unlikely to apply when the goods or intellectual property rights in question were built with money from the state or when the firm enjoyed a statutory monopoly. The defence is inapplicable to the owner of a port that was built when he had exclusive rights to sail ships, but would apply in a situation like that in *Oscar Bronner* where a private firm developed an innovative system from scratch. The Commission, however, raises one difficulty because it sees innovation not only as a 'defence' but also as a point of attack, as in *Microsoft*: if in its view access is likely to lead to more 'follow-on' innovation by other firms, then this will be a

---

[90] *BPB Industries plc* [1989] OJ L10/50 para. 146; Case T-65/89 *BPB v. Commission* [1993] ECR II-389 para. 94.
[91] *United Brands* [1978] ECR 207 para. 203; *Boosey & Hawkes: Interim Measures* [1987] OJ L286/76.
[92] *United Brands* [1978] ECR 207 para. 192.

factor that can count in favour of a decision to order a firm to help its competitors.[93]

3.7 Remedies

Once the Commission decides that a refusal to supply is abusive, it orders that the dominant firm cooperate with the competitor, but this gives rise to a number of risks. First, the dominant firm and the new entrant may collude so that the market conditions are no different. Second, the dominant firm may enter into a contract with the competitor at a high price, leading the new entrant to raise its prices to customers, allowing the dominant firm to keep its prices high also. Third, the dominant firm can operate a 'price squeeze' so that the rival cannot afford to remain in the market. In other words, the dominant firm that is forced to cooperate with a rival has no incentive to create a more competitive market. Forcing the dominant firm to allow market access without more is pointless, and the declaration that there is a duty to collaborate does not end the Commission's involvement. The upshot is that the regulatory burden on the Commission might be so heavy that the cost of administering remedies far exceeds the benefits to economic welfare. It has been suggested that when imposing an obligation to cooperate with competitors, the Commission should carry out a cost–benefit analysis that takes into account the following four factors: (1) the benefits to the requiring firm; (2) the costs on the dominant firms (which include the cost of granting access and the long-term disincentives to innovate); (3) the costs for the competition authority in monitoring the remedy; (4) the benefits to consumers.[94] It is worth considering how far these considerations have been taken into account when the obligation to supply is imposed: first when the Commission imposes it, and second when enforcement is in the hands of NRAs.[95]

In the case of Commission enforcement most of the costs and benefits have been borne in mind: the benefits in (1) and (4) are necessary for the obligation to be imposed in the first place and the costs on innovation are taken into account in the IP cases. The cost of making the facility available is not taken into account expressly; however, the Court has held that a refusal to grant access to a facility may be justified when it is impractical to grant access.[96] The cost to the competition authority is not mentioned expressly; however, in both *IMS Health* and *Microsoft* the Commission indicated that a third party should be appointed to

---

[93] DG Competition Discussion Paper on the Application of Article 82 of the Treaty to Exclusionary Abuses (December 2005) paras. 235–6.

[94] P. Larouche 'Legal Issues Concerning Remedies in Network Industries' in D. Geradin (ed.) *Remedies in Network Industries: EC Competition Law vs. Sector Specific Regulation* (Antwerp: Intersentia, 2004) pp. 28–9.

[95] An additional consideration is the interaction between the application of competition law and sector-specific regulation. This is examined in chapter 12.

[96] *BP v. Commission* [1978] ECR 1513.

monitor the supply obligations imposed by the Commission. This is a recognition that the cost of monitoring can be excessive and unpredictable and, as a result, enforcement is privatised. In most cases this privatisation means that a dispute about the grant or cost of access is referred to an expert for resolution.[97] In the *Microsoft* case monitoring is carried out by a trustee who may also take measures to ensure that Microsoft is complying with the obligation to grant access. This is tantamount to creating an *ad hoc* regulator for the firm.

In newly liberalised sectors instead, the EC has been able to delegate the task of regulating access to bespoke National Regulatory Authorities who are better resourced and in a better position to carry out the sort of day-to-day monitoring which the imposition of a duty to allow access requires.[98] Some of the sector-specific legislation requires that the NRA carry out a cost–benefit analysis. However, there is no obligation on the NRA to take into account the costs that it would incur in enforcing the remedy in question, but it might be argued that this consideration is for the NRA to carry out in order to decide which cases to investigate.

4 Regulatory competition law

The nature of competition law enforcement in this chapter has certain unique features. First, the Community is using competition law as a tool to benefit consumers in newly liberalised markets: its efforts in regulating prices in telecommunications are designed to put pressure on NRAs to act under sector-specific regulation. There is an institutional overlap between the Community's competition authorities and national regulators and the Commission has exploited this. The overlap was also used in developing the essential-facilities doctrine, amplifying Article 82 and then transposing a doctrine into more detailed sector-specific rules that are administered by NRAs (telecommunications) or the Commission (air transport).

However, it is not only in newly liberalised sectors that the case law reviewed in this chapter advances an industrial policy. The early refusal-to-supply doctrine was designed to safeguard the economic freedom of small players, and the more recent explanations of the doctrine suggest that the aim of imposing a duty to cooperate with competitors is designed to allow the entry of firms that are able to provide better products and services and more choice for consumers. This is laudable, but goes beyond what competition law is designed for: to deter firms from acting unlawfully. In contrast the cases in this chapter compel dominant firms to ensure that as many benefits as possible accrue to the consumer.

---

[97] E.g. *NDC Health/IMS Health* [2002] OJ L59/18.

[98] For an argument that only bespoke regulators are suited, see G. J. Werden 'The Law and Economics of Essential Facilities' (1986) 32 *Saint Louis University Law Journal* 433, 479–80.

Even those who agree with the Commission's policy, however, should accept that sometimes the Commission commits Type 1 errors. Access remedies are granted without proof of harm: for example, when it granted interlining rights, the victim's market share had been increasing during the alleged abuse.[99] Moreover, access remedies are granted with scant attention to trading off the benefit to consumers from the remedy with the deterrent effect on innovation. *Microsoft* suggests that the Commission is now aware that this trade-off is important. It remains to be seen whether this continues to be taken into consideration.

---

[99] *British Midland/Aer Lingus* [1992] OJ L96/34. Compare AG Jacobs in *Bronner* para. 67.

8

Merger policy

Contents

1. Introduction   *page* 246
2. Horizontal mergers: single-firm dominance   250
   2.1 Market shares   251
   2.2 Actual and potential competitors   252
   2.3 Strategic behaviour of the merged entity   253
   2.4 Countervailing buyer power   255
3. Market power without dominance?   256
   3.1 The economic problem: 'unilateral effects'   256
   3.2 The legal solution   258
   3.3 Implementing the new legal standard   261
4. Vertical mergers   264
   4.1 Vertical mergers and the ECMR   266
   4.2 Vertical mergers in the broadcasting sector   268
5. Conglomerate mergers   271
   5.1 Leveraging   272
   5.2 Strategic pricing and entry deterrence   280
   5.3 Eliminating a potential competitor   281
6. Merger remedies   283
   6.1 Structural remedies   283
   6.2 Behavioural remedies   286
   6.3 The nature of merger remedies   290
7. Widening the aims of merger policy?   291
   7.1 Efficiencies   292
   7.2 Rescuing a failing firm   296
   7.3 Industrial policy   298
8. A European merger policy?   300
   8.1 Thresholds   301
   8.2 National interests   302
   8.3 Protectionism   305

1 Introduction

The regulation of mergers and acquisitions[1] is the principal instrument by which competition authorities control the structure of an industry. In this chapter we are concerned with mergers that increase the market power of a single firm. It might be argued that since dominant firms can be regulated under Article 82, there is no need for a merger policy: one can allow mergers creating a dominant firm and regulate that firm's behaviour *ex post*. Furthermore, there is evidence that most mergers do not reduce competition, so that merger policy is a disproportionate response.[2] However, merger law is necessary for the following reasons First, once the market is dominated by one or a few strong firms, the competition authorities may not have the resources or the information to pursue every anticompetitive action so that preventing the merger is a more cost-effective way of maintaining competition. Second, merger policy may be to the benefit of the merging firms – it might be problematic if two firms are allowed to merge and become dominant only to be assiduously regulated after the merger, or even broken up by the competition authorities some years after the two businesses have been integrated. Third, even if fully resourced, the competition authorities might not be able to remedy all the anticompetitive effects of a change in market structure (e.g. mergers in oligopoly markets considered in chapter 9). Fourth, the anticompetitive effects of a merger extend beyond the parties: when a merger creates a dominant firm and it raises prices, it creates a 'price umbrella' and other competitors raise prices to the same level. Merger policy can prevent the creation of market structures that lead to anticompetitive effects outside the reach of competition law.

In spite of the potentially significant impact that mergers can have on competition, there are no powers to block mergers in the EC Treaty (whilst merger rules were present in Article 66 of the ECSC Treaty). Some have put this down to the fact that merger rules were perceived as more important in the coal and steel sector given the strategic significance of these industries in post-war Europe.[3] The Commission soon saw the need for

---

[1] A merger is when two independent undertakings fuse their businesses to create a new company; an acquisition (or takeover) is where one company obtains a controlling interest in another. See Article 3 Council Regulation (EC) No. 139/2004 of 20 January 2004 on the Control of Concentrations between Undertakings (hereinafter ECMR) [2004] OJ L24/1. In this chapter references to mergers are references to both mergers and acquisitions. Unless otherwise specified, references to the ECMR refer to the 2004 legislative text, not to the original 1989 ECMR, as amended in 1997.

[2] On the arguments for and against *ex ante* merger control, see K. George 'Do We Need a Merger Policy?' in J. A. Fairburn and J. A. Kay (eds.) *Mergers and Merger Policy* (Oxford: Oxford University Press, 1990).

[3] L. Brittan *Competition Policy and Merger Control in the Single European Market* (Cambridge: Grotius, 1991) p. 23. But see S. Bulmer 'Institutions and Policy Change in the European Communities: The Case of Merger Control' (1994) 72 *Public Administration* 423, arguing that the nature of the EC Treaty did not allow the inclusion of merger law.

merger rules,[4] but there was little political consensus to agree to a Regulation empowering the Commission to regulate mergers, in spite of repeated draft regulations tabled by the Commission in the 1970s and 1980s.[5] This is because Member States were keen to retain powers over mergers. These transactions can affect the distribution of resources in society, and may entail a national firm being acquired by a firm from abroad. Some Member States, therefore, wished to use merger policy as part of national industrial policy and were unwilling to relinquish their powers to the Community.[6] It is largely for these political reasons that Member States were reluctant to give up national control of mergers to the Commission, which only gained power to scrutinise mergers in 1990.[7] Even today, certain Member States remain reluctant to allow market forces to operate in all economic sectors. Only recently, for example, the French Prime Minister called for 'real economic patriotism' when issuing a decree to protect certain strategic French firms from foreign takeovers, based on employment and France's industrial strength.[8]

A combination of factors led to the adoption of the EC Merger Regulation (hereinafter ECMR) in 1989.[9] The first was that the Court of Justice found that some mergers fell under the jurisdiction of Articles 81 and 82. As far back as 1973 it held that if a dominant firm were to merge, thereby strengthening its dominance, this could constitute an abuse under Article 82.[10] However, this could not be the basis of a systematic Community merger policy. Of more concern for Member States was the 1985 ruling that some mergers (e.g. acquisitions of minority holdings) would fall to be considered under Article 81.[11] This widened the Commission's powers to review mergers to such an extent that Member States preferred to negotiate an ECMR rather than give the Commission unchecked freedom to develop a system of merger control under Articles 81 and 82. The second factor was demand from industry. In the late 1980s, there was a significant increase in merger activity, in part as a response

---

[4] H. W. de Jong 'Concentration in the Common Market: A Comment on the Memorandum of the EEC Commission' (1966–7) 4 *Common Market Law Review* 166.

[5] Commission Proposal for a Regulation of the Council on the Control of Concentrations between Undertakings [1973] OJ C92/1; Amended Proposal for a Council Regulation on the Control of Concentrations between Undertakings [1982] OJ C36/3 (11th Annual Competition Report p. 26); [1984] OJ C51 (14th Annual Competition Report p. 46); [1986] OJ C324 (16th Annual Competition Report). Several variations were drafted during negotiations: [1988] OJ C130/4; [1988] OJ C309; [1989] OJ C22/14.

[6] For background, see N. Levy 'Dominance versus SLC: A Subtle Distinction?' in G. Drauz and M. Reynolds (eds.) *EC Merger Control: A Major Reform in Progress* (Oxford: Oxford University Press, 2003) pp. 146–8.

[7] Regulation 4064/89 [1989] OJ L395/1.   [8] *The Times* 1 September 2005, p. 45.

[9] See generally Bulmer 'Institutions and Policy Change'; L. McGowan and M. Cini 'Discretion and Politicization in EU Competition Policy: The Case of Merger Control' (1999) 12 *Governance* 175; M. Armstrong and S. Bulmer *The Governance of the Single European Market* (Manchester: Manchester University Press, 1998) ch. 4.

[10] Case 6/72 *Europemballage and Continental Can v. Commission* [1973] ECR 215.

[11] Cases 142 and 156/84 *BAT and Reynolds* [1987] ECR 4487.

to the creation of the internal market, and firms found national merger review burdensome as each transaction had to be vetted by multiple competition authorities, each with different criteria and procedures. An industry preference for a one-stop merger control system arose.[12] Third, the internal politics in three key Member States led to pressures for adopting the ECMR.[13] The French saw the ECMR as a way of translating national policy of promoting national champions into an EC-wide policy of sponsoring European champions; moreover it felt that German merger laws had thwarted the expansion of French firms. Germany was reluctant to yield power to Brussels because it had a well-developed merger law, but lent support to the Commission because of a complex set of national events: first, domestic industry was concerned that the stricter German laws gave firms in other Member States a competitive advantage; second, the anticipated reunification of Germany meant that the government needed to obtain support of the Member States to implement controversial economic measures to facilitate the integration of the economies. Moreover, in 1989 the German government had controversially allowed a merger that the German competition authority had originally blocked and felt that backing a competition-based ECMR would act as a signal that the decision in question was an aberration. However, Germans remained cautious about European merger laws. The British supported a competition-based test for mergers but were reluctant to relinquish control over mergers without the EC also taking steps in the field of corporate governance. This was a result of concerns that British firms were more vulnerable to foreign takeovers than those in other Member States. Fourth, the anticipated completion of the internal market in 1992 gave the Commission a bargaining chip to press for the development of EC-wide merger rules, and in this context the negotiating skills of the Commissioner for competition policy (Lord Brittan) were crucial to the coming into force of the Merger Regulation[14] after 'arduous negotiations'.[15]

This chapter is mostly concerned with the EC Commission's substantive assessment of mergers, but a basic understanding of the procedures involved is essential and a sketch is provided here.[16] The basic principle of the ECMR is that mergers are scrutinised before they are implemented. The parties announce their plans to merge, but then put these on hold pending the Commission's decision.[17] The rationale for this is so that the Commission

---

[12] There were 115 mergers in 1982/3, 208 in 1984/5 and 622 in 1989/90: L. Tsoukalis *The New European Economy* 2nd edn (Oxford: Oxford University Press, 1993) p. 103.

[13] The following draws from E. Schwartz 'Politics as Usual: The History of EC Merger Control' (1993) 18 *Yale Journal of International Law* 607.

[14] His story of the birth of merger control is told in Brittan *Competition Policy*.

[15] *Twenty-third Report on Competition Policy* (1993) p. 35.

[16] For further detail on procedures, see C. J. Cook and C. S. Kerse *EC Merger Control* 4th edn (London: Sweet & Maxwell, 2006) chs. 4 and 7; L. Ortiz Blanco (ed.) *EC Competition Procedure* 2nd edn (Oxford: Oxford University Press, 2006) chs. 16–18.

[17] Art. 7(1) ECMR.

can 'deal with eggs, rather than omelettes'.[18] Upon notification, the merger is reviewed under phase 1 procedures (which are carried out within four weeks of notification).[19] During this period, interested parties are able to comment on the likely impact of the merger, and the Commission verifies the information it has received and consults Member States. At the end of phase 1, five outcomes are possible: (1) the transaction is found not to be a merger, so scrutiny under the ECMR is unnecessary; (2) the merger does not have a Community dimension, so it falls outside of the Commission's jurisdiction; (3) the merger is compatible with the Community and may go ahead; (4) the merger is compatible with the Community, but amendments are required before it may go ahead (e.g. parties must sell off some assets); (5) the merger raises doubts as to whether it is compatible with the Community, and a phase 2 investigation must be carried out to review the transaction in more depth.[20] A phase 2 investigation lasts for four months,[21] and in addition to the consultation processes in phase 1, there is an oral hearing where the Commission, the parties to the merger and interested parties participate. On top of the formal procedure, there are regular contacts between the parties to the merger and the Commission. Decisions in phase 2 cases are those of the Commission acting as a collegiate body and are discussed among all Commissioners, who also have to give attention to the opinion of the Advisory Committee (composed of representatives of national competition authorities).[22] Three outcomes are possible at the end of phase 2: (1) the merger is compatible with the Community and thus may proceed; (2) the merger is compatible with the Community but may only proceed if modifications are made; (3) the merger cannot go ahead because it is incompatible with the Community.[23] The vast majority of mergers have been cleared unconditionally in phase 1, and only nineteen mergers have been blocked, the last one in 2004.[24]

From 1990 to 2004, the test for evaluating mergers was the following:

> A concentration which creates or strengthens a dominant position as a result of which effective competition would be significantly impeded in the Common Market or in a substantial part of it shall be declared incompatible with the Common Market.[25]

This calls for a two-step analysis: first, the identification of a dominant position; second, a prospective analysis to determine whether the merger leads to a situation where effective competition is impeded. This test is designed to predict the 'effects of concentration on competition'.[26] However, since the early days the Commission presumed that a merger would impede effective competition if it created or strengthened a dominant position, thereby

---

[18] Brittan *Competition Policy* p. 27.   [19] Art. 10(1) ECMR.   [20] Art. 6 ECMR.
[21] Art. 10(1) ECMR.   [22] Art. 18(3)–(7) ECMR.   [23] Art. 8 ECMR.
[24] Case M.3440 *ENI/GDP/EDP*.   [25] Art. 2(3) Regulation 4064/89 [1989] OJ L395/1.
[26] Joined Cases C-68/94 and 30/95 *France v. Commission* [1998] ECR I-1375 paras. 221–2.

operating a single 'dominance test'. As of 1 April 2004 the ECMR was recast, and the new test for the substantive assessment of mergers is the following:

> A concentration which would significantly impede effective competition, in the common market or in a substantial part of it, in particular as a result of the creation or strengthening of a dominant position, shall be declared incompatible with the common market.[27]

The reasons behind this reformulation (which may seem to be nothing more than a rearrangement of the words in the old ECMR) are explored in section 3 below. For present purposes it need only be noted that the legislative intention is that the new test is not a fundamental reconsideration of the economic basis by which mergers are reviewed. On the contrary, for the vast majority of mergers, no change in analysis is envisaged.[28] The Commission has indicated that 'the creation or the strengthening of a dominant position is a primary form of . . . competitive harm'.[29] Accordingly, upon proof of dominance, one may presume that the merger substantially impedes effective competition.[30]

The chapter is organised in the following manner. Section 2 is a review of how the dominance test applies to horizontal mergers, that is mergers between competitors. The basic elements of dominance have been discussed in chapter 5, so only the distinguishing features of the dominance test carried out under the ECMR are reviewed here. Section 3 explains how horizontal mergers might cause anticompetitive effects without dominance and the motivation behind the reform of the substantive test in the ECMR. Section 4 considers vertical mergers (mergers where the products of one firm are supplies for the others' downstream activities) and section 5 analyses conglomerate mergers (where the products of the two firms are complementary or unrelated). If an anticompetitive effect is likely, it is possible for parties to offer concessions to assuage the Commission's concerns. 'Merger remedies' are explored in section 6. In section 7 we consider the scope for deploying merger policy to achieve a wider range of goals than those for the protection of the competitive process. Finally we review the limits of the Commission's powers.

2 Horizontal mergers: single-firm dominance

The most prominent risk posed by mergers arises when the merging firms are competitors and the merger creates or strengthens a dominant position. The analysis begins by considering the new firm's market share, the size and

---

[27] Art. 2(3) ECMR.   [28] Recital 26 ECMR.

[29] Guidelines on the Assessment of Horizontal Mergers under the Council Regulation on the Control of Concentrations between Undertakings (hereinafter Horizontal Merger Guidelines) [2004] OJ C31/5 part IV para. 2.

[30] On the reform generally, see J. Schmidt 'The New ECMR: "Significant Impediment" or "Significant Improvement"?' (2004) 41 *Common Market Law Review* 1555, 1567.

strength of its rivals, the potential competition faced by the merged entity and any countervailing customer power.[31]

One aspect that distinguishes the analysis of market power in merger cases from Article 82 cases is that in the latter the focus is often simply on the market power of the dominant firm, scant attention being paid to potential competition and the power of consumers. In contrast in merger cases the countervailing power of other market actors (competitors, potential competitors and buyers) is taken into account more fully. This is so for two reasons: the first is that the analysis in Article 82 cases is retrospective (*has* the firm abused its dominance?) while in merger cases the analysis is prospective (*will* the merger impede effective competition?). In Article 82 cases what other market players might have done is not helpful because one is analysing historical facts. The second reason is that to date there has been a different approach by the Commission in merger cases, whereby there is greater reliance on economic analysis, which has led to a more comprehensive appraisal of market power.

2.1 Market shares

Market shares allow for a quick look to gauge the possibilities of anticompetitive risk, and market shares above 50 per cent are prima facie evidence of dominance.[32] However, an added refinement in merger cases is that the market share analysis is dynamic; merely adding up the market shares of the merging parties today may not yield an accurate estimate of the parties' market power in the future. For example, in a market for raw materials account has been taken of the fact that a rival's reserves were soon to be depleted, which indicated that the market power of the merged entity would become more considerable as time went on.[33] Conversely, if the merging parties are developing new products, anticipated market shares are a more helpful indicator than the parties' current market position.[34] And in markets where market shares are unstable because of repeated and random bouts of innovation, market shares are unhelpful and a more comprehensive market analysis is necessary to measure market power adequately.[35]

A finding that the post-merger market shares of the merged entity are low will normally result in the merger being cleared, while if market shares are high, the inquiry extends to considering the competitive strength of rivals (e.g. if they are able to increase output to counter the merged entity's exploitation of

---

[31] Horizontal Merger Guidelines part IV.
[32] Case M.784 *Kesko/Tuko* [1997] OJ L110/53; Horizontal Merger Guidelines paras. 14 and 17.
[33] Case T-102 *Gencor v. Commission* [1999] ECR II-753.
[34] Case M.1806 *Astra Zeneca/Novartis* [2004] OJ L110/1 paras. 150–3, 188–98.
[35] Case M.1795 *Vodafone Airtouch/Mannesmann* (12 April 2000), where it was found that the merged entity was best placed to dominate an emerging market; Case M.2256 *Philips/Agilent Health Care Technologies* (2 March 2001) paras. 31–2, where the competitive strength of other firms was taken into account; Case M.2609 *HP/Compaq* (13 February 2002) para. 39, where the strength of other competitors and low switching costs were taken into account.

their greater market position, or whether the merger is with a firm that was a growing competitive force in the market),[36] the likely entry of new competitors, and the countervailing strength of consumers. These findings help to determine whether the merged entity is able to act independently of competitors, customers and consumers.[37]

2.2 Actual and potential competitors

Large market shares mean little if existing competitors are able to increase output when the largest firm raises its prices.[38] Accordingly, it is necessary to determine whether the merged entity's current competitors are able to react in such a way so as to remove the likelihood that the merged entity will raise price.[39]

In so far as potential competitors' entry prospects are concerned, the fears of future anticompetitive effects due to high market shares can be assuaged by proof that entry is 'likely, timely and sufficient to deter or defeat any potential anti-competitive effects of the merger'.[40] The Commission has been willing to accept potential competition from overseas, in contrast with the practice in Article 82.[41] In determining whether entry is *likely*, the test is whether a hypothetical market player would find entry profitable, taking into account the risks and costs of entry, the effects of entry on price, and the anticipated response of the other firms in the market.[42] The principal consideration is whether the new entrants face insuperable entry barriers. As we noted in chapter 5, the EC has favoured a broad conception of entry barriers.[43] In the Commission's practice entry is said to be *timely* if it occurs within two to three years.[44] Entry is *sufficient* if it is able to defeat or deter the merged entity's anticompetitive conduct. This approach suggests that the Commission does

[36] E.g. Case M.53 *Aerospatiale-Alenia/de Havilland* [1991] OJ L334/42 para. 53 (no lessening of competition if dominance were 'only temporary and would be quickly eroded because of a high probability of strong market entry').

[37] Case T-102 *Gencor v. Commission* [1999] ECR II-753 para. 200; Joined Cases C-68/94 and C-30/95 *France v. Commission* [1998] ECR I-1375 para. 221.

[38] E.g. Case M.222 *Mannesmann/Hoesch* [1993] OJ L114/34, where there was a market share of 70 per cent but the merger was cleared because of potential competition.

[39] Horizontal Merger Guidelines paras. 32–5.

[40] Ibid. para. 68, the language similar to that in Case M.190 *Nestlé/Perrier* [1992] OJ L356/1 para. 91.

[41] Compare Case M.9 *Fiat Geotech/New Holland* (8 February 1991), where large overseas tractor manufacturers were able to enter new markets, with Case 322/81 *Nederlandse Banden-Industrie Michelin v. Commission* [1983] ECR 3461, where large tyre sellers from outside the EU were disregarded.

[42] Horizontal Merger Guidelines para. 69. For a successful application, see Case IV/M.704 *Unilever/Diversey* (20 March 1996) paras. 26–8.

[43] See chapter 5 and the merger cases cited therein, and also Horizontal Merger Guidelines paras. 68–75.

[44] Case M.430 *Procter & Gamble/VP Schickedanz* [1994] OJ L211/1 para. 77; the Horizontal Merger Guidelines para. 74 suggest that entry is timely if it occurs two years after the merger, but this period may be longer or shorter depending on the characteristics of the market.

not trade off short-term anticompetitive price increases for long-term competitive effects, as a total welfare economic model might recommend. On the contrary, the threat of new entry must prevent all anticipated anticompetitive behaviour by the merged entity.[45] This means that although entry of the potential competitor may take two years, the merged entity should have no incentive to attract such entry by exploiting its temporary dominant position. This approach is consistent with the priority placed upon consumer welfare. The Commission rejects the view that welfare losses for today's consumers can be accepted if the market is more competitive in the future.

2.3 Strategic behaviour of the merged entity

In certain cases the Commission's analysis of a merger's effects is informed by considerations of whether the merged entity will raise rivals' costs after the merger, thereby considering whether the merged entity is itself likely to erect new entry barriers.[46] For example, in *Vodafone Airtouch/Mannesmann* the merged entity would be able, through its control of leading mobile phone networks in several Member States, to develop advanced, seamless pan-European mobile telecommunication services, while if competitors were to offer a similar service they would need to cooperate with the merged entity and gain access to part of its mobile telephone network. According to the Commission, the effect of the merger would be an 'increased ability and incentive of the new entity to eliminate actual and/or potential competition'.[47] The merged entity could either refuse to give others access to its network or allow access only on terms that would make competing services unattractive. Moreover, the merged entity might develop customised handset functionalities with manufacturers of mobile phones, which would be unavailable to other competitors, thereby strengthening the network's dominance further. Similarly, in *Worldcom/MCI* the Commission identified a market for top-level, universal internet connectivity and found that the merged entity's dominant position in that market 'would enable it to pursue various stratagems to reinforce its market position ... One would be to raise rivals' costs, and the other would be to price selectively to attract customers away from competing networks.'[48] As for the former, the merged entity could either refuse to connect rivals to their network (which is seen as essential to offer internet services) or grant access on unfavourable terms, thus controlling a large part of the competitors' costs. Moreover, the merged entity 'could influence their cost position by charging prices for paid peering or transit that were designed to prevent its

---

[45]   See e.g. Case COMP/M.1742 *Sun Chemical/TotalFina/Coates* (22 December 1999) paras. 24–30.
[46]   Horizontal Merger Guidelines para. 36. See also M. A. Utton *Market Dominance and Antitrust Policy* (Cheltenham: Edward Elgar, 1995) pp. 182–3.
[47]   Case M.1795 *Vodafone Airtouch/Mannesmann* (12 April 2000) para. 44.
[48]   Case M.1069 *Worldcom/MCI* [1999] OJ L116/1 para. 118.

"customers" (formerly competitors) from being able to offer prices competitive with those on offer from MCI WorldCom itself'.[49]

This extensive analysis of the anticipated exclusionary conduct of the dominant firm is only raised infrequently in horizontal merger cases, but there is a
pattern: these are cases of network industries where the concern is that the
holder of the network's access points has an 'essential facility' which the
Commission wishes to ensure is available to all competitors. This concern
also arises in other instances where the merged entity has control of an
upstream or a downstream market through which it can deny access to
competitors: for example, the ownership of vital intellectual property rights.[50]
By raising concerns over the merged entity's exclusionary tactics, the
Commission forces the parties to make commitments to ensure that competitors have access to the facilities as a condition for clearing the merger: for
example in *Vodafone Airtouch/Mannesmann* the merged entity promised to
give non-discriminatory access to its network to allow others to provide
advanced telecommunication services. The Commission was satisfied that
this commitment would preserve a competitive structure and have an overall
beneficial effect on the development of this market.[51] Note also how the
Commission uses merger control to ensure competitive markets in a way
similar to that we saw in chapter 7: access for competitors is required even if
the strict *Bronner* criteria are not met; the Commission's analysis does not
establish the presence of an indispensable facility. Instead, the Commission
uses merger policy strategically, to stimulate the development of industry. In
particular it notes that granting access will allow the creation of a competing
network so that in the future access to Vodafone's facility by its competitors
will become redundant. Community industrial policy is in play in these kinds
of cases.

This approach to defining dominance by virtue of likely post-merger anticompetitive conduct is unusual and may not be repeated because the Court has
recently held that if the Commission's fear of dominance is the result of
anticipated anticompetitive conduct, it should consider whether the merged
entity has an incentive to put such conduct into practice. In determining this
one should consider the anticipated gains that a firm would make by excluding
rivals together with factors that reduce this incentive, for example the fact that
the conduct is an abuse of a dominant position and may be punished under
Article 82.[52] This may place a limit to how far the Commission can use merger
control to pursue an industrial policy. In a scenario like *Vodafone* for example,

---

[49] Ibid. para. 123. For similar analysis, see Case M.1741 *WorldcomMCI/Sprint* [2003] OJ L300/1
paras. 153–64.

[50] E.g. Case M.1671 *Dow Chemical/Union Carbide* (3 May 2000): commitment to grant open
licences (paras. 176–8).

[51] Case M.1795 *Vodafone Airtouch/Mannesmann* (12 April 2000) paras. 58–60.

[52] Case C-12/03P *Commission v. Tetra Laval BV*, judgment of 15 February 2005, paras. 74–5 (we
explore this aspect of the ruling further below).

it would have to establish more evidence to determine the likelihood that the merged entity would engage in exclusionary conduct. On the other hand, parties in fast-moving businesses are keen to obtain quick regulatory clearance, and provided the remedy which the Commission seeks does not frustrate the reason for the merger, merging parties will make what commitments are necessary to gain phase 1 clearance. The Commission has the upper hand in negotiations.

2.4 Countervailing buyer power

When those who purchase the goods of the merged entity are able to thwart its efforts to increase prices, this undermines the merged entity's dominance.[53] For example, in *Enso/Stora* the merger would have led to a market with one dominant firm (with a market share above 60 per cent) and two smaller suppliers, but the buying side was also composed of one large and two small buyers, all of which would have sufficient power to prevent an exercise of dominance.[54] The Commission identified two tactics that the buyers could deploy to counteract anticompetitive behaviour. First, all three were able to switch some orders to other suppliers. This would be particularly painful for Enso/Stora because the industry in question relies on high-capacity utilisation to make satisfactory profits. Second, the largest buyer (Tetra Pak) was said to have the ability to develop new capacity with existing or new suppliers, and Enso/Stora would not wish to lose Tetra Pak's large orders. Moreover, Tetra Pak's power would also strengthen the position of the two smaller buyers, because Enso/Stora would be keen to keep their custom so as not to become totally dependent on Tetra Pak's orders. In the Commission's view, the buyers 'have sufficient countervailing buyer power to remove the possibility of the parties' exercising market power'.[55] Nevertheless, the Commission retained some concern that the two smaller buyers might be exploited and so the merger was allowed only under the condition that the merged entity would not raise prices to the smaller customers by more than it would raise prices to Tetra Pak. This suggests that powerful buyers can eliminate the risk of dominance if two conditions are met: (1) the buyers can obtain the goods elsewhere; (2) all buyers are able to exercise power so that the dominant firm is unable to price discriminate, offering low prices to the powerful buyers and high prices to the weak.[56]

However, buyer power is a conceptually suspect mechanism, for two main reasons.[57] First, a dominant firm can damage competition by slowing down

---

[53] See Horizontal Merger Guidelines paras. 64–7.

[54] Case M.1225 *Enso/Stora* [1999] OJ L254/9 paras. 84–97.

[55] Ibid. para. 97.   [56] Case M.2097 *SCA/Metsa Tissue* [2002] OJ L57/1 paras. 86–8.

[57] J. B. Nordemann 'Buying Power and Sophisticated Buyers in Merger Control Law: The Need for a More Sophisticated Approach' [1995] *European Competition Law Review* 270, considering that merger law should not place customers in a position where they are forced to exercise buyer power.

innovation or preventing new entry or exercising commercial pressure to eliminate other competitors (for example, through predatory pricing), three effects which powerful buyers are unlikely to be able to remedy. Second, the ability of buyers to thwart attempts by the dominant firm to raise prices depends upon the existence of actual or potential competitors, which means that if entry barriers are high and existing competitors weak, it becomes hard to see how buyers can exercise any power. Therefore, buyer power seems to be a redundant consideration unless buyers know that the seller is raising prices without good reason (e.g. not because the costs of raw materials have increased) and are able to find alternative sellers.[58] *Enso/Stora* might best be read more restrictively as a case where the buyers had the incentive and the ability to obtain alternative sources of supply.[59] In this view, buyer power serves to strengthen existing competitors and to lower entry barriers for potential competitors.[60] Therefore buyer power is better seen as an additional consideration to determine the strength of existing competitors and the viability of potential competition (which eliminates all risks posed by a dominant firm) and not as a stand-alone device that automatically eliminates the risk of anticompetitive effects.

Conversely, 'customer weakness' is often just another way of indicating that there are fewer alternative suppliers,[61] or that entry barriers are high because consumers face high switching costs (e.g. if customers are tied by long-term contracts, discounts for exclusivity, or have designed their production processes so that it would be costly to switch to buying products of other firms).[62] In the latter scenario, the concern that customers are vulnerable is also somewhat misplaced for the concern is primarily that competitors of the merged entity are weak.

3 Market power without dominance?

3.1 The economic problem: 'unilateral effects'

In the run up to the reform of the ECMR, questions were raised as to whether the 'dominance' standard was sufficient to capture all forms of horizontal merger.[63] It was suggested that there were certain market conditions where,

---

[58] See M. L. Steptoe 'The Power-Buyer Defense in Merger Cases' (1993) 61 *Antitrust Law Journal* 493.

[59] This is how buyer power was analysed in Case M.042 *Alcatel/Telettra* (12 April 1991) paras. 38–40.

[60] In the United States the possibility that a buyer will sponsor new entry is assessed under ease of entry: Joint Department of Justice and Federal Trade Commission Horizontal Merger Guidelines (1992, amended in 1997, available at: www.usdoj.gov/atr/index.html s. 3.0).

[61] E.g. Case M.877 *Boeing/McDonnell Douglas* [1997] OJ L336/16 para. 70.

[62] See Case M.986 *Agfa Gevaert/Du Pont* [1998] OJ L211/22 paras. 63–71.

[63] The reform process started with the *Green Paper on the Review of Council Regulation (EEC) No. 4064/89* COM(2001)745/6 final paras. 159–69.

even without dominance, a merged entity would be able to act in an anti-competitive manner.[64]

The major debate was in cases of mergers by producers of two close substitutes in a differentiated consumer product market. Assume that the market for chewing gum is an oligopoly, and each manufacturer makes gum of only one flavour, and that consumers of gum find that lemon and lime flavoured gums are very close substitutes. This means that the price of lemon gums is affected mostly by the competitive strategy of the lime gum manufacturer and vice versa. A merger between the lemon and lime manufacturers can have anticompetitive effects because it removes the principal competitive constraint: the merged entity can freely raise the price of lemon gums, knowing that the majority of buyers who will switch will buy the lime gums, thus the lost sales are recovered through sales in the other market and additional profits are gained by the higher prices. This effect can arise even if the market share of the lemon and lime gums on the chewing gum market is fairly low. And this effect may be followed by an overall increase in the price of all gums, as the lemon gum buyers switch to other, non-lime brands, the manufacturers of which in turn may find it profitable to raise prices.[65] Under this scenario, anticompetitive effects are also possible when the market is dominated by a third firm that is not a party to the merger, a scenario which confronted the US Federal Trade Commission in the *Heinz/Beech-Nut* case we discussed in chapter 4. The second and third largest manufacturers of baby foods proposed a merger in a market dominated by Gerber (which held a 60 per cent share of the market).[66] The two smaller manufacturers competed head to head to supply retail outlets with baby foods, Gerber seemingly oblivious to this as its market power was safeguarded by a strong brand image, which meant that retailers had to stock its products. In contrast, retailers demanded that Heinz and Beech-Nut had to pay them 'slotting fees' in order to have their goods displayed on the shelves. A merger would eliminate 'head-to-head' competition between Heinz and Beech-Nut, resulting in higher prices for consumers.[67] The merger would reduce economic welfare because the merged entity would face no competition for being the second choice supplier of baby food. It would act like its larger rival and reduce output, behaving unilaterally to reduce economic welfare even though it did not hold a dominant position. Retailers would still need to stock a second choice baby food product, but would now be faced with only one second choice supplier which could behave as if it had a monopoly. It was argued that the dominance test would not be sufficiently flexible to apply to this kind of merger. To the suggestion that one could simply redefine a

---

[64] See US Horizontal Merger Guidelines ss. 2.21 and 2.22, noting two kinds of unilateral effects. We focus on the first.

[65] Horizontal Merger Guidelines para. 24.

[66] *FTC v. H. J. Heinz Co.* 246 F 3d 708 (2001), the so-called *Baby Foods* case.

[67] *FTC v. Heinz & Co. and Milnot Holding Corp.* (14 July 2000) (www.ftc.gov/os/2000/07/heinz.htm).

narrower market (e.g. lime and lemon gums, or the supply of the second brand of baby food), some objected that these narrow markets would have adverse effects in subsequent cases.[68] This is an unconvincing objection because market definitions in one case do not bind the Commission in other decisions.[69] Nevertheless, the Commission had to decide what to do in the face of arguments about a gap in the ECMR. The reform of the ECMR's substantive test to encompass unilateral effects is a revealing episode about how deeply economic thinking now prevails in the Commission but also about how this is translated imperfectly.[70]

3.2 The legal solution

When the issue was first raised in the Green Paper on the ECMR in 2001, the Commission's response was dismissive, stating that 'while interesting as a hypothetical discussion, the Commission has so far not encountered a situation of this kind',[71] and adding that the dominance test had not revealed any loopholes.[72] Nonetheless it agreed to keep the issue under consideration. After commissioning a study on unilateral effects,[73] and as a result of a consultation exercise where interested parties, including several eminent economists, urged reform,[74] the Commission became more persuaded, and in its explanatory notes on the proposed new ECMR it recognised that 'the economic community seems to agree that such cases [unilateral effects] should indeed be covered'.[75]

However, the new test does not reflect fully the views of economists. Most economists would have been in favour of a standard that blocks mergers when they would 'substantially lessen competition', the so-called SLC test, which operates in the US and the UK. Under this approach, one would not have to look for dominance for any merger, but merely test the effects of the merger. This would have eliminated the mismatch between law and economics by

[68] E.g. J. Fingleton and D. Nolan 'Mind the Gap: Reforming the EU Merger Regulation' (29 May 2003) (www.tca.ie/press/articles/mercato_29may_03.pdf).

[69] Cases T-125 and 127/97 *The Coca-Cola Company and Coca-Cola Enterprises Inc. v. Commission* [2000] ECR II-1733 paras. 80–5.

[70] See also K. Fountoukakos and S. Ryan 'A New Substantive Test for EU Merger Control' [2005] *European Competition Law Review* 277, where two Commission officials summarise the history of the amendments.

[71] Green Paper para. 166.   [72] Ibid. para. 167.

[73] M. Ivaldi, B. Jullien, P. Rey, P. Seabright and J. Tirole *The Economics of Unilateral Effects* (Report for DG Competition, European Commission, November 2003) (available at http://europa.eu.int/comm/competition/mergers/others/#study). The study is wider than the title suggests, offering an overview of coordinated and unilateral effects.

[74] In particular, J. Vickers 'How to Reform the EC Merger Test?' in Drauz and Reynolds *EC Merger Control*, who argued that it could not be safely assumed that the dominance test covered all anticompetitive mergers of concern.

[75] Proposal for a Council Regulation on the Control of Concentrations between Undertakings [2003] OJ C20/4, Explanatory Memorandum, para. 53.

implementing the economic standard as the new rule. However, against such a radical reform were concerns that a wholesale replacement of the current test would create uncertainty. Moreover, as the Commission and the Courts had by now established fairly detailed means by which to test for single-firm and collective dominance, dropping the dominance-based test altogether would require a reconsideration of the application of EC merger law to all types of merger. This led to the majority of the Council agreeing a compromise test which rearranges the language of the old ECMR (where proof of dominance was necessary) so that the substantial impediment of competition is the key test but proof of dominance will be particularly helpful in establishing anticompetitive effects. It is evident from the Recitals to the ECMR that the Council was keen to retain the old approach to assessing horizontal mergers creating a dominant position, a collective dominant position, vertical mergers and conglomerate mergers, and that the only reason for the reform was to close the unilateral-effects gap:

> The notion of 'significant impediment to effective competition' in Article 2(2) and (3) should be interpreted as extending, beyond the concept of dominance, only to the anti-competitive effects of a concentration resulting from the non-coordinated behaviour of undertakings which would not have a dominant position on the market concerned.[76]

While economists were successful in making a case for extending the scope of merger control, the full thrust of the economic analysis behind the SLC test was tempered by the need to retain a legal standard which the Commission had felt comfortable in using. Economics is asked to work around the legal norm. So it appears that there are two legal standards in the ECMR: the dominance and the substantial impediment of effective competition (SIEC) tests.

Moreover, the reform fails to capture the real economic problem. The economic problem that was raised did not require a reconsideration of the 'dominance' test but required a reconsideration of the *methods* by which we identify dominance.[77] As we saw in chapter 5, the traditional, indirect, method for measuring dominance rests on market definitions, market shares and entry barriers. However, we also saw that this methodology can be displaced if there is direct evidence of market power. The economic debate about unilateral effects was framed as a legal question while what it required was the need to explore the variety of economic evidence that can lead a competition authority to consider the same economic question: whether the merged entity has substantial market power. The reason why the *Heinz/Beech-Nut* merger would not have been considered satisfactorily under the ECMR was not because of the dominance test, but because the Commission has tended to

---

[76] Recital 25 ECMR.

[77] Along similar lines, see L. Coppi and M. Walker 'Substantial Convergence or Parallel Paths? Similarities and Differences in the Economic Analysis of Horizontal Mergers in US and EU Competition Law' (2004) 49 *Antitrust Bulletin* 101, 128–33.

examine market power in a mechanistic manner by defining markets, adding up market shares and assessing entry barriers, and has not considered whether there are other means by which we can measure whether the merged entity is dominant. In sum, the 'gap' lay in the lack of sufficiently sophisticated economic tools to determine market power, not in an under-inclusive legal test.

We can illustrate this critique by reference to the *US v. Oracle* decision where the court considered both direct and indirect methods to analyse the presence of market power. The Department of Justice sought to enjoin a merger between two makers of 'high function enterprise resource planning computer packages' sold to 'large complex enterprises'.[78] This was a very narrow market definition, because it suggested that certain types of consumers only bought certain types of computer applications. The court began by considering whether such a narrow market existed and whether market power could be measured indirectly. The court set out a four-stage test: first, the market must be one where products are differentiated (that is, the products of the merging parties are not 'perfect' substitutes, e.g. Coca Cola and Pepsi are not perfect substitutes); second, the products of the two firms must be close substitutes (that is, if the price of one rises, consumers switch to the other); third, other products are so different from those of the merging parties that after the merger a small but significant non-transitory price increase would be profitable; fourth, the non-merging firms are unlikely to reposition their products after the merger so as to compete vigorously against the merged entity.[79] According to the court, this analysis allows the court to determine whether the merger creates a 'grouping of sales' which can be classified as a relevant market:

> In a unilateral effects case, a plaintiff is attempting to prove that the merging parties could unilaterally increase prices. Accordingly, a plaintiff must demonstrate that the merging parties would enjoy a post-merger monopoly or dominant position, at least in a 'localized competition' space. Unilateral effects analysis shares many similarities with standard coordinated effects antitrust analysis. But there are also notable differences. Relevant markets defined in terms of 'localized competition' may be much narrower than relevant markets defined in typical cases in which a dominant position is required.[80]

The method which the court applies here is to measure market power indirectly by determining whether there is a distinct market. The court's label of 'localised competition' is helpful: on the general market which includes all consumers it may well be that the parties to the merger compete with a wide range of other software solutions, but the Department of Justice's contention was that for a certain group of consumers, only the software made by the two parties to the merger would do. The merger would not harm competition in the general market, but in the local market comprising only those firms that find Oracle and PeopleSoft the only alternatives, then a merger impedes

---

[78] *US v. Oracle* 331 F Supp 2d 1098 (2004).   [79] Ibid. at 1117.   [80] Ibid. at 1118.

competition if the court finds that the two have a monopoly or a dominant position.[81] Instead of asking whether dominance exists in a market one asks whether there is dominance vis-à-vis certain consumers, and instead of asking if there are entry barriers one asks whether other firms can 'reposition' their products (e.g. by alterations on design) so that they can compete for the consumers of the merged entity.[82]

The court subsequently considered whether one could prove the market power of the merged entity directly: that is, by reviewing whether there was any indication that the sole competitive restraint for both parties was the other. As we saw in chapter 5, the Department of Justice failed to provide sufficient evidence to allow the court to find that Oracle's prices were low only through pressure from PeopleSoft. In sum, the court in *Oracle* considered both direct and indirect evidence to determine whether the merger would lead to anti-competitive effects. Both of these approaches could be carried out using a 'dominance' test.

This discussion suggests that switching from a 'dominance' test to a 'substantial impediment of effective competition' test in the EC was unnecessary.[83] Economists demanding reform did not appreciate the flexibility of the dominance criteria and advocated unnecessary legal change, while the legislator did not understand the demands of the economic community who favoured a direct test of market power over one based on structural characteristics. Moreover, the Commission had already begun to identify direct evidence of market power in decisions predating the amendment to the ECMR, so that the dominance test was already becoming more flexible and capable of taking into account unilateral effects. The relevant cases are examined below.

3.3 Implementing the new legal standard

Even if we assume that the Community now scrutinises mergers either under the old dominance approach or under a SIEC test, the Commission fails to provide guidance that is structured in this manner. We might have expected that in writing the Horizontal Merger Guidelines the Commission would first

---

[81] Ibid. at 1123.

[82] The US Horizontal Merger Guidelines provide a comprehensive framework for unilateral effects cases, considering both the closeness of the products and the ability of competitors to reposition their products: ss. 2.211 and 2.212. See also S. B. Völcker 'Mind the Gap: Unilateral Effects Analysis Arrives in EC Merger Control' [2004] *European Competition Law Review* 395, 401.

[83] The one instance where the reform is relevant, but which did not seem to be debated, is in mergers that allow a reduction in capacity by the merged entity. Assume a market of fungible goods (e.g. steel). A merger between two major suppliers might create an incentive for the merged entity to reduce output and raise prices when the merged entity can make enough sales at a higher price for it to make a profit even though the aggregate number of sales is down. Provided the other firms are unable to expand output and entry barriers are high, this tactic will be successful. The reduced output will also cause prices to rise in the whole market. Dominance is unnecessary provided that nobody can increase output.

summarise how the 'dominance' standard was applied and then in a separate section illuminate the reader on how a substantial impediment of competition would be identified in cases where there is no dominance. Instead, the Horizontal Merger Guidelines have a section entitled 'Non-coordinated effects' which purports to offer guidance for unilateral effects arising from single-firm dominance and for unilateral effects arising without proof of dominance.[84] So on the one hand the reason for reforming the merger test was because dominance was not wide enough to encompass all unilateral effects, but on the other the Guidelines do not differentiate between proof of dominance and proof of unilateral effects without dominance. The Guidelines are more in line with the critique we have provided here, that as dominance means the presence of substantial market power, there are two ways to prove this: directly and indirectly. There are not two types of market power but two types of routes to prove market power.

Nonetheless the Commission might have structured the Guidelines to emphasise what evidence is more useful to prove market power indirectly and what evidence might serve to show market power directly. For example, the first factor listed in the Guidelines, the market share of the merged entity relative to competitors, is more relevant to the indirect method. On the other hand, a factor which is considerably more significant when trying to show market power directly is whether the merging firms are close competitors.[85] This factor is particularly important for analysing the effect of a merger in a market of differentiated goods.

The Commission's decisions pre-dating the reform of the ECMR indicate that the Commission was already well on its way to filling the 'gap' of the old dominance test, making the reform of the ECMR unnecessary. First, the Commission had already gained some experience in determining whether the products of the merging firms are close substitutes, as this was the key factor in the Commission's analysis of Volvo's proposed mergers with Scania and Renault. These were part of Volvo's strategy to focus its energies on the truck markets and emerge as a strong global player.[86] The Volvo/Scania merger was blocked, not only because Volvo's market share in heavy trucks in Sweden was 44.7 per cent and Scania's 46.1 per cent and the next competitor lagged behind with 6.2 per cent, but also because Volvo and Scania were each other's closest competitors:[87] purchasers based their decisions about which truck to buy on a range of non-price factors (e.g. the reputation of the brand, the availability of a service network), and taking all these attributes together, the merging parties were the only ones able to offer an attractive package; post-merger a price increase in the Volvo brand would lead to consumers switching to Scania, not to other competitors. In contrast, in *Volvo/Renault* the merged entity would have had a combined market share

---

[84] Horizontal Merger Guidelines paras. 24–38.   [85] Ibid. paras. 28–30.
[86] Case COMP/M.1672 *Volvo/Scania* [2001] OJ L134/74 para. 7.   [87] Ibid. paras. 80–2, 107–8.

of 49 per cent in the market for heavy trucks in France, which raised the risk that the merger might create a dominant firm, but the Commission found that the two firms were not each other's closest competitors. Renault was losing sales to DAF, and Volvo trucks were seen by consumers as being of superior quality to those of Renault: in fact a price increase by Volvo in 1998 had not been matched by other competitors.[88] Accordingly, while market shares indicated dominance, a closer analysis of the market suggested that the merged entity had no greater power to raise the price of its trucks: a price increase in Renault trucks would have seen customers migrate to other truck manufacturers, not to Volvo. These two decisions show us that, as in the *Oracle* case, there are two ways of determining whether the merger is anti-competitive. One is to define markets, and in the *Volvo/Scania* merger we find that there is a 'localised market' of customers for whom only Volvo or Scania trucks will do. In contrast, in the *Volvo/Renault* case we find a localised market of Renault/DAF consumers and a market of consumers who favoured Volvo. The second merger does not allow the merged entity to raise prices on any localised market because there is no horizontal overlap. The second way of proving anticompetitive effects is to show that if Volvo and Scania were to merge, a price increase in Volvo trucks would not lead to any loss of profits by the merged entity because consumers would either pay more or switch to Scania. Instead, in the Volvo/Renault merger, a price increase in Renault goods would lead consumers to buy DAF. In sum, we can either define localised markets, or test for market power directly: the answer is the same. The difference is in the evidence used to prove the effects. More recently the Commission has used a vast range of qualitative studies to determine whether a merger would eliminate a significant competitor, and while so far these studies have been used to consolidate a finding of dominance,[89] the same methods could be used to establish whether the merged entity would be able to cause harm.

Second, the Commission was already departing from the old dominance approach by considering its analysis in a series of mergers in markets for complex medical equipment. In the *Philips/Agilent* merger, for example, the relevant market for cardiac ultrasound machines was oligopolistic, and while the combined market shares of the products sold by the merging parties were higher than those of competitors, evidence from an economic study revealed that the products of the merging parties were not close substitutes:

> The conclusion which can be drawn from the study is that for HSG's cardiac ultrasound machines [those which Philips was acquiring from Agilent] GE and Siemens/Acuson are the strongest challengers on both projects won and lost. ATL [machines made by Philips] is generally the third ranked. Therefore, it can be assumed that Philips/HSG would not be in a position to increase prices for

---

[88] Case COMP/M.1980 *Volvo/Renault* (1 September 2000) paras. 33–4.
[89] Most notably in Case COMP/M.3083 *GE/Instrumentarium* [2004] OJ L109/1 paras. 125–47.

one or both products without facing competitive constraints by the other first-tier suppliers.[90]

This methodology is more consistent with the first approach suggested in *Oracle* where what counts is not the determination of market shares but whether there would be consumer harm post-merger. Similarly, in the *Philips/Marconi* merger the Commission found that while the merger would allow Philips to strengthen its 'leading position', no anticompetitive risks arose because the merger eliminated neither of Philips's main competitors.[91] In these cases a precise definition of the market is unnecessary because there is direct evidence that shows that price competition would remain lively after the merger.

The methods in the trucks and medical equipment mergers reflect the Commission's opening statements in the Horizontal Merger Guidelines where it indicates that its policy is to prevent mergers that would be likely to deprive customers of economic benefits 'by significantly increasing the market power of firms'.[92] While the letter of the ECMR preserves the old 'dominance' standard, the spirit of the Commission's Guidelines embraces a more economics-based approach focused on market power. The upshot of this is that we might find that in future, mergers which the Commission originally scrutinised under the 'dominance' test are reclassified as unilateral effects cases under the SIEC test. For example, in *Barilla/BPL/Kamps*, the merged entity would have held a combined market share in the German market for bread substitutes (i.e. crispbread and crackers) of over 40 per cent, but decisive in the Commission's finding of anticompetitive risk was that the merger would bring together the two leading brands of bread substitutes, removing the closest substitute to the leading brand.[93] This evidence can prove 'dominance', but it can also go to show in a more direct manner that post-merger there is likely to be a significant impediment of competition because the merged entity faces no competitors.

4 Vertical mergers

A firm (say a manufacturer of ready-mixed concrete) may wish to integrate 'backwards' and acquire a cement plant, or it may wish to integrate 'forwards' and acquire a construction company. In competitive markets vertical mergers cause no competition concerns, but are dictated by the firm's desire to save costs. Cost savings may be of two kinds: a vertically integrated firm may be able

---

[90] Case COMP/M.2256 *Philips/Agilent* (2 March 2001) para. 33.
[91] Case COMP/M. 2537 *Philips/Marconi Medical Systems* (17 October 2001) paras. 30–4.
[92] Horizontal Merger Guidelines para. 8.
[93] Case COMP/M.2817 *Barilla/BPS/Kamps* (25 June 2002) paras. 34 and 38. The merger was cleared when Barilla undertook to divest Kamps' brand, retaining the pre-merger competitive structure.

to exploit certain technology more effectively; or it saves the costs of contracting with firms up- or downstream, guarantees that deliveries are made on time and thus saves all the costs that go with such contracts.[94] The increased efficiency of a vertically integrated ready-mixed concrete plant may increase its market share at the expense of non-integrated firms, but consumers benefit from the lower costs.

Whether a vertical merger that involves a dominant firm in the up- or downstream market warrants scrutiny is more controversial. The Chicago School view is that there can be no risks to competition, for if a firm is dominant upstream, it is already selling at an anticompetitive price, and by acquiring a downstream firm it is not able to raise that anticompetitive price further, so the effects of the merger are at worst neutral. Efficiencies realised through vertical integration suggests that some of the savings will be passed on to consumers.[95] However, competition authorities have not been as optimistic and recent economic analysis has revealed that some vertical mergers can reduce competition, in particular because a vertical merger may foreclose competitors. The foreclosure analysis is comparable to the leveraging one we have reviewed in chapter 6. Foreclosure can be of two sorts. First, foreclosure can occur in the non-dominated market. Take for example a firm dominant in the upstream (cement) market acquiring a firm in the downstream market (concrete). The merged entity could foreclose competition on the downstream market by limiting supplies, or raising the price of cement to competitors on the concrete market.[96] The effect of this is that the merged entity can use its dominance in the cement market to leverage its position in the concrete market.[97] Second, foreclosure can occur in the dominated market. Consider a dominant cement manufacturer merging with a non-dominant but significant ready-mixed concrete manufacturer again: if the merged entity refuses to buy cement from competitors, this could lead to the exit of competing cement manufacturers, consolidating the dominant position upstream. Foreclosure can also be achieved when a vertically integrated dominant firm refuses to sell to competitors on the downstream market. Say a downstream concrete firm buys 50 per cent of its cement supplies from the dominant firm and 50 per cent from a competitor. If the competitor is unable to increase supplies or find alternative customers, then once the dominant firm ceases supplying cement to the downstream firm, it can shut down competitors downstream (because they

---

[94] The seminal work on the latter is by R. H. Coase 'The Nature of the Firm' (1937) 4 *Economica* 386. See also O. Williamson 'Transaction-Cost Economics: The Governance of Contractual Relations' (1979) 22 *Journal of Law and Economics* 233.

[95] R. H. Bork *The Antitrust Paradox* (New York: Free Press, 1978) ch. 11. This argument is comparable to the Chicago School critique of tying discussed in chapter 6.

[96] See Case M.2317 *Lafarge/Blue Circle (II)* (1 March 2001) para. 17; Case M.1381 *Imetal/English China Clays* (26 April 1999) para. 68.

[97] See M. H. Riordan and S. C. Salop 'Evaluating Vertical Mergers: A Post Chicago Approach' (1995) 63 *Antitrust Law Journal* 513.

cannot find enough cement to keep the business running) and also upstream as the competing cement supplier has no more customers to sell to.[98]

4.1 Vertical mergers and the ECMR

The anticipated anticompetitive effects in a vertical merger depend upon the merged entity behaving in a specific manner. Unlike horizontal mergers where proof that the merger creates a dominant position or substantial market power is normally sufficient to establish that the merger will substantially impede effective competition, the Commission must show that the merged entity will have, post-merger, an incentive to foreclose and the capacity to foreclose, and that foreclosure can have significant anticompetitive effects.[99]

The Commission can satisfy the first element by showing that foreclosure of rivals would be in the merged entity's commercial interests.[100] However, the Commission is also bound to consider any disincentives that arise if the methods by which foreclosure is carried out constitute an abuse of a dominant position under Article 82. The potential fine could deter the firm from engaging in leverage.[101] The way the CFI has interpreted this requirement appears to suggest that if leverage would take the form of an abuse of dominance, it seems very unlikely that the merged entity will have the incentive to engage in leverage.

The second step is to evaluate the capacity to leverage. To prove this, the Commission should consider whether the market context makes leveraging profitable.[102] The majority of the case law suggests that the capacity to leverage depends upon the merged entity being dominant in one of the two markets.[103]

The final step is to prove that the merger will have anticompetitive effects. One legal question to be confronted is how to apply the old and new ECMR to this requirement. Recall that under the old ECMR, the merger had to create or strengthen a dominant position. Where the vertical merger has foreclosure effects on the dominated markets, then the application of the ECMR is unproblematic (the merger strengthens a pre-existing dominant position), but what if the fear is that the vertical merger allows the merged entity to leverage in a new market: must the Commission prove that the merger will lead to the creation of a dominant position in the non-dominated market?[104]

---

[98] Of course, in this example, there would be no foreclosure if there are other downstream concrete buyers to which the cement can be sold. See e.g. Case M.1759 *RMC/Rugby* (15 December 1999) paras. 18–19, where the market was sufficiently competitive that vertical integration raised no foreclosure risks. Compare the reasoning of the Supreme Court in *Brown Shoe Company v. United States* 370 US 294 (1962), where even small foreclosure effects were of concern. The strict approach by the Supreme Court has now been abandoned.

[99] Case M.2803 *Telia/Sonera* (10 July 2002) para. 91.

[100] Case T-210/01 *General Electric v. Commission*, judgment of 14 December 2005, para. 297.

[101] Ibid. paras. 303–12.   [102] E.g. Case M.1879 *Boeing/Hughes* (27 September 2000) para. 83.

[103] E.g. Case M.2803 *Telia/Sonera* (10 July 2002) para. 80.

[104] For a detailed examination of the case law, see A. Lindsay *The EC Merger Regulation: Substantive Issues* (London: Sweet & Maxwell, 2003) pp. 376–8.

Under the old ECMR, dominance somewhere had to be established, so if the merger did not strengthen a pre-existing dominant position, it follows that dominance elsewhere had to be established. However, the test in the new ECMR is different because the Commission has to show that a merger will substantially impede effective competition, not that the merger creates or strengthens a dominant position. Therefore, proof of significant foreclosure should suffice to establish that the merger has anticompetitive effects. The alternative view is that the preamble to the ECMR suggests that the new 'SIEC' test is designed to apply exclusively to horizontal mergers having 'unilateral' effects, so that for all other types of merger the old dominance test must be fulfilled. This argument, however, is unconvincing, because the aim of merger law must be to prevent all transactions that substantially impede effective competition, and the creation of dominance is but one example of that effect. Moreover, as we will see in chapter 10, the risk of foreclosure also occurs when a non-dominant firm enters into a vertical contract (e.g. a distribution contract) with a downstream firm. Accordingly, it seems unnecessary to demand the creation of a dominant position in the non-dominated market in the merger context. This view seems to be supported by two recent merger decisions which ignore the ECMR's Recital and find that a vertical merger creates anticompetitive effects without showing dominance. In one case the Commission found that the merged entity would be dominant in one upstream market and have a market share of 30–40 per cent on the downstream market, with one significant competitor downstream holding a market share of 40–50 per cent. The Commission feared that the merged entity would cease supplying the upstream product to downstream competitors and this would strengthen its position downstream. The Commission did not say that a dominant position would result on the downstream market.[105] A similar analysis was undertaken in E.ON/MOL.[106] MOL held a quasi-monopoly in the (upstream) market for wholesale gas and E.ON was a strong player downstream. The Commission feared that after the merger MOL would have an incentive to raise rivals' costs by making access to the upstream market more difficult, strengthening E.ON's position downstream. The merger would have substantially impeded effective competition downstream but there was no evidence that E.ON would obtain a dominant position.

One implication of this analysis and the two recent decisions is that the assessment of vertical mergers requires a consideration of two sources of competitive harm: 'anticompetitive foreclosure' or the creation or strengthening of a dominant position. It follows that a vertical merger can be blocked even if the parties are not dominant pre-merger in the up- or downstream markets and even if there is no post-merger dominance, provided there is foreclosure. And to return to our critique of the ECMR's reform, it is striking that the first

---

[105] Case M.3593 *Apollo/Bakelite* (11 April 2005) paras. 154–5.
[106] Case M.3696 *E.ON/MOL* (21 December 2005).

two cases where the SIEC test was applied are vertical mergers, while the debate about the gap in the old ECMR was about horizontal mergers.[107]

4.2 Vertical mergers in the broadcasting sector

Foreclosure risks have been particularly prominent in the broadcasting sector. In the United States this is exemplified by the agreement the FTC reached in allowing Time Warner to acquire Turner Broadcasting.[108] Together, Time Warner and Turner would produce 40 per cent of all cable programmes (the upstream market). Time Warner and Tele-Communications Inc. (TCI) would hold 44 per cent of the market for cable distribution (the downstream market). In addition, TCI had a long-term contract to carry Turner programming on its cable network. This gave the new company a leading position in the upstream market for cable programming and in the downstream market for cable distribution. In the eyes of the FTC this scenario would lead to foreclosure of both markets. Programme makers competing with Time Warner and Turner would have difficulties entering the distribution market – Time Warner would tend to favour its own programmes, TCI had a long-term contract with Turner, and the remaining distribution channels would not be big enough to allow the new programmer to distribute his product sufficiently widely to achieve profitability. Moreover, Time Warner could raise entry barriers to competing programme makers further by selling other cable distributors 'bundles' of Time Warner and Turner programmes, which would make it difficult for other cable programmers to sell their programmes. The merger would also make life difficult for downstream broadcasters who would compete with TCI – they would need access to programmes, and Time Warner would have an incentive to price discriminate in favour of its distribution network, raising the costs of other broadcasters.

This example shows that a vertically integrated firm with sufficient market power may adopt two strategies to raise entry barriers: first denying access to its upstream or downstream facilities, second raising rivals' costs, making their existence on the market less profitable. These concerns are reflected in the conditions the FTC imposed on the parties so that the merger could be consummated. In order to ensure that new programmes had access to a distribution network, the following remedies were accepted. First, TCI would sever its links with Time Warner and rescind its long-term contracts with Turner. These would give TCI the independence to select competing

---

[107] And it is surprising to read an article co-authored by the Commission's chief economist that refers to the *E.ON* case as a 'gap' case. L.-H. Röller and M. de la Mano 'The Impact of the New Substantive Test in European Merger Control' (2006) 2 *European Competition Journal* 9.

[108] See press release at www.ftc.gov/opa/1997/9702/twfinal.htm; S. M. Besen, E. J. Murdoch, D. P. O'Brien, S. C. Salop and J. Woodbury 'Vertical and Horizontal Ownership in Cable TV: *Time Warner–Turner* (1996)' in J. E. Kwoka Jr and L. J. White (eds.) *The Antitrust Revolution* 3rd edn (Oxford: Oxford University Press, 1999).

programmes. Second, Time Warner agreed not to raise rivals' costs by promising not to discriminate vis-à-vis other programmers who sought to distribute their programmes via its network, and by not 'bundling' its programmes with those of Turner so that other distributors could choose to broadcast other programmes. These remedies opened up the upstream market. In order to open the downstream market for new distributors, Time Warner was obliged not to discriminate against these when selling its cable programmes.

This reasoning appears to rest on the identification of two different types of entry barrier. First, a competitor of the merged entity on the up- or downstream part of the market would find it difficult to obtain access to the other level of the market. For example, a new programmer must find it impossible either to buy up a cable distribution network or to contract with enough cable distribution networks to be able to enter the market successfully. Thus if Time Warner and TCI do not give a new programmer access, he cannot find alternative access. Secondly, Time Warner and TCI can raise barriers by granting discriminatory access to their distribution network or act to reduce further the number of other distributors who are willing to buy the competitor's programmes. Seen in this light, the FTC's case is not dissimilar to an 'essential facilities' case, whereby even though Time Warner and TCI control only 44 per cent of distribution, this is sufficient, in the circumstances of the case, to conclude that access to their network is essential for the existence of other competitors. The analogy with essential facilities becomes even more striking when we consider that the remedies imposing a duty on Time Warner to deal with potential competitors are exactly the kinds of obligations imposed under the essential facilities case law. Inevitably this aggressive remedy raised the concern that the FTC was protecting competitors rather than competition.[109] Moreover, it has been argued that while there is evidence that vertical integration forecloses market access (i.e. integrated firms tend to favour their own programmes), it also leads to greater efficiencies in these markets, so that overall the effects of this kind of merger are positive. The efficiencies are assumed because vertically integrated firms sell more subscriptions.[110]

The EC Commission has also been concerned about foreclosure effects in media markets.[111] Initially the Commission blocked a number of mergers,[112]

---

[109] See the dissents of FTC Commissioners Azquenaga and Starek, www.ftc.gov/opa/1997/9702/twfinal.htm.

[110] T. Chipty 'Vertical Integration, Market Foreclosure, and Consumer Welfare in the Cable Television Industry' (2001) 91 *American Economic Review* 428.

[111] For a flavour of the Commission's perspective, see M. Mendes Pereira 'Vertical and Horizontal Integration in the Media Sector and EU Competition Law' (speech, April 2003, available at http://ec.europa.eu/comm/competition/index_en.html); G. B. Abbamonte and V. Rabassa 'Foreclosure and Vertical Mergers – The Commission's Review of Vertical Effects in the Last Wave of Media Mergers' [2001] *European Competition Law Review* 214.

[112] Case M.469 *MSG Media Services* [1994] OJ L364/1; Case M.490 *Nordic Satellite Distribution* [1996] OJ L53/20; Case M.709 *Telefónica/Sogecable/Cablevisión* (19 July 1996) (decision not adopted when parties withdrew their plans).

but more recently it has cleared mergers subject to commitments that are designed to remove the threat of foreclosure. This change in policy is a recognition of changed economic conditions: while in the early 1990s there were fears that new digital technologies would be monopolised, the current climate recognises the considerable difficulties faced by entrants in the digital broadcasting market.[113]

The *Vivendi/Canal+/Seagram* merger is illustrative of the Commission's regulatory approach and of the market conditions.[114] The merger affected markets for music and film. In the film market, the vertical concerns arose in this manner: before the merger, Canal + (controlled by Vivendi) already held a dominant position in the (downstream) pay-TV market in several Member States, in particular because it had managed to obtain exclusive output deals with the majority of US studios, giving it a 'de facto near monopoly position on premium films for pay-TV'.[115] The merger with Seagram would have strengthened Canal +'s position because Seagram owned Universal, one of the six major Hollywood studios. As a result, Canal + would have had exclusive access to Universal's films and this would have also allowed Canal + to negotiate further exclusive deals with other Hollywood major studios because Universal provided finance for several films produced by other studios. Moreover, the merger would have linked Canal + with two other major film producers, MGM and Paramount, because of a shared distributor, and, thanks to Vivendi's 25 per cent control of Fox, the merged entity would have had links with another major producer. The upshot would have been to strengthen Canal + and foreclose the pay-TV market as competitors of Canal + would have found it hard to obtain premium films. This reasoning is premised on the Commission's view that one of the principal selling points of a pay-TV platform is being able to show popular films, in particular Hollywood blockbusters (so-called premium films) and/or major sporting events. The merger therefore meant that the merged entity could refuse to allow competing pay-TV operators access to attractive content, undermining their ability to compete. The merger also affected two internet-based markets: that for internet portals (a gateway through which a user can have access to online services) and that for online music (where customers can download music from the Internet). Vivendi had joint control of Vizzavi, one of the leading internet portals, and the risk of foreclosure arose because Seagram owned Universal's large music library. Just as premium films are key to the success of pay-TV, music is a key to the emerging portal market, and the merger would have made access to this market more difficult. In addition, Vizzavi's large existing customer base would have made it easier for it to attract other music content providers. In the long term this would have led to higher prices for online music.

---

[113] See Case JV.37 *BskyB/KirchPayTV* (21 March 2000); Case IV/36.539*BiB/Open* [1999] OJ L312/1; Case M.2876 *Newscorp/Telepiú* [2004] OJ L110/73; Case M.1845 *AOL/Time Warner* [2000] OJ L268/28.

[114] Case COMP/M.2050 (13 October 2000).   [115] Ibid. para. 40.

The Commission did not oppose the merger because the parties made certain commitments that removed the foreclosure effects. On the pay-TV market the parties undertook not to grant to Canal + more than 50 per cent of Universal films for five years, and Vivendi agreed to divest its stake in BskyB (thereby severing its links with one of the majors, Fox). The effect was to reduce the number of films Canal + would have exclusive access to and to allow more competition on the pay-TV market. In the online markets the parties undertook to grant access to Universal's music content to others on a non-discriminatory basis. This would prevent Vizzavi having exclusive access to attractive content that could have foreclosed the emerging internet markets.

These interventions by the competition authorities in both the EC and US are somewhat problematic because the agencies appear to be taking the place of industry regulators.[116] There are two aspects to this observation. First, the competition agencies intervene to shape the transaction so as to achieve what they consider is the best outcome for the market. The authorities seem to ignore the potential efficiencies that may result from the merger and concentrate instead on providing what they consider is the outcome which mostly benefits consumers. The Commission's early regulatory efforts whereby mergers affecting the pay-TV markets were blocked were criticised for failing to allow this market to develop at all, so that the wish to ensure a competitive market has led to poorly developed markets instead.[117] A second dimension of this critique is that the authorities might be concerned not merely with competitive markets but also with the pluralism of the media. In the US case, one concern was that the merger would favour the parties' own twenty-four-hour news channel (CNN) at the expense of other new entrants in the market (MSBNC and Fox news),[118] and in the Community context, there are statements from Commission officials which suggest that concerns over pluralism have had a role to play in the merger case law. Unfortunately the real significance of pluralism in the Commission's regulatory efforts is unclear. Moreover, it has been argued that competition policy is a poor way of achieving media pluralism, because merely ensuring market access to other firms does not guarantee diversity in broadcasting.[119]

5 Conglomerate mergers

Mergers are conglomerate when they are neither horizontal nor vertical: the products of the parties may be complementary (e.g. photocopiers and ink) or

---

[116] See also T. E. Sullivan 'The Antitrust Division as a Regulatory Agency: An Enforcement Policy in Transition' (1986) 64 *Washington University Law Quarterly* 997.

[117] C. Veljanovski 'Competitive Regulation of Digital Pay TV' in J. Grayston (ed.) *European Economics and Law* (Bembridge: Palladian Law Publishing, 1999).

[118] Besen et al. 'Vertical and Horizontal Ownership' p. 462.

[119] For a lively discussion, see M. Ariño 'Digital War and Peace: Regulation and Competition in European Digital Broadcasting' (2004) 10 *European Public Law* 135.

completely unrelated. Conglomerate mergers are now rare. They peaked in the United States in the 1970s (when it was considered that diversification would give competitive advantages) but have become less fashionable in recent times as firms consider that it is more profitable to specialise in a core business. This explains the higher number of horizontal mergers and many de-mergers as large conglomerates sell off ancillary businesses.[120] At the same time, the economic profession has revised its originally hostile position on conglomerate mergers, emphasising instead the possibilities that these mergers may yield similar efficiencies to vertical mergers.

In contrast to these trends in business practice and economics, the Commission is increasingly interested in the potential anticompetitive effects of conglomerate mergers. According to the Commission's practice, these mergers raise no anticompetitive concerns when the products of the parties are unrelated – thus a merger between a car manufacturer and a wine producer cannot raise competition concerns. Of more worry for the Commission are mergers where the firms produce two complementary products, or products that consumers tend to buy together. The Commission's principal concern is that the merged entity may engage in leverage, by tying the two products and thereby harming firms that sell only one. In contrast, economists normally see ties as efficiency enhancing because they result in lower prices to consumers. In addition to tying concerns, the Commission fears a conglomerate merger because it may create a firm with an incentive to behave strategically and harm competitors. A third concern arises when a firm acquires a potential competitor, thereby safeguarding its market power. This last scenario is best seen as a horizontal merger. We consider each of these three theories of competitive harm in turn, paying particular attention to leveraging, which is the most controversial theory of harm.

5.1 Leveraging

In its first detailed analysis of a merger's conglomerate dimensions (*Guinness/ Grand Met*) the Commission observed how a merger combining the activities of the two leading suppliers of spirits in the world would confer upon the new firm (to be called Diageo) the ability to offer a wide portfolio of drinks to its customers.[121] The anticompetitive risks of this were noted on the Greek market, where Guinness had strong sales of whisky, rum and gin while Grand Met was strong in the market for brandy, ouzo (the Greek national drink), tequila and liqueurs. The Commission's concern was not that the

---

[120] F. M. Scherer and D. Ross *Industrial Market Structure and Economic Performance* 3rd edn (Boston, MA: Houghton Mifflin, 1990) pp. 90–1.

[121] [1998] OJ L288/24. The discussion of the conglomerate effects is to be found at paras. 38–46 (general considerations) and paras. 80–103 (application to the Greek market). For comment, see S. Baker and D. Ridyard 'Portfolio Power – A Rum Deal' [1999] *European Competition Law Review* 181.

parties would come to dominate one of these spirit sectors (the merger raised very few horizontal overlaps) but that by holding a strong position in so many types of spirits (and a dominant position in gin, rum and brandy) the portfolio held by the new company would create a position of dominance in the sales of all spirits. As one competitor remarked to the Commission: 'In short the market power deriving from a portfolio of brands exceeds the sum of its parts.'[122]

The Commission identified four effects of the merger. First, customers would prefer purchasing from the merged entity because it offered a wider range of goods, and would be able to offer appealing discounts. Second, the merged entity would have lower costs because of the economies of scale and scope that result from integrating two distribution networks. Neither of these advantages are a good reason for blocking the merger: they show instead that the merger leads to efficiencies. A third concern was more rational from an economic perspective: a firm with a powerful portfolio of brands can offer bundles of drinks or tie the sale of its popular drinks with the sales of other spirits, thereby increasing its sales. Alternatively, the firm could demand that bars promote the spirits sold by it, which the buyers would have to accept since they could not afford not to stock the famous brands sold by the new firm. Fourth, the firm could threaten not to supply the retailer with certain 'must stock' drinks if he did not buy all goods from it. These strategies would strengthen the position of the new firm in all product ranges and reduce the sales of other competitors who lack comparable portfolio power. Thus while the market leader for Vodka is Stolichnaya, its owner (Seagram) lacked a sufficiently strong portfolio to counteract any aggressive tactic by the new firm to increase its presence in the Greek market. The fact that both Guinness and Grand Met had already individually sought to use their current portfolio to increase their sales suggested that this strategy was likely to be continued.

The Commission allowed the merger by requiring the parties to eliminate the source of the anticompetitive risk, terminating Guinness's right to distribute Bacardi rum in Greece (sales of which accounted for 70–80 per cent of sales of rum), and by the divestiture of some whisky brands. The effect was that Diageo no longer had as wide a range of spirits to offer, tempering its market power. Nonetheless this still left Diageo in a stronger position than its rivals who remained considerably smaller; moreover its dominance in the brandy and gin sectors was unaffected, Diageo holding on to the most prominent brands in both sectors (Gordon's and Metaxa), so one may question whether the divestitures were sufficient to eliminate Diageo's dominance.[123] On the other hand, these relatively lenient remedies might indicate that dominance and the consequent risk of tying only arises in limited circumstances – when

---

[122] [1998] OJ L288/24 para. 38.
[123] Only a minority of the Advisory Committee considered that the undertakings would be sufficient to prevent the creation of a dominant position, [1998] OJ C329/3.

the portfolio of brands held by the dominant firm is sufficiently extensive to eliminate a substantial portion of other competitors; thus even a small reduction in Diageo's market power would suffice to restore competition in the market.

The Commission's concerns about leveraging in this decision can be interpreted in three different ways.[124] First, judged from an economic perspective, leveraging is anticompetitive only if the effects are the consolidation of monopoly power, either in the markets that the firm already dominates or in new markets.[125] However, there is no analysis in the *Guinness* decision to suggest that tying would disadvantage rivals so much that they would exit the market, giving Diageo a dominant position in every drink sector. A second perspective is to suggest that the Commission was interested in consumer welfare: Diageo's tactics could restrict the diversity of drinks available to consumers. Thus whilst a tie would allow a retailer to obtain cheaper goods, a market without tying would allow the retailer to select a broader range of products, satisfying a different aspect of consumer demand. As suggested in chapter 4, the Commission's interest in competition cases is not about generating total welfare, but about consumer welfare. *Guinness* could be an example where the two types of welfare measures diverge: a wider range of drinks sold at a slightly higher price is preferred to a narrower range of drinks sold for less. A third way of interpreting *Guinness* is to suggest that the decision protects rivals. On this perspective, safeguarding competitors' economic freedom is the basis upon which the decision is reached.

The controversial *Tetra Laval* and *GE/Honeywell* cases might offer some clues as to which of these three readings is the most accurate reflection of the Commission's policy. The *GE/Honeywell* decision is controversial because the Commission blocked a merger between two American firms that had been allowed by the US authorities, prompting severe criticism. The Commission's response to those criticisms allows us to explore the basis upon which leveraging is a concern. The *Tetra Laval* case instead is helpful because it is the first time that the ECJ has become involved in the regulation of these types of merger and it helps us explain what must be proven by the Commission to block a merger creating risks of leverage.

5.1.1 The Commission's policy on leveraging

In *GE/Honeywell* the Commission found that GE had a dominant position in the market for large commercial aircraft engines and large regional jet aircraft engines, while Honeywell had a leading (but not dominant) position *inter alia* in the markets for avionics and non-avionics (which are goods that are fitted

---

[124] E. R. Emch 'Portfolio Effects in Merger Analysis: Differences between EU and US Practice and Recommendations for the Future' [2004] *Antitrust Bulletin* 55, criticising the Commission for failing to articulate clearly the grounds upon which conglomerate mergers are challenged, and failing to deploy an economic approach.

[125] See pp. 187–92, where we distinguished between offensive and defensive leveraging.

onto aircraft: for example, wheels, brakes and auxiliary power units). The merger would result in a strengthening of the market position of the products of both firms. For Honeywell's products, the merged entity would come to hold a dominant position, on the basis of two considerations. First, the Commission identified the likelihood of tying GE engines with Honeywell products, a common form of leveraging. Second, the Commission found certain specific features of GE that increased the possibilities of leverage. It found that Honeywell would benefit from a number of the competitive advantages which GE has to strengthen its own position: GE's ability to obtain exclusive contracts for the supply of engines to certain airframe manufacturers would trickle down to Honeywell's products so that Honeywell would now also be in a position to gain exclusive rights for its products; GE's GECAS branch (which is the largest purchaser of aircraft in the world) would extend its GE-only purchasing policy to Honeywell parts, furthering Honeywell's position in the market. Moreover, GE's considerable financial resources (especially from GE Capital) would allow the company to cross-subsidise its business segments. These considerations meant that the merger would create a dominant position in Honeywell's product markets because the other competitors in these markets would see their market shares shrink and would not have comparable commercial advantages. The result of this is that the competitors would be marginalised and possibly eliminated, both as participants in the market and as sources of innovation.

Leveraging claims such as these have been criticised as implausible from a number of perspectives. On the one hand, a number of practical arguments can be made to suggest that leveraging is unlikely to be successful. First, leveraging is unlikely unless the majority of consumers buy both products and selective tying is unlikely to exclude rivals; second, even if the products are complementary they might not be purchased at the same time, so they cannot be sold with a tie; third, customers may prefer to obtain goods from multiple sources, either because they value non-price features of other goods, or because they foresee that leveraging can exclude other suppliers and harm them in the long term. In *GE/Honeywell* for example, there were two major buyers (Boeing and Airbus) who would be wary of accepting rebates today if they foresaw monopoly prices in the future. The fact that neither expressed concerns about foreclosure effects suggested that leveraging was unlikely.[126] Another line of criticism suggests that leveraging is an efficiency-enhancing strategy and that there are no extra monopoly profits that can be gained by tying one product to another.[127] A third critique is that even if leveraging is successful in eliminating current competitors, the anticipated anticompetitive effects occur in an uncertain future when new competitors might have entered the market, so one is

[126] S. B. Völcker 'Leveraging as a Theory of Competitive Harm in EU Merger Control' (2003) 40 *Common Market Law Review* 581, 597–601.
[127] This is the Chicago School critique which we reviewed in ch. 6, pp. 187–9.

preventing a merger on the off chance that the parties might do something that damages current competitors but benefits consumers in the short run, in the expectation that this might allow them to raise prices in the future, with the assumption that new competitors will not surface. It is suggested that this is an irrational exercise of power by competition authorities given the number of uncertainties involved. Granted, all merger law is about predicting the future, but what one is predicting in horizontal and vertical mergers is immediate consumer harm, whereas here the consumer harm occurs at an unspecified time in the future.

The major criticism of the Commission's regulation of conglomerate mergers is that, taking into account all the weaknesses summarised above, it protects competitors and not competition, in contrast to US merger law where the authorities recognise the efficiency of conglomerate mergers. However, closer inspection reveals that the schism between the EC and the US lies elsewhere. The Commission's concern in these cases was not so much the elimination of competitors per se, but the consequences of their elimi- nation. In *GE/Honeywell*, the Commission thought that the foreclosure of the market would lead to a reduction of competition in the future, in two respects: first, as the market power of the new company would grow even further it would be free to raise prices; second, the elimination of competitors would stifle innovation. In *Air Liquide/BOC* the Commission acknowledged that tying as a means of entering a new market is not always unlawful but becomes so when there is dominance in one market which is used to strengthen dominance in another market.[128] These concerns are about mar- ket failures and consumer welfare. If there is a philosophical split between the EC and the US it is not that the EC protects competitors while the US protects competition. Rather it is that the Commission focuses on the immediate negative impact of the merger (harm to competitors) and has a pessimistic attitude towards the ability of the market to restore competition when competitors exit the market. This is the converse of the position in the United States where authorities focus on the immediate benefits of the merger and rely on the market to ensure that the market remains compet- itive.[129] This sentiment was expressed clearly by the then Director of the Merger Task Force when defending the *GE/Honeywell* decision. In his view the decision preserved a competitive market structure, which was necessary because there can be no competition without competitors. He rejected what he labelled a 'Darwinian' theory of markets, where inefficient competitors exit and more efficient firms enter. In his view in some markets exit is not followed by entry of new competitors, and so protecting a competitive

---

[128] Case M.1630 *Air Liquide/BOC* (18 January 2000) para. 194.

[129] W. J. Kolasky 'Conglomerate Mergers and Range Effects: It's a Long Way from Chicago to Brussels' (speech, 9 November 2001, available at www.usdoj.gov/atr/public/speeches/ 9536.pdf).

market structure was important.[130] In sum, the Commission believes in competitors, the DOJ believes in markets.

The causes of this schism are political, economic and institutional. At a political level, the EC views a market as well functioning when there are many market participants, disciplined by law. Markets fail when one dominant participant disciplines others. From an economics perspective, the US belief in the self-correcting nature of markets is not shared by the EC to the same degree. In the US, the fact that a merger might possibly eliminate all competitors and may then raise prices is dismissed because it assumes that elimination is possible and that no entry is likely during this period.[131] At the institutional level, US authorities can rely more confidently on *ex post* regulation through section 2 of the Sherman Act and a more proactive use of that provision by state competition authorities and private parties. Given that to date the Commission has been the sole enforcer of Article 82, there can be little confidence that *ex post* control can be successful. Moreover, the Commission's view is that *ex post* enforcement cannot remedy market foreclosure,[132] an argument which is somewhat disingenuous given that, as we have seen in chapter 6, the Commission is entitled to bring an Article 82 action well before any foreclosure has occurred. These three reasons converge to yield a more aggressive conglomerate merger policy in the EC. More generally, the regulation of conglomerate mergers in the US reveals a preference for Type 2 errors: it is better to allow anticompetitive conglomerate mergers to take place (because the market can eliminate the bad effects or because these can be regulated with s. 2 of the Sherman Act) than to make Type 1 errors and block pro-competitive mergers. On the other hand, the EC approach reveals a preference to avoid Type 2 errors because of concerns about the power of competition law or of markets to cure anticompetitive effects resulting from conglomerate mergers.

A less charitable interpretation is that the Commission's belief in maintaining a healthy market structure was the result of 'bureaucratic capture':[133] that is, the institution deviated from its mandate. Two strands of evidence support this argument. First, the Commission is not susceptible to meaningful judicial review because of the delays of the appeal process. This gives the Commission greater bargaining power: if it says no to a merger then it is unlikely to be consummated. Second, the Commission has fewer economists than the US DOJ, it relied on economics models designed by GE's competitors, and it dismissed the

---

[130] G. Drauz 'Unbundling *GE/Honeywell*: The Assessment of Conglomerate Mergers under EC Competition Law' (2002) 25 *Fordham International Law Journal* 885, 904.

[131] Kolasky '*GE/Honeywell*: Continuing the Transatlantic Dialog' (2003) 23 *University of Pennsylvania Journal of International Economic Law* 513.

[132] Drauz 'Unbundling *GE/Honeywell*'.

[133] J. Grant and D. Neven 'The Attempted Merger between General Electric and Honeywell: A Case Study of Transatlantic Conflict' (2005) 1 *Journal of Competition Law and Economics* 595. The authors also note that the Commission had probably assumed that the standard for judicial review was lower than that which was subsequently set by the Court.

economics expert that it had recruited when he started to disagree with the Commission's case. Grant and Neven place these factors alongside the unconvincing economics of the decision to suggest that the institutional makeup was weak, facilitating bureaucratic capture. In this view the institution damages the effective use of economic theories. On the other hand, this analysis can be used to show that the Commission applies merger law to pursue a consistent policy: safeguarding economic freedom, a political vision that is in conflict with the economics of markets. From this perspective there is no bureaucratic capture. Rather, the Commission pursues the correct political agenda, one which is at odds with the more sophisticated economic analysis of the US agencies.

5.1.2 Judicial limits for leveraging claims

The ECJ has accepted that mergers may be blocked when leveraging concerns arise, but has placed some limits to the Commission's powers in regulating these mergers in *Tetra Laval*. This case concerned a merger between Tetra Laval, dominant in the market for carton packaging, and Sidel, which held a strong position in a related market (plastic PET bottles). The Commission opined that post-merger the firm would leverage its dominance in the cartons market to create a dominant position in the PET market. As in the earlier cases, leverage would take the form of tie-ins (whereby bottlers would have to buy both carton and PET packaging systems from the merged entity), or predatory pricing or rebates to induce customers to purchase exclusively from it, thereby weakening other competitors on the PET market.[134]

On appeal, the CFI and ECJ acknowledged that conglomerate mergers may be blocked, but installed a more rigorous standard for determining the anticompetitive risks from leveraging. The CFI suggested that, in contrast to horizontal mergers, it could not be presumed that conglomerate mergers would lead to anticompetitive effects; in fact these mergers might be beneficial to consumers.[135] And the ECJ complemented this sentiment by indicating that the Commission had to prove its theory convincingly:

> The analysis of a 'conglomerate-type' concentration is a prospective analysis in which, first, the consideration of a lengthy period of time in the future and, secondly, the leveraging necessary to give rise to a significant impediment to effective competition mean that the chains of cause and effect are dimly discernible, uncertain and difficult to establish. That being so, the quality of the evidence produced by the Commission in order to establish that it is necessary to adopt a decision declaring the concentration incompatible with the common market is particularly important, since that evidence must support the Commission's conclusion that, if such a decision were not adopted, the economic development envisaged by it would be plausible.[136]

---

[134] Case M.2416 *Tetra Laval/Sidel* [2004] OJ L43/13 para. 364.
[135] Case T-5/02 *Tetra Laval v. Commission* [2002] ECR II-4381 paras. 142 and 155.
[136] Case C-12/03 *Commission v. Tetra Laval* [2005] ECR I-987 para. 44.

The standard of proof set out by the Court is not different from that in other types of merger; however, because the analysis is more complex than merely deciding if a merger creates a dominant position, every step leading to a conclusion that the merger can lead to leveraging risks must be proven. The Court of Justice's judgment suggests a four-step inquiry: (1) determining whether leveraging is *possible*, i.e. whether the economics of the markets make it feasible in theory for one firm to use its dominance in one market to enhance its market position in another, related market; (2) determining whether the firm has an *incentive* to leverage (based on objective criteria as to whether it would be profitable to expand one's position in the new market); (3) proving that leveraging would result in the anticompetitive effects predicted (under the old ECMR as applied in this case it would require proof of the creation of a dominant position in the related market or a strengthening of a pre-existing dominant position); (4) considering the possibility that behavioural commitments would remedy the anticompetitive risks created by the merger. This is the same kind of analysis that is carried out in vertical merger cases.

This standard requires a more detailed inquiry than that carried out in the Commission's decisions to date. The decision in *Tetra Laval* was annulled by the ECJ because the Commission had failed to analyse whether behavioural commitments would remedy the anticompetitive concerns, and had failed to muster sufficiently convincing evidence that leveraging would have anticompetitive effects. (The Commission failed on steps 3 and 4.) We consider the significance of step 4 in section 6 below. As regards the third step, the test should be modified now. As we noted in vertical mergers, the new ECMR merely requires proof of a substantial impediment of effective competition, so that the acquisition of dominance through leveraging is no longer necessary. Nevertheless, the Court's test makes it difficult to bring a successful leveraging case as the Commission has to show convincingly that the merged entity has the power to foreclose, that competitors are likely to exit, that buyers are unlikely to thwart the leveraging strategy, and that new entry is unlikely.[137] This suggests that while in spirit the Court sympathises with the Commission's concern over conglomerate mergers, in practice the test makes it almost impossible to block conglomerate mergers.

There is one significant difference between the legal standard indicated by the CFI and that of the ECJ in this case. The CFI observed that many of the leverage tactics that would be necessary to achieve dominance in the PET market would constitute an abuse of a dominant position. Accordingly, in determining whether the merged entity would have had the incentive to leverage, the CFI held that the Commission should take into account the deterrent effect resulting from the likelihood that leverage might be penalised under Article 82 (so in its view the Commission had also failed on step 2). Had the CFI's approach been accepted by the ECJ, it would have had implications

---

[137] See Völcker 'Leveraging as a Theory of Competitive Harm' pp. 602–9.

for vertical mergers as well as those horizontal mergers where the Commission identifies post-merger exclusionary tactics as anticompetitive effects. This approach drew support from Advocate General Tizzano. In his view, while in usual merger cases the anticompetitive effects were the direct result of the merger, in conglomerate mergers the anticompetitive effects depended upon future conduct. Accordingly, one should consider both the economic and the legal incentives and disincentives to leverage one's dominant position.[138] However, this approach is problematic because it risks undermining the *ex ante* nature of merger control. As we noted at the start of the chapter, it is more cost effective to prevent anticompetitive mergers than to allow firms to merge only to subject them to strict regulation or even the risk of divestiture in the future. However, the Court's approach is muddled. In one paragraph the Court held that in considering the incentives to leverage the Commission should take into account factors that may reduce or eliminate those incentives, including the possibility that the conduct is unlawful.[139] Then, immediately after, it suggests that the assessment of the disincentives does not require a detailed analysis of the likelihood of detection, the action taken by a competition authority and the fines that may be incurred.[140] The Court seems to suggest that some attention should be paid to the illegality of leveraging strategies, but it does not set out a workable framework. The Court seems to wish to find a middle way between two extreme approaches, that of the Commission whereby the likely illegality should be irrelevant, and that which the CFI proposed, whereby likely illegality is relevant and its relevance must be calculated. However, the Court's standard is incompatible with its own analysis of the Commission's burden of proof by which the latter must support its arguments 'convincingly'.[141] It is not clear how convincing the Commission's analysis can be if it merely states that, having considered the illegality of the leveraging practices, it does not consider that these are likely to deter the merged entity from leveraging. Surely the Commission's belief must be based upon factual evidence, and the likelihood of detection plus the likely level of fines is precisely the kind of evidence that is relevant to determine whether the merged entity is likely to infringe the law.[142] Thus, the anticipated illegality can be either relevant or irrelevant to determining whether leverage is likely to occur, and the middle way chosen by the Court is unwise.

5.2 Strategic pricing and entry deterrence

A firm which merges to become dominant in two separate product or geographical markets might be able to act strategically in one market to send

---

[138] *Commission v. Tetra Laval* [2005] ECR I-987, Opinion of AG Tizzano paras. 119–25.
[139] Ibid. para. 74.   [140] Ibid. para. 75.   [141] Ibid. para. 41.
[142] R. Cooter and T. Ulen *Law and Economics* 3rd edn (Reading, MA: Addison Wesley Longman, 2000) ch. 11.

signals to competitors in the other markets – for example, a predatory pricing strategy in one market in the face of increased price competition will warn competitors in the other markets that they should not cut prices. These concerns animated the Commission's decision in *Air Liquide/BOC*, a merger of two large industrial gas suppliers.[143] In the market for the supply of industrial gas in bulk or by cylinders Air Liquide had a dominant position in France and BOC in the United Kingdom and Ireland. The merger is 'conglomerate' in that the dominance is in two separate geographical markets. The combined entity would also have strong positions in other Member States. The merger would allow the new firm to retaliate against competitors in their home markets should they seek to challenge for market share in France or the UK and Ireland – for example, by predatory pricing in the market of the potential entrant. Moreover, a new entrant in any of the dominated geographical markets would face a more powerful incumbent and the threat of counterattacks in the other markets. Finally, the Commission reasoned that a firm dominant in certain geographical markets might use this as a 'base to attack other markets' by drawing on its strong financial position in the dominated markets and undercutting competitors. These risks are reminiscent of the abuses perpetrated in *Akzo* and *Tetra Pak 2*. The Commission seems to argue that the anticipation of these strategies can in itself create a barrier to entry.

These considerations no longer inform merger policy in the United States: first, American courts are increasingly sceptical of the possibilities of predatory pricing, and in fact there appears to be no evidence that predatory pricing is a more acute risk when a firm has multiple markets.[144] Second, it is suggested that these mergers benefit consumers because of resulting efficiencies and any possible anticompetitive behaviour by the conglomerate can be checked *ex post*.[145] Nevertheless, in EC competition law, the risks raised in *Air Liquide* can continue to be assessed with the same standard as applied when the anticompetitive effects are likely to result from leveraging.

5.3 Eliminating a potential competitor

A conglomerate merger might be a strategy to buy a potential competitor and so avoid a damaging price war, or a substitute for the implementation of a collusive device. In the 1960s and 1970s the US courts blocked conglomerate mergers that would eliminate potential competitors: for example, Procter and Gamble, a manufacturer of many household cleaners except bleach, was prevented from taking over Clorox (which controlled 50 per cent of the national market for bleach), the Supreme Court finding that the merger would have removed the only potential entrant in the bleach market (namely

---

[143] Case M.1630 (18 January 2000).

[144] H. Hovenkamp *Federal Antitrust Policy* (St Paul, MN: West Publishing, 1994) p. 507.

[145] We return to this second argument in section 7.1.

Procter and Gamble).[146] However, the analysis was coloured by static economic analysis – a 'potential' competitor is in reality (viewed from the supply side) a real competitor whose presence acts as a check on the market power of the incumbent, for should they increase prices, the potential competitor would enter the market and undermine the profitability of the price rise. Therefore, a merger with a potential competitor has the same characteristics as a horizontal merger. For these reasons, the takeover of a potential competitor should be prohibited along the same lines as horizontal mergers.[147] The question to be asked is whether, after the merger, there remain any other potential competitors who can challenge the dominance of the merged entity. This approach was applied inconsistently in the *Air Liquide/BOC* decision: a merger between two firms both dominant in separate geographical markets. When assessing the degree to which the merger would eliminate Air Liquide as BOC's only potential competitor in the UK market, the Commission went to great lengths to establish first that Air Liquide was a potential entrant in the UK market, and second that it was the most credible potential competitor.[148] This second step is necessary, for if others may also enter with sufficient ease, the market will be contestable and the merger will pose no significant anticompetitive risks. However, in considering whether the elimination of BOC (dominant in the UK and Ireland) would eliminate the only potential rival of Air Liquide on the French market, the Commission only considered evidence that BOC had demonstrated its ability to expand in Europe and had also been an actual competitor to Air Liquide. However, the decision fails to consider whether there might have been other competitors able to enter the French market.[149] The Commission did note that another potential competitor had commercial links with Air Liquide/BOC, which eliminated the risk of its moving into the market, but the possibility of other entrants was not considered. However, in most cases the Commission must assess whether the target company is in fact the only likely entrant or whether other firms are able to enter the market after the merger.[150] These mergers are best seen as horizontal.

---

[146] *FTC v. Procter & Gamble Co.* 386 US 568 (1967).

[147] The Supreme Court treated the merger in *US v. El Paso Natural Gas Co.* 376 US 651 (1964) as a horizontal merger even though the target had not made any actual sales in the relevant geographical market. The US Department of Justice thus indicates that an analysis analogous to that in horizontal mergers will be undertaken. (Non-Horizontal Merger Guidelines (1984) para. 4.13, available at www.usdoj.gov.)

[148] Case M.1630 (20 January 2000) para. 219.

[149] Similarly in *Tetra Laval/Sidel*, Tetra's disappearance as a potential competitor by its decision to take over the dominant firm in that market was condemned without much analysis as to whether Tetra was the only potential entrant, nor of its likelihood of entry ([2004] OJ L43/13 para. 265).

[150] Horizontal Merger Guidelines paras. 58–60.

6 Merger remedies

As we have seen in some of the decisions discussed above, when the Commission is faced with a merger that substantially impedes effective competition it may, instead of blocking it, demand that the parties modify the transaction so as to remove the anticompetitive risks. This allows the parties to achieve their commercial objective and removes the Commission's concerns. We may distinguish between two types of remedies: structural and behavioural.

6.1 Structural remedies

Structural remedies demand that the parties divest some of their business units. For instance in *Masterfoods/Royal Canin*, the merger would have led to the creation of a dominant position in the market for pet food in several Member States, but the parties agreed to divest business units to allow a new competitor to enter this market. The divestiture reduced the market shares of the merged entity and created a new competitor, which would prevent the merged entity from exploiting consumers.[151] In particular the divestiture also included brand names, allowing the new competitor to benefit from the goodwill established by the products it was obtaining. Thus divestitures may include a behavioural element, for example an obligation to license trademarks or patents, to ensure that the buyer can operate the assets profitably.[152]

Structural remedies are preferred because they are an immediate solution to the anticompetitive risk: they remove any threat posed by dominance by creating a new competitor or strengthening an existing firm. No long-term monitoring by the Commission is required.[153] A study of divestitures in the United States suggests that in the majority of cases the remedy is successful in that a viable competitor is created.[154] However, the study also identifies two weaknesses. The first is that the merged entity has an incentive to ensure that the buyer of the assets will not be a competitive force. This may be achieved by reducing the value of the assets to be sold (e.g. by allowing the assets to depreciate), or by selecting as a buyer a firm which the merged entity considers will be a weak competitor, or by delaying divestiture so that the assets remain out of the market for long periods and in the meantime the merged entity gains market power. After divestiture the merged entity can also disrupt the business of the buyer, in two ways. First, it may refuse to cooperate with the buyer (e.g. by refusing to provide suitable information about how a divested plant operates),

---

[151] Case M.2544 *Masterfoods/Royal Canin* (15 February 2002).

[152] E.g. Case M.190 *Nestlé/Perrier* [1992] OJ L356/1; Case M.430 *Procter & Gamble/Schickedanz* [1994] OJ L354/32; Case M.623 *Kimberley-Clark/Scott Paper* [1996] OJ L183/1.

[153] Notice on Remedies [2001] OJ C68/3, para. 8.

[154] Federal Trade Commission *A Study of the Commission's Divestiture Process* (1999) p. 8 (noting a success rate of 75 per cent) (available at www.ftc.gov/os/1999/08/divestiture.pdf).

or it may behave strategically to thwart the commercial success of the new firm (e.g. if the remedy was a divestiture of a particular brand, the merged entity can launch a closely competing brand at the same time, or the merged entity may have good market contacts with customers and use these to dissuade them from buying the new entrant's goods).[155] Second, the prospective buyer may have little knowledge of the business and thus be unable to evaluate whether the assets he is purchasing are sufficient to allow him to operate profitably.

The weaknesses identified by the US study influenced the Commission's practice and greater controls have been put in place to monitor divestitures to ensure that the seller does not act opportunistically and to ensure that the buyer is a viable competitor. There are four types of control. First, the Commission considers whether the assets the parties propose to divest are likely to allow the purchaser to act as a competitive force. To achieve this the Commission has occasionally required that the merged entity divest a wider range of assets, including products where no competition concerns arise if their sale is necessary to create a viable competitor.[156] Second, it ensures that before the assets are divested the merged entity does not cause them to lose competitiveness pending the identification of a buyer and their sale. This is achieved by the so-called 'hold separate' commitment by which the parties agree to keep the assets viable and which is monitored by a trustee who may have the powers to impose any measure necessary to ensure the business remains viable.[157] Third, the Commission can reject the proposed buyers.[158] In *Total Fina/Elf* for example, the remedy consisted of the sale of some seventy petrol stations in France.[159] The Commission held that the first buyers proposed by the parties were unsuitable because they were unlikely to be a competitive force. The parties then proposed a second purchaser, which was accepted. The Commission claimed that this case was a success because the second purchaser's first move was to reduce the price of petrol.[160] However, this might be somewhat optimistic: we do not know whether the first purchaser would have lowered prices. More generally, except in clear cases it is difficult for the Commission to know whether a buyer is suitable, especially as the US study strongly suggests that small purchasers can be as successful as larger ones.[161] However, the Commission is keen to vet potential buyers and in

---

[155] The latter concern was aired in Case M.2060 *Bosch/Rexroth* [2004] OJ L43/1.

[156] E.g. Case M.1990 *Unilever/Bestfoods* (20 September 2000).

[157] Notice on Remedies paras. 50–2.   [158] Ibid. paras. 58–9.

[159] Case M.1628 *TotalFina/Elf* [2001] OJ L143/1. Upheld in Case T-342/00 *Petrolessence SA v. Commission* [2003] ECR II-1161.

[160] M. Monti 'The Commission's Notice on Merger Remedies' in F. Lévêque and H. Shelanski (eds.) *Merger Remedies in American and European Union Competition Law* (Cheltenhan: Edward Elgar, 2003) p. 8.

[161] See M. Motta, M. Polo and H. Vasconcelos 'Merger Remedies in the European Union: An Overview' in Lévêque and Shelanski *Merger Remedies*, who argue that there is no economic theory to allow one to decide what would make a suitable competitor.

some cases it wishes to see an 'upfront buyer'; that is, the parties undertake to identify a committed buyer which is acceptable to the Commission before going ahead with the merger.[162] The upfront buyer provision may be inserted when the Commission considers that the only way to safeguard competition is for the buyer to start operating on the market immediately, or if the Commission fears that nobody would be interested in buying the assets.[163] In addition, the Commission imposes a timetable for divestiture and appoints a trustee to oversee the sale of the assets and inform the Commission of the suitability of the purchaser. The trustee is also empowered to sell the assets at any price if, within the time specified, the parties have been unable to find a suitable buyer.[164] The Commission may also provide that if, within a given time, a buyer has not been found, the merged entity will have to make a more extensive divestiture (a so-called 'crown jewel' remedy).[165] A fourth step is to monitor the merged entity's behaviour after divestiture when there is a risk that it could act to thwart the purchaser. A particularly striking illustration of this last remedy is found in the *Bosch/Rexroth* decision.[166] The merged entity would have had a dominant position in the market for hydraulic piston pumps: Bosch manufactured radial pumps and Rexroth axial pumps. The parties committed to sell the radial pump business to a third party, thereby retaining competition that would have been lost with the merger. In addition, the parties agreed to 'a clause banning Bosch from competing in respect of radial piston pumps, a clause banning Bosch from poaching staff, and a clause requiring Bosch to make good any loss of profits if it attracts away customers'.[167] The Commission considered these commitments necessary to allow the buyer to have a 'running-in period' to establish itself successfully on the market. However, none of the behaviour that Bosch promised to avoid doing constitutes an infringement of competition law. This indicates that in imposing remedies, the Commission is able to regulate the market more intrusively than when applying competition law *ex post*.

Considered cumulatively, the process of divestiture has become complex and costly, in particular if *ex post* behavioural remedies are necessary to protect the new entrant. Moreover, it has been argued that while the Commission's current procedures are designed to ensure the commercial success of the buyer, insufficient attention is paid to the risk that the merged entity and buyer may collude tacitly.[168] For example, the remedy in *Bosch/Rexroth* effectively divides the customer base as Bosch promises not to compete with the new firm. This

---

[162] Notice on Remedies para. 20.
[163] E.g. Case M. 2060 *Bosch/Rexroth* (13 December 2000); Case M.2337 *Nestlé/Ralston Purina* (27 July 2001).
[164] Notice on Remedies paras. 53–4.
[165] Ibid. para. 23; e.g. Case M.2337 *Nestlé/Ralston Purina* (27 July 2001).
[166] Case M.2060 *Bosch/Rexroth* [2004] OJ L43/1.   [167] Ibid. para. 86.
[168] Motta et al. 'Merger Remedies in the EU'.

can give the new firm the incentive to raise prices, knowing it is not faced with competition from the major industry player.

6.2 Behavioural remedies

The most common behavioural remedy is to require the merged entity to cooperate with competitors, so as to ensure the continued presence of other market players.[169] For instance in *Ciba-Geigy/Sandoz*, the merger would have given the merged entity (Novartis) a dominant position in the market for products for the treatment of fleas in animals, in particular because the parties held patents over some of the key ingredients for the manufacture of these products. Novartis undertook to grant licences to competitors for the key ingredients. The Commission accepted this commitment because, as a result, competitors will no longer be dependent on Novartis for access to the market.[170]

It will be recalled that access remedies are also granted under Article 82 EC, and that these have been agreed in the vertical mergers reviewed above. However, when access remedies are provided in merger cases the Commission does not always assess whether the facilities to which access is granted are essential: the normal Article 82 safeguards are not applied in all cases.[171] In particular, recall that the licence of intellectual property rights is normally only compelled if the firm obtaining the licence is seeking to develop a new product. This safeguard is absent in merger remedies.

Another example of wide-ranging access remedies is *Piaggio/Aprilia*, where the Commission was concerned that the merger of the top two manufacturers of scooters below 50cc would create a dominant position in Italy and the merger was cleared when Piaggio undertook to make available its new 50cc engine to others wishing to manufacture competing scooters.[172] If one were to apply the Article 82 'refusal to supply' case law test to decide whether Piaggio's concession was necessary, the answer would appear to be in the negative. First, there is no evidence that the new engine is necessary for entry, given that Honda was planning to enter with its own new engine,[173] and that there were other market players, albeit less successful than Piaggio, whose new engine stole a march on its rivals. Second, the market for small scooters was shrinking and was bound to become a niche market for fourteen- to sixteen-year-olds in Italy, thus it seems optimistic to assume that there would be a competitor

---

[169] See also Case M.1439 *Telia/Telenor* [2001] OJ L40/1 (local loop unbundling); Case M.1601 *AlliedSignal/Honeywell* [2001] OJ L152/1 (facilitating interoperability).

[170] Case M.737 *Ciba-Geigy/Sandoz* [1997] OJ L201/1.

[171] Although in *WorldCom/MCI* [1999] OJ L116/1 top-level internet service providers were referred to as essential facilities (para. 126).

[172] Case M.3570 *Piaggio/Aprilia* (22 November 2004) (a similar remedy was adopted in *Mercedes-Benz/Kässbohrer* [1995] OJ L211/1 but this is only included in a letter in the annex and was not analysed in the decision).

[173] *Piaggio/Aprilia* (22 November 2004) para. 44.

willing to enter this shrinking market by taking advantage of the availability of Piaggio's engine. In this light, had the merger gone ahead without commitments, the market would have been dominated by the merged entity, with Honda about to enter with a competing engine. In this context it would not have been an abuse of Piaggio/Aprilia's dominance to refuse to supply its engine to other competitors, yet the commitment was given. This suggests that the scope of remedies is not limited to avoiding a market failure. Instead the Commission can seek commitments that may make the market operate more competitively.

A similar approach was taken in the *Vivendi/Canal+/Seagram* merger discussed above. There the merged entity would have controlled a significant portion of premium films and a wide range of music. Its control over film rights would have foreclosed access to the pay-TV market and so the merged entity agreed to supply to other pay-TV companies 50 per cent of its premium films for five years. This would allow other pay-TV companies to compete with Canal +. Again, there was no clear statement that this remedy was necessary because 'premium films' are tantamount to an essential facility for the survival of competitors. Moreover, the remedy is somewhat loosely drafted because it gives the merged entity complete control over which films to offer its competitors. As the FTC study showed, one of the risks in merger remedies is opportunistic behaviour by the merged entity – in this case it was not safeguarded. The access remedy for the music library was also designed to maintain a competitive structure but it was not necessary to establish that without access no other online portals would survive.[174] Perhaps, in this decision, the Commission's concerns were not solely about preserving competitive market structure but also about preserving diversified broadcasting channels, as a means to safeguard media pluralism.

The latter may well have had a role in informing the Commission's decision in *Newscorp/Telepiù* to allow a merger on the Italian pay-TV market, which led to a situation where the merged entity held a quasi-monopoly position, subject to a range of behavioural remedies. The behavioural remedies may be divided into two categories. First, the merged entity had considerable buying power, which allowed it to acquire exclusive rights to attractive content to broadcast via its channels (e.g. Hollywood films and sports events). The remedy was for the merged entity to relinquish the exclusive rights so as to allow other competitors to obtain some content, either by starting a competing satellite pay-TV network or through other forms of broadcasting (e.g. cable, internet, or via mobile phones). Second, the merged entity was able to foreclose access of competing digital TV

---

[174] Although some Commissioners have stated that there are types of content which are 'essential' for the success of downstream operators. See H. Ungerer 'Application of Competition Law to Media' (speech, 22 June 2004, available at http://europa.eu.int/comm/competition/index_en.html).

operators because it controlled the set-top box technology. A new entrant would require access to that set-top box in order to market his products, and the parties undertook to grant such access. The effect of these remedies was that the Commission allowed a merger which created a monopoly pay-TV supplier in Italy, and subjected it to a range of behavioural commitments designed to facilitate the entry of competitors. Examining this decision purely on the basis of the remedies imposed, the decision runs counter to the views expressed by the Commission in the Notice on Remedies, where behavioural remedies are seen as second best. Moreover, the remedies are unduly optimistic in the assumption that new competitors will enter. However, the decision is consistent with the Commission's policy in this market: to attempt to increase the amount of choice for the consumer by widening the range of channels available – in this extreme case, by tolerating a monopoly and subjecting it to strict regulation.

In order to guarantee the presence of competitors on the market, remedies have also been utilised that force the merged entity to subsidise competitors, as in *Bombardier/ADtranz*.[175] This was a merger that would create a firm dominant in the German market for regional trains and that for trams. ADtranz was a full line manufacturer (that is, it made both the electrical and the mechanical part of rolling stock) while Bombardier focused on the mechanical part and, before the merger, obtained the electrical parts from two firms, ELIN and Kiepe. Post-merger Bombardier would switch to sourcing electrical parts internally and this would harm ELIN and Kiepe. The Commission agreed a remedy package whereby ADtranz undertook to withdraw from a joint venture, Stadler, which manufactured certain trains. This created a new competitor to the merged entity. In addition, ADtranz agreed to maintain certain contractual relations to ensure that the new firm could operate on the market successfully. The parties also undertook to license a train and a tram product line to Stadler so that it could gain market share. Stadler would obtain electrical components from ELIN and Kiepe, but in order to ensure that these two firms remained on the market, the merged entity undertook to ensure the viability of ELIN and Kiepe by maintaining supply contracts with them for a time after the merger, allowing them time to adjust to the new market conditions where they would no longer have commercial relations with Bombardier. This would allow the two to adjust and continue to play an important role in the supply of electrical equipment in this market. There is no evidence that commercial cooperation with Bombardier/ADtranz was essential for the survival of the two firms, but the Commission considered that in the long run their continued competitiveness would facilitate the entry of new providers of rail vehicles in Germany who could team up with these two suppliers of electrical equipment.[176] The merger would have had negative effects on existing suppliers and might have foreclosed market access for new competitors. Accordingly, the

---

[175] Case M.2139 *Bombardier/Adtranz* (3 April 2001).   [176] Ibid. paras. 63–4.

remedy was for the merged entity to keep viable two firms that would have been key to creating more competition in its market.

A second type of behavioural remedy is for the merged entity to sever certain contracts that may foreclose entry. In *New Holland/Case* the merger would have created a dominant position in the market for some agricultural equipment, which would have been reinforced by a high degree of loyalty on the part of retailers, making new entry difficult as the distribution channel might be foreclosed. Accordingly, the merger remedy was a divestiture of some assets to create a viable competitor, together with a commitment to inform the dealers that they would be free to sell the goods produced by the new competitor and that the merged entity would not sell competing goods to those dealers. This remedy was designed to give the buyer access to the distribution network, absent which the sale of assets would not have been sufficient to create a viable competitor.[177] Conversely an appropriate remedy might be to make the upstream market available to competitors: in cases where the merged entity has exclusivity deals with suppliers, severing this would allow suppliers to sell to competitors of the merged entity.[178]

What these two types of behavioural remedy have in common is that they are designed to facilitate the presence of one or more competitors: in other words, they achieve the same objective as structural remedies. However, the Commission prefers structural remedies because behavioural ones require continuous monitoring to ensure compliance, e.g. by requiring parties to submit regular reports to describe how the remedy is being complied with.[179] The Commission has reduced monitoring costs in two ways: first, by asking that the parties establish an arbitration agreement whereby performance by the merged entity is monitored by the beneficiary;[180] second, by enlisting national regulatory authorities to monitor post-merger commitments on its behalf.[181]

It would seem that a commitment by a merged entity not to abuse its dominant position would not be acceptable because it does not restore effective competition – the structure of the market itself is not conducive to competition. Moreover, it has been said that such a remedy would make merger control redundant, because *ex post* monitoring of the merged entity would replace *ex ante* scrutiny.[182] However, this approach might be called into

---

[177] Case M.1571 *New Holland/Case* (28 October 1999). See also Case M.877 *Boeing/McDonnell Douglas* [1997] OJ L336/16, where one remedy was the termination of exclusive supply contracts between Boeing and three US airlines.

[178] For an illustration of exclusive contracts severed upstream and downstream, see Case M.986 *Agfa-Gevaert/Du Pont* [1998] OJ L211/22 paras. 110–16.

[179] Ibid.

[180] For example, the arbitration clause in Case M.3570 *Piaggio/Aprilia* (22 November 2004).

[181] For example, the role played by the Italian Communication Authority in monitoring some of the access remedies in Case M.2876 *Newscorp/Telepiù* [2004] OJ L110/73 para. 259.

[182] E. Navarro Varona (ed.) *Merger Control in the European Union* (Oxford: Oxford University Press, 2002) para. 11.59.

question by the analysis of the Court of Justice in *Tetra Laval*. Here the Court suggested that the Commission had a duty to consider whether a commitment not to abuse one's dominant position (in that case by not leveraging its dominance into another market) could have resolved the anticompetitive risk.[183] On the one hand, it may be argued that this ruling is unhelpful because it does not give the Commission the ability to consider whether its resources are sufficient to monitor the behavioural remedy. On the other, we have seen the Commission has increasingly made use of behavioural remedies, often jointly with structural ones, and the Court's judgment may be supported on grounds of proportionality: the Commission has an obligation to identify the least restrictive remedy that removes the anticompetitive risk. The key to merger remedies so far has been to guarantee the presence of one or preferably more actual or potential competitors to the merged entity. A promise by the merged entity not to cause the exit of rivals may thus be an acceptable merger remedy, in line with the Commission's policy.

6.3 The nature of merger remedies

When merger remedies are considered, the Commission's work is of a different nature from when it enforces EC competition law in more traditional scenarios like hard-core cartels. The power to impose remedies allows it to regulate markets in a detailed manner, a process achieved through negotiation with the parties to the merger. The parties may accept that the merger can only go ahead subject to the remedies required by the Commission, or simply withdraw the merger.

It is worth reflecting whether these are negotiations where the Commission or the parties have the upper hand. An early study of the operation of the ECMR suggested that the Commission clearing mergers subject to remedies meant that the parties had a stronger bargaining position because the Commission preferred to allow the merger.[184] Business thus expected that the Commission would be willing to engage in negotiations. Moreover, as we have seen above, the US study indicated that merging parties have some advantages in that they are in control of the divestiture. Finally, the recent case law of the CFI, which found that the Commission's decision to block certain high-profile mergers was unlawful, may create further incentives to agree to the remedies offered by the parties. However, the reforms brought about by the Commission (up-front buyers, crown jewel provisions, hold separate obligations and strict vetting of proposed buyers) suggest that the Commission has sought to regain the upper hand by controlling how divestitures take place. Another factor giving the Commission negotiating strength is the limited amount of time during which merger remedies may be discussed. It

---

[183] *Tetra Laval*, judgment of 15 February 2005, para. 85.
[184] D. Neven, R. Nuttall and P. Seabright *Merger in Daylight* (London: CEPR, 1993) p. 130.

has also been noted that merging parties keen to have the merger occur as quickly as possible may be willing to offer remedies which go beyond that which is strictly necessary to remove the risk to competition in order to have a quick solution, something which some of the decisions above clearly indicate.[185] This tends to suggest that while in the early years of the ECMR the parties may have had the upper hand, at present the Commission has regained some bargaining power.

In exercising its powers the Commission states that it does not 'assess the compatibility of business strategies with the common market' and 'restructure an individual firm's business strategy'.[186] This is true in so far as remedies are offered by the parties and not imposed by the Commission. However, the case law suggests that the Commission can have a profound influence on what remedies the parties propose by indicating what the competition problems are and so guiding the parties towards remedies that it wishes to see implemented. Structural remedies, for example, make parties restructure the industry in the way the Commission considers works in the best interest of consumers. And behavioural remedies are not limited to the parties' avoiding committing acts incompatible with EC competition law. In other words, if the merged entity refused to act on its behavioural commitments it would be in breach of its obligations under the ECMR but would not likely be in breach of Articles 81 or 82 by, for example, refusing to supply products to competitors, because often the obligation to supply is not premised on the existence of an essential facility owned by the merged entity. Thus, the behavioural remedies are designed to achieve a well-functioning market after the merger. This objective seems to go beyond the traditional role played by a competition authority. EC competition law is designed to remove market imperfections caused by the way parties behave on the market. Instead, the Commission seems to use merger remedies to improve market conditions even if this goes beyond the market failure. For example, in *Piaggio/Aprilia* a supply obligation was agreed even if there would be no abuse in a refusal to supply.

7 Widening the aims of merger policy?

The Commission's merger policy, consistently with Articles 81 and 82, is grounded in two concerns: that a merger may harm consumer welfare and that the merged entity might have the power to exclude rivals. It may thus be said that the aim of merger policy is to promote or ensure the maintenance of rivalry in the market. As we saw with *GE/Honeywell*, this was one reason for the

---

[185] A. Winckler 'Some Comments on Procedure and Remedies under EC Merger Control Rules: Something Rotten in the Kingdom of EC Merger Control?' in Lévêque and Shelanski *Merger Remedies* p. 78.

[186] G. Drauz 'Remedies under the Merger Regulation' 1996 *Fordham Corporate Law Institute* ch. 12 p. 200 (Hawk ed. 1997).

divergence with the US where merger policy is solely preoccupied with consumer welfare.

However, in some cases one can detect the wish to safeguard other interests. The broadcasting cases suggest a wish to guarantee media pluralism, and some decisions seem to be designed to protect the continued existence of particular firms, for example *ADtranz* and *Piaggio/Aprilia*. These decisions safeguard rivalry plus other interests. The recitals to the ECMR suggest that non-competition considerations may be taken into account,[187] but it is unclear how and how far they may affect the decision. The Commission has explicitly recognised that the application of the ECMR requires it to consider whether the merger yields efficiencies and whether the merger is with a failing firm. We first consider the significance of these two considerations and then examine the role of industrial policy considerations in merger cases.[188]

7.1 Efficiencies

As we explained in chapters 2 and 4, efficiencies in EC competition law are perceived to be a welcome result of the competitive process, and are only relevant in so far as they benefit the consumer. This means that if a merger creates or strengthens the market power of a single firm, it is impossible to declare the merger lawful on the basis that the efficiencies outweigh the harm to consumers. The so-called Williamson tradeoff model (whereby in a merger creating a monopoly a competition authority can trade off the loss of allocative efficiency with the gain in productive efficiency)[189] is not applicable in EC competition law because the law's emphasis is on consumer welfare, not economic welfare.[190] Moreover, it is not clear whether any other jurisdiction uses a total welfare model to incorporate efficiency claims in merger cases.[191] An attempt to do so in Canada led to calls for law reform to avoid this result.[192] The Commission is often accused of seeing efficiencies as a factor that counts

---

[187] Recitals 4, 23 and 29 ECMR (referring to the competitiveness of European industry, the fundamental objectives of the Community in Article 2 EC and efficiencies respectively).

[188] This section draws on G. Monti 'Merger Defences' in G. Amato and C.-D. Ehlermann (eds.) *EC Competition Law: A Critical Assessment* (Oxford: Hart Publishing, 2007).

[189] O. Williamson 'Economies as an Antitrust Defense: The Welfare Tradeoffs' (1968) 58 *American Economic Review* 18; but rejected as unsuitable for judicial application (e.g. R. A. Posner *Antitrust Law* 2nd edn (Chicago: University of Chicago Press, 2001) pp. 133–6).

[190] This was the Commission's view in *Danish Crown/Vestjyske Slagterier* [2000] OJ L20/1 para. 198.

[191] W. J. Kolasky and A. R. Dick 'The Merger Guidelines and the Integration of Efficiencies into Antitrust Review of Horizontal Mergers' (2004) 71 *Antitrust Law Journal* 207, noting that Williamson was influential in drafting the 1968 guidelines that set out his tradeoff model, but that the 1997 revision seems to require that efficiencies be passed on to consumers.

[192] *The Commissioner of Competition v. Superior Propane Inc.* [2003] FC 529. A private member's bill, Bill C-249, was tabled but the federal elections in May 2004 put an end to deliberations. But the debate continues. See generally Competition Bureau *Treatment of Efficiencies under the Competition Act* (September 2004) and Competition Bureau *Summary of the Consultations on Efficiencies* (2004–5), available at www.competitionbureau.gc.ca.

against the merger because they are evidence of market power, thus operating an efficiencies offence.[193] This undesirable position may be on the wane as the Commission reforms its approach to defining dominance, away from commercial power, as we saw in chapter 5.

While we have suggested how efficiencies should not apply in merger law, there is no consensus over how efficiencies should be considered.[194] The standard set in the ECMR is as follows: in addition to the anticompetitive effects of a merger, the Commission should consider the 'development of technical and economic progress provided that it is to the consumers' advantage and does not form an obstacle to competition'.[195] This phrase is a replica of Article 81(3) but it is not particularly helpful in explaining how to take efficiencies into consideration because it merely provides that they should be analysed alongside the assessment of anticompetitive risk. The Horizontal Merger Guidelines attempt to supply additional detail by specifying that efficiencies must be merger specific, verifiable and benefit the consumer. This approach may be criticised from two perspectives: first, that it is highly prescriptive and, second, because it does not explain how efficiencies can be taken into account after the Commission has gathered evidence that the merger creates or strengthens a dominant position or substantially impedes effective competition. By trying to follow the approach of Article 81(3), the Commission seems to suggest that some kind of balance can be achieved whereby a merger that restricts competition can be allowed provided the efficiencies outweigh the likely harm. However, this is not appropriate. As we saw in chapter 2, the Commission identifies a restriction of competition under Article 81(1) in such a way as to create a presumption of competitive harm, which the firms can rebut by the application of Article 81(3). However, the ECMR does not apply in this bifurcated manner: proof of dominance means that the merger should be prohibited, regardless of countervailing efficiencies. As merger policy protects rivalry, efficiencies cannot serve to allow a merger creating dominance.[196]

---

[193] F. Jenny 'EEC Merger Control: Economies as an Antitrust Defense or an Antitrust Attack?' 1992 *Fordham Corporate Law Institute* 591 (Hawk ed. 1993); W. J. Kolasky 'North Atlantic Competition Policy – Converging Towards What?' (speech, 17 May 2002, available at www.usdoj.gov/atr/public/speeches).

[194] For an overview of the debates, see D. Gerard 'Merger Control Policy: How to Give Meaningful Consideration to Efficiency Claims?' (2003) 40 *Common Market Law Review* 1367; C. Luescher 'Efficiency Considerations in Merger Control' [2004] *European Competition Law Review* 72; M. de la Mano 'For the Customer's Sake: The Competitive Effects of Efficiencies in European Merger Control' Enterprise Directorate-General Enterprise Papers No. 11 (2002); EC Commission, DG for Economic and Financial Affairs *The Efficiency Defence and the European System of Merger Control* (2001) European Economy No. 5; I. K. Gotts and C. S. Goldman 'The Role of Efficiencies in Mergers and Acquisitions Global Antitrust Review – Still in Flux?' 2002 *Fordham Corporate Law Institute* 201 (Hawk ed. 2003).

[195] Article 2(1)(b) ECMR.

[196] In contrast the Horizontal Merger Guidelines (para. 84) say such a finding is highly unlikely, leaving space for efficiencies even after proof of dominance.

One potentially fruitful interpretation of the role of efficiencies is to suggest that evidence of efficiency can be used to disprove the likely anticompetitive effects. This interpretation cannot help in a horizontal merger where the merged entity is likely to reduce output and increase prices but can be applied to conglomerate and vertical mergers. Recall that in these scenarios the anticompetitive effects result from the merged entity's subsequent conduct and that the Commission must show four elements: (1) that the merged entity is able to foreclose; (2) that it has the incentive to do so; (3) that foreclosure harms consumer welfare; (4) that no behavioural or structural remedy can remove the risk of harm. Efficiencies can be relevant to disprove the second limb of this test.

An example of this is found in the *Procter & Gamble/Gillette* merger.[197] This was a conglomerate merger between two sellers of a wide range of consumer goods. One of the Commission's concerns with this merger was foreclosure through 'category management'.[198] Category management is a phrase that describes a method by which supermarkets try to ensure that the categories of goods they sell meet consumer demand. Leading suppliers (like the two firms here) provide category management services to supermarkets free of charge. The person providing this service (sometimes known as the category captain) gathers data and advises supermarkets about what products to sell, how to shelve them, what prices to set and how to promote brands. The risk is that the category captain will favour its products and foreclose market access to competitors. There is also a risk of tacit collusion between the category captain and the supermarket: remember that many supermarkets now stock own-brand goods, so the relationship between the category captain and retailer has some horizontal dimensions, and the two could conspire to boycott a competitor's brands. On the facts, the Commission was concerned that because the merged entity had a wide range of popular brands, it might be able to exploit its role as category captain and foreclose rivals. However, the evidence suggested otherwise and the efficiencies of category management were noted. The Commission found that while category management tended to harm suppliers of non-leading brands, there were no anticompetitive effects because retailers would not follow the recommendations of their category captain, but merely take those findings into consideration together with its marketing plans and ideas. Thus, category captains did not determine what was sold, but provided retailers with additional information. Moreover, category captains have in the past seen the retailer de-list their products, so that the role did not even guarantee the continued presence of the captain's own brands. In sum, category management cannot have foreclosure effects: the category captain cannot exploit it unilaterally, and there is no evidence to suggest tacit coordination between the retailer and the category captain. However, the Commission went further and noted that category management

---

[197] Case M.3732 *Procter & Gamble/Gillette* (15 July 2005).   [198] Ibid. paras. 134–51.

generated efficiencies. First, retailers increase their sales because they obtain better information about consumer demand. ('As category management is based on shoppers' habits it leads as well to higher customer satisfaction as it meets better demand expectation.')[199] Second, retailers achieve economies of scale through category management because it reduces stocks and ensures that the optimal quantity of goods is available to consumers. Third, suppliers achieve economies of scale too because they are better able to anticipate demand.[200] It follows that it is not in the interest of either the retailer or the category manager to foreclose market access through misusing category management. The parties have an incentive to use category management to reduce costs and increase profits. This shows how efficiencies can serve to rebut the fears of anticompetitive effects. In this case the efficiencies served to show that the second limb of the four-part test noted above was not satisfied: there was no incentive to foreclose.

A second way to integrate efficiencies in the analysis of a merger is to consider whether imposing a remedy would allow the merger's efficiencies to materialise while avoiding the merger's anticompetitive effects. The other aspects of the *Procter & Gamble/Gillette* merger illustrate the use of structural remedies and are also significant for the Commission's explicit discussion of efficiencies. The merger raised concerns in the markets for battery and rechargeable toothbrushes. P&G was only active in the market for battery toothbrushes, and jointly the parties would have held a dominant position in several Member States, creating an 'oral care giant'.[201] The parties assuaged the Commission's dominance worries by divesting the battery toothbrush business owned by P&G. The Commission was satisfied by this commitment because the remedy removed the horizontal overlaps between the parties. The merger also had a conglomerate dimension: both parties own 'must stock' brands, and after the merger the parties would own twenty-one strong brands with a turnover of more than 1 billion dollars.[202] The Commission analysed the risk of foreclosure via bundling, whereby the merged entity might offer discounts conditional on the buyer obtaining a wide range of products sold by the merged entity, using the strongest brands as a lever. It dismissed these risks on four grounds: first, that the parties were unlikely to engage in bundling because it made little commercial sense; second, there was competition from other major suppliers, so that purchasers were not dependent on a single company with a broad portfolio; third, there was buyer power in the shape of large retailers who would be able to exert pressure on the merged entity; fourth, the Commission identified 'portfolio efficiencies'.[203] We concentrate on explaining this final finding, which stands in stark contrast to the Commission's earlier views on portfolio effects. The Commission said that there were two sources of efficiency in

---

[199] Ibid. para. 150.   [200] Ibid. para. 150.   [201] Ibid. para. 25.   [202] Ibid. para. 111.
[203] Ibid. paras. 115–33.

this case.[204] First, the retailers had only one partner to negotiate with, and this reduced transaction costs. Second, suppliers would be able to realise economies of scale and scope, for example by economising on distribution costs. The Commission also mentioned that the supplier would have stronger innovation capacities but it is unclear from the decision what evidence supported this finding. Two economists working in DG Competition noted that in this case buyer power was the key reason why the Commission did not find anticompetitive portfolio effects, not the efficiencies.[205] However, at a symbolic level, the Commission's acknowledgment that the merger was efficient is important for two reasons. First, it seems that this is the first case where efficiencies were mentioned explicitly. Second, it seems to be a direct response to those who criticised the Commission's antagonistic stance towards portfolio power. The Commission asserts that if there are efficiencies, these will be taken into account. As we saw above when discussing the risk of foreclosure through category management, efficiencies were seen as part of the reason why the foreclosure effect was unlikely to obtain. There are other cases which illustrate the Commission's use of remedies to maintain the efficient aspects of a merger: for instance, the remedies in *Vodafone/Mannesmann* and *Vivendi* were designed to allow the merged entity to enter new markets (hence benefiting consumers) while preventing the foreclosure of competitors.

These two methods of integrating efficiencies in merger assessment (finding that efficiencies minimise the risk of anticompetitive effects and using remedies to redesign the transaction so as to preserve the efficiencies and eliminate the harms to competition) are not in line with the Horizontal Merger Guidelines but can provide more realistic ways for integrating efficiencies in the analysis of mergers.

7.2 Rescuing a failing firm

In *CCE de Vittel & Others v. Commission* the CFI held that 'in the scheme of [the ECMR], the primacy given to the establishment of a system of free competition may in certain cases be reconciled ... with the taking into consideration of the social effects of that operation if they are liable to affect adversely the social objectives referred to in Article 2 of the Treaty'.[206] This suggests that the social (i.e. employment) consequences of a merger might lead to a merger being blocked even if there is no reduction in competition, and perhaps that positive social effects could also have a role to play in allowing a merger, so that if a merger rescues a failing firm and saves jobs it might be a factor that counts in favour of merger clearance.[207] However, the role of social

---

[204] The discussion of portfolio efficiencies is in one brief passage, in para. 131.

[205] Röller and de la Mano, 'Impact of the New Substantive Test'.

[206] Case T-12/93 [1995] ECR II-1247 para. 38.

[207] Joined Cases C-68/94 and 30/95 *France v. Commission* [1998] ECR I-1375, Opinion of AG Tesauro paras. 56–7.

considerations has been largely absent in the application of the ECMR. In considering mergers with a failing firm, the Commission has set out three cumulative criteria to evaluate whether the merger is the cause of anticompetitive effects: (1) if the failing firm would be forced out of the market in the near future; (2) if there is no less anticompetitive alternative purchaser than the party wishing to acquire the firm; (3) if without the merger the assets of the failing firm would inevitably exit the market.[208] This approach is not based upon the anticipated benefits that result from allowing a merger with a failing firm, in terms of saving employment or efficiency gains, but is a specific way of showing that the merger does not cause anticompetitive effects. However, considering how this test has been applied in a leading decision suggests that the Commission regulates mergers with failing firms in such a way as to ensure the most efficient outcome.

In *BASF/Eurodiol/Pantochim* the Commission received evidence that the two firms being acquired had been placed under a pre-insolvency regime in Belgium, and that the Belgian tribunal was unlikely to prolong the judicial suspension of debts; in fact the tribunal informed the Commission that if a buyer was not approved a declaration of insolvency was looming.[209] This established the first limb of the test. The Commission then reviewed the unsuccessful efforts to find a purchaser by those in charge of running the firms during the pre-insolvency stage as well as initiating its own search for alternative purchasers.[210] This demonstrated the absence of an alternative purchaser. Then the Commission moved to the final requirement: whether without the merger the assets would exit the market. It may be argued that this final consideration is redundant because if there is no willing buyer, and if the company is likely to exit without a purchase, then it follows that the assets will exit. However, the Commission under this criterion appears to take a long-term view of the future of the assets. Thus, it compares alternative, *pre-failure* purchasers under the second limb of the test, with the future of the assets *post-failure*. In *BASF* the latter assessment was grim: a takeover immediately after insolvency would be costly because of an obligation under Belgian law to take over the entire workforce and the high environmental risks of running the chemical plants; a later takeover would be even less attractive as start-up costs were high and finding new skilled labour would be difficult. Moreover, no firm would have an interest in buying part of the assets.[211] The Commission then contrasted the post-exit scenario with the post-merger scenario. With exit, there would be a significant capacity shortage with no firm able to meet the shortfall for a considerable period of time. Moreover, given inelastic demand, a significant price increase was likely. In contrast, the post-merger scenario looked more rosy: regular supplies would be maintained, and in the

[208] Horizontal Merger Guidelines para. 90.
[209] Case COMP/M.2314 *BASF/Pantochim/Eurodiol* [2002] OJ L132/45 para. 144.
[210] Ibid. paras. 146–7.   [211] Ibid. paras. 152–6.

circumstances it was unlikely that BASF would raise prices significantly post-merger because, according to the Commission, the main reason for the failing firm's problem was the under-use of its capacities, whereas BASF's business plan noted the importance to use the plant at full capacity in order 'to achieve profitability and to make use of the full cost reduction potential of the technology'. Thus 'it could be assumed that BASF will attempt to decrease costs after the merger'.[212] Accordingly 'the market conditions would be more favourable for the customers after the merger'.[213] The Commission therefore concluded: 'Under these conditions, considered cumulatively under the particular circumstances of this specific case, the market conditions can be expected to be more favourable than in case of the market exit of the assets to be acquired.'[214] The significance of this analysis lies in the Commission's consideration of the efficiencies that result from the merger, and it might be the first case where the efficiency defence as set out in the Horizontal Merger Guidelines was applied. However, the tradeoff that the Commission carried out is not between the merger's anticompetitive effects and its redeeming virtues. Rather, the efficiencies outweighed the harm that would result absent the merger, where the exit of the assets would reduce economic welfare more severely than the merger. Conversely, if the post-exit market is likely to be more competitive than the post-merger scenario, the merger will be prohibited.[215]

7.3 Industrial policy

In the *Twenty-sixth Report on Competition Policy* the Commission suggested that merger control will be used to foster 'the development of a powerful European industry that can meet the challenges of world competition'.[216] This goal can be achieved in two ways. One is by setting out predictable merger rules and by taking efficiencies into consideration. In these ways industrial policy is consistent with competition policy. A more aggressive industrial policy, which has some political support, would see the Commission allow mergers that strengthen European industry, regardless of their effect on consumer welfare, especially when the merger is in a sector of strategic importance.[217] There are some mergers where this more aggressive form of industrial policy may have played a role.[218]

---

[212] Ibid. para. 162.   [213] Ibid. para. 160.   [214] Ibid. para. 163.

[215] E.g. Case IV/M.774 *Saint-Gobain/Wacker-Chemie/NOM* [1997] OJ L247/1; Case IV/M.890 *Blokker/Toys 'R' Us* [1998] OJ L316/1.

[216] *Twenty-sixth Report on Competition Policy* (1996) para. 8.

[217] F. Ilkovitz and R. Meiklejohn 'European Merger Control: Do We Need an Efficiency Defence?' in EC Commission, DG for Economic and Financial Affairs *Efficiency Defence* pp. 10–11 (reviewing relevant statements by the Commission and Parliament).

[218] And recall the *de Havilland* affair discussed in chapter 1.

One early occurrence is *Alcatel/Telettra*.[219] This merger was viewed with concern by DG Competition but other Commissioners also saw the possibility of creating a strong European competitor in the supply of telecommunications equipment.[220] It is understood that similar considerations affected the decision in *Mannesmann/Vallourec/Ilva* even though DG Competition publicly stated that the decision to clear was based on economic considerations.[221] In neither of these cases does the decision refer to policy considerations. However, in both, the economic analysis was weak. In *Alcatel/Telettra* the considerations of 'buyer power' that led to the merger being cleared have not been found persuasive, for the buyer in question had little incentive to look for alternative suppliers.[222] In *Mannesmann/Vallourec/Ilva* the anticompetitive risks were said to be reduced by the presence of potential competition from outside the EU, but this is not quantified and is a consideration, as we noted earlier, that does not usually affect the analysis of mergers. More recently, in *Piaggio/Aprilia* a merger was cleared in the motorcycles market and the decision made reference to the global weakness of European firms vis-à-vis competition from Japan, and the possibility that this merger would strengthen the fourth largest European player.[223] Industrial policy considerations do not always win the day. For example, the MSG Media Services merger, which the Commission blocked on competition grounds, was supported on industrial policy grounds by DG Industry and DG Telecommunications who considered this merger necessary to develop a European multi-media sector.[224] And in *Volvo/Scania* the merger was blocked in spite of pleas by the Swedish government that the concentration was necessary to build a strong EC truck manufacturer against competition from overseas.[225]

In a policy document published in 2004 to explain how competition law can assist in making Europe the most competitive economic trading bloc (the key aim of the Lisbon strategy), the Commission emphasises that competitive markets are the key to strengthening European firms, making no reference to the strategic use of competition law to facilitate the creation of European champions. However, the institutional makeup allows for other Community policies and for national interests to infiltrate in merger decisions occasionally, suggesting divisions among EU officials about the proper

---

[219] [1991] OJ L122/48.

[220] G. Ross *Jacques Delors and European Integration* (Cambridge: Polity Press, 1994) pp. 132–3.

[221] E. M. Fox 'Antitrust, Competition, and the World Arena' (1996) 64 *Antitrust Law Journal* 725, 726; D. Banks 'Non-Competition Factors and their Future Relevance under European Merger Law' [1997] *European Competition Law Review* 182, 185.

[222] Neven et al. *Merger in Daylight* pp. 118–19.

[223] Case M.3570 *Piaggio/Aprilia* (22 April 2004).

[224] [1994] OJ L364/1. See M. Cini and L. McGowan *Competition Policy in the European Union* (London: Macmillan, 1998) p. 130.

[225] The arguments were couched in terms of widening the geographical market so as to avoid a finding of dominance. See Ilkovitz and Meiklejohn 'European Merger Control' p. 11; N. Levy 'Mario Monti's Legacy in EC Merger Control' (2005) 1 *Competition Policy International* 99.

scope of industrial policy, something which has dogged the ECMR since its inception.[226]

8 A European merger policy?

As noted in the introduction, the larger Member States supported the development of *a* merger regulation, but its final text gave little guidance as to whether the ECMR would become a tool to sponsor European champions (as France hoped) or a means to safeguard consumer welfare (as Germany and the UK wished). They gave the Commission the opportunity to shape merger policy, in particular because once a merger has a Community dimension, the Commission has exclusive competence over it and Member States cannot apply national law.[227] On the whole, the Commission's decisions suggest that for the vast majority of cases the governing principle is that mergers are prohibited when they stifle economic opportunities, whether of consumers or of competitors. While there are resonances of the 'economic freedom' concept, the tenor of the decisions taken as a whole is to support such freedom as a means to guarantee consumer welfare, not as an end in itself. The ECMR in this respect did not undergo the same paradigm shift we noted in the context of Article 81; instead the Commission pioneered an economics-based approach in this field of activity. Nevertheless, there are episodes when the Commission's decisions do more than protect consumer welfare: mergers are blocked or modified, or indeed even allowed in spite of their anticompetitive potential, in accordance with wider Community interests. As with the role of public policy considerations under Article 81 (considered in chapter 4), decisions which support other Community interests are opaque. That is, the policy context is implicit but not examined expressly.

Thus, the shape of Commission merger policy is as uneven as the political support that it received. It must be noted, moreover, that support was not for a European merger policy. Had the Member States wished to allow the Commission to regulate mergers in Europe, the ECMR would, like Articles 81 and 82 EC, have applied whenever the merger had an effect on trade between Member States. However, the Commission's jurisdiction is limited in two formal ways: first, only mergers above a certain turnover threshold may be reviewed at Community level; secondly, national interests may be invoked to refer a merger back to a Member State. Moreover, protectionism is on the increase and the Community is struggling to halt this, creating a third, informal means by which national interests can be safeguarded.

---

[226] One of the main reasons why the implementation of the ECMR was delayed was divisions over the role of industrial policy. See Levy 'Dominance versus SLC' pp. 146–8; L. Brittan 'The Law and Policy of Merger Control in the EEC' (1990) 15 *European Law Review* 351.

[227] Article 21 ECMR.

8.1 Thresholds

The Commission's first proposal for a merger regulation in 1973 was that the Commission would consider mergers where the firms had a worldwide turnover of 200 million ecus (1 ecu = 1 euro).[228] Realising the political impossibility of having such a low threshold accepted, the Commission raised the threshold to 1 billion ecus in its 1988 proposal. Germany and the UK countered this with a threshold of 10 billion ecus, and a Solomonic compromise was reached whereby the qualifying threshold was agreed at 5 billion ecus. However, the threshold is actually more complex, requiring (a) a combined aggregate turnover of 5 billion ecus *and* (b) aggregate Community turnover of each of at least two of the undertakings of more than 250 million ecus. And if each of the undertakings achieves more than two-thirds of its aggregate Community-wide turnover within one and the same Member State, the Commission does not have jurisdiction.[229] The thresholds show how jealously Member States wish to guard mergers having a predominantly national impact. In theory, the Commission could vet mergers below these thresholds by invoking Articles 81 and 82; however, at the time the ECMR was agreed Lord Brittan gave an undertaking that the Commission would not deploy Article 81 against mergers that fell outside the ECMR.[230]

While the Regulation provided for these thresholds to be reviewed (downwards), this has not occurred.[231] The Commission's proposal to lower the threshold to 2 billion ecus in 1996 was turned down because of Member States' reluctance to confer more powers on the Commission.[232] Nevertheless, in 1997 Member States agreed to a partial extension of the Commission's jurisdictional reach. Rather than revising the thresholds downwards, a new trigger for Commission jurisdiction was created (Article 1(3) ECMR) for mergers where the firms have substantial business in at least three Member States. However, this compromise solution has not led to a significant increase in the Commission's competence.[233] In the 2002–3 review of the ECMR, there was no call for lowering the thresholds, but a creative measure was put into place to allow for the re-allocation of cases from Member States to the Commission (and vice versa): the parties to a merger can make a request to national authorities that a merger that lacks an EC dimension and falls within their jurisdiction should be considered by the Commission (and conversely they may request that the Commission relinquish its jurisdiction in favour of

---

[228] Council Regulation (EC) No. 1103/97 of 17 June 1997 on Certain Provisions relating to the Introduction of the Euro [1997] OJ L162/1.

[229] Article 1(2) ECMR.

[230] New Ideas on European Merger Control (press release IP/89/200, 31 March 1989).

[231] The next review is due in 2009 (Art. 1(4) ECMR).

[232] *Green Paper on the Review of the Merger Regulation* COM(96)19 final.

[233] *Green Paper on the Review of Council Regulation (EEC) No. 4064/89* COM(2001)745/6 final (11 December 2001) paras. 22–8.

national scrutiny).[234] This complements the ability of one or more Member States to request that the Commission examine mergers that lack an EC dimension but affect trade between Member States.[235] These reforms have been advanced in the expectation that mergers will be reviewed by the most appropriate authority, although it is likely that they will increase the number of cases reviewed by the Commission.[236]

The thresholds are politically motivated attempts to safeguard national merger policy. On the one hand, they guarantee legal certainty, but they have perverse economic consequences. The major economic disadvantage is that the thresholds fail to take into consideration that industrial sectors vary in size, which means that the powers of the Commission are biased towards certain sectors with large players and against concentrations of smaller, more specialised industries.[237] The effect is that in some sectors too many mergers are referred to the Community whilst in others too many remain regulated by national law even though they have significant effects on trade between Member States. One study has revealed that in those industry sectors where anticompetitive risks are greatest, very few mergers fell under the jurisdiction of the Commission. Thus potential Community-wide market failures are not addressed at the appropriate level, but left to Member States.[238] This limits the effectiveness of European merger policy, and as such limits the effectiveness of the single market programme. A second perverse effect of the thresholds is that, with inflation, the 5 billion ecu threshold is not as high now as it seemed in 1989. According to John Vickers, 5 billion ecus in 1990 would now be worth 7.5 billion ecus, therefore the work of the Commission gradually increases every year even without any modification to the thresholds![239] Such arbitrary effects are mitigated by the ability to refer cases to and from the Commission and national authorities, but these provisions are no substitute for a negotiated bargain to reform the scope of application of the ECMR.

8.2 National interests

As if the provisions discussed above did not serve to preserve enough national control over mergers, the Merger Regulation also provides that mergers which meet the thresholds of the Regulation may be referred back to the Member States when the merger would have an anticompetitive effect in a distinct

---

[234] Article 4(4) and (5) ECMR.   [235] Article 22 ECMR.
[236] Commission Notice on Case Referral in Respect of Concentrations [2005] OJ C56/2 paras. 4–5.
[237] A. Jacquemin, P. Buigues and F. Ilkovitz 'Horizontal Mergers and Competition Policy in the European Community' (1989) 40 *European Economy* 50.
[238] European Commission 'Competition and Integration: Community Merger Control Policy' (1994) 57 *European Economy* 35–8.
[239] J. Vickers 'International Mergers: The View from a National Competition Authority' 2001 *Fordham Corporate Law Institute* ch. 10 (Hawk ed.).

market in a Member State, or when a Member State considers that its legitimate public policy interests would be adversely affected by the merger.

When the merger has an effect on a distinct market in a Member State, which might be overlooked by the Commission's assessment of the merger's impact on the Community market, Article 9 (the so-called German clause) allows the Member State to request that the merger be referred back to its competition authorities. If the distinct market is not a substantial part of the EC, the Commission must refer the merger to the Member State, but if the distinct market is EC-wide, then it has the discretion to handle the case itself. When the case is referred back, the Member State may only regulate the transaction to protect competition on the national market, and cannot apply non-competition criteria. In the first referral, the Commission opted to refer only parts of the transaction in question to the requesting Member State, even though the power to make partial referrals was expressly provided for only in the 1997 revision to the Regulation.[240] Partial referrals offer a convenient way of reviewing each aspect of the merger at the most appropriate level, although at the risk of inconsistent or irreconcilable decisions by the various competition authorities.[241] In the early years, the Commission interpreted Article 9 narrowly, holding on tightly to those few mergers that it had jurisdiction over. However, more recently there has been an increased willingness to refer mergers back to Member States. Some have attributed this to the merger wave of the late 1990s, which increased the number of mega-mergers which the Commission had to consider, leading to its willingness to relinquish its obligations towards certain transactions. The Commission has also articulated more clearly the grounds upon which it will decide to refer the merger to a Member State: in four cases it has based its decision on considering whether the National Competition Authority was 'best placed' to examine the transaction, and the criteria to judge this included the existence of national markets as well as that authority's expertise in the economic sector in question.[242] This clarification of the basis upon which referrals are made is to be welcomed because it allows the Commission to allocate cases to the most effective regulator.[243]

Member States may also invoke public interest grounds for demanding that the merger be referred to the national authorities so that the merger clearance respects national public policy considerations. Under Article 21(4) the range of public interests includes only three: public security, the plurality of the media and prudential rules. Member States may request that other public interests be

---

[240] Case IV/M.180 *Steetley/Tarmac* (12 February 1992).

[241] Case T-119/02 *Philips v. Commission* [2003] ECR II-1433 paras. 350, 380 and 381.

[242] Cases M.2533 *BP/E.ON* (6 September 2001); M.2234 *Metsäliitto Osuuskunta/Vapo OY/JV* (8 February 2001); M.2154 *C3D/Rhone/Go-Ahead* (20 October 2000); M.2044 *Interbrew/Bass* (22 August 2000).

[243] More detailed criteria have been set out in the EC Commission *Notice on Case Referral in Respect of Concentrations* [2005] OJ C56/2.

taken into account, but these requests have been scrutinised strictly, going so far as finding Portugal in breach of Article 21(4) when it invoked unconvincing public interest justifications in two cases. In both cases the Commission rejected the view that national interests and the protection of strategic sectors for the national economy would count as legitimate interests, so that once a merger has a Community dimension national industrial policy considerations cannot apply.[244]

The loser from these exceptions to 'one-stop shop' merger control is the single market programme. The development of a coherent European merger policy is stunted if the Commission's powers are limited only to the largest transactions. Smaller Member States also lost as they wished for greater scope for the Merger Regulation because, given their size, most mergers in their jurisdictions had Community-wide effects. In response to this, national competition authorities have devised soft law means of cooperating to facilitate multi-jurisdictional notifications,[245] and the network of competition authorities (discussed further in chapter 11) is likely to play a role in further coordination.[246]

The Commission's recent reforms, designed to facilitate the reallocation of merger cases, are a clever way of attempting to create a true European merger policy, by facilitating the review by the Commission of mergers that have an appreciable effect on trade between Member States. The reforms go in the same direction as John Vickers's suggestion that merger cases should move freely within the Community, depending upon which authority is best placed to address the anticompetitive risks. Those mergers that raise international competition issues are best handled by the EC, whilst those raising domestic competition problems should be handled at domestic level. If the Commission's recent reforms were to function well, one might hope that, in the long run, an effects-based test would be possible. To a certain extent, the Commission's recent clarification on the exercise of their discretion under Article 9 facilitates this transition. However, Vickers's suggestions rely upon National Competition Authorities and firms acting in good faith when deciding whether to seek national or Community control over a merger. And trust amongst national agencies is a prerequisite for the successful free movement of merger cases.

---

[244] Cases M.1616 *BSCH/A. Champalimaud* (20 July 1999) and M.2054 *Secil/Holderbank/Cimpor* (22 November 2000), upheld in Case C-42/01 *Portugal v. Commission* [2004] ECR I-6079.

[245] These mechanisms are informal and are not on a statutory basis. For example, the competition authorities of the UK, France and Germany have cooperated to enable businesses to use a common form for mergers that have to be examined in more than one of these countries. See Appendix on the Merger Control Procedures in the United Kingdom, available at www.oft. gov.uk. National authorities also cooperate over common issues like market definition.

[246] Recital 14 ECMR; EC Commission *Notice on Case Referral in Respect of Concentrations* [2005] OJ C56/2 paras. 53–8.

8.3 Protectionism

The Commission's exclusive competence in merger cases has recently come to be challenged by a new Member State: Poland. This ongoing dispute serves to signal the tensions that still exist between the economic policies of Member States and the Community. An Italian bank, Unicredit, owns a Polish bank, Pekao (the country's second largest bank). When this merger occurred a privatisation agreement was entered into between Poland and Unicredit in 1999 which prohibited Unicredit from investing in any of Pekao's competitors. The rationale for this was to safeguard the competitiveness of the Polish market.[247] In 2005 Unicredit acquired a German bank, HBV, and with this an interest in the third largest Polish bank (BPH). The merger was cleared by the EC Commission, but Poland found that it infringed the privatisation agreement and has blocked the merger. There are a range of political interests behind the government's move. First, the merger is likely to cut 9 per cent of jobs in the banking sector in Poland. Second, the merger would create Poland's largest bank, which will be operated from headquarters in Austria. Third, the merger undermines the strength of the state-owned bank, PKO BP, and it fears for its competitive position.[248] The Polish move is protectionist and the Commission has taken two actions to thwart it: first, it has begun a procedure to rule that Poland is in breach of Article 21 of the ECMR and, second, it has begun to take steps to challenge the agreement as restricting the free movement of capital (contrary to Article 56) and the right of establishment (contrary to Article 43).[249] A finding against Poland means it would be bound to allow the merger; however, the delay that is inherent in the application of these provisions means that the Polish government has some space to negotiate with Unicredit, which is eager to consummate the merger and exploit the business opportunities in Poland, so that a settlement between Unicredit and Poland, which safeguards Polish interests, is likely. The Commission is aware that this kind of action can compromise the process of economic liberalisation and it issued a declaration where it stated that cross-border mergers increase competition, benefit consumers and strengthen European competitiveness, allowing firms to compete globally. It also warned that protectionism by Member States would hamper these benefits and warned Member States that its central priority would be the enforcement of the competition and internal market rules to challenge 'undue interference' by national authorities.[250]

The Polish rules are not unique – several Member States have in place legislation that is designed to protect foreign takeovers of national companies.[251] For example, France has supported a takeover of Suez (a formerly

---

[247] IP/06/276.   [248] 'Tussles with Brussels' *The Economist* 21 January 2006, p. 76.
[249] See IP/06/276 and IP/06/277.
[250] Commission Declaration, Strasbourg Plenary 15 March 2006 (available on DG Competition's website), http://ec.europa.eu/comm/competition/index_en.html.
[251] 'To the Barricades' *The Economist* 4 March 2006, pp. 55–6.

state-owned water and power company) by Gaz de France to avoid a possible takeover of Suez by an Italian electricity firm, Enel. Conversely, the Italian government enacted a law forbidding takeovers of privatised Italian electricity and gas industries by state-owned firms to prevent a takeover from the French state-owned firms (which the ECJ has declared illegal),[252] and the Spanish government has taken steps, currently being challenged by the Commission, to prevent E.ON, a German energy company, from taking over Endesa, a Spanish energy firm.[253] The Italian government had tried to prevent foreign takeovers of Italian banks, and several states hold 'golden shares' in recently privatised firms which are designed to prevent a foreign takeover (e.g. over the Dutch telecommunications and post office).[254] Some might see this resurgence of national protectionism as a sign that the internal market is working in that these are episodic bouts of national protectionism, often carried out to curry favour in the name of domestic political expediency, while a more pessimistic interpretation suggests that these bouts of protectionism reveal that a European competition culture is still underdeveloped.

The Commission has taken several actions under Article 226 to challenge these national rules for infringing Articles 43 and 56, and the Court of Justice has backed the Commission in declaring that golden shares breach EC law, although the restrictions may be justified for public policy reasons.[255] Note that when declaring national law incompatible with the EC Treaty's single market rules, the courts are able to facilitate mergers even if they fall below the threshold for the application of the ECMR. This is an indirect way of shaping national merger control rules. While it does not harmonise national rules, so that mergers may be blocked by national authorities if they run counter to national merger rules, it reduces the scope of public interest considerations which can be taken into account, preventing protectionist measures. By 'negative integration' national merger rules converge to some extent.

While the Commission's willingness to act against state protectionism may serve to deter some, the practical effects of an enforcement action are unsatisfactory. Firms are keen to merge, and the slow process of the law means that a firm like Unicredit is better off negotiating with the Polish government to obtain a compromise that will allow it to enter the Polish market. The network

---

[252] Case C-174/04 *Commission v. Italy*, judgment of 2 June 2006. See para. 2 of AG Kokott's opinion of 3 March 2006, noting the Italian state's concerns about a takeover by French firms.

[253] IP/06/569. The Spanish law empowers the Spanish energy regulator to block mergers in these sectors.

[254] Cases C-282 and 283/04 *Commission v. Netherlands*, judgment pending, but see Opinion of AG Poiares Maduro of 6 April 2006 declaring these golden shares unlawful.

[255] Case C-367/98 *Commission v. Portugal* [2002] ECR I-4731 (for all privatised industries); Case C-483/99 *Commission v. France* [2002] ECR I-4781 (oil company); Case C-503/99 *Commission v. Belgium* [2002] ECR I-4809 (energy markets); Case C-463/00 *Commission v. Spain* [2003] I-4581 (petroleum, energy, telecommunications, banking, tobacco and electricity); Case C-98/01 *Commission v. UK* [2003] ECR I-4641 (airport administration). See E. Szyszczak 'Golden Shares and Market Governance' (2002) 29 *Legal Issues of Economic Integration* 255.

of National Competition Authorities might provide some 'peer pressure' for Member States to avoid such protectionism, and a robust way of overcoming national protectionism could be for the Commission to utilise Articles 81 and 82 to regulate mergers falling outside the scope of the ECMR when it is concerned about the application of national laws to thwart takeovers by foreign firms.[256]

[256] This option was noted by AG Kokott in Case C-174/04 *Commission v. Italy* para. 45.

9

Oligopoly markets

Contents

1. Introduction	*page* 308
2. Merger control	311
2.1 Concentration	316
2.2 Market facilitates tacit collusion	317
2.3 Deterrence mechanisms	320
2.4 Entry barriers	321
2.5 Causation and efficiencies	322
2.6 Assessment	323
3. Express collusion	324
3.1 The meaning of agreement and concerted practices	325
3.2 Evidence of express collusion	330
3.3 Incentives to confess	332
4. Tacit collusion	334
4.1 Tacit collusion as abuse of collective dominance	335
4.2 Facilitating devices under Article 81	339
4.3 Facilitating devices under Article 82	341
4.4 Oligopoly control: lessons from the US and UK	342
5. Conclusion: unenforceable competition	344

1 Introduction

The previous chapters were about the application of competition law to firms that dominate a market individually. We now turn to examine how competition law controls markets populated by a small number of firms. Economists are divided over the level of regulation required in oligopoly markets because while high degrees of concentration might make markets less competitive, it is also possible to find lively competition in an oligopoly market.[1]

A simple example can illustrate the principal competition concerns in oligopoly markets. Suppose we have a market with three large producers of a chemical in the EC. The product is standardised and competition is purely based on price, the three are protected from imports by anti-dumping duties and face constant but unchanging levels of demand, there are no other significant competitors in the EC and no technological developments are possible to reduce production costs. In this kind of market, the temptation for the three firms to come to an agreement to fix prices or subdivide markets is high. If they agree to fix prices they can behave like monopolists and earn more profit than if they competed. What is particularly worrying from the perspective of competition law enforcement is that the firms need not even communicate with each other to fix prices – one of the firms might 'lead' a price increase, for example it might raise its prices by €10. The other firms might see this as an opportunity to make profit in the first instance by keeping their prices low, but if the other firm persists in keeping the prices higher by €10, the others will realise that they can maximise profits by raising prices also, as customers need the goods and have no real alternatives but the three firms. The 'price leadership' exercised by one firm in an oligopoly is a recognised mechanism by which firms can 'tacitly collude' by sending signals to each other about their actual and anticipated conduct.[2] Most economists see no difference between express collusion (where the manufacturers meet to plan their anti-competitive strategies) and tacit collusion (where the parties behave anti-competitively by adapting to the actual and anticipated conduct of their competitors, e.g. via price leadership) because the effects are the same: prices rise and output falls. However, from a legal perspective, the distinction between express and tacit collusion is crucial: the former can be pursued under Article 81 EC (as an agreement restrictive of competition) but it is not clear how far tacit collusion can be regulated – in fact, it seems to be immune from Article 81.[3] The US Supreme Court expressed a similar sentiment: 'Tacit collusion, sometimes called oligopolistic price coordination or conscious parallelism, describes the process, not in itself unlawful, by which firms in a concentrated market might in effect share monopoly power, setting their prices at a profit-maximizing, supracompetitive level by recognizing their

---

[1] See F. M. Scherer and D. Ross *Industrial Market Structure and Economic Performance* 3rd edn (Boston, MA: Houghton Mifflin, 1990); C. F. Rule and D. L. Meyer 'Toward a Merger Policy that Maximises Consumer Welfare: Enforcement by Careful Analysis not by Numbers' (1999) 44 *Antitrust Bulletin* 251.

[2] For a clear example, see Case IV/M.2498 *Norske Skog/Parenco /Walsum* [2002] OJ L233/38 para. 129 where the Commission explains how the leading players would play a 'signalling game' by announcing their investment plans so as to coordinate the overall level of investment as a means of reducing capacity in the markets for newsprint and paper. But on the facts it found that signalling would not be practicable (paras. 134–5).

[3] The clearest statement of this is *Zinc Producer Group* [1985] OJ L220/27 paras. 62–3.

shared economic interests and their interdependence with respect to price and output decisions.'[4]

Price leadership is only one way in which firms in an oligopoly can facilitate tacit collusion; a rich vein of economic studies, in particular resting upon game theory, suggests other means through which coordination may be achieved.[5] Game theory is a mix of economics, mathematics and psychology, which helps in identifying the market conditions when firms in oligopoly markets are likely to cooperate.[6] For instance, cooperation is more likely when the parties play a 'repeated game': in the price leadership example above, this means that the parties determine their prices weekly or monthly so that there is a period when they observe each other's actions and then a subsequent period to react. Cooperation is also more possible when the parties know each other through repeated interaction and there are no new entrants whose behaviour is unknown, and when the parties know that none of them is able to 'win' the entire market so there is no incentive to compete. In short, the structure of the market can facilitate tacit collusion by creating conditions whereby firms can develop a coordinated approach to their actions on the market. It follows that if competition law can do nothing about tacit collusion, then there would be a significant gap. However, some question whether tacit collusion is a real concern. In the price leadership example, it might be argued that the rational response to price leadership is not to follow the leader, because by not follow-ing the price increase one can increase sales while the leader is charging higher prices. Only if failing to follow the leader causes a loss will price leadership work to secure anticompetitive effects. But a loss can only occur if the parties have established a mechanism to punish those that do not follow the price leader. If so, it is likely that there has been some express agreement. In short, monopoly pricing in oligopoly markets cannot be expected absent an explicit agreement.[7] However, antitrust authorities have not taken this critique to mean that tacit collusion cannot exist. In response to the above critique, antitrust authorities suggest that tacit collusion is only likely if there is a punishment mechanism, and that there may be markets where such punish-ment mechanisms exist without agreement: for instance, if the firms have spare

[4] *Brooke Group Ltd v. Brown & Williamson Tobacco Corp.* 509 US 209, 227 (1993).
[5] A helpful review is D. G. Baird, R. H. Gertner and R. C. Picker *Game Theory and the Law* (Cambridge, MA: Harvard University Press, 1994) pp. 165–78.
[6] Those seeking a more formal analysis can consult: K. Bagwell and A. Wolinsky 'Game Theory and Industrial Organization' in R. J. Aumann and S. Hart (eds.) *Handbook of Game Theory with Economic Applications* (Amsterdam: North-Holland, 1992); E. Kantzenbach, E. Kottman and R. Krüger *New Industrial Economics and Experiences from European Merger Control – New Lessons about Collective Dominance?* (Luxembourg: Office for Official Publications of the European Communities, 1995); S. D. Gurrea and M. Owen 'Coordinated Interaction and S.7 Clayton Enforcement' (2003) 12 *George Mason Law Review* 89 (a critical summary of the contribution of economics).
[7] G. J. Werden 'Economic Evidence on the Existence of Collusion: Reconciling Antitrust Law with Oligopoly Theory' (2004) 71 *Antitrust Law Journal* 719.

capacity to start a price war should one of them deviate from a tacitly agreed price increase.

Revisiting the example we began with, it might be argued that a merger between two of the three competitors makes collusion easier because with fewer firms tacit or express collusion is easier to achieve.[8] In this scenario the EC is well equipped to block a merger that might facilitate future collusion, whether express or tacit. While the original version of the ECMR only prohibited mergers that create or strengthen a dominant position as a result of which effective competition would be significantly impeded,[9] the Commission was quick to extend its scope to oligopoly markets causing coordinated effects by stating that in such markets the firms would be collectively dominant.[10]

In sum, while merger law allows the Commission to prevent the creation of market structures where express and tacit collusion are likely, *ex post* regulation of anticompetitive behaviour in oligopoly markets can only tackle express collusion. We begin by exploring how the economic theories of oligopoly behaviour have been integrated in merger control, by identifying conditions where collusion is likely, labelled collective dominance. In section 3 we consider how Article 81 applies to curb express collusion and in section 4 we explore how far tacit collusion might be addressed.

2 Merger control

The Commission was aware that the 'dominance' test of the original ECMR was defective in that it did not encompass mergers in oligopoly markets; it waited for a strong case to establish a legal basis for finding that mergers increasing concentration in oligopoly markets could be blocked.[11] The Commission considers that in an oligopoly market, the firms hold a collective dominant position if it can be shown that 'together, in particular because of correlative factors which exist between them, [the firms] are able to adopt a common policy on the market and act to a considerable extent independently of their competitors, their customers, and also of consumers'.[12] According to this approach, coordinated effects in oligopoly markets have similar effects to the exploitation of a dominant

---

[8] In fact some studies suggest that anticompetitive effects are most likely in duopolies and much less likely in oligopoly markets with more firms. See S. Huck, H.-T. Normann and J. Oechssler, 'Two are Few and Four are Many: Number Effects in Experimental Oligopolies' (2004) 53 *Journal of Economic Behavior and Organization* 435.

[9] Article 2(3) of Regulation 4064/89 on the Control of Concentrations between Undertakings [1990] OJ L257/31, as amended by Regulation 1310/97, [1997] OJ L180/1.

[10] The first decision was *Nestlé/Perrier* [1992] OJ L356/1. The Court backed the Commission in Joined Cases C-68/94 and C-30/95 *France v. Commission* (*Kali & Salz*) [1998] ECR I-1375.

[11] Accordingly, some early mergers in oligopoly markets escaped scrutiny: see D. Ridyard 'Joint Dominance and the Oligopoly Blind Spot Under the EC Merger Regulation' [1992] *European Competition Law Review* 161, who suggests that the Commission may have been under pressure by the German Bundeskartellamt to extend the reach of the ECMR to oligopoly markets.

[12] *Kali & Salz* [1998] ECR I-1375 para. 221; cited in Case T-102/96 *Gencor v. Commission* [1999] ECR II-753 para. 163; Case T-342/99 *Airtours v. Commission* [2002] ECR II-2585 para. 59.

position of a single firm, therefore – as with single-firm dominance – entry barriers must be high, and competitors and consumers weak. The distinguishing feature that is necessary to establish collective dominance is the *interdependence* of the oligopoly, which establishes the likelihood that the firms will coordinate behaviour. Following on from the game theoretical insights, a test to determine collective dominance includes the following four elements:[13]

- a highly concentrated market
- economic conditions which make it easy for the firms to coordinate their behaviour
- conditions that deter each firm from deviating from the common policy
- lack of power of the other firms and lack of potential competition or buyer power.

This structure provides a mechanism for explaining the Commission's decisions reached to date as well as being broadly in line with economic theory. The first two elements facilitate coordination so that prices are higher than under competitive conditions. But when prices are high, it would be profitable for one firm to 'cheat' and give some customers secret discounts, as this would increase its sales and profits at the expense of rivals. Tacit collusion can only be stable if those who cheat in this way are identified and can be penalised by the other firms. Lastly, tacit collusion can only be sustained if buyers are unable to find alternative supplies, and so are forced to pay the higher prices set by tacit collusion. Thus, the third and fourth conditions guarantee that the effects of tacit collusion are stable. The Commission's decisions have evolved to apply this standard.

We present the case law in two ways. First, we summarise the findings of four of the leading cases below. This allows us to show how the criteria that the Commission has identified have been codified in the *Horizontal Merger Guidelines*.[14] The factors enumerated to identify mergers likely to lead to coordinated effects are in tune with much of the economic theory.[15] The results are summarised in table 9.1. Having established the criteria, we comment on how they have been applied in the sections that follow.

---

[13] This draws roughly on *Airtours* [2002] ECR II-2585 para. 62.

[14] *Guidelines on the Assessment of Horizontal Mergers under the Council Regulation on the Control of Concentrations between Undertakings* [2004] OJ C31/5 paras. 76–91 (hereinafter Horizontal Merger Guidelines). It follows that the Commission will continue to use collective dominance even after the review of the ECMR. (See Recital 25, Council Regulation (EC) 139/2004 on the Control of Concentrations between Undertakings [2004] OJ L24/1. Regulation 139/2004 suggests that the SIEC test is not applicable when the dominance test has been invoked in the past.)

[15] The framework is comparable to that suggested by G. J. Stigler 'A Theory of Oligopoly' (1964) 72 *Journal of Political Economy* 44. It is also broadly consistent with the approach set out in the US Merger Guidelines. See also J. Vickers 'Merger Policy in Europe: Retrospect and Prospect' [2004] *European Competition Law Review* 455, 459 (suggesting that economists should approve of the criteria set out in *Airtours*). Some of the early decisions have been criticised for failing to look at markets dynamically: see J. S. Venit 'Two Steps Forward and No Steps Back: Economic Analysis and Oligopolistic Dominance after *Kali & Salz*' (1998) 35 *Common Market Law Review* 1101.

Table 9.1 Evidence of collective dominance

Case	Nestlé/Perrier	Kali & Salz	Gencor/Lonrho	Airtours	Guidelines
Post-merger concentration	Top two with 82%	Top two with 23% and 37%	Top two with 60–70% (between 30 and 35% each)	Top three with 32%; 27% 20%	Market shares and HHI (paras. 17–21)
Conditions facilitating coordinated effects	Transparency of prices and quantities	Transparency in relation to production and price	Transparency regarding both price and quantities	Market not transparent	Paragraphs 47 and 50
	Similarity in size and costs	Different competitive strength	Similarity in market share, reserves and cost structures	Fluctuating market shares	Paragraph 48
	Mature technology	No innovation	Mature technology	NA	Paragraph 45
	History of collusion and price leadership	NA	History of tacit collusion	No history of collusion	Paragraph 43
	NA	Homogeneous products	Homogeneous products	Homogeneous products	Paragraph 47
	Commercial links in other markets	Irrelevant commercial links in other markets	Multimarket contacts	Irrelevant commercial links in other markets	Paragraph 48
	NA	NA	Slow demand growth	Demand is growing and volatile	Paragraph 45
Conditions that deter deviation	Present	No express consideration	Present	Not found	Paragraphs 49–55
Power of other market participants	Lack of supply- and demand-side strength	Powerful supply-side substitutes	Lack of supply- and demand-side strength	Powerful supply- and demand-side forces	Paragraphs 56 and 57 and parts V and VI
Outcome	Collective dominance	No proof of collective dominance	Collective dominance, merger blocked	No proof of collective dominance	

The first merger where collective dominance was identified is *Nestlé/Perrier*, in the market for still, bottled mineral water in France.[16] Nestlé acquired Perrier and sold the Volvic brand to BSN. The Commission found that the merger created a position of collective dominance but it was cleared when the parties agreed to divest assets to create an additional competitor. The merged entity would have had a market share of 82 per cent. The following conditions facilitated tacit collusion: retail processes were transparent, there was a system for information exchange which permitted immediate detection of any deviation, the firms had similar sizes and costs creating a common interest to maximise profits, technology was mature, so no new development could give one firm a considerable advantage over rivals, there was a history of tacit collusion, parallel prices since 1987 and price leadership by Perrier. The two firms also cooperated in other food sectors. There were deterrence mechanisms because aggressive competitive action by one would trigger responses by the other which would hurt both firms. Other firms had no power: on the supply side, fringe firms were too small and dispersed and entry barriers were high; on the other side, demand was inelastic, and retailers lacked buyer power to force lower prices.

In *Kali & Salz* the Court affirmed the Commission's power to apply the ECMR in cases of collective dominance, but the Commission lost on the facts.[17] The merger in the market for potash-salt-based products for agricultural use in the EC (except Germany) did not create a position of collective dominance. The two main undertakings were the merged entity K&S/MdK with a 23 per cent market share and SCPA with 37 per cent. Some conditions facilitated collusion (e.g. transparency of prices, lack of innovation and product homogeneity). However, two factors suggested collusion was unlikely: there was no evidence of a causal connection between the structural links of the two firms (both participated in an export cartel with other producers, and the two owned 50 per cent of the capital of a Canadian potash producer) and anticompetitive behaviour, and differences in the positions of the two firms (K&S's industrial capacity is strengthened by the merger) reduced the common interest in cooperation. The Commission did not consider deterrence mechanisms. The Court noted that even if the parties had incentives to collude, they faced competition, as imports from Eastern Europe had been increasing and Coposa (in Spain) had excess capacity to maintain or increase its market share.

The Commission survived judicial scrutiny in *Gencor/Lonrho*, a merger in the worldwide market for platinum, and this was the first merger to be blocked on grounds of collective dominance.[18] The merger would have reduced the market to two main firms: Implats and Amplats jointly had 60–70 per cent of the market (between 30 and 35 per cent each) and the third leading player's

---

[16] [1992] OJ L356/1.   [17] Case IV/M.308 *Kali & Salz* [1994] OJ L186/38.
[18] Case IV/M.619 *Gencor/Lonrho* [1997] OJ L11/30.

reserves were in decline, so the market would have soon become a duopoly. Several factors facilitated tacit collusion: market transparency regarding both price and quantities because metals are sold in metal exchanges, statistics are publicly available, a small number of buyers means sellers are in contact with all purchasers, opening of new capacity is public information, similarity in market share, reserves and cost structures creates a common interest, no one party has a technological advantage, technology is mature, history shows tendency to tacit collusion so far restrained by waning Russian sales, homogeneous products, structural links through multimarket contacts (e.g. in the gold market), and slow demand growth that did not encourage vigorous competition. Price transparency allowed for 'retaliatory measures', and links between the undertakings in other markets discipline the oligopoly by 'multiplying the risks of retaliation'. The duopoly would be insulated from other firms: on the supply side, existing competitors were insufficiently strong, there were no significant mines of platinum outside the control of existing players, and recycled platinum is not an effective substitute; on the demand side, buyers were not powerful and demand was inelastic.

The cases above have three players and the merger creates a duopoly. In *Airtours* the Commission wanted to block a merger (in the market for short-haul package tours) with four players that would have been reduced to three (Airtours/First Choice (32 per cent); Thomson (27 per cent); Thomas Cook (20 per cent)) but its factual findings were found to be erroneous on appeal.[19] The Commission claimed the market was transparent, but the CFI held the market was insufficiently transparent; moreover, the CFI considered that the complexity of capacity planning made it difficult to interpret actions of competitors; the CFI found that market shares had been fluctuating and varied between seasons and so pre-merger the market was competitive and not tending to collective dominance as the Commission claimed; the Commission claimed there were commercial links (e.g. purchase of airline seats from competitors; vertical integration and use of each other's travel agency chains) but the CFI ruled that there is no reason why these commercial links increase interdependence; moreover, demand is growing and volatile, making collusion more difficult. The CFI also held that there were no deterrence mechanisms because there was insufficient transparency to detect deviation and the evidence suggested that possible retaliatory measures would be insufficient. Finally, the three had much to fear should they collude: on the supply side, small operators were able to increase capacity to undermine any anticompetitive action by the big three, and on the demand side consumers were well informed and able to obtain cheaper deals from small operators.

---

[19] Case IV/M.1524 *Airtours/First Choice* [2000] OJ L93/1, annulled by Case T-342/99 *Airtours* [2002] ECR II-2585. For analysis, see A. Nikpay and F. Houwen 'Tour de Force or a Little Local Turbulence? A Heretical View on the *Airtours* Judgment' [2003] *European Competition Law Review* 193.

2.1 Concentration

The degree of concentration among the firms is very high in all cases: this is an important condition as cooperation is possible only when the number of firms is small.[20] Concentration provides a prima facie indication of possible coordinated effects, requiring further scrutiny.[21] The majority of the Commission's decisions measure concentration by considering the market's 'concentration ratio': that is, what market share the leading firms in the oligopoly have. In the cases summarised above, the lowest concentration ratio considered by the Commission gives the oligopoly a 60 per cent share of the relevant market. The Horizontal Merger Guidelines have introduced the Herfindhal Hirschmann Index (HHI) as a means of measuring how concentrated the market is. This is said to be a more precise mechanism for measuring concentration in that it takes into account all the firms, not just the major players.

The utility of the HHI index

The HHI index was developed in the US Horizontal Merger Guidelines. At first the Guidelines had adopted another measure of concentration, known as the concentration ratio (CR). Thus CR4 was the sum of the market shares of the four leading firms. However, this was said to be uninformative because it did not take into account all the firms in the market, nor did it look at the relative size of each firm. A CR4 of 80 can mean that there are four firms with 20 per cent of the market, or that there is one firm with 50 per cent and three with 10 per cent each. Moreover, it tells us nothing about the other firms. As a result, in the 1992 Merger Guidelines the US authorities switched to the HHI index, which takes into account all the firms' market shares. However, rather than merely adding these up, it adds the sum of the squares of each firm. This has the effect of giving greater prominence to the larger firms and reducing the significance of smaller firms. Consider these two industries:

Market A: five firms, each with a market share of 20 per cent
Market B: nine firms, one with a market share of 20 per cent and eight with a market share of 10 per cent

In market A the HHI is 2,000 $= (20^2 + 20^2 + 20^2 + 20^2 + 20^2)$;
In market B the HHI is 1,200 $= (20^2 + 10^2 + 10^2 + 10^2 + 10^2 + 10^2 + 10^2 + 10^2 + 10^2)$

If two firms merge in market A and there is a merger between the firm with 20 per cent and one firm with 10 per cent in market B, the HHI indexes become:

In market A: 2,800 (an increase of 800 points)
In market B: 1,600 (an increase of 400 points)

The highest HHI is 10,000 where one firm has 100 per cent of the market; the HHI gets very close to zero when there are many small firms. Proponents of this index argue that it

---

[20] A factor which economists settled early on: Stigler 'Theory of Oligopoly'.
[21] See also Case COMP/M.2201 *MAN/Auwärter* [2002] OJ L116/35 para. 32; Case IV/M.1225 *Enso/Stora* [1999] OJ L254/9.

takes into account all firms and so all data is factored in, and that by emphasising the power of larger firms, it gives a better sense of where the competitive risks lie. The higher the HHI, the greater the risk. The US Guidelines use this approach to determine what degree of concentration creates a presumption of anticompetitive risk, and they distinguish the following three levels:

Unconcentrated markets: where the post-merger HHI is below 1,000
Moderately concentrated: where the post-merger HHI is between 1,000 and 1,800 and the increase in HHI is greater than 100 (the merger in market B falls into this bracket)
Highly concentrated: where the post-merger HHI is above 1,800 and the increase in HHI is greater than 50 (the merger in market A falls into this bracket).

A merger below these thresholds is deemed to be safe and no further scrutiny is required, while one above these thresholds calls for additional scrutiny.

The EC's Horizontal Merger Guidelines follow this method, and the only difference is in the numbers used for the three categories:

no risks below HHI of 1,000
no risks with a post-merger HHI between 1,000 and 2,000 and an increase less than 250
no risks with a post-merger HHI above 2,000 and an increase below 150.

According to the Commission, these numbers are 'initial indicators' of the absence of competition concerns, raising no presumptions. While the HHI method is widely praised, it seems fairly useless in the EC context. If we look at the mergers in table 9.1, mergers have been blocked when the HHIs have been well above the 2,000 level. Moreover, the competitive strength of other firms is taken into account already by considering the power of competitors and entry barriers. HHIs might be more useful in the US system, but seem another 'import' that provides little added value to EC competition law.[22]

2.2 Market facilitates tacit collusion

Upon determining that the market is sufficiently concentrated, the next crucial question is whether the market conditions facilitate tacit collusion. While this is an intimately fact-specific exercise (and, as can be seen from the table, not all the factors are considered in every case),[23] one feature is a necessary condition

---

[22] And even in the United States, the FTC's enforcement pattern is to challenge mergers with an HHI much higher than that set out in the guidelines. See H. Hovenkamp *The Antitrust Enterprise: Principle and Execution* (Cambridge, MA: Harvard University Press, 2005) p. 203.

[23] 'While these characteristics are often presented in the form of a list, it is necessary to examine all of them and to make an overall assessment rather than mechanistically applying a "check-list". Depending on the circumstances, the fact that one or another of the structural features usually associated with collective dominance may not be clearly established is not in itself decisive to exclude the likelihood of a co-ordinated outcome.' Case M.2499 *Norske Skog/Parnco/Walsum*, decision of 21 November 2001, para. 77; see the list of factors in the Horizontal Merger Guidelines paras. 42–8.

for a finding that anticompetitive effects may result: market transparency. Transparency is crucial for two reasons. First, parties must be able to work out their strategies on the basis of the performance of others: there can be no coordination unless the parties can see what the strategies of the others are. Second, transparency is necessary to detect any deviation from the agreed practice by one firm, thereby allowing the others to react.[24] The significance of transparency has evolved with the case law: in *Gencor* the CFI noted the importance of transparency as a mechanism necessary to facilitate retaliation and in *Airtours* the CFI confirmed the dual purpose of transparency. As a matter of evidence, market transparency may be proven in different ways: there may be close structural links between undertakings (e.g. membership in a joint venture in another market), or prices may be easily observable because the goods are sold on the open market,[25] or there may be reliable data that the parties are able to obtain which allows them to monitor each other's actions, for instance from customers,[26] or the parties may all be members of a professional association where information is available.[27] The parties can make the market transparent by their own efforts: for example, in one decision concerning a merger of stainless steel tube pipes, the price lists were publicly available and all constructed by reference to one particular type of tube pipe, and both consumers and competitors knew that prices for other tube pipes were calculated by reference to that one type, facilitating price comparisons and price leadership by one supplier.[28] Transparency can also be facilitated by the homogeneity of products, which allows firms to compare each other's market performance more easily than when products are highly differentiated. Perhaps the most dramatic demonstration that transparency has a determinative impact on the facility with which oligopolies are able to coordinate behaviour is the old Danish competition law which was designed to promote price transparency,[29] on the basis that perfect competition theory suggests that transparent markets lead to lower prices because consumers can make better choices if prices are visible. Instead, the promotion of transparency in the highly concentrated cement industry by the publication of price lists by the competition authority facilitated coordinated pricing by cement firms, seeing prices rise by 15–20 per cent![30]

While transparency is necessary, it is not sufficient to create the degree of interdependence that leads to collective dominance, and a range of other factors

---

[24] *MAN/Auwärter* [2002] OJ L116/35 para. 52. [25] E.g. *Gencor/Lonrho* [1997] OJ L11/30.

[26] E.g. *Nestlé/Perrier* [1992] OJ L356/1.

[27] E.g. Case M.2499 *Norske Skog/Parnco/Walsum*, decision of 21 November 2001, paras. 83–5, but here the degree of transparency was insufficient.

[28] Case IV/M.315 *Mannesmann/Vallourec/Ilva* [1994] OJ L102/15 paras. 85–8.

[29] Article 1 Danish Competition Act 1990 (this Act was replaced in 1997 by legislation which is closer to the EC model and which removed the priority given to market transparency as a means to enhance competition).

[30] S. Albaek, P. Møllgaard and P. Overgaard 'Government-Assisted Oligopoly Coordination? A Concrete Case' (1997) 45 *Journal of Industrial Economics* 429.

can be deployed to determine whether coordinated effects are likely. The Commission's decisions can be criticised for giving inconsistent messages about what other factors are also necessary. For instance, in one decision it stated that symmetrical cost structures were 'a precondition for the existence of a stable duopoly'.[31] This view finds favour in some economic quarters:[32] symmetrical market power means that the parties have less incentive to compete as they do not have a decisive comparative advantage over each other, and if the profits resulting from tacit coordination are similar for each member of the oligopoly this will induce cooperative strategies more easily than otherwise.[33] However, the Commission in *Danish Crown* found that a collusive duopoly would obtain when there were no such symmetries.[34] This was because the Commission found that while one firm had greater economic power than the other overall, the smaller firm had a comparative advantage in one important geographical market, thus neither had an incentive to compete aggressively.[35] Accordingly, it may be suggested that while cost symmetries are highly significant in creating incentives to coordinate behaviour, other factors that create similar incentives may suffice.

Certain market characteristics are more likely to lead to coordinated effects, but this does not prove that in their absence there can be no coordinated effects *a fortiori*. For instance, in many mergers markets were not growing. This factor facilitates coordination because existing firms have less incentive to compete for new markets, and may favour the stability afforded by coordinated behaviour.[36] However, when entry barriers are high, coordinated effects may occur even in growing markets.[37] Similarly in many cases there was little innovation in the market. Technological maturity makes it easier to coordinate behaviour because there is no risk of one firm gaining a superior cost advantage by research and development;[38] however, when other features in the market point strongly in favour of coordinated effects, these can eliminate the chances of competition presented by the possibility of developing

---

[31] *MAN/Auwärter* [2002] OJ L116/35 para. 56.

[32] O. Compte, F. Jenny and P. Rey 'Capacity Constraints, Mergers and Collusion' (2002) 46 *European Economic Review* 1.

[33] Accordingly mere difference in size and market share is in itself irrelevant and the analysis in some early cases can be criticised for failing to see this: see D. Ridyard 'Economic Analysis of Single Firm and Oligopolistic Dominance Under the European Merger Regulation' [1994] *European Competition Law Review* 255, 260–1.

[34] Case IV/M.1313 *Danish Crown/Vestjyske Slagterier* [2000] OJ L20/1 para. 177.

[35] Ibid. para. 178.

[36] Although, if prices were falling, tacit collusion would be less likely to work as all firms would try to fight for the shrinking market. See J. Haltiwanger and J. Harrington 'The Impact of Cyclical Demand Movements on Collusive Behavior' (1991) 22 *Rand Journal of Economics* 89.

[37] P. Christensen and V. Rabassa 'The *Airtours* Decision: Is there a New Approach to Collective Dominance?' [2001] *European Competition Law Review* 227, 232.

[38] For historical evidence that innovation disrupts collusion, see Scherer and Ross *Industrial Market Structure* p. 285.

innovative products.[39] Another regular finding in mergers that have been blocked is product homogeneity, and the economic literature confirms that coordination is more likely with homogeneous products than in cases of consumer goods.[40] Heterogeneity makes it more difficult to compare products and prices, and complicates enforcement efforts by reducing market transparency.

In some early decisions, it appeared that a necessary requirement for a finding of collective dominance was the presence of structural links among the oligopolists (e.g. that the firms were also members of an export cartel, or were the parent companies of a joint venture in a related market). It is true that structural links can facilitate cooperation and retaliation. For example, in a merger in the Danish market for fresh pork sold to retailers which would have created two main suppliers, it was found that the smaller of the two, Steff-Houlberg, would use the merged entity's export companies, creating both a more transparent market to facilitate collusion and also the risk of retaliation by the merged entity if Steff-Houlberg began to compete more aggressively (e.g. by making the use of its export companies more costly).[41] However, the Court has clarified that structural links are not necessary if other economic factors are sufficient to facilitate coordinated effects.[42] From an economic perspective, this is the correct conclusion: the key question is whether the market facilitates tacit coordination and allows the parties to monitor each other's behaviour. Commercial links might help establish these economic conditions but are not necessary.[43]

2.3 Deterrence mechanisms

Even if the conditions in the market are such that the parties have the ability and the incentive to coordinate behaviour, it is also important that there is no incentive to 'cheat' upon tacitly agreed practices. Accordingly, there must be a means of punishing those who deviate from the tacitly agreed course of action. The approach to deterrence mechanisms is evolving – there is little mention of this requirement in the early decisions (for example, there is a brief mention in *Nestlé/Perrier* and no discussion in *Kali & Salz*) but a more exacting consideration in later cases.[44] On the one hand, evidence of market transparency

---

[39] E.g. Case IV/M.580 *ABB/Daimler-Benz* [1997] OJ L11/1, where the far-reaching cooperation between the duopolists and the large number of buyers meant that cooperation was more plausible than competition.

[40] See e.g. G. A. Hay and D. Kelly 'An Empirical Survey of Price Fixing Conspiracies' (1974) 17 *Journal of Law and Economics* 13.

[41] *Danish Crown/Vestjyske Slagterier* [2000] OJ L20/1 para. 177.

[42] *Gencor/Lonrho* [1997] OJ L11/30.

[43] See J. Briones 'Oligopolistic Dominance: Is there a Common Approach in Different Jurisdictions?' [1995] *European Competition Law Review* 334, 339–40.

[44] E.g. *Danish Crown* [2000] OJ L20/1: the Commission noted that only one duopolist could retaliate against the other (para. 177); in *ABB/Daimler-Benz* [1997] OJ L11/1 there was no mention of retaliation.

without any further explanation as to how this allows parties to retaliate against a firm who decides to cheat is insufficient, but on the other hand the Commission is not bound to establish precisely what retaliation mechanisms exist, rather it must show that there are deterrents 'which are such that it is not worth the while of any member of the dominant oligopoly to depart from the common course of conduct to the detriment of the other oligopolists'.[45] Accordingly, if tacit collusion results in the parties reducing supplies as a way of inflating prices, it will be possible for retaliation to occur if it can be proven that the market is sufficiently transparent to discover if any firm is increasing output, and if the others can quickly increase their output and are able to target the increased output towards those customers of the cheating firm.[46] On the contrary, if the retaliation mechanism (e.g. an increase in capacity by the other firms) would come too late to harm the party who cheated, this will not constitute a credible retaliation strategy.[47] The Commission is of the view that retaliation need not damage the cheating firm, that it is sufficient if the effect of retaliation is to restore the market to the pre-collusive price levels. This appears satisfactory in that if the retaliation is quick enough then the cheater will gain very little by destroying the tacit collusive agreement. Significantly, the Horizontal Merger Guidelines fail to mention another important element of deterrence mechanisms, namely that all cheaters can be punished by the other firms. There would be no credible deterrence if only one firm was able to mete out punishment but nobody was able to penalise it should it choose to cheat.

2.4 Entry barriers

Upon determining that the firms are able to present themselves on the market as a collectively dominant entity, the analysis then turns (as in all merger cases) to considering the countervailing power of other suppliers and buyers. As we have noted in chapter 8, the merger case law adopts a more perceptive assessment of actual and potential competition than the dominance case law under Article 82.[48] In *Airtours* for example, the Court noted that a smaller firm or a new entrant need not be able to enter the market on equal terms with the incumbents, but need only be able to take advantage of the opportunities in the market resulting from the firms' output reduction.[49] The relevant question is whether a sufficiently vast number of small entrants can thwart the behaviour of the dominant oligopoly by offering a number of short haul holidays to neutralise the anticompetitive effects of the oligopoly's restriction in output.[50]

---

[45] *Airtours v. Commission* [2002] ECR II-2585 para. 195.
[46] E.g. Case M.2499 *Norske Skog/Parnco/Walsum*, decision of 21 November 2001, paras. 137–9.
[47] Ibid. para. 135.   [48] Ibid. paras. 140–8.
[49] *Airtours v Commission* [2002] ECR II-2585 paras. 210–69.   [50] Ibid. paras. 213–14.

2.5 Causation and efficiencies

One final, significant consideration is that the Commission must prove that the merger is the likely cause of an impediment of competition.[51] A causal link may be established when the merger eliminates a maverick competitor that had made coordination difficult, or the merger leads to more symmetrical cost structures, or greater transparency, or improved retaliation mechanisms, all of which enhance the capacity of the parties to coordinate their action. For instance, in *Gencor/Lonrho*, while the market already exhibited tendencies to tacit collusion, it was found that the duopoly would make it 'much easier for the main suppliers to adapt to each other's behaviour and . . . restrict output'[52] because of the elimination of the competitor with the greatest incentive to compete, and because the merger created two firms with similar cost structures.[53] It follows that if pre-merger the market already shows signs of collective dominance because of the economic features of the market reviewed above, it will be difficult to prove convincingly that the merger causes an even greater competitive threat.[54] The question of causation is not always given the weight it deserves. Some may be satisfied that higher post-merger concentration improves the possibility of tacit collusion, but this summary conclusion is unwarranted. Others have gone so far as to say that a merger in oligopoly markets should only be blocked if it eliminates the possibilities of a maverick firm unsettling tacit collusion.[55] This would restrict the application of merger control significantly because the merger could only be regulated upon proof that there is some competition pre-merger that is caused by a firm declining to collude tacitly and that this firm would either exit the market (because it is taken over) or lose its ability to disrupt collusion. Instead in EC competition law it seems that, provided the Commission can show that the merger facilitates tacit collusion, it may be blocked, and this can occur even if there is already evidence of collusion on the market.

Conversely, if the merger yields efficiency gains, this might negate the causal link between increased concentration and tacit collusion. If a merger creates a more efficient firm, then it will have less incentive to coordinate its behaviour with others, and have an incentive to use the efficiencies to extend its market position. This is the one type of merger where the Horizontal Merger Guidelines provide for the application of efficiency considerations: 'In the context of coordinated effects, efficiencies may increase the merged entity's incentive to increase production and reduce prices, and thereby reduce its incentive to coordinate its market behaviour with other firms in the market. Efficiencies may therefore lead to a lower risk of coordinated effects in the

---

[51] Ibid. para. 82.   [52] *Gencor/Lonrho* [1997] OJ L11/30 para. 181.
[53] Ibid. para. 190.   [54] See also Nikpay and Houwen 'Tour de Force' p. 199.
[55] See J. B. Baker 'Mavericks, Mergers and Exclusion: Proving Coordinated Competitive Effects under the Antitrust Laws' (2002) 77 *New York University Law Review* 135.

relevant market.'[56] Notice how in this context efficiencies are not used as a defence, rather they are evidence that rebuts the presumption that firms in tight oligopolies would coordinate behaviour post-merger. The role of efficiency considerations in alleviating concerns in oligopoly markets had already been considered by the Commission in *Airtours*. After discussing the factors that facilitated tacit collusion, the Commission referred to efficiencies:

> it should also be noted that the merger is only expected to lead to overall synergies of less than 1 per cent of the overall costs of the combined entity. Furthermore, the cost savings mostly relate to overhead and other fixed costs. Consequently, the merger would not cause any material change in the overall cost structure of Airtours/First Choice. Therefore, changes to the cost structure would not *increase the incentives to compete*.[57]

The italicised passage illustrates that the Commission would have reached a different conclusion as to the anticompetitive effects had efficiencies been more substantial. It would have ruled that tacit collusion was unlikely because the efficiencies would have given the merged entity the ability and the incentive to reduce prices.

2.6 Assessment

In general, the approach taken to regulate coordinated effects is economically sound – it translates the economic insights of oligopoly and game theory into a workable legal formula. The fact that two out of the three merger decisions we considered in detail were overturned on appeal is not evidence of misconceived economics by the Commission. In both cases the decisions were criticised for the inability to comprehend the evidence: in *Kali & Salz* the links between the parties were not explored sufficiently closely, in *Airtours* the analysis was vitiated by a series of errors of assessment as to the evidence. This indicates that the flaws in the current system are procedural, not substantive. After the Commission lost *Airtours* it devised more rigorous checks to ensure that its economic theories match the facts, and one merger was cleared when the newly recruited economists questioned the economic rigour of the Commission's initial case.[58] However, even this upgraded level of scrutiny proved insufficient as the Commission's clearance was later challenged successfully on appeal, which casts doubts on the Commission's ability to manage evidence.[59]

---

[56] Horizontal Merger Guidelines para. 82 (this passage appears to contradict the position taken by the Commission in *Gencor/Lonrho* [1997] OJ L11/30 para. 214).

[57] *Airtours* [2000] OJ L93/1 para. 146.

[58] Case M.3333 *Sony/BMG* (19 July 2004): products insufficiently homogeneous, market insufficiently transparent, no evidence to indicate retaliation was likely should one cheat. See *Financial Times* 20 July 2004, p. 26 (reporting that the chief economist, L.-H. Röller, expressed reservations about whether the firms would tacitly collude).

[59] Case T-464/04 *Independent Music Publishers and Labels Association (Impala) v. Commission*, judgment of 13 July 2006.

It will be argued that the multi-factor approach used by the Commission is uncertain. However, legal certainty is not as pressing when the parties are negotiating *ex ante* with the competition authorities; in contrast certainty is much more important when regulation is *ex post* where the parties must be able to self-assess whether their activities will infringe the competition rules. In merger cases the parties are able to offer commitments, which remove the risk of coordinated effects while at the same time allowing the merger to be consummated. For instance, in *Nestlé/Perrier* the parties secured clearance by removing the causes of oligopolistic interdependence: first they promised to sell enough brands of bottled water to allow a new firm to enter the market (which would have restored the pre-merger market structure of three major sellers) and then Nestlé undertook not to provide sales data to any association which would allow other firms to find out what its sales volumes were, thereby reducing transparency in the market and making tacit coordination more difficult post-merger.[60] Moreover, the criticism of legal uncertainty is less compelling when, as noted above, the Commission's approach is relatively consistent in that a similar range of factors are regularly considered in order to assess the risks posed by mergers in oligopoly markets.

3 Express collusion

The economic analysis used to identify situations of collective dominance in merger cases is also helpful in examining the behaviour of cartels (that is, agreements among manufacturers of competing goods that reduce output, raise prices or allocate territories to each cartel member). Cartels are the major concern of competition authorities, described as 'cancers' in the economy.[61] Most cartels have been uncovered in oligopoly markets where the possibilities to coordinate behaviour are significantly facilitated by the market structure: a relatively contained number of firms, fungible goods, a falling market, the lack of innovation, and weak buyers.[62] And cartels can collapse when there is no deterrent effect,[63] as happened for instance to the cartel between the four major providers of electrical equipment in the United States (General Electric, Westinghouse, Allis-Chalmers and Federal Pacific). The cartel self-destructed when in 1957 one major customer (the Florida Power and Light Company)

---

[60] *Nestlé/Perrier* [1992] OJ L356/1 paras. 136–7. See also *Danish Crown* [2000] OJ L20/1 paras. 236–7, approving commitments that removed those factors which facilitated coordination.

[61] M. Monti 'Fighting Cartels: Why and How?' Third Nordic Competition Policy Conference, 11–12 September 2000. Metaphors abound: Justice Scalia referred to cartels as the 'supreme evil of antitrust': *Verizon Communications Inc. v. Law Offices of Curtis V. Trinko LLP* 540 US 398 (2004).

[62] For example: *Polypropylene* [1986] OJ L230/1 (fifteen manufacturers, four holding 64 per cent of the market in a chemical product); *Zinc Phosphate* [2003] OJ L153/1 (five manufacturers in the EC, foreign firms having an insignificant share of sales in the Community).

[63] E.g. in *Zinc Phosphate* [2003] OJ L153/1, while there were no punishment mechanisms, sales quotas were enforced through peer pressure and via the reallocation of customers (para. 62).

pressurised Westinghouse to reduce its prices in exchange for a promise that it would buy all its requirements from Westinghouse. However, General Electric found out and matched the lower price offered to Florida Power. This led to a price war until discounts in the winter of 1957–8 reached 60 per cent.[64] General Electric and Westinghouse learned the lesson of the 1950s when in the 1970s they coordinated again in the turbo-generator market. This time the parties included a mechanism of deterrence: they both offered a 'price protection plan' to their customers by which a discount on new orders would also apply retrospectively to all orders for the past six months. The effect of this was to make cheating highly expensive.[65] This suggests that if the cartel is poorly designed, it is likely to end by itself, without the intervention of a competition authority.

However, economic insights about the conditions for successful collusion are irrelevant for competition authorities in cartel cases. First, competition authorities distinguish between express and tacit collusion and indicate that they are merely empowered to catch the former. Second, a finding of express collusion is based only upon whether there is evidence to show that the parties have communicated directly with each other: the conditions for successful collusion we discussed in section 2 are irrelevant. Express collusion is per se unlawful (bar the possibility of exemption for crisis cartels noted in chapter 4). The per se rule is justified because the risk of Type 1 errors is low: when competitors agree to fix prices or allocate territories, it is unlikely that this has a pro-competitive justification. Conversely, the harm from Type 2 errors is significant: if the cartel is successful, it can cause severe harm.

The Commission's policy in cases of express collusion is strengthened by three interrelated features: a wide meaning to notions of the words 'agreement' and 'concerted practice'; wide powers to obtain information and the possibility to infer an agreement from market behaviour; and the availability of incentives on parties to cartels to inform the Commission of their complicity in an infringement of competition law.[66]

3.1 The meaning of agreement and concerted practices

Article 81 applies to three forms of coordination: agreements, decisions by associations and concerted practices. In the present context only the concepts of agreement and concerted practice are relevant.[67] An agreement is found

---

[64] W. K. Viscusi, J. E. Harrington Jr and J. M. Vernon *Economics of Regulation and Antitrust* 4th edn (Cambridge, MA: MIT Press, 2005) p. 127.

[65] The Department of Justice obtained an undertaking from the parties that they would drop the price protection plan. Ibid. p. 141.

[66] On the Community's cartel policy, see generally C. Harding and J. Joshua *Regulating Cartels in Europe – A Study of Legal Control of Corporate Delinquency* (Oxford: Oxford University Press, 2003).

[67] An association which represents the interests of all firms in a given sector can be the means through which anticompetitive agreements are carried out. In *Fenex* [1996] OJ L181/28 for example, the association representing freight forwarders in the Netherlands had been active

when parties express their joint intention to act on the market in a specific way.[68] It is not limited to contractual agreements, nor to any form of communication. A concerted practice differs from an agreement for two reasons. First, it is less intense: it is 'a form of coordination between undertakings which, without having been taken to a stage where an agreement ... has been concluded, knowingly substitutes for the risks of competition practical cooperation between them'.[69] Second, a concerted practice requires conduct on the market after the coordination and a causal link between coordination and subsequent conduct.[70] In an early case the Court drew a distinction between concerted action (collusion) and the concerted practice (the implementation of collusion).[71] The difference might be illustrated in this way: if two competitors enter into a contract to set the same price for their goods, this is an unlawful agreement from the moment the contract is signed. In contrast, if two competitors meet and exchange information about their intended commercial strategy for the following year, this is a concerted practice only when the parties take this information into account in devising their future commercial strategy. In the first example the parties express a wish to act in a particular manner, while in the second, the parties may not behave in the same way but will take the other person's statements into account when planning their conduct and this can lead to a reduction in output and higher prices. The difference between agreement and concerted practice should not be analogised to that between murder and manslaughter in the criminal law. That is, an agreement is not more serious and deserving of greater punishment than a concerted practice. Instead, there is only one offence in Article 81, express collusion, and it may take different forms.[72] As the ECJ put it, the concepts of agreement and concerted practice 'are intended to catch forms of collusion having the same nature and are only distinguishable from each other by their intensity and the form in which they manifest themselves'.[73]

In long-running cartels the Commission has observed both forms of express collusion, with some rounds of coordination taking the form of agreements and others the form of concerted practices. This reflects economic studies,

---

[68] Case C-49/92 *Commission v. Anic Partecipazioni SpA* [1999] ECR I-4125 para. 130; Case 41/69 *ACF Chemiefarma v. Commission* [1970] ECR 661 para. 112; Case T-1/89 *Rhône Poulenc v. Commission* [1991] ECR II-867 para. 120; Case T-141/94 *Thyssen Stahl v. Commission* [1999] ECR II-347 para. 262; Joined Cases T-305/94 etc. *Limburgse Vinyl Maatschappij NV and Others v. Commission* [1999] ECR II-931 para. 715.

[69] Case C-199/92P *Hüls AG v. Commission* [1999] ECR I-4287 para. 158, citing Joined Cases 40/73 to 48/73, 50/73, 54/73, 55/73, 56/73, 111/73, 113/73 and 114/73 *Suiker Unie and Others v. Commission* [1975] ECR 1663 para. 26.

[70] *Anic* [1999] ECR I-4125 paras. 115 and 118; *Hüls* [1999] ECR I-4287 para. 161.

[71] See in particular *Suiker Unie* [1975] ECR 1663 paras. 179–80.

[72] *Anic* [1999] ECR I-4125 para. 108. See generally I. Lianos 'La confusion des infractions de l'article 81(1): quelques interrogations sur l'utilité de la notion d'infraction unique' (2000) 36 *Revue trimestrielle de droit européen* 239.

[73] *Anic* [1999] ECR I-4125 para. 131.

which suggest that cartels may be unstable and that differing levels of coordination might be expected throughout the lifetime of a collusive endeavour.[74] In these situations, the Commission can characterise a long-running cartel as an agreement and/or concerted practice. That is, just because the parties' cooperation varies, this does not mean that each round of cooperation is a distinct infringement. Rather, while the collusive scheme is a complex cartel, containing various forms of cooperation,[75] it is a 'single infringement'.[76] This facilitates the Commission's investigation in two ways. First, it allows the Commission to catch collusion which manifests itself sometimes in the form of an agreement and sometimes in the form of a concerted practice. Otherwise the Commission would be forced to take separate actions against the firms for each round of collusion. Second, this allows the Commission to hold each firm responsible for the whole agreement even if they did not take part in every aspect of it.[77] For example, in the *PVC* decision a firm was held responsible for an anticompetitive agreement even if it did not attend all the meetings where the anticompetitive policy was made. The CFI affirmed, holding that a firm can be held responsible even without proof of complete participation in all elements of a cartel 'if it is shown that it knew or must have known that the collusion in which it participated was part of an overall plan intended to destroy competition and that the plan included all the constituent elements of a cartel'.[78]

The concept of concerted practice is particularly helpful in the context of oligopoly markets. As we saw above, a collusive equilibrium depends upon a particular market structure and is characterised by interdependence among the firms. Concerted practices can be one route to facilitate collusion by increasing the degree of transparency in the market. However, there is one flaw and one ambiguity in the current conceptualisation of concerted practice.

The flaw is that the two limbs of the definition of concerted practice are formalistic. The first limb has been summarised in this way: 'direct or indirect contact which is designed or has the effect of reducing uncertainty about [the firm's] future conduct'.[79] This is problematic because in the case law there is little analysis of the market where the concerted practice takes place. Contact can only reduce uncertainty if the market in question is one where the circumstances make the information valuable. In a market with very low entry barriers, or a market with thousands of firms, a concerted practice is hardly likely to have an anticompetitive effect. Nor can it have an anticompetitive

---

[74] See generally R. H. Porter 'Detecting Collusion' (2005) 26 *Review of Industrial Organization* 147.

[75] Case T-7/89 *Hercules v. Commission* [1991] ECR II-1711 para. 264; *Zinc Phosphate* [2003] OJ L153/1 para. 203.

[76] *Anic* [1999] ECR I-4125 para. 83.   [77] Ibid. paras. 84–9.

[78] *Limburgse Vinyl Maatschappij NV and Others v. Commission* [1999] ECR II-931 para. 773.

[79] J. Faull and A. Nikpay *The EC Law of Competition* (Oxford: Oxford University Press, 1999) para. 2.49.

object: in competitive markets with many players or low entry barriers a concerted practice is not obviously capable of harming competition.[80] It is only in oligopoly markets that a concerted practice can serve to reduce uncertainty. This is the market structure that has been found in the majority of the cases where concerted practices have been uncovered, but the Court's definition fails to declare this to be an essential element.[81]

The second limb of the definition of concerted practice is that the efforts to coordinate behaviour have an effect on the firms' future conduct. However, the burden of proof for the second limb is very low. First, provided the firm stays in the market, the Commission is entitled to presume that its conduct was influenced by the coordination efforts.[82] Second, Article 81 prohibits collusion whose object is the restriction of competition, and so a concerted practice can be prohibited regardless of the effects.[83] Third, the Commission does not have to prove that the subsequent conduct has an anticompetitive effect, but only that the firm's subsequent conduct is caused by the cooperation, which can be presumed.[84] It seems impossible for a firm to provide evidence to disprove the second limb unless it ceases trading altogether. Moreover, a party who attends meetings where a concerted practice takes place cannot say that it did not agree with the discussions or chose not to follow them unless it indicates to the others 'that it was participating in those meetings in a spirit that was different from theirs'.[85] Private dissent from collusion is insufficient to escape liability. This makes it impossible for firms to rely on the fact that they did not follow the recommendations of the meeting in their subsequent behaviour – for example, if they lowered prices contrary to what had been negotiated. The test is so easy to satisfy by the Commission and so hard to rebut by the firm that it has little practical value. Moreover, it adds little to the first limb and should be discarded.

The ambiguity stems from an uncertainty over how far the concept of concerted practices can stretch. A simple example can help visualise the uncertainty. Say there is a duopoly: two petrol stations in a deserted road in France, opposite each other, one operated by Nicole and the other by Odette. Consider the following scenarios.

(a) Nicole and Odette make an appointment to meet in a café in Switzerland and both disclose their marketing strategy for the coming year.

---

[80] Opinion of AG Tizzano, Case C-551/03 *General Motors Nederland and Opel Nederland v. Commission* (25 October 2005) para. 71, suggesting that in determining 'object' under Article 81 one should ask if the agreement is obviously capable of infringing Article 81.

[81] Save for one vague reference to the need to have regard to the nature of the products, the size and number of firms and the volume of the market without any elaboration: see *Anic* [1999] ECR I-4125 para. 117.

[82] Ibid. para. 121; *Hüls* [1999] ECR I-4287 para. 162.

[83] *Anic* [1999] ECR I-4125 para. 123; *Hüls* [1999] ECR I-4287 paras. 163–4.

[84] *Anic* [1999] ECR I-4125 para. 124; *Hüls* [1999] ECR I-4287 para. 165.

[85] *Anic* [1999] ECR I-4125 para. 96; *Hüls* [1999] ECR I-4287 para. 155.

(b) Nicole and Odette make an appointment to meet in a café in Switzerland and Nicole tells Odette about her plan to raise prices by €1. Odette remains poker faced. They then talk about the weather.

(c) Odette phones Nicole and says 'Raise your prices by 10 per cent; I'll raise mine the next morning. You will make more money and I will too.'[86] She hangs up, and there is no further communication.

(d) Odette regularly opens her petrol station an hour earlier than Nicole and displays her prices prominently so that Nicole as well as the motorists can see them.

In all of these scenarios it is possible that prices will rise, but which constitute concerted practices? There is no doubt that (a) is covered because both parties help each other reach a collusive outcome. The case law suggests that (b) is also caught because a participant in a meeting where coordination is discussed does not have to play an active role. The firm that receives information can be presumed to act upon it. The case law suggests that in scenario (b) Odette should 'publicly distance' herself from the information she has received or else she will be party to an anticompetitive concerted practice.[87] Moreover, the Court might imply that the recipient's silence is helpful to the firm that disclosed the information: it can plan knowing that its suggestions were not opposed. Scenario (c) is less clear. The difference is that in (a) and (b) the parties agreed to meet and in the case law upon which (b) is a stylised example, the parties were aware that these meetings were not social occasions: their purpose was anticompetitive.[88] As Adam Smith put it, 'people of the same trade seldom meet together, even for merriment and diversion, but the conversation ends in a conspiracy against the public, or in some contrivance to raise prices'.[89] In (c) however there is no agreement to meet, merely a unilateral and unsolicited offer to collude. Some have suggested that this is enough to find an infringement because the recipient of this information can ring back and say she does not agree, thus publicly distancing herself from the communication. Failure to do so implies acquiescence.[90] However, there is as yet no case law to support a finding of collusion in this setting, although given the Commission's tough anti-cartel policy, it would be reasonable to suppose that this would be their conclusion.

---

[86] This paraphrases the telephone conversation between two managers in the airline industry in *US v. American Airlines* 743 F 2d 1114 (5th Cir. 1984).

[87] Case C-291/98 P *Sarrió v. Commission* [2000] ECR I-9991 para. 50.

[88] E.g. Joined Cases T-202/98, T-204/98 and T-207/98 *Tate & Lyle and Others v. Commission* [2001] ECR II-2035 para. 58; S. Stroux *US and EC Oligopoly Control* (The Hague: Kluwer Law International, 2004) pp. 157–9.

[89] A. Smith *An Inquiry into the Nature and Causes of the Wealth of Nations* (1776; Modern Library Edition, New York: Random House, 1937) p. 128.

[90] O. Odudu *The Boundaries of EC Competition Law* (Oxford: Oxford University Press, 2006) pp. 85–8. Opinion of AG Cosmas in *Anic* [1999] ECR I-4125 paras. 41–2.

Scenario (d) falls outside the scope of Article 81. This can be explained in several ways. First, there is no direct communication with competitors: the prices are announced to consumers so they can decide whether or not to buy petrol. In this way communications that are exclusively intended for the competitors (examples (a), (b) and (c)) fall within Article 81, and public information does not. A second reason is that the Court has held that firms have a right to adapt themselves intelligently to the existing and anticipated conduct of their competitors provided there is no contact between the two firms.[91] It seems to follow from this that following a price leader cannot be evidence of collusion.[92] Therefore, if one party makes its anticipated behaviour public, its competitors have a right to use that information. However, a third explanation might allow one to apply Article 81 to scenario (d) in some circumstances. The rationale is as follows: public price announcements are allowed when this is the only way to communicate prices to consumers and to prohibit this would be irrational and inefficient. This would suggest that if we found a scenario where public communication of prices was unnecessary because consumers already had access to the information in question, then scenario (d) could fall within Article 81. However, it would be undesirable to apply Article 81 to this example because it would implicate all competitors, perhaps even those unaware of the announcement.

Whether or not the concept of concerted practices can extend to the behaviour in example (c) is of particular importance in evaluating how far Article 81 can regulate oligopoly behaviour. This is because the scenarios in (c) and (d) come closer to what some regard as examples of tacit collusion, lacking as they do any reciprocity.[93]

3.2 Evidence of express collusion

3.2.1 Tangible evidence

In the majority of cases, the Commission proves agreements and concerted practices by obtaining documentary evidence of collusion: for example, faxes, emails or recorded conversations.[94] These documents must show either that the parties agreed to behave in the market in a specific way (so that the documents can prove the presence of an agreement), or that the parties have exchanged information about their future intentions, thereby facilitating coordination and showing the presence of a concerted practice. The Commission's standard of proof is low, because all that has to be shown to find an infringement is that a firm has participated in a meeting where

---

[91] *Suiker Unie* [1975] ECR 1663 para. 174.   [92] Ibid. para. 285.

[93] According to some, reciprocity is a feature of express collusion. See AG Darmon in Joined Cases 89, 104, 114, 116, 117 and 125–129/85 *A. Ahlström Osakeyhtiö and Others v. Commission* (*Woodpulp*) [1993] ECR I-1307.

[94] E.g. *LdPE* [1989] OJ L74/21.

anticompetitive activities were discussed.[95] The principal legal issue that has arisen when the Commission relies on documentary evidence has been about the powers that the competition authority has exercised to obtain this information and the degree to which these infringe the firm's fundamental rights. This has given rise to extensive case law that has circumscribed the Commission's powers somewhat. Nevertheless, the Commission has considerable powers to look for evidence, which are set out in Regulation 1/2003. These include the power to enter premises of firms that are suspected of engaging in anticompetitive activities and to seize relevant documents, as well as the power to interview employees.[96]

3.2.2 Economic evidence

Even with extensive powers to search, there will be cases where cartel members are able to hide the evidence of collusion so well that insufficient documentary evidence is found. In this context we distinguish two scenarios: first when there is some documentary evidence and second when there is none.

In certain circumstances an agreement may be inferred because the behaviour witnessed on the market, plus other evidence, allows the competition authority to infer that there has been collusion. Neither the other evidence nor the behaviour are sufficient, but together they allow an inference of collusion. In the United States, this is described as the use of plus factors. Proof of conspiracy is based upon parallel behaviour 'plus' documentary or other evidence that allows the court to infer that the behaviour is caused by agreement and is not unilateral. In the US, plus factors are of two sorts: communications among the conspirators and action that appears to be irrational but for the presence of an agreement.[97] An example of plus factors in the EC can be seen in the sugar cartel case of the 1970s, in particular with reference to the way the concerted practice between Dutch and Belgian sugar producers was proven. The Commission proved a concerted practice to protect the Dutch market based on the conduct of Dutch firms (their failure to export into Belgium in spite of excess supplies) and correspondence between the Belgian producers and their distributors in Belgium forbidding the latter to export into the Netherlands.[98] The documents made some references to a cartel between the sugar manufacturers but there was no direct evidence of this cartel. However, seeing market behaviour consistent with the cartel that manufacturers and distributors referred to was sufficient to establish a concerted practice.

---

[95] Van Bael and Bellis *Competition Law of the European Community* 4th edn (The Hague: Kluwer Law International, 2005) p. 54. See Joined Cases C-204/00P, C-205/00P, C-211/00P, C-213/00P, C-217/00P and C-219/00P *Aalborg Portland A/S and Others v. Commission* [2004] ECR I-123 para. 81.

[96] It is beyond the scope of this book to review the Commission's powers and procedures. For an outline, see D. Chalmers, C. Hadjemannuil, G. Monti and A. Tomkins *European Union Law: Text and Materials* (Cambridge: Cambridge University Press, 2006) ch. 21.

[97] For a review of the case law see Werden 'Economic Evidence' pp. 746–51.

[98] *Suiker Unie* [1975] ECR 1663 paras. 131–80.

The second scenario is when the Commission has no documents. Can it infer the existence of an agreement only from the way the firms behave? (This returns to example (d) discussed above.) An affirmative answer was provided in an early judgment, *Dyestuffs*.[99] The Commission had found proof of a cartel in the market for dyes and established this with evidence that the producers met and discussed prices. It also inferred the presence of an agreement from the fact that the producers increased prices simultaneously by similar percentages and used similar words in communicating the price instructions to their subsidiaries. On appeal the Court focused only on the behaviour of the firms and suggested that one can infer the presence of an agreement when the behaviour of the firms results in a state of affairs that is different from that which would obtain without collusion. However, the Court's ruling is an unreliable precedent because there was evidence of express collusion, and it should also be read subject to the provisos found in subsequent cases whereby if the Commission tries to find collusion by relying exclusively on market conduct, the parties are entitled to provide alternative explanations for the parallel behaviour.[100] This way they can show that there are good economic reasons, unrelated to collusion, that account for cartel-like conduct. The key ruling is *Wood Pulp* where the Commission tried to infer a price-fixing conspiracy based on similar prices, simultaneous price announcements and a system of regular price announcements. The Court explained that the Commission may infer express collusion if this is the only plausible explanation for the conduct.[101] The Court appointed two economics experts to review the market and examine whether the parties' parallel conduct could be explained only by express collusion, and the economists reported that there were other explanations for parallel conduct. In particular, the price announcements were seen as a rational response to the needs of consumers and the market had 'oligopolistic tendencies'.[102] This finding is a reminder that the Commission can use Article 81 to address express collusion only. Tacit collusion in oligopoly markets is immune from a frontal attack under Article 81. Returning to Odette and Nicole's example (d): signalling of prices is not enough to show an agreement or a concerted practice because the price announcements inform road users of the price of petrol.

3.3 Incentives to confess

While wide definitions of agreement and concerted practices and the power to infer agreement from economic evidence could facilitate the Commission's burden of proving express collusion, the most successful plank of the Commission's anti-cartel policy has been the use of 'leniency programmes'

---

[99] Cases 48–57/69 *ICI v. Commission* (*Dyestuffs*) [1972] ECR 619.
[100] See also Case 172/80 *Züchner v. Bayerische Vereinsbank* [1981] ECR 2021.
[101] *Woodpulp* [1993] ECR I-1307 para. 71.   [102] Ibid. para. 126.

that offer firms who confess to having participated in an anticompetitive agreement and provide the Commission with sufficient evidence to challenge the other parties to the cartel an immunity from fines, or at least a substantial reduction on the fine that would otherwise be set.[103] Immunity from fines is available if a firm is the first to provide evidence that enables the Commission to adopt a decision to carry out an investigation or enables the Commission to find an infringement.[104] Fines can be reduced for firms that provide evidence that strengthens the Commission's ability to prove the infringement, and the reduction is more generous for the first firm that provides this evidence.[105] The benefits of immunity can be substantial given that the Commission has the power to impose a fine of up to 10 per cent of the firm's turnover.[106]

Leniency programmes are based upon the same economic logic as collusion. According to game theory, collusion makes sense because it is the way for profit to be maximised. Leniency policy uses the same logic to suggest to firms that it is in their interests to confess. Consider table 9.2 below. Say firms 1 and 2 are the sole members of a cartel and the Commission has accused them of collusion. They have two choices: to confess that the cartel exists or to stay quiet. Leniency programmes mean that the choice one firm makes has an effect on the other firm. Four possibilities arise.

Table 9.2 The prisoners' dilemma created by leniency programmes

Firm 2 Firm 1	Confess	Do not confess
Confess	Penalty reduced for both firms, but by not as much as if only one confessed	Firm 1's penalty reduced, Firm 2's penalty not reduced
Do not confess	Firm 2's penalty reduced, Firm 1's penalty not reduced	Neither firm's penalty is reduced if the Commission proves the cartel

If both firms confess then both avoid the full weight of the fine. If only one firm confesses then it avoids the full impact of the fine while the other firm gets

[103] EC Commission *Notice on Immunity from Fines and Reduction of Fines in Cartel Cases* [2002] OJ C45/3 (hereinafter Leniency Notice). This replaces the *Notice on the Non-Imposition of Fines in Cartel Cases* [1996] OJ C207/4. The first leniency award was made before the notices in *Cartonboard* [1994] OJ L243/1.

[104] Leniency Notice (2002) paras. 8–11. Immunity is not available for a firm that coerced others to participate in the cartel.

[105] Ibid. paras. 20–3 (30–50 per cent for the first firm, 20–30 per cent for the second firm, up to 20 per cent for each subsequent firm).

[106] In *Fine Art Auction Houses* (30 October 2002) Christie's confession earned it immunity while Sotheby's fine was reduced by 40 per cent for its cooperation, but this still meant it had to pay a fine of €20.4 million (6 per cent of its worldwide turnover); in *Methylglucamine* [2004] OJ L38/18 Merck was granted total immunity while the other party to the cartel was hit with a fine of €2.85 million.

fined. But why confess at all? After all, if both refuse to confess they can earn profit from collusion unless the Commission finds other proof of the cartel. The reason why firms have an incentive to confess is that they see the probability that the Commission will uncover the infringement as relatively high. Therefore, while not confessing is profitable, these profits are discounted by the probability of being caught and paying a fine. If that probability is sufficiently high, a party will find it more rational to confess. And because the first party to confess 'wins' the greatest reduction, with a strong possibility of immunity, then the leniency programme can lead to a 'race' to confess. Several cartels have been uncovered as a result of leniency policies, and in several cases more than one firm has provided information to benefit from leniency.[107] More generally, leniency programmes are probably more effective in uncovering collusion than any increase in the Commission's power to search for incriminating documents and any extension of the meaning of agreement and concerted practice.[108] However, too strong a leniency policy may overdeter and cause firms to spend excessive amounts in monitoring employees to ensure no one in the organisation engages in collusion, which can increase cost and paradoxically lead to higher prices.[109]

4 Tacit collusion

There is a gap in competition law: *ex ante* merger control prevents tacit and express collusion, but *ex post* competition law controls only express collusion. When the Commission uses economic evidence to infer the existence of an agreement, parties can rely on evidence that the market structure was conducive to tacit collusion to escape a finding of collusion. As the Court has repeated frequently, Article 81 'does not deprive economic operators of the right to adapt themselves intelligently to the existing and anticipated conduct of their competitors'.[110] The upshot is that oligopoly acts as a 'defence' against an attempt by the Commission to characterise this behaviour as an infringement of Article 81.

Some find this position unnecessarily legalistic. They argue that behind every successful episode of collective anticompetitive pricing must lie an agreement of some form, and that therefore seeing anticompetitive parallel

---

[107] See, for example, *Fine Art Auction Houses* (30 October 2002); *Vitamins* [2003] OJ L6/1; *Electrical and Mechanical Carbon and Graphite Products* [2004] OJ L125/45; *Graphite Electrodes* [2002] OJ L100/1.

[108] As a result of Regulation 1/2003, it seems that a leniency applicant should make a leniency application to all NCAs that allow it, as he does not yet know which one may act against the cartel. Cooperation Notice [2004] OJ C101/43 para. 37.

[109] B. H. Kobayashi 'Antitrust, Agency, and Amnesty: An Economic Analysis of the Criminal Enforcement of the Antitrust Laws against Corporations' (2000–1) 69 *George Washington Law Review* 715, 735–6.

[110] *Hüls* [1999] ECR I-4287 para. 160; *Suiker Unie* [1975] ECR 1663 para. 174; *Züchner* [1981] ECR 2021 para. 14.

pricing is evidence that there must have been efforts to coordinate behaviour, and a competition authority should be willing to penalise collusion when it sees its effects.[111] However, this view has not been embraced in the EC, nor has it found any favour in the United States. The reason is that it is based on a different economic premise from that which we described at the start of the chapter. Findings of tacit collusion are based on the belief that a market's structure determines economic performance (a position we associate with the Harvard School's SCP paradigm). On the contrary, some argue that an oligopoly market is not sufficient for there to be tacit collusion: the parties must do something to achieve collusive results, so that penalising parallel behaviour without more is justified because we can infer that the parties must have taken steps to coordinate behaviour. This is a position we associate with the Chicago School. While the Chicago School position received some support from the US Supreme Court when it opined that more than oligopoly market structure was needed to achieve anticompetitive effects,[112] US courts still rely only upon hard evidence of collusion in order to prove a conspiracy in restraint of trade and still consider that there are forms of tacit collusion that fall outside the scope of antitrust law. Nevertheless, the Chicago arguments have raised awareness of the fact that firms in an oligopoly can take steps to facilitate the process of tacit collusion. As we saw in section 2, tacit collusion requires very specific kinds of market attributes: if some are missing the firms might enter into agreements or concerted practices to create an oligopoly market where tacit collusion can result. These agreements can then be caught as 'facilitating devices'. That is, the agreement is not designed to fix prices directly but to create the economic conditions where tacit collusion can occur.[113] It seems that Articles 81 and 82 can both apply to prohibit the use of certain facilitating devices. We consider facilitating devices in sections 4.2 and 4.3. Beforehand we ask whether tacit collusion can be characterised as an abuse of collective dominance.

4.1 Tacit collusion as abuse of collective dominance

Article 82 applies to the abuse of dominance by one or more firms, but the Commission has made little use of the notion of collective dominance to date.[114] As we saw in section 2, one manifestation of collective dominance is the presence of a tight oligopoly. The definition of collective dominance deployed in the context of the ECMR can be transposed to Article 82.[115] If

---

[111] R. A. Posner *Antitrust Law* 2nd edn (Chicago: University of Chicago Press, 2001) ch. 6.

[112] *Brooke Group* 509 US 209 (1993): the Court was discussing a scheme for post-predation recoupment, but its general scepticism about tacit collusion caused by market structure is clear.

[113] The clearest analysis is S. C. Salop 'Practices that (Credibly) Facilitate Oligopoly Co-ordination' in J. E. Stiglitz and G. F. Mathewson (eds.) *New Developments in the Analysis of Market Structure* (London: Macmillan, 1986).

[114] For an overview, see Stroux *US and EC Oligopoly Control* ch. 5.

[115] See Case T-193/02 *Piau v. Commission* (26 January 2005); DG Competition Discussion Paper on the Application of Article 82 of the Treaty to Exclusionary Abuses (December 2005) pt 4.3;

so, it would seem to follow that the anticompetitive effects resulting from an oligopoly could be labelled as exploitative abuses of collective dominance.[116] This would close the oligopoly gap, but while this approach is attractive because of its apparent simplicity, it should be rejected because it conceals several difficulties. The first is how to characterise oligopoly behaviour as abusive. As we saw in chapter 7, the Court has struggled to define excessive prices and the regulation of such behaviour is relegated to newly liberalised markets.

The second difficulty relates to the remedy. If we believe that tacit collusion is the result of the market's structure, neither a fine nor a behavioural remedy is appropriate. It follows that a structural remedy is appropriate, such as in *Nestlé/Perrier* where the divestiture of assets eliminated the risk posed by collective dominance. Today the Commission has the power to impose a structural remedy, but only in very limited circumstances. Article 7 of Regulation 1/2003 provides that the Commission may impose:

> any behavioural or structural remedies which are proportionate to the infringement committed and necessary to bring the infringement effectively to an end. Structural remedies can only be imposed either where there is no equally effective behavioural remedy or where any equally effective behavioural remedy would be more burdensome for the undertaking concerned than the structural remedy.[117]

Three conditions must be satisfied to impose a structural remedy: it must be proportionate, necessary and effective.[118] The recitals provide some guidance on when a structural remedy will be proportionate: 'changes to the structure of an undertaking as it existed before the infringement was committed would only be proportionate where there is a substantial risk of a lasting or repeated infringement that derives from the very structure of the undertaking'.[119] This could suggest that the abuse must have caused a change to the market structure, and so the remedy can only apply to restore the market to its pre-abuse position. However, in the scenario of oligopoly pricing, there is no change in the structure. The abuse is exploitative in nature: the firms take advantage of an existing structure.

A structural remedy is 'necessary' when there is no other effective behavioural remedy. However, it might be argued that since the effect of tacit collusion is high prices, a behavioural remedy is available, even if it is one

---

G. Monti 'The Scope of Collective Dominance under Article 82 EC' (2001) 38 *Common Market Law Review* 131, 132–8.

[116] In this vein, see S. Stroux 'Is EC Oligopoly Control Outgrowing its Infancy?' (2000) 23 *World Competition* 3, 43.

[117] Regulation 1/2003 on the Implementation of the Rules on Competition laid down in Articles 81 and 82 of the Treaty [2003] OJ L1/1.

[118] A. Tajana 'If I had a Hammer . . . Structural Remedies and Abuse of Dominant Position' (2006) 1 *Competition and Regulation in Network Industries* 3.

[119] Recital 12, Regulation 1/2003.

the Commission seldom uses.[120] It is not clear what an effective remedy is. The Regulation implies that the structural remedy must be more effective, or as effective but cheaper to implement, than a behavioural remedy. On the one hand, it might be argued that a remedy is effective if it stops the infringement. Satisfying this requirement may be problematic and the Commission must be sure that the divestiture eliminates the risk of tacit collusion. For example, if a duopoly is broken up and both firms are forced to divest some assets to create a third competitor, one must be sure that the three-firm oligopoly is not susceptible to tacit collusion. On the other hand, effectiveness could be read in a more forward-looking manner to mean that the remedy not only must solve the competition problem, but also must not cause any harm to the market. Put another way, effectiveness is judged with a cost–benefit analysis: are the benefits of the remedy outweighed by any costs that the remedy causes? This would be more difficult to show. In the box below we analyse proposals for deconcentration legislation in the United States, which suggest that the Commission may struggle to prove that a structural remedy would lead to more efficient market performance.

Anti-concentration legislation

In the early 1970s, when the SCP paradigm dominated antitrust thinking, the Federal Trade Commission began to take action against a number of concentrated industries, invoking a theory of 'shared monopoly' which has affinities with the EC's collective dominance label.[121] The FTC targeted the breakfast cereal, petroleum and car industries.[122] The remedy sought in many cases was a 'deconcentration' of the industry to bring its structure closer to a competitive market. These actions had the backing of a number of influential legal and economic experts.[123] In 1959, Carl Kaysen and Donald Turner published one of the early and most influential works on competition policy where they lamented that: '[t]he principal defect of present antitrust law is its inability to cope with market power created by jointly acting oligopolists'.[124] In their view the answer lay in new legislation to dismantle economic sectors whose structure led to poor economic performance. This was followed up by the influential Neal Report commissioned by the government which made similar recommendations,[125] and by several legislative proposals to target highly concentrated industries.[126]

---

[120] See ch. 7 pp. 218–20.   [121] See generally Stroux *US and EC Oligopoly Control* pp. 57–70.

[122] See T. J. Muris 'Improving the Economic Foundations of Competition Policy' (2003) 12 *George Mason Law Review* 1, 3–4.

[123] See generally W. E. Kovacic 'Failed Expectations: The Troubled Past and Uncertain Future of the Sherman Act as a Tool for Deconcentration' (1989) 74 *Iowa Law Review* 1105.

[124] C. Kaysen and D. Turner *Antitrust Policy: An Economic and Legal Analysis* (Cambridge, MA: Harvard University Press, 1959) p. 110.

[125] White House Task Force on Antitrust Policy, reprinted in (1968–9) 2 *Antitrust Law and Economics Review* 11.

[126] Note, 'The Industrial Reorganization Act: An Antitrust Proposal to Restructure the American Economy' (1973) 73 *Columbia Law Review* 635.

However, the FTC's actions and the legislative initiatives were abandoned as economics pointed to certain fallacies at the root of these enforcement efforts. Most significantly, it was shown that while many industry sectors were highly concentrated, this was because of the efficiencies that could be reaped as a result of large-scale production.[127] Thus, any reduction in the size of industry would raise production costs and increase prices, the opposite result to what those clamouring for deconcentration were seeking. In addition to undermining productive efficiency, deconcentration could act as a disincentive to grow because it would penalise firms that are successful. The purported benefit of breaking industry up (removing tacit collusion) was outweighed by fears that the consequences would be more costly (losses in allocative, productive and dynamic efficiency).

This short review of the rise and fall of the shared monopoly theory in the United States is a cautionary tale for any endeavour to impose structural remedies in oligopoly firms. The authority in charge of deconcentration simply does not know in advance whether the remedy makes the market work better or whether it destroys the efficiencies that exist.

In addition to practical and economic difficulties in developing a sound theory of abuse of collective dominance, there is also a procedural risk: that the Commission uses Article 82 to catch express collusion. As we saw in section 3, the Commission must obtain convincing documentary evidence to prove an agreement or concerted practice. It could avoid this difficult exercise by identifying an oligopoly market and then finding parallel conduct to be an abuse of collective dominance. There are two risks here. The first is that the Commission uses collective dominance to overcome the higher burden of proof in Article 81.[128] The second is that, having done so, the Commission can impose a structural remedy on a market where coordination had been achieved through express collusion that went undetected, imposing unnecessarily onerous remedies.

It follows that while applying Article 82 to tacit collusion is attractive because it would eliminate the gap in EC competition law, it is a move that should be resisted because the risks of damaging a competitive market structure are significantly greater than the possible benefits of creating a more competitive market.

---

[127] For example, in the car sector this was shown in J. S. McGee 'Economies of Size in Auto Body Manufacture' (1973) 16 *Journal of Law and Economics* 239. See also more generally: Y. Brozen *Concentration, Mergers, and Public Policy* (London: Macmillan, 1982); H. Demsetz 'Two Systems of Belief about Monopoly' in H. J. Goldschmid, H. M. Mann and J. F. Weston (eds.) *Industrial Concentration: The New Learning* (Boston, MA: Little, Brown, 1974) p. 164; J. S. McGee *In Defense of Industrial Concentration* (New York: Praeger, 1971).

[128] Opinion of AG Fennelly, Case C-395-6/96P *Compagnie Maritime Belge Transports SA and Others v. Commission* [2000] ECR I-1365 para. 29.

4.2 Facilitating devices under Article 81

The least controversial route to prevent tacit collusion by using Article 81 is to regulate information exchanges. In EC competition law, traders in highly concentrated markets are forbidden to exchange information (e.g. business secrets, individual output, planned increases in capacity) likely to facilitate tacit collusion. As we saw in section 3 above, disclosure of such information at meetings with competitors can constitute a concerted practice. A systematic procedure to exchange information constitutes an agreement. In the leading case, *UK Agricultural Tractor Registration Exchange*, the Commission was concerned that detailed information about past sales could be an effective means of foreseeing future behaviour, especially in a highly concentrated market (four firms with 80 per cent of the market) with high entry barriers and weak buyers.[129] The Commission said:

> The Exchange restricts competition because it creates a degree of market transparency between the suppliers in a highly concentrated market which is likely to destroy what hidden competition there remains between the suppliers in that market on account of the risk and ease of exposure of independent competitive action. In this highly concentrated market, 'hidden competition' is essentially that element of uncertainty and secrecy between the main suppliers regarding market conditions without which none of them has the necessary scope of action to compete efficiently. Uncertainty and secrecy between suppliers is a vital element of competition in this kind of market. Indeed active competition in these market conditions becomes possible only if each competitor can keep its actions secret or even succeeds in misleading its rivals.[130]

The Commission's analysis of information exchanges in this case was premised upon a view that the object of exchanging information was not anticompetitive, but its effects might be. This explains why the Commission went on to explain that the information was exchanged in a highly concentrated market so that tacit collusion was a likely result of the agreement to exchange information. In contrast, as we saw in section 3, when the agreement has as its object the restriction of competition, the Commission is not required to show that collusion has anticompetitive effects.[131]

Another facilitating device can stem from agreements between the members of the oligopoly and their distributors. For example, say that all three manufacturers in an oligopoly, without discussion among themselves, appoint distributors and demand that they sell at prices fixed by the manufacturer (so-called resale price maintenance). It has been argued that this obligation

---

[129] *UK Agricultural Tractor Registration Exchange* [1992] OJ L68/19, upheld by the CFI in Case T-35/92 *John Deere v. Commission* [1994] ECR II-957 and the ECJ in Case C-7/95P *John Deere v. Commission* [1998] ECR I-1311. For a detailed review, see A. Capobianco 'Information Exchange under EC Competition Law' (2004) 41 *Common Market Law Review* 1247.

[130] *UK Agricultural Tractor Registration Exchange* [1992] OJ L68/19 para. 37.

[131] Case T-6/89 *Anic v. Commission* [1991] ECR II-1623 paras. 200–1.

makes it easier to monitor tacit collusion because the oligopoly manufacturers are able to see if any of them deviate from the anticompetitive price. Without resale price maintenance, a low price charged by a distributor may be the result of that distributor wishing to expand its market share, and not necessarily the result of his obtaining the goods more cheaply from a cheating manufacturer.[132] Other aspects of a distribution agreement between oligopoly manufacturers and distributors can also facilitate collusion: for example, if all oligopoly manufacturers insert an 'English clause' which requires the distributor to report any better offers and allow its supplier to match that offer. This can also be a means whereby the tacitly agreed anticompetitive price can be maintained: the clause creates transparency so that cheating can be detected and punished.[133] It can also be argued that agreements whereby distributors are forced to buy all their requirements from one supplier can facilitate tacit collusion upstream, because if all oligopoly suppliers have similar clauses, then the distribution market is foreclosed for new entrants, and the high entry barriers facilitate tacit collusion. As we shall see in chapter 10, even though distribution agreements are largely lawful, the Commission reserves the right to declare them unlawful when anticompetitive effects materialise, and this could occur when the Commission sees that the distribution contracts are an effective means to prevent tacit collusion.[134]

In these instances Article 81 is not applied to address tacit collusion directly, but it might be an effective preventative tool. One advantage of proceeding under Article 81 is that the firms utilising the contractual clauses under scrutiny may justify these clauses by reference to Article 81(3). An exclusive purchasing obligation can be justified by efficiencies. Therefore the Commission is able to consider whether the risks that the restraint facilitates tacit collusion are outweighed by efficiencies in the distribution agreements. A second benefit is that a much less aggressive remedy is needed than under a theory of abuse of collective dominance: the Commission can request that the offending contract clause be removed. However, there is one weakness in this analysis: while resale price maintenance clauses and exclusive purchasing obligations can arguably infringe Article 81, it is less clear how an English clause restricts competition. That is, in traditional Article 81 cases, the restriction of competition is caused as between the parties to the agreement. The English clause may facilitate tacit collusion among manufacturers but it is not clear how it restricts competition between manufacturer and distributor. For contract clauses that can operate as facilitating devices while not infringing Article 81, a better avenue is to consider them under Article 82.

---

[132] EC Commission, *Green Paper on Vertical Restraints* COM(96)721 para. 61; M. Motta *Competition Policy* (Cambridge: Cambridge University Press, 2004) p. 158.

[133] EC Commission *Guidelines on Vertical Restraints* [2000] OJ C291/1 para. 152.

[134] The benefit of the Block Exemption may be withdrawn when anticompetitive effects are felt. See pp. 361–3.

4.3 Facilitating devices under Article 82

The case law suggests that a position of collective dominance need not be abused collectively – even abuse by one firm designed to safeguard a collectively dominant position can be regulated under Article 82.[135] This possibility is in line with the classical case law on abuse by which a causal link between dominance and abuse is unnecessary, so that the anticompetitive effects need not result from dominance.[136] Several possibilities for tackling oligopoly markets are opened up by this.

First, it might be possible to challenge price leadership. As we suggested above, public price announcements are not sufficient to constitute agreement and private, unilateral price announcements might not qualify as concerted practices. However, acting under Article 82 one can accuse the price leader of an abuse: his tactics facilitate tacit collusion to his benefit. The other firms escape punishment because they are merely reacting intelligently to what signals they pick up. The abuse is also easy to remedy by an order banning forms of price announcements that facilitate tacit collusion.

Second, contract clauses that serve as facilitating devices can be characterised as abuse of collective dominance when they do not infringe Article 81: for example, a most-favoured-nation (MFN) clause. This clause is a promise to buyers that if the seller offers any discounts to other buyers, the same discount will be offered retroactively to the buyers that had not received the discount. If all firms in an oligopoly market use this clause then prices can be stabilised at anticompetitive levels, because discounts are discouraged.[137] Moreover, even if only one firm uses the MFN clause, collusion is facilitated. The MFN clause is a signal to other competitors that they can raise their prices to similar levels, and that the price leader will retaliate if they do not follow (by fighting a price war) but will not lower his prices if they keep theirs high.[138] So price leadership plus an MFN clause can be described as a credible cooperative gesture, which it is in the other manufacturers' interests to accept as prices can be raised profitably. Agreements between firms and customers that facilitate tacit collusion and are not caught by Article 81 can be regulated as individual abuses of a collective dominant position. The anticompetitive effects can be of two sorts: first, a reduction of competition among the existing firms, and second, entry deterrence – if the facilitating device shows existing firms are willing to fight a price war, entrants may be discouraged. Both types of harm are within the ambit of Article 82.[139]

---

[135] Case T-228/97 *Irish Sugar plc v. Commission* [1999] ECR II-2969 para. 66. For detail, see Monti 'Scope of Collective Dominance' pp. 141–5.

[136] Case 85/76 *Hoffmann La Roche v. Commission* [1979] ECR 461.   [137] Salop 'Practices' p. 274.

[138] See further T. E. Cooper 'Most-Favoured Customer Pricing and Tacit Collusion' (1986) 17 *Rand Journal of Economics* 377. For an example of the unilateral use of MFN clauses, see Scherer and Ross *Industrial Market Structure* pp. 212–13.

[139] *Hoffmann La Roche* [1979] ECR 461 para. 91.

However, the Commission has yet to apply Articles 81 and 82 to facilitating devices. One reason why price leadership is hard to catch is that the price leader can justify public price announcements by saying that customers must be informed of the prices so that they can plan. Similarly, MFN clauses seem pro-competitive at first because they are a guarantee of lower prices and thus evidence that the market is competitive. In these circumstances, demanding that the firms stop these practices may harm the competitive process. As we saw when discussing structural remedies, it seems that the Commission must weigh up the anticipated benefit of removing some preconditions for tacit collusion against the likely loss in competition and efficiency should these practices be prohibited. This might be too hard an assessment to make when collusion might break down anyway if it is unstable.

4.4 Oligopoly control: lessons from the US and UK

Above we have sketched some ways through which EC competition law can be applied to stop or prevent tacit collusion. However, caution is warranted, and a brief overview of two other jurisdictions suggests that tackling oligopoly behaviour *ex post* may be too difficult to achieve.

In the US the most direct challenge against oligopoly was a lawsuit launched by the Federal Trade Commission after it noted that three producers of tetraethyl lead enjoyed high profits and prices were uniform, despite a fall in demand resulting from government regulations. A price war should have erupted, so the FTC assumed that the parties had engineered a situation to avoid losses. It found that the three quoted uniform delivered prices (that is, prices set regardless of the shipping distance); gave ample notice of price changes; and offered buyers most-favoured-customer clauses, promising that if prices were cut for any customer, they would be reduced for all.[140] The FTC held that the use of facilitating devices was unlawful, applying s. 5 of the Federal Trade Commission Act which prohibits 'unfair methods of competition'.[141] But this ruling was overturned on appeal because these practices were already in place when one of the defendants, Ethyl Corporation, was the sole seller, and were imitated by the others for sound business reasons. Moreover, the Court said that the FTC failed to 'define the conditions under which conduct claimed to facilitate price uniformity would be unfair so that businesses would have an inkling as to what they can lawfully do'.[142] This objection captures the policy dilemma: if anticompetitive effects are facilitated by practices that are normally seen to be acceptable, how can one regulate markets without creating uncertainty among firms as to what they can and cannot do?

UK competition authorities have a unique power. They can carry out an investigation into given markets where there are perceived market failures and

---

[140] *E. I. Du Pont de Nemours Co. et al. v. Federal Trade Commission* 729 F 2d 128, 130 (1984).
[141] 15 USC 45.   [142] 729 F 2d 128, 139.

impose a range of orders on the firms, even when none have been found to have acted in breach of competition law.[143] Market investigations are carried out by the Competition Commission (CC), a competition authority whose powers are mostly engaged when the principal competition authority, the Office of Fair Trading (OFT), calls upon the CC to act by way of a 'reference'. In the context of market investigations, the OFT has stated that a reference will only be made if no other powers at its disposal are capable of addressing the market failure and if it considers that the CC has the powers to remedy the market failure.[144] In turn the CC has published notes that indicate its belief that market investigations are a suitable means of regulating oligopoly markets. It identifies the same structural features noted in section 2 above as being conducive to behaviour likely to harm consumer welfare.[145]

The CC's market investigations are different from the sector inquiries that the EC Commission is empowered to carry out.[146] The major difference is that EC sector inquiries are designed to identify whether Articles 81 and 82 are infringed,[147] whereas CC market studies empower the CC to devise remedies to address the market failures that it has identified in its market investigation merely upon proof that the market conditions cause a substantial lessening of competition, and the remedies that the CC prescribes are designed to affect the entire market.

The standard by which the CC analyses markets is based upon discovering whether any feature, or combination of features, in a market prevents, restricts or distorts competition.[148] If there is harm to competition, the CC must decide whether to take action to protect consumers. As with EC competition law, the CC's concept of harm to consumers is wide, and it includes: higher prices, lower quality, less choice and less innovation.[149] The Enterprise Act 2002 provides an impressive array of remedies that may be imposed, and the CC is bound to select the remedies that achieve as comprehensive a solution as is possible to remedy the anticompetitive effects.[150] It is said that this kind of

---

[143] Originally these were carried out under the Monopolies and Restrictive Practices (Inquiry and Control) Act 1948, replaced by the Fair Trading Act 1973. The current law is found in Part 4 of the Enterprise Act 2002. For more detailed discussion of the procedures, see R. Whish *Competition Law* 5th edn (London: Lexis Nexis, 2003) ch. 11. On the background to the new law, see *White Paper on Productivity and Enterprise – A World Class Competition Regime* Cm 5233 (2001).

[144] Office of Fair Trading *Market Investigation References* (March 2006) para. 2.1 (available at www.oft.gov.uk).

[145] Competition Commission *Market Investigation References: Competition Commission Guidelines* (June 2003) paras. 3.58–3.64.

[146] Article 17 Regulation 1/2003.

[147] E.g. Energy Sector Inquiry – Draft Preliminary Report (16 February 2006) and N. Kroes 'Towards an Efficient and Integrated European Energy Market – First Findings and Next Steps' (16 February 2006) (available at http://europa.eu.int/comm/competition/antitrust/others/sector_inquiries/energy/). Actions against firms are said to be imminent.

[148] S. 134 Enterprise Act 2002.   [149] S. 134(4)(b) Enterprise Act 2002.

[150] S. 134(6) Enterprise Act 2002.

action is a helpful complement to other competition law norms because it focuses on industry-wide features rather than on certain types of behaviour, and that its remedies are forward looking, so consumers gain a direct benefit.[151]

Several of the remedies available to the CC seem ideal to address tacit collusion. For example, structural measures can be imposed so as to divide a business, and orders can be imposed to supply goods or services in a particular manner, or to regulate prices, or to prohibit firms from withholding goods or services.[152] In spite of the considerable potential that market investigations have for regulating tacit collusion, they appear to have been used more frequently as a means to protect consumers in markets where a lack of information allows firms to exploit weak parties or where systemic market failures produce markets that work less than perfectly.[153] Even when powers exist, it is difficult to address tacit collusion.

5 Conclusion: unenforceable competition

This chapter shows the resilience of the SCP model. While some economists would suggest that tacit collusion is either non-existent or so exceptional as not to warrant consideration, so that competition law should only be concerned about express collusion and look for smoking gun type evidence (e.g. communications among conspirators),[154] competition authorities have only taken into account the Chicago School's major criticisms of the SCP model so as to refine the market analysis. In particular, the requirement for a retaliation mechanism to guarantee the stability of tacit collusion is a direct response to the critique that without retaliation there can be no collusion. In the EC context, the weight accorded to theories of collective dominance is also in line with the political concern over concentration of economic power.

The chapter also reveals some important limitations of the interaction between law and economics. The most significant is that even if economics teaches us to predict harm (tacit collusion) there may be no remedy available, because we cannot design a remedy where the authority can be confident that the gain (eliminating tacit collusion) is greater than the loss (harm to allocative, productive and dynamic efficiency as a result of the market's structure and the firm's actions). This explains why *ex ante* we can design merger law to prevent the creation of market structures prone to tacit collusion, but *ex post* competition authorities are more sceptical about the benefits of law

---

[151] P. A. Geroski 'The UK Market Inquiry Regime' (7 October 2004) (available at www.competition-commission.org.uk).

[152] For a full list, see Schedule 8 Enterprise Act 2002.

[153] E.g. Competition Commission *Store Cards Market Investigation* (6 March 2006); *Extended Warranties on Domestic Electrical Goods* Cm 6089 (2003) (see ch. 11, pp. 422–3).

[154] See e.g. K. G. Elzinga 'New Developments on the Cartel Front' (1984) 29 *Antitrust Bulletin* 3, 25.

enforcement: any rule to block efforts at tacit collusion seems likely to yield significant Type 1 errors and to be expensive to enforce.

Conversely, economic analysis is jettisoned when the cost of carrying out an economic assessment is higher than the risk of Type 1 errors (over-enforcement). Thus, when the Commission proceeds against forms of express collusion a per se rule applies, and firms are found to have infringed Article 81 even if their attempts at coordination were doomed to be unsuccessful. The fact that a market's structure makes express collusion improbable is no bar to a finding that there has been an infringement.

Taken together, these conclusions strengthen the position taken in chapter 1 that an effective competition law must minimise the cost of errors and the costs of enforcement. The upshot of such cost–benefit analysis is that sometimes, when faced with anticompetitive behaviour, it is prudent not to enforce competition law.

10

Distribution agreements

Contents

1. Introduction   *page* 347
2. The economic debate   348
   2.1 Stimulating v. deterring entry   349
   2.2 Benefits v. losses for consumers   351
   2.3 Intentional exclusion   355
   2.4 Policy implications   355
3. Community policy towards vertical restraints   357
   3.1 The original, non-economic approach   357
   3.2 The primacy of the Block Exemption   358
   3.3 The application of the Block Exemption   359
   3.4 Withdrawal   361
4. Market integration in the regulation of distribution agreements   363
5. Individual appraisal under Article 81   366
   5.1 The analytical framework   366
   5.2 Selective distribution   369
   5.3 Vertical restraints by dominant firms   371
6. Distributors' power   372
   6.1 France: abuse of economic dependence   377
   6.2 United Kingdom: market investigations   380
7. The politics of distribution: the car sector   384
   7.1 Opening the car distribution market   385
   7.2 Opening the repair and service market   386
   7.3 From protection to a regulated competitive market?   387
8. Conclusion   390

1 Introduction

Compared to collusion or abuse of dominance, a distribution agreement, where neither manufacturer nor distributor holds a dominant position, seems to be conduct that should not worry competition authorities. While a cartel is an alliance where parties' shared aim is damage to the competitive process by reducing output and increasing price, a distribution agreement (in the jargon, a 'vertical restraint')[1] is an alliance where the parties' shared aim is to increase output and reduce price to the benefit of consumers.[2] This abstract point can be illustrated by the ECJ's observations in *Delimitis v. Henninger*.[3] The dispute concerned a contract between a brewery and a publican: in exchange for the brewer offering the publican a lease of a pub on favourable terms as well as equipment and furniture necessary to operate the pub, the publican undertook to buy a certain quantity of beer exclusively from the brewery. The Court recognised that this agreement did not have as its object the restriction of competition because of the benefits to brewer, publican and consumer: the contract guaranteed that the brewer had certain outlets that would sell its beer, allowing it to plan sales and to organise production and distribution effectively; the publican gained access to the beer distribution market under favourable conditions and with the guarantee of beer supplies, and their 'shared interest in promoting sales of the contract goods likewise secures for the reseller the benefit of the supplier's assistance in guaranteeing product quality and customer service'.[4] The consumer gains from joined efforts of supplier and distributor.

However, even vertical agreements can have anticompetitive effects. The Court went on to say that these would occur if all brewers were to adopt a similar distribution system, locking all pubs into exclusive purchasing agreements, which would make it impossible for new brewers to enter the market, for there would be no outlets for them to sell beer. Vertical restraints might foreclose market access just as effectively as a dominant firm's strategies to raise rivals' costs. Granted, the degree of economic harm will be less: in a market that is foreclosed but where several breweries are able to find outlets there is competition among the existing brands which drives costs and prices down, to the benefit of consumers. While greater access to more breweries would allow for greater variety of goods, there are diminishing returns to variety. Even so, antitrust intervention is warranted, especially if there is a

---

[1] Vertical restraints are 'agreements or concerted practices entered into between two or more undertakings each of which operates, for the purpose of the agreement, at a different level of the production or distribution chain, and relating to the conditions under which the parties may purchase, sell or resell certain goods or services': Article 2(1) Regulation 2790/99 on the Application of Article 81(3) of the Treaty to Categories of Vertical Agreements and Concerted Practices [1999] OJ L336/21.

[2] D. Neven, P. Papandropolous and P. Seabright *Trawling for Minnows: European Competition Policy and Agreements Between Firms* (London: CEPR, 1998) pp. 20–1.

[3] Case C-234/91 *Stergios Delimitis v. Henninger Bräu AG* [1991] ECR I-935.   [4] Ibid. para. 12.

risk that significant numbers of brewers are foreclosed and the remaining sellers are able to engage in tacit collusion. Likewise, if a competition authority seeks to guarantee economic freedom of market participants in addition to consumer welfare, foreclosure is an evil to be remedied no matter how irrelevant the extra supply is to consumer satisfaction.

The facts of *Delimitis* also suggest (although this issue was not considered in the judgment) that vertical restraints by large breweries that own several pubs may endanger the continued existence of small, local breweries. From a policy perspective then, distribution agreements may warrant regulation to safeguard certain Community interests, for instance the protection of small and medium-sized firms or the protection of regional economies. Moreover, given the Commission's interest in protecting consumers, vertical restraints that reduce the diversity of goods available on the market may raise competition law concerns.

There are various types of distribution agreement. The manufacturer may deploy an exclusive dealing contract which forbids the retailer to sell competing goods, or he may select only distributors that agree to provide certain additional services to consumers (e.g. pre-sale services by trained staff). Alternatively a manufacturer may restrict the way the distributor does business, for example by requiring the distributor to sell the goods only from one retail outlet, or by fixing resale prices. A distribution contract can restrict both whom the manufacturer deals with and what the distributor can do. For example, a manufacturer may distribute via franchising contracts, by which an aspiring retailer is supplied with know-how on the marketing of the manufacturer's goods and sells only the manufacturer's products using the instructions specified by the manufacturer. This contract guarantees uniformity at all points of sale so that the consumer can expect the same quality at all retail outlets. The reason for imposing these restraints is to give the distributor incentives to market the goods more aggressively. If the distributor sells only the manufacturer's products, he will devote all energies to that task, for example. If prices are fixed, the retailer must ensure the goods are sold by advertising or providing non-price benefits to consumers (e.g. free demonstrations). Moreover, vertical restraints also set out contractual obligations to act in specific ways (e.g. the franchise contract).

2 The economic debate

Presently, there is a broad consensus among economists that vertical restraints are neither always harmful nor always beneficial, and that a determination of whether a vertical restraint reduces economic welfare requires an appraisal of all relevant facts.[5] But beyond this broad consensus lie different shades of

---

[5] In the 1970s scholars of the Chicago School suggested rules of per se legality, but since the 1990s, most economists have taken the view that per se legality is not warranted. For the current

opinion about how to regulate vertical restraints, because the borderline between restraints that enhance and those that restrict competition is uncertain. In what follows we explore the economic arguments from the perspective of two groups that are affected by vertical restraints: third parties wishing to enter the markets of either the manufacturer or the distributor, and consumers.[6] This mirrors the analysis carried out in previous chapters, distinguishing between harm caused by exclusionary practices and harm caused by exploitative practices.

One caveat must be entered at this stage: determining whether or not a distribution system or the retail market is economically efficient is as difficult a task as determining whether any other market is working efficiently.[7] The few empirical economic studies that have been carried out suggest that in general vertical restraints are efficiency enhancing, but do not allow one to identify *a priori* all necessary and sufficient conditions to be able to identify when vertical restraints are beneficial.[8] Accordingly, the economic debates rely on speculation about anticipated effects and the resulting regulatory scheme is an attempt to regulate markets as well as possible given limited knowledge.

2.1 Stimulating v. deterring entry

Distribution agreements are necessary for manufacturers to reach consumers: the distributor has a comparative advantage over the marketing of the goods, and the manufacturer may be unable or unwilling to integrate vertically and acquire a distribution network, in which case distribution contracts are necessary to bring goods to the market. Moreover, vertical restraints can enhance efficiencies in distribution: for instance, a manufacturer may prefer to sell large quantities to a few dealers rather than small quantities to many dealers as a way of reducing transportation costs. For new entrants at the manufacturing stage, the freedom to enter into distribution agreements is the means to market access. On the other hand, vertical restraints can also be used to make entry of new competitors more difficult. This can occur intentionally: a leading manufacturer wishing to preclude entry by a new and more efficient competitor can enter into exclusive agreements with major distributors and prevent effective entry by others.[9] However, this effect might also manifest itself accidentally – say that all existing manufacturers have exclusivity contracts with dealers (e.g. all breweries have exclusive purchasing agreements with all pubs, whereby each pub agrees to source most of its supplies from one brewery). A new brewery

---

economic consensus, see M. Motta *Competition Policy* (Cambridge: Cambridge University Press, 2004) ch. 6.

[6] Neven et al. *Trawling for Minnows* ch. 2.

[7] S. Howe (ed.) *Retailing in the European Union: Structures, Competition and Performance* (London: Routledge, 2003) ch. 8.

[8] For a review, see J. L. Cooper, L. M. Froeb, D. O' Brien and M. G. Vita 'Vertical Antitrust Policy as a Problem of Inference' (2005) 23 *International Journal of Industrial Organisation* 639; L. M. Froeb, J. L. Cooper, M. W. Frankena, P. A. Poulter and S. Silvia 'Economics at the FTC' (2005) 27 *Review of Industrial Organization* 223, 246–9.

[9] See ch. 6 pp. 183–6.

will find it very difficult to enter the market if no pubs are available for it to distribute its beers. In this scenario, the cumulative effect of efficient distribution networks operated by several brewers is that the market is foreclosed to new entrants. This foreclosure effect is accentuated when it is impossible for a new distributor to enter the market to assist the entry of new competitors (e.g. planning or licensing regulations limit the number of pubs that can be opened).

Vertical restraints can also be used to accelerate the commercial success of a new product: a manufacturer of, say, a new videogame wishes to ensure that distributors engage in promotional campaigns and offer pre-sales advice to potential buyers. However, these activities are costly and a distributor will be reluctant to take these steps for fear of the 'free-rider' effect. This manifests itself where distributor 'A', who is considering investing resources in promoting the new product, is reluctant to do so for fears that consumers will buy the product from a competing distributor ('B') who takes advantage of A's marketing efforts and pre-sales advice, and is therefore able to sell at a lower price because it has no advertising costs to recoup. Thus consumers might view A's advertisements, take advantage of its pre-sales services offered in comfortable premises located conveniently in the town centre, and then purchase the product at an out-of-town warehouse or an internet site owned by B who free rides upon A's marketing efforts and can afford to set a lower price as there are no promotional costs to recoup. In this situation, merely selling the videogame to retailers creates no incentives to provide pre-sale services, and the videogame will not be as commercially successful. The manufacturer can avoid the free-rider effect by offering a distributor an exclusive territory in which to sell the products, so that the distributor is guaranteed a steady return on the investment.[10] The distributor knows that if he invests money in publicising the new product, he will reap the benefits because he is the sole seller. The free-rider effect can also result in manufacturers being reluctant to engage in certain pre-sale activities, for example in training the distributors' staff, if the knowledge thus imparted can be used by the staff to promote competitors' goods. Nor will a manufacturer wish to invest in enhancing the reputation of certain distributors if other competing manufacturers will then free ride on the reputation of those outlets (so-called certification free-riding).[11] In this context the manufacturer may wish to restrict sales of competing products by securing obligations from distributors not to market these, through an exclusive purchasing obligation.

But these arguments cannot be taken to mean that the free-rider effects and the need to give distributors incentives to market products aggressively justify

---

[10] The classic analysis of the free-rider effect is L. Tesler 'Why Should Manufacturers Want Fair Trade?' (1960) 3 *Journal of Law and Economics* 86. See also H. P. Marvel 'The Resale Price Maintenance Controversy: Beyond the Conventional Wisdom' (1994) 63 *Antitrust Law Journal* 59.

[11] H. P. Marvel and S. McCafferty 'Resale Price Maintenance and Quality Certification' (1984) 15 *Rand Journal of Economics* 346.

all vertical restraints. The restraints described above can damage both inter-brand competition and intra-brand competition. Inter-brand competition is that between products of different manufacturers (e.g. Nintendo versus Sony videogames). If one manufacturer prohibits distributors from stocking competing videogames, this may reduce market access to competitors. Intra-brand competition is that between distributors who sell the same product. If a manufacturer grants one dealer the exclusive right to sell its videogame in a territory, then that dealer has a 'monopoly' over that market and rather than have an incentive to advertise aggressively, he may be tempted to exploit that monopoly power. Exclusivity can also prevent the entry of more efficient distributors. This suggests that the free-rider justification for vertical restraints can be successfully invoked only when the manufacturer is selling a new product requiring promotional activities or the need for pre-sale services. If the manufacturer is selling a well-known product (e.g. carbonated water) then there is no need to suffocate intra-brand or inter-brand competition: the consumer reaps no benefit.

Entry of new distributors is further facilitated by vertical restraints when these can resolve the 'hold-up problem'. This occurs where a manufacturer or a distributor has to make considerable sunk investments in order for the goods to be sold. This investment will not be made unless there are reassurances that the goods will be distributed. A franchise agreement illustrates hold-up risks on both sides: the franchisor communicates certain know-how to the franchisee and is concerned about this know-how being used to sell competing goods – a non-compete obligation will reassure the franchisor that the know-how will be used to promote only its goods. On the other hand, the franchisee will invest money in setting up a shop that matches the characteristics wanted by the franchisor only with a guarantee that enough sales will be possible to recoup the investment, thus it will insist on being allocated certain customers or an exclusive territory. In this way both sides use the contract to demonstrate commitment to each other, facilitating the development of diverse distribution channels. There is a risk of course that if the franchisee's non-compete obligation extends for longer than the contract, or the franchisee is unable to redeploy his skills to sell competing products, market access for competing manufacturers may be foreclosed.

In sum, for each pro-competitive justification for a vertical restraint (facilitating entry, resolving the free-rider problem, or removing 'hold-up' risks), there can be an adverse effect on distributors and competing manufacturers, suffocating intra- and inter-brand competition.

2.2 Benefits v. losses for consumers

Vertical restraints can reduce the price of goods. It is said that when both manufacturer and supplier have market power there is a risk of double marginalisation: the manufacturer sets a price above marginal cost and the distributor sets its price above marginal cost (which includes the cost of purchasing the goods from the manufacturer) so two parties raise the price.[12] Vertical integration (the manufacturer merging with the distributor) can eliminate double marginalisation (prices are raised only once) but so can vertical restraints limiting the distributor's ability to raise prices (e.g. the manufacturer imposing a price cap on the retailer).[13] However, certain other vertical restraints might induce higher prices: for instance, if a manufacturer uses a system of selective distribution to sell only to retail outlets that meet certain criteria (e.g. a manufacturer of cosmetics selling only through pharmacies which, because of planning laws, are never located in proximity to each other) he can reduce competition among retailers selling the same product (intra-brand competition) and where inter-brand competition is weak then distributors are able to raise prices.[14] In this scenario a manufacturer with market power might even be able to facilitate double marginalisation by committing to sell exclusively to one distributor who will be certain that no other distributors sell the same goods at a lower price.[15] It is also possible that allocating exclusive territories to distributors (a technique which might be pro-competitive when free-rider effects are present) can become disadvantageous for consumers when the market is oligopolistic and distributors have no incentives to pass on price cuts that result from a reduction in the wholesale price of goods if these would be matched by dealers of competing products. This eliminates incentives for manufacturers to reduce prices, to the detriment of consumers.[16] The impact of a vertical restraint on price depends upon the nature of the restraint, the market structure and arguably the kinds of products involved. In relation to the products involved, studies suggest that the removal of vertical restraints in markets like toys and jeans reduced prices and increased output.[17] This is explained by the fact that when consumer demand is not affected by pre-sale promotion or services, then there is no need to create a distribution network to generate incentives for promotion, and that restrictions on intra-brand competition are more likely the result of powerful retailers wishing to increase profits.[18]

Consumers also benefit from information about the goods they wish to purchase. As we noted above, vertical restraints can create incentives for

---

[12] J. Spengler 'Vertical Integration and Antitrust Policy' (1950) 58 *Journal of Political Economy* 347.

[13] Of course if there is no market power at the retail level, then there is no risk of double marginalisation, for retailers' incentives to keep prices low stem from the competition among them.

[14] S. Bishop and M. Walker *The Economics of EC Competition Law* 2nd edn (London: Sweet & Maxwell, 2002) paras. 5.36–5.43.

[15] Ibid. para. 5.46.

[16] P. Rey and J. Stiglitz 'Vertical Restraints and Producers' Competition' (1988) 32 *European Economic Review* 561; D. Besanko and M. K. Perry 'Exclusive Dealing in a Spatial Model of Retail Competition' (1994) 12 *International Journal of Industrial Organisation* 297.

[17] R. L. Steiner 'Sylvania Economics – A Critique' (1991) 60 *Antitrust Law Journal* 41.

[18] W. S. Grimes 'The Seven Myths of Vertical Price Fixing: The Politics and Economics of a Century-long Debate' (1992) 21 *Southwestern University Law Review* 1285.

distributors to provide the information that consumers value, and by guaranteeing sales to a distributor provided his investments are successful create an environment where the distributor has incentives to maximise his sales efforts: for instance, a franchise contract whereby the franchisor, a manufacturer of wedding dresses, confers upon one person the franchise contract for one city, guarantees the distributor the ability to reap the profits of successful investment while providing consumers with an enhanced shopping experience. Likewise, a distribution system whereby the goods are sold only to those who offer pre-sale services can ensure that the consumers receive adequate information.

To this purported benefit, Professor Comanor has raised an intriguing objection: not all consumers require the pre-sale services offered by the shops. The aim of certain distribution techniques is to increase sales by targeting the marginal consumer who is attracted by the added services and who might not have purchased the goods without them, but the consumers for whom the services are irrelevant (say because they are already sufficiently well informed) will be forced to pay a higher price (because the provision of added services necessarily raises the costs of distribution and therefore the price of goods).[19] In reply it can be argued that if there is a healthy degree of interbrand competition, then the consumer who does not need the high level of services will probably be able to find the same product by another manufacturer which is not sold via a distribution network that targets marginal consumers, but this might not obtain when all manufacturers are trying to vie for the custom of the marginal consumer.

An even more radical way of questioning whether consumer information improves through vertical restraints is that excessive product differentiation through advertising may hinder, rather than help, the consumer. This point was noted by the ECJ in its seminal *Consten and Grundig* decision which we examined in chapter 2. In replying to Grundig's argument that the appointment of an exclusive distributor on the French market helped Grundig market its goods, the Court replied: 'the more producers succeed in their efforts to render their own makes of product individually distinct in the eyes of the consumer, the more the effectiveness of competition between producers tends to diminish'.[20] Following this line of reasoning, some have argued that increased product differentiation comes close to deceiving the consumer.[21] Moreover, the use of various means of informing the consumer can paradoxically leave consumers less well informed because their search costs increase – a visit to one outlet will not be enough to compare different products if all sell

---

[19] W. S. Comanor 'Vertical Price Fixing, Vertical Market Restrictions and the New Antitrust Policy' (1985) 98 *Harvard Law Review* 983.

[20] Cases 56/64 and 58/64 *Consten/Grundig v. Commission* [1966] ECR 299, 343.

[21] W. S. Grimes 'Spiff, Polish, and Consumer Demand Quality: Vertical Price Restraints Revisited' (1992) 80 *California Law Review* 817.

through different retail outlets.[22] However, these arguments seem to ignore the way consumer goods markets work in modern society. Ever since the explosion of the so-called consumer society, there have been those who argue that demand for goods is 'created' by manufacturers.[23] Two products can be used to illustrate how this phenomenon has been analysed: Listerine and bottled water. Listerine was a hospital disinfectant used to clean walls in operating theatres until the owner of the business, Gerard Lambert, noted the term 'halitosis' in a medical journal and began to write advertisements for Listerine showing a woman losing the man of her dreams because of her bad breath. The conclusion is that Lambert did not invent Listerine but created halitosis.[24] Critics rely on examples like this to show how demand is fuelled by manufacturers. As we saw in chapter 9 with *Nestlé/Perrier*, consumers believe that bottled water is different from tap water. Each brand advertises its water to appeal to a particular segment of society, so that, as James Twitchell remarks, 'holding Evian in your hand is like waving a wand. You are too special for tap water.'[25] Importantly, he argues that Evian does not create this irrational desire (tests regularly show consumers' inability to distinguish the taste of tap and mineral water), rather it taps into our wishes, codifies and quenches our needs as consumers. Distribution agreements that help differentiate goods are necessary to satisfy consumers' wishes to have distinctive products. The critique in *Consten/Grundig* seems to assume that consumers could, in a perfectly competitive market, merely base their purchases on price and needs, but we know full well that there is no such innocent state of nature: product differentiation satisfies consumers' desires. The social construction of halitosis by advertising is not creating a non-existent desire, but awakening a latent wish to be more attractive.

Finally, it has been argued that vertical restraints are a means to support tacit collusion: for instance, selective distribution or franchising agreements are a means by which intra-brand competition is reduced, and if all manufacturers use this mechanism, this can be a way of softening price competition. Moreover, it has been suggested that vertical restraints are the means to police an express agreement (e.g. in a horizontal price-fixing cartel, using resale price maintenance (RPM) clauses that require the distributor to sell at a fixed or minimum price ensures that manufacturers do not offer secret discounts). However plausible these arguments are, there is little empirical support for RPM being used to strengthen upstream cartels.[26]

---

[22] See generally P. Klemperer 'Markets with Consumer Switching Costs' (1987) 102 *Quarterly Journal of Economics* 375.

[23] T. Veblen *The Theory of the Leisure Class* (1899; reprint, New York: Basic Books, 1962); J. K. Galbraith *The Affluent Society* (New York: Houghton Mifflin, 1958).

[24] J. B. Twitchell *Adcult USA: The Triumph of Advertising in American Culture* (New York: Columbia University Press, 1996) pp. 144–5.

[25] J. B. Twitchell *Living It Up: Our Love Affair with Luxury* (New York: Columbia University Press, 2002) p. 159.

[26] F. M. Scherer and D. Ross *Industrial Market Structure and Economic Performance* 3rd edn (Boston, MA: Houghton Mifflin, 1990) p. 550.

In sum, there are circumstances where consumers may receive more information and lower priced goods when vertical restraints are deployed, but there may also be circumstances where consumers receive unnecessary amounts of information and find that goods have higher prices because of vertical restraints.

2.3 Intentional exclusion

We have so far considered harmful effects that may result when the manufacturer does not intend to harm competitors, distributors or consumers. However, the economic literature suggests that manufacturers may use vertical restraints as strategic devices to harm competitors. An example is when a manufacturer knows that because of economies of scale, competitors must sell a given number of units to make a profit. The manufacturer may enter into several exclusive dealing agreements so as to prevent the competitor from finding enough purchasers to sell his good profitably, thereby excluding him from the market.[27] More generally, it has been argued that exclusive distribution can be used to raise entry barriers, by forcing new entrants to establish their own distribution networks.[28] However, these considerations require that the firm using vertical restraints to exclude a competitor gain some advantage, and if the market is competitive the exclusion of one competitor is not harmful, while if the firm is dominant, exclusion is more problematic.

2.4 Policy implications

The above synopsis indicates that no vertical restraint can be judged *a priori* to be lawful or unlawful by merely reading the distribution contract. This point can be illustrated by the vast amount of economic literature on resale price maintenance (RPM), a practice condemned in competition law both in the EC and in the US.[29] Economists have long argued that RPM is just one mechanism to avoid the free-rider effect and to give retailers an incentive to promote the manufacturer's brand.[30] However, others have challenged this argument by observing that RPM is used in markets where no pre-sale services are offered to consumers, and therefore the efficiency justification is not substantiated in all cases.[31] The first policy implication therefore is that every vertical restraint should be analysed in its specific market context to determine its legality,

[27] E. B. Rasmussen, J. M. Ramseyer and J. S. Wiley Jr 'Naked Exclusion' (1991) 81 *American Economic Review* 1137.
[28] W. S. Comanor and H. E. Frech 'The Competitive Effects of Vertical Agreements' (1985) 75 *American Economic Review* 539.
[29] Article 4 Regulation 2790/99; *Dr Miles Medical Co. v. John D. Park & Sons Co.* 220 US 373 (1911).
[30] Bishop and Walker *Economics* ch. 5 n. 69.
[31] R. L. Steiner 'The Nature of Vertical Restraints' (1985) 30 *Antitrust Bulletin* 143.

considering the contractual restraint, the competitiveness of the market (both the upstream production market and the downstream distribution market) and the kinds of goods distributed. A framework for assessing the effects of a vertical agreement in the round may be based upon the consideration that from the consumer's perspective most restraints reduce intra-brand competition (by limiting the number of distributors that handle the manufacturer's products), hence the losses to consumers result from the disincentives of distributors to compete, but consumers gain because by facilitating entry, vertical restraints stimulate inter-brand competition. In assessing the overall impact on consumers, a competition authority can weigh up the reduction in intra-brand competition with the increase in inter-brand competition. Likewise from the perspective of economic actors that are foreclosed by vertical agreements, one can trade off the degree to which a vertical restraint promotes new entry with its adverse effects on new entrants.

However, the first policy implication is unhelpful because it reduces legal certainty. Competition law must encourage parties to enter into vertical agreements, and offer them as much freedom as possible to design the contract according to their commercial desires. However, given the difficulty of predicting the effects of vertical restraints, this is easier said than done. Thus the second policy implication, to maximise the ability of business to plan, is in tension with an effects-based analysis of vertical restraints.

In the United States, the solution reached by the Supreme Court since the mid-1970s is to suggest that all vertical restraints (except RPM fixing minimum prices) should be considered under a rule of reason analysis under which they should be prohibited only when there is an adverse effect on inter-brand competition.[32] This approach was influenced by the Chicago School's view that all vertical restraints are designed to give distributors incentives to promote goods more efficiently. The upshot of this is that provided the manufacturer has no market power, he will invest in the most commercially effective distribution network to keep up with rivals. As a unanimous Supreme Court put it, 'the primary purpose of the antitrust laws is to protect interbrand competition'.[33] Only when there is a lack of inter-brand competition (or, which amounts to the same thing, the presence of market power) should vertical restraints be considered unlawful. The effect of this approach is that few vertical restraints are challenged.[34]

---

[32] The major decision that overrules the earlier, more restrictive, approach is *Continental TV Inc. v. GTE Sylvania Inc.* 433 US 36 (1977).

[33] *State Oil Co. v. Kahn* 522 US 3 (1997).

[34] Some suggest that no vertical restraint should be challenged: see R. A. Posner 'The Next Step in the Antitrust Treatment of Restricted Distribution: Per Se Legality' (1981) 48 *University of Chicago Law Review* 6.

3 Community policy towards vertical restraints

3.1 The original, non-economic approach

In contrast to the American application of Chicago economics (not wholly uncontroversial given the alternative theories we canvassed above),[35] the Community's early response to vertical restraints failed to take into consideration both of the policy implications identified above. Rather than considering the effects of vertical agreements, the Commission distinguished pro- and anticompetitive agreements by their form, and rather than facilitating flexibility, the Commission's policy led to an approach whereby distributors operated under a regulatory scheme that was described as a 'straitjacket'. A brief review of the original approach is helpful to explain and appreciate the magnitude of the reform carried out in 1999.[36] As we saw in chapter 2, the ECJ had in some cases suggested that an analysis of whether agreements infringed competition had to be carried out by considering the economic context,[37] but this case law had two limitations. First, in the same year that the Court advocated a flexible, economics-oriented approach to vertical restraints, it also held that when a vertical restraint threatened to disintegrate the common market, this would be deemed anticompetitive.[38] So the Court sent mixed messages: on the one hand applying what came close to an economic cost–benefit analysis of vertical restraints, while on the other applying a per se prohibition towards restraints segmenting the market: the core value of market integration took precedence over considerations of economic efficiency. The second limitation of the Court's case law was that it had little impact on the Commission, who refused to follow the Court. Instead the Commission relied upon findings that vertical restraints were restrictions of competition because they restricted the distributors' economic freedom.[39] This meant that an exemption was necessary for the vast majority of vertical restraints. However, under Regulation 17/62 the sole way of obtaining exemption was to notify the agreement to the Commission.[40] The Commission's resources meant that it was unable to cope with the number of notifications, so parties suffered from an administratively inefficient system. The response was that the Community

---

[35] See generally Steiner 'Sylvania Economics'.

[36] The finest summary and critique of the old law is B. Hawk 'System Failure: Vertical Restraints and EC Competition Law' (1995) 32 *Common Market Law Review* 973.

[37] Case 56/65 *Société Technique Minière v. Maschinenbau Ulm GmbH* [1966] ECR 235; Case 23/67 *Brasserie de Haecht v. Wilkin-Janssen* [1967] ECR 407.

[38] *Consten and Grundig* [1966] ECR 299.

[39] One former Advocate General lamented this approach in colourful terms: 'Is it not striking for competition law that the Commission's Decisions and the Court's case-law have systematically treated all restrictions of competitors' freedom as a restriction of competition? That is a very legalistic approach, considering the right to compete as a basic human right.' W. van Gerven 'Panel Discussion' in C. -D. Ehlermann and L. L. Laudati *Proceedings of the European Competition Forum* (Chichester: Wiley, 1997) p. 183.

[40] Article 4 Council Regulation No. 17 of 6 February 1962, First Regulation Implementing Articles 85 and 86 of the Treaty [1962] JO L13/204.

drafted 'Block Exemption' regulations for the more common types of vertical restraints. These provided a list of contractual restrictions which would benefit from exemption (a white list) and a list of restrictions that would not qualify for exemption (a black list). Firms able to draft agreements to fall within the four corners of a Block Exemption benefited from automatic exemption. However, while the Block Exemption resolved the administrative inefficiency for some (it had no impact upon those using vertical restraints that were not covered by a Block Exemption), it created a new problem: the black lists were very extensive and they reduced the ability of parties to draft vertical restraints according to their commercial needs. Professor Hawk condemned the policy as embodying systemic failures.[41] For firms, the choice was between redrafting their contracts to try and fit within the Procrustean bed of a block exemption, or notifying the agreement to the Commission in the hope of obtaining an exemption, which would normally result in the Commission issuing a 'comfort letter' that did not provide sufficient legal security.[42] From the perspective of consumer welfare, the Commission's approach led to Type 1 errors (that is, it prevented efficient behaviour) for two reasons. First, the Block Exemptions were so prescriptive that they probably prohibited some efficient agreements. Second, the uncertainty of the notification system discouraged firms from experimenting with more efficient forms of distribution. It also caused Type 2 errors (that is, it failed to punish inefficient behaviour) because the Block Exemptions were form-based and not premised on economic analysis and could protect inefficient agreements.

In sum, rather than considering the effects of vertical agreements, the Commission distinguished pro- and anticompetitive agreements by their form, and rather than facilitating flexibility, the Commission's policy stifled freedom of contract for no good reason.[43] In 1996 the Commission signalled a change to this policy: as we noted in chapter 4, it was with vertical restraints that the Community kicked off the modernisation of competition law by abandoning the emphasis on economic freedom in favour of an emphasis on economic efficiency. In what follows we trace how successfully the new law implements this policy direction.

3.2 The primacy of the Block Exemption

The linchpin of the new approach is a market power screen. The Commission promises to 'limit the scope of application of Article 81 to undertakings

---

[41] B. E. Hawk 'System Failure: Vertical Restraints and EC Competition Law' (1995) 32 *Common Market Law Review* 973.

[42] Case 99/79 *Lancôme v. Etos* [1980] ECR 2511, where the ECJ maintained that comfort letters did not bind national courts. The effect was that if a contractual dispute arose, the distributor could challenge a non-exempted agreement as infringing Article 81 in the national courts.

[43] EC Commission 'Follow-up to the Green Paper on Vertical Restraints' COM(98) 544 final, 4.

holding a certain degree of market power where inter-brand competition may be insufficient'.[44] This premise has been welcomed by many economists – most of the damage that consumers suffer results when the manufacturers have, solely or collectively, enough market power to foreclose entry, which leads to limited inter-brand competition; conversely when there are many manufacturers, consumer choice is high and price competition is enhanced.[45] Limiting intra-brand competition is less harmful when there is strong inter-brand competition. For example, an exclusive distribution agreement designed to avoid the free-rider problem is unlikely to allow the distributor to raise prices or provide unnecessary pre-sale services because it is competing with distributors of other brands that keep it in check. This approach tallies with the policy in the US we summarised above.

The way this policy has been implemented is curious from a legal perspective. It might have been suggested that vertical agreements where firms lack market power do not restrict competition and that therefore many vertical agreements escape the application of Article 81(1).[46] This option would have conferred the maximum amount of freedom to firms to plan their business strategies without restrictions. Instead, the Community drafted a Block Exemption Regulation which exempts from the application of Article 81 those agreements where the market share of the manufacturer does not exceed 30 per cent and where the contract does not contain certain black-listed clauses.[47] This approach sidesteps the Court's ambiguous case law on the interpretation of Article 81(1), buries the Commission's overly aggressive past policy and offers a method that enhances planning opportunities and targets the use of vertical restraints only when there is market power, and hence less inter-brand competition. Theoretically it seems wrong and cumbersome because the Regulation 'exempts' and *a fortiori* assumes that vertical restraints restrict competition when instead economic theory suggests there is no such harm if the firm lacks market power. However, in practice, it guarantees a safe haven for firms that comply with the Block Exemption's requirements and legal security is more important than doctrinal purity.

3.3 The application of the Block Exemption

The Block Exemption applies to vertical agreements where the market share of the manufacturer does not exceed 30 per cent.[48] Above this market share, the manufacturer is taken to have sufficient market power to damage the interests

---

[44] Ibid. para. 102.

[45] See e.g. Bishop and Walker *Economics* para. 5.50; M. Hughes, C. Foss and K. Ross 'The Economic Assessment of Vertical Restraints Under UK and EC Competition Law' [2001] *European Competition Law Review* 424.

[46] This was an option considered in the *Green Paper on Vertical Restraints in EC Competition Policy* COM(96)721 final.

[47] Articles 3, 4 and 5 Regulation 2790/99.   [48] Article 3 Regulation 2790/99.

of consumers and competitors. In cases of exclusive purchasing agreements, the market share of the distributor is taken into account because the concern is about how much of the distribution market is foreclosed by the agreement. The market share level was a compromise – prior discussions mentioned thresholds of 20 to 40 per cent.[49] It might be argued that the threshold is too low, or that it is improperly cast. Those who argue that the threshold is too low point out that the anticompetitive risks can arise only when there is a dominant firm. A non-dominant firm cannot raise rivals' costs and cannot harm consumers because they still benefit from inter-brand competition. Those who argue that the threshold is improperly cast would agree with the above criticism but recall that anticompetitive effects can manifest themselves when there is the risk of oligopolistic interdependence (as we saw in chapter 9). Accordingly, an assessment of the market's concentration would be more useful than the assessment of one player's market share.[50] Some go further and argue that given the uncertainties over market definition, a market share threshold is no substitute for a detailed analysis of whether the consumers suffer as a result of a particular practice,[51] but this would undermine the procedural efficiency of the current system which creates a safe harbour so that investigative resources are allocated to those cases where anticompetitive effects are most likely to arise. Compared to the earlier system, a market power screen is an economical way to minimise Type 1 and 2 errors because it is designed to exclude from enforcement those firms who have too little power to do harm.

Contracts where the market share does not exceed 30 per cent can be designed as the parties wish, provided the clauses prohibited in Articles 4 and 5 of the Block Exemption are not included. Article 4 provides a 'black list' of clauses whose presence deprives the agreement of the benefit of the Block Exemption. The black list mostly prohibits various types of market segmentation (these prohibitions are analysed below). It also prohibits resale price maintenance (RPM) and clauses that restrict the sale of spare parts to repairers or other service providers. The exclusion of RPM can be disputed on the basis that, according to economists, it is just one method of creating incentives for the distributor to market goods aggressively. However, the view might legitimately be taken that there are other, less intrusive ways of obtaining the distributor's commitment to engage in active marketing of the products (e.g. exclusive distributorships, express contractual commitments); accordingly RPM is black-listed because it is not the least restrictive way to achieve distributional efficiencies. Another black-listed restriction is that the manufacturer cannot be prevented from selling spare parts to independent

[49] *Green Paper on Vertical Restraints.*
[50] *Vertical Restraint Guidelines as Adopted by the National Association of Attorneys General* (1995) § 4.7 (www.naag.org/issues/pdf/at-vrest_guidelines.pdf).
[51] B. Bishop and D. Ridyard 'EC Vertical Restraints Guidelines: Effects-Based or Per Se Policy?' [2002] *European Competition Law Review* 35, 37.

repairers or end users. This reflects the Community's interest in preventing the exercise of power in after markets and in promoting the presence of independent repair outlets.[52]

Article 5 of the Block Exemption provides that three types of non-compete clauses do not benefit from the Block Exemption – although the remainder of the agreement may do so if it can be severed from the non-exempted clauses.[53] The first are non-compete obligations lasting for more than five years which require a distributor to buy more than 80 per cent of his requirements from the manufacturer. This is designed to prevent the market being foreclosed to new sellers. (Two sectors are implicitly excluded: beer and petrol, where it is common for the manufacturer to lease premises to the distributor. Here, non-compete obligations for the duration of the lease are exempted.) The second are post-contract non-compete obligations, which are not exempted unless this is necessary to protect know-how that has been transferred to the distributor. In this case, which is likely to arise in franchise agreements, a one-year non-compete obligation is exempted. Lastly, selective distribution agreements that prevent members from selling the brand of particular competitors do not benefit from the Block Exemption. The Guidelines on Vertical Restraints suggest that this provision is designed to prevent a group boycott by several manufacturers of the goods of a competitor.[54] It is common for a selective distribution contract for the sale of luxury perfumes or cosmetics to require that the retail outlet sell competing products from other luxury brands,[55] but the manufacturer may wish to foreclose access by a *specific* brand that it wishes to oust. However, it is difficult to see how any of these non-compete obligations can foreclose market access given the low threshold of market power necessary for the application of the Block Exemption.[56] It appears then that the concern is more about safeguarding business opportunities for competitors and distributors than about eliminating real entry barriers.

3.4 Withdrawal

To counter the risk that the block exemption is too permissive and results in Type 2 errors, the Commission or a National Competition Authority may withdraw the benefit of the block exemption in an individual contract where the effects of the agreement are incompatible with Article 81(3).[57] The

---

[52] See ch. 5 pp. 148–50.

[53] Whether the agreement is severable is a matter for the applicable national law. See *Société Technique Minière* [1966] ECR 235.

[54] Guidelines on Vertical Restraints para. 61.   [55] E.g. *Parfums Givenchy* [1992] OJ L236/11.

[56] As the US Supreme Court noted, while a group boycott is an antitrust problem (and is properly dealt with as a horizontal agreement), a single non-dominant firm boycotting a rival is unlikely to reduce economic welfare. *NYNEX Corp. v. Discon Inc.* 525 US 128 (1998).

[57] Articles 6 and 7 Regulation 2790/1999.

Commission is also empowered to withdraw, by regulation, the benefit of the Block Exemption from an entire market where a series of unrelated vertical agreements cover more than 50 per cent of the relevant market and all contain specific restraints.[58] The primary preoccupation that underpins the powers of withdrawal is that networks of similarly worded vertical agreements by many different firms can foreclose the markets, both for suppliers and for distributors, because of their cumulative effects.[59]

However, the Community's preoccupation with foreclosure is ambivalent. On the one hand, the concern seems to be based on efficiency criteria, so the Commission indicates that vertical restraints that select certain distributors might exclude efficient distributors or reduce innovation in distribution, to the detriment of consumers.[60] Provided that this is the only basis for withdrawal, the only remaining concern is about choosing which firms' contracts should no longer receive the benefit of the Block Exemption (it seems likely that those contracts that make the most significant contribution to the anticompetitive effects will not benefit from the Block Exemption).[61] On the other hand, in certain instances the interest in withdrawing the exemption is motivated merely by the concern that the vertical restraints foreclose entry, without any reflection as to whether new entry is to the advantage of consumers. This approach can be counterproductive: if current manufacturers all use an efficient mechanism for distributing goods and there is lively inter-brand competition among them, then it may be inefficient to withdraw the benefit of the Block Exemption merely to facilitate the entry of a new competitor – the Commission would force the person whose exemption is withdrawn to compete using a less efficient (and potentially less competitive) distribution contract and skew the competitive process. Even more worrying are remarks suggesting that a withdrawal of the Block Exemption may arise when certain types of distribution outlets are foreclosed. For example, the Commission notes the risk that vertical restraints may prevent access to other distributors capable of selling the products adequately, especially price discounters, 'thereby limiting distribution to the advantage of certain existing channels and to the detriment of final consumers'.[62] The difficulty with this foreclosure argument is that on the one hand the Block Exemption allows for the foreclosure of certain types of outlets: thus if sellers of high definition TVs prefer to sell these through specialised shops rather than supermarkets, they are free to do so. On the other hand, the Commission seems to reserve the right to second guess that business choice when, in its mind, other distributors are capable of selling the goods in question, even when the firms involved do not think so.

[58] Article 8(1) Regulation 2790/1999.

[59] This has been a long-standing concern of the Court, e.g. Case 75/84 *Metro v. Commission* (*Metro 2*) [1986] ECR 3021; *Delimitis* [1991] ECR I-935.

[60] Guidelines on Vertical Restraints para. 199(3).   [61] Ibid. para. 189.   [62] Ibid.

There has only been one withdrawal decision to date: *Langanese-Iglo* where withdrawal occurred for a set of exclusive purchasing obligations because the leading ice cream manufacturer's contracts foreclosed market access in a duopoly market, preventing the entry of a third large manufacturer.[63] However, it is not clear from the decision whether the withdrawal occurred because of a market failure (i.e. the duopoly acting anticompetitively by setting high prices for ice cream) or merely upon proof of foreclosure (i.e. Mars's difficulty in penetrating the market given the network of pre-existing contracts).[64] Moreover, as the Commission Guidelines suggest, there is an even wider discretion to withdraw the Block Exemption when certain distributors are excluded for what in the Commission's judgment are not good reasons. This reveals a tension between adopting, respectively, an economic efficiency, a consumer interest or an economic freedom rationale for applying the power to withdraw the benefits of the Block Exemption. An economic efficiency rationale would admit withdrawal only when there is evidence that the distribution agreement causes a reduction in output and an increase in prices. A consumer welfare rationale gives the Commission the discretion to determine what consumer interests are and to regulate the way goods are distributed accordingly, substituting the Commission's opinion for the business acumen of the manufacturers. An economic freedom rationale would withdraw the benefit of the Block Exemption when market access to others is limited, regardless of economic consequences. The Commission's stance suggests a preference for the latter two approaches; however, its practice (only one withdrawal) suggests a preference for the first, which would be in line with the economic approach of the Block Exemption.

4 Market integration in the regulation of distribution agreements

The Commission claims that even after five decades of the EC's existence the single market is still not a reality. One oft-cited piece of evidence for this proposition is that price differences among Member States remain high. The desire to integrate the market has led to the Community experimenting with various forms of regulation addressed to Member States. In the context of competition law, the aim of market integration has resulted in strict regulation of business practices that contribute to market segmentation. In the context of vertical agreement, this strict approach is in direct tension with the free-rider argument, which suggests that market segmentation can be a useful technique to guarantee that distributors act to maximise sales. One may go so far as to say that the Commission's policy is counterproductive to market

---

[63] *Langanese-Iglo* [1993] OJ L183/19 (confirmed in Case T-7/93 *Langanese Iglo GmbH v. Commission* [1995] ECR II-1533).

[64] Ibid. (at para. 146 it is merely presumed that price competition is weak).

integration, as we suggested in chapter 2 by looking at *Consten and Grundig*: a territorial restraint designed to avoid the free-rider effect was banned with the consequence that the manufacturer integrated vertically, an option which is anticompetitive because it forecloses the market for other manufacturers as one distribution channel is now owned by a competing manufacturer. The Commission's new approach resiles from the per se condemnation of territorial segmentation and offers a more flexible framework which takes into account the free-rider arguments even though the manner by which this is achieved is somewhat untidy.

First, the Guidelines on Vertical Restraints indicate that when the manufacturer wishes to penetrate a new market or introduce a new product, the distributor may be afforded absolute territorial protection for two years without this infringing Article 81(1).[65] This means that the distributor may be prohibited from selling the contract goods outside its territory and other distributors can be prohibited from selling in that territory. From an economic perspective, this is a welcome recognition of the circumstances where the free-rider effect is strongest: a distributor offering a new product or entering a new market faces considerable risks that the venture may fail; the guarantee of a market where it has exclusive selling rights is a reward that encourages the taking of such risks. The reasoning in *Consten and Grundig* is therefore unlikely to be repeated by the Commission.

Second, less absolute forms of territorial protection benefit from an exemption, but only under strictly specified conditions. In an exclusive distribution contract, or a franchise agreement where the manufacturer has granted a distributor an exclusive territory, the manufacturer may prevent other distributors from making *active sales* into the territory reserved to another distributor.[66] In order to qualify for exemption all the manufacturer's distribution contracts must be assessed, so as to discover which territory or territories are allocated to an exclusive distributor and then to check that all other distributors are unable to make active sales into those territories. To benefit from this exemption, other distributors must be able to make *passive* sales into the protected territories. Active sales occur when a distributor approaches customers in the protected territory or establishes outlets in that territory, while passive sales are those made in response to requests from consumers in the protected territory to import the goods from a distributor outside the territory.[67] The distinction between forbidding active sales (allowed) and forbidding passive sales (not allowed) seems to be the creative manner by which the Commission balances the benefits of distribution agreements (eliminating the free-rider effect) and their potential risks (higher prices). This is because a free rider is usually only going to be successful if he can actively solicit custom. Say

---

[65] Guidelines on Vertical Restraints para. 119, point 10.   [66] Article 4(b) line 1 Regulation 2790/99.

[67] See Guidelines on Vertical Restraints paras. 51–2 for a comprehensive explanation of this distinction.

the manufacturer forbids active sales into Greece. It is unlikely for most consumer goods that the Greek shopper would free ride on local stores' pre-sales services and then travel to Italy or Hungary to purchase the good there. The Italian free rider can operate most effectively if he is able to make active sales into Greece. Instead, if the Greek stores take advantage of their market power and raise prices, this will encourage entrepreneurs in Greece to purchase goods more cheaply from abroad (as passive sales cannot be forbidden) and sell them in Greece.

Third, the Commission tolerates agreements that divide the market when they are necessary to safeguard the integrity of the distribution system in question. First, the contract may prevent wholesalers from selling directly to end users.[68] Second, in a selective distribution contract active and passive sales by distributors to unauthorised outlets may be prohibited.[69] This is necessary because the manufacturer selects dealers based on the quality of the shop, and does not wish its brand to be devalued by being sold in shabby stores, or stores where there is inadequate pre-sale service. However, restrictions of cross supplies among distributors and the restriction of active and passive sales by distributors in a selective distribution scheme are black-listed.[70] A selective distribution contract allows the manufacturer to prohibit distributors from operating out of unauthorised establishments. This indirectly restricts most active sales in other territories, for usually selective distribution is used for luxury products where consumers wish to enter the premises where the goods are sold.

In sum, the importance of market integration wanes as economic analysis shapes competition policy. However, it may be argued that the Commission's refusal simply to declare territorial segmentation *per se* lawful is not only dictated by a political desire to pursue market integration for its own sake, but rests upon a sound economic rationale, embracing those who have criticised the Chicago School's overly lenient position. This is particularly so for absolute territorial protection, which is only tolerated when free-rider effects are most likely to be felt: when the manufacturer introduces new goods or enters new markets, necessitating promotional expenses by the distributor. In other cases, when territorial restrictions seem unnecessary the Commission regulates which restrictions may be imposed more strictly. An example of this is the refusal of the Commission to accept the justifications offered by Yamaha when its scheme of territorial protection was challenged. Yamaha distributed musical instruments through a selective distribution network and forbade retailers to buy goods from each other. It argued that it offered each retailer quantity rebates as a means of giving them an incentive to sell more goods in their territories, so forbidding sales to other retailers was necessary to maintain that incentive. If parallel trade was allowed, it meant that the rebates would be offered to the parallel traders who bought more goods (but exported them) and not to the retailer who sold them in the end.

---

[68] Article 4(b) line 2 Regulation 2790/99.   [69] Article 4(b) line 3 Regulation 2790/99.
[70] Article 4(c) Regulation 2790/99.

However, the Commission rightly rejected this argument as the retailer who bought the goods from a fellow retailer engaging in parallel trade clearly figured he was going to get these goods more cheaply than if he bought directly from Yamaha, even taking the possible rebate into account. Moreover, the Commission suggested that Yamaha could achieve its commercial objectives less restrictively by setting a sales target for each dealer.[71] On the other hand, the Commission's findings might be questioned on the basis that Yamaha submitted that few retailers would have an incentive to engage in parallel trade given the cost of transport and the low volume of goods involved, so one may query whether the Commission's action is likely to have had any tangible effect on market integration and reducing the price differences.[72] In other words, Yamaha probably inserted a superfluous clause and paid €2.56 million in fines for attempting to restrict parallel trade. Perhaps the Commission's scarce resources should be invested in cases where there is evidence that vertical restraints are the cause of price differences.

5 Individual appraisal under Article 81

For firms whose market shares are above the safety zone of the Block Exemption, or which contain black-listed clauses, the mechanics of the application of Article 81 are of crucial importance, in particular given that notification to the Commission is now impossible and parties need to be able to predict whether their planned distribution agreement is antitrust compliant.[73] To cater for this, and in line with the economic approach taken in the Block Exemption, the Commission has published *Guidelines on Vertical Restraints* which set out the Commission's analytical framework for assessing the economic effects of distribution agreements. The Guidelines pay little attention to distinguishing finely between agreements which are lawful because they do not infringe Article 81(1) and those which are lawful because they benefit from Article 81(3), as the effect on the parties is the same, albeit the burden of proof is upon complainants to show an infringement of Article 81(1) and upon defendants to show that Article 81(3) applies.[74] In what follows we begin by considering how the Commission determines the agreement's effects and then examine two scenarios where the analytical framework seems problematic: selective distribution and vertical restraints by dominant firms.

5.1 The analytical framework

The Commission fears four types of negative effects from distribution agreements: (1) foreclosure of suppliers or distributors; (2) reduction in inter-brand

---

[71] Case 37.975 *PO/Yamaha*, decision of 16 July 2003, paras. 175–9.   [72] Ibid. paras. 91–5.
[73] Regulation 1/2003 abolishes the notification/exemption route although there is an informal consultation mechanism: see chapter 11.
[74] Article 2 Regulation 1/2003.

competition; (3) reduction in intra-brand competition; (4) the creation of obstacles to market integration.[75] The first three effects are consistent with the economic analysis canvassed above. Economists would be concerned about the fourth effect only if it contributed to the three other negative effects; for the Commission the latter is unlawful per se.[76] Focusing on economic effects, the starting point for determining whether these materialise is an evaluation of the market power of the firm as well as the position of its competitors, the market position of the distributor, and entry barriers.[77] The result of this exercise is that if there is sufficient inter-brand competition then the firm in question lacks market power and no competition problems arise, while if the agreement restricts inter-brand competition this facilitates foreclosure and price increases. The significance of the Guidelines is that the Commission is increasingly willing to find that distribution agreements may not infringe Article 81(1); however, in instances where the market is highly concentrated it also keeps a close eye on whether the effects of the agreement harm consumers or foreclose entry.

The type of consumer harm depends on the type of distribution agreement. In the context of *single branding* (where a buyer purchases exclusively from one manufacturer) consumer harm may result either from the fact that if these agreements are used by all suppliers tacit collusion is facilitated, or from a loss of inter-brand competition. To test the risk of tacit collusion the analysis focuses on the concentration in the market. The loss of inter-brand competition is measured by the level of trade and the degree of product differentiation: if single branding is imposed on retailers in a market selling branded goods with high degrees of product differentiation, consumer harm is likely in a highly concentrated market.[78] Applying this methodology to the market for the sale of beer in public houses, the Commission in *Bass* held that a single-branding agreement reduces inter-brand competition when the person operating the pub is unable to sell competing beer brands, and the high level of concentration resulting from the cumulative use of single branding meant that the restriction harmed consumers.[79] In *Van den Bergh Foods*, the Commission found that a contract between a manufacturer of ice cream and retailers offering each a free refrigerator with the obligation that only its ice cream be stored in it reduced inter-brand competition by making entry of other competitors more costly, thereby causing consumers to suffer 'both from a poorer choice of competing products and from the effects of weaker price competition'.[80] In *exclusive distribution* contracts, where the manufacturer appoints one distributor for a specific geographical region, the main risk is a reduction in intra-brand competition. The methodology adopted here is to gauge

---

[75] Guidelines on Vertical Restraints para. 103.   [76] *Yamaha*, decision of 16 July 2003.

[77] Ibid. para. 121.   [78] Ibid. para. 159.

[79] *Bass* [1999] OJ L186/1 paras. 121–55 (but the focus was more on foreclosure than on the restriction of inter-brand competition). Upheld in Case T-231/99 *Joynson v. Commission* [2002] ECR II-2085.

[80] *Van den Bergh Foods* [1998] OJ L246/1 para. 198 (upheld in Case T-65/98 *Van den Bergh Foods Ltd v. Commission* [2003] ECR II-4653).

the market power of the manufacturer and to measure the level of inter-brand competition. The higher the level of inter-brand competition, the less important is the reduction in intra-brand competition, while weaker inter-brand competition means that consumers would benefit from intra-brand competition.[81]

The Commission's analysis of foreclosure is less satisfactory. Following the post-Chicago theories explored in chapter 6, an evaluation of foreclosure requires first a determination that the rival's costs have been raised by the practice in question and secondly a determination that foreclosure harms consumers. Consumers can be hurt by foreclosure because it raises the costs of certain market players, and this permits the excluding firms to raise their prices.[82] Accordingly, the foreclosure of some competitors does not necessarily mean that anticompetitive effects follow automatically – there may be sufficient numbers of highly motivated competitors that consumers will not suffer. It is not clear from the Commission's Guidelines whether this approach is followed or whether proof of foreclosure is sufficient. The Commission provides much guidance on measuring foreclosure but nothing on how to measure its effects. It seems that the Commission and the Court are too ready to condemn distribution agreements purely upon proof of foreclosure. This problem is one we have already encountered in the context of the analysis of abuse of dominance. There too, exclusion of a competitor was the basis of a finding of abuse, based upon the EC's economic freedom rationale.[83]

The style of analysis in the Guidelines reflects the Commission's new approach described in chapter 2: rather than merely identifying a restriction of economic freedom of consumers or competitors or other economic actors, the Commission seeks to measure the restriction whereby only appreciable restrictions of economic freedom are found to infringe Article 81(1). The weakness of this approach in the context of distribution agreements is that proof of such restriction is not always enough to show harm to consumer welfare. However, all agreements that yield anticompetitive effects may also gain exemption if the four criteria in Article 81(3) are met.[84] Therefore, even if the approach under Article 81(1) remains more aggressive than is necessary, Article 81(3) can be used to measure whether the efficiency gains outweigh the restrictions of economic freedom.

Even agreements that are anticompetitive by object may benefit from exemption: very severe forms of territorial restriction can be characterised as pro-competitive.[85] Similarly, there is no per se rule against resale price

---

[81] Guidelines on Vertical Restraints paras. 161–4.

[82] S. C. Salop 'Analysis of Foreclosure in the EC Guidelines on Vertical Restraints' 2000 *Fordham Corporate Law Institute* 177 (Hawk ed. 2001).

[83] See ch. 6 pp. 183–6.   [84] Case T-17/93 *Matra Hachette v. Commission* [1994] ECR II-595.

[85] Paragraph 119(10) of the Guidelines appears to formalise the approach adopted by the Commission in relation to Distillers' attempts to introduce whisky on the continent: while initially prohibiting an export ban from the UK distributors (*Distillers* [1978] OJ L50/16), the Commission gave the company a period of grace to launch its products on the market. See

maintenance: the Court has indicated that RPM may be justified in the distribution of newspapers and periodicals. RPM might be the only means to support the financial burden of having to take back unsold copies, if taking back newspapers is the only way in which a wide selection of newspapers are made available to readers.[86] The Court does not guarantee an exemption but suggests that the pluralism of the media is a consideration which is relevant in determining whether the agreement is exempt. In this market, the interests of the purchaser as citizen in addition to the interests of the purchaser as consumer are taken into consideration.[87]

Efficiencies are the basis for the application of Article 81(3). The burden is placed on the parties to prove these: speculative evidence will not satisfy the Commission and efficiencies must benefit the consumer. Accordingly, proof of efficiencies is fact-specific: for instance, in the context of exclusive distribution, one usual claim is that exclusivity is necessary to facilitate investment by the distributor to build the image of the product. The Commission indicates that this efficiency claim is more easily accepted in the case of a new product, or for a complex product where giving the distributors incentives to promote the goods by providing pre-sale services is important.[88] To date, the Commission has exempted the vast majority of distribution agreements, at times by recommending some modifications. It may be instructive to explore one significant instance when an exemption was not granted. In *Van den Bergh Foods*, the Commission found that contracts obliging retailers to stock only the manufacturer's ice cream in the freezers that it supplied to retailers did not generate sufficient distributional efficiencies to compensate for the losses: retailers would benefit from not having to worry about stock or repairing the freezers, while the manufacturer would benefit from economies of scale generated in the purchase and repair of the freezer cabinets and distributional efficiencies. However, retailers would lose the ability to select competing products and the size of the freezer might be inefficiently large for their shops. Moreover, given the manufacturer's economic strength, the cost savings would be unlikely to be passed on to consumers.[89] The decision shows how efficiencies are estimated and balanced against the perceived restrictions of competition.

5.2 Selective distribution

For some types of vertical restraints the Commission drafted Block Exemptions in the 1970s and 1980s (e.g. on franchising, exclusive distribution and exclusive purchasing), and in the absence of a Block Exemption for

---

A. Jones and B. Sufrin *EC Competition Law: Text, Cases and Materials* 2nd edn (Oxford: Oxford University Press, 2004) pp. 678–9.

[86] Case 243/83 *SA Binon & Cie v. SA Agence et Messageries de la Presse* [1985] ECR 2015 para. 46.

[87] As we noted in chapters 4, 5 and 8, media pluralism plays an ambiguous role in the legal reasoning of the Commission.

[88] Guidelines on Vertical Restraints para. 174.

[89] *Van den Bergh Foods* [1998] OJ L246/1 paras. 238–40.

selective distribution, the Court had developed criteria to test its legality.[90] Selective distribution is a system often used to exclude discount stores from a distribution network. The contracts often provide that the distributors must ensure staff hold certain qualifications or undergo training, and that the location and appearance of the retail outlet are suitable for the goods in question. In *Metro* the Court held that selective distribution systems constitute:

> an aspect of competition which accords with Article [81(1)], provided that resellers are chosen on the basis of objective criteria of a qualitative nature relating to the technical qualifications of the reseller and his staff and the suitability of his trading premises and that such conditions are laid down uniformly for all potential resellers and are not applied in a discriminatory fashion.[91]

This statement encapsulates a rule whereby so-called 'simple' selective distribution networks that satisfy the criteria set out above do not restrict competition, provided there are no anticompetitive effects, which only materialise if there is a cumulative effect when all manufacturers use similar distribution networks.[92] The rule applies only to certain goods where selective distribution benefits the consumer, and has been applied to luxury goods (e.g. perfumes) because the aura of prestige surrounding the brand is an essential factor in competition among brands, to technically complex products because trained staff would facilitate consumer choice, and to newspapers and periodicals because the consumer expects each outlet to offer a representative selection of publications.[93] The advantage of falling within this rule was that an exemption was unnecessary. However, given that the new Block Exemption applies to selective distribution, this procedural benefit is redundant and the Block Exemption is considerably wider in scope: it tolerates the use of selective distribution for all types of goods, and allows the manufacturer to limit the number of distributors, while the case law allowed only selection based on qualitative criteria.

However, the *Metro* doctrine is not limited by a market share threshold; accordingly it may be advantageous for parties whose market share does not allow them to benefit from the Block Exemption to fit their contract under the

---

[90] The Commission decided not to design a Block Exemption because selective distribution is practised only in certain markets, so it preferred to develop its practice by issuing decisions on typical cases. J. Dubois 'Selective Distribution: The European Community's Stance' in Ehlermann and Laudati *Proceedings* p. 125.

[91] Case 26/76 *Metro v. Commission (Metro 1)* [1977] ECR 1875 para. 20.

[92] *Metro 2* [1986] ECR 3021 para. 40.

[93] For a useful insight into the commercial practices in the luxury goods sector, see Case T-19/92 *Groupement d'Achat Edouard Leclerc v. Commission* [1996] ECR II-1851; for an insight into the mechanics of newspaper distribution, see Case 243/93 *SA Binon & Cie v. SA Agence et Messageries de la Presse* [1985] ECR 2015. For a detailed review of the Commission's practice, see Dubois 'Selective Distribution'.

Metro standard, thereby avoiding the requirement of proving that the agreement satisfies the four conditions of Article 81(3). This represents disharmony between the case law and the Block Exemption. Arguably the *Metro* doctrine originated in 1977 as part of the Court's effort to restrict the overly wide application of Article 81(1) so as to avoid the procedural discomfort of the old system of notification/exemption; it was one of those unusual cases where the Court balanced the restriction of economic freedom on the one hand with the gains that consumers obtained through increased quality of service under Article 81(1) rather than under Article 81(3).[94] However, the application of the *Metro* rule today is at odds with the economic philosophy underpinning the Block Exemption because the rule is not limited by a market power test. Accordingly, the rule should be quietly abandoned. This is likely to happen in practice, as parties will shape their agreements according to the Block Exemption and the Guidelines rather than the case law. However, some aspects of the Court's jurisprudence may be worth retaining, for instance the criterion that selective distribution is only appropriate for certain types of goods. Firms should not be allowed to quell intra-brand competition when consumers gain no added benefit from the distribution system.[95] It remains to be seen whether the Commission or a National Competition Authority will remove the benefit of the Block Exemption when a manufacturer uses selective distribution for products that do not need specialised outlets.

5.3 Vertical restraints by dominant firms

Last, it is worth considering how distribution agreements by dominant firms are regulated. Dominant firms are subject to both Articles 81 and 82.[96] The Commission may apply either provision, and as we have seen in chapter 6 some vertical restraints have been governed strictly by Article 82: exclusive supply agreements, rebates and tying.[97] The Guidelines on Vertical Restraints take a similarly harsh line if the Commission were to apply Article 81: 'Where an undertaking is dominant or becoming dominant as a consequence of the vertical agreement, a vertical restraint that has appreciable anti-competitive effects can in principle not be exempted.'[98] Unless the vertical restraints do not infringe Article 81(1) an exemption will not be available, irrespective of whether the practice infringes Article 82. The justification for this position is that the last criterion under Article 81(3) is that the agreement must not eliminate competition and that dominance means that competition is

---

[94] *Metro 1* [1977] ECR 1875 para. 21.

[95] This is hinted at in the Guidelines on Vertical Restraints para. 186.

[96] Case 85/76 *Hoffmann La Roche v. Commission* [1979] ECR 461 para. 116; *Compagnie Maritime Belge and Others v. Commission* [2000] ECR I-1365 paras. 33–4.

[97] See pp. 183–95 for a detailed summary of the case law.

[98] Guidelines on Vertical Restraints para. 135, and in the context of tying the position is even more categorical: 'the question of a possible exemption under Article 81(3) arises as long as the company is not dominant' (para. 222).

eliminated. *A fortiori*, dominant firms cannot benefit from Article 81(3).[99] This means that dominant firms have an incentive to integrate vertically to avoid the application of Article 81, leading to a situation where form rather than substance dictates business plans.[100]

In more recent statements, however, the Commission has softened its stance on the application of Article 81(3) to dominant firms. This is because the CFI corrected the Commission's opinion on the role of the final condition of Article 81(3). As noted above, the Commission's view is that dominant firms cannot benefit from an exemption even if their activities may bring economic benefits because their dominance 'eliminates competition'. However, the CFI has held that the phrase 'elimination of competition' in Article 81(3) has an autonomous meaning which is unrelated to the concept of dominance. Accordingly, while Article 81(3) cannot apply where the dominant firm abuses its dominant position, an exemption may be granted when a dominant firm's agreement falls under Article 81(1).[101] In the *Guidelines on Article 81(3)* the Commission rescinds its position in the Vertical Restraints Guidelines so as to be consistent with this judgment.[102] This means that dominant firms are now treated like non-dominant firms so that the Commission will adopt the same economic rationale weighing up the positive and negative effects of agreements entered into by dominant firms, allowing exemptions even for vertical restraints by dominant firms.[103]

6 Distributors' power

The EC's regulation of distribution agreements is mostly based upon scenarios where suppliers impose terms on distributors to ensure that the latter do not frustrate the commercial interests of the former (thus resolving the principal–agent problem).[104] In this section we consider retailers with commercial power who dictate terms to suppliers. In some instances, this is desirable: when the

[99] L. Peeperkorn 'EC Vertical Restraints Guidelines: Effects-Based or Per Se Policy? – A Reply' [2002] *European Competition Law Review* 38, 39–40.

[100] Bishop and Walker *Economics* para. 5.53.

[101] Joined Cases T-191/98, T-212/98 and T-214/98 *Atlantic Container Line v. Commission*, judgment of 30 December 2003, para. 939; Case T-395/94 *Atlantic Container Line* [2002] ECR II-875 para. 330. Arguably the ECJ suggested a similar interpretation in *Hoffmann La Roche* [1979] ECR 461 para. 120.

[102] *Guidelines on the Application of Article 81(3) of the Treaty* [2004] OJ L101/97 para. 106. At footnote 92 the Commission suggests that this is how the Vertical Restraints Guidelines should be interpreted. However, it is hard to avoid the conclusion that there has been a U-turn.

[103] See also E. Rousseva 'Modernising by Eradicating: How the Commission's New Approach to Article 81 EC Dispenses with the Need to Apply Article 82 to Vertical Restraints' (2005) 42 *Common Market Law Review* 587, 617–18 and 632–6, where she notes that the Commission has deployed Article 81(3) with respect to the distribution agreement of a dominant firm in *Van den Bergh Foods* [1998] OJ L246/1.

[104] This is a label used when the principal (here the manufacturer) has to motivate the agent it has hired (here the distributor) by offering incentives to undertake tasks that are in the interests of the principal.

selling market is highly concentrated or dominated by one firm, powerful buyers can counterbalance the anticompetitive risks posed by manufacturers because they can keep prices low.[105] For example, a powerful buyer can refuse exclusive distribution contracts that would foreclose market access to other manufacturers,[106] and buyers that create associations to purchase goods and then compete independently when selling these on to the consumer lead to lower prices.[107]

However, matters are different if the distributors are powerful as buyers *and* as sellers, because then even though they may be able to put pressure on suppliers to reduce prices, these are not passed on to consumers. The power of buyers, especially retailers, is high on the policy agendas of some Member States, especially because of Europe-wide consolidation of food retail out-lets.[108] The major concern is that large retailers can impose disadvantageous terms on suppliers. For example, the distributor may levy an extra charge to suppliers who wish to have their goods distributed (a listing charge); impose an extra charge for placing the supplier's products in highly visible shelves (a slotting charge); insert a clause obliging the supplier not to sell the goods at lower prices to other distributors (an MFN clause);[109] demand that suppliers contribute to the distributor's promotional expenses; and make requests for exclusivity.[110] How should competition law respond to contracts that contain these terms?

From an economic perspective, two undesirable effects can arise. The first is that powerful retailers that have market power in buying and selling can raise prices, at the expense of consumers. Second, even when retailers do not have power over consumers, the exercise of buyer power can foreclose market access to suppliers unable to bear the higher costs of distribution. This can occur because certain suppliers cannot afford to deal with powerful retailers that impose onerous obligations on manufacturers. The effect is to reduce con-sumer choice. Moreover, selecting suppliers on the basis that they are willing to

---

[105] This tallies with the role of buyer power in mergers (see ch. 8 pp. 255–6).

[106] Guidelines on Vertical Restraints para. 145 (the same argument applies in relation to tying, para. 221). On the other hand, if buyers agree to an exclusive distribution agreement, this may foreclose market access for other distributors, and facilitate collusion among retailers (see Guidelines paras. 166–7, and a similar argument for selective distribution (para. 191) and exclusive supply (para. 204)).

[107] For example, the Court's analysis in Case C-250/92 *Gøttrup-Klim e.a. Grovvareforeninger v. Dansk Landbrugs Grovvareselskab AmbA* [1994] ECR I-5641.

[108] This phenomenon is prevalent in Northern European states: see e.g. Case IV/M.784 *Kesko/Tuko* [1997] OJ L110/53; Case IV/M.1221 *Rewe/Meinl* [1999] OJ L274/1; Case COMP/M.1684 *Carrefour/Promodes*, 25 October 2000.

[109] Most-favoured-nation clause, so called because it was originally included in trade agreements where country A agreed to treat imports of country B in the same way that it treated those of A's most-favoured nation.

[110] See P. Dobson, R. Clarke, S. Davies and M. Waterson 'Buyer Power and Its Impact on Competition in the Food Retail Distribution Sector of the European Union' (2001) 1 *Journal of Industry, Competition and Trade* 247 for a helpful overview.

submit to the retailer's demands does not necessarily mean that the most efficient suppliers are selected.[111] These harms must be traded off against the likely efficiencies of having powerful distributors: transport may be cheaper if deliveries are made to one rather than several buyers, and information about consumer demand is enhanced when the retail market is more concentrated, thus allowing supply to meet demand more effectively. More specifically, the relationship between a powerful retailer and its suppliers is not necessarily antagonistic, rather it can create reciprocally beneficial effects: for instance, the retailer's ability to collect information about consumer demand (through loyalty card schemes) can be valuably sold to the suppliers who in turn are able to respond to consumer demand more effectively, thereby increasing their and the retail outlet's profits and enhancing consumer welfare. This dynamic distribution relationship leads to increases in productive and allocative efficiencies.[112] These efficiency gains are comparable to those obtained in distribution contracts between powerful suppliers and weak retailers (e.g. pub leases). Accordingly, the risks of foreclosure for some suppliers should be balanced against the resulting efficiencies of the dynamic relationship between manufacturers and retailers.

In addition to balancing the economic costs and benefits that result from buyer power, one should (considering 'consumer welfare' implications as opposed to merely 'economic welfare' implications)[113] identify other negative effects on consumers. For instance, large retail outlets can suffocate small local stores, or eliminate suppliers of niche products that cannot lower prices faced with pressure from powerful distribution chains. From this perspective, the harm resulting from distributors' buyer power is more severe: a price war between large retailers who in turn place pressure on suppliers might lead to lower priced wines for example, but if makers of Pouilly Fumé are unable to sell to supermarkets at the low prices which American Sauvignon and Australian Chardonnay producers can set, then the consumer's gains from lower prices must be weighed against the loss of good wines. While there is a flavour of protectionism in this line of argument, the Community's approach to competition law is premised upon consumer welfare, and not merely economic welfare, and this legitimates a wider definition of consumer harm whereby these considerations may be legitimate in determining the shape of competition policy in this area.[114]

---

[111] P. W. Dobson 'Exploiting Buyer Power: Lessons from the British Grocery Trade' (2005) 72 *Antitrust Law Journal* 529, 557.

[112] J. Stuyck and T. Van Dyck 'EC Competition Rules on Vertical Restrictions and the Realities of a Changing Retail Sector on National Contract Laws' in H. Collins (ed.) *The Forthcoming EC Directive on Unfair Commercial Practices* (The Hague: Kluwer Law International, 2004) pp. 134–47.

[113] On the significance of this distinction, see ch. 3 pp. 83–6.

[114] See L. Vogel 'Competition Law and Buying Power: The Case for a New Approach in Europe' [1998] *European Competition Law Review* 4, 5.

Whichever stance we take on the types of harmful effects of buyer power, we require a more nuanced definition of market power when analysing the behaviour of powerful retailers, because the presence of buyer power can obtain even with very low market shares. The reason is this: a major retailer stocks between 20,000 and 30,000 products, and so they can easily afford not to sell one supplier's goods. In contrast suppliers are much more dependent on making sales to the retailers they have contracts with: if a supplier loses a contract with a major retailer this can lead to a considerable loss of sales (in the UK, for example, this can lead to a loss of sales of between 10 and 30 per cent)[115] and it may be difficult to find other large buyers. Given the high fixed costs facing a supplier, the loss of one major contract can have very serious consequences for the viability of its business.[116] Even if a retailer has a fairly small market share when it sells goods onto the market, and therefore has little power over price, it has power over suppliers. The UK Competition Commission suggests that a retailer with 8 per cent of grocery purchases for resale can have sufficient market power over producers (whereby losing one such contract would cause harm to a producer),[117] and the EC Commission has reached similar findings in the merger context, suggesting that a producer cannot afford to lose a buyer where sales account for 22 per cent of its turnover.[118] In addition, there are other, indirect, benefits for a supplier if he is present in certain stores; for instance a store's loyalty card system facilitates monitoring of consumer demand and passes valuable information to the manufacturers. Another relevant factor is the presence of stores' own-brand goods, which can be used as a bargaining tool to force the supplier to reduce the price of their goods, or to exclude suppliers of branded goods altogether.[119] These attributes also suggest that powerful buyers have advantages over less powerful retailers, allowing them to obtain cheaper supplies.[120] While in the short term this benefits consumers, in the long term there is a risk that these practices reduce competition as weaker retailers exit.[121] Moreover, not only are existing retailers powerful, but entry barriers are high because planning laws prevent the construction of new large retail outlets.[122]

---

[115] Competition Commission *Supermarkets: A Report on the Supply of Groceries from Multiple Stores in the United Kingdom* Cm 4842 (2000) para. 6.72.

[116] Dobson 'Exploiting Buyer Power' pp. 534–5.

[117] Competition Commission *Supermarkets* para. 2.458.

[118] Case COMP/M.1684 *Carrefour/Promodes*, 25 October 2000, paras. 52–9. See also P. Dobson *Buyer Power and its Impact on Competition in the Food Retail Distribution Sector of the European Union* 1999, available at http://europa.eu.int/comm/competition/publications/studies/bpifrs/ pp. 34–5: 'For the supplier, the retailer may represent a significant proportion of its overall sales (say 15%), but for the retailer that 15% may represent say only 1% or 2% of turnover, and thus the real power may lie with the purchaser and not the supplier.'

[119] Competition Commission *Supermarkets* paras. 2.518–2.521.   [120] Ibid. para. 2.448.

[121] See e.g. *Kesko/Tuko* [1997] OJ L110/53 paras. 133–4.

[122] Dobson 'Exploiting Buyer Power' p. 539.

So far we have considered how to identify market power when the risk is the exclusion of suppliers or retailers and suggested that buyer power need not manifest itself only when the buyer purchases all or almost all of the goods on the market. If the focus is upon *exploitation* of retailer power against consumers, then one needs to identify not only retailer buyer power, but also retailer selling power. This may warrant narrower market definitions of the retail market, focusing upon consumers' substitutability among different types of stores. Accordingly, a vast supermarket may be in a different market from a small inner city shop, given that consumers prefer shopping here owing to the range of products available.[123]

In sum, large retailers have market power in two distinct but interrelated ways. First, when retailers are powerful vis-à-vis suppliers they are able to impose costs on suppliers which can have exclusionary effects, both on suppliers and on other retailers. Second, large retail outlets have market power vis-à-vis consumers and are able to exploit this position by raising prices and reducing output. A framework for examining the compatibility of vertical restraints imposed by powerful distributors is therefore necessary.

Using 'economic welfare' as their starting point (and thus ignoring considerations about wider consumer welfare notions), Dobson, Clarke, Davies and Waterson suggest the following approach to tackle exclusionary practices.[124] The first step is to identify markets where the risk of anticompetitive effects is most severe. This is when the distributor has both buyer power vis-à-vis the manufacturer and seller power vis-à-vis the consumers. However, harm can also occur when there is no seller power, if the exercise of buyer power is likely to eliminate certain suppliers, increasing concentration at the supply level, which can lead to higher prices in the long term. Then one can consider whether the agreement contains terms that damage economic welfare by raising prices or foreclosing entry. Of particular concern are clauses that dampen competition among suppliers: thus MFN clauses and slotting allowances are problematic as they reduce intra-brand competition. Against these anticompetitive risks one can explore whether productive efficiencies resulting from improved distribution outweigh the economic losses. Their analysis is particularly helpful because it fits within the analytical framework used in the context of seller power in Article 81: balancing the anticompetitive effects with possible efficiencies. Exploitative behaviour by retailers is more difficult to control: as we noted in chapter 6, the Commission is reluctant to use Article 82 as a mechanism to control prices; however, merger control can be used to prevent increases in concentration that create risks of higher consumer prices.

The Commission has considered retailer buyer power only in some merger decisions, and has not applied Article 81 to the kinds of practices we have discussed. There are three reasons for this inaction. First, the growth of retailer

---

[123] See generally *Carrefour/Promodes*, 25 October 2000, paras. 9–12.
[124] Dobson et al. 'Buyer Power'.

buyer power is relatively recent. Second, it is not an EC-wide phenomenon: the retail sector is highly concentrated in the UK and France, but less so in other Member States.[125] Third, the traditional tools of competition law focus on the immediate effects of business tactics on consumers, and the exercise of retail buyer power in this context is usually beneficial: prices fall and distribution is more efficient. Only by adopting a longer-term perspective do the anti-competitive risks from foreclosure and reduction in the diversity of products arise. This final reason may explain why some Member States have enacted specific competition rules that are designed to address the distinct problems of retailer buyer power. The French and UK laws are illustrative examples of two different methods and of the limits of using competition law to curb buyer power.

Before we explore these models, it needs to be borne in mind that the economic analysis summarised above excludes considerations of distributive equity: thus if powerful retailers cause the elimination of regional products, or cause a reduction in the number of small shops in city centres, then the consumer harms that some suffer as a result of these effects are ignored. They can be incorporated easily, however, by widening the notion of harm and by considering more qualitatively how consumer interests are affected by the exercise of buyer power. The risk of course is that factors like product choice, product quality and store choice are difficult to measure objectively, thereby giving the competition authority considerable flexibility. The French law in particular takes this wider perspective of the role of competition law into account and seeks to protect small traders, while the British competition authority has resisted calls for similar protection for suppliers and small retailers.

6.1 France: abuse of economic dependence

The French law arose as a direct response to the concerns arising from 'la grande distribution' (i.e. large retail outlets). The French Competition Commission noted that while large distributors held a relatively small market share, they exercised considerable power over manufacturers, as if they held a dominant position. Retailers' power was perceived as a particular threat to agricultural and food suppliers.[126] In response, the concept of abuse of dominance was extended in the following manner:

> also prohibited is the exploitative abuse of one enterprise or a group of enterprises, of the state of economic dependence in which another enterprise finds itself with respect to it, whether as a client or as a supplier, provided it may affect

---

[125] Dobson 'Exploiting Buyer Power' p. 549.

[126] Commission de la concurrence *Avis relatif à la situation des centrales d'achat et de leur regroupements* Rapport au Ministre de l'Economie et des Finances et du budget pour l'année 1985, annexe 1.

the functioning or the structure of competition. This abuse may consist for example of refusals to sell, in tied sales, or discriminatory practices.[127]

The section creates an antitrust offence called 'abuse of economic dependence'. The focus is on the retailer's actions against its distributors, the exclusionary effect of retailer power. The law was first introduced in 1986 and was amended in 2001. Its principal rationale is the protection of small and medium-sized suppliers faced with powerful buyers. The Ministry of Economics and Finance suggested that the law was designed to protect the producer who sells most of his goods through a large buyer so that without those sales his entire business is in jeopardy.[128] Several abusive tactics have been identified: for example, requests for retroactive rebates, requests for free supplies, making excessive demands of suppliers and using the failure to comply as grounds for rescinding contracts, asking suppliers to make financial contributions when the buyer is acquiring another retail chain, requiring sellers to reduce supplies to the buyer's competitors, and threatening to break off commercial relations if the supplier fails to comply with the retailer's demands. According to the legislature, thousands of enterprises live in a state of economic dependence and require protection.[129]

In the original version of the law, a finding of illegality required the following: (1) proof of a position of economic dependence; (2) the absence of alternative buyers; (3) an abuse restricting competition. The major limitation of the old law was the final requirement: proof that competition was restricted. Often the abuse would be against a very small supplier and damage to it was unlikely to harm the process of competition, because even if it was forced to exit the market, there would be several competitors left.[130] Likewise, given the small market shares of the buyer, it was always arguable that the seller would be able to find another outlet for his goods, thus denying a finding of a position of economic dependence. In fact some decisions suggest that the existence of alternative buyers is presumed as soon as there are other retail networks.[131] The current version of the law removes these two requirements to make the application of the rule easier. One merely has to show that the abuse 'may' affect the structure of the market. It was impossible for the legislature to remove any reference to effects on the market because otherwise the competition authority would have become involved in mere commercial disputes and would be acting outside its remit.

---

[127] Article L420–2, line 2, Code de Commerce (Law number 2001-420 of 15 May 2001).
[128] J.-Y. Le Déaut *Rapport d'information n. 2072 sur l'évolution de la distribution: de la cooperation à la domination commerciale* Assemblée Nationale 11 January 2000, p. 117. For a general overview in English (predating the 2001 reforms) see Ehlermann and Laudati *Proceedings* ch. 9.
[129] Le Déaut *Rapport* p. 118.   [130] Ibid. p. 118.
[131] Conseil de la Concurrence, Decision n. 91-MC-03, Recueil Lamy n. 457 (comments of V. Selinsky); confirmed by the Court of Appeal in Paris, 23 October 1991, *Gazette du Palais* 26–28 January 1992 (comments of J. P. Marchi).

However, the law is still difficult to apply because the Courts adopted a restrictive definition of economic dependence. This is a question of fact where the competition authority looks at the following: the percentage of revenue which the seller makes with the buyer, the distributor's importance in the sales of the seller's goods, and the factors which led the seller to concentrate his sales with the buyer.[132] Moreover, the absence of alternative buyers is likely to remain a factor in determining whether there is a state of economic dependence even if this requirement has been intentionally removed from the statute, because, logically, there can be no dependence on someone if there are alternatives. A striking illustration of the stringent definition of economic dependence can be seen in the *Cora* decision. The alleged abuse occurred when the defendant retailer was acquiring another retail outlet and it demanded financial contributions from those selling goods through its stores to help finance the merger. It threatened to stop dealing, or to reduce the amount of goods it bought, or to invest less in promoting their goods unless payments were made. The suppliers made between 22 per cent and 67.5 per cent of their sales through the Cora group, but the court held that this was insufficient evidence to show economic dependence because there were alternative retail outlets. One puzzled commentator noted that no firm could afford to terminate a contract with a supplier with whom it made 5–10 per cent of its sales, at 22 per cent one would be hard pressed to find any businessman willing to forego commercial relations, and if a manufacturer sold 67.5 per cent of its goods through one retail outlet it seems incomprehensible to deny that he is economically dependent on that one retailer.[133]

Therefore, even with the recent amendments, it does not seem that the law has, to date, been successful in curbing the perceived power of large retail outlets. In addition to problems of establishing a relationship of economic dependence, a major reason is that few manufacturers have made complaints because they fear reprisals from the retailer.[134] One of the few successful cases (*Société Prodim v. Duval*) arose in the context of a franchise contract when, after contractual relations had broken down, the franchisor sued the franchisee under the contract and the franchisee counter-claimed that the franchisor had abused his position. The court identified the following abuses: the franchisor raised the fee owed by the franchisee when he took over the accounting services; he set up a computerised system for delivery which made it difficult for the franchisee to know in advance the prices of the goods ordered; and he obtained the power to pay the franchisee's invoices and following this delayed payment to other suppliers.[135] These are particularly egregious forms of abuse, but were carried out by a powerful supplier against a weak retailer. The aim of

---

[132] Decision n. 96-D-44 Carat, 18 June 1996, Recueil Lamy n. 698 (comments of P. Arbel).
[133] X. de Mello 'L'affaire Cora: un coup pour rien' *Gazette du Palais* 3 November 1994, 1224, 1227.
[134] R. Germain and L. Vogel *Traité de droit commercial* vol. I, 17th edn (LGDJ, 1998) para. 839.
[135] Bulletin des arrêts de la Cour de Cassation, chambre civile, 1997, parties 4 and 5, n. 337 p. 291.

the law was to protect weak suppliers against powerful retailers, but most of the case law is composed of claims by retailers against suppliers.[136]

6.2 United Kingdom: market investigations

As we saw in chapter 9, UK competition law contains a distinctive regime whereby the Competition Commission (CC) is able to carry out investigations in markets where there is evidence of a systemic market failure.[137] Potentially this approach can provide a comprehensive remedy for buyer power in the retail sector. In 2000 the CC published its investigation of the supermarkets sector. This was spurred by three concerns: that the price of groceries in the UK was higher than that in the EU and US; that supermarkets were paying farmers too little for their produce, judged by the difference between the farm-gate and the retail price; and that the growth of large out-of-town retail outlets was having adverse effects on small retailers in city centres.[138] As with the French legislation, the CC found that a retailer need not have a high market share to be able to exercise considerable power over suppliers and found that supermarkets holding a market share of 8 per cent or above in the purchase of groceries were likely to have buyer power.[139]

The CC found that the supermarkets operated in a competitive environment, but that they engaged in a number of unfair practices vis-à-vis suppliers: for example, asking suppliers to pay for consumer complaints, requiring that suppliers make a contribution to the retailer's marketing costs, retrospective reductions in prices without notice, delaying payment. It found that the sustained use of these methods could raise two competition concerns. First, because the supermarkets' requests increased the costs of suppliers, the suppliers would spend less on innovation and product development and this would harm consumers. Moreover, suppliers' increased costs could lead some to leave the sector and deter new suppliers from entering. This would also harm consumers by reducing choice. Second, the exercise of buyer power by supermarkets would imperil smaller retail outlets unable to obtain similar advantages from suppliers and this would reduce competition at the retail level of trade, harming consumers by reducing choice and potentially leading to price increases as the retail market became more concentrated. The upshot was a Code of Practice agreed in March 2002, which binds the four major retailers,[140] and is a blueprint for how retailers should deal with suppliers. The code lists a number of obligations which retailers have, forcing them to refrain from taking steps that raise suppliers' costs: for example, retrospective reductions in prices agreed with suppliers are forbidden unless reasonable notice is given (Clause 4); supermarkets cannot make unreasonable requests

---

[136] F. Jenny 'Panel Discussion' in Ehlermann and Laudati *Proceedings* p. 178.
[137] See pp. 342–4.   [138] Competition Commission *Supermarkets.*   [139] Ibid.
[140] The parties gave a statutory undertaking under s. 88(2) Fair Trading Act 1973.

to suppliers to contribute to marketing costs (Clause 5); supermarkets cannot demand lump sum payments from suppliers who seek to gain better shelf space or an increase in shelf space (Clause 10); changes in the quantity of goods required by a supermarket from a supplier must be requested by giving reasonable notice in writing and the supermarket must compensate the supplier for losses that may be incurred (Clause 16). According to the CC, measures like these are designed to guarantee the efficiency of suppliers by ensuring that their costs are not increased. Thus, while the code is couched in terms about 'supermarkets and their suppliers being reasonable in their dealings with each other',[141] its motivation is the guarantee of competitive conditions.

The Office of Fair Trading (OFT) has carried out two reviews of the code's operation, which broadly indicated that it had been complied with.[142] Two aspects of the OFT's reviews are worth noting. The first is that the OFT's priority when reviewing this industry is about whether the retail market is competitive. On this point the evidence shows that prices are low and consumers benefit from the availability of a wide range of goods.[143] The second is that the OFT has no evidence of lack of compliance with the code. The OFT commissioned a study by an accountancy firm which revealed infrequent infringements of the code.[144] Moreover, representations made to the OFT about breaches have been anecdotal: no supplier provided the OFT with concrete examples of the code being breached.[145] Part of the reluctance to take formal enforcement procedures is probably due to fears of reprisals, as in France. In fact 73 per cent of respondents to the OFT's first review suggested that the code was unlikely to work because suppliers feared that demanding compliance with the code would place their entire contract in jeopardy and it was reported that even among large suppliers, some of which are multinational companies, there was a reluctance to use the code.[146] However, it is remarkable that only one formal complaint under the code has been brought and that the supply industry is reluctant to take any formal action or advise the OFT of any infringements. Perhaps these fears are exaggerated; in fact the OFT observed that the fears were based on a perception of what supermarkets may do rather than on observations about what supermarkets have done in the past.[147] Moreover, the OFT invited trade associations to compile dossiers of breaches but none have agreed to do so, which renders enforcement impossible.[148]

---

[141] Code of Practice, Preamble paragraph (d).

[142] Office of Fair Trading *The Supermarkets Code of Practice* (February 2004) (OFT 697); Office of Fair Trading *Supermarkets: The Code of Practice and Other Competition Issues: Conclusions* (August 2005) (OFT 807).

[143] OFT 807 part 4.

[144] Office of Fair Trading *Supermarkets: The Code of Practice and Other Competition Issues* (March 2005) (OFT 783).

[145] OFT 697 paras. 2.3–2.10.   [146] Ibid. paras. 5.9–5.12.

[147] Ibid. para. 7.9.   [148] Ibid. para. 7.16.

An independent empirical study carried out to measure the success of the code was concerned with gauging whether it had delivered 'justice' in two ways: first from a distributive justice perspective, whether producers were better protected, and second from a procedural justice perspective, whether the producers were less subject to the whims of the retailers.[149] Most of the findings relate to procedural justice and the responses suggested that suppliers did not view the code as having had much of an impact on the conduct of retailers.[150] This study is likely to fuel calls for more aggressive regulation of supermarkets even if all that the study reveals is that suppliers do not believe that the code is functioning.

Those pressing for reform, however, have a different understanding of the role of competition policy from that of the CC and the OFT and have had to frame their concerns in terms that would allow the competition authorities to respond positively. The British competition authorities see their principal task as maintaining competitive markets in the supply of goods and in the retail sector. Provided that costs of production are minimised and prices are low, the competition authorities are reluctant to intervene. Other social problems caused by powerful retailers are for other government departments.[151] In contrast, those clamouring for further regulation wish to deploy competition law to guarantee fairness in the relationship between suppliers and supermarkets, and others have concerns that supermarkets deal unfairly with suppliers in general, and that there can be long-term damage to certain suppliers as a result of the hard bargaining by supermarkets. In addition, several other issues of distributive justice are raised, for example the adverse effects of supermarkets on local traders and on suppliers from developing countries. However, the British organisations seeking additional regulation to safeguard these interests often 'frame' their representation in the language of consumer welfare. For example, Friends of the Earth speak of a lack of consumer choice as a result of buyer power by large supermarkets, even if they also widen their concerns, identifying threats to environmental and social standards.[152] Similarly, the Association of Convenience Stores frames its concerns using the language of competitive markets and consumer choice, but also expresses wider social benefits resulting from small stores.[153] This strategy is probably what enabled the CC and OFT to draft the Code of Practice, because they were

---

[149] R. Duffy, A. Fearne and S. Hornibrook 'Measuring Distributive and Procedural Justice: An Exploratory Investigation of the Fairness of Retailer–Supplier Relationships in the UK Food Industry' (2003) 105 *British Food Journal* 682.

[150] A. Fearner, R. Duffy and S. Hornibrook 'Justice in UK Supermarket Buyer–Supplier Relationships: An Empirical Analysis' (2005) 33 *International Journal of Retail and Distribution Management* 570, 577.

[151] OFT 807 points 2.4 and 5.2.

[152] Friends of the Earth Press Release, 26 November 2004 (available at www.foe.co.uk).

[153] Letter to Jim Dowd MP, All Party Parliamentary Group for Small Shops, 30 June 2005 (available at www.thelocalshop.com).

able to explain it in terms of its capacity to safeguard consumer welfare even if it can also be read as designed to safeguard wider distributive justice concerns.

The British approach contrasts with the intentions of the French legislator in drafting the rules on abuse of a position of economic dependence to achieve a wider range of policy ambitions, for example protecting suppliers regardless of whether there is an adverse impact on competition. One reason for the narrow interpretation of competition policy in Britain has to do with the relatively recent amendments to the competition rules, where one of the principal aims was to remove political intervention from the regulatory process.[154] The CC and OFT are now independent agencies that need to establish non-political processes to guarantee their legitimacy. Thus, those in the UK wishing for increased regulation and calling for further reviews must frame issues in narrow, consumer welfare terms and are therefore unlikely to succeed in obtaining more wide-ranging regulation from the competition authorities. However, even in France, where such lobby groups have been more successful in obtaining law reform, there are practical hurdles in leaving enforcement in the hands of weak retailers.

This brief comparative excursion suggests that a successful enforcement strategy towards buyer power would be for a competition authority to apply an 'abuse-type' provision and enforce this itself rather than leaving the initiative with weak suppliers. However, the need for this enforcement strategy depends upon the political interests one wishes to promote. If the role of competition policy is cast narrowly in terms of safeguarding economic welfare, there is no need for augmenting the powers of competition authorities. The evidence from the UK suggests that by and large the market is competitive, although the market may require monitoring to ensure that retailer concentration does not increase. In this market context, where quality and consumer choice are not under serious threat, additional enforcement is unnecessary. Only if competition policy is understood as a means of guaranteeing a wider range of distributive justice considerations is reform necessary (e.g. to ensure that small farmers using sustainable methods can survive, that small retailers are able to thrive, and that overseas exporters from developing countries are treated fairly by retailers). The prospects of EC competition law applying the latter perspective, whether to safeguard the interests of small retailers or the interests of weak suppliers, seem remote given the narrow, economics-oriented reform of the law on vertical restraints. Nevertheless, as we have seen above, the Commission's interest is in consumer welfare defined more widely than mere economic efficiency, and as we shall see in the following section, it is possible for the Commission to devise 'sector-specific competition laws' to address specific market failures.

---

[154] See pp. 401–2.

7 The politics of distribution: the car sector

The regulation of vertical restraints discussed above applies to all goods and services covered by EC competition law, unless another Block Exemption exists,[155] and the one sector to which special distribution rules apply is the motor vehicle market. In contrast to the process of reform that took place in the context of distribution agreements for other goods, where the Commission's motivations were to facilitate business planning and to introduce an economically sound basis for regulating vertical restraints, the reform of the rules regulating car distribution contracts was characterised by a tension between the Commission's desire to liberalise car distribution and lobbying by interested parties to retain a system of distribution operating outside the rules of competition. It should come as no surprise that the car sector has enjoyed a privileged position under EC competition law: after all the automobile industry has been one of the most important in the EU both for its contribution to the Union's economic wealth and for the vast number of persons employed in the sector, and it has also benefited from a range of protectionist measures designed to curb imports of Japanese cars, notably a voluntary export restraint that expired in 1999.[156]

In the competition context, the power of the car lobby was evident with the first Block Exemption in the motor vehicle sector of 1985: this allowed manufacturers to appoint exclusive dealers and to prevent them from selling competing cars; exclusivity could be linked with a system of selective distribution to ensure that retail outlets conformed to the manufacturers' requirements. Moreover, manufacturers could tie up car sales and repair services, so that a distributor wishing to sell cars would be obliged to offer repair services as well.[157] This link was justified as being more efficient and in the interest of consumers; moreover, a manufacturer's reputation depended on providing effective repair services.[158] The 1985 Block Exemption formalised the practices that existed in this sector at that time. It was premised on the belief that cars were a special product, which necessitated a different distribution network with close cooperation between the manufacturer and a small number of dealers. The Commission tolerated methods of distribution that restricted inter-brand competition (by allowing manufacturers to demand that dealers do not sell competing cars), prevented intra-brand competition (by allowing the allocation of exclusive territories), and thereby damaged the internal market.

The regulatory philosophy under the current Motor Vehicle Block Exemption Regulation (hereinafter MVBER), which came into force on

---

[155] Article 2(5) Regulation 2790/99.
[156] See P. A. Messerlin *Measuring the Costs of Protection in Europe: European Commercial Policy in the 2000s* (Washington, DC: Institute of International Economics, 2001) ch. 2.
[157] Regulation 123/85 [1985] OJ L15/16, amended by Regulation 1475/95 [1995] OJ L145/25.
[158] Recital 4 Regulation 1475/95.

1 October 2002, is very different.[159] The premise is that dealers have little bargaining power vis-à-vis car manufacturers and that by increasing the independence of dealers as well as their number, the market will become more competitive.[160] Moreover, the Commission observed that car owners should also benefit from competitive conditions when seeking to repair their car, and the old argument that sales and repair were carried out most efficiently by the same firm was abandoned. The MVBER is designed to inject more competition at both levels: car sales and car repairs and maintenance. As a result, the new regulatory structure is *stricter* than that under the Regulation on Vertical Restraints because the Commission sees its task as creating a competitive market rather than merely preventing market failures.[161] It was accompanied by increased action against manufacturers who attempted to prevent parallel trade in cars by their dealers.[162]

7.1 Opening the car distribution market

Regarding car sales, the MVBER has three objectives: first, to increase competition among dealers selling the same brands (intra-brand competition), in particular by facilitating sales from one Member State to another; second, to facilitate the entry of new retail forms, especially supermarkets and internet retailing; and third, to increase competition among different brands of car.

In order to facilitate competition among dealers, manufacturers wishing to benefit from the Block Exemption must choose between three types of distribution system: (a) exclusive distribution (i.e. appointing one dealer for a given territory); (b) quantitative selective distribution (i.e. selecting a discrete number of distributors that meet the manufacturer's criteria); (c) qualitative selective distribution (i.e. selecting all dealers that are able to meet the manufacturer's criteria). This differs from the earlier Regulation (and from the general policy on vertical restraints) that allowed a combination of exclusive and selective distribution which insulated dealers from competition. Now, dealers who opt for exclusive distribution must have a market share below 30 per cent to benefit from exemption, while manufacturers who opt for quantitative selective distribution must have a market share of less than

---

[159] EC Commission *Report on the Evaluation of Regulation 1475/95 on the Application of Article 85(3) [now 81(3)] of the Treaty to Certain Categories of Motor Vehicle Distribution and Servicing Agreements* COM(2000)743 final; Explanatory Brochure for Commission Regulation (EC) 1400/2002 of 31 July 2002 on the Application of Article 81(3) of the Treaty to Categories of Vertical Agreements and Concerted Practices in the Motor Vehicle Sector (available at http://ec.europa.eu/comm/competition/index_en.html).

[160] Explanatory Brochure (this document is comparable to the Guidelines on Vertical Restraints).

[161] Recital 2 Regulation 1400/2002 on the Application of Art. 81(3) EC to Categories of Vertical Agreements and Concerted Practices in the Motor Vehicle Sector [2002] OJ L203/30 (MVBER).

[162] E.g. *Volkswagen AG* [1998] OJ L124/60; *Opel* [2001] OJ L59/1; *Volkswagen AG* [2001] OJ L262/14; *Daimler Chrysler* [2002] OJ L257/1.

40 per cent, and no maximum market share applies if manufacturers opt for qualitative selective distribution, which is the option that allows for the widest number of dealers to gain access to the market.[163] Intra-brand competition is most difficult when there is one exclusive dealer in one territory. As a result, exemption is only available when the manufacturer has little market power and the loss in intra-brand competition is compensated by the presence of inter-brand competition.[164] When manufacturers opt for selective distribution instead, the possibilities of intra-brand competition are greater because there are more dealers per territory and dealers are free to make sales in other territories. In particular, a dealer appointed via a selective distribution network is able to establish additional outlets in other locations in the EC, something unavailable to selective distribution networks under the general Block Exemption.[165]

To increase inter-brand competition the MVBER makes the establishment of multi-brand distribution outlets easier. The manufacturer is not allowed to impose a non-compete obligation on dealers,[166] and while in general competition law jargon a non-compete obligation is one where the dealer must purchase more than 80 per cent of its requirements from the manufacturer,[167] in this sector, it is an obligation to purchase more than *30 per cent* of the dealer's total purchases.[168] Moreover, the manufacturer may not prevent dealers from purchasing cars from a particular competing car manufacturer.[169]

Finally, the MVBER tries to make entry into the retail market easier for new kinds of distributors by preventing the manufacturer from forcing dealers to have their own repair facilities. Instead, the manufacturer must allow them to sub-contract the provision for repair and maintenance to repairers that are authorised by it.[170] Under the general vertical restraint rules instead, this obligation could be imposed. The anticipated effect of the MVBER is to lower the cost of entering the retail market, making it possible for supermarkets to sell cars since they do not need to provide after-sales services and for cars to be sold via the Internet.[171] Moreover, the MVBER facilitates the role of 'intermediaries' who shop for cars around the EU on behalf of customers by forbidding the imposition of any obligation on dealers not to sell to such persons.[172]

7.2 Opening the repair and service market

Regarding the repair and maintenance sector, the major innovation of the MVBER is that it disaggregates the retail and repair businesses. As we saw

---

[163] Article 3(1) MVBER.
[164] Some intra-brand competition is possible in that exclusive dealers located in other territories are able to make passive sales into other territories (Article 4(1)(b)(i) MVBER).
[165] Article 5(2)(b) MVBER.   [166] Article 5(1)(a) MVBER.
[167] Article 1(b) Regulation 2790/1999.   [168] Article 1(b) MVBER.
[169] Article 5(1)(c) MVBER.   [170] Article 4(1)(g) MVBER.
[171] However, there is no specific provision about internet sales in the MVBER, except at Recital 15.
[172] Recital 14 MVBER.

above, retailers cannot be obliged to offer repair services, and to complement this, a supplier may appoint 'authorised repairers' and must allow these businesses to limit their activities to providing repair and maintenance.[173]

Moreover, the MVBER facilitates market access for independent repairers. These are repairers that are not appointed by the supplier (e.g. an independent garage or an automobile club) and that carry out a significant proportion of repairs.[174] Under the MVBER, no exemption is granted where the supplier refuses to give independent repairers 'access to any technical information, diagnostic and other equipment tools ... or training required for the repair and maintenance of these motor vehicles'.[175] The reader should note how remarkable this provision is. First it imposes an obligation akin to the one we have seen in chapter 7 when considering refusals to contract by dominant firms. As we saw there, the Court was cautious in circumscribing the obligation to deal to limited circumstances.[176] No limits are provided here: the supplier loses the benefit of the Block Exemption if it refuses to deal with third parties. This leads us to the second special feature: the obligation imposed is to deal with strangers. Under the general Block Exemption for vertical restraints, the supplier selects its distributors and the Block Exemption places limits upon what terms may be inserted in the contract. Here, instead, the supplier has a duty to deal with any independent repairer and if he refuses to do so he loses the benefit of exemption for the entire distribution network. Granted, the manufacturer may be able to justify a refusal to deal with a wholly incompetent independent repairer; nevertheless the commercial freedom of the supplier is severely restricted.

7.3 From protection to a regulated competitive market?

The Commission devised an aggressive regulatory scheme for the car sector. We have seen examples of this in other chapters (e.g with regard to broadcasting rights to sports events in chapter 4, where obligations to deal with specific broadcasters were also imposed).[177] 'Sector-specific competition laws' empower the Commission to design rules to inject more competition and to redesign markets. This approach presents opportunities and risks. On the one hand, it can be argued that the MVBER creates novel distribution channels which are likely to benefit consumers, but on the other hand, one may question whether such detailed 'micro-management' of the industry is really necessary

---

[173] Article 4(1)(h) MVBER.

[174] S. Norberg 'Car Distribution in the 21st Century: The European Commission's New Draft Block Exemption Regulation' 5 July 2002 (http://ec.europa.eu/comm/competition/index_en.html).

[175] Article 4(2) MVBER.

[176] See pp. 223–40. In Case 238/87 *Volvo v. Veng* [1988] ECR 6211, the Court addressed the refusal of a car manufacturer to license parts for its vehicles to independent repairers under Article 82; however, the obligation imposed by the MVBER is more extensive.

[177] See pp. 105–10.

when the manufacturing side of the market is not highly concentrated, suggesting that there should be sufficient inter-brand competition to undermine any attempts by manufacturers or dealers to exploit their position to harm consumers. Moreover, if there are new, profitable, models of distribution one would expect industry to exploit these, particularly given the vibrant competition from Japanese car manufacturers. It has been suggested that the car manufacturing industry needs to revise its distribution strategy to yield greater efficiencies; as a result the market might well have been able to resolve market imperfections by forcing manufacturers to redesign their distribution network.[178]

In addition to concerns about competitive markets, the Block Exemption also regulates the contracts between suppliers and dealers, so that no exemption is available unless: (i) the supplier who wishes to terminate gives notice in writing and gives 'detailed, objective and transparent' reasons for wishing to terminate the contract;[179] (ii) the contract has a minimum duration of five years or is for an indefinite period, and notice of termination is two years;[180] (iii) the contract provides for an arbitration procedure in case of disputes.[181] It may be argued that these compulsory terms are necessary to guarantee the independence of dealers and to prevent retaliation by suppliers, for example when dealers take advantage of the MVBER to sell in other Member States.[182] On this view, the compulsory terms are necessary to achieve competitive markets. On the other hand, these terms have little to do with competitive markets and are more about protecting dealers from unfair business tactics.[183] As we have seen before, including compulsory contract terms is part of a pattern of sector-specific competition law.[184] Moreover, many dealers are small enterprises (61 per cent of dealers sold fewer than 150 cars in 2001)[185] so the contractual restrictions seem to be designed to protect a vulnerable party.

How might one account for the imposition of such an aggressive regulation on the car sector when it was one of Europe's most protected sectors? First, the competition Commissioner, Mario Monti, took a tougher negotiating stance and was less willing to accept a pragmatic solution than his predecessor. It was under his leadership that the interests of the consumer became a paramount consideration in the enforcement of competition law, and the price differences

---

[178] See S. M. Knupfer, R. K. Richmond and J. D. Van Der Ark 'Making the Most of US Auto Distribution' (2003) 1 *McKinsey Quarterly* 1.

[179] Article 3(4) MVBER.   [180] Article 3(5) MVBER.   [181] Article 3(6) MVBER.

[182] Recitals 9 and 11 MVBER.

[183] D. Gerard 'Regulated Competition in the Automobile Distribution Sector: A Comparative Analysis of the Car Distribution System in the US and EU' [2003] *European Competition Law Review* 518. See also the distinction drawn between antitrust law and other private law provisions in *NYNEX v. Discon* 525 US 128 (1998).

[184] See for example the compulsory terms in the Block Exemption in the insurance sector, ch. 4 p. 102.

[185] Norberg 'Car Distribution'.

in the car sector were a prominent symbol of the consumer harm that competition law should eradicate.[186] As he put it: 'If they [consumers] want to buy their vehicle over the Internet, through an intermediary, or from another country, why should we stand in their way?'[187] Fighting restrictive practices in the car sector thus became a symbol of DG Competition's work in the interests of the European consumer. Second, Akbar suggests that the lobbying positions of the interested parties shifted so that the Community was able to go forward with its single market programme.[188] Originally, Member States supported domestic manufacturers, and both manufacturers and dealers had a shared interest in maintaining the status quo. By 2000 the configuration of interests changed and facilitated a reform that aligned car distribution rules to the EC's interests. The support of Member States waned, in large part because of the growth of foreign ownership of 'national' car manufacturers, but also because the voluntary export restraint for Japanese vehicles expired. The 1985 Block Exemption was seen as helpful in controlling the flow of Japanese cars into the Member States that had secured protection from imports. With no export restraint, the restrictions in the Block Exemptions were no longer necessary. This facilitated the overhaul of the 1985 Block Exemption even if the main association representing car manufacturers objected.[189]

It remains to be seen whether the Commission's reform is successful. In the Commission's favour is the fact that the law is cast without evidence of regulatory capture: the Commission consulted all stakeholders and designed rules which it believed would benefit consumers. This is unlike the earlier Block Exemptions, which favoured car manufacturers. On the other hand, the Commission's highly prescriptive approach may have adverse effects as it increases manufacturers' costs. By giving greater power to dealers, it makes it difficult for manufacturers to terminate ineffective dealers and to generate incentives for efficient dealers. It is too soon to determine whether the MVBER is successful; however, preliminary indications suggest a bleak picture. To date the vast majority of manufacturers have opted for selective distribution systems because they allow them to control the dealers' sales outlets.[190] When manufacturers sell via exclusive distribution systems they can control the dealer's sales outlet but cannot control the quality of other retail outlets to which the dealer may sell the goods, while with selective distribution, dealers may sell only to other authorised dealers.[191] The effect of this choice is that

---

[186] See M. Monti 'Who Will Be in the Driver's Seat?' 11 May 2000 (http://ec.europa.eu/comm/competition/index_en.html).

[187] M. Monti 'The New Legal Framework for Car Distribution' 6 February 2003 (http://ec.europa.eu/comm/competition/index_en.html).

[188] Y. Akbar 'Slip Sliding Away? The Changing Politics of European Car Distribution' (2003) 5 *Business and Politics* 175.

[189] See ACEA's position paper (www.acea.be).

[190] S. Vezzoso 'On the Antitrust Remedies to Promote Retail Innovation in the EU Car Sector' [2004] *European Competition Law Review* 190.

[191] Article 4(1)(c) MVBER.

alternative forms of distribution (e.g. internet sales or sales via supermarkets) cannot emerge when selective distribution is used. This is because the criteria for joining a selective distribution network can be onerous (e.g. standards of presentation in the shop, an obligation to offer test drives, and duties to advertise). This explains why some, including the UK's Competition Commission, have called for a ban on selective distribution to allow for the creation of innovative distribution channels.[192] More generally, while there has been some reduction in price differences between Member States, it is not clear how far this can be attributed to the new distribution regime, nor whether the still significant price differences will be affected as new distribution networks emerge.[193]

8 Conclusion

Judging the effectiveness of competition policy towards vertical restraints requires us to determine what policy objectives we have in mind. Judged from the perspective of economic efficiency, the new-style Block Exemption Regulation reflects economic thinking in that it provides a market power screen to filter out those firms whose behaviour has no effect on the market. The analytical framework for agreements that require individual exemption is also by and large consistent with economic theory. Nevertheless, there remain a number of systemic barriers that prevent the complete economic conversion of EC competition law in this field. The first is that the role of market integration remains, although in a less dogmatic form. An economic approach would suggest that if a firm has no market power, efforts to segment the market are unlikely to reduce economic welfare. Thus, the central political imperative of EC competition law continues to stifle the use of economics. The second barrier is that the Commission retains an interest in consumer welfare as opposed to economic welfare. Accordingly, aspects of distributive justice inform the decision-making process. The Commission, for example, reserves the right to withdraw exemption if it considers that consumer interests are not well served even if the distribution network is economically efficient. The third barrier is that the Commission retains an interest in the other core value, economic freedom. Accordingly, the analysis of foreclosure is premised upon the elimination of suppliers or retailers rather than upon the adverse economic effects that may arise as a result of excluding certain market players; similarly, the right of access to spare parts for independent repairers is premised upon granting them market access rather than upon any risk to competition that may result from their absence.

---

[192] See Competition Commission *New Cars: A Report on the Supply of New Motor Cars within the UK* Cm 4660 (2000); Vezzoso 'Antitrust Remedies'.

[193] See generally http://ec.europa.eu/comm/competition/car_sector/price_diffs/ (containing detailed studies on car price trends in Europe).

These three barriers to a full economic analysis suggest that the Commission retains an allegiance to political values. As we have observed in the last section of this chapter, the role of politics is diminishing, in large part because the Commission wished to position competition policy at the service of consumers and protectionist lobbies saw national support vanish. Nevertheless, as we saw in the context of buyer power, new lobby groups can astutely capture the regulatory process and may succeed in obtaining special, sector-specific rules. This has occurred in France and to a much lesser extent in the UK, but matters may change in the UK as the OFT has been required to carry out further reviews[194] and is under political pressure to take a more robust stance to protect small retailers.[195] In the Community context the recent focus on consumer interests by DG Competition noted in chapter 4 opens up an avenue for influencing the direction of competition policy towards distributive justice concerns.

More generally, whether or not the Commission identifies new markets where sector-specific competition law is necessary, one may query whether EC-wide regulation of distribution agreements is beneficial, because national markets retain local particularities. As Dawson puts it: '[r]etailing in Europe remains . . . a response to local European culture . . . As the European political ideal progresses to encompass Central Europe so the pressures for divergence in consumer values and cultures increase, with a plurality of consumer cultures from Poland to Portugal. Many aspects of retailing show features of divergence rather than convergence.'[196] This conclusion is borne out by differences in the concentration levels of retail networks (small-scale retailers still prominent in the south of Europe, larger retail chains more prominent in the north), and by the fact that consumer preferences for different types of stores remain, and certain forms of retailing are more successful in certain countries.[197] The implication is that business strategies will differ between Member States and a successful competition policy should take this into consideration rather than straitjacket distribution agreements into a Euro-distribution template. From this perspective, should one not galvanise national competition laws instead of reforming European policy? In response, it may be argued that the Commission's new approach is sensitive to this diversity, in particular by creating a more flexible regulatory framework under the Block Exemption Regulation (thus allowing suppliers and distributors to adapt to local particularities), and by allowing National Competition Authorities to withdraw the benefit of the Block Exemption when anticompetitive effects materialise in their country. Institutionally, this partial decentralisation of competition law appears sufficient to cater for national diversity.

---

[194] *The Association of Convenience Stores v. OFT* [2006] CAT 36.
[195] House of Commons All Party Parliamentary Small Shops Group 'High Street Britain 2015' (2006).
[196] J. Dawson 'Retailing at Century End: Some Challenges for Management and Research' (2000) 10 *International Review of Retail, Distribution and Consumer Research* 119, 120.
[197] See generally Howe *Retailing*.

11

Institutions: who enforces competition law?

Contents

1. Introduction   *page* 392
2. The background to modernisation   395
   2.1 The Commission's perspective   395
   2.2 Europeanisation of national laws   401
   2.3 Regulation 1/2003   404
3. The new enforcement structure   409
   3.1 The Commission   409
   3.2 National Competition Authorities   414
   3.3 The European Competition Network   415
4. Side effects   419
   4.1 Juridification   420
   4.2 Europeanisation of economic governance   421
   4.3 The rebirth of national laws?   421
5. Private enforcement   424
   5.1 The protective scope of competition law statutes   424
   5.2 Which consumers should claim?   431
   5.3 Practical difficulties for claimants   434
   5.4 Private actions and modernisation   436
6. The challenges of institutional resettlement   438

1 Introduction

So far, we have observed one institution's enforcement of EC competition law: the European Commission. The discussion of controversial mergers in chapters 1 and 8 provided strong indications that the institutional makeup of the Commission plays a determining role in the final outcome. To some, this is evidence of the way EC competition law is corrupted to serve illegitimate aims, while to others, the deliberative process of decision-making is justified by the way competition law is embedded within the EC Treaty and should be used to serve the wider aims of the Community, not merely to preserve consumer welfare. While the political aspect of competition decisions came under severe scrutiny in the 1990s, in particular by German scholars and practitioners,[1] developments since that time within DG Competition (that segment of the Commission that carries out the operational aspect of law enforcement) have brought some changes to the nature of competition law enforcement. These include increased economic sophistication and growing attention to new theories of anticompetitive effects. These trends were caused by DG Competition interacting with US antitrust enforcers, and by the increased number of economists working in DG Competition, culminating in the creation of the post of Chief Competition Economist in 2003.[2]

The growth of economic analysis and expertise is analogous to that which occurred in the United States in the early 1960s, where increasing numbers of economists in the DOJ and FTC affected the direction of antitrust law, facilitating the success of the Chicago School views in the 1970s.[3] However, the increased reliance on economic theories by DG Competition is unlikely to have the same radical effects that a similar process had in the United States. This is because the Commission, not DG Competition, has the last word in controversial cases, and it has not embraced the economics-oriented approach of DG Competition, while US antitrust agencies have greater policy and operational independence. Thus, as we observed in chapters 2 to 4, while DG Competition is clearly committed to a 'more economics based approach', this has not led to the complete exclusion of public policy considerations in competition cases.

If one accepts the premise hinted at in the above paragraphs, that the composition of institutions enforcing the rules can shape the law, the upshot must be that if the institution in charge of competition enforcement is altered radically, the substantive interpretation and application of competition law will be affected. In this chapter we examine this claim by considering the potential impact of Regulation 1/2003, the so-called Modernisation Regulation, on competition law.[4] This Regulation makes three significant changes to the enforcement of Article 81.[5] The first is that Article 81(3) is

---

[1] For a concise review of the German criticisms, see M. Dreher 'Do We Need a European Competition Agency?' in G. Wilson and R. Rogowski (eds.) *Challenges to European Legal Scholarship: Anglo-German Essays* (London: Blackstone Press, 1996) pp. 95–101.

[2] See ch. 3.

[3] See generally M. A. Eisner *Antitrust and the Triumph of Economics* (Chapel Hill: University of North Carolina Press, 1991).

[4] Regulation 1/2003 on the Implementation of the Rules on Competition laid down in Articles 81 and 82 of the Treaty [2003] OJ L1/1. This is based on EC Commission *White Paper on Modernisation of the Rules Implementing Articles [81] and [82] of the EC Treaty* (28 April 1999) COM(99)101 final (hereinafter White Paper on Modernisation).

[5] Only the second of these changes affects Article 82, and there are no effects on the application of the ECMR even if the White Paper on Modernisation had suggested that the scope of the ECMR

deemed to have direct effect, and so can be applied by national institutions (namely competition authorities and courts).[6] The second is to 'Europeanise' competition law by requiring that National Competition Authorities apply EC competition law when reviewing business activities that affect trade between Member States.[7] This means that from 1 May 2004, when Regulation 1/2003 came into force, the Community moved from having one competition authority (DG Competition) to twenty-six (DG Competition plus all National Competition Authorities). The third change is that the system of *ex ante* notification and exemption is abolished (firms cannot notify agreements to the Commission or to National Competition Authorities to obtain an individual exemption).[8] It means that parties bear the burden of determining on their own whether the conduct they are planning complies with EC competition law, and risk fines if their assessment of their measures' competitive impact is wrong. Taken together, this means that enforcement of competition law changes in two ways: the identity of the enforcer (EC Commission, or National Competition Authorities, or national courts) and the nature of enforcement (*ex post* enforcement by the competition authorities, and claims for damages by parties injured by anticompetitive behaviour).

The background to Regulation 1/2003 is sketched in section 2. The Regulation is often presented as a revolutionary and welcome change.[9] A slightly different view is taken here. In section 2.1 we note that the Commission had been attempting to change its enforcement procedures since the early days of competition law enforcement, and so the Regulation is merely the final and decisive step towards a different policy model from that which had been put in place in 1962. In section 2.2 we note that even before Regulation 1/2003 there had been a trend among the Member States to redraft national competition laws in ways that mimic the EC rules. This development helps to explain why Member States accepted Regulation 1/2003: most had already anticipated the primacy of Community competition law in their national laws.[10] In section 2.3 we consider in more detail the key features of

---

should be widened to allow more joint ventures to be considered under the merger procedures (para. 79).

[6] Articles 1, 2 and 6 Regulation 1/2003. Some have questioned whether giving Article 81(3) direct effect by declaration is sufficient and have indicated that Treaty reform was necessary. See T. Wissmann 'Decentralised Enforcement of EC Competition Law and the New Policy on Cartels' (2000) 23 *World Competition* 123, 139–40; M. Gustafsson 'Some Legal Implications Facing the Realisation of the Commission White Paper on Modernisation of EC Antitrust Procedure and the Role of National Courts in a Post-White Paper Era' (2000) *Legal Issues of European Integration* 159.

[7] Article 3 Regulation 1/2003.

[8] German Monopolies Commission *Cartel Policy Change in the European Union?* 16 September 1999, para. 80 (available at www.monopolkommission.de).

[9] C.-D. Ehlermann 'The Modernisation of EC Antitrust Policy: A Legal and Cultural Revolution' (2000) 37 *Common Market Law Review* 537.

[10] J. Temple Lang 'Decentralised Application of Community Competition Law' (1999) 22 *World Competition* 3, noting that the developments at national level allowed the formulation of the Commission's proposals in the White Paper on Modernisation.

the Regulation and assess the degree to which this so-called revolution was necessary and sufficient to achieve more effective enforcement of EC competition law.[11] In section 3 we consider the new actors in the field of public enforcement, considering the roles of the Commission, National Competition Authorities and the European Competition Network. In section 4 we canvass three possible consequences of modernisation. The first is the elimination of politics from competition law, probably a desired consequence of modernisation. The second is the erosion of national sovereignty over economic policy: competition law is one tool that Member States may utilise to steer national industrial development, but modernisation reduces the possibilities of this; instead the application of EC competition law means all Member States must accept the Community's economic vision for the role of competition law. The third consequence is that Member States might react against these two developments and undermine the modernisation of competition law by applying other rules of law to govern industrial behaviour. Finally, in section 5 we consider what role private enforcement may play in EC competition law and suggest that although the ECJ's jurisprudence has only developed recently, the Court has started on the wrong foot, failing to filter meritorious and unmeritorious plaintiffs.

2 The background to modernisation

2.1 The Commission's perspective

Until 1 May 2004, competition law enforcement was based on Regulation 17/62.[12] The main rule that served to centralise enforcement in the hands of the Commission was in Article 9(1), which provided that the Commission was the only body able to grant exemptions under Article 81(3). It meant that while national courts and NCAs (the latter only if empowered to do so by national law) could apply Article 81(1), they had no competence once the firm had notified the agreement to the Commission. And once the Commission had granted an exemption, one could not apply stricter national competition laws to prohibit the agreement.[13] The effect of this was to incapacitate national courts and NCAs because they were unable to apply Article 81 in full.

---

[11] Those looking for a more upbeat assessment can consult: J. S. Venit 'Brave New World: The Modernisation and Decentralisation of Enforcement under Articles 81 and 82 of the EC Treaty' (2003) 40 *Common Market Law Review* 545.

[12] Council Regulation No. 17 of 6 February 1962, First Regulation Implementing Articles 85 and 86 of the Treaty [1962] JO L13/204.

[13] See Case 14/68 *Walt Wilhelm v. Bundeskartellamt* [1969] ECR 1. One difficulty with the Court's approach is that while it is clear that the grant of an individual exemption prevents the application of national law, the Court did not clarify whether the grant of negative clearance following a notification would prevent the application of national competition law, and the grant of a comfort letter was something that national courts might have regard to but did not bind them. Thus the Court's approach did not preclude the parallel application of EC and national competition law in all circumstances.

Moreover, the Commission's wide interpretation of Article 81(1) contributed to centralising enforcement in the Commission's hands. In chapter 2 we argued that the Commission interpreted a restriction of economic freedom as a restriction of competition. There we suggested that this was in line with an ordoliberal interpretation of the role of competition law. Another possible explanation of this reading is that it served the Commission's desire to centralise enforcement.[14] Had the Court in *Consten and Grundig* accepted the arguments in favour of a rule of reason, this would have made it possible for national courts to apply Article 81(1) more effectively because only agreements whose overall effect was anticompetitive would require assessment and exemption under Article 81(3). The effect of this could have led to significantly fewer notifications, less intervention by the Commission, and greater involvement by national authorities.[15] Moreover, it could have led to the application of stricter national competition law and to regulatory diversity among Member States. Instead, centralised enforcement would facilitate the application of a uniform competition law across the EC, something of value in a Community where historically Member States had supported cartels.[16] In fact, the Commission's White Paper on Modernisation in 1999 (which proposed the current regime) noted that the utility of centralised enforcement lay in the creation of a 'culture of competition' throughout the Community.[17] This serves as an extreme example of how an institution shaped the development of substantive law principles to favour its policy choices, opting for a controversial interpretation of Article 81(1) to facilitate the uniform application of EC competition law and the development of the internal market characterised by free competition.

Nothing in the Treaty required the institutional makeup established in 1962: centralisation was a conscious decision by the Member States.[18] Today the work of DG Competition might be taken for granted by many, but one must bear in mind that the powers which the Commission obtained under Regulation 17/62 were (and to a certain extent still are) unique.[19] The Commission can

---

[14] See I. S. Forrester 'The Modernisation of EC Antitrust Policy: Compatibility, Efficiency, Legal Security' in C.-D. Ehlermann and I. Atanasiu (eds.) *European Competition Law Annual 2000: The Modernisation of EC Antitrust Policy* (Oxford: Hart Publishing, 2001) pp. 77, 97; B. Van Houtte 'A Standard of Reason in EEC Antitrust Law: Some Comments on the Application of Parts 1 and 3 of Article 85' (1982–3) 4 *Northwestern Journal of International Law and Business* 497, 509; D. Waelbroeck 'Antitrust Analysis under Article 85(1) and Article 85(3)' 1997 *Fordham Corporate Law Institute* 693, 696 (Hawk ed. 1998).

[15] I. Forrester and D. Norall, 'The Laicization of Community Law: Self-Help and the Rule of Reason' (1984) 21 *Common Market Law Review* 11, 41.

[16] H. G. Schröter 'Cartelization and Decartelization in Europe, 1870–1995: Rise and Decline of an Economic Institution' (1996) 25 *Journal of European Economic History* 129.

[17] White Paper on Modernisation, Executive Summary, para. 4.

[18] Ehlermann 'Modernisation' pp. 538–40; G. Tesauro 'Some Reflections on the Commission's White Paper on the Modernisation of EC Antitrust Policy' in Ehlermann and Atanasiu *European Competition Law Annual 2000*.

[19] As suggested in chapter 7, there are certain other provisions that empower the Commission to regulate firms that are designed in a manner similar to competition laws.

implement competition policy largely independently of the Council and the Member States, and impose financial penalties on firms for breach of the rules. This contrasts with the traditional Community method whereby the EC legislates and leaves implementation and enforcement to Member States and national courts. However, centralised Commission enforcement faced two challenges: one practical and one political.

The practical challenge arose as early as one year after the introduction of Regulation 17/62: by then the Commission had received notifications of over 35,000 agreements.[20] It did not have the staff to address all these notifications in an efficient manner, and in many cases there were significant delays between notification and decision. As the years went on the number of notifications increased but DG Competition's resources did not. This had two consequences. First, competition enforcement was inefficient. For example, in the period 1994–7 the Commission managed to reach a formal decision in only 95 cases, while 1,755 cases were closed informally, so only approximately 5 per cent of cases received full treatment.[21] Moreover, at the time the White Paper on Modernisation was published, only nine notified agreements had been subsequently prohibited by the Commission between 1962 and 1999.[22] This small figure suggests that most agreements that were notified were largely innocuous and the Commission's resources were wasted. (In part of course this wastage was the Commission's own doing given its interpretation of Article 81(1).) Second, the Commission was unable to develop its enforcement priorities because it had to react to notifications. Again taking the 1994–7 period, the Commission received 1,022 notifications and 620 complaints about anticompetitive behaviour but commenced only 251 cases on its own initiative.[23] The Commission adopted a range of mechanisms to counter these problems, but none were deemed to be completely satisfactory. We can discern three phases in the Commission's attempts to reduce its workload while attempting to ensure the uniform application of EC competition law.

In the first phase, from the mid-1960s to the 1980s, the Commission deployed three strategies to reduce the time spent on notifications. First, it developed a de minimis rule whereby agreements of minor importance were deemed not to infringe Article 81.[24] This removed some agreements from its

---

[20] D. G. Goyder *EC Competition Law* 4th edn (Oxford: Oxford University Press, 2003) p. 41.

[21] EC Commission *Twenty-seventh Report on Competition Policy* (1998) pp. 337–8.

[22] Wissmann 'Decentralised Enforcement' p. 128. However, this number does not take into account how many conditional exemptions were granted, that is cases where the Commission required amendment to the agreement before approval. As we saw in chapter 3, this is a very powerful tool for the Commission.

[23] *Twenty-seventh Report on Competition Policy* (1998) pp. 337–8.

[24] The first was Commission *Notice on Agreements of Minor Importance* [1970] OJ C64/1. The current version is Commission *Notice on Agreements of Minor Importance which do not Appreciably Restrict Competition under Article 81(1) of the Treaty establishing the European Community (de minimis)* [2001] OJ C368/15.

reach, which also facilitated the Commission's policy of favouring cooperation among small and medium-sized firms. Second, it drafted Block Exemption Regulations (the first regulation was in 1967). These identified certain types of agreement and detailed which contract clauses were contrary to EC competition law and which were lawful. Parties whose agreements fell within the four corners of the Block Exemption were granted automatic exemption.[25] However, as discussed in chapter 10, the early Block Exemptions were highly prescriptive, so that firms wishing to benefit from these would have to rewrite their contract to ensure that it complied. Their commercial interests were compromised by the need for legal security.[26] Third, it developed procedures for settling notifications informally. These took the form of 'comfort letters' issued to firms that had notified their agreements. A comfort letter was designed to provide the firms with reassurance that their agreement did not infringe EC competition law or that it would probably benefit from an exemption. However, this practice was criticised for offering firms little comfort: the letter did not bind national courts or competition authorities so the firm still faced the risk of its agreement being challenged under national competition law.[27] Thus firms faced a stark choice: modify their agreement so as to fit within a highly prescriptive Block Exemption (and therefore potentially skew the commercial purpose of their agreement), or notify to the Commission and face uncertainty either because of delays should the Commission decide to issue a decision granting exemption under Article 81, or because the response took the form of a comfort letter. It is little wonder that some advised firms not to notify and to hope that the Commission would not challenge the agreement.[28] These measures failed in two respects: they did not reduce the Commission's workload, and they did not provide a workable system for firms.

In the early 1990s the Commission attempted a new route to reduce its workload, trying to deflect complainants from contacting DG Competition by galvanising enforcement at national level by involving NCAs and national courts.[29] It obtained support from the Court of First Instance, which ruled that the Commission did not have an obligation to investigate all complaints that it received, but could set its own enforcement agenda by taking up cases

---

[25] Regulation 1967/67 on the Application of Article 85(3) of the EC Treaty to Categories of Exclusive Distribution Agreements [1967] OJ L84/67.

[26] M. Siragusa 'Rethinking Article 85: Problems and Challenges in the Design and Enforcement of the Competition Rules' 1997 Fordham Corporate Law Institute 271, 282 (Hawk ed. 1998).

[27] Joined Cases 253/78 and 1 to 3/79 Procureur de la République and Others v. Bruno Giry and Guerlain SA and Others [1980] ECR 2327 paras. 12–13 and 18.

[28] C. Bright 'EU Competition Policy: Rules, Objectives and Deregulation' (1996) 16 Oxford Journal of Legal Studies 535.

[29] EC Commission Notice on Co-operation between National Competition Authorities and the Commission in applying Articles 85 and 86 of the EC Treaty [1997] OJ C313/3; EC Commission Notice on Co-operation between National Courts and the Commission in applying Articles 85 and 86 of the EC Treaty [1993] OJ C39/6.

that had Community interest.[30] The Commission thus indicated that it would focus its enforcement principally on cases that raised a new point of law and cases involving Article 86(1), while NCAs should consider cases where the effects are felt within their territories and those unlikely to qualify for exemption under Article 81(3).[31] However, these moves were unsuccessful: complainants were reluctant to seek remedies in the national courts (we explore the reasons in section 5 below), and NCAs were not as active as the Commission desired. According to the German Federal Cartel Office and the Federal Ministry of Economics, the following reasons explain why. First, the NCA could not apply Article 81 to controversial agreements which might require appraisal under Article 81(3) because only the Commission could at that time grant exemptions. This relegated the NCA to dealing with 'run of the mill' cases, a job that NCAs were not eager to take up. Second, in 1993, only a few Member States empowered the NCA to apply EC competition law, so decentralised application could not occur. And even in Germany, where the Federal Cartel Office had the power to apply Articles 81 and 82, the NCA preferred to apply German competition law.[32]

The third and final attempt to reduce workload occurred in the late 1990s and, in contrast to the two previous phases, the Commission engineered a substantive rather than a procedural change in policy: it reconsidered its system of Block Exemptions. As we noted above, the Block Exemptions that had been drafted so far were criticised for creating a 'straitjacket effect'; that is, parties had to make significant modifications to their contracts to 'fit' within the scope of a Block Exemption.[33] As we saw in chapter 10, the Commission embraced a radically different approach with the Block Exemption on vertical restraints in 1999. First, the Block Exemption has a market power screen whereby its application is restricted to firms below a given threshold. Second, the Block Exemption is significantly more permissive in that it contains only a brief list of agreements that are forbidden and gives the parties considerable latitude in designing agreements according to their commercial necessities. A similar approach has been applied to all other Block Exemptions. It had been suggested that this approach was likely to reduce the Commission's burden considerably as more firms would take advantage of the new Block

---

[30] Case T-64/89 *Automec Srl v. Commission* [1990] ECR II-2223 paras. 71–98. The Commission's decision not to take up a case is justiciable: see Case T-37/92 *Bureau Européen des Unions des Consommateurs and National Consumer Council v. Commission* [1994] ECR II-285, where the Commission's decision not to institute proceedings was quashed.

[31] *Notice on Cooperation between National Competition Authorities and the Commission* paras. 26 and 34–6.

[32] House of Lords Select Committee on the European Communities *Enforcement of Community Competition Rules* Session 1993–4, Memorandum by the Federal Cartel Office pp. 197–202.

[33] B. Hawk 'System Failure: Vertical Restraints and EC Competition Law' (1995) 32 *Common Market Law Review* 973.

Exemptions and so the number of notifications would fall.[34] However, it was impossible to judge the significance of this final effort on the Commission's workload because the Commission was eager to implement a more radical reform in the shape of Regulation 1/2003, which we consider more fully below. Nevertheless, the number of new cases between 1999 (the year of the first new-style Block Exemption) and 2004 (the final year when notifications were possible) shows a significant downward trend in the number of notifications when compared to the period 1989–98. In the latter period, the Commission received over 200 notifications a year, peaking at 368 notifications in 1995. In 1999, the number of notifications fell to 162, and in the first years of the new century, notifications fell significantly: 101 (in 2000); 94 (in 2001); 101 (in 2002); 71 (in 2003); and 21 (in 2004).[35] Moreover, the Commission had been working hard at reducing the backlog of cases: over 3,000 notifications were pending in 1980, but this figure had fallen to 1,204 in 1998 and 473 in 2004.[36] The Commission never clarified whether its limited resources would have remained insufficient even with this significant reduction in notifications that seems to have been caused, in part, by the new-style Block Exemptions.

The need to reform Regulation 17/62 resulted not only from what the Commission diagnosed as the inadequacy of the system of notification in an enlarging European Union. There was also a political challenge that arose in the mid-1990s soon after the Commission gained powers to regulate mergers. Certain Member States, in particular Germany, expressed concern about the infusion of politics in competition decisions, and the lack of transparency in the Commission's decisions.[37] German commentators began to demand a radical institutional reform: the creation of a European Cartel Office, operating independently of the EC Commission and able to deliver decisions based exclusively on legal principles.[38] This request is in line with the position taken in this chapter: that the institutional change can have an effect on the direction of competition policy, both in its priorities and in its interpretation of the rules.[39] While the proposal for a European Cartel Office was never likely to be implemented, in particular because few Member States backed the project and because of the legal difficulties in creating independent regulatory agencies at Community level, Regulation 1/2003 can be read as a response to

---

[34] W. Möschel 'Guest Editorial: Change of Policy in European Competition Law?' (2000) 37 *Common Market Law Review* 495.

[35] See EC Commission *Twenty-sixth Report on Competition Policy* (1996) pp. 341–2; *Thirty-third Report on Competition Policy* (2003) p. 63; *Thirty-fourth Report on Competition Policy* (2004) p. 63.

[36] EC Commission *Thirty-third Report on Competition Policy* (2003) p. 63.

[37] See Dreher 'Do We Need a European Competition Agency?' pp. 95–101, reporting strongly worded criticisms from the German Cartel Office.

[38] C.-D. Ehlermann 'Reflections on a European Cartel Office' (1995) 32 *Common Market Law Review* 471.

[39] See also S. Wilks and L. McGowan 'Disarming the Commission: The Debate over a European Cartel Office' (1995) 32 *Journal of Common Market Studies* 259.

these criticisms: by surrendering enforcement to NCAs, the Commission was sending a signal that the political meddling by the Commissioners would wane.[40] Moreover, given that the Commission's workload seemed to be steadily diminishing since the late 1990s, it can be argued that the political demand for reform was stronger than the practical arguments which were at the forefront of the White Paper on Modernisation. In sum, the Commission's portrayal of an overworked Directorate General for Competition, unable to engage in a proactive competition policy, was overstated.

2.2 Europeanisation of national laws

In 1962, only Germany had a credible system of competition law. However, this picture changed radically from the mid-1980s. At the same time that the Commission was attempting to decentralise enforcement, significant moves were afoot within the Member States: a number of them amended national laws, aligning them to the EC provisions.[41] By 1999 all Member States except Germany had adopted national competition laws that were similar to Articles 81 and 82 and eight out of fifteen Member States (Belgium, France, Germany, Greece, Italy, the Netherlands, Portugal and Spain) conferred express powers on National Competition Authorities to apply Articles 81 and 82.[42] They were not compelled to take either of these measures by the Community and their reasons for reform are varied. Some Member States (e.g. Italy and Ireland) had no national competition laws; some (e.g. Spain, Greece and Sweden) adopted such laws in anticipation of joining the EC; others had an unsatisfactory competition policy. Among this last camp was the United Kingdom, where reform of the rules had been raised several times but the law was changed only in 1998.[43] The old rules were perceived to be too weak, and the role of ministers in competition decisions too prominent.[44] While existing Member States 'Europeanised' national competition laws without any obligations stemming from Community law, the countries seeking to gain access to the EU were required to put into place a system to enforce competition law and used the EC

---

[40] At the time Regulation 1/2003 was agreed Germany objected to it and wished for a Regulation that allowed for the application of stricter national law, with Article 81 serving as a minimum standard, but it was unable to gain enough support to block the coming into force of the Regulation. See L. McGowan 'Europeanisation Unleashed and Rebounding: Assessing the Modernization of EU Cartel Policy' (2005) 12 *Journal of European Public Policy* 986, 995.

[41] I. Maher 'Alignment of Competition Law in the European Community' [1996] *Yearbook of European Law* 223.

[42] U. Zinsmeister, E. Rikkers and T. Jones 'The Application of Articles 85 and 86 of the EC Treaty by National Competition Authorities' [1999] *European Competition Law Review* 275.

[43] I. Maher 'Juridification, Codification and Sanction in UK Competition Law' (2000) 63 *Modern Law Review* 544.

[44] S. Eyre and M. Lodge 'National Tunes to a European Melody? Competition Law Reform in the UK and Germany' (2000) 7 *Journal of European Public Policy* 63.

model to achieve this.[45] The effect of all this legislative activity was that the norms of EC competition law were spreading into the national laws of the Member States even before Regulation 1/2003 was being discussed.

Some have suggested that the reason for this kind of spontaneous harmonisation was the emergence of an 'epistemic community' of legal professionals which cajoled Member States into updating national laws and bringing these into line with EC competition law.[46] Moreover, it has been suggested that pressure from business associations, like the Confederation of British Industry, the EU branch of the American Chamber of Commerce, the European Round Table of Industrialists and the German Business Association, also affected national governments and led to calls for the alignment of national competition law to the EC model.[47] Certainly businesses would favour this kind of harmonisation because it reduces their risks and costs by having one set of rules applied consistently. However, business did not obtain a complete harmonisation, rather a hybrid model: some rules (notably those relating to agreements under Article 81) were aligned but Member States retained their own merger rules, special sector-specific exemptions, and other competition provisions different from Articles 81 and 82.[48] Accordingly, it might be best to summarise these legislative developments as the result of a common competition culture across Europe rather than as harmonisation,[49] and yet this would be to ignore the significant efforts of some Member States to ensure that national law did not contradict EC competition law. In several national laws, interpretive provisions were inserted to guarantee a high degree of uniformity in the application of the law. Three examples will illustrate this. The Italian Act (which entered into force in 1990) sets out rules that are worded like Articles 81 and 82 (save the effect on trade requirement), and provides that if the practice in question is one to which Articles 81 and 82 apply, then only EC competition law is applicable.[50] This means that the Italian Act is only applicable in cases that have no effect on inter-state trade, and even in those

---

[45] See generally J. Fingleton, E. Fox and D. Neven *Competition Policy and the Transformation of Central Europe* (London: Centre for Economic Policy Research, 1996); F. Vissi 'Challenges and Questions around Competition Policy: The Hungarian Experience' (1995) 18 *Fordham International Law Journal* 1230.

[46] F. van Waarden and M. Drahos 'Courts and (Epistemic) Communities in the Convergence of Competition Policies' (2002) 9 *Journal of European Public Policy* 913.

[47] McGowan 'Europeanisation Unleashed' p. 998; H. Vedder 'Spontaneous Harmonisation of National (Competition) Laws in the Wake of the Modernisation of EC Competition Law' (2004) 1 *Competition Law Review* 5, 10.

[48] Eyre and Lodge 'National Tunes'; D. Hay 'Is More Like Europe Better? An Economic Evaluation of Recent Changes in UK Competition Policy' in N. Green and A. Robertson (eds.) *The Europeanisation of UK Competition Law* (Oxford: Hart Publishing, 1999).

[49] Vedder 'Spontaneous Harmonisation'.

[50] Article 1(1) Law No. 287 of 10 October 1990 (Gazzetta Ufficiale del 13 Ottobre 1990, n. 240). The NCA has powers to apply Articles 81 and 82 under Article 54(5) Law No. 52 of 6 February 1996 (Gazzetta Ufficiale del 10 Febbraio 1996, n. 34). English language texts are available at www.agcm.it/index.htm. For commentary, see M. Siragusa and G. Scassellati-Sforzolini 'Italian and EC Competition Law: A New Relationship' (1992) 29 *Common Market Law Review* 93.

instances when Italian law applies, the Act provides that the law should be interpreted by reference to legal principles established by the EC.[51] A softer harmonising approach is taken by the Irish competition legislation (which was first enacted in 1991) which merely provides in the long title of the Act that the legislation is designed to prohibit anticompetitive practices 'by analogy with Articles 81 and 82'.[52] An intermediate route was selected by the UK. After setting out prohibitions worded like Articles 81 and 82, the Competition Act 1998 incorporates a 'consistency principle' in section 60 whereby the decision-maker must ensure that the substantive application of UK law follows the legal principles established in the EC Treaty and by the European Court, and also has regard to decisions and statements made by the Commission.[53]

Another significant development in the Member States is that NCAs grew in prestige. It has been suggested that the creation of independent National Competition Authorities was to a large extent a symbolic exercise, demonstrating commitment to free market values by the state, with the expectation that the agencies would not be very active. But governments' expectations were confounded: several national competition agencies have become powerful and highly regarded enforcement institutions.[54] This is because the agencies were given enough political independence to be insulated from national politics and they developed technocratic expertise in law and economics, thereby narrowing the criteria they used to enforce the laws, further excluding political considerations. This development (uneven across the Member States) is significant because it served to embed the 'culture of competition' in the Member States, and it made the Member States support an enhanced profile for NCAs.

If we take these national developments together (alignment of national laws along the EC standard, conscious efforts to ensure that laws are interpreted in line with EC competition law, the growth of prestige and expertise of NCAs), the implementation of Regulation 1/2003 by the Council of Ministers becomes both possible and palatable. It is possible because the Community is able to trust NCAs: they have developed independently of government and are highly professionalised. In other words, they can be trusted to apply competition law in a non-political manner. Moreover, the spontaneous convergence of national laws minimised the risks of the application of stricter national competition law, so creating a level playing field of decentralised competition law enforcement was feasible. Implementation of Regulation 1/2003 is palatable, to Member States, because the NCAs had already been applying rules with a view to ensuring that the application of national law was comparable to that of EC law, so the Regulation would not be seen as revolutionary by the NCAs or

---

[51] Article 1(4) Law No. 287 of 10 October 1990.
[52] Irish Competition Act 2002.
[53] A. Robertson 'UK and EC Competition Laws: Will They Operate in Complete Harmony?' in Green and Robertson *Europeanisation*.
[54] S. Wilks and I. Bartle 'The Unanticipated Consequences of Creating Independent Competition Agencies' (2002) 25 *West European Politics* 148.

by the electorate. On the contrary, Regulation 1/2003 complements and strengthens the pre-existing Europeanisation of competition law. Some have seen these national developments more cynically, however, and argued that business support for the reforms was a tactical ploy designed to remove from the statute books strict national competition laws, and governmental acqui-escence to business demands was a means to rein in the power and activism of National Competition Authorities.[55]

2.3 Regulation 1/2003

So far we have seen that the key reforms in Regulation 1/2003 are the last chapter in a series of attempts by the Commission to decentralise enforcement and give DG Competition greater autonomy to set its enforcement priorities, and that the Commission was able to press for such radical change at least in part because of Europeanisation of competition law at national level, and possibly as a response to criticisms about the political meddling of the Commission in competition cases. We now query the extent to which these changes were necessary and sufficient to achieve a more efficient enforcement process by reviewing in detail the three key aspects of the reform: direct effect of Article 81(3); abolition of the notification/exemption system; and applica-tion of EC competition law over national law. In the White Paper on Modernisation three objectives were canvassed by which we might measure the effectiveness of the new system: rigorous enforcement of competition law; effective decentralisation and consistent enforcement; and easier administra-tive burdens on firms without sacrificing legal certainty.[56]

Declaring the direct effect of Article 81(3) was seen as necessary to galvanise NCAs, as this was the major stumbling block to decentralised enforcement. Their involvement would allow the Commission to increase its ability to take on cases of Community interest and become more proactive. The result is to multiply the number of agencies able to enforce EC competition law, leading to more rigorous enforcement. As we noted in chapters 2 and 4, this reform by itself was insufficient because of the risk that NCAs would reach divergent results by applying this provision in different ways, so that the Commission has had to intervene to narrow down the interpretation of Article 81(3). However, it remains to be seen whether all NCAs will apply the law in the same way or if divergences make competition law enforcement less predictable for firms, and thus less efficient. We consider additional mechanisms that the Commission has developed to avoid this risk below: suffice it to note that merely conferring direct effect was not sufficient. Moreover, as NCAs were already applying national competition law moulded upon the EC norms, it is not clear why

---

[55] H. Ullrich 'Harmonisation within the European Union' [1996] *European Competition Law Review* 178, 182.

[56] White Paper on Modernisation para. 42.

empowering them to apply EC competition law enhances the effectiveness of competition law enforcement.

Abolishing the notification procedure was seen as essential for the Commission to redeploy its resources and develop a proactive enforcement policy. This argument seems overstated, for several reasons. First, the backlog of notifications which the Commission had received was falling in the years leading up to Regulation 1/2003,[57] and more efficient management of the backlog could have eliminated the Commission's heavy workload. Second, the claim was not consistent: why does *ex ante* notification under the ECMR not cause comparable harm to the Commission's priorities?[58] Moreover, as we suggested earlier, the Commission's work priorities could have been streamlined automatically with the coming into force of the new Block Exemptions. Wernard Möschel, then Chairman of the German Monopolies Commission, suggested that the argument that the abolition of notification was necessary because of the Commission's limited resources was probably not intended to be taken seriously, referring to a comment by a Commission official that the proposed modernisation would go ahead even if the personnel in DG Competition was doubled.[59] Therefore it is wrong to say that the lack of direct effect of Article 81(3) and the notification procedure were jointly responsible for an ineffective and reactive competition policy. It was the Commission's inefficient management of notifications, combined with its unreasonably wide conceptualisation of what restricts competition under Article 81(1), that led to the system's ineffectiveness. This means that the reason why Regulation 1/2003 was implemented had little to do with abandoning a system that could not work, but rather the Commission was refusing to make the current system work well, and it wished to opt for a solution that brought EC antitrust law in line with a US-style enforcement policy of *ex post* application of competition law coupled with deterrence elements.[60] A substantive policy change is inherent in the procedural reform.

However, a working, efficient system of notification/exemption would have been worth keeping. If the number of notifications was bound to fall with the new-style Block Exemptions, the Commission would have been able to respond to parties entering into novel types of agreements where the ability to self-assess was more limited.[61] Administrative ease and legal certainty are more consistent with a limited scope for notification than with no notification system at all.

---

[57] *Twenty-fourth Report on Competition Policy* (1994) Annex III, reporting a drop from over 3,000 pending cases in 1980 to 1,052 in 1994; *Thirty-third Report on Competition Policy* (2003) p. 63, reporting a fall from 1,204 pending cases in 1998 to 473 in 2004.

[58] Möschel 'Guest Editorial'.   [59] Ibid. p. 496.

[60] This is the gist of the critique of the German Monopolies Commission *Cartel Policy Change in the European Union?*

[61] For similar arguments, see M. Paulweberer 'The End of a Success Story? The European Commission's White Paper on the Modernisation of European Competition Law' (2000) 23 *World Competition* 3, 36–41.

The third major plank of Regulation 1/2003, the application of EC competition law at national level and the exclusion of divergent national competition rules, can be said to be crucial to ensure coherent enforcement across the Member States. To a certain extent, one might query whether Regulation 1/2003 needed to make express provision for this because the vast majority of Member States had already aligned their competition laws with those of the Community, so substantive divergence resulting from the application of national law might have been minimal. Moreover, as we suggest below, a degree of substantive divergence might well be beneficial. Nevertheless, when the Commission originally proposed that EC competition law should apply exclusively (as in the Italian model summarised above), the larger Member States that had retained certain distinctive features in their national laws vetoed this, so a compromise was necessary.[62] The first two paragraphs of Article 3 provide as follows:

> 1. Where the competition authorities of the Member States or national courts apply national competition law to agreements, decisions by associations of undertakings or concerted practices within the meaning of Article 81(1) of the Treaty which may affect trade between Member States within the meaning of that provision, they shall also apply Article 81 of the Treaty to such agreements, decisions or concerted practices. Where the competition authorities of the Member States or national courts apply national competition law to any abuse prohibited by Article 82 of the Treaty, they shall also apply Article 82 of the Treaty.
>
> 2. The application of national competition law may not lead to the prohibition of agreements, decisions by associations of undertakings or concerted practices which may affect trade between Member States but which do not restrict competition within the meaning of Article 81(1) of the Treaty, or which fulfil the conditions of Article 81(3) of the Treaty or which are covered by a Regulation for the application of Article 81(3) of the Treaty. Member States shall not under this Regulation be precluded from adopting and applying on their territory stricter national laws which prohibit or sanction unilateral conduct engaged in by undertakings.

Article 3(1) contains an obligation to apply Articles 81 and 82 in parallel with national competition law (so there is no exclusive application of EC competition law). The first sentence of Article 3(2) is designed to ensure the supremacy of EC competition law in cases of parallel proceedings – thus stricter national law cannot be applied. So if an agreement does not infringe Article 81, stricter national competition law cannot apply to enjoin it. However, this was not enough to satisfy all Member States, and the French government in particular insisted on the second sentence of Article 3(2). This is because French competition law has two special rules that are stricter than Article 82. One, which we considered in chapter 10, is the abuse of economic dependence, and the

---

[62] H. Gilliams 'Modernisation: From Policy to Practice' (2003) 28 *European Law Review* 451, 463.

other is a rule that prohibits the sale of consumer goods at a price that is significantly below cost even when the firm has no dominance.[63] Back in 1993 this latter provision was the subject of the famous *Keck* ruling and Advocate General van Gerven explained the policy behind this prohibition:

> French experience in detecting and penalizing sales at a loss shows that this type of sale is primarily used as an offensive technique by the big distribution networks which are highly concentrated in France. Furthermore, most of the infringements committed against the prohibition of resale at a loss do not in practice involve newly-launched products but well-known consumer products (washing powder, coffee, drinks, jams) the usual price of which is known by consumers. It would therefore follow that the rules on resale at a loss ... are general rules for regulating the market which do not have as their purpose the regulation of trade flows between the Member States but are the result of a choice of economic policy, which is to achieve a certain level of transparency and fairness in conditions of competition.[64]

In *Keck* the law survived the challenge of the EC's internal market rules, and the French fought hard to preserve this law during the negotiations leading to Regulation 1/2003 even though it is seldom invoked.[65] Germany's competition law also embodies rules that regulate unilateral conduct more aggressively than Article 82, and Article 3(2) means that these rules too have survived Regulation 1/2003.[66] In so far as national competition laws are concerned then, Article 3(2) limits the possibility of divergence in so far as Article 81 is concerned, but tolerates stricter competition laws that apply to unilateral conduct.

The third paragraph of Article 3 goes further by allowing national laws that prohibit acts that constitute 'unfair trading practices' whether they are unilateral or not:[67]

> 3. Without prejudice to general principles and other provisions of Community law, paragraphs 1 and 2 do not apply when the competition authorities and the courts of the Member States apply national merger control laws nor do they preclude the application of provisions of national law that predominantly pursue an objective different from that pursued by Articles 81 and 82 of the Treaty.

This provision codifies the Court's views in two cases that arose from Germany where the Court held that a rule of German 'unfair competition law' (not

---

[63] Article L420–5 Code du Commerce.

[64] Joined Cases C-267/91 and C-268/91 *Criminal proceedings against Bernard Keck and Daniel Mithouard* [1993] ECR I-6097, Opinion of Advocate General Van Gerven of 28 April 1993, para. 3.

[65] The two provisions (abuse of economic dependence and the rule against below-cost selling) are applied in less than 1 per cent of the competition law cases. L. Idot 'France' in D. Cahill (ed.) *The Modernisation of EU Competition Law Enforcement in the EU* (Cambridge: Cambridge University Press, 2004) 151, 155.

[66] S. 19 Act Against Restraints of Competition, as amended 1 July 2005 (an English version of the Act is available at www.bundeskartellamt.de).

[67] Recital 9 Regulation 1/2003.

German antitrust law) could be applied by national courts to declare an agreement void even if that agreement was lawful for the purposes of Article 81. The background to the dispute is a rule in German unfair competition law whereby a selective distribution system can only be enforced between the manufacturer and the distributor if the distribution system is 'impervious'; that is, the manufacturer must ensure that no unauthorised distributor can sell the goods in question. If the manufacturer fails to ensure that the distribution system is impervious so that the authorised distributors face competition from unauthorised distributors, the former are no longer bound by the sale restrictions in their contract. This rule is designed to protect the distributors who are subject to the selective distribution agreement. The rule is based on fairness considerations: distributors in a selective distribution network have onerous obligations (e.g. to have attractive premises and expert staff) which means they must set high retail prices to recoup costs. It would be unfair on them if the manufacturer were then to sell the same goods to members outside the network who can set lower retail prices because they have no comparable obligations. The ECJ held that the criterion of 'imperviousness' was irrelevant for the application of Article 81, but that national courts could still apply this criterion under national law to declare the agreement void.[68] This means that when there is a 'diagonal' conflict (that is, a conflict between EC competition law and a national rule of law that is not based on national competition law) the national law rule can apply to declare a contract invalid even if the contract is not void under Article 81.[69] To give an example based on English law, if two parties enter into an agreement which is lawful under Article 81, but void under national contract law because of economic duress, then the national rule applies to render the agreement unenforceable.

The difficulty in applying Article 3(3) is to determine which rules of national law are not to be considered 'competition law' rules. The examples used here are borderline: economic duress could be compared to the abuse of a dominant position by a situational monopoly, so perhaps similar policies animate that doctrine; the German example is more borderline (the rule can be rationalised on the basis of free-rider arguments familiar to competition lawyers), and the ECJ seems to have assumed that national law could apply because the rule in question did not fall within the statute on what in Germany is called 'cartel law'. Moreover, the borderline between what is competition law and what is not might be the subject of greater controversies in the future, especially as the current vogue is to see EC competition law as designed to promote 'consumer welfare'. Could this mean that rules of national consumer law can no longer apply to regulate agreements if these agreements are lawful under Article 81?

---

[68] Case C-41/96 *VAG-Händlerbeirat eV v. SYD-Consult* [1997] ECR I-3123 paras. 12–14.
[69] R. Wesseling 'The Commission White Paper on Modernisation of EC Antitrust Law: Unspoken Consequences and Incomplete Treatment of Alternative Options' [1999] *European Competition Law Review* 420, 429–30.

Alternatively, can Member States circumvent the primacy of EC competition law by drafting stricter national laws and labelling them 'consumer protection' or 'unfair practices' laws? If the latter, one might be excused for questioning whether the effects of these exceptions to the primacy of EC competition law are potentially so extensive as to frustrate the goal of excluding the application of national competition laws.

Taking all that has been said in this section together, it is debatable whether Regulation 1/2003 was necessary to achieve efficient enforcement and that it will actually lead to more effective enforcement. More generally, in the White Paper on Modernisation the Commission presented four other options for reform but none were given any serious consideration.[70] One option, for example, which had been suggested by the German competition authorities, was to empower NCAs to grant exemptions, so that the burden of the notification/exemption system was shared. This was rejected in the White Paper because the allocation of notifications could be troublesome and new Member States might struggle.[71] However, these two problems also affect the system that has been put in place, as we will see below when we look at case allocation. This option would have served to resolve the Commission's overload and allowed it to pursue an active competition policy while guaranteeing parties who were bona fide uncertain as to the legality of their agreement a better opportunity of having this reviewed and exempted. Another option, reading Article 81(1) in a more economically enlightened manner, as the Court of Justice had repeatedly suggested, was rejected because it would have rendered Article 81(3) redundant, although as we noted in chapter 2 this argument is not convincing. On the contrary, had the Commission begun to interpret Article 81(1) so as to catch only agreements truly likely to harm economic welfare, fewer parties would feel the need to notify and obtain exemptions. However, as Rein Wesseling put it, the Commission was 'married to one idea' and paid scant attention to alternative reform projects, avoiding any meaningful debate over alternative solutions to achieve more effective enforcement of the law.[72]

3 The new enforcement structure

3.1 The Commission

The major implication of modernisation is that the Commission has freed itself from the burden of reviewing harmless agreements and is capable of setting its priorities. It intends to focus upon serious infringements (e.g. cartels) and enforce state aid rules with more rigour. This could be a significant change. In the period 1989–96 the Commission had begun 'own initiative' enforcement

---

[70] Wissmann 'Decentralised Enforcement' pp. 149–53.
[71] White Paper on Modernisation paras. 58–62.
[72] R. Wesseling 'The Draft Regulation Modernising the Competition Rules: The Commission is Married to One Idea' (2001) 26 *European Law Review* 357.

action in only 13 per cent of the cases; the rest of its activity was reactive (the result of either complaints or notifications).[73] The Commission's new policy priority is complemented by greater enforcement powers. First, Regulation 1/2003 empowers the Commission to carry out unannounced inspections in private homes as well as company headquarters; it may seal premises and offices to ensure evidence is not destroyed, ask for oral explanations and even, if the parties consent, carry out interviews.[74] It has been suggested that the increase in investigatory powers that the Council granted to the Commission is a tacit endorsement of the Commission's commitment to prioritise cartel enforcement.[75] Second, the Commission has been increasing the level of fines set for cartel infringements,[76] a policy which has been backed by the ECJ.[77] Third, as we saw in chapter 9, it has imitated the United States in offering leniency to firms that 'confess' to being party to an anticompetitive agreement. While the enforcement powers and the penalties are not as significant as those provided for in the United States and in some EC Member States (e.g. criminal penalties are available for infringements of UK competition law) they provide a coherent shape to the Commission's new enforcement policy.[78] As we suggested above, it is arguable that a major reason for Regulation 1/2003 is to shift the Commission's enforcement policy towards a US-style model based on deterrence. This, rather than the inadequacy of the old system, is a better explanation for Regulation 1/2003. To a certain extent, this change in enforcement policy pre-dates the reform. In a major speech the competition Commissioner, Neelie Kroes, noted that in the four years after 2001 (that is, three years before the coming into force of Regulation 1/2003) the Commission adopted thirty-one decisions against cartels, imposing fines of nearly 4 billion euros. These numbers amount to 35 per cent of all cartel cases since 1969.[79] Thus the deterrence-based model had already been embraced while the Commission was supposedly locked into the inadequacies of Regulation 17/62.

---

[73] EC Commission *Twenty-sixth Report on Competition Policy* (1996) pp. 341–2.

[74] Procedures fall outside the scope of this book. For an outline, see D. Chalmers, C. Hadjemmanuil, G. Monti and A. Tomkins *European Union Law: Text and Materials* (Cambridge: Cambridge University Press, 2006) pp. 940–57. For greater detail, see C. S. Kerse and N. Kahn *EC Antitrust Procedure* 5th edn (London: Sweet & Maxwell, 2005); L. Ortiz Blanco (ed.) *EC Competition Procedure* 2nd edn (Oxford: Oxford University Press, 2006).

[75] Venit 'Brave New World' p. 568.

[76] EC Commission *Guidelines on the Method of Setting Fines Imposed Pursuant to Article 23(2)(a) of Regulation No. 1/2003* (2006) (available at http://ec.europa.eu/comm/competition/antitrust/legislation/fines.html), which increase the amount of fines to enhance the deterrent effect of competition law.

[77] E.g. Joined Cases C-189/02P, C-202/02P, C-205/02P – C-208/02P and C-213/02P *Dansk Rørindustri A/S and Others v. Commission*, judgment of 28 June 2005 upholding the Commission's fine even though it deviated from the fining Guidelines.

[78] EC Commission 'A Proactive Competition Policy for a Competitive Europe' COM(2004)213 final para. 4.1.

[79] N. Kroes 'The First Hundred Days' speech, 7 April 2005, available at http://ec.europa.eu/comm/competition/index_en.html.

In addition to acting as a cartel buster, the Commission also has three major additional tasks to perform. The first is to dictate the development and direction of EC competition law.[80] This is accomplished by the publication and renewal of soft law instruments and Block Exemptions. The second task is to assist firms that are planning agreements but are uncertain about the competition law implications, and the third is to monitor the performance of NCAs. We have seen examples of the first task in earlier chapters, and we consider the second task here and the third in sections 3.2 and 3.3 below.

Recall that one major gap in the new system is that parties are unable to notify agreements *ex ante*. While the notification/exemption system was not perfect (it was time consuming and laden with uncertainty) it offered parties some legal security, which they now lack. As we suggested above, if the notification system had been managed efficiently, there would have been no case for abandoning it. It is amusing that the Commission itself recognised the value of *ex ante* notification in a recent case before the CFI. The parties had been granted an exemption in 2003 but were dissatisfied because it was not granted for a long enough period, so they appealed to the CFI to have the Commission's exemption quashed, principally on the grounds that the Commission had misinterpreted Article 81(1). One of the Commission's arguments was that the parties should be content with the exemption because it gave them 'legal certainty' which they would have to forgo if the appeal was successful because Regulation 1/2003 brought to an end the system of prior notification.[81] This is an extraordinary (if not scandalous) admission that a system of *ex ante* regulation brings benefits to some kinds of agreement, but it has now been lost. It also reveals that the Commission is still aware that firms find it next to impossible to understand what constitutes an anticompetitive agreement under Article 81(1), so the claim that the absence of a notification system can be traded off because parties have enough legal certainty to assess for themselves whether the agreement complies with Article 81 is one which even the Commission now doubts. Moreover, in this case, presumably decided while the Commission was busy writing its Guidelines on the interpretation of Article 81(3), the CFI disagreed with the Commission's own assessment of what is meant by a restriction of competition. So even the principal enforcer is still struggling to work out what triggers Article 81(1). This is in striking contrast to what the Commission was saying in the White Paper on Modernisation about the increased degree of legal certainty that has now emerged that would allow firms to plan. The upshot is that firms will require ever increasing legal and economic advice

---

[80] Based on Article 85 EC and Case C-344/98 *Masterfoods Ltd v. HB Ice Cream Ltd* [2000] ECR I-11369 para. 46.

[81] Case T-328/03 *O2 (Germany) GmbH & Co. OHG v. Commission*, judgment of 2 May 2006, para. 42, discussed above at pp. 37–9.

before implementing agreements, and this favours larger firms with greater economic resources.[82]

The Council and the Commission responded to the risk of legal uncertainty in two ways: by attempting to clarify the substantive meaning of Article 81, and by creating procedures that allow for a substitute to *ex ante* notification. The substantive clarification of Article 81 can be witnessed by the fact that the Commission used the final years of Regulation 17/62 to publish a vast number of individual exemptions in a range of markets so that parties and NCAs are aware of how Article 81(3) operates.[83] In addition, it sought to restrict the scope of Article 81(3) so that public policy considerations are excluded from its ambit. These are designed to make the application of Article 81 more predictable and to aid business in a system without *ex ante* notifications. Nevertheless these two measures are unlikely to be of help when parties engage in practices not foreseen by the guidelines. Moreover, because competition cases are intimately fact specific, it has been argued that general guidelines and precedents are unlikely to provide sufficient legal security to those planning an agreement.[84]

At a procedural level, Regulation 1/2003 provides three additional substitutes for the now defunct notification system. The first is in Article 9 under which firms are able to offer 'commitments' to the Commission whereby they promise to modify their behaviour when the Commission intends to take action against them. This allows the parties to negotiate a solution with the Commission after the agreement has been implemented and investigated by the Commission. Thus, there is still scope for some form of consultation with the Commission. However, the paradox is that the Commission has settled highly controversial cases where a formal decision would perhaps have been preferable for the sake of transparency to indicate the nature of the Commission's policy.[85] Moreover, as with comfort letters, commitment decisions do not appear to bind National Competition Authorities.[86] Nevertheless, the Article 9 route seems to be the functional equivalent of a notification/exemption system.[87]

---

[82] Gilliams 'Modernisation' p. 472; F. Montag and A. Rosenfeld 'A Solution to the Problems? Regulation 1/2003 and the Modernization of Competition Procedure' (2003) *Zeitschrift für Wettbewerbsrecht* 106 (also available at: www.freshfields.com/practice/comptrade/publications/pdf/Regulation12003.pdf).

[83] E.g. *Simulcasting* [2003] OJ L107/58; *Austrian ARA* [2004] OJ L75/59; *CECED* [2000] OJ L187/47; *UEFA Champions League* [2003] OJ L291/25.

[84] Möschel 'Guest Editorial'.

[85] Case COMP/37.214 *Joint Selling of the Media Rights to the German Bundesliga* [2005] OJ L134/46; Case COMP/39.116 *Coca-Cola* [2005] OJ L253/21.

[86] Recital 22 Regulation 1/2003. But see Montag and Rosenfeld 'A Solution to the Problems?' p. 152, who argue that national courts should be bound.

[87] See L. Ritter and W. D. Braun, *European Competition Law: A Practitioner's Guide* 3rd edn (The Hague: Kluwer Law International, 2004) p. 227.

The second substitute for *ex ante* notification is Article 10, which is worth citing in full:

> Where the Community public interest relating to the application of Articles 81 and 82 of the Treaty so requires, the Commission, acting on its own initiative, may by decision find that Article 81 of the Treaty is not applicable to an agreement, a decision by an association of undertakings or a concerted practice, either because the conditions of Article 81(1) of the Treaty are not fulfilled, or because the conditions of Article 81(3) of the Treaty are satisfied. The Commission may likewise make such a finding with reference to Article 82 of the Treaty.

The preamble suggests that the intention behind this provision is to clarify the law, in particular when the parties engage in practices for which there is no precedent. Thus, the 'public interest' is to promote legal certainty and to ensure coordinated enforcement.[88] However, this phrase is quite elastic and may allow the Commission to protect agreements which benefit the economy or on other public policy grounds. Having attempted to seal off the use of Article 81(3) as a tool for public policy, the Commission might reintroduce this risk with Article 10 of Regulation 1/2003.[89]

The third substitute is a suggestion in the Regulation's preamble that the Commission is still able to offer informal guidance to parties where a case gives rise to 'genuine uncertainty'.[90] Such informal guidance is reminiscent of the 'comfort letters' that the Commission would issue, and while the Commission has emphasised that this guidance would be provided only when the legal issues are novel and unresolved and of Community interest, the guidance, like comfort letters, does not bind national courts or competition authorities.[91] This procedure allows for continued dialogue between industry and the regulator but it is a further recognition that a shift to an *ex post* enforcement policy needs to be balanced by an effective *ex ante* notification system.

It remains to be seen whether these methods of granting some form of guidance are going to be workable. They present three challenges. The first is whether the guidance is sufficient for parties. The second is the extent to which they can be used to negotiate or impose upon parties obligations that have nothing to do with the anticompetitive effects but are designed to open markets. As noted in chapter 4, the first Article 9 settlement on football broadcasting rights raised questions as to the relevance of cultural and industrial policy. The third risk is whether the Commission's workload might be

---

[88] See also Draft Regulation implementing Articles 81 and 82 EC [2000] OJ C365E/284, Explanatory Memorandum Article 10.

[89] Montag and Rosenfeld 'A Solution to the Problems?' p. 115, who note that the European Parliament was in favour of interpreting Article 10 as a public policy measure to achieve wider Community ambitions.

[90] Recital 38 Regulation 1/2003.

[91] Commission *Notice on Informal Guidance relating to Novel Questions concerning Articles 81 and 82 of the EC Treaty that Arise in Individual Cases* [2004] OJ C101/78 paras. 5, 24 and 25.

affected so that these procedures remove resources from its central activity, fighting hard-core cartels.

3.2 National Competition Authorities

National Competition Authorities are expected to take on more cases than the Commission, and the UK government suggests this places NCAs in the 'driving seat for much competition law enforcement'.[92] In particular they will address local competition law infringements where they have a comparative advantage because of their familiarity with the local markets and are better placed to regulate national markets than the Commission.[93] The degree to which this division of labour will provide effective enforcement depends on three variables: whether the Commission has managed to save resources with Regulation 1/2003; whether enforcement among the twenty-six competition authorities can be coordinated effectively; and whether NCAs enforce competition law with equal determination. On the first point, we have seen above that the Commission has considerable responsibilities under the new system. We consider the second variable, coordination, in section 3.3 below. It is too soon to make any observations about the third variable, but some preliminary observations may be attempted. First some NCAs are less politically independent than others,[94] second some have fewer resources and less expertise (e.g. it was reported that the seven members of the Belgian competition authority had resigned in protest because resources were woefully inadequate),[95] and third, as a result, some will have more prestige than others. The upshot is that enforcement may be more intensive and sophisticated in states with stronger and more well-resourced competition authorities (e.g. the UK, Germany and Italy) and less so in states where competition authorities lack the resources or expertise to enforce competition law actively. In less than two years since the operation of the network began differences were already beginning to appear. Between 1 May 2004 and 30 June 2006, the three busiest competition authorities were the French (ninety-four cases), the German (sixty-four cases) and the Dutch (forty-four cases); while twelve Member States' NCAs initiated fewer than ten cases.[96] Diversity in the composition of NCAs is acknowledged under Regulation 1/2003 so long as the NCA is able to carry out the tasks under the Regulation.[97]

---

[92] Department of Trade and Industry 'Modernisation – A Consultation of the Government's Proposals for Giving Effect to Regulation 1/2003 and for Re-alignment of the Competition Act 1998' (April 2003).

[93] Temple Lang 'Decentralised Application'.

[94] A. Riley 'EC Antitrust Modernisation: The Commission Does Very Nicely – Thank you!' [2003] *European Competition Law Review* 659–61, suggesting that there is less political independence in the new Member States' authorities.

[95] Forrester 'Modernisation' p. 106.

[96] Statistics are complied at the ECN's homepage: http://ec.europa.eu/comm/competition/antitrust/ecn/ecn_home.html.

[97] Article 35 Regulation 1/2003.

Whether this diversity will continue and whether it can cause damage to the Community interests remains to be seen.

Even if NCAs are equal in terms of resources, however, it may be questioned whether creating twenty-five additional authorities can lead to more effective enforcement. It has been suggested that difficult cases always require lengthy appraisal whether at national or Community level, so that the application of competition law by NCAs is not likely to lead to faster or cheaper enforcement at least in the short run. Difficult cases in front of inexperienced authorities can also lead to diverging interpretations; moreover, the NCAs are entitled to set diverse enforcement priorities. This suggests that under the new system there may not be, at least for a transitional period, a level playing field for firms.[98]

Moreover, the involvement of NCAs is subject to one further uncertainty even in the easy cases of a flagrant breach of competition law. In order for the application of EC competition law to be engaged, the practice must affect trade between Member States. It follows that the anticompetitive effects will occur in the Member State where the NCA is located and in other Member States as well. However, the penalties that the NCA can impose seem to be restricted to effects felt in its territory, and the NCA has powers to enforce the law only against firms located in its territory. If so, this would risk undermining the rigorous enforcement of EC competition law because the NCA would not be able to impose a fine reflecting the entire harm of the infringement.[99] The alternative, that once the first NCA reaches a decision, the other NCAs where the agreement causes harmful effects will institute their own proceedings, may violate the firm's rights (in breach of the *ne bis in idem* rule which prevents multiple prosecution and punishment for the same offence),[100] but moreover seems a highly inefficient use of resources. It remains to be seen whether the European Competition Network will elaborate solutions to this issue.

3.3 The European Competition Network

The European Competition Network (hereinafter the ECN) was established in 2002, when Regulation 1/2003 was agreed.[101] The ECN is not an administrative body, but a forum where the Commission and NCAs meet to carry out two formal tasks: allocating cases among the NCAs (coordination of enforcement) and ensuring the coherent application of the rules (coordination of results).[102]

---

[98] Gilliams 'Modernisation', noting the transitional problems.

[99] See further R. Smits 'The European Competition Network: Selected Aspects' (2005) 32 *Legal Issues of Economic Integration* 175, 184–8.

[100] W. Wils 'The Principle of "Ne Bis in Idem" in EC Antitrust Enforcement: A Legal and Economic Analysis' (2003) 26 *World Competition* 131.

[101] Council of the European Union, Joint Statement of the Council and the Commission on the Functioning of the Network of Competition Authorities, 10 December 2002, available at http://register.consilium.eu.int; document number 15435/02 ADD1.

[102] A. Schaub 'Continued Focus on Reform: Recent Developments in EC Competition Policy' 2001 *Fordham Corporate Law Institute* 31 (Hawk ed. 2002).

These two kinds of coordination are necessary because Regulation 1/2003 did not establish a system whereby the decision of one NCA binds others. Instead, to use the Commission's jargon, there is a system of 'parallel competences'.[103] This means that, in theory, an agreement could be reviewed independently by more than one NCA and each could reach a different result. To avoid this outcome, which would frustrate the aims of the reform programme, the Commission expects that cases can be allocated via the ECN and has published a prescriptive notice to regulate case allocation, and there are safeguards to ensure rules are applied consistently. We consider these two forms of coordination in turn.

Coordination of enforcement is provided for in the Notice on Cooperation within the Network of Competition Authorities. The basic principle is that each case should be taken up by either a single NCA, or several NCAs acting jointly, or the Commission.[104] This leads to one decision per case and avoids inconsistent outcomes (but, as suggested above, it is not clear whether from a deterrence perspective the NCA is able to impose fines for all the anticompetitive effects). The reason why a system of exclusive competences was not established is probably because Member States wanted to remain free to apply competition law independently of other NCAs.[105] This is confirmed by the political declaration establishing the ECN, where, while Member States agree to cooperate with other NCAs and the Commission on the basis of 'equality, respect and solidarity', they also declare the independence of each NCA.[106]

In practice, the ECN will not operate to allocate cases, but to reallocate them, because a competition case will first be taken up by one NCA whose first duty is to notify the Commission and other NCAs that it has commenced an investigation.[107] Only at that moment might a case be reallocated, and this can occur for two reasons: first, the NCA itself seeks reallocation (e.g. because it realises that there is another NCA that is better placed or because it wishes to cooperate with another NCA); second, another NCA or the Commission might request that it address the case in question. In order to decide which NCA should act, it is determined which NCA is 'well placed' on the basis of three criteria: the effects of the infringement in question occur in its territory; it is capable of issuing an appropriate remedy; it is able to obtain the relevant

---

[103] Commission *Notice on Cooperation within the Network of Competition Authorities* [2004] OJ C101/43 (hereinafter Notice NCA) para. 1.

[104] Ibid. para. 5.

[105] The most that was agreed is that if one NCA is acting, then other NCAs and the Commission are entitled to use that fact to reject a complaint on the same infringement. Article 13 Regulation 1/2003.

[106] Joint Statement of the Council and the Commission para. 7.

[107] Article 11(3) Regulation 1/2003 (NCA's duty to inform the Commission); Article 11(2) (Commission's obligation to inform other NCAs) and Notice NCA paras. 16–17 (NCA's duty to inform the ECN).

information.[108] The Commission is deemed to be better placed than NCAs when the agreements have effects covering more than three Member States or when the case raises issues of Community interest or a new legal issue.[109] Cooperation among NCAs continues once the case has been allocated in that information that NCAs have about the firms under investigation may be exchanged.[110]

While these efforts to coordinate enforcement are designed to make allocation predictable,[111] certain potential risks arise. First, there is a risk of under-enforcement: a well-placed competition authority may take no action, either because the anticompetitive behaviour in question is seen to be in the national interest (e.g. an export cartel) so the NCA refuses to prohibit it, or because, while willing to address the issue, it lacks resources to take action. Second, there is a risk of duplication of enforcement: if two or more NCAs want to act on the same infringement, there is nothing in the ECN procedures that establishes a formal way to allocate a case to one NCA. The risk for a firm is that its actions are evaluated in an uncoordinated manner, with different results in different Member States.[112] However, some have suggested that parallel enforcement is incompatible with the principle that penalties cannot be imposed twice for the same infringement, so that while it is possible for NCAs to investigate a case jointly, only one NCA is entitled to impose a penalty.[113] These risks of duplication and under-enforcement should make one query the degree to which Regulation 1/2003 can lead to a more effective application of EC competition law.[114] The Commission had predicted that reallocation would be rare and it reported that in the 180 new cases in 2005 there were few reallocations (without unfortunately reporting the number of reallocations).[115]

In contrast to the informal 'network' structure put into place to ensure coordination of enforcement, the process for coordination of outcomes is hierarchical, because while there is little to ensure cooperation among the NCAs, the Commission controls the decision-making practice of each NCA. First, an NCA may not reach a decision that is contrary to a Commission decision.[116] Second, before adopting a decision, the NCA must send a draft to the Commission, and at this stage the Commission may make comments or take the drastic step of removing the case from the NCA and initiate proceedings itself.[117] Formally, there seems to be more scope for the ECN to comment on case allocation than on the substantive application of the law. In fact, the

---

[108] Notice NCA para. 8.   [109] Ibid. paras. 14 and 15.

[110] Article 12 Regulation 1/2003; Notice NCA paras. 26–30.

[111] Joint Statement of the Council and the Commission para. 13.

[112] See S. Bammer 'Concurrent Jurisdiction under Regulation 1/2003 and the Issue of Case Allocation' (2005) 42 *Common Market Law Review* 1383, 1402–8.

[113] Wils 'Principle of "Ne Bis in Idem"'.

[114] In 2004 reallocation occurred in fewer than 1 per cent of 298 cases. EC Commission *Thirty-fourth Report on Competition Policy* (2004) para. 105.

[115] EC Commission *Thirty-fifth Report on Competition Policy* (2005) paras. 210–14.

[116] Article 16(2) Regulation 1/2003.   [117] Article 11(4)–(6) Regulation 1/2003.

ECN seems to be sidelined by provisions that certain anticipated decisions may be referred (by an NCA or a Member State) to the Advisory Committee.[118] Thus the ECN seems to have little role to play in the development of substantive law, where the Commission plays a monitoring role.

The system affords the possibility of coordination to a much greater extent than the powers available to federal competition authorities in the United States.[119] This might be necessary given the relative inexperience of certain Member States with competition law, although it does undermine the Commission's claim in the White Paper on Modernisation that there is a 'culture of competition' in the EU. Arguably such control mechanisms would be less relevant if this culture were better embedded in national laws. In fact in 2005 the Commission said that the ECN was serving as a means to create a competition culture among the Network members.[120] Moreover, the Commission's determination to control the results that NCAs reach stands in contrast to the assertion in the White Paper on Modernisation that there is 'abundant case law, clearly established basic principles and well-defined details'.[121]

A more general reflection is warranted about the functioning of the ECN, and that is to consider what assumptions underlie networks and how far the Commission has designed a system with the potential to contribute to delivering effective enforcement. On one level, it has been argued that a well-functioning network requires three conditions: mutual trust and cooperation; professionalism; and a common regulatory philosophy.[122] Judged against these standards, the ECN is not perfect. While there is some degree of trust (the members are committed, at a political level, to the idea of one NCA per case), the Commission's right to veto NCAs by taking a case away from them and the ability of one NCA to institute independent proceedings should it disagree with another NCA point to a lack of complete trust among the members of the ECN. There is a good degree of cooperation (especially with the provisions for exchanging information) but the Commission seems to retain its role as principal. All NCAs are increasingly professionalised, although Regulation 1/2003 does not require that an NCA should be independent of government control, which could weaken the role of the network. The Commission believes that there is a common regulatory philosophy after forty years of centralised competition law enforcement; however, as we said before, this statement is not consistent with its re-interpretation of

---

[118] Article 14(7) Regulation 1/2003; Notice NCA paras. 61–2.

[119] T. Calvani 'Devolution and Convergence in Competition Enforcement' [2003] *European Competition Law Review* 415, 422; P. J. Slot 'Is Decentralisation of Competition Enforcement Dangerous? Drawing Lessons from the US Experience' 2001 *Fordham Corporate Law Institute* 101 (Hawk ed. 2002).

[120] EC Commission *Thirty-fifth Report on Competition Policy* (2005) para. 204.

[121] White Paper on Modernisation para. 3.

[122] G. Majone 'The Credibility Crisis of Community Regulation' (2000) 38 *Journal of Common Market Studies* 273, 297–8.

Article 81(3). While the conditions for a successful network might not be perfect, it may be suggested that the presence of the ECN itself will make each NCA accountable to the others and eager to ensure the success of the network and the effective enforcement of competition law. Thus the network might strengthen itself as the members have an incentive to maintain their reputation in the eyes of their colleagues.[123] Trust, cooperation and a common regulatory philosophy can emerge through the working of the network.[124] However, one flaw in the Commission's design for the ECN is its excessive zeal in holding NCAs to account, which may lead to too much homogeneity in the performance of NCAs.[125] This criticism is based on the fact that the ECN gives the Commission hard law powers to control the NCAs when a less rigid scheme of accountability would be preferable, so as to allow a degree of regulatory diversity. It has been suggested, for example, that the ECN could function as a forum for comparing and evaluating the performance of the NCAs and that this would allow each NCA to have greater autonomy while creating a system where, incrementally, the methods of enforcement can converge by the dissemination of 'best practices'. Moreover, diversity may be necessary as conditions of each market vary, requiring diverse regulatory efforts. In the latter case, it is worth remembering that one argument for Regulation 1/2003 is that NCAs have a better understanding of local markets. This should imply greater autonomy when such markets are regulated, and less oversight by the Commission.

4 Side effects

We noted some of the practical challenges that the current system of enforcement faces above. We suggested that Regulation 1/2003, far from being necessary and revolutionary, was part of an incremental re-orientation of competition law enforcement, and a response to a more complex set of factors than just Commission overload, in particular a response to pressures from those wanting a European Cartel Office, and an interest in developing a new set of enforcement priorities. We also noted that the Commission's tasks go beyond the pursuit of hard-core cartels and extend to designing policy, guiding uncertain firms planning agreements that are not in their nature anticompetitive, and monitoring NCAs. As for the latter, we suggested that the coordination among NCAs is incomplete and that the ECN might not be designed in an ideal manner because, rather than devising some form of network governance, whereby the ECN becomes a locus for the development of competition policy, the Commission seems to retain a primary role. In this section the net is cast a

[123] Ibid. p. 298.
[124] D. Marsh and M. Smith 'Understanding Policy Networks: Towards a Dialectical Approach' (2000) 48 *Politics* 4.
[125] P. Nicolaides 'The Political Economy of Multi-tiered Regulation in Europe' (2004) 42 *Journal of Common Market Studies* 599.

little wider, to consider how far Regulation 1/2003 challenges the nature and role of competition law.

4.1 Juridification

Some scholars have argued that one feature of modern states is the increased 'juridification' of social and economic life. By this they mean that more areas of human activity are subjected to legislation, enforcement by regulatory authorities and judicial control.[126] Imelda Maher has used this concept to reflect upon the reform of UK competition law in 1998, where the juridification of competition policy seems to have occurred in a fairly dramatic manner: gone is discretionary ministerial control over how to regulate restrictive practices, gone is a 'public interest' standard in the legislation and in come agencies freed from state control, with increased investigatory powers and applying legal standards that are more easily susceptible to judicial review.[127] Regulation 1/2003 can be said to force the juridification of competition law across the EU in that it requires that Member States designate independent competition authorities to apply Articles 81 and 82.[128]

If juridification replaces politics with law (or, to use Professor Teubner's more elaborate words, it constitutionalises the economic system) it also gives greater prominence to technocratic methods for addressing competition problems, and economic theories come to the fore. Doctrine becomes subservient to the insights of economics, and the 'public interest' goals of competition law as administered by a state-centred system vanish. This phenomenon is clearly visible in the British system and is likely to repeat itself across Europe as a result of Regulation 1/2003. It might be argued that there is nothing serious at stake: after all, markets are best governed by rules that are sensitive to the way markets work, and if juridification of competition law is necessary to allow institutions to regulate markets more effectively, it should be welcomed. Juridification might even be what the Commission wished to achieve with Regulation 1/2003: by placing the bulk of enforcement in the hands of independent agencies, it responded to the criticisms of its own politicised decision-making institutional makeup. The problem is that while NCAs may well apply legal standards in a narrow technical manner, the Commission remains the supreme enforcer and public policy considerations can still be identified, either via Article 81(3) decisions, or via the procedures that the Commission has under Articles 9, 10 and 16 of Regulation 1/2003 that we discussed above. Juridification is incomplete.

---

[126] See generally G. Teubner 'General Aspects' in G. Teubner (ed.) *Juridification of Social Spheres* (Berlin: De Gruyter, 1987).
[127] Maher 'Juridification'.   [128] Article 35(1) Regulation 1/2003.

4.2 Europeanisation of economic governance

Professor Wilks has suggested a provocative perspective from which to challenge Regulation 1/2003: modernisation is not about empowering national competition authorities, rather a strategic move through which the Community's economic policy (based on neoliberal ideas about how markets work) is imposed on Member States.[129] The argument is plausible in that, as we noted above in section 3, NCAs must first and foremost apply EC competition law, they must subject their decisions to scrutiny by the Commission, and considerable soft law measures have been put into place to secure a uniform interpretation of EC competition law among the NCAs. This deprives governments of the power to apply national law to carry out various forms of industrial policy. This critique suggests that Regulation 1/2003 places DG Competition in a position comparable to the European Central Bank. Just as the ECB dictates monetary policy for national central banks, so the Commission dictates the direction of competition policy for NCAs to implement. Thus, the decentralisation of enforcement achieved by Regulation 1/2003 gives the Commission more power over the development of competition law in the EC than the system of compulsory notification in Regulation 17/62. In effect, this Regulation can be characterised as forcing 'convergence by stealth', turning NCAs into branches of DG Competition.[130] As Möschel had put it, the effect of modernisation is that 'the organs of the Member States mutate into auxiliaries of the Commission'.[131] From this perspective, Regulation 1/2003 is part and parcel of the Community's industrial policy, premised upon the promotion of free markets.

This vision is not a threat for Member States whose economic policy is broadly in tune with the Commission's but it can provide a source of tension with Member States who see their sovereignty over economic policy taken away by the Commission's increased efforts to remove economic governance from the Member States. The anticipated risk that this creates is of tension and conflict between the Commission and Member States who are antagonistic to the Commission's policy. It remains to be seen whether some reaction akin to that of the Polish government in response to EC merger law (which we discussed in chapter 8) will manifest itself in controversial Article 81 cases.

4.3 The rebirth of national laws?

In a provocative reflection which tallies with the two themes broached above, Professor Ullrich has suggested that the reduction in the scope of EC

---

[129] S. Wilks 'Agency Escape: Decentralisation or Dominance of the European Commission in the Modernisation of Competition Policy?' (2005) 18 *Governance* 431; see also Riley 'EC Antitrust Modernisation'.

[130] McGowan 'Europeanisation Unleashed' pp. 1001–2.

[131] Möschel 'Guest Editorial' p. 497.

competition law which has been brought about by the substantive changes that we discussed in earlier chapters (i.e. the use of the consumer welfare standard and economic theories of anticompetitive harm), combined with the marginalisation of national competition law brought about by Regulation 1/2003, could in turn stimulate the growth or rebirth of other doctrines in the Member States, in particular laws of unfair competition. That is, courts and Member States might react against the dominance of the Commission by recourse to other norms to reassert their understanding of what competition is about. This might occur with rules of law that may apply to contradict Article 81 but are in conformity with EC law by virtue of Article 3(3) of Regulation 1/2003. He argues, with reference to German law, that this development would complement EC competition law, in particular by protecting competitors and granting each their 'basic freedom of individual competition'.[132] These reflections are a reaction against the increasing use of economics in EC competition law and the abandonment of ordoliberal principles of discipline and pluralism.

A similar example that supports this analysis can be seen in the approach taken by the British Competition Commission (CC) acting under the powers of the Enterprise Act 2002. In two recent market investigations (over store cards and warranties for electrical goods) the CC concluded that there was a market failure that required regulatory intervention in scenarios where no action would be warranted under EC competition law.[133]

In the case of store cards, the concern arose when large department stores offered consumers a store credit card (which can normally be used only to make purchases in the store which issues it) with very high APRs (average percentage rates, a standard measure for the cost of a credit agreement). All store cards had high APRs, although there was no agreement among the stores to fix high rates. The CC found that there was no competitive pressure on retailers to reduce the APR; and while credit card APRs were much lower, this did not exert any competitive pressure on store cards. There was simply a market failure which harmed consumers. The remedy imposed was to require store cards to provide clearer and greater information for consumers about the APRs and the charges they were likely to incur.

In the case of warranties for domestic electrical goods, concerns arose about the sale of extended warranties in store. The larger retail outlets had their own electrical warranty which they offered to consumers. It was noted that unless the warranty was bought in store, consumers were unlikely to obtain warranties for the goods. The CC found little price competition on warranties (although there was considerable competition for the sale of the electrical

---

[132] H. Ullrich 'Anti-Unfair Competition Law and Anti-Trust Law: A Continental Conundrum?' EUI Working Paper in Law 2005/01 (available at http://cadmus.iue.it/dspace/) pp. 45–6.

[133] Competition Commission *Store Cards Market Investigation*, 7 March 2006; Competition Commission *Extended Warranties on Domestic Electrical Goods* Cm 6089 (2003).

goods) and concluded that the five largest retailers made excessive profits when selling warranties as a result of the market's imperfections (estimated at between £116 and £152 million more than would have been earned in a competitive market). This meant that consumers would pay a third less for the warranty in a competitive market. This market failure was remedied by imposing requirements on retailers to provide transparent information about the price of warranties, and to allow consumers to cancel a warranty easily, so as to facilitate their search for better offers.[134]

The puzzle with both of these decisions is that traditional competition law norms could not apply. This might suggest, as we have already hinted in chapter 9, that the market investigation powers of the Enterprise Act are a way of filling in the gaps of other competition rules. On the other hand, it might suggest that the perspective through which the CC acted in these two cases is quite different from that which would be adopted by a competition authority. Rather, the actions of the CC are more reminiscent of those of a consumer protection agency: consumers are portrayed as weak and ill informed and in need of safeguards to avoid incurring debts. It is a much wider conception of consumer welfare than that displayed by competition law enforcement. A competition lawyer would ask whether the store selling the card had market power and answer this in the negative: the consumer should shop around for the best credit deal; the fact that many consumers fail to do so is their fault, or a problem with the market, but not something for which the retailer is responsible. The excess profits earned by retailers are not a major antitrust worry either: in fact, as we noted in chapter 7, the EC Commission hardly bothers with pursuing excessive pricing cases. Likewise the remedies are quite remote from that which we see in competition cases and they look more like the kind of regulatory remedy one sees in consumer law, which prizes the provision of clear information to the consumer and the ability to cancel contracts freely. On the other hand, according to some economists, this is the direction that competition law should take, by focusing on factors that determine consumer habits.[135]

Just as Professor Ullrich noted how German unfair competition law might be deployed to extend the concept of competition beyond economic efficiency to guarantee economic freedom of businesses, the CC extends the notion of consumer welfare by considering a different kind of market failure (lack of information), which causes the same kind of harm that competition law safeguards. The expansion of national law may result in a richer domestic culture of competition than that which DG Competition is keen to create.

---

[134] The Supply of Extended Warranties on Domestic Electrical Goods Order SI 2005 No. 37.

[135] M. Waterson 'The Role of Consumers in Competition and Competition Policy' (2003) 21 *International Journal of Industrial Organization* 129 for an illuminating account.

5 Private enforcement

Modernisation envisages an increased role for damages claims by parties suffering from anticompetitive conduct.[136] While the European Courts proclaimed that Articles 81(1) and 82 have direct effect and granted actionable rights as early as 1974,[137] to date there has been little recourse to the courts. A major study in 2004 suggested that there was 'total underdevelopment' of damages actions for breaches of competition law, with approximately sixty cases since 1962.[138] This is a paltry record if compared with the United States where private actions outnumber public enforcement by a ratio of ten to one,[139] and where some commentators suggest that there is under-enforcement in spite of these larger numbers.[140]

We explore the possible role of private enforcement in the EC in the following way. First, we argue that the ECJ has failed to address a crucial question about the protective scope of competition law, by stating that anyone is free to claim damages. The effect of this is to allow claims by parties whose success frustrates the aims of competition law. Instead, we argue that only certain parties should claim: consumers and competitors. In section 5.2 we consider the difficulties in compensating consumers adequately. In section 5.3 we explore some of the reasons why a culture of private litigation might not emerge readily in the EC, and in section 5.4, we consider the relationship between modernisation and private enforcement.

5.1 The protective scope of competition law statutes

In any tort liability rule, the law imposes certain limitations on the right to claim. Some of the limits are created by rules of causation, but first the courts decide the kinds of plaintiffs that have a right to seek damages: the protective scope of tort. A well-known English tort case can help explain what this means. A ship-owner agreed to carry a number of sheep belonging to the defendant. The sheep were washed overboard because the ship-owner failed to secure them in pens, in breach of the Contagious Diseases (Animals) Act 1869. The owner of the sheep sought damages on the basis that the ship-owner was in

---

[136] See Recital 7 (noting that national courts have 'an essential part to play') and Article 6 Regulation 1/2003.

[137] Case 127/73 *Belgische Radio en Televisie and Société Belge des Auteurs, Compositeurs et Editeurs de Musique v. SABAM* [1974] ECR 51 para. 16; the right to damages was restated in Case C-282/95P *Guérin Automobiles v. Commission* [1997] ECR I-1503 para. 39.

[138] Ashurst Study on the conditions of claims for damages in case of infringement of EC competition rules, 31 August 2004 (available at http://ec.europa.eu/comm/competition/antitrust/others/actions_for_damages/study.html).

[139] B. E. Hawk and J. D. Veltrop 'Dual Antitrust Enforcement in the United States' in P. J. Slot and A. McDonnell *Procedure and Enforcement in EC and US Competition Law* (London: Sweet & Maxwell, 1993) p. 27.

[140] See generally C. A. Jones *Private Enforcement of Antitrust Law in the EU, UK and USA* (Oxford: Oxford University Press, 1999).

breach of his statutory duties, but the court did not allow the claim. The aim of the statute was to protect the animals from disease, not to guarantee their safety. Had the sheep died from illness, a claim would have been allowed, but the loss in question did not fall within the protective scope of the statute.[141] An action for damages under Articles 81 and 82 is also an action for breach of statutory duty, so it is relevant to explore what the protective scope of these measures is.

There are two ways to explore the protective scope of competition law statutes. The first begins by suggesting that private litigation has a dual function: it protects the plaintiff and it deters further anticompetitive conduct.[142] This is supported by the fact that the plaintiff must prove both that the defendant's act restricts competition (now understood as a harm to consumer welfare), and that he has suffered a personal loss. Competition law does not protect an individual, but the market. Private litigation then should be allowed when the plaintiff's action helps to deter anticompetitive behaviour.[143] The second way to justify a right to damages is to explore what classes of person EC competition law protects. On this basis, all consumers should be entitled to claim because EC competition law protects consumer welfare. This was made quite clear in the Court's explanation of the harm caused by a cartel:

> Participation by an undertaking in anti-competitive practices and agreements constitutes an economic infringement designed to maximise its profits, generally by an intentional limitation of supply, an artificial division of the market and an artificial increase in prices. The effect of such agreements or of such practices is to restrict free competition and to prevent the attainment of the common market, in particular by hindering intra-Community trade. Such harmful effects are passed directly on to consumers in terms of increased prices and reduced diversity of supply. Where an anti-competitive practice or agreement is adopted in the cement sector, the entire construction and housing sector, and the real-estate market, suffer such effects.[144]

Note how the Court argues that the individuals harmed by a cartel are all those who purchased cement, and all consumers further down the line that suffer as a result of the higher prices in the industry. It follows from this that consumers should have a right to damages because they are the direct beneficiaries of

---

[141] *Gorris v. Scott* (1874) LR 9 Exch. 125.

[142] The Commission erroneously says that private lawsuits only safeguard the plaintiff's rights. EC Commission *Notice on Cooperation between National Courts and the Commission in applying Articles [81] and [82] of the Treaty* [1993] OJ C39/6 para. 4; EC Commission *Notice on the Cooperation between the Commission and the Courts of the EU Member States in the Application of Articles 81 and 82 EC* [2004] OJ C101/54 para. 4.

[143] See Case C-453/99 *Courage v. Crehan* [2001] ECR I-6297 paras. 26 and 27. On the significance of this case generally, see A. P. Komninos 'New Prospects for Private Enforcement of EC Competition Law: *Courage v. Crehan* and the Community Right to Damages' (2002) 39 *Common Market Law Review* 447.

[144] Joined Cases C-204/00P, C-205/00P, C-211/00P, C-213/00P, C-217/00P and C-219/00P *Aalborg Portland and Others v. Commission* [2004] ECR I-123 para. 53.

Article 81. Until recently, the Italian courts had refused to recognise the consumer's right to secure damages, but in a path-breaking judgment Italy's highest court has now recognised that competition law safeguards consumer interests.[145]

In sum, we can justify the right to damages for consumers on two alternative grounds: they have a 'subjective right' which is within the protective scope of Article 81, or their lawsuits deter unlawful agreements.[146]

The same two justifications can be invoked to establish that competitors have a right to seek damages. Recall that Article 82 is designed to protect competitors from the exclusionary tactics of dominant firms. Note also that, as we saw in chapter 10, vertical restraints can foreclose market access to other competitors. In these two scenarios the person that the law seeks to protect should have a right to damages. From a deterrence perspective, granting a right to damages to a person that is so directly injured by the anticompetitive action serves to protect those who are less directly affected, for example consumers or would-be entrants who may be deterred because of the dominant firm's exclusionary reputation.

However, the Court of Justice has not examined what the protective scope of the competition laws is in the manner suggested above, and has said that other parties are also able to claim damages for infringements of Article 81. In a recent judgment the Court simply proclaimed: 'any individual can claim compensation for the harm suffered where there is a causal relationship between the harm and an agreement of practice prohibited under Article 81 EC'.[147] With this conclusion the Court appears to suggest that there is no need to ask who is protected by Article 81, because anyone whose loss is caused by the breach of Article 81 can claim damages. However, this is an unreasonably wide basis upon which to ground liability. Suppose members of a cartel supplying a safety device to factories boycott one factory because it is trying to buy competing goods from outside the cartel and as a result an employee of that factory suffers injury. Can the Court really have intended that this victim (whose loss is caused by the cartel) should be entitled to make a claim against the cartel members under Article 81? While this example is deliberately far-fetched, a real scenario has occurred where the Court's failure to consider the protective scope of Article 81 has negative repercussions. This is the scenario in the litigation between Crehan and Inntrepreneur. Mr Crehan entered into a

---

[145] See R. Incardina and C. Poncibò 'The Corte di Cassazione takes "Courage". A Recent Ruling Opens Limited Rights for Consumers in Competition Cases' [2005] *European Competition Law Review* 445.

[146] In the United States, the 'protective scope' inquiry is carried out by considering whether the plaintiff has suffered 'antitrust injury'. This requires the court to decide what economic effects the law seeks to prevent followed by a determination of whether the plaintiff's injury flows from the effects that the law condemns. See generally R. W. Davis 'Standing on Shaky Ground: The Strangely Elusive Doctrine of Antitrust Injury' (2003) 70 *Antitrust Law Journal* 697.

[147] Joined Cases C-295-298/04 *Manfredi and Others v. Lloyd Adriatico and Others*, judgment of 13 July 2006, para. 61.

lease for two pubs owned by Inntrepreneur. One term of the lease was a 'beer tie' by which Crehan agreed to purchase beers specified by Inntrepreneur. Crehan's business failed, suffering losses between 1991 and 1993, when he surrendered the properties. He sought damages on the grounds that the beer tie infringed Article 81.

When his claim arrived in the English courts, the first doubt was whether a party that had entered into an anticompetitive agreement was entitled to damages, as under English law the right to damages is denied in these circumstances. The Court of Appeal sought guidance from the Court of Justice as to whether the same applied in EC competition cases, and the ECJ ruled that 'anyone' could seek damages, except if they were significantly responsible for the agreement. The Court advanced two hypotheses to illustrate which plaintiff was not significantly responsible: first when the plaintiff is in a weak position vis-à-vis the other party to the contract so that his freedom to negotiate is negated, second when the plaintiff is a distributor in a vast distribution network and the cumulative effect of all the contracts that the defendant manufacturer has entered into lead to an infringement of Article 81. In this context, the responsibility of avoiding the network effects is on the manufacturer, not on the individual distributors.[148] So Crehan could claim, being in a weaker position. The dispute then returned to the English courts for resolution. At first instance, the judge concluded that the agreement was not in breach of Article 81(1) and so damages could not be claimed.[149] In the Court of Appeal the plaintiff won damages because the Court relied on a decision of the Commission (*Whitbread*) that had ruled that a similar agreement was in breach of Article 81(1).[150] But the House of Lords quashed that ruling and reinstated the decision of the High Court, holding that the English courts were not bound to reach the same decision as the Commission in an analogous case.[151] As the House of Lords made no substantive analysis of the right to damages, it is worth returning to that part of the judgment of the Court of Appeal. It held that Crehan was entitled to damages on two grounds: first the losses incurred while running the two pubs, and second the value of the hypothetically successful pubs in 1993 had there been no unlawful beer tie. This calculation seems to be in line with recent case law of the ECJ, which provides that an injured party has a right to damages both for actual loss and for loss of profit.[152]

---

[148] *Courage v. Crehan* [2001] ECR I-6297 paras. 31–3.
[149] [2003] EWHC 1510 (Ch).
[150] [2004] EWCA Civ 637, relying on *Whitbread* [1999] OJ L88/26. It seems unusual to impose liability on Inntrepreneur by relying on *Whitbread* where the Commission decided that beer ties benefited consumers. As we saw in chapter 2, the Commission makes a partial competition assessment in Article 81(1) and a complete assessment under Article 81(3). Therefore, by applying only part of the *Whitbread* decision, the Court of Appeal failed to consider the overall effects of the beer tie. This point was not noted on appeal to the House of Lords.
[151] [2006] UKHL 38.   [152] *Manfredi*, judgment of 13 July 2006, para. 95.

The upshot of this protracted test case is that both the European and English courts believe that a person like Crehan has a right to damages. However, it is not clear why a distributor should have a claim against the supplier for breach of Article 81. The reason why the beer ties were found unlawful was that they foreclosed market access to other brewers. As we saw in chapter 10, foreclosure is one of the key harms that are caused by distribution agreements, so it would seem appropriate that the protective scope of Article 81 should extend to parties that are unable to enter the market. It is less clear why Crehan should fall within the protection of Article 81. As we did when considering the right to damages of consumers and competitors, we can use two methods to discover why Crehan has a right to damages: either he is within Article 81's protective scope, or his claim deters anticompetitive agreements.

To say that Article 81 protects distributors as well as competing brewers can be justified by reference to the Commission's views on beer ties in the *Whitbread* decision.[153] The Commission, considering a distribution contract similar to that between Crehan and Inntrepreneur, noted that under the beer supply agreement in question the lessee obtained a relatively inexpensive pub lease, while paying higher prices for the tied beer. The Commission was concerned that the beer tie could give the brewer the opportunity to 'cash in on his leverage vis-à-vis the tied customers' with the effect 'that the lessee who faces (unjustified) price differentials may not be in a position to compete on a level playing field'.[154] However, on the facts the Commission granted an exemption because the price charged to tied pubs was only slightly higher than that charged to other pubs and the lessee obtained other benefits to compensate for the higher beer price.[155] The lesson from these findings is that, according to the Commission, Article 81 protects distributors against sharp practices by powerful manufacturers. However, if we accept this, it means that Article 81 is not merely designed to protect consumer welfare, but also designed to safeguard weak parties who enter an anticompetitive agreement. Read in this way, the protective scope of Article 81 becomes very similar to that of Article 82: the protection of weaker parties. This goes against the Commission's attempts in recent years to narrow down the scope of Article 81 to a tool that safeguards consumer welfare. So if we were to say that Crehan's right to damages exists because distributors are protected by Article 81, then this would call into question, if not frustrate, the Commission's reorientation of Article 81 away from safeguarding economic freedom and towards protecting consumer welfare.[156]

---

[153] [1999] OJ L88/26.   [154] Ibid. paras. 156 and 158 respectively.   [155] Ibid. para. 168.

[156] The better view is that '[i]mprovident contracts are not antitrust problems simply because they were carelessly or naively made. The tenant who stupidly signs a lease permitting the landlord to vary the rent has not turned the landlord into a monopolist. To accept the contrary position turns antitrust into an engine for resolving contract disputes.' H. Hovenkamp *The Antitrust Enterprise: Principle and Execution* (Cambridge, MA: Harvard University Press, 2005) p. 203.

The second way of justifying Crehan's right to damages is to find that EC competition law protects competition in the sale of beer to pubs, and that by foreclosing competitors through beer ties, the price of beer is inflated and this higher price causes damage to beer purchasers, which in turn harms consumer welfare by pushing up the price of beer. And so Crehan has a right to damages because his lawsuit deters brewers from entering into agreements that cause foreclosure effects. According to this argument, anyone can claim damages provided that their action has a direct or indirect impact on parties who infringe Article 81, in that the award of damages deters them. If this is so, however, then the employee who suffers personal injury because a cartel boycotts his employer's firm should also be entitled to claim damages because that too would deter cartel members.

Of these two justifications (Crehan is a protected party or deterrence), the ECJ in *Courage v. Crehan* seemed to apply the latter. While the Court began by saying that Crehan has 'rights which the court must safeguard' its emphasis is not on why these rights should accrue to the individual, but rather that conferral of these rights strengthens the effectiveness of Article 81:

> Indeed, the existence of such a right strengthens the working of the Community competition rules and discourages agreements or practices, which are frequently covert, which are liable to restrict or distort competition. From that point of view, actions for damages before the national courts can make a significant contribution to the maintenance of effective competition in the Community.[157]

The upshot of this is that the reason why damages claims exist is to deter. This explains why in *Manfredi* the ECJ did not say anything about the 'protective scope' of Article 81, but merely held that 'any individual' (a phrase it repeated three times in as many paragraphs) can claim provided they can show that the breach caused them harm.[158]

The argument that we should allow anyone to claim damages provided that we believe that their lawsuit deters anticompetitive agreements seems too extensive, and undermines competition law. Consider the litigation in *Crehan* again. There, Inntrepreneur had been in constant discussion with the Commission, trying to come to an understanding as to how it could comply with EC competition law. In this scenario, can we really say that allowing a claim in damages by the distributor enhances the deterrent value of Article 81? Second, the passage quoted from *Crehan* above speaks of covert agreements; however, in this case the contract was far from covert. In fact, most distribution agreements are not covert, so it is not clear how many anticompetitive practices can be identified by giving distributors a right to damages. Third, as we saw above, in distribution contracts the effect is to harm the manufacturer's competitors, so the distributor does not necessarily suffer any

---

[157] *Courage* [2001] ECR I-6297 para. 27; see also paras. 23–6.
[158] *Manfredi*, judgment of 13 July 2006, paras. 59–61.

loss, consequently the incentive for him to seek damages stems from something other than the market foreclosure. The distributor will seek damages when the business does not go well, but if the manufacturer's foreclosure efforts are successful, distributors may well be the winners as competing shops close down. A fourth question, which the ECJ did not answer, is whether, having successfully obtained damages, the distributor can be sued in turn. Say a foreclosed brewer seeks damages, can this person obtain damages only from the other brewers or also from the distributors that accepted the anticompetitive agreement? In the United States it has been suggested that the distributor's right to damages does not give him immunity from claims by third parties.[159] If so, one must doubt whether any distributor would have an incentive to uncover an anticompetitive agreement as a way of claiming damages if this opens up the possibility of subsequent claims against him.[160] More generally, as we have seen in previous chapters, vertical restraints are among the least harmful of practices from a competition law perspective and lawsuits alleging infringements in this context should be viewed with suspicion.[161] Granting any individual the right to secure damages does not make any sense.

Another reason why we can object to the use of deterrence as the reason for allowing a person to secure damages is that it increases the obligations on the defendants and distorts the meaning of Article 81. It seems from *Courage* that a person who enters into a contract which might infringe Article 81 cannot bargain hard to close the deal (because if he does so then it follows that the other party is not significantly responsible for the breach and can later seek damages), and he must observe the market to make sure that the cumulative effect of all his contracts does not foreclose market access, otherwise any of his distributors can sue him for damages.[162] It seems that giving parties to a contract a right to damages creates a range of special responsibilities on the potential defendant that are quite alien to the nature of Article 81 and closer to those we find in Article 82 but more extensive: the manufacturer has a duty to negotiate with care.

Finally, a word of caution is necessary about the motivations of a plaintiff's actions. Competition law can be used as a strategy to harm competitors.[163] This is the converse of the theory that the Court and Commission have embraced whereby the use of the legal process can be an abuse of

---

[159] *Perma Life Mufflers v. International Parts Corp.* 392 US 134 (1968).

[160] These points are discussed in more detail in G. Monti 'Anticompetitive Agreements: The Innocent Party's Right to Damages' (2002) 27 *European Law Review* 282.

[161] T. E. Kauper, E. Thomas and E. A. Snyder 'An Inquiry into the Efficiency of Private Antitrust Enforcement: Follow-on and Independently Initiated Cases Compared' (1985–6) 74 *Georgetown Law Journal* 1163, 1164.

[162] The second obligation already exists but it merely empowers the Commission to withdraw the Block Exemption, if it originally applied. Article 6 Regulation 2790/99 on the Application of Article 81(3) to Categories of Vertical Agreements and Concerted Practices [1999] OJ L336/21.

[163] See generally W. J. Baumol and J. A. Ordover 'The Use of Antitrust to Subvert Competition' (1985) 28 *Journal of Law and Economics* 247.

dominance.[164] One has to be careful lest the right to damages is offered to parties who use it for their personal gain. In fact, this is a risk that has already been observed in several cases in the past. Many parties to anticompetitive agreements have used the courts to secure a declaration that the contract is void as a way of escaping liability for breach of contract, a practice known as a Euro-defence.[165] If it is inappropriate to use competition law to secure an avoidance of contractual liability, it is even more inappropriate to allow a claim in damages.[166]

In sum, the few judgments of the ECJ suggest that the right to damages for breaches of EC competition law has a private and a public dimension but that the two are indissoluble: the individual who has suffered loss is allowed to sue only because his claim safeguards the market by increasing the deterrent effect of the competition law. However, it may be queried how far claims by disgruntled distributors contribute to deter anticompetitive behaviour. It is unfortunate that the Court did not investigate more fully the protective scope of competition law and saw a claim in damages as merely a means to strengthen the application of EC competition law without seeing that its decision may well have the opposite effect: distorting the obligations imposed by Article 81.

5.2 Which consumers should claim?

It is not controversial that consumers should be entitled to secure damages, but it is more difficult to decide which consumers should have a right to damages. A hypothetical example can help visualise the difficulties. Say there is a cartel in the market for cement that causes the price to rise. A builder, Bob, buys cement from the cartel and builds a house for Aisha. Bob was also about to enter into a contract to build an extension to Charlie's house; however, once Bob gave Charlie the new quotation for the work (which took into account the higher cost of cement as a result of the cartel price) Charlie decided not to build the extension.

If we are committed to protecting consumer welfare, all three parties suffer loss as a result of the cartel. Bob, the builder, suffers two losses: first he pays more for the cement he buys, and second he loses business as a result of the higher price. Aisha pays more for her house, and Charlie suffers because he is unable to build his extension. Do they all have a claim?

---

[164] For example, in Case T-111/96 *ITT Promedia v. Commission* [1998] ECR II-2937 the Court said that vexatious litigation could be an abuse; in *Generics/Astra Zeneca* (decision of 15 June 2005) the Commission ruled that misuse of the patent system to delay market access to competitors constituted an infringement of Article 82.

[165] See R. Whish *Competition Law* 4th edn (London: Lexis Nexis, 2001) pp. 266–7 for a review of the attitude of UK courts to this tactic.

[166] Granted, this line of argument is also one that militates against claims by competitors of the defendant firm, but at least in this context we first have established that the competitor is directly protected by the competition laws.

Under US federal law the only person who can claim damages is the direct purchaser (Bob the builder who bought the goods directly from the cartel), but only for the extra price of the cement he buys, not for the lost contracts. The indirect purchaser (Aisha) cannot claim.[167] Moreover, it might be argued that the direct purchaser can mitigate his losses by 'passing on' the higher cement price to the homeowner, so that Bob would mitigate his losses by charging Aisha a higher price. However, US federal law does not reduce the damages awarded to the builder even if some of the losses have been avoided. In the jargon, there is no passing-on defence.[168] More generally, there is no evidence that would-be purchasers who are put off by the higher price (Charlie) have ever sought damages, or that a person like Bob has ever thought of claiming for lost business opportunities.[169] These legal principles sound perverse: if the aim of competition law is to safeguard consumer welfare, the law should provide that the indirect purchaser has a claim, and concomitantly that the passing-on defence applies to reduce the damages payable to the direct purchaser. Moreover, the person who is priced out of the market deserves compensation. Instead of compensating everyone for the losses suffered, the US system seems to overcompensate a few 'lucky' plaintiffs. But the seeming arbitrariness of the US rule is justified by the administrative ease with which it can be operated. The example we considered is quite simple. Imagine the effect of a cement cartel across the entire industry and with more vertical links: the number of indirect purchasers is immense, and each of their losses is quite small. How many indirect purchasers are likely to mount an action in these circumstances? Moreover, there is a 'floodgates' concern: should courts be deployed to safeguard each of these relatively small losses? And if indirect purchasers have a right to secure damages, it is only fair that the passing-on defence applies to reduce the amount that the defendant has to pay, otherwise the defendant is paying excessive damages.[170] Moreover, apportioning the damages among all plaintiffs would be cumbersome and increased complexity would reduce the incentive to litigate.[171] Therefore, the complex and costly logistics of a fair compensation system outweigh the benefits of a less fair system. In contrast, a more blunt rule that overcompensates some but leaves others uncompensated is more administratively efficient. The US federal rules have also been supported on grounds that they are more efficient from a deterrence perspective: first, the direct purchaser is the more effective enforcer because he is aware of the source of the loss and has better information regarding the infringement and his losses; second, if the loss is divided among several plaintiffs each

---

[167] *Illinois Brick Co. v. Illinois* 431 US 720 (1977).

[168] *Hanover Shoe Inc. v. United Shoe Machinery* 392 US 481 (1968).

[169] R. H. Lande 'Why Antitrust Damage Levels Should Be Raised' (2004) 16 *Loyola Consumer Law Review* 329, 338.

[170] Plus the difficulties of calculating how much of the losses are passed on, described as an insurmountable task by the Supreme Court in *Hanover Shoe*.

[171] *Hanover Shoe* 392 US 481 (1968) 492–3.

person's loss is so small that, given the difficulties in making a successful lawsuit against the defendant, the incentive to sue is diminished. Instead, if one plaintiff can expect a windfall upon success, then that person has a greater incentive to sue.[172]

Critics of the US position point out that it denies compensation to a wide range of victims,[173] and it places the right to sue on parties with the least incentive to make use of it, because direct purchasers are able to pass on the higher prices. As a result, many states have allowed indirect purchasers to claim under state antitrust laws.[174] This has added an intolerable layer of complexity because litigation on the same case takes place in different courts with different laws. The upshot is that the consensus among US commentators is that the mixture of conflicting federal and state systems is confusing and inefficient to such an extent that 'no rational person ever would have designed it from scratch in its current form'.[175]

The debate about whether indirect purchasers should be entitled to sue shows that there are three conflicting attributes that we seek in a damages regime: that it compensates fully, that it deters adequately and that it is simple to operate. Ease of operation is inconsistent with full compensation, and adequate deterrence is hard to achieve unless all harms caused by the anti-competitive behaviour are caught.[176] According to these considerations, the decision of the German legislator to allow claims only to direct purchasers and to abolish the passing-on defence on grounds of administrative ease is understandable even if it sacrifices the aim of full compensation.[177] The guidance from the ECJ as to whether the German approach is correct is unclear. On the one hand, given that the ECJ has ruled that 'anyone' is entitled to claim provided the losses are caused by the defendant, this means that both direct and indirect purchasers should be entitled to claim, and that also non-purchasers, who refuse to buy at the higher price, should have a right to damages. On the other hand, the ECJ's basis for conferring a right to damages

---

[172] W. M. Landes and R. A. Posner 'Should Indirect Purchasers Have Standing to Sue under the Antitrust Laws? An Economic Analysis of the Rule in *Illinois Brick*' (1979) 46 *University of Chicago Law Review* 602.

[173] See M. Denger and D. J. Arp 'Does Our Multifaceted Enforcement System Promote Sound Competition Policy?' (2001) 15 *Antitrust* 41.

[174] *California v. ARC America* 490 US 93 (1989), ruling that *Illinois Brick* does not pre-empt state laws allowing indirect purchaser suits. For discussion, see R. W. Davis 'Indirect Purchaser Litigation: ARC America's Chickens Come Home to Roost on the Illinois Brick Wall' (1997) 65 *Antitrust Law Journal* 375.

[175] Lande 'Why Antitrust Damage Levels Should Be Raised' p. 330.

[176] But see J. E. Lopatka and W. H. Page 'Indirect Purchaser Suits and the Consumer Interest' (2003) 48 *Antitrust Bulletin* 531 part IV, arguing that deterrence works less well when indirect purchasers are allowed to claim.

[177] S. 33(1)–(3) Act Against Restraints of Competition (as amended, in force from 1 July 2005). See N. Reich 'The "Courage" Doctrine: Encouraging or Discouraging Compensation for Antitrust Injuries?' (2005) 35 *Common Market Law Review* 35 for a discussion of the case law predating the amendment.

is that the plaintiff's action serves to deter future anticompetitive behaviour. Then it may be argued that if deterrence is best achieved by reserving the right to sue for direct purchasers, this could support the choice made by the German legislator. Unfortunately, there is insufficient empirical evidence to demonstrate what liability rule best deters.

The debates summarised above will sound very familiar to tort lawyers. Any liability rule is imperfectly designed: its deterrence value is never explored, its ability to compensate fully is always compromised, and the operation of the tort system is extraordinarily expensive.[178] One solution often advocated in tort circles is to abolish liability rules in favour of a compensation scheme. An interesting variation of this is the policy of some US states to apply so-called *parens patriae* (i.e. the state as father of the people) powers to secure damages on behalf of the state's citizens.[179] When exercising these powers, the burden of litigation is upon the state but it secures damages on behalf of the citizens and then distributes the proceeds. In some cases the damages awards are distributed to persons that have suffered damage (whether direct or indirect purchasers) and sometimes the money is distributed in ways so as to benefit the injured consumers indirectly, a so-called *cy pres* (from French, meaning as close as possible) recovery procedure. For example, as part of the settlement against a price-fixing conspiracy for music CDs, $78.5 million worth of CDs was donated to libraries, schools and colleges; in a case against toy manufacturers and retailers $37 million was used to buy toys for needy children in the state.[180] This procedure allows for a more successful mix of full compensation, deterrence and administrative ease than the tort law avenue, although it depends on states being well financed and willing to take this kind of action.

5.3 Practical difficulties for claimants

We can divide claimants into two groups: those whose claim is a 'follow on' action after a competition authority has made an infringement decision and who thereby use the factual findings of the authority to help their claims, and 'stand alone' claims by parties who identify a breach of competition law without a prior finding by a competition authority. The Commission is eager to encourage both, and has recently identified some of the major hurdles in a Green Paper.[181] It is not yet clear whether some of the options canvassed by

---

[178] See generally P. Cane *Atiyah's Accidents, Compensation and the Law* 6th edn (Cambridge: Cambridge University Press, 2003) for an evaluation of the UK tort system.

[179] 15 USC 15(c).

[180] Comments of the Attorneys General of California, Arizona, Connecticut, the District of Columbia, Illinois, Louisiana, Massachusetts, Mississippi, New Mexico, the Northern Mariana Islands, Ohio, Oregon, Rhode Island, Utah, Washington and West Virginia on the Review of Damages Actions for Breach of the EC Antitrust Rules, available at www.naag.org/issues/pdf/EUCommentsLetter.pdf pp. 2–4.

[181] EC Commission *Green Paper – Damages Actions for Breach of the EC Antitrust Rules* SEC (2005) 1732.

the Commission will translate into a legislative proposal. The principal points are summarised below.

Follow-on claimants have a somewhat easier route to claim. In some jurisdictions (e.g. the UK and Germany) the national court is bound by the findings of a competition authority.[182] In Germany, a national court hearing a follow-on damages claim is bound by decisions of the EC Commission, the Bundeskartellamt and even of the competition authorities of other Member States.[183] This means that the plaintiff in a follow-on action merely has to show that the breach caused loss and to quantify that loss. Thus UK and German rules seem to be sufficient to encourage follow-on actions.[184] Follow-on lawsuits can make a significant dent in the profits of a firm embroiled in a cartel: for instance, actions in the aftermath of the prosecution of the vitamins cartel in the US gave rise to $1 billion in damages paid by seven plaintiffs (plus $122 million for counsel's fees), and in another case the defendants settled for $512 million before the prosecution had even been brought.[185]

The plaintiff in a stand-alone action instead bears the burden of identifying the breach. In order to promote stand-alone actions, one would need to facilitate access to information held by the parties and by competition authorities.[186] This can be problematic because access to evidence is restricted, in particular in civil law Member States, where the discovery rules are less generous than in common law countries. Moreover, even if information is available, a stand-alone action is more risky than a follow-on lawsuit because the result is uncertain. Accordingly, additional measures might be needed to encourage stand-alone claims. These might include altering the rules on cost awards (whereby the losing party need not pay the defendant's costs) and awarding punitive damages (e.g. double or treble damages),[187] which is said to increase deterrence and also to increase the number of willing litigants.[188] Nevertheless, the US experience leads us not to expect much from stand-alone actions, in particular in cases that are not hard-core cartels, as few plaintiffs have the resources to mount actions where a full economic analysis must be deployed to prove harm.

---

[182] S. 58A Competition Act 1998 (as amended by the Enterprise Act 2002). See B. Rodger 'Private Enforcement and the Enterprise Act: An Exemplary System of Awarding Damages?' [2003] *European Competition Law Review* 103.

[183] S. 33(4) German Act Against Restraints of Competition.

[184] An EC-wide application of this rule is canvassed in Option 8 of the Green Paper.

[185] S. W. Waller 'The Incoherence of Punishment in Antitrust' 78 *Chicago-Kent Law Review* 207. The reasons for settling beforehand are twofold: (1) one can settle for less since the outcome is uncertain; (2) the DOJ will not demand restitution of ill-gotten gains since compensation has already been paid.

[186] Options 1–7 and 9–19 of the Green Paper.   [187] Options 16 and 27 of the Green Paper.

[188] S. C. Salop and L. J. White 'Economic Analysis of Private Antitrust Litigation' (1985–6) 74 *Georgetown Law Journal* 1011, 1020–1.

5.4 Private actions and modernisation

On one view, private actions are necessary in order to ensure all the antitrust enforcement objectives are met. According to Harding and Joshua, enforcement has three objectives: injunctive (ending anticompetitive behaviour); restorative/compensatory (remedying the financial losses); and penal (punishing and deterring the firms).[189] Public enforcement cannot achieve the restorative/compensatory objective in its present form. Moreover, in the eyes of the Commission, private enforcement serves to achieve all three goals; thus it enhances the injunctive and penal roles of enforcement as well as compensating victims. In this light, private actions complement public enforcement of competition law.[190] In particular, the Commission is eager to see growth of both follow-on and stand-alone actions on the basis that NCAs do not have the resources to reach decisions on every private dispute. From this perspective, the Green Paper on damages is seen as a starting point for debates at national and Community level to decide how best to facilitate the growth of private litigation.

A less optimistic analysis is to suggest that the majority of damages actions against firms guilty of the more serious violations of competition law (e.g. cartels and abuses of dominance) are likely to be follow-on lawsuits. That is, parties will wait for a competition authority to make a finding and then use this as the basis for a claim in damages. This means that private enforcement is not an alternative to public enforcement but merely a way of compensating those who suffer harm.[191] However, it has been suggested that fines are too low, so that follow-on actions can increase the deterrent value of competition law. On this view, follow-on actions complement the activities of public authorities by increasing the scale of punishment, not the scope of enforcement. Moreover, given the procedural difficulties we have seen above, it is unlikely that stand-alone private lawsuits will unearth hard-core cartels. If so, this undermines the Commission's stated policy of seeing private enforcement supplementing public enforcement via stand-alone actions.[192] Instead, one is more likely to see stand-alone actions like Crehan's: Euro-defences and counterclaims for damages when business relations turn sour. As was suggested above, lawsuits by parties to anticompetitive contracts based on competition law are undesirable. This less optimistic appraisal is justified by looking at trends in the United

[189] C. Harding and J. Joshua *Regulating Cartels in Europe – A Study of Legal Control of Corporate Delinquency* (Oxford: Oxford University Press, 2003) pp. 229–30; see also K. Yeung 'Privatizing Competition Regulation' (1998) 18 *Oxford Journal of Legal Studies* 581, 586–92.

[190] Recital 7 Regulation 1/2003, a point repeated by Commission officials. See e.g. N. Kroes 'The Green Paper on Antitrust Damages Actions: Empowering European Citizens to Enforce their Rights', speech of 6 June 2006 (available at http://ec.europa.eu/comm/competition/antitrust/others/actions_for_damages/index_en.html).

[191] K. Holmes 'Public Enforcement or Private Enforcement? Enforcement of Competition Law in the EC and the UK' [2004] *European Competition Law Review* 25.

[192] EC Commission Memo/05/489, What Types of Infringement does the Commission Think Private Damage Actions Should Enforce?

States where frequently the victims of a price-fixing conspiracy are follow-on claimants, taking advantage of the findings of a public enforcer,[193] and most stand-alone cases instead are launched by competitors in actions that look more like business tort suits.[194] If so, then the Commission's interest in encouraging private litigation should be tempered: stand-alone actions can risk undermining the substantive modernisation of EC competition law (e.g. *Crehan* runs against the reform of Article 81), and efforts should only be devoted to facilitating follow-on lawsuits.[195]

Another perspective from which to examine the relationship between private enforcement and modernisation is to consider how court proceedings interact with those of competition authorities. First, it seems that courts are not bound by commitment decisions that the Commission enters into under Article 9 of Regulation 1/2003. This recreates the same problem of uncertainty that existed with comfort letters. Second, courts are not bound by leniency schemes. So a party that settles with the Commission may still face private lawsuits. This problem is particularly poignant because it creates a risk that facilitating private litigation diminishes the incentive for parties to make leniency application (e.g. when the reduction of a fine through leniency programmes is less than the damages that the party is likely to have to pay).[196] Accordingly, the Commission is investigating how to reconcile leniency programmes with damages claims.[197] Some have also doubted the extent to which national courts will be capable of applying Article 81(3) given that it calls for complex economic analysis.[198] The standard response to this question is that courts have been asked to interpret Articles 81(1) and 82 for some time and that there is not a quantum leap between these and Article 81(3). However, this debate misses the point that national courts have little experience in applying competition law at all, so the difficulties of national courts are over the application of all parts of Articles 81 and 82.

---

[193] Taking advantage of 15 USC 16(a): 'A final judgment or decree heretofore or hereafter rendered in any civil or criminal proceeding brought by or on behalf of the United States under the antitrust laws to the effect that a defendant has violated said laws shall be prima facie evidence against such defendant in any action or proceeding brought by any other party against such defendant . . .'

[194] Waller 'Incoherence' p. 210.

[195] An even more pessimistic position is taken by W. Wils 'Should Private Antitrust Enforcement Be Encouraged in Europe?' (2003) 26 *World Competition* 473, suggesting the superiority of public enforcement by NCAs. See the robust response by C. A. Jones 'Private Antitrust Enforcement in Europe: A Policy Analysis and a Reality Check' (2004) 27 *World Competition* 13.

[196] In the United States this risk was resolved by s. 213 Antitrust Criminal Penalty Enhancement and Reform Act of 2004 (Pub. L. No. 108–237), which provides that a firm which has made a successful leniency application is spared the burden of paying treble damages, and merely compensates victims for the losses they suffered.

[197] One option is to allow the defendant who has provided evidence under a leniency programme to gain a rebate on damages claims, another is not to make that defendant jointly and severally liable for the losses caused (Options 29 and 30 of the Green Paper).

[198] Gilliams 'Modernisation' p. 457.

Last, coordination between courts and the Commission is established to ensure consistent enforcement. However, unlike the ECN, where the Commission possesses considerable powers to prevent inconsistent decisions, the independence of the courts prevents comparably aggressive checks on national courts. Regulation 1/2003 provides for three forms of cooperation. First, the court may seek some assistance from the Commission (access to documents in its possession, or the Commission's opinion on economic, factual or legal matters); second, the court must transmit a copy of its judgment to the Commission; third, the Commission may act as amicus curiae to provide its opinion to the court.[199] The last is the closest the Commission can get to influencing the national court, and there may be a risk of less confident courts following the Commission's opinions. It is not clear whether, if the Commission is dissatisfied with a national court's decision declaring a practice lawful, it may begin its own procedures and declare the activity in breach of EC competition law.[200] These more lax forms of control suggest, paradoxically, that a more subtle 'network' is in place among the national courts: on the one hand, their autonomy allows courts to explore different solutions to comparable problems, and on the other, courts will be referred to judgments of foreign courts and this will facilitate an exchange of ideas which is not as likely under the ECN with the Commission's more hands-on control to ensure uniformity.

6 The challenges of institutional resettlement

Competition policy has been described as the EC's 'first truly supranational policy' because the Commission operates as an autonomous agency, free from interference from Member States, the Council or the European Parliament.[201] Regulation 17/62 gave the Commission more powers than the Member States foresaw and it allowed the Commission to design a competition policy for the EC largely free from adverse judicial scrutiny, the ECJ backing most of the Commission's interventions. After 1985 competition enforcement grew in volume and in diversity and the success of competition law led to calls for reform. The Commission wished for modernisation, ostensibly because of an overload of cases, but more probably in order to redirect its enforcement policy away from scrutinising notified agreements and towards regulating cartels. Certain Member States were concerned about the politicisation of decision-making, and decentralised enforcement was seen as a means of resolving this criticism, by placing independent NCAs at the front line of competition enforcement.

---

[199] Article 15 Regulation 1/2003.
[200] The Commission thought this was possible in the White Paper on Modernisation para. 102, but Regulation 1/2003 does not provide for this.
[201] L. McGowan 'Safeguarding the Economic Constitution: The Commission and Competition Policy' in N. Nugent (ed.) *At the Heart of the Union: Studies of the European Commission* 2nd edn (London: Macmillan, 2000) p. 148.

The procedural change comes together with a substantive change for competition law, at two levels: the priorities for enforcement have changed (away from reviewing cooperative contracts and towards hidden collusive agreements) and the substantive interpretation of the law is narrowed down, recourse to public policy considerations being replaced by an emphasis on effects on consumer welfare.

This substantive policy change is reinforced by the provisions of Regulation 1/2003 that strive to compel NCAs and national courts to apply Articles 81 and 82 in a harmonised manner and to the exclusion of national competition law. Whether or not enforcement is more efficient, control over the enforcement of competition law by the newly galvanised NCAs and courts is considerable. The so-called 'network' of NCAs seems to be a forum to facilitate the Commission's policy, by ensuring that there is only one authority in charge of any case and allowing the Commission the final word on any anticipated ruling of NCAs. Thus, while the institutional resettlement appears to decentralise enforcement, it merely decentralises the operational aspect of enforcement, leaving the policy aspect to the Commission. If we recall, looking back over the previous chapters on the substantive law, that the Commission is increasingly keen to view competition law as a means to achieve consumer welfare through competitive markets, then the effect of the kind of decentralisation we witness is to displace national economic policies in favour of a neoliberal, pro-consumer economic policy favoured by the Commission. This might be challenged by the growth of national competition cultures that safeguard a wider range of interests, and by private litigation which, in the aftermath of *Courage v. Crehan*, supports the launching of lawsuits that undermine the pro-consumer bias of modern EC competition law.

12

Competition law and liberalisation

Contents

1. Introduction	*page*	441
2. Initiating liberalisation		442
2.1 Market context		442
2.2 Legislative tools		444
2.3 The Court and the market		446
3. Introducing competition in network industries		451
3.1 Airlines		452
3.2 Telecommunications		456
3.3 Electricity		460
4. Re-regulation		463
4.1 National Regulatory Authorities		463
4.2 Sector-specific regulation in electronic communications		464
4.3 Sector-specific regulation or competition law?		468
4.4 Monitoring National Regulatory Authorities		471
5. Sector-specific competition law		474
5.1 Electricity: merger control		474
5.2 Air transport: regulating airline alliances to open up slots		476
5.3 Postal monopolies: regulating Deutsche Post's cross-subsidies		478
5.4 Testing the legitimacy of sector-specific competition law		484
6. Public services		485
6.1 Exclusion		486
6.2 Exemption		488
6.3 Universal service obligations		491
7. More markets, more law		494

1 Introduction

In the 1980s, states began to relinquish control in a number of economic sectors that had been under their ownership since at least the post-war era (e.g. telecommunications, energy, transport, postal services).[1] For economic reasons (the industries were considered natural monopolies) and/or political considerations (the industries provided public services that all should have a right to as citizens, not as consumers) competition was excluded and in many countries the industries operated as a single, vertically integrated, state-owned monopoly. However, state monopolies were called into question by three considerations: economic (increasing dissatisfaction with the performance of these sectors under state management and an understanding that competition could inject greater efficiency), technological (innovations weakened the natural monopoly argument) and political (a shift in the conception of the role of the state, perhaps best encapsulated by the catchphrase 'rolling back the state'). Today, the provision of public services does not allow one to make a prima facie case for excluding competition. Instead '[t]he traditional approach to public life, based on stewardship and public duty, has been replaced by a market-oriented approach to the delivery of public goods and services'.[2] One useful way to describe the changed relationship between the state and newly liberalised industries is to deploy the concept of the regulatory state. That is, the relationship between the state and industry is no longer characterised by state ownership, support and control but by the following four features: privatisation (i.e. the sale of state-owned industries), liberalisation (allowing new entrants to compete in markets which were reserved to one player), re-regulation (necessary in particular to control the former holder of exclusive monopoly rights so that new entrants are able to compete), and the use of independent bodies to carry out regulatory tasks in the public interest.[3]

The aim of this chapter is to explore the role of EC competition law in shaping the regulatory state. First, we explain how liberalisation in the EC occurred: what economic, political and institutional configurations shaped

[1] For an illuminating study, see M. Thatcher 'From Industrial Policy to Regulatory State: Contrasting Industrial Change in Britain and France' in J. Hayward and A. Menon (eds.) *Governing Europe* (Oxford: Oxford University Press, 2002). The snapshot in this paragraph applies to all industries, although there are differences in detail for each sector. See P. D. Cameron *Competition in Energy Markets: Law and Regulation in the European Union* (Oxford: Oxford University Press, 2002) ch. 1; P. Larouche *Competition Law and Regulation in European Telecommunications* (Oxford: Hart Publishing, 2000) ch. 1; D. Geradin (ed.) *The Liberalisation of State Monopolies in the European Union and Beyond* (The Hague: Kluwer Law International, 2000). For an overview of the different ways through which Member States reduced state intervention, see J. Clifton, F. Comín and D. Díaz Fuentes *Privatisation in the European Union* (Dordrecht: Kluwer Academic, 2003) ch. 2.

[2] J. McEldowney 'Public Management Reform and Administrative Law in Local Public Service in the UK' (2003) *International Review of Administrative Sciences* 69, 79.

[3] Thatcher 'From Industrial Policy'.

this development. We do this in two stages: in section 2 by sketching legal and economic features that underpin the process of liberalisation; in section 3 by applying these to trace the process of liberalisation in three markets (air transport, telecommunications and electricity) where we suggest that the tension between the aim of achieving competition (embraced by the Commission and firms eager to compete) and the interests of some Member States to control the development of competition accounts for 'selective liberalisation' – that is, a gradual and differentiated pace of liberalisation among Member States and economic sectors.[4] In section 4 we explore re-regulation, and address the development of sector-specific regulation that draws on competition law norms and is enforced by national regulatory authorities. We focus on the content of regulation and on how the work of national regulators is monitored.[5] Then in section 5 we examine how EC competition law is applied in a 'sector-specific way' to regulate markets. This section brings us back to the discussion in chapter 7, and reveals that seeing competition law as one set of norms designed to remedy market failures is inaccurate, given that competition law is applied in a sector-specific manner as an industrial policy tool. This application of competition law can be challenged as illegitimate, but the application requires study. Having sketched how formerly protected industries have 'joined the mainstream of market-oriented change in Europe',[6] we consider how the introduction of competition affects and is affected by the requirement to deliver public services in section 6. Having created competitive markets, can one guarantee that citizens receive the public services they are entitled to?

2 Initiating liberalisation

2.1 Market context

Professors Armstrong, Cowan and Vickers have designed an illuminating analytical framework that explains the process of liberalisation and its economic and regulatory implications: we reproduce their diagram below.[7] The diagram works particularly well in network industries. Take the telephone system: pre-liberalisation one vertically integrated firm provides all services in all markets – infrastructure, handset, telephone calls and other services that can be routed via the network. Liberalisation occurs by identifying which of the several

---

[4] M. P. Smith 'In Pursuit of Selective Liberalisation: Single Market Competition and its Limits' (2001) 8 *Journal of European Public Policy* 519.

[5] Other important themes in the growth of sector-specific regulation are the lack of accountability and the lack of a coherent regulatory philosophy. On these, see T. Prosser 'Regulation, Markets and Legitimacy' in J. Jowell and D. Oliver (eds.) *The Changing Constitution* 4th edn (Oxford: Oxford University Press, 2000).

[6] Cameron *Competition in Energy Markets* p. 29.

[7] M. Armstrong, S. Cowan and J. Vickers *Regulatory Reform: Economic Analysis and British Experience* (London: MIT Press, 1994) p. 6.

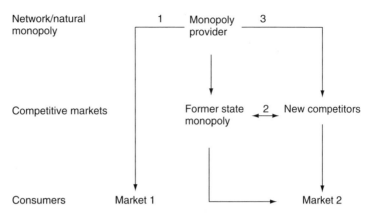

Figure 12.1 Liberalisation of network industries

components of the state monopoly can afford to have more than one supplier, and abolishing the monopolist's exclusive rights in these segments. On this premise, there is no reason why many firms cannot compete to sell more attractive and useful handsets to make calls, or provide cheaper services. Conversely, some other market segments would not work better with competition; as we noted in chapter 7, the local loop is one such market. The first step for liberalisation is identifying markets that would benefit from the entry of more players and abolishing state-granted monopoly rights in these segments, tolerating monopoly in sectors where competition would not make a difference or would be undesirable.

However, merely creating competitive markets does not guarantee competition. Arrow number 1 shows that there are consumers that may be subject to monopoly prices if there is no competition. Arrow number 2 points to a second risk: after liberalisation, the former state monopoly remains in the markets that have been opened to competition and, for a transitional period at least, has significant market power. Think of telephones again: on the day the market is liberalised, every customer has a supply contract with the former state monopolist for telephone services. New entrants must persuade consumers to switch. However, the incumbent monopoly provider may engage in practices that harm the new entrant. Finally, arrow number 3 points to another risk: often the new entrant needs access to facilities operated by the incumbent (e.g. the local loop). However, as the owner of that facility competes with the new entrant downstream, he is tempted to engage in exclusionary tactics to raise rivals' costs by denying access or granting access on unfavourable terms. The tactics that the incumbents can deploy to thwart competitors are those we covered in chapters 6 and 7 when considering Article 82, but the degree of regulatory intervention is more intense in the economic sectors considered in this chapter. As we saw in chapter 7, a specialised agency regulates prices and access to essential facilities in the telecommunications sector and detailed rules apply to ensure access in certain airline markets. Those special rules are risk-based: the remedy is imposed upon proof of market power and risk of harm, not upon proof of misconduct.

2.2 Legislative tools

The introduction of competition requires the creation of new markets by stripping down state monopolies. Markets need three kinds of legal support: property rights, governance structures and rules of exchange.[8] Property rights in this context determine whether the state can continue to own certain enterprises, and whether a monopoly must surrender some of its property rights and give access to competitors. Governance structures are the rules that allow for competition, and rules of exchange determine the terms under which firms can trade with each other and with the consumer (e.g. consumer safety legislation). Judged against these prerequisites, the legal tools that the Community has at its disposal are incomplete. In particular, the Community cannot designate property rights widely. This is due to Article 295 EC which provides that the 'Treaty shall in no way prejudice the rules in Member States governing the system of property ownership'. Therefore state ownership (but not necessarily state monopoly) is lawful. Article 295 means that the Community cannot compel Member States to privatise an industry.[9] However, it can challenge the exercise of property rights when this goes against the Treaty, so, for example, as we saw in chapter 7, property owners may have to share essential goods or services.

The Community has the power to alter governance structures and so liberalise markets. Two articles are of particular importance in giving the Community the legislative power to create markets.[10]

Article 86 EC

1. In the case of public undertakings and undertakings to which Member States grant special or exclusive rights, Member States shall neither enact nor maintain in force any measure contrary to the rules contained in this Treaty, in particular to those rules provided for in Article 12 and Articles 81 to 89.
2. Undertakings entrusted with the operation of services of general economic interest or having the character of a revenue-producing monopoly shall be subject to the rules

---

[8] N. Fligstein and I. Maria-Drita 'How to Make a Market: Reflections on the Attempt to Create a Single Market in the European Union' (1996) 102 *American Journal of Sociology* 1.

[9] But see W. Devroe 'Privatizations and Community Law: Neutrality versus Policy' (1997) 34 *Common Market Law Review* 267.

[10] In addition, Article 31 EC provides that state monopolies of a commercial character must be adjusted so that there is no discrimination between Member States – again no abolition of monopolies is required. These are monopolies over the sale and purchase of goods, for instance the Swedish alcohol retail monopoly, examined and declared lawful in Case C-189/95 *Franzén* [1997] ECR I-5909.

> contained in this Treaty, in particular to the rules on competition, in so far as the application of such rules does not obstruct the performance, in law or in fact, of the particular tasks assigned to them. The development of trade must not be affected to such an extent as would be contrary to the interests of the Community.
>
> 3. The Commission shall ensure the application of the provisions of this Article and shall, where necessary, address appropriate directives or decisions to Member States.

This provision is ambiguous: Article 86(1) may be said to oblige Member States to ensure that state monopolies are subject to competition law – it is a liberalisation provision; on the other hand it provides that state monopolies are permitted, moreover when read with Article 86(2) the conclusion is that state monopolies are not subject to competition law if this would prevent the provision of services of general economic interest. Given that historically the basis for having state control over network industries was precisely to guarantee the provision of a service to all citizens in the public interest, Article 86 can be read to justify the continued existence of state monopolies. The ambiguous drafting reflects a political compromise between Member States in favour of continued public sector presence and the more liberal states.[11] Nevertheless, Article 86(3) gives the Commission the power to legislate, and with appropriate judicial support (which arrived in the early 1990s), this can provide a route to inject competition in sectors shielded by national law. As we show in section 3, this provision played a particularly important role in kick starting liberalisation of the telecommunications sector and in cajoling Member States to agree to liberalisation of the electricity sector.

The second tool is Article 95, which has been the legal basis for the vast majority of the Community's liberalisation initiatives. Legislation under Article 95 is designed to improve the conditions for the establishment and functioning of the internal market.[12] It does so by harmonising national laws. Under this provision the Community can write laws that allow, say, a British courier company to deliver post to Spain. This is achieved by 'harmonising' the laws about which types of postal services are excluded from competition, thereby banning state monopolies outside those markets.[13] Harmonisation is justified by finding evidence that diversity of national regulation hampers the functioning of the internal market. This allows for an indirect challenge to national laws: they are not attacked for their protectionism, but because diversity frustrates the single market.

---

[11] G. Marenco 'Public Services and Community Law' (1983) 20 *Common Market Law Review* 495.

[12] Case C-376/98 *Germany v. Parliament and Council (Tobacco Advertising)* [2000] ECR I-8419 para. 84.

[13] Article 7 Directive 97/67 on Common Rules for the Development of the Internal Market of Community Postal Services and the Improvement of Quality of Service [1998] OJ L15/14, amended by Directive 2002/39 with regard to Further Opening to Competition of Community Postal Services [2002] OJ L176/21.

Of these two legal grounds for liberalisation legislation, Article 86(3) is less politically correct because the Commission enacts the directives independently of other Community organs. In contrast, Article 95 legislation requires approval of legislation by the European Parliament and a qualified majority of the Council.[14] The conventional distinction between Articles 86(3) and 95 is that the former is a liberalisation instrument (requiring Member States to remove special or exclusive rights) and the latter a harmonisation instrument (whereby the market is regulated so that the aims of liberalisation are met). However, such a neat relationship is not accurate. First, the Court suggests that there is some overlap,[15] so that the Commission would be able to use Article 95 for the purposes of liberalisation; second, the early telecommunications directives show that some harmonisation was carried out with Article 86(3);[16] finally, Article 86(3) was not used to dismantle exclusive rights in sectors other than telecommunications. As we suggest below, Article 86(3) directives are better seen as a tool that the Commission can use to force liberalisation strategically when political agreement under Article 95 is stalled by Member States. This is well encapsulated by one MEP's reproach to the Commission after the latter had just promulgated yet another Article 86(3) directive in telecommunications: 'Legally you are right, but politically you are wrong.'[17]

2.3 The Court and the market

Two doctrines developed by the ECJ have been an important complement to the legislative powers in the Treaty because the Court provided a legal basis to challenge anticompetitive state regulation, which allowed the Commission and Council to legislate to open markets to competition. Court rulings have also led to individual traders challenging anticompetitive state legislation that hampered their economic opportunities. The Court's case law contributes to the construction of markets by facilitating positive integration (i.e. the rulings provide justification for Community legislation which authorises competitors to enter the market) or by achieving negative integration (i.e. rulings that declare the denial of market access by national laws unlawful).[18] In the sectors considered in this chapter, negative integration attacks were one of the means pursued by the Commission and private litigants to demand that markets should be opened to competition.

---

[14] Article 251 EC.

[15] Case C-202/88 *France v. Commission* (*Telecommunications Terminal Equipment*) [1991] ECR I-1223.

[16] See Larouche *Competition Law*, ch. 2, esp. pp. 60–70.

[17] Quoted in L. Conant *Justice Contained: Law and Politics in the European Union* (Ithaca: Cornell University Press, 2002) p. 102.

[18] On positive and negative integration generally, see G. Majone *Dilemmas of European Integration* (Oxford: Oxford University Press, 2005) ch. 7.

2.3.1 Article 10 and Articles 81 and 82

Article 10 EC obliges Member States to abstain from measures that could jeopardise the attainment of the objectives of the Treaty. The Court has decided that the obligation in Article 10 may be read jointly with Articles 81 and 82 and so prohibit any action by a Member State which encourages firms to infringe the competition rules.[19] This interpretation has been particularly useful in challenging state meddling in the air transport sector. One illuminating case is *Ahmed Saeed*.[20] The defendants, two travel agents based in Germany, obtained airline tickets from airlines or travel agents established in another state. Although the starting point for the journey mentioned in those tickets was situated outside Germany, passengers who bought tickets from the defendants boarded their flight at a German airport where the scheduled flight made a stopover. In spite of the longer flight, these tickets cost less than tickets for flights departing from Germany. The travel agents' antics were challenged by the association for the campaign against unfair competition, who argued that by selling cheap tickets the defendants contravened German law which prohibits the sale of tickets at prices which are not approved by the competent federal minister. It transpired that air tariffs for flights from Germany were agreed among airlines flying from German airports and the government then approved those fees, which made tickets expensive. In other words, it was a government-sanctioned cartel. The Court of Justice held that the tariff agreements were in breach of Article 81, and that the German government was also acting unlawfully (in breach of Article 10 read jointly with Article 81). The Court ordered that the state must 'refrain from taking any measure which might be construed as encouraging airlines to conclude tariff agreements contrary to the Treaty'.[21] The effect of this finding is significant: not only can travel agents now buy cheap tickets from abroad as the defendants had done, but as the government is no longer able to protect the airlines' cartel, this can be challenged by a competition authority, which will cause prices to fall as airlines are forced to compete against each other for customers. This is an example of using EC competition law to achieve negative integration, as the judgment necessarily reverberated in every Member State that supported airline cartels: all became subject to legal challenge and, as we shall see below, the Commission seized on this to press for liberalisation.

In *Ahmed Saeed* the defendants probably infringed the law deliberately so as to raise the EC competition law point as a defence, but it is also possible to challenge national law on the basis of Articles 10 and 81 directly. For example, a German match manufacturer complained to the Italian Competition Authority that national legislation relating to a consortium of Italian match manufacturers was hindering trade by supporting an unlawful agreement. In this

---

[19] For greater detail, see D. Chalmers, C. Hadjemmanuil, G. Monti and A. Tomkins *European Union Law: Text and Materials* (Cambridge: Cambridge University Press, 2006) pp. 1116–22.

[20] Case 66/86 *Ahmed Saeed Flugreisen and Silver Line Reisebüro GmbH v. Zentrale zur Bekämpfung unlauteren Wettbewerbs eV* [1989] ECR 803.

[21] Ibid. para. 49.

scenario the competition authority is obliged to disapply national law so as to allow the trader to compete on the national market.[22] The Commission can also challenge anticompetitive national laws by issuing a reasoned opinion finding a Member State in breach of EC law, but this route has been used only once.[23]

The Article 10 doctrine is based on the need to ensure the effectiveness of competition law: the competition rules prohibiting anticompetitive conduct would be emasculated if firms could lobby national governments and ask for legislation that legitimises cartels. But the doctrine has two limits. First, it only applies if one can establish a link between state action and an agreement or an abuse of a dominant position. Either state law requires firms to breach Articles 81 and 82, or it encourages anticompetitive behaviour, or it allows firms to enter into a collusive agreement and then ratifies their decisions. On the contrary, if a national law has the effect of stifling price competition (e.g. by preventing an insurer from passing on certain financial advantages, or by granting a monopoly right) this is insufficient to invoke the rule. There must be a breach of competition law by the firms, which is causally connected to the action of the state.[24] Second, the doctrine is inapplicable if the state allows a group of firms to enter into certain agreements, for example lawyers agreeing to fix fees for legal services, but the state then actively supervises the fees that have been agreed to make sure that they are compatible with the public interest. In this case the doctrine does not apply because the fees are subject to effective supervision by the state according to clearly articulated public interest considerations.[25] In this scenario, when public interest considerations are inherent in the procedure that restricts competition, competition law does not apply.[26]

2.3.2 Articles 86(1) and 82

The Commission's liberalisation strategy was legitimated and strengthened by a radical set of judgments in the early 1990s interpreting Article 86(1) where the Court fashioned standards to test the legality of state monopolies. The Court regularly says that the creation of a monopoly by the grant of an exclusive right is not contrary to Article 86(1); however, it also attacks state monopolies when national legislation undermines the effectiveness of Articles 81 and 82.[27] One does not have to search for an infringement by the firm, but

---

[22] Case C-198/01 *Consorzio Industrie Fiammiferi v. Autorità Garante della Concorrenza e del Mercato* [2003] ECR I-8055.

[23] Case C-35/96 *Commission v. Italy* [1998] ECR 3581 (customs agents' tariffs).

[24] Case C-2/91 *Wolf W. Meng* [1993] ECR I-5751: see especially the Opinion of AG Tesauro.

[25] Case C-39/99 *Criminal Proceedings against Arduino* [2002] ECR I-1529. Cf. the US state action doctrine in *California Retail Liquor Dealers Association v. Midcal* 445 US 97 (1980).

[26] H. Schepel 'Delegation of Regulatory Powers to Private Parties under EC Competition Law: Towards a Procedural Public Interest Test' (2002) 39 *Common Market Law Review* 31.

[27] Case C-179/90 *Merci Convenzionali Porto di Genova v. Siderurgica Gabrielli* [1991] ECR I-5889, Opinion of AG van Gerven para. 14. This goes much further than what can be done using Article 10. See K. Bacon 'State Regulation of the Market and EC Competition Rules' [1997] *European Competition Law Review* 283.

only for whether the creation of a monopoly has or may have anticompetitive effects. The Court has identified three ways in which the grant of special or exclusive rights undermines competition.[28]

First, the grant of an exclusive right is unlawful when the beneficiary is not efficient.[29] In the leading case, *Höfner*, Germany had granted a monopoly in the market for recruitment services, banning private recruitment agencies. This had been done in the public interest, to ensure a well-functioning employment market where recruitment agencies were widely available. However, it transpired that the state services were inadequate. In these circumstances, the state could be in breach for its 'regulatory or decisional intervention'.[30] That is, there is no infringement merely because the firm is managed badly, but there is an infringement if the state grants the monopoly to a firm that it knows is poorly managed or under-resourced, or if the state fails to take steps once it sees that the firm is inept. Under this rule the state breaches Article 86(1) only if the provision of the service by the state monopoly is *manifestly* inadequate, providing the state a margin of appreciation as it carries out its regulatory tasks.[31] The German government was bound to take these criteria into account to test whether the exclusive right was justifiable or if the market for employment services should be opened to competition. According to some authors, this doctrine embodies a powerful message from the Court in favour of liberalisation when state intervention leads to an inefficient allocation of resources.[32] However, the case law does not demand liberalisation; rather the state that chooses, for public policy reasons, to grant an exclusive right is under an obligation to monitor the performance of firms to which it grants these rights on a regular basis, for the service may be satisfactory at its inception but become unable to meet demand as circumstances change. If the state monopoly is inefficient the state may cure the inefficiency (e.g. by increasing its finances through taxation) but liberalisation is not compulsory, although it may become necessary if the cost of financing the service through taxation is politically unpalatable.

Second, the case law prohibits the grant of exclusive rights when this creates a conflict of interest and makes it likely that the firm will use these rights to

---

[28] For more conventional interpretations of the case law, see D. Edward and M. Hoskins 'Article 90: Deregulation and EC Law: Reflections Arising from the XVI FIDE Conference' (1995) 32 *Common Market Law Review* 157; Case C-67/96 *Albany International BV v. Stichting Bedrijfspensioenfonds Textielindustrie* [1999] ECR I-5751, Opinion of AG Jacobs paras. 388–439. The focus here is on 'exclusive' rights as the Courts have had little to say in relation to special rights.

[29] Case C-41/90 *Höfner and Elser v. Macrotron* [1991] ECR I-1979; *Porto di Genova* [1991] ECR I-5889.

[30] Case C-475/99 *Ambulanz Glöckner v. Landkreis Südwestpfalz* [2001] ECR I-8089, Opinion of AG Jacobs para. 148.

[31] *Höfner* [1991] ECR I-1979.

[32] N. Reich 'The Single Market and "Public Service" – Reflections on a Current Controversy' ZERP, DP 7/91, pp. 15–22 (reprinted and translated in H. W. Micklitz and S. Weatherill *European Economic Law* (Aldershot: Ashgate, 1997) pp. 182–6).

exclude rivals. For example, in *RTT v. GB INNO*, Belgium had granted the company holding a monopoly over the operation of the public telecommunications network (RTT) the sole power to lay down standards for telephone equipment and to check whether suppliers of equipment met those standards. RTT was also active in the market for telephone equipment. The upshot was that RTT was regulating market access of its competitors. The Court held that this would undermine equality of opportunity between economic operators, placing the firm in charge of regulating access at an obvious advantage over its competitors as it could raise entry barriers to competitors.[33] Using a similar approach in *ERT*, the Court reviewed the Greek radio and television monopoly. The monopolist enjoyed exclusive rights over both the transmission of its own programmes and the retransmission of third party programmes, including those produced in other Member States. The Court held that Article 86(1) prohibits the grant of such exclusive rights where they are liable to create a situation in which the undertaking is led to infringe Article 82 as a result of a discriminatory broadcasting policy in favour of its own programmes.[34] Generalised, these two cases suggest that vertical integration in network industries is problematic: it can allow the owner or controller of the network to exclude competitors, or at least raise their costs to the advantage of its upstream goods or services. Referring back to the diagram on page 443, the Court's case law suggests that there should be unbundling between the monopoly and competitive segments.

Third, the Court held that a Member State would infringe Article 86(1) by granting unnecessarily wide monopoly rights to one firm.[35] In the leading case, a Belgian law granted a monopoly over a wide range of postal services to the Régie des Postes. Mr Corbeau flouted the law by offering an express postal service in the city of Liège, in competition with the state monopoly. When criminal charges were brought against him for breaching the Belgian postal monopoly, he challenged it under Article 86. The Court of Justice condemned the existence of the overly extensive monopoly rights granted to the Régie des Postes, but added that the grant of an extensive monopoly over several service markets to one firm could be tolerated if this was necessary to guarantee the provision of a universal postal service.[36] For example, if Belgium wished to reserve the (profitable) market for express delivery of mail to the same firm that also operates the (unprofitable) nationwide postal service, then the grant of both monopoly rights could be justified because operating the profitable sector helps to pay for the provision of a public service. However, if this justification is absent, then excessive monopoly rights are conferred

---

[33] Case C-18/88 *RTT v. GB-INNO-BM SA* [1991] ECR I-5941 paras. 20–8; *Telecommunications Terminal Equipment* [1991] ECR I-1223 para. 51.

[34] Case C-260/89 *ERT v. Dimotiki Etairia Pliroforissis* [1991] ECR I-2925 para. 37.

[35] J. Pelkmans 'Making EU Network Markets Competitive' (2001) 17 *Oxford Review of Economic Policy* 432, 434.

[36] Case C-320/91 *Corbeau* [1993] ECR I-2533.

unlawfully. This ruling builds on the *RTT* and *ERT* cases. There the Court condemned vertical integration, the grant of exclusive rights up- and downstream, because the firm was in a position to raise rivals' costs. In *Corbeau* the Court considered the denial of market access that results when the state grants monopoly rights across too many markets, suffocating competition in potentially competitive markets.

The upshot of these rulings is twofold. First, the grant of a monopoly in one market is subject to an efficiency benchmark: Member States must ensure that the privileged firm is able to meet demand. Second, the grant of a monopoly to a firm present in more than one market is unlawful in two circumstances: when it creates temptations for the firm to use its market power to exclude others in related markets, and when granting a portfolio of monopolies to one operator is not necessary to finance the provision of a public service. These doctrines have the following effects. First, they legitimate liberalisation, by showing that Member State laws granting exclusive rights are incompatible with the principles of an open market economy. Second, they establish principles that find their way into the legislation. Third, they create incentives for private litigants and the Commission to pursue individual Member States, which can serve as a catalyst towards EC-wide liberalisation.

3 Introducing competition in network industries

The Court's aggressive case law of the 1990s is in contrast with its earlier position that public utilities were justifiably excluded from the internal market project,[37] and even the Commission ignored state monopolies in the 1985 White Paper on the Single Market (which announced the 1992 internal market programme).[38] However, the Commission soon saw the liberalisation of national monopolies and the introduction of cross-border trade as a logical corollary to the internal market programme and as a policy which would foster the competitiveness of European industry.[39] For instance, reducing the price of electricity would lower costs for the manufacturing industry, and a thriving telecommunications market would spur an innovative economy. Below we sketch the Community's involvement in the liberalisation of three industries. This serves to identify certain common themes: markets are opened in phases, EC competition law is used as a 'can opener'[40] in the process of transition from monopoly to competition, the Commission bargains with Member States to

---

[37] The Court backed this position in Case 6/64 *Costa v. ENEL* [1964] ECR 585; Case 155/73 *Sacchi* [1974] ECR 409 (supporting, respectively, ENEL's electricity and RAI's broadcasting monopoly).

[38] EC Commission *White Paper on Completing the Internal Market* COM(85)310.

[39] K. van Miert 'Engineering Competition: The European Approach' in E. F. M. Wubben and W. Hulsink (eds.) *On Creating Competition and Strategic Restructuring* (Cheltenham: Edward Elgar, 2003).

[40] The metaphor is by the former Director General for Competition. K. van Miert 'Liberalisation of the Economy of the European Union: The Game is Not (Yet) Over' in Geradin *Liberalisation*.

accelerate the pace of liberalisation, and the current market condition in the three sectors, while better than two decades ago, does not allow us to find that any market is fully competitive. These themes underpin a wider debate among political scientists about the nature of the Community. Some see the EC, especially the Commission, as the engine of integration, pressing Member States towards Community goals (the supranational view); others see the EC as a forum where Member States negotiate their preferences (the intergovernmental view);[41] while some have suggested that liberalisation shows a partnership between Member States and Community.[42] The results of liberalisation to date suggest each of these three visions contains a kernel of truth: the fact that the Community only began to attack state monopolies in earnest at the same time that the economic and political winds began to change in the Member States suggests that the relationship between national and supranational institutions was cooperative;[43] moreover, the Commission, even when legislating with Article 86(3), always made sure that there was broad political consensus over liberalisation. This also explains why liberalisation of telecommunications has been faster than electricity even if from a legal perspective the Commission's market-creating powers could be deployed with equal force: political consensus over telecommunications liberalisation was more easily obtained than in electricity markets.[44] However, the lack of a systematic process of deregulation, and the gradual opening of markets so as to allow Member States time to adjust, points towards the intergovernmental interpretation. And the strategic use of competition law to put pressure on Member States, the way the Commission negotiated with Member States to overcome domestic pressures (coming from well-organised public sector unions fearful of liberalisation) plus the recourse to Community law by private litigants as a means of securing market access favours the supranational interpretation: what political partnership there existed between the Commission and Member States was in large part formed by the Commission's efforts.[45] The process of liberalisation suggests that the Community's deployment of competition law was one causal factor in achieving liberalisation and in the rate and scope of this process.

3.1 Airlines

Originally the airline sector operated in a highly restrictive manner: states owned a national 'flag carrier' and national aviation policy was conducted to

---

[41] For a refreshingly accessible and robust review and critique, see R. Alesina and R. Perotti 'The European Union: A Politically Incorrect View' (2004) 18 *Journal of Economic Perspectives* 27.

[42] M. Thatcher 'The Commission and National Governments as Partners: EC Regulatory Expansion in Telecommunications 1979–2000' (2001) 8 *Journal of European Public Policy* 558.

[43] Ibid.

[44] For an illuminating account, see Conant *Justice Contained* chs. 4 and 5.

[45] On the Commission's role, see C. Scott 'Changing Patterns of European Community Utilities Law and Policy: An Institutional Hypothesis' in J. Shaw and G. More (eds.) *New Legal Dynamics of European Union* (Oxford: Oxford University Press, 1995) pp. 199–210.

support it, with minor competition from charter airlines or regional airlines. International flights were arranged bilaterally with other states through Air Service Agreements, resulting in duopolistic market structures, where capacity was shared and tariffs agreed. Given the desire to maintain national champions, the application of EC competition law by the Commission was blocked.[46] Similarly, action against exclusive rights granted to national airlines on the basis of Article 86(1) EC was made difficult by Article 51(1) EC, which provides that freedom to provide services in the field of transport is governed by the Transport Title of the Treaty, making it hard for the Commission to act against individual Member States, or to legislate to remove exclusive rights on the basis of Article 86(3).[47] Public ownership was used as a tool of industrial policy: airlines created employment, they bought their requirements locally, strengthening other segments of the economy, and strong public-sector unions pressed governments for job security and high pensions.[48]

Inspired by the economic gains that had been made in the United States by the deregulation of air transport (entry of new airlines, increase in passenger numbers, reduction in the cost of air travel), and galvanised by lobbying from consumer groups, business users (e.g. the European Roundtable of Industrialists), and new non-state-owned airlines that had entered the market in the UK (where the market was already liberalised), the Commission tabled proposals for gradual deregulation. However, its success was modest. In 1983 the first directive liberalising the provision of air transport services provided access for new competitors only to 3 per cent of intra-Community air traffic and limited the size of aircraft that could serve the routes that were opened to competition.[49] A ruling by the Court in 1985 strengthened the Community's hand because it held that the competition rules applied to the transport sector.[50] The case made it possible for the Commission to initiate proceedings against ten airlines for infringement of competition rules (e.g. challenging tariff coordination agreements and slot exchanges, clear breaches of Article 81) as a means of inviting consensus on the application of competition law to the sector to facilitate its liberalisation. The actions were dropped once progress was made on the legislative front.[51] The Court's judgment is significant

---

[46] Regulation 141/62 Exempting Transport from the Application of Council Regulation No. 17 [1962] JO 124/2751.

[47] B. Van Houtte 'Air Transport' in Geradin *Liberalisation* p. 85.

[48] D. O'Reilly and A. Stone Sweet 'The Liberalisation of European Regulation of Air Transport' in W. Sandholtz and A. Stone Sweet (eds.) *European Integration and Supranational Governance* (New York: Oxford University Press, 1998) p. 165.

[49] Council Directive 83/416/EEC of 25 July 1983 concerning the Authorisation of Scheduled Inter-regional Air Services for the Transport of Passengers, Mail and Cargo between Member States [1983] OJ L237/19. For comment see O'Reilly and Stone Sweet 'Liberalisation' pp. 167–8.

[50] Joined Cases 209 to 213/84 *Ministère Public v. Asjes* [1986] ECR 1425 para. 45.

[51] See N. Argyrs 'The EEC Rules of Competition and the Air Transport Sector' (1989) 26 *Common Market Law Review* 5, 8–11; *Seventeenth Report on Competition Policy* (1987) para. 45.

not merely for what it ruled, but because of the way it came about, which resembles *Ahmed Saeed*: the defendants were private and charter airlines and travel agents that sold tickets in France at prices below those that were approved by the Minister for Civil Aviation. They knew this to be a criminal offence, and when prosecuted in the criminal court argued that the French law was invalid because ticket prices were fixed by agreements among the airlines (a clear breach of Article 81) and the French government, in ratifying these anticompetitive agreements, was in breach of its obligations under the EC Treaty, based upon Article 10. The Court agreed.[52] The effect was that in addition to actions by the Commission against airlines, national policy in this sector could be challenged in the domestic courts. Rather than face multiple legal battles which would have led to uncertainty over the continued existence of national flag carriers, Member States preferred to negotiate and so attempt to protect some of their interests while conceding that the market had to be opened to competition.[53] In parallel, some Member States had already introduced measures to liberalise air transport independently of the Community. The pioneers were the UK and the Netherlands who signed an agreement in 1984 to allow any airline to offer flights between the two countries. This was followed by similar bilateral agreements between the UK and Ireland, Belgium and Germany.[54] As increasing numbers of Member States became convinced of the benefits of liberalisation, action at Community level became politically possible by 1986. The speed by which the Community was able to initiate liberalisation in this sector was due to a mixture of liberal Member States that anticipated Community measures, lobbying at national and Community level, and the strategic use of EC competition law that is said to have been decisive to bring France and Germany to agree to negotiate.[55]

The liberalisation of the air transport sector necessitated the break up of a system of bilateral agreements. The agreements were international trade agreements between states, which specified the routes to be flown between two states, the airlines that could operate (normally in the EC context the two national airlines of the states), the capacity allowed, and a system of pricing controls. This cartel-like arrangement supported the national, state-owned airlines.[56] The market was liberalised in three phases (1988, 1991 and 1993), each phase allowing greater scope for competition in the provision of flights. In the first phase bilateral agreements were still tolerated but the freedom of airlines to set fares was increased (Member States retained the power to approve the fares) and access for competing airlines was improved so that 60 per cent of the market (by capacity) could be served by airlines other than

---

[52] *Asjes* [1986] ECR 1425 para. 77.   [53] O'Reilly and Stone Sweet 'Liberalisation' p. 175.
[54] Ibid. p. 178.   [55] Ibid. p. 179.
[56] For a helpful overview, see European Commission *The Single Market Review Subseries II: Impact on Services Volume 2: Air Transport* (1997) ch. 3.

the national ones.[57] Freight services were liberalised during the second phase, while it was only in the third phase that international passenger air routes were completely opened to any EC airline, dismantling the bilateral system.[58] And in 1997 airlines from one Member State were allowed to offer flights within another Member State (e.g. enabling a Dutch airline to offer flights from London to Manchester).[59] Today, firms set airfares freely.[60] The relevant legislation is addressed to Member States, reflecting their ownership of the airspace[61] and airport infrastructure (which is usually owned by local authorities). In addition, the Commission is able to enforce some of the obligations imposed upon Member States: for example, Member States have an obligation to regulate the distribution of air traffic without discrimination on the grounds of nationality and the Commission is empowered to issue decisions to prevent such discrimination, and has acted against some who had favoured national airlines.[62]

Perhaps one reason why, even if liberalisation was phased, the three stages occurred in relatively quick succession lies in the fact that the legislation has failed to tackle slot allocation and transatlantic flights.[63] In order for an aircraft to fly and take off, it requires a slot of time in which to do so. Slots are scarce resources because new runways are not built regularly. They constitute an insurmountable entry barrier for a new entrant. The allocation of slots is in the hands of an independent slot coordinator, who pools all the available slots annually and distributes them to airlines. The major problem with this system is that if an airline has utilised a given slot during the year, then it is automatically entitled to keep that slot.[64] In the trade, it is known as the 'grandfather right' that an airline has over a slot. Established airlines hold several grandfather rights given their former monopoly status and are reluctant to relinquish their slots voluntarily. The effect is that while 50 per cent of available slots must be made available to new entrants,[65] the number of slots is limited. In spite of

---

[57] Directive 87/601/EEC on Fares for Scheduled Air Services between Member States [1987] OJ L374/12; Council Decision 87/602/EEC on the Sharing of Passenger Capacity between Air Carriers on Scheduled Air Services between Member States and on Access for Air Carriers to Scheduled Air-Service Routes [1987] OJ L374/12. The preambles of both directives state that these are the first steps towards full liberalisation. For a summary, see *Seventeenth Report on Competition Policy* (1987) paras. 43–5.

[58] Council Regulation 2408/92 of 23 July 1992 on Access for Community Air Carriers to Intra-Community Air Routes [1992] OJ L240/8.

[59] Ibid., Article 3.

[60] Council Regulation 2409/92 on Fares and Rates for Air Services [1992] OJ L240/15.

[61] Article 1 Chicago Convention, 1944.

[62] The basis for this is Article 8 Regulation 2408/92. See e.g. *TAT* [1994] OJ L127/32 (access to Orly airport), upheld in Case T-260/94 *Air Inter SA v. Commission* [1994] ECR II-997 paras. 106–13.

[63] A. Gleijm 'Competition in Transport on the Move' in J. Eekhoff (ed.) *Competition Policy in Europe* (Berlin: Springer-Verlag, 2004) pp. 133–4.

[64] Article 10(3) Council Regulation 95/93 of 18 January 1993 on Common Rules for the Allocation of Slots at Community Airports [1993] OJ L14/6.

[65] Ibid. Article 10(7).

the market-opening efforts of the Commission, and the increased competition in several routes, further progress is impossible unless there is a more significant availability of slots.[66] Moreover, while the market for European flights is more competitive now than a decade ago, the market for transatlantic flights remains highly concentrated because of bilateral agreements between Member States and the US, which were only successfully challenged in 2002; agreement over a more liberal multilateral scheme to establish an 'Open Aviation Area' has just been reached.[67]

3.2 Telecommunications

To describe the structure of the telecommunications market we can distinguish between an upstream level (e.g. infrastructure) and a downstream market (telephone services). The economic necessity for liberalisation was set out emphatically in the 1987 Green Paper which noted increased demand for telecommunication services, the dramatic technological leaps forward, and the need for the Community to remain competitive in this crucial sector.[68] This was against a background of poor performance by national telecommunication providers throughout the EU. While Member States seemed to agree that reform was necessary, it was the Commission, acting under the legislative powers conferred upon it in Article 86(3), which issued two important directives in the telecommunications field that kick-started market opening in the early 1990s, and which were at the heart of the first phase of liberalisation.[69] The Commission opened the telecommunications equipment and value-added telephone services to competition, leaving the state provider a monopoly in the upstream market for infrastructure and in the downstream market for voice telephony.[70] Satellite networks were liberalised in 1994,[71] mobile telephony and alternative infrastructure in 1996,[72] and, when public voice telephony and networks were opened to competitors in 1998, the market was fully liberalised.[73] The 1998 regulatory model was replaced in 2002 by a fresh regulatory framework with a less intrusive set of obligations, modelled on competition law, which applies to

---

[66] *Twenty-eighth Report on Competition Policy* (1998) p. 49.

[67] E.g. Case C-466/98 *Commission v. UK* [2002] ECR I-9427. For an overview of Commission activity since the cases, see http://ec.europa.eu/transport/air/index_en.htm.

[68] *Towards a dynamic European economy: Green Paper on the Development of the Common Market for Telecommunications Services and Equipment* COM(87)290 final.

[69] The phases are described in detail in Larouche *Competition Law*.

[70] Directive 88/301 on Competition in the Markets in Telecommunications Terminal Equipment [1988] OJ L131/73; Directive 90/388 on Competition in the Markets for Telecommunication Services [1990] OJ L192/10.

[71] Directive 94/96 Satellite Directive [1994] OJ L268/15.

[72] Directive 96/2 Mobile Directive [1996] OJ L20/59; Directive 96/19 Full Competition Directive [1996] OJ L74/13.

[73] Directive 96/19 Full Competition Directive [1996] OJ L74/13.

all forms of electronic communications (this includes telecommunications, the Internet and cable TV).[74]

The story of the two early Article 86(3) directives that were crucial to market opening is helpful in tracing the politics of liberalisation. The Terminal Equipment Directive required that Member States remove exclusive rights for the importation, marketing, connection and bringing into service of terminal equipment (e.g. telephones, telex machines, switchboards) from the national telecommunications provider. This was designed to facilitate imports of this equipment from other Member States – as matters stood (recall the *RTT* judgment above),[75] the national telecommunications provider was also supplying terminal equipment and was in charge of importing competitors' equipment. In this scenario the opportunities for favouring one's own goods and preventing competition are obvious, and the directive, by removing this exclusive right from the national operator, injected competition into the market for equipment.[76] The directive was probably motivated by technological advances: innovative forms of terminal equipment were being developed, with high costs. Makers could only be successful if they were able to sell large quantities so as to recover their costs, so while national equipment manufacturers had originally been happy with national monopolies (the state bought exclusively from them), they began to support liberalisation to increase sales, once sales to 'their' state were insufficiently profitable.[77] The second major Article 86(3) directive was designed to introduce competition in the market for telecommunication services, excluding voice telephony, which would remain in the hands of the national monopolist for a transitional period to facilitate adjustment. Member States were obliged to withdraw the exclusive rights conferred on the national monopolist over all other telecommunication services (e.g. data transmission services and e-mail).[78] This preserved the most profitable sector to the state monopoly, affording it time to adjust, while allowing new players to enter the market.

Certain Member States challenged the two directives, and while the litigation looks like a constitutional squabble about whether Article 86 or Article 95 is the appropriate legal basis, at the heart of these disputes was the reluctance of certain Member States to liberalise at the speed and magnitude that the

---

[74] See generally L. Garzaniti *Telecommunications, Broadcasting and the Internet* 2nd edn (London: Sweet and Maxwell, 2003) ch. 1; M. Cave 'Economic Aspects of the New Regulatory Regime for Electronic Communications' in P. A. Buigues and P. Rey (eds.) *The Economics of Antitrust and Regulation in Telecommunications: Perspectives for the New European Regulatory Framework* (Cheltenham: Edward Elgar, 2004).

[75] See p. 450.

[76] Article 2 and Recitals 1, 5, 13–14 Directive 88/301 on Competition in the Markets in Telecommunications Terminal Equipment [1988] OJ L131/73.

[77] W. Sandholtz 'The Emergence of a Supranational Telecommunications Regime' in Sandholtz and Stone Sweet *European Integration* p. 141.

[78] Article 2 Directive 90/388 on Competition in the Markets for Telecommunication Services [1990] OJ L192/10.

Commission wished. The Court's judgments did not follow the spirit of the earlier case law that upheld state monopolies in the public interest, nor did the Court explain why a monopoly that had been in existence for some time was now contrary to Article 86.[79] The Court was able to change its position because of the opaque language of Article 86, and its policy shifted from one of supporting Member States to one of supporting the Commission's efforts. Following these judgments, which were a victory for the Commission, the Council agreed a raft of measures under Article 95 to speed up the process of liberalisation. These measures included harmonised standards for telecommunications equipment and a framework to guarantee Open Network Provision, i.e. access to the monopoly infrastructure by new entrants on the competitive markets.[80] Member States were more willing to negotiate politically to retain control of the process of liberalisation after the Commission's legal powers under Article 86(3) had been galvanised by the Court.

Having established the basis for market opening, the Commission was eager to cut down the scope of national monopolies further. As summarised above, liberalisation was achieved in phases, and it was the Commission that dictated the pace of market opening. A telling illustration of how this was achieved is the liberalisation of alternative infrastructure. This includes cable TV, or railway networks that could be used to route telecommunications services, or existing infrastructure that was not owned by the state monopoly. Opening this market would weaken the state monopoly over traditional telecommunications infrastructure. The Commission was eager to move on this (supported by the UK, Sweden and Finland) but other Member States opposed this initiative and wanted to give the state monopoly more breathing space. The Commission used competition decisions to 'convince' the other Member States. The clearest example is the Commission's review of the *Atlas* joint venture.[81] This was an agreement between France Telecom and Deutsche Telekom (at the time both state owned) for a joint venture that would provide advanced telecommunications services to companies. The Commission granted an exemption under Article 81(3), but one of the conditions was that France and Germany liberalise alternative infrastructure so as to allow market access for competitors of the joint venture. So the Commission applied the conditional legality approach (which we identified in chapter 4 as one of the techniques by which public policy is pursued through Article 81) as a means of achieving its regulatory ambition; and similar steps were undertaken

---

[79] Case C-202/88 *France v. Commission* [1991] ECR 1223; Joined Cases C-271/90, C-281/90 and C-289/90 *Spain and Others v. Commission* [1992] ECR I-5833 (but both judgments annulled certain Articles of the directives on technical grounds). F. Blum 'The Recent Case Law of the European Court of Justice on State Monopolies and its Implication for Network Industries' (2000) 1 *Journal of Network Industries* 55, 57–8.

[80] For a review, see A. Bavasso *Communications in EU Antitrust Law* (The Hague: Kluwer Law International, 2003) ch. 2.

[81] *Atlas* [1996] OJ L239/23.

vis-à-vis other Member States.[82] Having thus 'persuaded' reluctant Member States, the Commission legislated to open all national markets for alternative infrastructure to competition.[83] While liberalisation was achieved with the consent of Member States, this was obtained by striking a bargain, trading a joint venture clearance in exchange for liberalisation.[84] This move can be questioned from a legal basis (the remedy is not addressed to the parties) but the political sagacity of the Commission can only be admired.

Measuring the results of liberalisation thus far, consumers have made gains as prices have fallen and a variety of new services are available. However, in fixed telecommunications, the degree of concentration remains high, especially as former state monopolies devise new schemes to win back customers that had been lost,[85] and have a large (albeit declining) share of the market for broadband services.[86] On the other hand, old and new providers are suffering a downturn, mostly due to the vast sums many spent buying 3G mobile phone licences from Member States only to find that consumer demand is weak and the costs cannot be recouped. Moreover, a number of strategic alliances entered into at the beginning of the process of liberalisation have failed to yield any real benefits and have been abandoned. Finally, the resilience of the incumbent suggests that the deregulatory effort has not been sufficiently robust. Regarding the last point, Professor Larouche has suggested that the regulatory model which introduced competition in the 1990s was problematic in the following ways.[87] First, it focused on giving new entrants access to provide new services by using the upstream infrastructure owned by the incumbent, but created few incentives for newcomers to build alternative infrastructure and concomitantly allowed the incumbent to make access costly or difficult, thereby raising rivals' costs. While the new regulatory framework provides some recognition that European regulation should encourage 'efficient investment and innovation',[88] there is little detail on how this policy is to be implemented while at the same time promoting competition. Second, the regulatory structure was inflexible, formalistic and uncertain.[89] Third, there was no 'regulatory bargain' by which old state monopolies were given

---

[82] The case law is explored in depth by Larouche *Competition Law* pp. 53–60 and 302–16 and A. de Streel 'Remedies in the Electronic Communications Sector' in D. Geradin (ed.) *Remedies in Network Industries: EC Competition Law vs. Sector Specific Regulation* (Antwerp: Intersentia, 2004).

[83] Directive 95/91 amending Directive 90/388 with regard to Cable TV [1995] OJ L256/49; Directive 96/2 and Directive 96/19.

[84] Thatcher 'Commission and National Governments' p. 572.

[85] *Communication on Market Reviews under the EU Regulatory Framework* COM(2006)28 final p. 7.

[86] EC Commission *European Electronic Communications Regulations and Markets* 2005 (11th Report) COM(2006)68 final.

[87] P. Larouche 'What Went Wrong: The European Perspective' *TILEC Discussion Paper* (DP 2003–001) pp. 11–27.

[88] Article 8(1)(k) Directive 2002/21/EC on a Common Regulatory Framework for Electronic Communications, Networks and Services [2002] OJ L108/33 (Framework Directive).

[89] This is addressed in the 2002 framework, which we review briefly below.

incentives to comply with the rules on access. That is, there was no promise of profits in other markets should the firms comply. Fourth, while each national market has been liberalised, there is no Community market for telecommunications. Perhaps a good illustration is the absence of pan-European phone networks, with expensive international roaming charges for many consumers who travel. And in this context the Commission's most recent proposal, to regulate roaming charges by promising to cut these by 70 per cent, treats the symptoms but not the cause of the high prices: fragmented markets and firms that plan locally.[90]

3.3 Electricity

The electricity market consists of four vertically interdependent markets: (1) *generation* of electricity; (2) *transmission* of electricity through high voltage grids; (3) *distribution* through lower voltage grids; (4) *supply* to final customers. Of these markets, the transmission and distribution systems are natural monopolies. Competition is possible at the generation and supply ends of the market, provided that generators and suppliers have access to the network. In most Member States, the four sectors were vertically integrated with local or national monopolies designed to maintain security of supply and public service obligations;[91] however, the consumer had no choice and the monopolist bore no risks if the system was not managed well.[92] The market was liberalised by giving increasing numbers of consumers the ability to choose suppliers. Under the first liberalisation directive in 1996, only large industries that consumed considerable amounts of electricity were eligible to choose suppliers.[93] This meant that only 27 per cent of the retail market was open to competition.[94] With the second directive, all non-household customers were eligible from 2004, and from 1 July 2007 all customers may choose suppliers freely.[95] Concomitantly, there is provision of access to the network by new generators.

The Commission introduced proposals for liberalisation in 1988, which were boosted by the success of British liberalisation, but it faced opposition from many Member States. So the Commission (as with airlines and

---

[90] Proposal for a Regulation of the European Parliament and of the Council on Roaming on Public Mobile Networks within the Community and amending Directive 2002/21/EC on a Common Regulatory Framework for Electronic Communications Networks and Services COM(2006)382 final.

[91] L. Hancher 'Slow and Not So Sure: Europe's Long March to Electricity Liberalisation' (1997) *Electricity Journal* 92, 93.

[92] Cameron *Competition in Energy Markets* pp. 6–7.

[93] Directive 96/92 concerning Common Rules for the Internal Market in Electricity [1997] OJ L27/20.

[94] A. Schaub 'Liberalisation of the European Energy Markets: The Perspective of Competition Policy' in A. von Bogdandy, P. Mavroidis and Y. Mény (eds.) *European Integration and International Coordination: Studies in Transnational Economic Law in Honour of C.-D. Ehlermann* (The Hague: Kluwer Law International, 2002) p. 407.

[95] Article 21 Directive 2003/54 concerning Common Rules for the Internal Market in Electricity [2003] OJ L176/37.

telecommunications) pressed for market opening by taking legal action against certain Member States and hinted that it would use Article 86(3) to legislate. However, the Article 86(3) route proved risky given that the degree of opposition (in particular from two major Member States, France and Germany) was stronger than that faced in telecommunications. The Commission used the threat of Article 86(3) regularly during negotiations, but it was also worried about Member States demanding a revision of the Treaty to axe this provision, so the threats were not as powerful as in the telecommunications sector.[96] The Commission's fortunes turned in 1995 when Germany moved to support liberalisation (explained by some as a result of policy learning by seeing the UK model and through discussions about liberalisation in the EU, and by others as a response to lobbying from German consumers who faced the highest electricity bills in Europe and the support of liberalisation by German utilities).[97] This isolated the French, whose main interest was in protecting the national electricity giant Electricité de France but who were worried about the Commission's legal challenges[98] and agreed to negotiate a liberalisation package so that they would be able to control how this came about. The Commission too compromised, by redrafting one aspect of the first directive to accommodate French demands. The compromise was about access obligations. Giving consumers the right to choose suppliers is meaningless unless a supplier has access to the transmission and distribution networks. The Commission had proposed two access routes: negotiated third-party access (access is negotiated with the network operator) or regulated third-party access (access prices are published and there is no negotiation). The French proposed an alternative, the single-buyer model (that is, one wholesale buyer of electricity in the Member State), and the Commission accepted this, even though this option was not then taken up in France.[99]

The results of liberalisation to date have been limited, mostly because while final consumers have a choice, this is relatively limited: the upstream market is highly concentrated with high entry barriers. At national level, for example, there has been an increase in competition (six Member States, for example, have opened the supply market fully already)[100] but in most Member States supply is still highly concentrated, and the former state monopolist has the lion's share of the market. In terms of generation, the market share of the biggest generator (normally the former state monopolist) has shrunk in many

---

[96] Conant *Justice Contained* ch. 5, esp. p. 132.

[97] See, respectively: R. Eisig and N. Jabko 'Moving Targets: National Interests and Electricity Liberalization in the European Union' (2001) 34 *Comparative Political Studies* 742, and J. Greenwood 'Electricity Liberalisation' in R. Pedler (ed.) *European Union Lobbying* (Basingstoke: Palgrave, 2002) pp. 271–2.

[98] Case C-159/94 *France v. Commission* [1997] ECR I-5815 (see commentary by P. J. Slot (1998) 35 *Common Market Law Review* 1183). The Commission lost but the threat of further action, either from the Commission or from private litigants, meant that liberalisation was inevitable and France preferred to control this politically via the EC.

[99] Under the new directive, all Member States must provide regulated access.

[100] Austria, Denmark, Finland, Spain, Sweden and the UK.

Member States but not proportionately.[101] Consumer prices have fallen, but the number of customers that have switched supplier is low: in the best performing Member State, the UK, only 12 per cent of small commercial and domestic users have switched suppliers, although switching by large users has been more considerable (45 per cent of large users have switched in Denmark, 20 per cent have switched in Germany, Ireland, the Netherlands and Spain).[102]

Viewed from the Community level, the first directive was criticised for allowing some liberalisation at national level but failing to create the conditions for an internal market,[103] and cross-border trade was 10.7 per cent of total consumption in 2004, representing only a 4 per cent increase since 2000.[104] As a result, national markets are shielded from competition. There are two major reasons that explain the fragmented nature of markets: weak unbundling and lack of interconnection capacity.

The industry is vertically integrated, so while a company that only operates the transmission or distribution market would be willing to sell access to any supplier, it has no incentive to do so when new suppliers become its competitors. The second directive has imposed more significant unbundling requirements: each Member State must nominate a Transmission System Operator (TSO) and a Distribution System Operator (DSO) whose task is the maintenance and monitoring of electricity flows. The market is unbundled by the requirement that TSOs and DSOs that are vertically integrated (in generation or supply) must operate transmission and distribution independently from other services, but the directive does not require divestiture.[105] The separation is reinforced by the duty to keep separate accounts for transmission and distribution functions to prevent distortions of competition from cross-subsidisation.[106] Having created a quasi-independent network, the directive entitles all customers (including suppliers) to have access to the grid based on non-discriminatory tariffs.[107] It was politically impossible to agree full divestiture, so the TSO and DSO must put in place a compliance programme to ensure that there is no discrimination and that unbundling is carried out.[108] It remains to be seen whether, once this framework has been implemented, trade among Member States will increase.

Trade is also stifled by the low levels of interconnection capacity between states and the lack of obligations in the directive to compel the creation of new

---

[101] For a detailed breakdown, see DG TREN *Draft Working Paper, Third Benchmarking Report on the Implementation of the Internal Electricity and Gas Market* (1 March 2004).

[102] Ibid.

[103] B. Eberlein 'Regulation by Cooperation: The "Third Way" in Making Rules for the Internal Energy Market' in P. D. Cameron (ed.) *Legal Aspects of EU Energy Regulation* (Oxford: Oxford University Press, 2005) p. 64.

[104] *Report on Progress in Creating the Internal Gas and Electricity Market* COM(2005)568 final p. 5.

[105] Articles 10(1), 15(1) Directive 2003/54. The same firm can combine the tasks of DSO and TSO (Article 17).

[106] Ibid. Article 19.   [107] Ibid. Article 20.

[108] Ibid. Articles 10(2)(d) TSO, 15(2)(d) DSO and 17(d) combined operators.

interconnection capacity.[109] In 2002, the European Council committed each Member State to develop interconnection capacity so that at least 10 per cent of its requirements could be sourced from overseas, but this has not yet been achieved.[110] This is unsurprising given that vertical integration deprives the owner of the network of any incentive to build infrastructure that may harm profits downstream. The Commission has threatened to use Article 82 to force the owners of some interconnection networks to grant non-discriminatory access to third parties (e.g. opening capacity between the UK and France (previously reserved to EdF's exports to the UK) and between Germany and Scandinavian countries).[111] Moreover, the Court has held that in certain circumstances, the historical preference given to long-term contracts for access to interconnection capacity may be contrary to EC law, and this might serve to open the existing network to new suppliers further.[112]

In sum, unless deeper regulatory efforts are undertaken to create competition, either by unbundling generation and transmission, and forcing generators to compete, or by increasing interconnection between Member States, it is unlikely that the single-market project will progress further merely through episodic challenges to restrictive practices under the competition rules.[113]

4 Re-regulation

Liberalisation is accompanied by the creation of independent National Regulatory Authorities (NRAs) to monitor newly created markets. We begin by outlining the role of the NRA; then, using electronic communications as an example, illustrate how the substance of much sector-specific regulation (SSR) draws on competition law principles and discuss the relationship between SSR and competition law. Last, we examine how the application of SSR is kept in check.

4.1 National Regulatory Authorities

From a political science perspective, there are three reasons why governments delegate regulation to an independent authority: first, the agency can specialise

---

[109] EC Commission *Communication on Infrastructure and Security of Supply* COM(2003)743 p. 5, noting that the target for cross-border trade in electricity (10 per cent of installed generation capacity) was unlikely to be met by the 2005 deadline.

[110] *Report on Progress in Creating the Internal Gas and Electricity Market* p. 5.

[111] Press releases IP/01/30 and IP/01/341.

[112] Case C-17/03 *Vereniging voor Energie, Milieu en Water and Others v. Directeur van de Dienst uitvoering en toezicht energie*, judgment of 7 June 2005; Commission Staff Working Document on Case C-17/03 SEC(2006)547.

[113] See generally D. Newbery 'Regulatory Challenges to European Electricity Liberalisation' (2002) 9 *Swedish Economic Policy Review* 9; L. Bergman, G. Brunekreeft, C. Doyle, B.-H. von der Fehr, D. M. Newbery, M. Pollitt and P. Regibeau *A European Market for Electricity?* (London: Centre for Economic Policy Research, 1999).

in the sector and gain expertise, making for better regulation; second, governments can shift the blame to the agency when the liberalised market does not work well; third, creating the agency demonstrates a credible commitment to efficient markets.[114] As we saw in chapter 11, similar reasons motivated the creation of National Competition Authorities, but an unexpected effect was that many NCAs grew in prestige, distanced themselves from political control and increased their powers, well beyond those which states anticipated.

It is likely that these effects will also occur for NRAs. First, the liberalisation directives prescribe that NRAs must be independent of the firms they regulate.[115] Second, the directives entrust specific tasks to the NRA. These two elements make it less possible for government to circumscribe the NRA's powers. However, it is likely that some NRAs are weaker than others: for example, the role of agencies is better understood in UK public law than in Germany, where the competition authority has a much higher status; and in the case of telecommunications, the UK regulator has greater power and autonomy than the German regulator.[116] Third, NRAs are monitored by other NRAs via European networks, and peer pressure through these is likely to enhance their independence from national politics further. In the field of electronic communications for example, the European Regulators Group was established by the Commission,[117] and has agreed a harmonised approach to remedies.[118] Fourth, as we explain below, in the field of electronic communications, the Commission can control the application of SSR, limiting the scope for national control.

4.2 Sector-specific regulation in electronic communications

The regulatory framework empowers NRAs to impose obligations on certain market players, with considerable guidance from the Commission.[119] The most burdensome obligations can be imposed on operators that have significant

---

[114] M. Thatcher 'Delegation to Independent Regulatory Agencies: Pressures, Functions and Contextual Mediation' (2002) 25 *West European Politics* 125, 133.

[115] *RTT* [1991] ECR I-5941 suggests that the regulator's independence from the firms it regulates is a principle of EC law; Article 22 Directive 97/67 on postal services. In electronic communications, Article 3 Framework Directive provides that if the Member State owns firms in the market, it must ensure effective structural separation of regulation and activities. In air transport there is no overall NRA as the majority of the liberalisation provisions are addressed to Member States, but a 'coordinator' must be established for the allocation of landing slots in airports. Little guidance is given save that he shall act in an 'independent, neutral, non-discriminatory and transparent manner'. Article 4 Council Regulation 95/93.

[116] D. Coen 'Managing the Political Life Cycle of Regulation in the UK and German Telecommunications Sectors' (2005) 76 *Annals of Public and Cooperative Economics* 59.

[117] Decision establishing the European Regulators Group for Electronic Communications Networks and Services [2002] OJ L200/38 (amended by Decision 2004/3445, [2004] OJ L293/20).

[118] Revised ERG Common Position (ERG (06) 33), available at http://erg.eu.int/.

[119] This is a necessarily brief overview: those seeking more detailed treatment can start with A. de Streel 'The Integration of Competition Law Principles in the New European Regulatory Framework for Electronic Communications' (2003) 26 *World Competition* 489 for a clear and thoughtful presentation.

market power. The regulatory process begins with the Commission publishing a recommendation on relevant markets it believes may warrant NRA intervention,[120] and guidelines for the assessment of market power.[121] NRAs then take these two soft law instruments into account and review national markets to determine whether there are any instances where one or more firms have significant market power.[122] The concept of significant market power (SMP) is analogous to the concept of dominance,[123] and the procedure described resembles the start of an Article 82 inquiry, whereby markets are defined and dominance analysed. If the NRA finds that there is no SMP, then it must remove any regulatory obligation, while if it finds that certain firms hold SMP, then it is empowered to regulate the markets.[124] This process can be characterised as a risk-based assessment whereby a finding of SMP triggers the application of the law, not unlike the procedure we have seen in the context of vertical restraints where the lack of market power allows for the application of a Block Exemption, or in the context of merger cases where thresholds are used to signal the potential presence of anticompetitive risk. The NRA's draft analyses of market definition and market power are subject to review and veto by the Commission, while the NRA has greater independence in designing the appropriate remedy.[125] The Commission has identified eighteen markets where regulation might be warranted but two examples in the mobile phone sector will suffice to offer a practical illustration of how the process summarised above works in practice.

The first is 'access and call origination'. In simple terms, assume that firm B wants to offer mobile phone services. It might want to do so by using the upstream network of another existing mobile phone operator (e.g. firm A).

There is a risk to competition if the upstream network owner does not allow new entrants access, because it can reserve the downstream market to itself, or it can operate a 'price squeeze' to make entry by firm B less profitable. If the NRA finds that there is SMP on the upstream market, it may impose one or more remedies on firm A drawn from the Access Directive.[126] Table 12.1 sets out the remedies and the rationale for them in ascending order of intrusiveness.[127]

---

[120] Article 15(1) Framework Directive and Commission Recommendation on Relevant Product and Service Markets within the Electronic Communications Sector Susceptible to Ex Ante Regulation in accordance with Directive 2002/12/EC of the European Parliament and of the Council on a Common Regulatory Framework for Electronic Communication Networks and Services [2003] OJ L114/5.

[121] Article 15(2) Framework Directive and Commission *Guidelines on Market Analysis and the Assessment of Significant Market Power under the Community Regulatory Framework for Electronic Communications Networks and Services* [2002] OJ C165/6.

[122] Articles 15(3) and 16(1) Framework Directive.

[123] Article 14(2) and (3) Framework Directive (see ch. 5).

[124] Article 14(3) and (4) Framework Directive.

[125] Article 7(3) and (4) Framework Directive.

[126] Directive 2002/19/EC on Access to, and Interconnection of, Electronic Communications Networks and Associated Facilities (Access Directive) [2002] OJ L108/7.

[127] This analysis draws on Cave 'Economic Aspects'.

Table 12.1 Remedies under the Access Directive

Remedy	Rationale
Article 9 Transparency: publish data on technical specifications, network characteristics and prices.	Information on technical specifications is necessary in order to ensure interoperability between the services of the person requiring access and the network. Price transparency can allow the new entrant to make informed decisions on entry.
Article 10 Non-discrimination: a duty to treat each firm requiring access equally and in particular to provide competitors the same terms and conditions as it offers to its own vertically integrated services.	Designed to prevent foreclosure by ensuring that the firm does not favour its own downstream providers (e.g. by setting different prices). Prevents margin squeezes.
Article 11 Accounting separation: a duty to make its wholesale prices transparent when the firm is vertically integrated and competes in the same downstream market as the firm requiring access.	This can allow the NRA to observe whether the firm is cross-subsidising monopoly profits upstream to finance exclusionary tactics on the downstream market.
Article 12 Obligation of access to, and use of, specific network facilities where the denial of access would 'hinder the emergence of a sustainable competitive market at the retail level, or would not be in the user's best interests'.[128]	This can be used if there is a fear that the firm will not merely make access difficult (for which the above remedies apply) but may refuse to grant access point blank.
Article 13 Price control and cost accounting obligations: when the operator is able to harm end users by excessive prices.	To protect (1) consumers from high prices; (2) competitors from a price squeeze that would exclude them.

The Finnish NRA wished to intervene in this sector because the leading mobile network operator (TeliaSonera) held a 60 per cent market share in the downstream market. The NRA wished to impose remedies to require the leading firm to provide interconnection to its network and not to discriminate against new entrants. However, the Commission disagreed with the Finnish regulator and said that TeliaSonera lacked SMP. The upstream market included two other mobile network operators and there were over ten downstream service providers, some of which had concluded agreements with mobile network operators to provide their services, so there seemed to be no obstacles to new entrants gaining access to a network. Moreover, mobile network operators found themselves competing to offer network coverage to new entrants, so there was little risk that TeliaSonera would raise the costs of new downstream providers or prevent their entry. Moreover, the evidence suggested that new entrants would negotiate network access with all the mobile network operators and select the most lucrative deal. This suggested that TeliaSonera lacked the power to reduce output and increase

---

[128] Article 12(1) Access Directive.

price.[129] A comparable trend is present in several Member States, so regulatory obligations have been phased out in this market.[130]

The second example is in the market for voice call termination. Following on from the first example, firm B, having obtained access to a network, must enter into contracts with other providers of telephone services so that its customers can call those in other networks. In Figure 12.2 a telephone call 'originates' on B's network but 'terminates' on A's network. At retail level, the call is paid for by the caller (the so-called calling party-pays principle) and B must negotiate a termination charge with A, the cost of which is passed on to the consumer. In all the Member States, the regulators have said that each mobile network operator like A has SMP. This is because when the customer who uses B's network makes a call (say he uses Orange) to a person who is using A's network (say Vodafone), that call can only terminate on that network (Vodafone) and so A has the power to raise the termination charges. Neither the person making the call nor his supplier can get round this: the call has to terminate on A's network.

Client of (B) makes a call ⟶ Call origination (B) ⟶ Call termination (A) ⟶ Call received by user of A's network

Figure 12.2 Voice call termination

The UK regulator, for example, has determined that every mobile network operator has SMP because their market shares are 100 per cent for the market of calls to its network.[131] This approach (which the Commission calls 'one network, one number') has been followed by all regulators, and termination charges have fallen as a result of regulatory intervention.[132] In the UK, for example, the NRA imposed a wide range of obligations, including an obligation to allow for access to call termination, a duty not to discriminate, and price controls.[133]

The key focus of SSR, as the two examples above show, is on the upstream wholesale market (involving the relationship between network owners and providers of services), with the assumption that provided more market players can enter to provide competing services to consumers, then this removes the need to regulate the retail market (involving the relationship between the provider of services and the final consumer). This is confirmed in the Universal Service Directive which allows the NRA to impose remedies on retail markets only (1) upon proof of SMP and (2) when wholesale regulations

---

[129] Case FI/2004/0082 *Access and Call Origination on Public Mobile Telephone Networks in Finland*, Commission Decision of 5 October 2004 (available at http://ec.europa.eu/comm/competition/liberalization/decisions/).

[130] EC Commission *Communication on Market Reviews under the EU Regulatory Framework Consolidating the Internal Market for Electronic Communications* SEC(2006)86 p. 8.

[131] Office of Communications (Ofcom) *Wholesale Mobile Voice Call Termination* 1 June 2004.

[132] EC Commission *Communication on Market Reviews* p. 8.

[133] Ofcom *Wholesale Mobile Voice Call Termination*.

would not serve to promote competition.[134] The remedies that may be imposed at retail level 'may include requirements that the identified undertakings do not charge excessive prices, inhibit market entry or restrict competition by setting predatory prices, show undue preference to specific end-users or unreasonably bundle services'.[135] They mirror the regulatory scope of Article 82.

However, SSR is not limited to players that have substantial market power. There are also obligations that the NRA may impose upon all market operators without proof of SMP so as to guarantee that the market is more competitive. These include the obligation on all network operators to negotiate interconnection so that they can accept incoming calls from other networks. This ensures that all operators can deliver the calls originating in their network to any other.[136] The policy underpinning these obligations is to ensure that there is a complete network, which benefits users and also each operator: as the value of a network increases the more persons one can communicate with through that network. Another example of SSR that applies across the industry is number portability, which we discussed in chapter 7.[137] The NRA must ensure that users who switch from one service provider to another can keep the existing number.[138] This is an effective means of facilitating consumer choice, which could not be achieved by competition law.

4.3 Sector-specific regulation or competition law?

In regulating electronic communications, the NRA acts like a competition authority, and it is difficult to draw clear boundaries between 'regulatory' and 'antitrust' functions.[139] The overlap is not surprising because the economic problems in network industries are similar to those we saw in chapters 6 and 7 when there is a dominant firm. The major distinction between SSR and competition should be this: 'while competition policy tells firms what not to do, regulation involves telling them what they are to do'.[140] However, as we saw in chapter 7, this distinction breaks down because the Commission has used competition law in a sector-specific manner, to guide firms to reduce excessive prices and to grant access to essential facilities. Accordingly, it is legitimate to ask whether sector-specific regulation is necessary, given

---

[134] Article 17(1) Directive 2002/22/EC on Universal Service and Users' Rights relating to Electronic Communications Networks and Services (Universal Services Directive) [2002] OJ L108/51.
[135] Article 17(2) Universal Services Directive.   [136] Articles 4 and 5 Access Directive.
[137] See p. 222.   [138] Article 30 Universal Services Directive.
[139] For some attempts at line drawing, see M. J. Trebilcock, R. A. Winter, P. Collins and E. Iacobucci *The Law and Economics of Canadian Competition Policy* (Toronto: University of Toronto Press, 2002) pp. 712–14; A. Perrot 'Régulation et politique de concurrence dans les réseaux électriques' (2004) 14 *Economie publique* 3.
[140] H. Ergas, quoted in Cave 'Economic Aspects' p. 25.

that competition law seems sufficiently broad in scope to achieve regulatory functions.

There are a number of ways to defend the role of SSR when it overlaps with competition law. First, we can condemn the Commission for corrupting competition law and extending it illegitimately to carry out the task of sector-specific regulation (we discuss this below in section 5). Second, an NRA has a comparative advantage over competition authorities, based on expertise and resources, making the NRA a better institution for regulating price and determining access. A competition authority intervenes in markets episodically; it lacks the resources for day-to-day management. It also lacks adequate remedial tools: as we saw in chapter 7, when access remedies are imposed the Commission often subcontracts supervision to third parties. NRAs are better equipped to review systemic market failures. However, this is an argument in favour of empowering the NRA to apply competition law and it does not make a case for SSR. Third, according to the Commission, there is a need for risk-based regulation. That is, rather than wait for a dominant firm to refuse to supply, it is necessary to establish obligations to avoid further deterioration of the market.[141] However, this justification is weak in that often Article 82 is applied prudentially before the abuse has caused harm, and conversely SSR remedies are likely to be imposed when the NRA has some experience that a firm with SMP is acting anticompetitively. A fourth justification is that SSR can be more aggressive than competition law. For example, the obligation not to discriminate is probably wider under SSR than under Article 82,[142] and SSR applies to regulate price, something that general competition law eschews. The obligation to provide access is also more extensive under SSR than under Article 82. In the field of electronic communications NRAs may compel access when refusal would either 'hinder the emergence of a sustainable competitive market at the retail level, or would not be in the user's best interests'.[143] The first ground is similar to the *Oscar Bronner* doctrine where the Court required that the refusal eliminate competition in the downstream market, but it is phrased in a significantly different manner: under Article 82 a refusal is abusive if it eliminates competition, and an access remedy does not necessarily make the downstream market workably competitive, it may just lead to the addition of another market player. However, the NRA can force the grant of access rights to as many downstream competitors as it wants until it considers that the retail market is 'sustainably competitive', a phrase that eschews precise definitions, giving the regulator considerable flexibility. Moreover, the NRA has a second ground upon which it can require access: the interest of users, which seems to give it even more power in imposing an access remedy. The

---

[141] Recital 25 Framework Directive, identifying SSR with *ex ante* regulation.
[142] E. Pitt 'Competition Law in Telecommunications' in I. Walden and J. Angell *Telecommunications Law and Regulation* 2nd edn (Oxford: Oxford University Press, 2005) p. 318.
[143] Article 12 Access Directive.

flexibility afforded to the regulator poses a risk that decisions will focus on short-term consumer interests at the expense of long-term interests: granting access too frequently risks denting incentives of new entrants on upstream markets.[144] The more aggressive approach under SSR can be justified by the fact that in newly liberalised markets entry barriers are higher and this requires more intrusive regulation.

These four justifications suggest that there is no neat borderline that divides the task of SSR and that of competition law: both address similar market failures with similar rules. Accordingly, the Commission's view that SSR should apply only where 'competition law remedies are not sufficient to address the problem' is not a workable distinction.[145] Rather, when there is an overlap, consideration might be given to whether SSR is better, given the NRA's comparative institutional advantage, and given the transitional state of the market. For example, access remedies are best imposed using SSR because the NRA is in a better position to determine access conditions and access prices.

The Commission also takes the view that SSR should be phased out in the long term as markets become workably competitive, so that only competition law will apply.[146] However, Professor Larouche has challenged this assumption on the basis that SSR is more than just a more robust application of competition law.[147] The legislative mandate for the NRAs is threefold. They must apply the law in order to promote competition, contribute to the development of the internal market, and promote the interests of citizens in the European Union.[148] In addition, they may also use SSR to promote cultural and linguistic diversity and media pluralism.[149] These goals suggest a long-term future for SSR. Moreover, the economic and non-economic goals indicate that the regulation of this industry cannot be carried out solely by reference to modified competition law rules. In Larouche's view, a more coherent political vision of SSR is that a well-functioning electronic communications network across the EU is necessary for the Union's economic development. SSR, in brief, might be best aligned with industrial policy rather than competition policy. We can then characterise SSR as having a role to perform beyond merely guaranteeing competitive markets, in the maintenance of a viable communications network as a means for sustaining other economic activities. However, the legislation upon which the regulatory framework is constructed is ambiguous: while the recitals make reference to wider industrial and social policies, the detailed regulation of markets is solely grounded in competition policy,

---

[144] M. Cave and P. Crowther 'Pre-Emptive Competition Policy Meets Regulatory Antitrust' [2005] *European Competition Law Review* 481, 484.

[145] Recital 27 Framework Directive.

[146] Commission Recommendation on Relevant Product and Service Markets [2003] OJ L114/45, Recital 1.

[147] P. Larouche 'A Closer Look at Some Assumptions Underlying EC Regulation of Electronic Communications' (2002) 3 *Journal of Network Industries* 129, 142–5.

[148] Article 8(2), (3) and (4) Framework Directive.

[149] Ibid., Article 8(1) para. 3.

so the industrial policy considerations can only be achieved by Member States. The limitations of the legislation tally with the critique we made of the market above: liberalisation has opened national markets, but there is no Community market yet.

4.4 Monitoring National Regulatory Authorities

NRAs operate in a complex environment, where three possible conflicts may arise. Again, we illustrate these with reference to electronic communications. The first is a 'horizontal' conflict between the decision of an NRA and principles of national competition law. The second is a 'vertical' conflict where the approach of the NRA may be inconsistent with the Community's regulatory framework. The third is a 'diagonal' conflict between one set of supranational rules (EC competition law) and one set of national rules (SSR).

Beginning with the vertical conflict: the Commission is able to exercise control over NRAs in a number of respects provided for in Article 7 of the Framework Directive. In brief, each NRA is called upon to make three determinations: define relevant markets, determine if a firm has SMP, and impose remedies. The NRA must communicate any draft measure (market definition, determination of SMP, or proposed remedies) to the Commission and Member States who have one month to comment. The Commission may consider that the definition of markets outside those identified by the Commission or the determination of SMP creates a barrier to the single market or is otherwise incompatible with the aims of the law, in which case it has two additional months to analyse the draft determination further and may veto the measures. There are no veto powers regarding the remedies that the NRA selects. Instead, a coordination mechanism has been put into place so that Member States and the Commission agree on suitable remedies. Article 7 procedures are carried out by DG Competition and DG Information Society, which enables the Commission to pool its expertise in market analysis and the development of the markets.

The control mechanisms are not exactly the same as those established under Regulation 1/2003. In the latter National Competition Authorities are free to decide what investigations to carry out, but their final decision is subject to veto as the Commission can review the draft decisions. However, the objectives of the review processes are the same: to guarantee consistency and provide legal certainty. The Commission has yet to apply its veto power to draft competition decisions notified under Regulation 1/2003 and has exercised its veto power in the electronic communications field only four times to date. However, potentially more significant than the exercise of veto power are the Commission's informal prompts to Member States to take certain action. Moreover, the network of NRAs is likely to furnish further peer pressure on recalcitrant NRAs, so that informal means are likely to be more useful in avoiding vertical conflicts.

As far as horizontal conflicts go, the Community has left Member States to manage these. In the field of electronic communications Member States must ensure that competition authorities and NRAs consult each other, cooperate and share relevant information.[150] In the postal sector in contrast the directive provides that the NRA 'may' be charged with the application of competition law in this sector.[151] A single agency in charge might be better able to manage SSR and competition rules by selecting the most appropriate remedy. A related horizontal conflict is between the NRA and a national court. A plaintiff seeking a remedy (e.g. access) can have recourse to the NRA, NCA or court simultaneously to try and obtain a favourable solution. Moreover, as the plaintiff can use EC and national competition law, this gives rise to diagonal conflicts. And to complete the picture, an additional diagonal conflict may arise when the Commission wishes to apply competition law in a market where the NRA has already taken action.

The general rule in diagonal conflicts is this: unless the directives on which SSR is based provide that competition law does not apply when SSR does, then it is possible to apply competition law even if the market has already been regulated under SSR. This approach was taken in *Deutsche Telekom*.[152] In this case the Commission found that Deutsche Telekom (DT) had abused its dominant position by deploying a 'price squeeze'. DT held a dominant position in the upstream market for the local loop, and was active in the downstream market for broadband internet connections. Would-be competitors sought access to the local loop, but DT charged them a wholesale price that was higher than the retail price that DT set for its broadband services. In this setting, competitors would be unable to mount any meaningful challenge since they could not offer end users a broadband connection cheaper than DT. It did not matter that the German NRA had already regulated both wholesale and retail prices: DT was not required to set prices fixed by the NRA and was still capable of selecting price levels that would not have squeezed competitors from the market.

The effect of this approach to diagonal conflicts is that the Commission is able to supplement its supervisory powers. Under the electronic communications directives the Commission can monitor what the NRAs choose to do, and using EC competition law the Commission can take action when NRAs fail to do so. This might be welcomed on the basis that some NRAs are very weak and some may be 'captured' by interest groups or by the incumbent. Professor Geradin has thus suggested that competition law should apply when the NRA

---

[150] Ibid., Article 3(4) and (5).

[151] Article 22(4) Directive 97/67/EC on Common Rules for the Development of the Internal Market of Community Postal Services and the Improvement of Quality of Service OJ L15/14, as amended by Directive 2002/39/EC with regard to the Further Opening to Competition of Community Postal Services [2002] OJ L176/21.

[152] *Deutsche Telekom* [2003] OJ L263/9.

fails to act but not when the NRA has applied SSR correctly.[153] However, this leaves out a situation where the NRA has applied SSR but not as the Commission would have liked, or has failed to apply SSR for what it thinks is a good reason. And given that the NRA ought to have a comparative advantage in regulating this economic sector, it is not clear on what grounds the Commission can decide that the NRA has failed to apply SSR, or has applied it erroneously. The Commission is not a Europe-wide regulatory authority: Member States rejected the creation of such an agency. It is problematic to argue that the Commission should assume such powers and become a 'regulator of regulators' in this context.[154]

Moreover, *Deutsche Telekom* deviates somewhat from previous 'margin squeeze cases' that we considered in chapter 6. There we saw that margin squeeze was used to oust competitors. Here the abuse consists of denying competitors access. So the Commission is *extending* the abuse doctrine to cure a regulatory failure. An important judgment of the US Supreme Court, *Verizon Communications v. Trinko*,[155] offers some cautionary tales in this respect. The Court was faced with a claim whose essential facts may be summarised like this: Verizon is the owner of the upstream telecommunications network and has obligations under federal law to share the network with firms wishing to compete downstream. Verizon did not comply, hampering the entry of new firms, *inter alia* AT&T. The regulator investigated Verizon and the latter settled, promising to comply. The plaintiff, Trinko, was a law firm that had entered into a supply contract with AT&T and sought damages as a result of the inferior service that it received from AT&T, caused by Verizon's infringement of antitrust law: its refusal to deal with AT&T. The Court had to consider whether Verizon had infringed s. 2 in making AT&T's access to the market more difficult. It began by noting that the American SSR (the Federal Telecommunications Act of 1996) explicitly provided that the Act did not supersede the application of antitrust law.[156] So far the position is as in the EC. But then the Supreme Court held that while the Act allowed the Court to apply existing antitrust law to Trinko's lawsuit, its provisions militated against developing antitrust doctrines further. The Court found that the 1996 Act's regulation of access was sufficiently comprehensive ('an effective steward of the antitrust function') that antitrust law should not be expanded. Moreover, the Court noted the risk of Type 1 errors: antitrust liability might undermine Verizon's incentives to invest and add yet more regulatory burdens. These considerations suggest that while applying well-established antitrust rules to behaviour that could also be subject to SSR is acceptable because the legislation allows it, antitrust agencies should be reluctant to read antitrust doctrine

---

[153] D. Geradin 'Limiting the Scope of Article 82 EC: What the EU Can Learn from the US Supreme Court's Judgment in *Trinko* in the Wake of *Microsoft*, *IMS*, and *Deutsche Telekom*' (2004) 41 *Common Market Law Review* 1519.

[154] De Streel 'Remedies' pp. 98–9.   [155] 504 US 398 (2004).   [156] 47 USC 152.

expansively merely to cure what they think is a regulatory failure. This might be a fruitful way of limiting the application of competition law in regulated sectors. Applied to *Deutsche Telekom*, it would counsel against action because the Commission extended the law on margin squeeze to cure what it perceived to be a failure by the German NRA. However, the Commission has regularly used competition law to 'patch up' regulatory gaps that arise, and not only in electronic communications, as we shall see in the following section. Nevertheless, it is worth reflecting upon whether certain regulators' decisions should not be worthy of greater respect. As we noted above, regulation is an industrial policy task carried out by NRAs in the interest of the Community. In this context, might not one wish to tolerate seemingly anticompetitive regulation if this might facilitate more competitive markets in the future?[157]

5 Sector-specific competition law

In the previous section we argued that while SSR may resemble competition law, and some have suggested that SSR codifies competition law principles, SSR is best seen as a distinct set of rules. The similarity between SSR and antitrust has more to do with the fact that they address similar economic problems than with any transfer of principles developed in one field. Moreover, SSR has a broader economic mandate: to inject competition (not merely to prevent anticompetitive behaviour).

Conversely, a more preoccupying phenomenon is the application of competition law in a sector-specific manner.[158] This manifests itself in two ways: first, the Commission uses competition law to set out its legislative intentions and anticipates the liberalisation of markets (e.g. *Atlas*); second, competition law is used to supplement or correct SSR (e.g. *Deutsche Telekom*). We illustrate this use of EC competition law with examples drawn from a range of industrial sectors that have undergone liberalisation in the sections that follow.[159] These examples show how competition law is a strategic industrial policy tool.

5.1 Electricity: merger control

Foot dragging by Member States has so far been successful in limiting the liberalisation of the electricity sector, but, anticipating the liberalisation of the sector, the major electricity firms in Europe have adjusted by diversification

---

[157] A case in point is the *O2* litigation we considered in chapter 2 (pp. 37–9). While network sharing might appear to infringe Article 81, it is arguable that in the circumstances that was the only way to increase competition.

[158] Along similar lines, see Larouche *Competition Law*.

[159] For comprehensive treatment, see Geradin *Remedies*; Garzaniti *Telecommunications* chs. 6 and 8.

through mergers. Accordingly, the Commission has attempted to use merger control to try and create the conditions for more competition and overcome the political stalemate. We review two decisions where the Commission devised extensive remedies.[160]

In *VEBA/VIAG* the merger would have led to a dominant duopoly in the market for electricity via the interconnected grid in Germany. The parties agreed a range of structural remedies, which prevented the market being monopolised by two firms (the merged entity and RWE/VEW). However, in addition the merged entity also agreed to release some capacity on its electricity grid to facilitate exports of electricity from Scandinavia (where prices are low) into Germany.[161] The latter remedy seemed unnecessary to remove the competition problems caused by the merger, but is helpful in achieving the Community's wider objective of creating a single market for electricity, by facilitating cross-border trade, especially as interconnection capacity is scarce and limits cross-border trade.

In *EnBW/EDP/Cajastur/Hidrocantábrico* the Commission considered the acquisition of Hidrocantábrico (a firm active in the supply of electricity in Spain) by a consortium composed of EnBW (active in the supply of electricity in Germany), EDP (the Portuguese electricity operator) and Cajastur (a bank). EnBW was jointly controlled by Electricité de France (EDF), the French electricity giant.[162] The Commission's sole concern was caused by EDF's connection with one of the acquiring firms. The Commission noted that the Spanish market for the generation and wholesale supply of electricity was a duopoly – Endesa and Iberola – and they enjoyed a position of collective dominance. The only potential competitor was EDF, which could transmit its electricity into Spain. However, after the merger EDF would lose the incentive to compete on the Spanish market because it would harm Hidrocantábrico's profits, which EDF had an interest in after the merger. The effect would be to strengthen the duopoly of Endesa and Iberola. The first point to note in this assessment is that while the merger strengthens the collectively dominant position of Endesa and Iberola, they are not parties to the merger. However, the Commission thinks the ECMR applies provided that the merger causes anticompetitive effects: it does not matter that the market where these effects are felt is not one which the merger affects directly. The Commission's justification for applying the ECMR in this case is that it is similar to a merger that creates collective dominance, where the anticipated

---

[160] For a thorough analysis, see M. Piergiovanni 'EC Merger Control Regulation and the Energy Sector: An Analysis of the European Commission's Decisional Practice on Remedies' (2003) 4 *Journal of Network Industries* 227.

[161] Case M.1673 *VEBA/VIAG* [2001] OJ L118/1 para. 247.

[162] Case M.2684 *EnBW/EDP/Cajastur/Hidrocantábrico*, 19 March 2002, paras. 57 and 58. See EC Commission *European Energy Infrastructure* COM(2001)775 final, noting the isolation of the Spanish market and acknowledging that competition rules could facilitate the creation of a single market.

lessening of competition arises through tacit collusion among all firms, even those who are not party to the merger.[163] This is a poor argument. In mergers to oligopoly the merged entity is one of the parties which is collectively dominant. In this case, the merger strengthened the collective dominance of parties that were not privy to the merger. However, this finding was necessary for the Commission to have a basis for imposing remedies. The Commission cleared a merger subject to one of the firms agreeing to build extra interconnection capacity between France and Spain, thereby facilitating the emergence of a single market. With increased interconnection, another electricity supplier (other than EDF) would be able to penetrate the Spanish market and modify the collective dominance of the duopoly.

In both cases the remedies go beyond that which is necessary to remove the anticompetitive effects caused by the merger. More generally, they turn the Commission into an industry regulator which uses its powers to improve the way markets work. This seems misplaced given that normally an industry regulator has specific knowledge of the industry in question and is able to regulate the entire industry, not merely segments of it when disputes arise. Nevertheless, the policy pursued by the Commission in the electricity mergers is clear: they are used to accelerate the liberalisation of the market and the creation of the single market. However, in a damning assessment, Professor Helm has found that in tolerating a number of mergers and acquisitions in the sector, the Commission has undermined any attempt at liberalisation because there are not enough players to have effective competition; instead the market is an oligopoly dominated by French, German and Italian firms.[164] If so, in relation to the *EnBW/EDP/Cajastur/Hidrocantábrico* merger, one must question what firm there is on the market that will use the new interconnection built by EDF. And the creation of an internal energy market via merger remedies seems like a Pyrrhic victory if there are no firms taking advantage of it.

5.2 Air transport: regulating airline alliances to open up slots

The Commission's regulation of alliances in the airline sector is an illustration of the Commission's use of competition law to encourage entry by new competitors, in particular by increasing the number of slots available for new entrants. As noted above, the ability to provide air services between two destinations is negated if there are no slots available for the aeroplanes to take off and land. As capacity (e.g. new runways) is not extended regularly, those who have been granted slots in the pre-liberalisation days (normally the former flag carriers) have a significant advantage over new entrants because of grandfather rights and the Commission to date has not been very successful in changing the pattern of slot allocation through legislation. However, when

---

[163] See pp. 311–24.
[164] D. Helm *Energy, the State and the Market* (Oxford: Oxford University Press, 2002) pp. 382–4.

airlines enter into alliances where they integrate their networks (that have been notified either under the ECMR or under the procedures for exemption under Article 81) the Commission has made authorisation conditional on the airlines giving up some slots. For example, say that airlines A and B enter into an alliance and have thirty slots a day each for flights between Vienna and Paris. The Commission tends to identify each city pair (Vienna to Paris) as a relevant market and requires that in this market A and B surrender some of their slots so that after the alliance, a new player is able to offer flights between the two cities. This speeds up the process of liberalisation, in an area where the Community has had less success on the legislative front.[165] Most airline alliances have taken the form of agreements vetted under Article 81. In these cases the Commission has ordered slot divestiture for a limited number of years, but in a more recent alliance that took the shape of a merger, the divestiture of slots was made for an unlimited period, and accompanied by the possibility that the entrant could gain grandfather rights over the slot and then use it to provide flights to other destinations as market conditions changed.[166] In approving this, the Commission noted that the effect on competition would be wider than on the specific routes where anticompetitive problems were felt.[167] So the remedy injects competition into the air transport market as a whole.

Moreover, the airline alliance decisions also demonstrate how, in order to facilitate the entry of new firms, the Commission imposes remedies that look like, but go well beyond, those that can be imposed under traditional EC competition law. Three remedies exemplify this, and in several decisions these have been imposed as a package.[168] First, in some decisions the alliance is asked to reduce the frequencies of flights or to freeze frequencies between certain city pairs. This is designed to allow the new entrant who has obtained slots on that city pair the opportunity to establish itself on the market, and to avoid a situation where the dominant firm can thwart entry by increasing supply.[169] However, this is not the kind of remedy that could be imposed by applying Article 82. Second, in *Lufthansa/Austrian Airlines* the alliance gave an undertaking that if it were to reduce prices on a market where it faced competition from a new entrant, it would also have to reduce prices on three other markets on which it did not face competition.[170] This was designed to avoid predatory pricing by the alliance that could cut prices selectively on one market, recouping the losses on other markets where it did not face

---

[165] See e.g. *Austrian Airlines/Lufthansa* [2002] OJ L242/25 para. 108. For a summary of the case law, see G. Goeteyn 'Remedies in the Air Transport Sector' in Geradin *Remedies* pp. 244–50.

[166] Case M.3280 *Air France/KLM*, 11 February 2004.   [167] Ibid. para. 161.

[168] The package also includes other remedies: an obligation on the alliance to interline (that is, offer a passenger the option of making one leg of his journey on one of its airlines and the other on the competitor's); and blocked space agreements (allowing the new entrant to buy seats on the alliance's airlines for its customers). These packages are standard in all airline alliances: see e.g. *Air France/Alitalia*, 7 April 2004, paras. 170–5.

[169] E.g. *Austrian Airlines/Lufthansa* [2002] OJ L242/25 para. 109.

[170] Ibid. para. 110; similar remedy in Case M.3280 *Air France/KLM*, 11 February 2004, para. 166.

competition. Again, it is not clear how far this kind of strategy could be caught by traditional competition law principles, in particular since the undertaking was not merely about avoiding below-cost pricing but about discounts in general. A third remedy is to require alliances to offer new entrants the possibility of joining the alliance's frequent-flyer programmes. The rationale behind this is that an airline that operates a wider network has a competitive advantage over a new entrant who, at least initially, offers more limited services. A new entrant would be unable to offer a frequent-flyer programme that is as attractive as that of the alliance and so is allowed to join that of the alliance. This 'essential facility' type of remedy goes well beyond what can be achieved by applying the formula in the *Oscar Bronner* case. While these three remedies may appear like *ex ante* applications of competition law concepts (the aim is to prevent dominant firms foreclosing new entrants) the remedies go well beyond those that are available under Article 82 as it has been interpreted thus far. There is evidence that in certain cases, new entrants have begun to compete against the alliance;[171] however, it is not clear whether the package of remedies that are required is necessary to guarantee the growth of competition. Moreover, in some of these decisions, the Commission also designs the market. A particularly striking example is the remedy imposed upon airlines to facilitate the provision of intermodal transport: that is, the airline alliance was required to enter into agreements with railway firms to provide a mixed rail/air ticket.[172] This can help a new entrant but seems also to assist firms operating in other markets, a remedy that goes well beyond the traditional scope of merger control.

The central objective of remedies in the airline alliance cases is to rectify a regulatory failure: slot reallocation cannot be negotiated at a political level and it is achieved as a condition for clearing alliances. The parties to these alliances have no interest in querying the legal basis of the Commission's requests as the difficult economic climate means they are eager to merge as quickly as possible. Nor are third parties interested in challenging the Commission's clearance, except in demanding even greater remedies to secure more market access.[173]

5.3 Postal monopolies: regulating Deutsche Post's cross-subsidies

Cross-subsidisation occurs when a firm has one business activity where the revenues are insufficient to cover costs, but it is able to draw upon earnings from other business ventures where its earnings are greater than its costs to subsidise the less profitable activity. In general, this practice is not objectionable because it is a way of ensuring that a firm can offer a wide range of services.

---

[171] *Austrian Airlines/Lufthansa* [2002] OJ L242/25 paras. 114–15.
[172] Ibid. para. 113; *Air France/KLM*, 11 Febuary 2004.
[173] Case T-177/04 *Easyjet Airline Co. Ltd v. Commission*, judgment of 4 July 2006 (unsuccessful challenge of *Air France/KLM*).

For instance, an airline company that sells flights to several destinations cross-subsidises losses on flights to unpopular destinations with revenue from profitable routes. It makes business sense to offer a wide range of routes so that passengers are attracted to that airline because of its breadth of coverage. In the postal services sector, the uniform price of a stamp for delivery within a country means that the cost of letters delivered to remote destinations is subsidised by the prices charged for letters delivered in densely populated areas. So cross-subsidisation allows the provision of a universal postal service.

In newly liberalised industries, however, cross-subsidisation can be more problematic. The *Deutsche Post* case provides a clear illustration of why this is so.[174] Before privatisation in 1989, a state-run administrative body provided all post and telecommunication services in Germany, but at the time of the decision Deutsche Post AG (hereinafter DPAG) held a statutory monopoly only in the market of letters up to 200 grammes, and other firms could enter freely in other postal service markets. United Parcel Services (UPS) complained that DPAG was using the revenue in the letter market (the so-called reserved sector) to subsidise an exclusionary pricing campaign in the market for parcel services (that is, the delivery of parcels from a business, say Amazon, to households) whose effect was the exclusion of UPS from the parcels market. Cross-subsidisation in this context is anticompetitive because it prevents efficient entry into the parcel services market by keeping DPAG's prices in that sector below cost. This kind of predatory campaign is sustainable and effective because entry barriers are significant (a company like UPS would have to ensure that it has contracts with several mail order companies so as to be able to recover the significant sunk costs that are necessary to enter this market) and the source of profits that serve to subsidise the exclusionary activities cannot be challenged so long as DPAG retains its statutory monopoly in the letter market. The Commission found that DPAG used the revenues in the reserved sector to carry out two kinds of abuses: below-cost pricing and offering loyalty rebates to the biggest mail order firms. The Commission observed how these practices foreclosed market access, allowing DPAG to retain a market share of over 85 per cent during the 1990s.[175] The Commission also noted specifically that a successful entrant would need to distribute 100 million parcels a year to recover its sunk costs and that this meant that it would need to serve at least two of Germany's six mail order firms. This was made impossible by the pricing schemes of DPAG.[176] The significance of the Commission's observations is to prove that the market for parcels could be contestable and had no natural monopoly characteristics. Moreover, the Commission went on to explain the four reasons why the practice was inefficient: DPAG's failure to cover the cost of the parcel services meant that there was a permanent need for cross-subsidisation, so the parcel service would never operate efficiently; efficient entrants were foreclosed; as a result of foreclosure, DPAG deployed

---

[174] *Deutsche Post AG* [2001] OJ L125/27.   [175] Ibid. para. 32.   [176] Ibid. para. 37.

more resources than would be necessary to provide mail order parcel services (if the market was competitive each firm would be striving to economise); and consumers in the reserved service were forced to finance the waste of resources.[177]

The Commission's use of Article 82 is a standard application of the abuse doctrine.[178] The Commission does not find that cross-subsidisation is an abuse, but shows that it can be the means by which well-recognised abuses (below-cost pricing and loyalty rebates) can be carried out. However, in a departure from the standard abuse analysis, the Commission provides details of the foreclosure effects and of the inefficiencies that result from the abuse. In part this may be to illustrate that the market was contestable, and in part perhaps to issue a general warning that the findings in this case can serve as a precedent in other liberalised industries.

The remedies that the Commission obtained and imposed show the regulatory streak in this decision. First, DPAG entered into a voluntary undertaking to divest its parcel service business. This was in response to the Commission's Statement of Objections (the document issued to the parties when the Commission starts infringement proceedings) where it noted that structural separation would prevent cross-subsidisation. DPAG's undertaking is complex but worth summarising in detail. A new firm (Newco) would be created to carry on the parcel business. If Newco were to source any part of its activities from DPAG (e.g. using DPAG's sorting facilities for processing parcels) then it would pay for these at market prices. Moreover, DPAG undertook that any service that Newco sourced from it would also be available, at the same price, to any other parcel service firm. Finally DPAG undertook to provide the Commission with reports on prices and Newco's costs and revenues and guaranteed to keep the accounts of DPAG and Newco separate to ensure full transparency.[179] The effects of this remedy are to prevent cross-subsidisation, to facilitate its detection, and to facilitate the entry of new competitors. It is not certain whether the Commission had the power under Regulation 17/62 to order the break-up of a firm.[180] Note that the remedy goes beyond preventing the recurrence of the abuse, however. It also establishes a means to monitor the prices charged by Newco and facilitates market access by ensuring that new entrants can have access to some elements of DPAG's infrastructure should these be seen as essential by Newco. This means that if any segment of the parcel delivery market has natural monopoly qualities, access is guaranteed to new entrants, *ex ante*.

The Commission also imposed a second set of regulatory remedies. DPAG must submit a statement of Newco's costs and revenues, and an itemised

---

[177] Ibid. para. 37.

[178] Bar the fact that to calculate predatory pricing it used incremental as opposed to variable costs: see chapter 6, p. 180 n. 75.

[179] Ibid. paras. 20–2.

[180] The remedy is now explicitly available: see Article 7 Regulation 1/2003.

statement of any prices that Newco paid for services that it procured from
DPAG. DPAG must also submit details of any rebate schemes that Newco
concluded with its six largest mail order customers.[181] These reporting obligations allow the Commission to ensure Newco's prices are not predatory and
its rebates not loyalty inducing. These remedies are remarkable because no
comparable obligations are imposed when firms commit these abuses in
competitive markets. The Commission's intervention is usually an order to
cease and desist from the practice.

The remedies go further than what is normally achieved in an Article 82 case:
they are designed to prevent future abuses (not merely to deter them by
imposing a fine); to facilitate entry by allowing access to DPAG's facilities
even without a finding that the facility is essential; and to prevent cross-
subsidisation by structural separation. Moreover, the remedies also go beyond
what had been achieved by the Postal Services Directive in 1997. The directive
merely tried to prevent cross-subsidisation by requiring that the firm with a
reserved sector must keep separate accounts for non-reserved services.[182] The
Commission's decision seems to cure a regulatory failure that plagues many
other sectors. The liberalisation directives seek to prevent cross-subsidisation
by providing for accounting separation but the Commission has been unable
to press Member States to agree to more radical structural measures that would
make cross-subsidisation more difficult to practise and easier to detect.
However, some have queried how far the structural separation in DPAG is
effective given that Newco will still be owned by the shareholders that control
DPAG, so the possibility of cross-subsidies remains and can only be eliminated if
Newco is sold to an independent buyer.[183]

There is another important, political, dimension to the DPAG decision that
must not be ignored. UPS had originally complained about DPAG in 1994, and
the Commission's decision was issued on 21 March 2001.[184] Why the delay?
According to Mitchell Smith, when the Commission received UPS's allegations, it 'confronted a tension between the apparent merits of the complaint
and its inappropriate timing'.[185] In 1994 the Commission had only just begun
to act to inject competition into the postal services sector. It had tackled some
cases where states had granted exclusive rights to national post offices that
prevented the entry of express courier services.[186] These were relatively easy
cases because the states were preventing competition by denying market access
via legislation, while in DPAG proof of the abuse required information about

---

[181] [2001] OJ L125/27 Article 2(2).   [182] Article 14(2) Directive 97/67.

[183] See D. Geradin and D. Henry 'Regulatory and Competition Law Remedies in the Postal Sector'
in Geradin *Remedies* p. 171.

[184] In 1999 the CFI found the Commission had failed to act on this complaint in a timely manner.
Case T-127/98 *UPS Europe SA v. Commission* [1999] ECR II-2633.

[185] Smith 'In Pursuit of Selective Liberalisation' p. 532.

[186] *Netherlands Express Delivery Services* [1990] OJ L10/47 (overruled on procedural grounds in
Joined Cases C-48 and 60/90 *Netherlands and Others v. Commission* [1992] ECR 565); *Spanish
International Express Courier Services* [1990] OJ L233/19.

costs which would take time to obtain and process. However, the technical difficulties have little to do with the delay. The Commission was under pressure from several lobby groups (in particular parcel operators in the United States) to step up the process of liberalisation,[187] but it tried to achieve this with the consensus of all the Member States by legislating to liberalise the sector rather than with recourse to competition law. However, the first directive in this sector was disappointing. It declared that Member States must reduce the exclusive rights that national postal operators had, but only for a small portion of the market, amounting to 3 per cent of the revenues of national mail carriers (although this figure does not take into account the fact that the market for value-added services was already liberalised).[188]

The Commission wished to press on with liberalisation and in 2000 tabled a directive that would have opened an additional 20 per cent of the monopolised market to competition, and in negotiating this new phase in the liberalisation process, there were tensions between Member States eager to see further liberalisation and those wishing to protect the sector. Germany's position on further liberalisation was ambiguous, so the Commission was reluctant to act on UPS's complaint in this delicate political environment. Moreover, the Commission's hands-off approach vis-à-vis Deutsche Post can also be seen in its relaxed attitude to DPAG's expansions through mergers. In order to prepare itself for liberalisation DPAG spent $6.5 billion between 1998 and 2000 acquiring US and European firms in the transport, distribution and express delivery services to become a powerful, global player in the postal services market.[189] However, the 2000 liberalisation initiative failed because the Commission lost the support of two significant players, Britain (who preferred to carry on with liberalisation of the Post Office under national law) and Germany. Germany was ready for further liberalisation but was concerned that the French would delay opening their markets and, as they had done with EDF in electricity, move into the German market. They refused to liberalise without the guarantee of reciprocity. Upon the failure of these negotiations, the Commission resumed the use of Article 82 as a means of trying to achieve liberalisation through competition law. The *Deutsche Post* decision showed that the Commission could probably go quite far in opening up postal services markets via Article 82. As it showed in its analysis of the

---

[187] J. I. Campbell Jr 'Couriers and the European Postal Monopolies: Policy Challenges of a Newly Emerging Industry' in R. H. Pedler and M. P. C. M. Van Schendelen (eds.) *Lobbying in the European Union* (Aldershot: Dartmouth, 1984).

[188] 'Europe's Last Post' *The Economist* 13 May 2000.

[189] E.g. Case IV/M.1168 *DHL/Deutsche Post*, 26 June 1998 (joint venture with a cross-border express delivery firm); Case IV/M.1347 *Deutsche Post/Securicor* 23 February 1999 (joint venture with an express parcel and document delivery firm); Case IV/M.1513 *Deutsche Post/Danzas/ Nedlloyd*, 1 July 1999 (acquisition of a firm in the fields of freight forwarding and parcel services, mainly active in Benelux and Germany); Case IV/M.1549 *Deutsche Post/ASG*, 8 July 1999 (acquisition of a firm active in road transport (including parcel delivery), air and sea freight logistics, operating mainly in Sweden, Norway, Finland and Denmark).

anticompetitive effects of DPAG's actions, all postal services can, in theory, be provided via competitive markets, and the foreclosure of competitors has prima facie anticompetitive effects. Faced with a potentially far reaching and unpredictable spate of Commission decisions that could have removed much of the postal monopoly's reserved sector, the Member States were able to agree to further liberalisation in 2002 when 16 per cent of the reserved market was opened to competition.[190]

In retrospect, the Commission's tactical delay in *Deutsche Post* was unsuccessful. Delay did not serve to persuade Germany to agree to further liberalisation and while the decision did force parties back to the negotiating table, the degree of liberalisation obtained in 2002 was less than that sought in 2000. Moreover, the fine of 24 million euros that the Commission imposed on DPAG is tiny compared to the vast sums that the firm used to buy up other companies so as to become a leading world player in the postal services markets. With this background, it becomes less surprising that DPAG agreed to divest the parcel delivery business – by 2001 DPAG had the means to remain a profitable competitor without the need for the exclusionary tactics that it deployed to maintain its dominance in the 1990s.

The background to the decision demonstrates the ambiguities and inconsistencies in the Community's approach to liberalisation. In spite of the powerful legal tools that the EC has to create markets, its efforts depend upon Member States agreeing to reforms. In this market, powerful domestic interests prevailed over the strategic use of competition law that UPS attempted. Nor is the tension merely one between a Commission bent on liberalising markets and protectionist Member States. At the same time that the Commission was seeking to open up the market, it tolerated the growth of DPAG through merger: after the Commission approved the joint venture between DHL and DPAG, UPS launched an action against the Commission complaining that DPAG had financed its acquisition of DHL through its revenues in the reserved sector and that this was an unlawful use of its monopoly position in breach of Article 82. However, the CFI disagreed, ruling that so long as the revenues used for the joint venture did not come from abusive practices (e.g. excessive pricing) DPAG was free to use the funds as it wished.[191] On a formal level, the CFI's ruling is unproblematic in that, as we noted before, cross-subsidisation per se is not an abuse of a dominant position. Nevertheless, if the Community is seriously interested in enhancing competition in the postal services market, it should recognise that the effect of DPAG's acquisition with money raised from the universal services is as inefficient as its financing of predatory pricing campaigns. There is also some conflict between the Commission insisting on structural separation in DPAG while, in clearing

---

[190] Directive 2002/39 amending Directive 97/67 with regard to Further Opening to Competition of Community Postal Services [2002] OJ L176/21.

[191] Case T-175/99 *UPS Europe v. Commission* [2002] ECR II-1915 para. 66.

the DHL joint venture, it was satisfied with an undertaking from DPAG that it would not use revenues from the reserved sector to finance the operational costs of DHL.[192] The Commission's tolerance of DPAG's growth through mergers may be interpreted in two ways. One is to see it as part of the Commission's industrial policy, whereby it supports the creation of global players (as with the *Atlas* joint venture we discussed above). A second reading is that tolerating DPAG's actions can be a means to press for greater liberalisation later: mergers allow former monopolies a means to adjust to a competitive market by diversifying their activities and once DPAG and other former postal monopolies become financially secure, the Commission can have more leverage in negotiating further liberalisation.[193] However, tolerating the creation of a highly concentrated market as a means of injecting greater competition seems to be a high-risk strategy.

5.4 Testing the legitimacy of sector-specific competition law

In the instances we considered above, as well as in chapter 7, the application of competition law is sensitive to the relevant sectors in many ways: the Commission launches cases strategically and interprets the law expansively to achieve regulatory ends. In many cases the remedies are 'agreed' with the parties, not imposed by the Commission. This seems to be done in good faith. That is, the Commission sees a political failure and steps in to get the market working. In the mid-1990s a similar trend was noted in US antitrust laws. Commentators noted that the agencies were increasingly settling cases by which firms agreed to modify their conduct to avoid a trial. Commentators were worried that competition law was moving from a 'law enforcement' model to a 'regulatory' model.[194] In a law enforcement model, the focus is on identifying an infringement, while a regulatory model focuses on the remedy. A comparable pattern is exhibited in the examples we have considered above. According to American critics, this change in the way enforcers thought about antitrust problems was undesirable for the following reasons. First, the remedies that the antitrust agency can get with a settlement are much more extensive than those it could get through litigation. Second, a settlement means that the firm is under constant supervision by the agency because if the firm wants to alter its conduct given changes in the marketplace, it may need approval from the agency should the proposed conduct infringe the settlement. Third, settlements avoid litigation and so pretermit the need to

---

[192] Case IV/M.1168 *DHL/Deutsche Post*, 26 June 1998, para. 33.

[193] The Commission noted the trend to consolidation without criticising it. See *Report from the Commission to the European Parliament and Council on the Application of the Postal Directive* COM(2002)632 final, 27.

[194] A. D. Melamed 'Antitrust: The New Regulation' [1995] *Antitrust* (Fall) 13; H. First 'Is Antitrust "Law"?' [1995] *Antitrust* (Fall) 9.

show that the behaviour was unlawful. The upshot of this is that settlements are more about what the government wants than what the law prohibits.[195]

These comments strike a chord in the light of the cases discussed above. The remedies in the electricity merger cases and in *Atlas* would not withstand judicial scrutiny, and the theories of competitive harm in the airline merger cases are suspicious. Moreover, the Commission's decisions tend to be appeal-proof because the Commission has the upper hand. The parties in the vast majority of controversial cases we have studied were eager to get on with their transaction, thus willing to trade off invasive remedies in favour of quick regulatory clearance. For example, Deutsche Post was willing to accept an invasive set of remedies because it had redirected its market strategy and could afford to accept the Commission's demands. However, now that the remedies have been agreed, they form precedents that the Commission is able to use to challenge similar types of behaviour in the future. The upshot is that the Commission is gaining increasing powers, without corresponding political authority and lacking appropriate procedures.[196]

6 Public services

The Community's attempt to create a competitive, Europe-wide market for utilities has regularly been opposed by those concerned that efficiency is in conflict with the public service obligations that utility companies have had, in particular under certain national traditions.[197] A trite aphorism from France's former Prime Minister, Lionel Jospin, captures the tension: 'Oui à l'économie de marché, non à la société de marché' (yes to a market economy, no to a market society).[198] The EC has managed the relationship between the economic objectives of the internal market and the social objectives of public service provision in three ways: first, by stating that certain public services, in particular those closely associated with the welfare state (e.g. social security and insurance schemes), fall outside the scope of EC competition law; second, by tolerating certain anticompetitive arrangements when these are necessary to finance the provision of public services; third, by imposing minimum public service obligations to be provided in all Member States. The first two approaches allow Member States to implement national policies to safeguard public services, while the third approach establishes public service obligations at a European level, and it is notable for two related features: first, the belief

[195] Melamed 'Antitrust' p. 14.   [196] Larouche *Competition Law* pp. 353–8.

[197] T. Prosser *The Limits of Competition Law* (Oxford: Oxford University Press, 2005) ch. 5; R. Kovar 'Droit communautaire et service public: esprit d'orthodoxie ou pensée laïcisée' [1996] *Revue trimestrelle de droit européen* 215; J. Bell 'The Concept of Public Service under Threat from Europe. An Illustration from Energy Law' (1999) 5 *European Public Law* 189.

[198] Quoted in J.-B. Nadeau and J. Barlow *Sixty Million Frenchmen Can't Be Wrong* (London: Chysalia Books, 2004) p. 276.

that public services can normally be delivered through competitive markets,[199] and so suspending competition should be exceptional; second, an emphasis on consumer choice as a means to monitor public service delivery.[200]

6.1 Exclusion

The subject of competition law is the firm. In the jargon of the EC Treaty, a firm is known as an 'undertaking', and the Courts have defined it as 'any entity engaged in economic activity, regardless of the legal status of the entity or the way which it is financed. Any activity consisting in offering goods and services on a given market is an economic activity.'[201] This means that a self-employed person or a multinational corporation are both undertakings. According to Advocate General Jacobs, an activity falls within the scope of competition law if 'it could, at least in principle, be carried out by a private actor in order to make profits'.[202] If we were to apply this approach literally, however, there is almost nothing that cannot be traded and no economic activity which is not carried out by an undertaking. Instead, the Court has elected to exclude two types of activity from the scope of competition law.

First, when the activity falls within the essential prerogatives of the state it is excluded. No matter how much sovereignty is relinquished as a result of continuing economic and political convergence in the EU, certain aspects of statehood are not subjected to EC law. We find these in the EC Treaty (e.g. Article 296 in relation to defence) and in the case law of the Court of Justice, which has extended this exclusion to activities deemed to be part of the essential function of the state, such as air navigation and certain antipollution services. The focus is on the activity, not the actor – thus a body may act as an undertaking for some functions but not others. For instance, an antipollution service exercises state-like powers when it provides antipollution services and collects charges for these, and probably also when it purchases equipment necessary to provide these services.[203] But it would be treated as an undertaking when carrying out acts unrelated to its state-like powers, for example if it also provided consultancy services for private firms wishing to install antipollution devices in their factories.

---

[199] See E. Szyszczak 'Public Service Provision in Competitive Markets' (2001) 20 *Yearbook of European Law* 35.

[200] G. Napolitano 'Towards a European Legal Order for Services of General Economic Interest' (2005) 11 *European Public Law* 565, 571–2.

[201] Joined Cases C-180–184/98 *Pavel Pavlov and Others v. Stichting Pensioenfonds Medische Specialisten* [2000] ECR I-6451 paras. 74–5.

[202] *Albany International* [1999] ERC I-5751 para. 311, restated in *Ambulanz Glöckner* [2001] ECR I-8089 para. 67.

[203] Joined Cases C-264, 306, 354 and 355/01 *AOK Bundesverband and Others v. Ichthyol-Gesellschaft Cordes, Hermani & Co.* [2004] ECR I-2493; Case C-205/03P *Federación Española de Empresas de Tecnología Sanitaria (FENIN) v. Commission*, judgment of 11 July 2006.

Second, the Court has restricted the application of competition law to certain aspects of the welfare state, especially when compulsory social security schemes have been challenged.[204] The dynamics of the litigation that has allowed the Court to exclude competition law from the welfare state are similar: a person is required to make payments towards a state-run social security scheme (normally operated by an administrative authority empowered to collect funds by the state), but finds that there are better insurance provisions in the private sector, so she stops making compulsory contributions and obtains the relevant insurance from the private sector. When her failure to pay is challenged, she relies on the EC Treaty to argue that the state-run scheme restricts competition, so she is able to disregard it and buy the relevant service in the private sector. Faced with these disputes, national courts sought the advice of the ECJ whose answer is that if a national scheme operates on the basis of the principle of solidarity, then the administrative authority is not acting as an undertaking, so the competition rules are inapplicable, provided that compulsory membership in the scheme is necessary to ensure the scheme's financial equilibrium. On the contrary, if the scheme is not solidarity based, then the operator is an undertaking and it can be challenged under the competition rules. Two early cases (*Poucet* and *FFSA*) set out the Court's interpretation of solidarity.[205] In *Poucet* the Court analysed sickness and maternity insurance schemes for self-employed persons and a basic pension scheme for skilled workers, while in *FFSA* the Court analysed a supplementary old-age insurance scheme for self-employed farmers. The schemes in *Poucet* were not operated by undertakings because they were compulsory; the sickness and maternity insurance scheme conferred equal benefits irrespective of contributions, and contributions were proportionate to income. The old-age pension scheme was financed by current workers, pension rights were not linked to contributions and the schemes that were in financial difficulty were subsidised by those that had a surplus. Accordingly, there were several manifestations of solidarity: between rich and poor workers, between high-risk and low-risk workers, between today's workers and those who had retired, and between profitable and non-profitable schemes. Solidarity was not present in *FFSA*: the scheme was optional, benefits depended on the contributions made by each individual and on the financial results reached by the body operating the scheme. While the scheme was designed to pursue a social objective and it had to operate on a non-profit basis, these elements were insufficient to declare the operator not an undertaking, so the scheme was subject to competition law.

The major difficulty with the Court's case law is the imprecise nature of solidarity, so that the Court looks for manifestations of solidarity and declares

---

[204] For a perceptive critique, see S. Giubboni 'Social Insurance Monopolies in Community Competition Law and the Italian Constitution' (2001) 7 *European Law Journal* 69.

[205] Joined Cases C-159/91 and C-160/91 *Poucet v. AGF* and *Camulrac and Pistre v. Cancava* [1993] ECR I-637; Case C-244/94 *Fédération Française des Sociétés d'Assurance and Others v. Ministère de l'Agriculture et de la Pêche* [1995] ECR I-4013.

that the scheme falls outside the scope of EC competition law when there is a sufficient degree of solidarity. The risk is that state social security policy occasionally falls to be regulated by EC competition law. A related criticism is that solidarity is inherent in many other activities (e.g. uniform tariffs for postal services mean that those posting letters within a large city support those who send letters to remote parts of the country) so that the special exclusion for social security schemes based on the principle of solidarity is hard to justify.[206] Another problem is that proof of solidarity is insufficient: the Court also demands that the alleged restriction of competition (compulsory affiliation) must be essential for the financial balance of the scheme.[207] This suggests that the Court is exempting certain schemes rather than excluding the application of competition law, so that the analysis in the following section might be more appropriate.[208]

6.2 Exemption

Public services were usually provided by the state because it is difficult to tempt the private sector: the cost of providing a universal electricity or postal service to all citizens at affordable rates is usually higher than the profits that can be generated. Accordingly, public services are financed in ways that restrict competition, in particularly by facilitating cross-subsidisation. A clear example is the *Corbeau* litigation: in order to finance a universal postal service for all Belgian citizens, the government had granted the Régie des Postes a monopoly over a number of other profitable postal services, in the belief that the revenue generated in the profitable sector would pay for the cost of running a universal service. This method of finance goes against the policy of liberalisation, since it reserves monopoly rights over potentially competitive markets. The Court has recognised that financing public services through restrictions of competition may be unavoidable, and it has interpreted Article 86(2) EC in an increasingly complex manner to accommodate this method of financing. Article 86(2) provides a defence for firms and Member States whereby Treaty obligations are disapplied to allow the delivery of public services. In order for state laws to benefit from this exemption, the following must be shown:[209] first, that there is a service of general economic interest, the performance of which is entrusted to the firm(s) in question; second, that the anticompetitive effects are necessary to allow the operator(s) to ensure the performance of the service of general economic interest under economically acceptable

---

[206] J. Winterstein 'Nailing the Jellyfish: Social Security and Competition Law' [1999] *European Competition Law Review* 324.

[207] Case C-218/00 *Cisal di Battistello Venanzio and C. Sas v. Istituto Nazionale contro gli infortuni sul lavoro (INAIL)* [2002] ECR I-691 para. 44.

[208] See J. Holmes 'Fixing the Limits of EC Competition Law: State Action and the Accommodation of the Public Services' (2004) 57 *Current Legal Problems* 149.

[209] Case C-320/91 *Corbeau* [1993] ECR I-2533 para. 14.

conditions;[210] third, that the service provider is able to offer the services in question efficiently.[211]

The first criterion allows Member States to define what 'economic services' they believe to be of 'general interest'. That is, the service is of an economic nature, so that Article 86(2) does not apply when the activity in question is not that which can be carried out by an undertaking (like those discussed in section 6.1 above) and the service in question is one which the state deems to be of general interest. The right of Member States to nominate services is subject to two limitations: the first is if the nomination is manifestly erroneous,[212] and the second is that the public service mission must be clearly defined and explicitly entrusted to the undertaking in question by the state.[213] In addition to the services provided by network industries (e.g. water, electricity, postal services, telecommunications),[214] the Court has recognised that there is a general interest when an airline serves routes that are not commercially viable but which provide connections to remote areas of a country,[215] when mooring services for ships are made available around the clock to ensure safety,[216] and where a waste management scheme is operated to address environmental risks.[217]

Second, the restriction of competition is subjected to a proportionality test. In the context of cross-subsidisation, the state can justify the grant of monopoly rights in a potentially competitive market (e.g. parcel services) when the profits earned by the firm in the reserved market facilitate its performance of the service of general economic interest (e.g. delivery of letters throughout the territory of the state). Without foreclosing profitable markets, private firms would cherry pick profitable services, leaving the unprofitable sector to be covered by the state (which might entail considerable rises in taxation) or not provided at all. The effect of Article 86(2) is to allow states to attract private firms to offer public services and, in exchange for their agreement to offer these services, to gain certain advantages in the form of profits in some profitable markets reserved to them. The proportionality requirement has been read increasingly leniently by the Court and the Commission: in the early years a restriction of competition was only tolerated when it was the only feasible way of performing the service of general economic interest. Now the

---

[210] Ibid. paras. 14–16.

[211] This condition was introduced in *Ambulanz Glöckner* [2001] ERC I-8089, and is analogous to the standard set out for Article 86(1) by *Höfner* [1991] ECR I-1979.

[212] For example, the Court doubted that dock work could qualify in *Merci Convenzionali* [1991] ECR I-5889 para. 27.

[213] Case 127/73 *BRT v. SABAM* [1974] ECR 313.

[214] EC Commission *Green Paper on Services of General Interest* COM(2003)270 final para. 17.

[215] Case T-260/94 *Air Inter v. Commission* [1997] ECR II-997.

[216] Case C-266/96 *Corsica Ferries France v. Gruppo Antichi Ormeggiatori del Porto di Genova Coop.* [1998] ECR I-3949 paras. 45 and 60.

[217] Case C-209/98 *Entreprenørforeningens Affalds/Miljøsektion (FFAD) v. Københavns Kommune* [2000] ECR I-3743 paras. 75–6.

Courts grant the exemption without the need to show that there are no less restrictive means of achieving the state goal, provided that the restriction allows the firm to provide the relevant service under 'economically acceptable conditions'.[218] This change is attributed to the increasingly strict interpretation of Article 86(1), which has led the Court to expand the possibilities for states to defend the grant of exclusive rights.

The third requirement indicates that the derogation is granted conditionally – the firm must provide the services efficiently. If the firm is manifestly unable to do so, then the derogation will become invalid. This requirement was introduced by the Court in *Ambulanz Glöckner*. One German administrative district had granted non-profit organisations the exclusive right to provide emergency ambulance services and non-emergency patient transport services. Certain organisations complained that this denied them access to the market for non-emergency transport, thus stifling competition, but the Court held that the grant of monopoly rights over the (profitable) non-emergency patient transport market was necessary to finance the provision of the (non-profitable) emergency transport; in fact the Court even opined that injecting competition into the profitable sector might 'jeopardise the quality and reliability' of the emergency services.[219] However, the exemption would be rescinded if it transpired that the organisations entrusted with the public service mission were manifestly unable to satisfy demand in the two reserved markets.[220] It was for the national court to determine whether the organisations in question 'are in fact able to satisfy demand and to fulfil not only their statutory obligation to provide the public emergency ambulance services in all situations and 24 hours a day but also to offer efficient patient transport services'.[221]

The efficiency condition to the Article 86(2) exemption can be compared to the approach that the ECJ has taken in situations where the Member State decides to finance the public service provider out of public funds. Generally, subsidies provided by states are regulated by the rules on state aid,[222] but the Court of Justice has declared that subsidies which merely compensate a firm for providing a service of general interest do not constitute state aid. In reaching this conclusion the Court has set out four requirements: first that the public service obligation is clearly defined, second that the compensation is established objectively and transparently, third that it does not exceed the cost of providing the service plus a reasonable profit, and finally that ideally the provider should be selected through a competitive tendering procedure (so

---

[218] *Albany International* [1999] ECR I-5751 para. 107. Commentators agree that the interpretation of Article 86(2) has become more lax. See M. G. Ross 'Article 16 EC and Services of General Interest: From Derogation to Obligation?' (2000) 25 *European Law Review* 22; L. Moral Soriano 'How Proportionate Should Anti-Competitive State Intervention Be?' (2003) 28 *European Law Review* 112.

[219] *Ambulanz Glöckner* [2001] ECR I-8089 para. 61.   [220] Ibid. para. 62.   [221] Ibid. para. 64.

[222] Articles 87–8 EC. This topic is outside the scope of the book. See generally A. Biondi, P. Eeckhout and L. Flynn *The Law of State Aid in the European Union* (Oxford: Oxford University Press, 2003).

that the most efficient provider is chosen).[223] The last condition is important because it means that the state must 'auction' the right to provide the public service to the most efficient firm. In contrast, under Article 86(2), there is no need to show that the most efficient provider has been selected, only that the firm offering the service is able to do so efficiently; which means that the public service is not necessarily offered at its lowest cost when Article 86(2) is applied, so that an auction model should also be developed in this context.[224] After all, the Community's objective is the 'efficient provision of services of general economic interest'.[225]

6.3 Universal service obligations

As the Court has recognised the right of Member States to suspend the application of competition law to ensure the efficient provision of public services, the Council, in its liberalisation directives, has begun to establish EU-wide public service obligations. This serves two distinct legitimising functions. First, it legitimises Community intervention by pointing to the necessity to safeguard the general interest at Community level. Second, it is used to show the sceptical European citizen how Community law impacts their daily life.[226] The importance of legitimising public services is so significant that the directives liberalising postal services and energy begin by defining universal services before dismantling restrictions of competition. While respectful of national concerns, 'EU public service law' has two features that distinguish it from national public service law: an emphasis on consumer interests, and a preference for market solutions.[227]

The European notion of public services (at EC-level, these are labelled universal services) embodies the following characteristics: universality (that is, the service must be available to all consumers throughout the territory); continuity; quality; affordability; user and consumer protection.[228] The liberalisation directives identify universal service obligations in each sector.[229] In the field of electronic communications, European universal service obligations are most well defined, and consumers have a range of entitlements as well as means to enforce their rights. Each end user has a right to the following:

---

[223] Case C-280/00 *Altmark Trans GmbH* [2003] ECR I-7747.

[224] See P. Nicolaides 'Towards More Competition in Services of General Economic Interest' in Eekhoff *Competition Policy in Europe.*

[225] *Ambulanz Glöckner* [2001] ECR I-8089, Opinion of AG Jacobs, para. 188. But see M. Ross 'The Europeanisation of Public Service Provision: Harnessing Competition and Citizenship?' (2004) 23 *Yearbook of European Law* 303, 310–11, criticising the case law as setting out 'pretty flaky yardsticks by which to measure the compatibility of public service provision with Union law'.

[226] C. Boutayeb 'Une récherche sur la place et les functions de l'intérêt général en droit communautaire' [2003] *Revue trimestrelle de droit européen* 587, 607–8.

[227] Napolitano 'Towards a European Legal Order'.

[228] *Green Paper on Services of General Interest* ch. 3.

[229] Article 3 Postal Services Directive; Article 3(3) Electricity Directive.

connection to the telephone network at a fixed location to make local, national and international telephone calls, use fax machines and access the Internet; a comprehensive telephone directory updated once yearly and a comprehensive telephone directory inquiry service; access to public pay telephones.[230] The right to these services is universal, meaning not only across the territory, but that Member States must also ensure that disabled users have access to them; that tariffs are regulated so that all social groups are able to afford these rights (which may include the duty to set tariff rates that depart from those set under normal commercial conditions when necessary to allow those on low incomes or special needs to gain access); and that there is no other form of discrimination among users.[231] Public service obligations are monitored in two ways. First, the National Regulatory Authority has powers to check the quality and prices of the universal services, and set quality targets; the NRA may impose financial penalties on firms that fail to provide universal services satisfactorily and may even withdraw the licence to operate; the NRA also protects users from arbitrary actions of their provider (e.g. disconnection).[232] Second, end users are afforded a range of means to protect their interests and rights: service providers must publish information on prices, standard terms and conditions;[233] the contract with a user must specify the service and quality level, types of maintenance offered, conditions for terminating and renewing the contract, compensation schemes if the quality levels are not met and procedures for dispute settlement;[234] consumers must receive information to control expenditure (e.g. itemised billing).[235] Subscribers also have the right to cancel without a penalty if the supplier changes the terms of the contract, and must receive one month's notice regarding any proposed contract modification.[236] The emphasis on consumer rights is a distinctive feature of the European model of public services because it makes the end user a part of the regulatory infrastructure: his or her choices give suppliers incentives to provide improved services. This fits with the market-oriented approach to universal services to which we now turn.

The second distinctive feature of European universal services law is the preference for market delivery. This is a significant departure from certain national systems where the state's legitimacy is based at least in part on its ability to provide certain services personally. Public service provision must now be delivered by the market whenever possible.[237] The clearest manifestation of this principle is in electronic communications. First, Member States must allow any firm to offer the universal services, and the Recital to the

---

[230] Articles 4, 5 and 6 Universal Services Directive.
[231] Articles 7 and 9 Universal Services Directive.
[232] Articles 4, 9, 11 and 29(3) Universal Services Directive.
[233] Article 21(1) Universal Services Directive.   [234] Article 20 Universal Services Directive.
[235] Article 10(2) and Annex I, pt A Universal Services Directive.
[236] Article 20(4) Universal Services Directive.
[237] Napolitano 'Towards a European Legal Order' p. 572.

directive goes so far as to suggest that the universal service obligations could be 'allocated to operators demonstrating the most cost-effective means of delivering access and services'.[238] This means that there would be competition for entering the universal services market. Second, in terms of financing the universal service in cases where the cost exceeds profits, the directive provides that universal service providers may be compensated in a 'competitively neutral way'. Member States have two choices: the firms receive compensation from the state in the form of subsidies, or other telecommunications companies pay a levy which goes to finance the universal service provider.[239] Accordingly, no restrictions on competition are allowed to finance universal services in the electronic communication sector.

In contrast, the Postal Services Directive provides for two means to finance the public service obligation: the grant of an exclusive right over the provision of a set of services defined by the directive, or the creation of a compensation fund.[240] In the former, a monopoly is created to allow the provider of universal services to cross-subsidise losses in the universal services market with profits in other markets, while under the latter scheme, all firms that offer postal services pay a given sum into a fund that is handed over to the firm(s) providing universal services so as to compensate them. The latter is less restrictive of competition in that all markets operate competitively. It may be argued that the compensation fund route is preferred by the legislator because the directive allows for the grant of monopoly rights only when this is 'necessary to ensure the maintenance of universal service'.[241] It follows that if the maintenance of the universal service can be achieved in less restrictive ways (through the compensation fund) then exclusive rights cannot be granted. This interpretation would be consistent with the competition preference we find in electronic communications.[242]

The powerful message of the liberalisation directives is that public services should be provided, but through competitive markets. This vision is out of line with that of a number of commentators, who rely on Article 16 to put forward a less market-oriented view.[243] Article 16 was inserted in the Treaty of Amsterdam amidst concerns about the Community's application of competition law to public services, with some Member States wishing for a means to exclude the application of competition law to public services. However, it is not immediately clear what this Article can deliver, as it gives the Commission no extra legislative powers, nor can it have direct effect, so the purported duty

---

[238] Recital 14 Universal Service Directive.
[239] Recitals 4 and 21, Article 13 Universal Service Directive.
[240] Article 7 (defining what services may be reserved); Article 9(4) (compensation fund) Postal Services Directive.
[241] Article 7(1) Postal Services Directive.
[242] In contrast, the Electricity Directive expresses no preference on the methods of financing: see Article 3(4).
[243] See also T. Prosser 'Competition Law and Public Services: From Single Market to Citizenship Rights?' (2005) 11 *European Public Law* 543.

on the Community and Member States to take care that public service missions are accomplished seems unenforceable.

> ## Article 16
>
> Without prejudice to Articles 73, 86 and 87, and given the place occupied by services of general economic interest in the shared values of the Union as well as their role in promoting social and territorial cohesion, the Community and the Member States, each within their respective powers and within the scope of application of this Treaty, shall take care that such services operate on the basis of principles and conditions which enable them to fulfil their missions.

In the seminal analysis of this provision, Professor Ross put forward the view that Article 16 serves to 'upgrade general interest services into positive horizontal policy-shaping considerations for both member States and the Community institutions'.[244] Accordingly, he has suggested that this might serve to trump the application of competition law to ensure public service delivery, and to afford citizens with the opportunity to 'attack the under-provision or poor quality of public services'.[245] However, this view is in contrast to the tone of the liberalisation directives under which competitive markets provide the best means for delivering public services and consumers are well placed to attack deficient public service delivery, by choosing among other providers. The trend in Community legislation is to apply non-market solutions only when the market fails to protect the general interest.[246]

7 More markets, more law

In this chapter we have considered how European Union law was used to create markets (through the application of Article 95 and the competition provisions in the Treaty), and then how it was used to regulate markets (through the development of sector-specific regulation and the application of competition law). We can evaluate these two processes from the perspective of institutions, economics and politics.

Turning to market creation, whilst it cannot be doubted that the EC and its Member States have taken significant steps towards the liberalisation of the economic sectors covered in this chapter, significant differences remain among the Member States' commitment to deeper liberalisation. The creative legal routes devised by Commission and Court to create markets are remarkable but they have ultimately proven inadequate to persuade all Member States to follow the path to liberalisation in a uniform, speedy

---

[244] Ross 'Article 16 EC' p. 34.   [245] Ross 'Europeanisation' p. 319.

[246] H.-P. Schwintowski 'The Common Good, Public Subsistence and the Functions of Public Undertakings in the European Internal Market' (2003) 4 *European Business Organization Law Review* 353.

manner.[247] Accordingly, the Lisbon competitiveness agenda is threatened by the reluctance of Member States to achieve open markets and by increased protectionism. Judged from the perspectives adopted in this book, market creation may be assessed as a process where the relevant institutions (Council, Commission, European Courts and Member States) faced several moments of disagreement which led to delicate and laborious negotiations in certain instances (e.g. energy and postal services), or to unilateral action to accelerate liberalisation (e.g. in kick-starting telecommunications liberalisation). Interested actors tried to use certain institutions (through litigation (the ECJ) or lobbying (the Commission)) to achieve liberalised markets. The institutional disagreements have to do with the economic and political configurations in the institutions. Some, like the Commission and the Court, have been more easily convinced that markets can function to deliver goods and services more efficiently than state monopolies. (For example, a recent study carried out by the Commission suggests that market opening has caused prices to fall by 8 per cent in electricity and by 22 per cent in telecommunications, as well as increases in employment and productivity.)[248] On the other hand, some Member States have resisted this economic prescription, at times in good faith, seeking to safeguard public services, but more often their resistance is premised on protectionism (wishing to maintain national champions) or reciprocity (reluctance to liberalise when other Member States may fail to do so, thereby weakening national firms).

Turning to market regulation, we have seen the emergence of a European regulatory state. An institutional perspective on the regulatory state suggests that decentralised regulation through National Regulatory Authorities, combined with cooperative networks and supervision by the Commission, is clumsy. A centralised, EC-wide regulatory structure would have two benefits. First, the Community regulator can make decisions by considering the interests of the Community as a whole and steer the industry in a coordinated manner. Second, the Community regulator may be less prey to government capture (as we noted earlier, some national regulators are not wholly independent of government). The 'functional need' for European agencies is difficult to challenge;[249] however, an alternative suggestion is to leave national regulators with greater freedom to experiment with different regulatory models and use networks as a means of identifying best practices.[250] The lack of comprehensive liberalisation has led the Commission to use competition law

---

[247] Pelkmans 'Making EU Network Markets Competitive', criticising the Lisbon targets.

[248] EC Commission *Evaluation of the Performance of Network Industries Providing Services of General Economic Interest 2005 Report* SEC(2005)1781.

[249] G. Majone 'The Politics of Regulation and European Regulatory Institutions' in Hayward and Menon *Governing Europe*, making the wider case for more regulatory agencies on the basis of a mismatch between the specialisation required of agencies and the administrative instruments that the Community currently has, but noting national resistance to this.

[250] P. Nicolaides 'The Political Economy of Multi-tiered Regulation in Europe' (2004) 42 *Journal of Common Market Studies* 599.

in ways that turn it into a regulator, or a regulators' regulator, substituting its judgment for the perceived inaction at national level. In the vast majority of the competition cases considered in this chapter, the Commission has deployed competition law in ways different from those in other sectors, motivated by the wish to create more competitive structures. The institutional gap (that is, the lack of a single regulator for each industry) is the result of political reluctance to apply market rules completely, and causes the Commission to act beyond its powers.

An interesting economic repercussion of liberalisation is the increase in Europe-directed investment of many firms, market structures shifting from national monopoly to regional oligopolies.[251] This structural effect suggests that the idea (espoused clearly in the electronic communications field) that sector-specific regulation can give way to competition is misconceived, as markets are likely to remain highly concentrated for the foreseeable future. Moreover, one of the weaknesses of EC liberalisation has been the emphasis on market access for competitors at the expense of creating incentives to introduce more investment in infrastructure which could increase market opening further.[252] This gap also militates in favour of retaining, and strengthening, sector-specific regulation. Finally, from the perspective of politics, the role of competition principles is affected by concerns relating to the protection of citizens' rights to have access to certain public services. The Community has provided a variety of responses to accommodate public services and competition, in a manner reminiscent of its approach to the relationship between public policy and Article 81. Accordingly, there are instances where competition law is deemed inapplicable so as not to interfere with national welfare systems (by reference to the principle of solidarity), others where an exemption from competition law obligations is granted, provided public services are offered in an efficient manner (by applying Article 86(2) EC), at times by defining public service obligations as a matter of Community law, and then assuming that competitive markets are the best way to ensure citizens' rights. This last approach shows how Member States have succeeded in recasting national worries about public services as matters that fall to be considered at European level.[253] Just as there is no harmonious thinking on the process of market liberalisation, there is much progress to be made to strike an adequate balance between competition and public service delivery.

---

[251] N. Fligstein and F. Merand 'Globalization or Europeanization? Evidence on the European Economy Since 1980' (2002) 45 *Acta Sociologica* 7.

[252] However, the Commission suggests that this aspect of regulation is a matter for Member States: *2005 Report* SEC(2005)1781.

[253] A. Héritier 'Market Integration and Social Cohesion: The Politics of Public Services in European Regulation' (2001) 8 *Journal of European Public Policy* 825.

13

Conclusions

Contents

1. Institutions   *page* 497
2. Economics   500
3. Politics   503

At the beginning of the book, I suggested that the study of competition law could be enriched by trying to do more than decode ambiguous Treaty Articles and Regulations, increasing volumes of soft law notices, and Delphic judgments. In addition, one should inquire about the forces that agitate the development of the law. For convenience, these forces were distilled into the trio of institutions, economics and politics. We take these in turn one final time to wrap up our inquiry and bring together the major themes which have been discussed in the preceding chapters.

1 Institutions

The Commission has been at the centre of law enforcement since Regulation 17/62 came into force. It has deployed three methods to enforce law: adjudication, legislation and soft law.[1] In the early days it relied exclusively on decisions to proscribe certain forms of conduct, while since the late 1970s and increasingly in the 1980s, it used legislative powers to draw up block exemptions to steer firms, and since the mid-1990s and in particular since 2004, it has relied on soft law notices. For firms this development may provide a greater degree of legal certainty, allowing them to plan in advance. However, it also removes the courts from the legal process, leaving the Commission free to establish, and alter, the rules of competition as its enforcement priorities shift. This is undesirable as there is no scrutiny over the Commission's

---

[1] On the shift from adjudication to legislation, see D. J. Gerber 'The Transformation of European Community Competition Law?' (1994) 35 *Harvard International Law Journal* 97, 133–4.

activities, especially as most parties prefer to negotiate and settle with the Commission rather than test its decisions in the courts. As we noted in relation to Article 9 of Regulation 1/2003, two recent settlements have been in areas where the law is evolving (football broadcasting rights and rebates), where a formal, judicially reviewable decision might have been preferred, and the remedies imposed in merger cases seem to go beyond what might be obtained if the parties were not under such pressure to agree to the Commission's competition concerns. Even less desirable is the phenomenon of regulation by information whereby parties comply with soft law notices to avoid confrontation with the Commission rather than test the Commission's interpretation of the law. The legitimacy of this sort of regulation is doubtful.[2]

The Court's lax review of Commission policy in the early years facilitated the impact of competition law by nurturing the growth of several doctrines, and today's soft law method of regulation achieves similar results (at a time when the Court keeps a more watchful eye over the Commission's decisions that are appealed), widening the scope of competition law, in particular sector-specific competition law, applied to achieve open markets.

Modernisation through Regulation 1/2003 changes the nature of Commission involvement but probably increases its powers. The Regulation is likely to reduce the volume of Article 81 cases that the Commission takes up, and also allows it to set enforcement priorities on the basis of market failures that are best regulated at Community level, continuing a trend that began in the 1990s. Moreover, the Commission has also gained a leading role in shaping competition policy at national level. Paradoxically, decentralised enforcement by National Competition Authorities gives the Commission more powers than before, because NCAs seem to have become its foot soldiers: their actions are scrutinised by the Commission and are subject to its veto. Moreover, the switch from centralised to decentralised enforcement has an impact on the substantive law. Most notably, the Commission's codification of the interpretation of Article 81 has meant that the discretionary powers that the Commission used to exercise over Article 81(3) to safeguard agreements that promote Community policies are being phased out to ensure that the rules are applied in a mechanical manner by national authorities, so as to ensure equal treatment and legal certainty for firms. Accordingly, the institutional resettlement has an effect on the policy perspectives through which competition law is applied: some elements of discretion recede (Article 81(3) exemptions), while others increase (settlements in merger cases and sector-specific enforcement).

The Commission, however, is not an institution in a bubble. It interacts with other institutions via a web of networks. Of particular importance in shaping substantive law has been the link between DG Competition and US antitrust

---

[2] H. C. H. Hoffmann 'Negotiated and Non-Negotiated Administrative Rule-making: The Example of EC Competition Policy' (2006) 43 *Common Market Law Review* 153.

agencies. Political scientists would say that there has been 'policy learning'. That is, the Commission has gained knowledge about enforcing the law by looking at a more experienced agency. It is likely that much of the emphasis on a 'more economics-oriented approach' to competition law has come through this link. Indeed, at times US antitrust acts as the bell-wether for EC competition policy, with several references to 'convergence' in speeches of the Commissioners. This discourse is unwise, for two reasons. First, it generates mistaken expectations that EC competition law is trying to assimilate all of US antitrust policy while, as we have shown, there are some cases that are likely to be handled differently in the long term. In particular, divergence is likely because American agencies are happier with Type 2 errors, while Europeans prefer Type 1 errors; US antitrust believes in markets as the key to economic welfare (so under-enforcement is acceptable), while EC competition law believes in rivalry as the key to consumer welfare (so under-enforcement would remove the seeds from which competition blossoms). Second, the discourse is unwise because convergence can prevent the EC from developing law in ways that may perhaps be better than the US standards. For instance, the scepticism of the Commission over vertical restraints that segment markets might be more justifiable than the Americans' laissez-faire approach, if only the Commission implemented the law from the perspective of post-Chicago economics rather than pursuing every practice that might segment the internal market.

The increased involvement of NCAs in competition law enforcement might serve to increase the deterrent effect of competition law by multiplying points of enforcement, but it is not clear how far this will affect the interpretation of competition law. An optimistic scenario is that national authorities draw strength from their obligations under Regulation 1/2003 and from their interactions via the European Competition Network to gain prestige and power so as to distance themselves from government interference. Thus liberated, they enforce competition assiduously and complement the Commission's enforcement efforts. A less rosy forecast is that some competition authorities will vigorously defend EC competition law, others will remain underfunded or overly subservient to governments, or even corrupt, while others may rebel against over-centralisation and develop national competition law in their own directions, increasing diversity among European states.

The national court is another institution that will increasingly be involved in enforcing competition law. According to the ECJ, anyone who has suffered injury as a result of a competition violation can seek damages. This is inappropriate. First, courts should only be open to plaintiffs who deserve protection and claims that risk undermining the principles of competition law should not be entertained. Second, the cost of operating the judicial system suggests that limits on claims should also be put in place lest the system cannot cope. Moreover, saying that anyone may claim is misleading because the costs and risks of litigation are so high that only a few will use the courts. But even a small number of cases can have a profound impact on the substance of competition law. Should courts reaffirm the view in *Courage v. Crehan* that large firms have a duty to negotiate with care in their contractual relations with smaller firms for example, this risks creating a set of obligations beyond those created by the Commission's interpretation of competition law. Accordingly, the more economics-oriented approach to competition championed by the Commission in soft law notices might run into conflict with damages claims where fair dealing is protected.

Accordingly, while decentralised enforcement is a reason for the Commission narrowing the scope of competition law to avoid reference to non-economic considerations, decentralisation creates the risk that the newly empowered bodies may undermine the economics-based approach that the Commission has promoted since the mid 1990s. Moreover, the Commission's own policy in newly liberalised industries and merger cases retains a public policy dimension out of line with the approach taken in Article 81.

2 Economics

If we asked economists to write a competition code starting with a clean slate, could they do any better than the draftsman of the EC Treaty? They might be tempted to draft only one commandment: 'conduct that harms economic welfare is prohibited'.[3] After all, the legal squabbles over technicalities about what 'agreement' or 'dominance' mean are far removed from the real issue, which is to deter firms from harming economic welfare. However, this single code is unhelpful because it would require one to 'ramble through the wilds of economic theory'[4] for every practice that is under assessment to decide if behaviour is harmful. The cost of running this method of enforcement would not reduce the cost of mistaken decisions commensurably.

Instead, economics is best translated into rules of law by ignoring express reference to that dismal science.[5] Economics can provide guidance to design rough rules of thumb that allow us to find safe harbours on the one hand and behaviour that must always be condemned on the other, without using economic analysis directly. In this respect certain aspects of EC competition law are designed according to this approach. In mergers and vertical restraints there are safe harbours based on market concentration and market share. This is not to say that the behaviour of firms who benefit from safe harbours cannot harm economic welfare, but it is highly unlikely that it will and it is more costly to find out which of those firms will harm economic welfare than to experience the cost of their anticompetitive acts. Safe harbours mean we tolerate Type 2

---

[3] For a similar discussion, see R. A. Posner *Antitrust Law* 2nd edn (Chicago: University of Chicago Press, 2001) ch. 9.

[4] *US v. Topco Associates Inc.* 405 US 596, 610 (1972).

[5] This description of economics is attributed to Thomas Carlyle.

errors. There are also kinds of action that are always rebuked, for example cartels and absolute territorial restraints. All attempts to fix prices are unlawful, even those that are unsuccessful. It is highly unlikely that price fixing or territorial division among competitors has an efficiency rationale, and it is too costly to find out if there is such a rationale. Per se rules mean we tolerate Type 1 errors. If enforcement costs are relevant, a safe harbour worth considering for any competition authority is that some anticompetitive effects have no remedy. Tacit collusion is a prime candidate for conduct that competition law can do little about: it is too costly to find an answer as to whether the parties' conduct is inefficient and facilitates collusion or enhances efficiency.

More problematic is behaviour which we cannot place in the per se or safe harbour boxes. Here the cost of enforcement must be incurred to apply the law. But even in these cases the hypothetical economists' one command (prohibit what causes harm to economic welfare) is an unhelpful recipe for enforcement. First, proving harm is costly and complex. Second, often competition law is enforced before the harm has taken place: in Article 82 cases where we suspect an exclusionary abuse, we chastise the dominant firm while it is committing the abuse, we do not wait until it has finished and begins to raise prices having eliminated rivals. In distribution agreements, the agency acts when it sees competitors being foreclosed, not after the foreclosure causes prices to rise, and in merger cases action is required before the merger even takes place. This makes proof of anticompetitive effect even less appealing as a legal standard. The discussions over the reform of Article 82 shed an interesting light on how we might handle cases where the welfare effects are anticipated but are too complex to subsume under the per se or safe harbour slots. Some, including the Commission, believe that a helpful standard is to ask if the dominant firm's conduct harms a competitor who is 'as efficient' as the dominant firm. This standard can be used to assess any exclusionary conduct (including vertical restraints and vertical or conglomerate mergers). It is premised on the belief that efficient competitors have a right to participate in the market because their presence enhances economic welfare. Others, including the US Department of Justice, take the view that exclusionary behaviour should only be condemned when it makes no economic sense. This occurs when the defendant's act can only be profitable if it harms rivals. These two approaches allow one to design competition rules that eschew complex economic analysis. Applied to predatory pricing, the 'as efficient competitor' standard would condemn all prices below cost because a competitor who is as efficient as the dominant firm would be unable to set prices below cost. The 'no economic sense' standard instead would require proof that predation allows the defendant to recover its losses from below-cost pricing because predatory pricing makes no economic sense unless competitors exit so that losses can be recovered. The 'as efficient competitor' test is more aggressive: any act harming a rival is an abuse, while under the 'no economic sense' test, acts that harm rivals are tolerated when the defendant's profits do not hinge on the rival's exit. While these standards are premised upon economic considerations, they ignore detailed effects-based analyses in favour of less precise but cheaper to handle standards.

However, even if one were to appraise competition law on the basis of whether the rules achieve an appropriate balance between maximising accuracy and limiting enforcement costs, it remains the case that the economic theory one begins with determines the choice and design of rules of thumb. Accordingly, managing tacit collusion is more of a problem from the perspective of the Harvard School, according to which structure drives performance, and less so from the perspective of the Chicago School, according to which collusion is highly unlikely absent some agreement. And the Commission's favoured test for Article 82 abuses is more in line with its wish to avoid Type 2 errors, and the political belief that competition requires the presence of competitors.

Finally, what of the efficiencies that may result from seemingly anticompetitive conduct? If enforcement agencies deploy rules that are mere proxies for determining market power and competitive harm, can a defendant rebut accusations of anticompetitive conduct by proof of efficiencies? The Commission wishes to streamline the efficiency defence by transposing the criteria in Article 81(3) to mergers and abuse of dominance. But this is misguided. The relative success of Article 81(3) in considering efficiencies since the 1960s is explained by the fact that the concept of a restriction of competition in Article 81(1) was read too widely, so that innocuous agreements were caught. The proxy that the Commission has used to find a restriction of competition (economic freedom) did not allow it to filter out efficient agreements: there were too many Type 1 errors in the application of Article 81(1), which were remedied by a more effective analysis under Article 81(3). A shift to a market power proxy for Article 81(1) is likely to render Article 81(3) less relevant as Type 1 errors diminish when this proxy is applied to Article 81(1). Moreover, in merger and Article 82 cases, the Article 81(3) type of defence breaks down because the Community places more emphasis on the process of competition, which by definition has been harmed by a merger creating dominance or the presence of a dominant firm. As suggested in chapters 8 and 9, a more fruitful role for efficiencies in merger cases arises when the efficiencies remove the incentive of the merged entity to cause harm. For example, a merger in an oligopoly market that creates efficiencies can reduce the firms' incentives to collude tacitly. Moreover, running an efficiency defence in this case does not require the same control factors as in Article 81(3) (for example, it is unnecessary to show that the merger is the sole route to efficiency when the efficiencies eliminate the anticompetitive risk). In Article 82, the only plausible role for an efficiency defence arises if the tests for dominance and abuse are too easily satisfied and over-inclusive. Then, efficiencies, as with Article 81 cases, serve as a safety valve to exclude the application of Article 82 to harmless conduct. This limited role for efficiency is based upon the political foundations of EC competition law: the rules are there, first and foremost, to ensure 'disciplined pluralism' among economic actors. This is why the Williamson trade-off model has no place in EC competition law: a merger to monopoly where productive efficiencies outweigh allocative inefficiencies is prohibited because it is a merger to monopoly. A competitive structure is the foundation of EC competition law not because the Commission is married to the SCP paradigm, but as a guarantee of economic freedom. Politics limits the application of economics-based rules and standards.

3 Politics

It is still not clear who the primary beneficiary of competition law is. An interesting 'conversation' over the role of competition law occurred when the Presidents of the CFI and ECJ were considering interim measures in the *IMS* case. In the CFI, the President said that 'the primary purpose of Article 82 EC . . . is to prevent the distortion of competition, and especially to safeguard the interests of consumers, rather than to protect the position of particular competitors'.[6] However, the President of the ECJ disagreed with this passage 'in so far as it could be understood as excluding protection of the interests of competing undertakings from the aim pursued by Article 82 EC, even though such interests cannot be separated from the maintenance of an effective competition structure'.[7] The former embraced a consumer welfare prescription, the latter a position closer to the ordoliberal vision of competitive market structures as the reason for competition law. I have suggested that originally, competition law was primarily interested in economic freedom and market integration (favouring the ECJ President's position), while today it is more interested in consumer welfare and efficiency (supporting the CFI President's views). However, even in the current paradigm, efficiency remains subordinate to economic freedom, as witnessed by the reluctance to consider efficiencies as a defence.

The change in priorities among what I labelled the three core values (efficiency, economic freedom and market integration) is further complicated by the opaque role that other policies play in EC competition law. According to some, the Commission's early Article 81 case law displayed an industrial policy dimension in that agreements among small and medium-sized undertakings and other alliances deemed to be in the Community interest received little scrutiny.[8] And others have suggested that more contemporary manifestations of EC competition law also embody concerns over the development of a Community industrial policy, not always in ways that are compatible with the focus on competitive market structures, although in most instances the

[6] Case T-184/01R *IMS Health Inc. v. Commission* [2001] ECR II-3193 para. 145.
[7] Case C-481/01P(R) *NDC Health GmbH & Co. KG v. Commission* [2002] ECR I-3401 para. 84.
[8] See E.-J. Mestmacker 'Concentration and Competition in the EEC' (1972) 6 *Journal of World Trade* 615.

Commission sees competitive markets as the key to promoting industrial development.[9] Moreover, the application of sector-specific competition law, either through focused enforcement in certain sectors, or where law is designed and enforced to achieve reorganisations of industrial market structures, suggests that the substance of the law is amplified when necessary to create competitive markets and develop Europe's industrial policy. Accordingly, sometimes the letter of competition law is not applied, to favour anticompetitive agreements in the Community interest, and at other times competition law is applied even more aggressively than it is normally, so as to facilitate economic development. But the institution doing this (the Commission) denies these trends, emphasising that the contribution that competition law makes to competitiveness rests on a transparent and unified legal framework based on an analysis of economic effects, where enforcement is focused on the most significant restrictions of competition.[10]

Beyond industrial policy, the substance of competition law is also affected by other, non-economic considerations. Here the law has responded in three ways. First, it has found that EC competition law does not apply, so that other non-economic benefits can accrue (e.g. labour relations, social security benefits, pluralism in book publishing, social security systems, safeguarding the integrity of the legal profession). Second, it has exempted agreements that bring non-economic benefits (notably agreements that are environmentally friendly, or grants of exclusive rights that are necessary to supply citizens with a public service). Third, it has imposed obligations designed to secure non-economic benefits (e.g. exempting crisis cartels on the condition that staff are retrained, allowing media mergers on conditions that protect pluralism, or imposing directives compelling Member States to provide certain universal services through competitive markets).

There are benefits in excluding competition law when it would harm the pursuit of other valuable objectives, and also benefits when citizens' rights are safeguarded at the expense of competition, but there are risks in using EC competition law to patch up incomplete political agreements over the direction of industrial and other non-economic policies. On the one hand, the Treaty demands that competition law fit within the broad framework of the Community (recall for example that Articles 81 and 82 and the ECMR all proclaim that certain practices are banned when 'incompatible with the common market', so that a holistic assessment of all Community interests is required to declare a practice illegal under the competition rules), but, on the other, it behoves other political agents to take over the regulation of

[9] W. Sauter *Competition Law and Industrial Policy in the EU* (Oxford: Oxford University Press, 1997) pp. 191–3, suggesting that at times anticompetitive effects may be tolerated in exchange for stronger EU firms, and pp. 227–30, suggesting that as a whole competition and industrial policies are complements.

[10] EC Commission *A Pro-active Competition Policy for a Competitive Europe* COM(2004)293 final pp. 7 and 16.

markets, as DG Competition has no comparative advantage in the design of industrial or other Community policies.

However, it seems impossible to exclude 'politics' from the implementation of competition law: not only because the institutional makeup of the Commission may often compel the consideration of non-competition factors, but also because any non-political version of competition law is a sham. An independent regulatory agency may be less prey to capture, but its interpretations of the rules rest upon normative foundations that reflect one's views about how markets work. Accordingly, agency independence does not eliminate the need for the agency to select a political vision over the role of competition, and a matching economic approach. Moreover, the recent trend whereby consumer welfare is perceived to be the centre around which EC competition law gravitates (and so might arguably narrow down agency discretion) is problematic in that it embodies distributional concerns (e.g. protecting vulnerable consumers, or infra-marginal consumers) that might motivate a more aggressive stance against certain practices than recent reforms suggest (e.g. in the field of distribution agreements), or the non-application of competition law in newly liberalised markets, against the trend in the liberalisation directives. Accordingly, a focus on consumer welfare may run against the more economics-oriented approach premised on a less aggressive competition policy that the Commission has sought to develop.

To suggest that the substance of EC competition law changes with the institution that enforces it, its economic vision and the politics that animate the enforcer is not to condemn the rules or their enforcement. On the contrary, the enforcement of EC competition law and the way competition is a basic anchor of European business life has been one of the European Union's success stories. The aim was to suggest that EC competition law is not merely a system that progressively and incrementally self-improves as it embraces new economic theories and different institutional designs.[11] Its decisions and policies are, necessarily, informed by a vast variety of complementary and conflicting interests, which change over time, and which form a constituent part of its identity.

---

[11] Similarly, Gerber 'Transformation', which also suggests a historical and institutional perspective on the development of EC competition law.

Index

abuse of dominance. *See also* dominance;
  market power
  British Airways/Virgin
    aftermath, 204
    anticompetitive exclusion, 164–6, 232
    case study, 162–72
    context, 169
    court approach, 167–9
    economic freedom paradigm, 166–7, 168
    neoclassical analysis, 163–4
    post-Chicago paradigm, 164–6, 167–8
    scope of Article 82, 170–2
    US litigation, 168–9, 171
  Commission reassessment, 130
  defences, 203–11
    burden of proof, 203
    economic efficiency, 208–10, 211–12
    economic justification, 204–5
    meeting competition, 205–8
    public policy, 210–11
  distribution agreements, 183–6, 371
  economic freedom, 128, 170
    above-cost discounts, 183
    discrimination, 201–2
    harm to other participants, 197
    reform, 177, 211
  electricity market, 463
  EU policy, 171
  exclusion of rivals, 173–95
    above-cost discounts, 182–3
    distribution agreements foreclosing
      entry, 183–6
    leverage, 186–95, 279–80
    predatory pricing, 177–82
    raising rivals' costs, 173–7
  exploitative abuse, 217–23. *See also* refusal
    to supply
    excessive pricing, 218–20, 376
  price control by regulators, 220–3
  extending concept
    economic freedom, 211
    leverage, 192
    regulatory failures, 473
  French retail sector, 377–80
  generally, 160–2
  harm to market participants, 195–8
    discriminatory treatment, 196
  market sharing, 198–203
  mergers
    use of Article 82, 246
    vertical mergers, 266
  objectives, 161
  pluralism, 196
  price control and, 218–20, 376
  protection of competitors, 175
  rationale, 162–72
  reform, 161–2, 171–2, 211–15
    exclusion of rivals, 173
    foreclosing distribution agreements,
      185–6
    new policy directions, 211–13
    unifying economic paradigm,
      213–15
  regulation role, 243–4
  remedies, 217
  statutory monopolies, 447–8, 480
  tacit collusion, 335–8, 341–2
  total welfare analysis, 212
abuse of economic dependence, 377–80
advertising
  distribution agreements and, 350–1
  entry barrier, 147
  product differentiation, 353–4
  refusal to supply, 224–5
  social construction, 354
Aer Lingus, 231–2

aerospace industry
  Boeing/McDonnell Douglas case, 22–3
  civil helicopters, 12
  De Havilland case, 6–15
  GE/Honeywell, 87, 129–30, 274–7
  global market, 139
  rivalry without competition, 22–3
  turbo-propeller markets, 7, 10
Aerospatiale, 6
aftermarkets
  market power, 148–50
  tying, 189, 191–2
agreements
  anti-competitive. *See* Article 81
      (anti-competitive agreements)
  meaning, 41–4, 325–7, 396
air services agreements, 453
Airbus, 22–3, 275
airlines
  British Midland/Aer Lingus, 231–2
  competition law, 476–8
  computer reservation systems, 234–5
  EU regulation, 234–7
  German tickets, 447
  liberalisation, 169, 231–2, 452–6
    freight services, 455
    slot allocation, 455–6, 476–8
    transatlantic flights, 456
  uneconomic routes, 489
  US predatory pricing, 72–3
airport services, 200–1, 235–7
Akbar, Y., 389
Alenia, 6
allocative efficiencies
  aftermarkets, 149
  cartels, 56
  case law, 45, 46
  economic welfare and, 26
  meaning, 45
  monopolies, 56
Amato, G., 97
ambulance services, 490
ancillary restraints, 33–6
anti-competitive agreements. *See* Article 81
      (anti-competitive agreements)
anti-doping, 114–15
Armani, 150
Armstrong, M., 442–3
Article 81 (anti-competitive agreements)
  agreement, meaning, 41–4, 325–7, 396
  agreements creating competition, 36–9

agreements of minor importance, 154–5
ancillary restraints, 33–6
direct effect, 47, 394, 404–5, 424
distribution. *See* distribution
    agreements
ECJ approach, 31–9
economic efficiency, 45–6
  increasing importance, 52
  pluralism, 50
  v market integration, 41, 50–1
economic freedom, 80
  ancillary restraints, 33–6
  concept of competition, 25–9
  market power screen, 48–50
  measuring restrictions, 31–3
  recasting, 48–50
elimination of competition, 372
exemptions. *See* Article 81 exemptions
fines, 40, 43
market integration, 39
  v economic efficiency, 41, 50–1
market power and, 153–7
  evolving analysis, 156–7
  quasi *per se* illegality, 155–6
  safe harbours, 154–5
objectives, 48, 50
price fixing, 155, 309–11, 448
rule of reason, 29–31
tacit collusion, 339–40
vertical integration, 41, 372
vertical restraints. *See* distribution
    agreements
void agreements, 431
Article 81 exemptions
  agreements of minor importance, 154–5
  block exemptions. *See* block exemptions
  burden of proof, 46, 49
  Commission role, 395–6
  conditions, 25–6
  consumer policy, 99–102
  culture, 102–10
  decentralisation of decisions, 213, 394
  direct effect, 47, 394,
      404–5, 424
  distribution agreements, 366–72
  economic efficiency, 45–6
  employment conditions, 97–9
  employment protection, 96–7, 121
  environmental policy
    guidelines, 92
    voluntary agreements, 91–2

Article 81 exemptions (cont.)
  guidelines
    effectiveness, 122
    efficiency, 93, 115, 120
    objectives, 48–50
    vertical restraints by dominant firms, 372
  industrial policy, 94–6
  narrowing interpretation of Art. 81(3), 119–22
  national interests and, 103, 110–13
  notifications, 29, 154, 357
    abolition, 394, 405
    comfort letters, 358, 398, 413
    reform option, 411–12
    workload, 397–400
  public policy considerations, 89, 210
    balance of factors, 115
    conditional exemptions, 115–16
    consequentialism, 116–17
    elimination, 119–22, 412
    exclusionary method, 113–17
    formalism, 116
    future, 122–3
    institutional legitimacy, 118–19
    methodology, 113–17
    redefining economic efficiency, 93, 115
    statutory agreements, 448
  railways joint ventures, 233–4
Article 82. See abuse of dominance
AT&T, 67, 473–4
Augusta, 12
Austria
  medicines, 152
  newspaper delivery services, 225–6

baby food market, 151–2, 257–8, 259
Bain, J. S., 64, 144–6
Baker, J. B., 54, 72
bananas, 128–9, 135–6, 197, 202, 219
Bangemann, Martin, 8, 11
banking
  Italy, 306
  Poland, 305
Baxter, William, 65
Bayer, 43–4, 152
beef packing, 66–7
beer supply agreements, 31, 36–7, 205, 347,
    367, 427–9
Belgium
  air transport liberalisation, 454
  Competition Authority, 414
  EU competition law jurisdiction, 401

failing firm mergers, 297–8
postal service monopoly, 450–1, 488–9
telecommunications, 222, 450
TV advertising, 224–5
Bishop, S., 148, 202
block exemptions
  application, 359–61
  Commission strategies, 399–400
  distribution agreements, 370, 399
  insurance, 102
  motor vehicles, 384–8
  non-compete clauses and, 361
  origins, 358
  rationale, 154
  resale price maintenance and, 360–1
  strategy, 358–9, 398, 411
  types of vertical restraints, 369
  withdrawal, 361–3, 390
Boeing, 22–3, 129, 275
Bolton, P., 181
Bork, Robert, 3, 55, 77, 81
branded goods, 150–3
  mergers, 257–8, 283
Breyer, Justice, 78
brick structure, 227–8
British Aerospace, 11, 12
British Airways/Virgin
  aftermath, 204
  anticompetitive exclusion, 164–6, 232
  case study, 162–72
  context, 169
  court approach, 167–9
  economic freedom paradigm, 166–7, 168
  facts, 162–3
  neoclassical analysis, 163–4
  post-Chicago paradigm, 164–6, 167–8
  scope of Article 82, 170–2
  US litigation, 168–9, 171
British Midland, 231–2
Brittan, Leon, 8, 9, 13, 248, 301
broadcasting
  advertising, 224–5
  cable TV, 457, 458
  geographic markets, 140
  Greek monopoly, 450
  liberalisation, 106
  mergers, 268–71, 292
  pay-TV, 142, 158, 271, 287–8
  sports broadcasting, 105–10, 143, 413
  TV listings, 227–8
Brodley, J. F., 79, 80, 181

BskyB, 109
business associations, 402
business software, 153
buyer power, mergers and, 255–6
buying pools, 45–6

cable TV, 457, 458
Canada, merger policy, 292
Canal+, 32, 38, 142, 270–1
Carlsberg, 27–8, 30, 50
cars. *See* motor vehicles
cartels
    agreements, meaning, 325–7
    cheating members, 63
    concerted practices, 325–7
    crisis cartels, 95, 96, 115
    dyestuffs cartel, 332
    effect, 56
    European Cartel Office, 419
    evidence, 330–2
        documentary evidence, 330–1
        economic evidence, 331–2
    fines, 410
    football clubs, 106
    generally, 324–34
    illegality, 156, 325
    incentives to confess, 332–4
    investigatory powers, 331, 410
    leniency programmes, 332–4,
        410, 437
    market structures, 324
    priority, 409, 410
    resale price maintenance, 354
    state-sanctioned, 447
    sugar cartel, 331
    wood pulp, 332
Carter, Jimmy, 78
CASE, 78
cash register market, 148–9
category management, 294–5
cellophane fallacy, 134
cement industry, 66
Chicago Convention 87, 455
Chicago School
    competition approach, 4, 6
    entry barriers, 64, 66, 147
    generally, 63
    government ineffectiveness, 64
    laissez faire politics, 81
    market power and, 158
    mergers, 65–7, 265

oligopolies, 335, 344
policy prescriptions, 65–8
predatory pricing, 67–8, 87, 178
principles, 63–5
translation into law, 74, 76–8, 393
    judicial appointments, 77–8
    politics, 78
tying, 188, 189
vertical restraints, 77, 348, 356
civil law systems
    discovery rules, 435
    economics and, 79
    legal reasoning, 80
Coca-Cola, 204
collusion
    express collusion. *See* cartels
    tacit. *See* tacit collusion
Comanor, W. S., 353
comfort letters, 92, 358, 398, 413
commercial power, 125–6, 128–30,
    157–8, 209
commercial solvents, 224, 225
competence, legislative competence, 142
competition, concepts
    Article 81, 25–9
    competing concepts, 2, 22–5
    neoclassicism, 23–4, 26
    ordoliberalism, 23–4
competition authorities. *See* National
        Competition Authorities
competition law
    market failures, 55–7, 442
    objectives, 2, 3–4, 5
        market improvement, 217
    policy. *See* competition policy
    principal rules, 2
    role, 2–3, 243–4
    sector-specific, 474–85
competition policy
    Commission role, 411–12, 421
    EU objectives, 52, 81
    EU policy and economics, 79–87
    EU themes, 21, 83
        consumer interests, 83–6
        market power, 86
        pluralism, 87
    requirements, 15–18
        predictability, 15–16
        rules v standards, 16–18, 81
    shaping factors, 4–6
        economics. *See* economics

competition policy (cont.)
  institutions. *See* institutions
  politics. *See* politics
  transformation, 20–2, 51–2
  values. *See* core values
computer software
  entry barriers, 146
  innovation defence, 241
  licensing refusal, 229–31
  mergers, 260–1
  tying, 189–90
concerted practices, meaning, 325–7
conduct, meaning, 57
conglomerate mergers
  anti-competitive effects, 272
  category management, 294–5
  elimination of competition, 281–2
  entry barriers, 280–1
  generally, 271–82
  leveraging, 272–80
    Commission policy, 274–8
    ECJ approach, 278–80
    market forces, 276–7
    Tetra Laval, 278–80
    US v EU, 276
  meaning, 250, 271
  SIEC test, 278–80
  strategic pricing, 280–1
Constitutional Treaty, 91
Consumer Liaison Officer, 86, 99
consumer welfare
  abuse of dominance and, 197, 212–13
  Article 81, 48, 171
    exemptions, 25, 26, 27, 28, 46, 99–102
  block exemptions, 358
    withdrawal, 363
  competition objective, 5, 21, 52, 83–6, 171
  concept, 85–6, 423
  cooperation obligations and, 223, 224–6
  distribution agreements, 351–5
  electricity liberalisation, 461–2
  Europeanisation of consumer law, 99–100
  focus, 53
  guarantees, 101
  IPR licensing obligations and, 229–31
  market power and, 86
  merger policy, 291–2, 300
  new entrants and, 186
  pre-sale services, 352–3
  predatory pricing, 181
  proportionality, 210

public services, 492
  rebates and, 184
  retail power and, 374, 377
    UK supermarkets, 382
  telecommunications liberalisation, 459
  total welfare v, 83–4, 274, 390
  tying, 189–90
  US economics, 79
  vacuity, 10
consumers
  customer weakness and mergers, 256
  private enforcement, 425–6, 431–4
  views and market definition, 136
  welfare. *See* consumer welfare
Cooke, C. J., 15–16
cooperation. *See also* refusal to supply
  agreements, increasing competition, 37–9
  merger conditions, 286–8
  oligopolies, 310
cooperatives, 34
core values
  changing relationships, 20–1, 48–51
  economic efficiency. *See* economic efficiency
  economic freedom. *See* economic freedom
  single market. *See* single market
  tensions, 48
  transformation thesis, 20–2, 51–2
Cowan, S., 442–3
crisis cartels, 96, 115, 325–7
cross-subsidies, 478–84, 493
culture
  book prices, 103–5, 122
  EU competition and, 102–10
  sports broadcasting, 105–10

DAF, 262–3
damages
  categories of claimants, 431–4, 499–500
  competitors, 426
  consumers, 425–6, 431–4
  Courage v Crehan, 427–9
  distributors, 427–9
  follow-on claims, 434–5, 436
  practical difficulties, 434–5
  punitive damages, 435
  scope of competition law, 424–31
Darwinism, 276–8
Dawson, J., 391
De Havilland case
  economics, 9–12
    dominance, 10–11

relevant market, 10
significantly impeding competition, 11–12
turbo-propeller markets, 7
facts, 6
false negatives and positives, 18
generally, 6–15
institutions, 13–14, 118
politics, 8–9, 16
defence, 486
demand substitutability, 132, 138
Denmark
electricity liberalisation, 462
pork market, 320
price transparency, 318
Deringer, Arved, 26–7, 195–6
Deutsche Post, 479–84, 485
Diageo, 272–4
Directorate General for Competition
Consumer Liaison Officer, 86, 99
developments, 393
economists, 82
lawyers, 80–1
legal nature, 118
role, 2, 13, 421
disabled, access to services, 492
discounts
above-cost discounts, 182–3
abuse of dominance, 195, 196
defences, 207
distribution agreements, 371
economic efficiency defence, 209
economic justification, 204–5
meeting competition defence, 206
British Airways/Virgin, 162–3
distribution agreements, 183–6, 195, 371
leverage, 186
retroactive rebates, 378
target rebates, 183
top-slice rebates, 183
discovery rules, 435
distribution agreements
abuse of dominance, 195–8
economic justification, 203–11
foreclosing entry, 183–6
anticompetitive effects, 347–8
Article 81, 366–72
analytical framework, 366–9
dominant firms, 371–2
efficiencies, 369
foreclosure, 368

negative effects, 366–7
selective distribution, 369–71
block exemptions
application, 359–61
Commission strategy, 399
market shares, 359–61
origins, 358
primacy, 358–9
withdrawal, 361–3, 390
car market, 384–90
Chicago School, 77, 348, 356
damages, 427–9
definition of vertical restraint, 347
distributors' powers, 372–83
economic debate, 348
consumer welfare, 351–5
intentional exclusion, 355
policy implications, 355–6
stimulating v deterring entry, 349–51
economic freedom, 348, 357, 358, 368, 390
efficiency, 209–10, 349
EU policy, 357–63
analytical framework, 366–9
application of block exemption, 359–61
market power screen, 358–9
original approach, 357–8
political values, 391
Green Paper, 82–3
Guidelines, 366–7
dominant firms, 371
new approach, 368
non-compete clauses, 361
territorial segmentation, 364–6
withdrawal of block exemptions, 363
hold-up problem, 351
market power, 125, 358–9, 399
meaning, 347
non-compete clauses, 361
single market and, 363–6
tacit collusion, 339–40, 354
territorial agreements, 364–6
types, 348
vertical mergers, 267
distributive justice
Article 81(3), 80
Chicago School disregard, 6
competition law role, 383
distribution agreements and, 390
EU competition policy, 26
UK supermarkets and, 382
US antitrust and, 79

Dobson, P. W., 376
dominance. *See also* abuse of dominance
    collective dominance
        evidence, 313
        merger case law, 314–15
        merger control, 311–12
        tacit collusion, 335–8, 341–2
    De Havilland case, 10–11
    EU competition law, 127–30
        measuring, 259
        reassessment, 130
        US differences, 130
    firms' obligations, 160
    horizontal mergers, 250–6
    merger test, 250
    Michelin case, 127
doping, 114–15
drinks market, 272–4
DuPont, 67
duress, 125, 408
dyestuffs cartel, 332
dynamic efficiencies
    competition role, 55
    intellectual property rights and, 229,
        230, 231
    meaning, 45
    monopolies and, 56
    telecommunications cooperation and, 237

Easterbrook, P., 64, 77
EC Treaty, cross-sectional clauses, 91, 102
econometric studies, 70
economic duress, 125, 408
economic efficiency
    allocative. *See* allocative efficiencies
    Article 81 exemptions, 45–6, 369
    Article 81 objective, 48
    block exemptions, withdrawal, 363
    burden of proof, 46
    Chicago School and, 65
    core value, 46–8
        increasing importance, 52
        widening concept, 93, 115
    defence, abuse of dominance, 208–10,
        211–12
    distribution agreements, 349, 369
    distributors' power and, 374
    dynamic. *See* dynamic efficiencies
    environmental protection, 91, 93
    Kaldor–Hicks measure, 24
    market integration v, 41, 50–1

merger policy, 292–6
    monopolies and, 56
        statutory monopolies, 451
    neoclassicism, 23–4
    oligopolies, 322–3
    pluralism v, 50, 87
    productive. *See* productive efficiencies
    public service monopolies, 490–1
    typology, 45
    vertical mergers, 264–5
    X-inefficiency, 56
economic freedom. *See also* small business
        freedom
    abuse of dominance and, 128, 170
        above-cost discounts, 183
        discrimination, 201–2
        harm to other participants, 197
        predatory pricing, 181
        reform, 177, 211
    aftermarkets, 149
    Article 81, 25–9, 80
        agreements creating competition, 36–9
        ancillary restraints, 33–6
        case law, 31–9
        market power screen, 48–50
        measuring restrictions, 31–3
        recasting, 48–50
    block exemptions, withdrawal, 363
    British Airways/Virgin, 166–7, 168
    conglomerate mergers and, 278
    cooperation obligations and, 223, 224–6
    core value, 22–39
    EC concern, 81, 87, 128
    market power and, 126, 128
    merger policy, 300
    ordoliberalism, 23–4, 44, 87, 396
    pluralism, 186, 196
    rule of reason, 29–31
    US antitrust, 128
    vertical restraints and, 348, 357, 358,
        368, 390
economic policy, sovereignty, 395, 421
economics
    civil law systems and, 79
    competition and
        approaches, 4
        conclusions, 500–3
        limits, 87–8
    De Havilland case, 9–12
    environmental value, 93
    EU competition policy and, 79–87

lack of analysis, 79–82
nature of approach, 82–7
new approach, 10, 21, 53–4, 81–2, 393
EU themes, 21, 83
consumer interests, 83–6
market power, 86
pluralism, 87
expert evidence, 78
juridification of competition and, 420
lack of consensus, 3
market power and, 157–8
politics and, 54
structural approaches. *See* market structures
US antitrust and, 73–9, 393
institutions, politics and law, 75–9
politics, 81
US–EU shared premises, 55–7
US models, 54
Chicago School. *See* Chicago School
post-Chicago model, 68–73
SCP model, 57–63
translation into law, 73–5
vertical restraints, 348
economies of scale
Chicago School, 63
mergers, 296
SCP theory, 58, 64
Eisner, M. A., 76–7
electrical warranties, 422–3
electricity
liberalisation, 460–3
consumer welfare, 461–2
internal market, 462–3
price falls, 495
speed, 452
vertical integration, 462
merger control, 474–6
sectors, 460
electronic communications
monitoring NRAs, 471–4
regulation, 237–9, 464–8
v competition, 468–71
universality condition, 491–3
empirical evidence
econometric studies, 70
post-Chicago paradigm, 69–71
employment
collective agreements, 97–8
EU competition and, 96–9, 121
German recruitment monopoly, 449
pension funds, 97–9

protection and promotion, 96–7
working conditions, 97–9
endovascular stents, 152
enforcement of EU competition
centralised, 395–401
decentralisation
assessment, 404–9
coherence, 406–9
Europeanisation of economic
governance, 421
fines, 415
impact, 499–500
juridification, 420
Modernisation Regulation, 401–4
monitoring, 415–19
new structure, 409
objectives, 439
rebirth of national laws, 421–3
side effects, 419–23
legal certainty, 405
new structure, 409
Commission role, 409–14
European Competition Network, 415–19
National Competition Authorities,
414–15
penalties. *See* fines
private enforcement, 424–38
categories of claimants, 431–4
claimants' practical difficulties, 434–5
competitors, 426
consumers, 425–6, 431–4
Courage v Crehan, 427–9
distributors, 427–9
follow-on claims, 434–5, 436
modernisation and, 436–8
scope, 424–31
English clauses, 340
entry barriers
broadcasting vertical mergers, 268–9
Chicago School, 64, 66, 147
conglomerate mergers, 280–1
definitions, 144–6
distribution agreements and, 349–51
exclusive distribution, 355
Harvard School, 58, 59
horizontal mergers, 252–3
buyer power, 256
intellectual property rights, 64
market power and, 131, 132, 144–8
oligopolies, 319, 321
postal services, 479

entry barriers (cont.)
  refusal to cooperate, 216
  supermarket power, 375, 380
  telecommunications, 220–3
  tying, 187
  US merger policy, 66–8
environmental policy
  economical value of environment, 93
  electricity efficiency, 92, 120
  EU competition and, 91–4
  horizontal agreements, guidelines, 92
  sustainable development, 93
  voluntary agreements, 91–2
errors
  abuse of dominance, 175
  access remedies, 244
  block exemption approach, 358, 360
  De Havilland merger and, 18
  false negatives (Type 2), 17
  false positives (Type 1), 17
  legal rules and, 88
  market shares, 126–7
  oligopoly control, 309, 345
  US antitrust policy, 18
essential facilities
  air transport regulation, 234–7, 478
  airport services, 235–7
  computer reservation systems, 234–5
  electronic communications regulation, 237–9
  EU regulation, 234–9
  ferries, 232–3
  liberalisation case law, 240
  mergers, 254
  railways, 233–4
  refusal to supply, 231–4
Euro-defence, 431, 436
European Central Bank, 421
European Commission
  assessment, 497–9
  autonomy, 438
  bargaining power, mergers, 277, 290–1
  College of Commissioners, 13, 118
  competition powers, 2, 201
  De Havilland case, 6–15, 118
  delegation to domestic authorities, 21
  DG Competition. *See* Directorate General
    for Competition
  ECJ, relation with, 43
  exemptions. *See* Article 81 exemptions
  guidelines, legitimacy, 10–11
  investigatory powers, cartels, 331, 410

judicial review, 277
  Merger Task Force, 13
  obiter dicta, 117
  politics and law, 18
  post-modernisation role, 409–14
    coordination, 438
    informal guidance, 413–14
    policy direction, 411–12, 421
  pre-modernisation role, 395–401
    workload, 397–400
  reputation, 13
European Competition Days, 100
European Competition Network, 415–19, 438
European Convention on Human Rights, 103
European Court of First Instance, 44
European Court of Justice
  failure to filter cases, 395
  relation with Commission, 43
European Parliament
  book prices, 103
  merger and industrial policy, 14
Evian, 354
exclusive distribution agreements
  abuse of dominance, 371
  block exemptions, 369
  creating competition, 36
  distributors' power, 373
  English clauses, 340
  entry barriers, 355
  inter-brand competition and, 367
  motor vehicles, 385–6
  purpose, 355
  restriction of competition, 27
exclusive purchasing agreements
  block exemptions, 360, 369
  efficiencies, 340
  entry barriers, 349
exclusive territorial agreements
  Commission policy, 364–6
  consumer welfare, 352
  single market and, 39–41
  temporary protection, 51
expert evidence, 78

failing firms, mergers, 3, 296–8
false negatives and positives. *See* errors
ferries, 232–3
film market, 270–1, 287
fines
  Article 81 breaches, 40, 43
  cartels, 410

decentralisation of competition, 415
  levels, 436
  market sharing agreements, 198
Finland, telecommunications, 458, 466–7
firms. *See* undertakings
Fokker, 11, 12
football broadcasting rights, 107–9, 115,
      143, 413
force majeure, 240
Ford, 42, 97, 115–16
Fox, E. M., 2
France
  abuse of economic dependence, 377–80, 406
  aerospace industry, 9
  airline tickets, 454
  airport services, 200–1
  book prices, 103
  collecting societies, 219
  competition workload, 414
  economic patriotism, 247
  electricity liberalisation, 461
  EU competition law jurisdiction, 401
  merger policy, 248, 300, 305
  mineral water, 314
  Modernisation Regulation and, 406
  predatory pricing, 407
  retail sector, 383
    abuse of economic dependence,
        377–80, 406
    concentration, 377
    product choice and quality, 377
  telecommunications, 458–9
  truck market, 263
  tyre market, 198–9, 204
  utilities, 305
franchises, 348, 351, 353, 361, 369
Frazer, T., 90
free movement principle
  airport services, 200
  capital, 305
  fundamental principle, 201
  national interest exceptions, 111–12
  scope, 104
free supplies, 378
freedom of expression, 103

game theory, 310, 333
General Electric, 46, 129–30, 274–7
geographic markets, 139–41
Geradin, D., 473
Gerber, D. J., 197

Germany
  air transport liberalisation, 454
  airline tickets, 235, 447
  airport services, 236–7
  ambulance services, 490
  book prices, 104–5
  bread substitutes, 264
  competition authorities, 399
    resources, 414
    workload, 414
  competition law, 401, 407
    damages, 433, 435
    void agreements, 407–9
  critique of EU competition law,
      393, 400
  electricity, 461, 462
  EU competition law jurisdiction, 401
  football broadcasting, 109
  judicial debt collecting, 111
  liberalisation and, 461, 462, 482
  market reports, 227–8
  mergers
    electricity, 475
    media, 141
    policy, 248, 300, 303, 311, 318
  Modernisation Regulation and, 401, 409
  National Regulatory Authorities, 464
  ordoliberalism, 23
  parcel delivery market, 199
  pay-TV, 142
  politics of competition, 14
  postal services, 478–84, 485
  rail transport, 173
  recruitment monopoly, 449
  telecommunications, 220, 458–9, 472
  train manufacture, 288–9
globalisation, 9
good faith defence, 206
governance, liberalisation and, 444–6
Grand Metropolitan, 27–8, 272–4
Grant, J., 278
Greece
  broadcasting monopoly, 450
  competition law, 401
  drink market, 272
  EU competition law jurisdiction, 401
Grundig, 40–1, 51, 353, 354
guarantees, 101, 422–3
guidelines, legitimacy, 10–11
Guinness, 272–4
Gyselen, Luc, 115–16, 117, 122

Harding, C., 436
Harvard School
  Chicago School critique, 63–5
  competition theory, 57–63
  conduct, 57
  market power, 65, 158
  market structures, 57, 86, 335
  mergers, 59–61
  performance, 57–8
  pluralism, 87
  policy prescriptions, 59–63
  political influence, 73, 337
  predatory pricing, 61–3
  principles, 57–9
  resilience of SCP model, 344
  small business freedom, 78, 81
  tacit collusion, 502
Hawk, Professor, 358
Hay, George, 76
Heinz, 151–2
Helm, D., 476
Herfindhal Hirschmann Index (HHI),
    316–17
Hoffman La Roche, 127
hold-up problem, 351
Honeywell, 274–7
horizontal mergers
  customer weakness, 256
  essential facilities, 254
  guidelines, 261–2
    efficiencies, 293, 298, 322–3
    Herfindhal Hirschmann Index (HHI),
      316–17
    oligopolies, 312
    tacit collusion, 321
  market power without dominance, 256–64
    guidelines, 261–2
    implementing SIEC test, 261–4
    SIEC test, 258–61
    substantial lessening of competition,
      258–9
    unilateral effects, 256–8
  single firm dominance, 250–6
    actual and potential competitors, 252–3
    countervailing buyer power, 255–6
    market shares, 251–2
    strategic behaviour, 253–5
Hovenkamp, H., 75, 79
Hugin, 148–9
hypothetical monopolist test, 136, 137,
    139, 157

IBM, 67
industrial policy
  abuse of dominance and, 243
  crisis cartels, 95
  EU competition and, 14, 94–6, 117
  merger control and, 254, 298–300
informal guidance, 413–14
innovation
  dominance and, 255
  mergers, 296
  refusal to supply and, 241–2
institutions. See also Directorate General
    for Competition; European
    Commission; National Competition
    Authorities; National Regulatory
    Authorities
  conclusions, 497–500
  De Havilland case, 13–14, 118
  legitimacy, 118–19
  shaping competition law, 4–5, 393, 396
  US antitrust economics and, 75–9
insurance, block exemption, 102
integration. See single market
intellectual property rights
  compulsory licensing, 283, 286
  economic objectives, 228
  entry barriers, 64
  mergers and, 254, 283, 286
  refusal to license, 227–31
Interbrew, 205
internal market. See single market
International Competition Network
    (ICN), 14
Internet
  broadcasting, 106, 110, 143
  car sales, 386, 390
  horizontal mergers, 253–4
  regulation of connection services, 220
  regulatory framework, 457
  vertical mergers, 270–1
investigatory powers, cartels, 331, 410
Ireland
  air transport liberalisation, 454
  competition law, 401, 403
  electricity liberalisation, 462
  sugar market, 173
  TV listings, 227–8
Italy
  banks, 306
  broadcasting mergers, 287–8
  Coca-Cola distribution, 204

competition authorities, resources, 414
competition law, 401, 402–3
consumer damages, 426
electricity market, 140
EU competition law jurisdiction, 401
Genoa docks, 175–6, 218
merger policy, 306
scooter market, 286–7
utilities, 306

jeans, 352
joint ventures, 140
Joliet, R., 161
Joshua, J., 436
Jospin, Lionel, 485
juridification, 420

Kaldor–Hicks standard, 24, 26
Kallaugher, J., 185–6
Kay, John, 23
Kerse, C. S., 15–16
Keynes, John Maynard, 54
Keysen, Carl, 337
Kjolbye, Lars, 121
Kovacic, W. E., 77
Krattenmaker, T. G., 174, 175
Kroes, Neelie, 109, 410

Lambert, Gerard, 354
Larouche, P., 459, 470
lawyers
    competition laws and, 402
    DG Competition, 80–1
    lawyer–accountant partnerships,
        110–12
    price fixing, 448
    professional regulation, 110–12
legal certainty
    Article 81 exemptions, 49
    comfort letters and, 358, 413, 437
    competition policy, 15–16, 81
    decentralisation of enforcement and, 405,
        411–12, 413
    merger control, oligopolies, 324
    rules and standards, 16–18
    vertical restraints, 356
legal profession. *See* lawyers
legal systems, integrity, 112
legislative competence, 142
leniency programmes, 332–4, 410, 437
Lenz, AG, 36

Lerner index, 130–1
leverage
    abuse of dominance, 186–95, 279–80
    anti-competitiveness, 187–92
    conglomerate mergers, 272–80
        Commission policy, 274–8
        ECJ approach, 278–80
        GE/Honeywell, 274–7
        market forces, 276–7
        US v EU, 276
    defensive leverage, 190, 193
    extending concept of abuse, 192
    Hilti case, 187–9
    refusal to supply, 193
    strategies, 186
    Tetra Pak 2, 192–5
    vertical mergers, 266
Levy, D., 142
liberalisation
    abuse of dominance, 231–4, 240
    broadcasting, 106
    car distribution, 384
    essential facilities, 240
    network industries
        airlines, 169, 231–2, 452–6
        electricity, 460–3
        introduction of competition, 451–63
        postal services, 482–3
        telecommunications, 456–60
    Poland, 305
    post-liberalisation regulation, 463–74
        electronic communications, 464–8
        monitoring NRAs, 471–4
        National Regulatory Authorities, 463–4
        price control, 220–3
        sector specific v competition, 468–71
    process, 442–51
        case law, 446–51
        legislative tools, 444–6
        market context, 442–4
    public services, 485–94
    sector-specific competition law, 474–85
        airlines, 476–8
        electricity mergers, 474–6
        legitimacy, 484–5
        postal services, 478–84
    selective liberalisation, 442
licensing, IPRs, 227–31, 283, 286
Liptons, 148–9
Lisbon agenda, 47, 299, 495
Listerine, 354

localised competition, 260–1, 263
Lufthansa, 10, 235

Maher, Imelda, 420
market definition
  Commission Notice, 134, 136
    aftermarkets, 149
    consumers' views, 137
    criticism, 138–9
    economic analysis, 142
    geographic markets, 139
    substitutes, 137
  De Havilland case, 10
  demand substitutability, 132, 138
  EU competition law, 135–7
  example, 131–2
  geographic markets, 139–41
  hypothetical monopolist test, 132–5, 136
    cellophane fallacy, 134
    Commission use, 157
    user views, 137
  irrelevance, 150–3
  policy-driven, 141–3, 158
  post-Chicago model, 70–1
  product markets, 135–9
    consumers' views, 136
  supply substitutability, 138–9
market economy, EU, 1–2
market failures
  competition law and, 55–7, 442
  conglomerate mergers, US v EU, 276–7
  market structures and, 59
  post-Chicago paradigm, 68–9
  UK electrical warranties, 422–3
  UK store cards, 422
market integration. *See* single market
market investigations, 342–4, 380–3, 422–3
market partitioning, 156, 198–203
market power
  aftermarkets, 148–50
  Article 81 and, 153–7
    agreements of minor importance, 154–5
    evolving analysis, 156–7
    exemptions, 48–50
    quasi *per se* illegality, 155–6
    safe harbours, 154–5
  Chicago School, 65, 158
  concepts, 57, 124–7
    ability to increase prices, 125
    commercial power, 125–6, 128–30, 157–8
    jurisdictional concept, 126–7, 154

    neoclassicism, 125
    post-Chicago concept, 126, 128
  consumer welfare and, 86
  distribution agreements, 358–9, 399
  distributors, 372–83
  economic analysis, 157–8
  economic freedom and, 126, 128
  EU theme, 86, 127–30
  Harvard School, 65, 158
  litmus test, 19, 124
  measuring, 130–48
    entry barriers, 131, 132, 144–8
    Lerner index, 130–1
    market definition. *See* market definition
    market shares, 131, 143–4
  mergers, power without dominance, 256–64
  post-Chicago paradigm, 126, 128, 144, 158
  product differentiation and, 150–3
  relational power, 197
  US–EU differences, 130
market reports, 227–8
market shares
  agreements of minor importance, 154
  block exemptions, 359–61
  calculation, 144
  horizontal mergers, 251–2
  market power and, 131, 143–4
  oligopolies, 316
  relevance, 74
  significance, 126–7
  stability, 144
  thresholds, 16–17
  UK supermarkets, 380
market structures
  Article 82 protection, 170
  cartels, 324
  Chicago School, 64
  economics, 5
  EU competition policy, 86
  Harvard School, 59, 86, 335
  meaning, 57
  structural remedies, 283–6, 295, 336–7
meat products market, 137–8
media. *See also* broadcasting
  EU regulation, 141
  pluralism, 141–3, 271, 292
Mediaprint, 225–6, 239
medical equipment, mergers, 263–4
Member States
  See also National Competition Authorities;
    National Regulatory Authorities

competition laws, 401–3
  EU model, 394, 402–3, 406
  rebirth, 421–3
EU competition role, 118
sovereignty over economic policy, 395, 421
undermining modernisation, 395
mergers
  Article 82 alternative, 254
  Chicago School, 65–7, 265
  Commission powers, 277, 290–1
  competition effect, 246
  conglomerate. *See* conglomerate merges
  consumer welfare, 291–2, 300
  De Havilland case, 6
  definitions, 246
  dominance test, 250
  ECMR, 247–9, 300–7
  economic analysis, 251
  economic efficiency v pluralism, 87
  economic freedom, 278, 300
  electricity sector, 474–6
  European policy, 300–7
  failing firms, 3
  geographic markets, 140
  Harvard School, 59–61
  horizontal. *See* horizontal mergers
  legal history, 246–50
  market share thresholds, 16–17
  media mergers, 142
  national interests, 302
  oligopolies. *See* oligopolies
  overview, 248–50
  policy objectives
    efficiencies, 292–6
    European policy, 300–7
    industrial policy, 298–300
    non-competition considerations, 292
    rescuing failing firms, 296–8
    social policy, 296
    tradeoff model, 292
    widening, 291–300
  post-Chicago model, 71
  procedure, 248–50
  protectionism, 305–7
  reasons, 246
  referrals to Member States, 302, 305
  remedies, 283–6
    behavioural remedies, 286–90
    Commission powers, 290–1
    contract severance, 289–90
    cooperation conditions, 286–8

divestment, 283–6, 295
  hold-separate commitments, 284
  monitoring, 289–90
  nature, 290–1
  structural remedies, 283–6, 295
rules v standards, 17
single market and, 304, 305
technical and economic progress, 8
test, 249–50
thresholds, 301–2
unilateral effects, 151
United States
  1968 guidelines, 60
  1982 guidelines, 65–6, 132
  branded products, 151–2, 257–8
  broadcasting sector, 268–9
  Chicago School, 65–7, 265
  conglomerate mergers, 272, 281–2
  consumer welfare objectives, 292
  divestments, 283–4
  guidelines, 76
  HHI index, 316
  market definition, 132, 134
  media pluralism, 271
  US v EU, 276, 292
  vertical mergers, 60–1, 66, 71, 76
vertical. *See* vertical mergers
MFN clauses, 341–2, 373, 376
Michelin, 127, 140, 195, 196, 198–9
Microsoft, 4
  EU case law
    innovation defence, 241
    IPR licensing refusal, 229–31
    remedy, 242–3
    tying, 189–90
  US case law
    defensive leverage, 190–1
    definition of monopoly, 128
    entry barriers, 146
Miert, Karel van, 9, 14, 105
mineral water, 314, 354
mobile telecommunications
  3G licensing, 459
  access and call origination, 465–7
  broadcasting, 106, 110, 143
  Germany, 37–9, 50
  horizontal mergers, 253
  liberalisation, 456
  mergers, 254
  roaming charges, 460
  voice call termination, 467–8

Modernisation Regulation
  alternative options, 409
  assessment, 404–9, 498
  background, 395–409
  behavioural commitments, 412
  damages and, 436–8
  direct effect of Article 81, 47, 393–4,
      404–5, 424
  Europeanisation of competition law,
      394, 401–4
  impact, 393–5
  legal certainty, 405, 411–12, 413
  new institutional structure, 409
    Commission, 409–14
    European Competition Network, 415–19
    National Competition Authorities,
      414–15, 471
  objectives, 439
  political impetus, 400–1
  pre-existing centralisation, 395–401
  private enforcement, 424–38
  public interest exemptions, 413
  side effects, 419–23
    Europeanisation of economic
      governance, 421
    juridification, 420
    rebirth of national laws, 421–3
  undermining, 395
monopolies
  effect, 56
  hypothetical monopolist test, 132–5, 136
    cellophane fallacy, 134
    Commission use, 157
    United States, 139
  meaning, 58
    US definitions, 128
  monopolistic competition, 58, 150
  state monopolies. *See* state monopolies
  statutory monopolies, 210, 218
    abuse of dominance, 447–8
    efficiency, 451
    exclusive rights, 449
Monti, Mario, 82, 100, 388–9
Möschel, Wernard, 29, 405, 421
motor vehicles
  block exemptions, 384–8
  certification, 199–200
  importance of industry, 384
  liberalisation
    distribution market, 385–6
    repair and service market, 386–7

mergers, 262–3
multi-brand distribution, 386
politics of distribution, 384–90
protectionism, 384
regulated competition, 387–90
spare parts, 227
Muris, T. J., 75, 79

nail guns, 187–9
National Competition Authorities
  centralisation policy and, 399
  common regulatory philosophy, 418
  decentralisation to, 21, 119, 213, 394
    Art. 81 application, 404–5
    background, 401–4
    coherence, 406–9
    control mechanisms, 417–18
    Europeanisation of economic
      governance, 421
    fines, 415
    impact, 499–500
    juridification, 420
    monitoring, 415–19, 471
    objectives, 439
    rebirth of national laws, 421–3
    role, 414–15
    side effects, 419–23
  growing authority, 403, 464
  independence, 414, 420
  pre-modernisation role, 395–6
  resources, 414–15
national interests
  EU competition and, 110–13
  free movement exceptions, 111–12
  integrity of legal systems, 112
  merger policy, 302
National Regulatory Authorities
  electronic communications, 464–8
  independence, 464
  monitoring, 471–4
  post-liberalisation, 463–4
  price control, 220–3
nationalised industries. *See* state monopolies
Neal Report, 337
neoclassical economics
  ancillary restraints, 35
  British Airways/Virgin case, 163–4
  concept of competition, 26, 49, 170
  definition of monopoly, 128
  dominance, 130
  economic efficiency, 23–4

economic freedom, 49
EU policy, 52
market power and, 125, 128, 130
Nestlé, 133, 314, 354
Netherlands
   air transport liberalisation, 454
   book prices, 104
   competition workload, 414
   digital TV, 143
   electricity liberalisation, 462
   EU competition law jurisdiction, 401
   lawyers–accountants partnerships, 110–12
   pension funds, 97–9
network industries
   introduction of competition, 451–63
      airlines, 452–6
      electricity, 460–3
      telecommunications, 456–60
   liberalisation, market context, 442–4
   sector-specific competition law, 474–85
      airline slots, 476–8
      electricity mergers, 474–6
      legitimacy, 484–5
      postal services, 478–84
Neven, D., 278
non-compete clauses, 33–4, 35, 361

obiter dicta, 117
OECD, 14, 49
Olesen, 197
oligopolies
   example, 309–11
   express collusion. *See* cartels
   market investigations, 342–4
   meaning, 58
   merger control, 311–24
      assessment, 323–4
      causation, 322–3
      collective dominance, 311–12, 314–15
      concentration ratio, 316–17
      deterrence mechanisms, 320–1
      efficiencies, 322–3
      electricity, 475
      entry barriers, 319, 321
      Herfindhal Hirschmann Index (HHI), 316–17
      legal certainty, 324
      price transparency, 315, 318–19
      scope, 311
      structural links, 320
      tacit collusion, 309–11, 314–15, 317–20

price leadership, 309–11, 341
tacit collusion, 334–44
UK control model, 342–4
US anti-concentration legislation, 337–8
US cases, 342
optical fibres, 95
Oracle, 153, 260–1
ordoliberalism, 23–4, 44, 87, 396
Ordover, J. A., 164

package holidays, 315
packaging market, 278–80
parallel imports, 40–4, 51
parens patriae jurisdiction, 434
partnerships, lawyers–accountants, 110–12
penalties. *See* fines
pension funds, 97–9
perfect competition, 58, 124
performance, meaning, 57–8
Perrier, 133, 314, 354
pharmaceutical products, 44, 51, 203
Pitofsky, R., 24, 147
planning laws, 375
plastic wastes, 91
pluralism
   Commission policy, 277
   economic efficiency v, 1, 50
   economic freedom and, 186, 196
   EU theme, 87
   media, 141–3, 271, 292
Poland, merger policy, 305, 421
politics
   car market, 384–90
   Commission powers and, 400–1
   concealment of policies, 19
   conclusions, 503–5
   De Havilland case, 8–9, 16
   distribution agreements, 391
   distributive issues. *See* distributive justice
   economic theories and, 54
   EU competition law and
      critique, 393
      elimination, 395
      factor, 4, 118
   National Competition Authorities, 414
   US antitrust economics and, 75–9, 81
   values, 3
Portugal
   airport charges, 201
   employment promotion, 97

Portugal (cont.)
    EU competition law jurisdiction, 401
    merger policy, 304
Posner, Richard, 9, 64, 77, 165
post-Chicago paradigm
    aftermarkets, 149, 150
    British Airways/Virgin case, 164–6,
        167–8
    empirical evidence, 69–71
    EU future, 88
    exclusionary tactics, 79
    foreclosure, 368
    market power, 126, 128, 144, 158
    mergers, 71
    policy prescriptions, 71
    political influence, 74, 75, 78
    predation by reputation, 160, 215
    predatory pricing, 71–3, 87, 179–82
    principles, 21, 68–71
postal services
    Belgian state monopoly, 450–1, 488–9
    cross-subsidies, 493
    exclusive rights, 481–2, 493
    German cross-subsidies, 478–84, 485
    liberalisation, 482–3
    regulation, 472
    solidarity principle, 488
Pratt & Whitney, 46
precedents, 77
predatory pricing
    abuse of dominant position, 177–82, 194
        reform, 181–2
    Chicago School, 67–8, 87, 178
    conglomerate mergers, 281
    definition, 177–8
    empirical evidence, 69–70
    France, 407
    Harvard School, 61–3
    leverage, 186
    market power, 125
    post-Chicago model, 71–3, 87, 179–82
    strategies, 178–9
    US policy, 61–3, 67–8, 74
price fixing agreements
    legal profession, 448
    oligopolies, 309–11
    per se illegality, 155
    price leadership, 309–11
prices. *See also* predatory pricing
    book prices, 103–5, 122
    conglomerate mergers, 280–1

control by regulators, 220–3
    universal services, 222–3
cross-elasticity, 133, 136
discrimination
    defences, 208
    territorial discrimination, 195–8, 200, 202
excessive pricing
    abuse of dominance, 218–20, 376
    Commission neglect, 423
    market partitioning, 199–200
    fixing. *See* price fixing agreements
    predatory. *See* predatory pricing
    price correlation studies, 133, 136
    price leadership, 309–11, 341
    price umbrellas, 246
    RPM. *See* resale price maintenance
    transparency, 315, 318–19
product differentiation
    advertising, 353–4
    horizontal mergers, 217
    market power and, 150–3
product markets, 135–9
productive efficiencies
    case law, 45, 46
    competition role, 55
    consumer welfare and, 84
    meaning, 45
    monopolies and, 56
property rights, 444
proportionality
    ancillary restraints, 34
    consumer welfare, 210
    defence, 206
    public policy exceptions, 113
    public service exemptions, 489–90
protectionism
    car market, 384
    measures, 39
    mergers, 305–7
    national champions, 495
public policy
    abuse of dominance, defence, 210–11
    Article 81 and. *See* Article 81 exemptions
    concealment, 19
    consumer policy, 99–102
    culture, 102–10
    economics v, 420
    employment policy, 96–9, 121, 449
    environmental protection, 91–4
    EU competition law and, 89–91
        balance of factors, 115

conditional exemptions, 115–16
consequentialism, 116–17
elimination of public policy, 119–22, 412
EU policy context, 113–22
exclusionary method, 113–15
formalism, 116
future, 122–3
institutional legitimacy, 118–19
methodology, 113–17
Modernisation Regulation, 413
redefining economic efficiency, 93, 115
industrial policy, 94–6, 117
market definition and, 141–3, 158
national interests, 110–13
political aims of competition, 4
predictability and, 15–16
tensions, 21
public services
competition law and, 485–94
exclusion, 485, 486–8
exemptions, 488–91
consumer focus, 492
market delivery, 492–4
regulatory state, 441–2
state monopolies, 441
universality obligations, 222–3, 485, 491–4
welfare state, 485, 487–8
punitive damages, 435

Quick, P. D., 78

railways, 233–4, 458, 478
Reagan, Ronald, 67, 78
rebates. *See* discounts
refusal to supply
abuse of dominance, 223–43, 286
defences, 240–2
innovation, 241–2
objective justification, 240–1
economic freedom and consumer welfare, 224–6
entry barriers, 216, 217
essential facilities
competition v regulation, 231–4
EU regulation, 234–9
French competition law, 378
IPR licensing, 227–31
Oscar Bronner case, 225–6, 239
remedies, 242–3
synthesis, 239–40

regulation, Chicago School and, 64
regulatory state
concept, 441–2
electronic communications, 464–8
emergence, 495–6
former state industries, 463–74
National Regulatory Authorities, 463–4
sector-specific regulation v competition, 468–71
telecommunications model, 459–60
remedies
abuse of dominance, 217
mergers, 283–6
refusal to supply, 242–3
structural remedies, 283–6, 295, 336–7
Renault, 262–3
Rennie, 152
reputation effects, 73
resale price maintenance
anti-competitive effect, 103
Article 81 and, 368–9
block exemptions and, 360–1
distribution agreements, 354
economic debate, 355
United States, 77
research and development, 44, 120
restraints of trade, 35
retailers
consumer welfare, 374, 377
French abuse of economic dependence, 377–80
local cultures, 391
power, 372–83
UK market investigations, 380–3
retroactive rebates, 378
Riordan, M. H., 181
roaming charges, 38–9, 460
Rocard, Michel, 9
Roche, 152
Rolls Royce, 46
Ross, M. G., 494
Rousseva, Ekaterina, 206
RTL, 224–5
rule of reason, 29–31, 36, 111, 112, 356

SABRE, 235
Salop, S. C., 164, 174, 175
Scalia, Justice, 77
Scania, 262, 263
Schaub, Alexander, 48, 90
Seagram, 270–1

selective distribution agreements
    Article 81 control, 369–71
    consumer welfare and, 352
    Germany, 408
    motor vehicles, 386, 389
    non-compete clauses, 361
    purpose, 370
    territorial segmentation, 365–6
Sher, B., 185–6
significant impediments to competition
    De Havilland case, 11–12
    horizontal mergers, 258–64
    vertical mergers, 267, 277
single branding, 367
single market
    concept of agreement and, 41–4
    core value, 39
    disintegrating practices, 39–41
    distribution agreements and, 363–6, 390
    economic efficiency v, 41, 50–1
    electricity liberalisation and, 462–3
    first EC principle, 39, 81
    French competition law and, 407
    harmonisation of laws, 445–6
    market sharing agreements and,
        198–203
    merger control, 304, 305
    motor vehicles, 389
    negative integration, 446, 447
    positive integration, 446
slotting allowances, 376
small business freedom
    car dealers, 388
    French retail sector, 377
    Harvard School, 78, 81
    United Brands, 196
    US giants v. European firms, 224
Smith, Adam, 329
Smith, Mitchell, 481
social construction, 354
social policy
    Agreement, 97
    mergers and, 296–8
social security services, 485, 487–8
solidarity principle, 487–8
sovereignty, economic policy, 395, 421
Spain
    competition law, 401
    electricity, 462, 475
    EU competition law jurisdiction, 401
    utilities mergers, 306, 475

sport
    anti-doping, 114–15
    Bosman case, 107
    broadcasting, 105–10, 143, 413
    Declaration on Sport, 107
    Helsinki Report, 107
    UEFA Champions League, 107–9, 115
standards, rules v, 17–18, 81
state aids, 409, 490
state monopolies. See also specific services
    ECJ challenge, 448–51
    EU law and, 444
        Article 86, 444–5
        Article 95, 445–6
    liberalisation. See liberalisation
    post-liberalisation regulation, 463–74
    privatisations, 231–4
    public services, 441
    sector-specific competition law,
        474–85
Stena, 232–3, 234
Stigler, G. J., 63, 144–6
store cards, 422
Structure–Conduct–Performance. See
        Harvard School
structures. See market structures
subsidies, 490, 493
    cross-subsidies, 478–84, 493
substantial lessening of competition, 258–9
sugar cartel, 331
supermarkets
    car sales, 390
    market power, 375
    own brand goods, 375
    planning laws, 375
    UK market investigations, 380–3
supply substitutability, 138–9
sustainable development, 93
Sweden
    competition law, 401
    telecommunications, 458
    truck market, 140, 262, 299
switch selling, 169

tacit collusion
    abuse of collective dominance, 335–8
    Article 81 devices, 339–40
    Article 82 devices, 341–2
    cheating, 312, 320–1
    distribution agreements, 367
    express collusion v, 325

gap in competition law, 334–5, 336
generally, 334–44
merger control, 314–15, 317–20
oligopolies, 309–11
price leadership, 309–11, 341
stability, 312
structural remedies, 336–7
vertical restraints, 339–40, 354
Talcid, 152
target rebates, 183
technical and economic progress
Article 81 exemptions, 25–8, 45–6
burden of proof, 46
direct effect, 47
industrial policy, 95
merger policy, 293
narrowing interpretation, 119–22
Tele-Communications Inc., 268–9
telecommunications. *See also* electronic
communications; mobile
telecommunications
excessive pricing, 220
exclusive statutory rights, 450
liberalisation, 456–60
market context, 442–4
market downturn, 459
satellite networks, 456
speed, 452
terminal equipment, 457
regulation
model, 459–60
National Regulatory Authorities, 463–4
price control, 220–3
television. *See* broadcasting
Télévision par Satellite, 32–3, 38, 50
Temple Lang, John, 128
Tetra Laval, 278–80
Tetra Pak, 192–5, 255–6
Teubner, G., 420
Thomas, Justice, 77
Time Warner, 268–9
top-slice rebates, 183
torts, limitation of liability, 424–5, 434
total welfare
abuse of dominance and, 212
consumer welfare v, 83–4, 274, 390
merger policy, 292
toys, 352
train manufacture, 288–9
transparency, 81
truck market, 140, 262–3, 299

Turner, Donald, 60, 75, 337
Turner Broadcasting, 268–9
Twichell, James, 354
tying
abuse of dominance, 193
distribution agreements, 371
efficiency defence, 209
aftermarkets, 189, 191–2
beer ties, 427–9
conglomerate mergers, 272
GE/Honeywell, 275
French competition law, 378
Hilti case, 187–9
leverage strategy, 186
Microsoft cases, 189–91

UEFA, 107–9, 112, 115, 120
Ullrich, H., 421–2, 423
undertakings
meaning, 486
terminology, 11
unfair competition laws, 422
United Brands, 128–9, 130, 135–6, 137
United Kingdom
airlines, liberalisation, 453, 454
car market, 199–200
competition authorities, 343
legitimacy, 383
objectives, 382
resources, 414
competition law, 401
criminal liability, 410
EU model, 403
juridification, 420
void agreements, 408
damages claims, 435
electricity liberalisation model,
460, 461
consumer choice, 462
ferries, 232–3
market investigations, 342–4, 422–3
electrical warranties, 422–3
store cards, 422
supermarkets, 380–3
media pluralism, 141
merger policy, 248, 300
National Regulatory Authorities, 464
postal services, 482
retail sector
Code of Practice, 380–2
concentration, 377

United Kingdom (cont.)
 market investigations, 380–3
 supermarket power, 375
 sports broadcasting, 109
 sugar market, 174
 telecommunications
 liberalisation, 458
 mobile telecoms, 467
 tort law, 424–5
 US antitrust law roots, 80
United States
 abuse of dominance, 214
 airlines, 72–3, 453
 antitrust law
 controversies, 2
 economic freedom and, 24–5, 128
 English roots, 80
 model, 410, 498–9
 objectives, 217
 antitrust law model, 54
 British Airways/Virgin, 168–9, 172
 cartels, 324–5, 331
 CASE, 78
 cement industry, 66
 competition authorities, 60
 economists, 5, 75–9
 FTC head, 76, 79
 economics
 approaches, 4, 21
 Chicago School. *See* Chicago School
 effect on antitrust law, 73–9
 institutions and politics, 75–9
 models, 54
 politics and, 81
 post-Chicago model. *See* post-Chicago
 paradigm
 SCP. *See* Harvard School
 entry barriers, 146, 147
 essential facilities, 232
 European Union and
 competition policy pressure, 1, 81–2
 influence, 498–9
 shared premises, 55–7
 excessive pricing, 218–19
 expert evidence, 78
 false negatives and positives, 18
 market definition, 132
 cellophane fallacy, 134
 consumers' views, 136
 hypothetical monopolist test, 133, 139
 supply substitutability, 138–9

market power, 157
 branded products, 153
 definition, 125
 dominance, 143
 EU–US differences, 130
 meeting competition defence, 205
 mergers. *See* mergers
 Microsoft. *See* Microsoft
 oligopolies, 335
 anti-concentration legislation,
 337–8
 case law, 342
 predatory pricing, 61–3, 67–8, 71–3, 74,
 178, 180
 price discrimination, 197–8
 private enforcement of competition, 424
 consumers, 432–3
 follow-on claims, 436
 parens patriae jurisdiction, 434
 stand-alone actions, 435
 restraints of trade, 35
 rule of reason, 29–31, 36, 111, 112, 356
 state action doctrine, 448
 Supreme Court, Justices, 77
 telecommunications, 473–4
 vertical restraints, 356
universal services, 222–3, 491–4
utilitarianism, 56, 80
utilities. *See also* essential facilities
 electricity. *See* electricity
 geographic markets, 140
 introduction of competition, 451
 mergers, 305–6
 refusal to supply, 231–4
Utton, M. A., 10

vertical integration, 41, 352, 372
vertical mergers
 broadcasting sector, 268–71, 292
 Chicago School, 265
 cost savings, 264–5
 distribution agreements, 267
 ECMR approach, 266–8
 foreclosure, 265–8
 generally, 264–71
 leverage, 266
 SIEC test, 267, 277
vertical restraints. *See* distribution
 agreements
Vickers, John, 55, 302–4, 442–3
Villepin, Dominique de, 247

Virgin/British Airways. See British Airways/Virgin
Visa International, 33
Vivendi, 270–1, 287
Volkswagen, 97, 115–16
Volvo, 262–3

Walker, M., 148
waste, plastic wastes, 91
websites, methodology, 11
welfare state services, 485, 487–8
Wesseling, Rein, 409
Westland, 12

Wilks, S., 421
Williamson, Oliver, 75, 292
Willig, R. D., 164
wine market, 374
Wish, Richard, 22
wood pulp cartel, 332

X-inefficiency, 56

Yamaha, 365–6

Zoja, 224, 225, 226